NEW HAMPSHIRE PRACTICE

Volume 4

CIVIL PRACTICE
AND PROCEDURE

by

RICHARD V. WIEBUSCH

Sections 1.01–28.08

LEXIS® Law Publishing

8204611

AUTHOR'S PREFACE

This is a book about the rules which are applied to the processing of civil matters through the courts and administrative agencies of the State of New Hampshire. It is intended to organize the subject into a comprehensible unit, to explain the relationships amongst the various procedural devices, and to assemble and make readily accessible the many authorities which have come to define civil practice as we know it today.

The greatest challenge in a project of this sort is to find and organize all the authorities and to explain how the various procedural devices relate to each other. I discovered early on that no one digest, set of annotations, or other secondary source in New Hampshire contains a reference to every New Hampshire authority on these subjects. Five digests—Gilchrist's (1846), Bell's (1858), Morrison's (1891), Hening's (1926), and West's (1951)—have, at one time or another, been compiled for use in New Hampshire, and I began my research on each procedural device by consulting all of these for references to the most significant cases. Although West's is updated periodically, its organization of topics does not correspond neatly to New Hampshire practice, and it occasionally misses cases of interest in the period prior to the Second World War. Of the five digits, I found that Hening's is by far the best and can safely be relied upon to identify all cases prior to 1926.

Most of New Hampshire civil practice cannot be understood without reviewing the history of its development. Simply plucking the language of an opinion out of the 1870s and attempting to apply it to a modern problem often is both confusing and misleading. This is not to say that the principles and even the language of our old cases have no modern application—on the contrary, the depth, flexibility, and common sense of our modern civil practice is based upon hundreds of such cases. But our heritage is so rich that a great deal of time must be devoted to reading all the cases and statutes in an area to understand how these principles have developed. I found, therefore, that the best method of researching each topic was to arrange, read, and abstract the cases in chronological order. In that way, I was able to see how procedural devices evolved to meet changing needs, to understand why statutes and rules were first enacted and later amended, and to perceive how various procedures were originally intended to relate to each other. This method of research led to some exciting discoveries—e.g., the advent of Special Appearances in 1858—and, I think, to a more accurate perception of the effect which such factors as the periodic expansion and contraction of the court system and the expansion of litigation in the federal courts have had on the development of New Hampshire practice. While the process of learning the principles of New Hampshire's civil practice may take longer than simply reading a code, in the end it provides us with a broader, deeper and more powerful system of thought with which to confront the problems of processing cases through the courts and administrative agencies of New Hampshire.

At one time, the principles of New Hampshire practice were learned by reading the law in preparation for admission to the Bar. But times have changed, and modern practice leaves most of us with little time to research anything but the narrow issues important to our immediate problems. I have attempted, therefore, to research this area once for everyone and to set down in a comprehensible format the rules which I discovered and the principles that bind them together. I hope this will prove useful to the Bench and Bar and, in the end, will promote a broader understanding of the richness and common sense of our New Hampshire heritage.

I am very grateful to Justice David Souter for his constant encouragement and many thoughtful comments on my drafts. His steadfast belief in the value of this project has helped make this book a reality. My thanks also to the staff at Equity Publishing Corporation for their inexhaustible patience and close attention to my drafts and for the many useful suggestions. I also want to acknowledge the kind assistance of John Safford and his successor as Clerk of the Merrimack County Superior Court, Jim Starr; of Carole Ingraham, Clerk of the Concord District Court; and of Carol Belmain, Deputy Clerk of the New Hampshire Supreme Court, in helping me put together a comprehensive Appendix of Forms.

I am also pleased to acknowledge the generous and unstinting support of my partners at Sheehan, Phinney, Bass & Green. My particular thanks to Jack Sheehan and Bill Green who had the vision and professional pride to create a law firm in which a person's professional interests could be so extensively pursued and to Jim Higgins and Jim Shirley for their specific suggestions on pretrial and trial procedure. My thanks, too, to my secretary, Susan Hume, for her dedicated work in typing drafts, checking citations, and keeping the thousands of pages of notes, drafts, and galleys organized.

Finally, I owe a debt of incalculable gratitude to my wife Margaret and to our three children, Kimberley, Alice, and Katrina, who for years have put up with my absence while I researched and wrote this book. More than any other people, they are responsible for the existence of this book.

Richard V. Wiebusch, Esq.

May 1984
Manchester, New Hampshire

PREFACE TO THE SECOND EDITION

In the thirteen years since this book was first published, New Hampshire civil procedure has continued to develop, based on principles of fairness and common sense and a recognition that the delivery of justice requires attention to the unique circumstances of each case. Some subject areas have gone through an active period of development; others remain as they were in 1984. But, on the whole, this period has seen a refinement and deepening of the system of civil procedure and a dedication by the courts to molding that system to fit the needs of present day litigation. New Hampshire continues to possess one of the most responsive and flexible systems of civil procedure in the country.

The production of this second edition has required the help of many hands. At various times, Scott O'Connell, Don Williamson, Mary Tenn, and others formerly associated with the New Hampshire office of Hale and Dorr have assisted in revising the chapters. More recently, Anne O'Reilly performed an extensive review of approximately half the chapters. Finally, Gordon MacDonald has undertaken to review and revise all of the proposals for change and to revise the balance of the book. The revisions of this second edition are largely the result of Gordon's thoughtful and tireless efforts.

I want to acknowledge, with gratitude and admiration, my partners at Hale and Dorr LLP who have generously supported annual updates of this book and the preparation of this second edition.

Richard V. Wiebusch, Esq.

November 1997

Manchester, New Hampshire

vii

PUBLISHER'S PREFACE

Civil Practice and Procedure—a multivolume treatise—is the third title in the New Hampshire Practice Series, a series which is designed to provide a comprehensive outline of selected subject areas of New Hampshire law.

Civil Practice and Procedure offers a panoramic view of New Hampshire civil litigation, beginning with the commencement of a civil action, proceeding through trial, and concluding with appellate review. The subjects traditionally covered in treatises on civil procedure—jurisdiction; parties; process; pleadings and motions; discovery; trial; verdict and judgment; and appellate review—are covered; in addition, coverage is afforded to other nontraditional topics of importance to the attorney engaged in general civil practice—among them arbitration, settlements, equity proceedings, and administrative agency proceedings. The breadth of scope of the treatise is matched by its depth of analysis, which blends history, theory, exposition of legal principles, and "rules" and practical guidance.

The author of Civil Practice and Procedure, Richard V. Wiebusch, is a partner in the Manchester law firm of Hale and Dorr LLP. Mr. Wiebusch served as an Assistant Attorney General with the State of New Hampshire until 1977 where he was Chief of the Division of Legal Counsel.

Mr. Wiebusch received his law degree from Cornell University and graduated "with high distinction" with an A.B. in English from Dartmouth College. He is a member of the State Ballot Law Commission, the New Hampshire Bar Association's Continuing Legal Education Committee and the Advisory Committee to the New Hampshire Law Library and has been admitted to the practice of law in New Hampshire since 1973.

Library References: This publication includes references to sections of CJS and ALR annotations. They are designed to aid an attorney who wishes to undertake further research on a given subject.

Forms and Samples: An Appendix of Forms, containing forms and sample pleadings, is included in Volume 6 of this publication. Where appropriate, references have been included in notes following the text to pertinent forms in the Appendix.

Cross References: Where appropriate, internal cross references to other portions of the text have been included in notes following the text.

Tables: Volume 6 of this publication contains several important distribution tables. The first table lists in alphabetical order all of the cases cited in the publication and indicates the sections in which references to each appear.

The second table lists provisions of the United States Constitution, New Hampshire Constitution, New Hampshire Revised Statutes Annotated, United States Code, Rules of Court, and other materials cited in the publication and indicates the sections in which references to each appear.

Index: Volume 6 of this publication includes a thorough and accurate subject-word index.

Upkeep Service: New Hampshire Practice: Civil Practice and Procedure will be kept current by means of regular cumulative supplementation.

LEXIS® Law Publishing
Charlottesville, Virginia

November 1997

SUMMARY OF CONTENTS

VOLUME 4

VOLUME 5

VOLUME 6

TABLE OF CONTENTS

PART I. THE JUDICIAL SYSTEM

CHAPTER 1. STRUCTURE OF THE JUDICIAL SYSTEM

PART II. JURISDICTION AND VENUE

CHAPTER 2. PRINCIPLES OF JURISDICTION

TABLE OF CONTENTS

TABLE OF CONTENTS

CHAPTER 4. VENUE

A. PRINCIPLES OF VENUE

B. ORIGINAL VENUE

C. PROPER VENUE

CHAPTER 5.   THE DOCTRINE OF FORUM NON
CONVENIENS

TABLE OF CONTENTS

PART III. PARTIES

CHAPTER 6.   PARTIES

A. INTRODUCTION

B. CAPACITY TO SUE AND BE SUED

C. JOINT OR SEPARATE ACTIONS

D. OBJECTING TO NONJOINDER

E. OBJECTING TO JOINDER (MISJOINDER)

F. CLASS ACTIONS AND REPRESENTATIVE SUITS

G. MISNOMER AND MISDESIGNATION

TABLE OF CONTENTS

H. INTERVENTION

I. SUBSTITUTION OF PARTIES

J. DEATH OF A PARTY

K. THIRD-PARTY PRACTICE

TABLE OF CONTENTS

PART IV. PLEADINGS AND MOTIONS

CHAPTER 7. POLICIES AND RULES REGULATING PLEADINGS

A. NATURE OF PLEADINGS

B. GENERAL RULES OF PLEADING

C. HOW TO DRAFT PLEADINGS

D. BARS TO FURTHER ACTION

TABLE OF CONTENTS

E. SPECIAL RULES AND PROCEEDINGS

TABLE OF CONTENTS

TABLE OF CONTENTS

TABLE OF CONTENTS

PART V. COMMENCEMENT OF A CIVIL ACTION

CHAPTER 13. FORMS, PREPARATION, AND FILING OF WRITS

A. FORMS AND PREPARATION

B. FILING

CHAPTER 14. SERVICE OF PROCESS

A. ON NATURAL PERSONS

B. ON CORPORATIONS

TABLE OF CONTENTS

C. ON GOVERNMENT OFFICIALS AND AGENCIES

D. ON MUTUAL ASSOCIATIONS

E. ON PARTNERSHIPS

F. ON LIMITED LIABILITY COMPANIES

G. OTHER SERVICE

H. RETURN OF SERVICE

I. EXEMPTIONS FROM SERVICE

TABLE OF CONTENTS

CHAPTER 15. APPEARANCE

A. GENERAL APPEARANCE

B. SPECIAL APPEARANCE

TABLE OF CONTENTS

TABLE OF CONTENTS

CHAPTER 18. REPLEVIN

TABLE OF CONTENTS

CHAPTER 19.   INJUNCTIONS

xxxi

TABLE OF CONTENTS

TABLE OF CONTENTS

PART VII. DISCOVERY AND DEPOSITIONS

CHAPTER 22. GENERAL PRINCIPLES OF PRETRIAL DISCOVERY

A. IN GENERAL

B. METHODS OF DISCOVERY

C. SCOPE OF DISCOVERY

TABLE OF CONTENTS

TABLE OF CONTENTS

CHAPTER 28. DEPOSITIONS IN PERPETUAL REMEMBRANCE

Chapters 29 through 64 appear in Volume 5; Forms, Tables, and Index appear in Volume 6

Part I

THE JUDICIAL SYSTEM

CHAPTER 1. STRUCTURE OF THE JUDICIAL SYSTEM

§ 1.01. Introduction

The judicial powers[1] of the State of New Hampshire are distributed amongst trial courts of limited and general jurisdiction, administrative

---

1 Despite the fact that pt. 2, art. 72-a of the Constitution of the State of New Hampshire provides that "the judicial power of the State shall be vested in the Supreme Court, a trial court of general jurisdiction known as the superior court, and such lower courts as the legislature may establish under Article fourth of Part 2," "judicial powers" are, in fact, exercised by every branch of state government. In this treatise, the term "judicial powers" is used to refer to any authority to hear and determine disputed issues in an adversary proceeding. The term "judiciary" is used to more narrowly designate that portion of the state's "judicial system" which is managed solely by judges and courts. In adopting this distinction, the author takes some comfort in noting that the Supreme Court has experienced some confusion of terminology in this area as well. In the case

1

agencies of state and local government, the two houses of the Legislature, the Governor and Council, and the Supreme Court.

Library References

CJS Constitutional Law § 144

A. *Judicial Powers Not Exercised by the Judiciary*

§ 1.02. Bodies Exercising Judicial Power—Generally

Administrative agencies of state and local government, the Governor and Council, the House and Senate, and the Governor and Council together with the House and Senate all have authority to exercise judicial powers in limited areas.

§ 1.03. —Administrative Agencies of State and Local Government

Many officers, boards, commissions, and agencies of the Executive Branch have statutory authority over matters that come within the ambit of their regulatory authority. Some of these agencies have the power to grant or to withhold licenses, permits, and certificates, and can otherwise prescribe the prerequisites for undertaking a particular activity. Cases coming before them usually involve issues regarding the completeness and accuracy of application materials, the character of the participants, and the appropriateness of the project. Enforcement of postpermission requirements is accomplished by the threat of censure or revocation of the license, permit, certificate, or other prerequisite which the agency controls.[2]

---

of In re Mussman, 112 N.H. 99, 289 A.2d 403 (1972), the Court held that a trial of impeachment in the Senate was not a "judicial" function, while in Bennett v. Thomson, 116 N.H. 453, 360 A.2d 187 (1976), *appeal dismissed*, 429 U.S. 1082 (1977), and King v. Thomson, 116 N.H. 838, 367 A.2d 1049 (1976), it followed the more traditional view adopted by Chief Justice Doe in Boody v. Watson, 64 N.H. 162 (1886), and referred to proceedings for the removal of unclassified state officers by the governor and council as "judicial functions." While the "judiciary" is unquestionably the main arm of the state's "judicial system," a great deal of "judicial power" is exercised by the other two branches of government as well. See also Smith Ins., Inc. v. Grievance Comm., 120 N.H. 856, 861, 424 A.2d 816, 819 (1980) ("The State Constitution provides that the three branches of government should be 'kept as separate from, and independent of, each other, as the nature of a free government will admit' N.H. Const. Pt. 1, art. 37. This court has consistently recognized, however, that the three branches cannot be completely separate.").

2 " '[W]hen an executive board has regulatory functions, it may hear and determine controversies which are incidental thereto. . . ' " Appeal of Plantier, 126 N.H. 500, 512, 494 A.2d 270, 277 (1985) (citing Opinion of the Justices, 87 N.H. 492, 493, 179 A.2d 357, 359 (1935)).

Other agencies, although not endowed with licensing powers, enjoy broad powers of investigation and have the authority to hold hearings and to issue administrative orders to enforce their statutes. Issues heard by this type of agency tend to be framed by the agency's investigation rather than by the checklist of its forms, and review can vary greatly depending upon the situation.

General rules of procedure and suggested methods of approaching administrative agency hearings are discussed in Part XVII. However, two points are worth noting here. First, although administrative agencies are granted only limited and special subject matter jurisdiction, the doctrine of exhaustion of administrative remedies and the statutory limits of the superior and Supreme Courts to review their decisions often result in agencies exercising authority which is outside any practical scope of judicial review.[3] Second, despite the requirements of the Administrative Procedures Act (RSA 541-A) and the Right-To-Know Law (RSA 91-A), the actual rules of procedure and "common law" doctrines of such agencies are, for the most part, unwritten and hard to discover. Administrative agencies of state and local government are, in a very real sense, a separate arm of the state's judicial power, and must be approached with that in mind.[4]

Library References

CJS Public Administrative Bodies and Procedures §§ 114, 115

§ 1.04. —The Governor and Council

The Governor and five Executive Councilors sit as one body with two parts at the head of the Executive Branch.[5] Each has a negative vote on the

---

3 See, e.g., Smith Ins., Inc. v. Grievance Comm., 120 N.H. 856, 862, 424 A.2d 816, 819 (1980) ("[If] the duty of an executive board is primarily to decide questions of legal rights between private parties that are unconnected to any regulatory function . . . such function belongs to the judiciary.").

4 See Gould v. Director, N.H. Div. of Motor Vehicles, 138 N.H. 343, 347, 639 A.2d 254 (1994) ("Actions by administrative agencies are quasi-judicial if the adjudicatory process provided by statute requires notification of the parties involved, a hearing including receiving and considering evidence, and a decision based upon the evidence presented.") (citing Winslow v. Holderness Planning Board, 125 N.H. 262, 266–267, 480 A.2d 114, 116 (1984)).

5 The phrases "Governor and Council," "governor with consent of the council," "governor . . . , by and with the advice and consent of the council," "governor, with advice of council," "governor, and a majority of the council for the time being," and "governor with the advice and consent of the council" are variously used to refer to this single body. See, e.g., N.H. Const. pt. 2, arts. 5, 34, 43, 46, 47, 50, 52, 56, 58, 68, 73, 74, 85, and 94 and RSA 21:31-a.

other[6] and must vote in the affirmative for the body to take any action. The Constitution confers upon the Governor and Council[7] the power to punish, by a term of imprisonment not exceeding ten days, any person guilty of disrespect in its presence, obstruction of its deliberations, infringement of the privileges of its members, interference with its officers in the execution of its orders, assault on a witness or other person called before it, or knowingly rescuing a person arrested by its order.[8] In addition, various statutes grant the Governor and Council power to hear and to determine specific civil cases.[9]

The Governor and Council may require the opinion of the Justices of the Supreme Court upon any "important questions of law" in the exercise of these functions. The Justices will give their opinion if the inquiry is "related to action awaiting the consideration of the inquiring body in the course of its executive duty."[10] However, the Justices will not give their opinion when it appears that private interests not adequately represented before the Court may be involved in the question,[11] or where it appears that the question may later come before the Court in the course of litigation.[12] When giving their opinion under part 2, article 74, the Justices act as "constitutional advisors"

---

6 Pt. 2, art. 47.

7 Whether the Governor and the Executive Council possess separate powers of imprisonment or must act jointly has not been settled. The language of pt. 2, art. 23 is ambiguous, referring as it does to the "senate, governor and council," and later stating that "no imprisonment *by either*" (emphasis supplied) may exceed 10 days. However, because the Executive Council has no other power which it can exercise alone, and in fact has no authority even to initiate an official action of the Governor and Council together, it seems more reasonable to construe art. 23 as conferring the power to punish by imprisonment upon the Governor and Council together.

8 Pt. 2, arts. 22 and 23.

9 RSA 4:1 (removal of certain unclassified officers); 6:19 (removal of the State Treasurer). It is not clear whether a hearing similar to that required by RSA 4:1 must be provided under RSA 6:19. However, as the State Treasurer is a legislative, rather than an executive officer, the provisions of RSA 4:1 do not apply to his removal and any requirement for a hearing must be founded in constitutional guarantees of due process, past administrative practices, or implication from the words of the statute. See also RSA 6:28 (removal of assistant treasurers.)

10 See Opinion of the Justices, 96 N.H. 517, 83 A.2d 738 (1950); Opinion of the Justices, 74 N.H. 606, 609, 68 A. 873, 874 (1907); Opinion of the Justices, 67 N.H. 600, 601, 43 A. 1074 (1892).

11 See, e.g., Petition of Turner, 97 N.H. 449, 91 A.2d 458 (1952); In re School Law Manual, 63 N.H. 574, 575, 4 A. 878 (1885).

12 See Opinion of the Justices, 67 N.H. at 601, 43 A. at 1074 (1892); Opinion of the Justices, 81 N.H. 563, 565, 128 A. 684, 685 (1925).

4

of the Governor and Council, rather than as a court,[13] and neither receives evidence nor determines issues of fact.[14]

§ 1.05. —The Senate and House of Representatives

Each legislative house has the same power as the Governor and Council to punish for contempt.[15]

Certain legislative officers and committees are also entrusted with authority to hear and to determine disputes regarding specific subjects. For example, the Secretary of State[16] is permitted to determine the right to do business under particular names,[17] trademarks, or service marks.[18] There is at least a question of whether part 1, article 15 of the Constitution and RSA 541-A do not require the Secretary of State to promulgate rules of procedure and to hold hearings on his determinations under these statutes.[19]

RSA 14:15-b vests in the Committee on Mileage authority to arbitrate "all disputes and claims involving payment of mileage to members of the House and Senate."[20] The Legislature has the power to remove some state officers.[21]

---

13 Piper v. Town of Meredith, 109 N.H. 328, 251 A.2d 328 (1969).

14 In re Probate Blanks, 71 N.H. 621, 52 A. 861 (1902).

15 The only difference is in the maximum term of imprisonment. While the Senate and the Governor and Council are limited to imposing a maximum term of 10 days, the House of Representatives may impose a longer or indefinite sentence. Compare pt. 2, arts. 22 and 23.

16 The Secretary of State and State Treasurer are legislative, rather than executive, officers. Pt. 2, art. 67; RSA 5:1 and 6:1.

17 With regard to trade names, see RSA 349:1.

18 With regard to service marks and trademarks, see RSA 350-A:2–4.

19 In part, the question turns on whether the Secretary of State, as a legislative officer, is exempt from the requirements of RSA 541-A by virtue of the provisions of RSA 541-A:1(II), which excludes "the legislature" from the definition of "agency." The Justices of the Supreme Court have already given their opinion that the Secretary of State has executive, as well as legislative, duties (see Opinion of the Justices, 106 N.H. 402, 213 A.2d 415 (1965)), but whether this takes him out of the meaning of "the legislature" as used in RSA 541-A:1(II), has not yet been determined. Regardless of how that issue is decided, in cases where property rights have been acquired in a name or mark, pt. 1, art. 15, should require notice and an opportunity to be heard to each person who is likely to be affected by the Secretary of State's decision.

20 The requirements of the Administrative Procedures Act (RSA 541-A) do not apply to such arbitration because the committee is part of the Legislature. RSA 541-A:1(II).

21 Pt. 2, arts. 17, 38, 39, 40, and 63. Pt. 2, art. 38 of the New Hampshire Constitution conveys the power to impeach an officer of the state for bribery, corruption, malpractice or maladministration. See In re Mussman, 112 N.H. 99, 289 A.2d 403 (1972) (the judiciary has the power to impeach).

In performing all of its judicial functions, each house of the Legislature can require the opinion of the Justices of the Supreme Court in the same manner and subject to the same limitations as the Governor and Council.[22]

§ 1.06. —The Governor and Council and the House of Representatives and Senate Together

The House of Representatives and Senate acting together may petition the Governor and Council for removal of any other commissioned officer of the state.[23] Presentation of a petition requesting such removal is referred to as an "address." The petition must state a reasonable cause for removal which is, nevertheless, not a sufficient ground for impeachment, and must not be presented to the Governor and Council until the officer involved has "had an opportunity to be heard in his defense by a joint committee of both houses of the legislature."[24]

B. Judicial Powers Exercised by the Judiciary

§ 1.07. Introduction

The New Hampshire system of courts and judges is a confused amalgam of courts with deep common law roots and tribunals of only recent legislative invention. Although there is no intermediate appellate court, some cases before judges of probate[25] and state and local administrative agencies[26] can be reviewed or retried by the superior court before being transferred to the Supreme Court for final review. While the distinction between law and equity is recognized in forms of pleading[27] and by the application of certain equitable principles to the granting of relief, the same procedural rules apply to the trial of both law and equity cases[28] and issues of law and equity may be freely joined in one case.[29]

---

22 See § 1.04; Opinion of the Justices, 121 N.H. 423, 430 A.2d 187 (1981); Opinion of the Justices, 123 N.H. 510, 463 A.2d 891 (1983).

23 Pt. 2, art. 73.

24 *Id.*

25 See RSA 558.

26 See, e.g., RSA 231:34 and 356-A:14(I).

27 See, e.g., Super. Ct. R. 118, 121, 132, and 134.

28 Super. Ct. R. 116.

29 See generally Owen v. Weston, 63 N.H. 599, 4 A. 801 (1886), and cases there cited. Chief Justice Doe wrote: "In a suit at law, either party may be allowed to file a bill in equity or an amendment of this pleading; and in a suit in equity, either party may be allowed to file a declaration at law."

§ 1.08. Constitutional v. Statutory Courts and Judicial Officers

A constitutional court cannot be abolished by legislative act; a statutory court can be. One of the weaknesses of New Hampshire's original constitution was its failure to provide for the establishment of specific courts with general trial and appellate jurisdiction. This deficiency led to nearly a century of legislative experimentation with the forms and jurisdiction of the state's courts,[30] ending finally in 1901 with a plan which was formalized in 1966 by the addition of article 72-a to part 2 of the Constitution. That article now provides:

> The judicial power of the state shall be vested in the supreme court, a trial court of general jurisdiction known as the superior court and such lower courts as the legislature may establish under article fourth of Part II.

The Constitution also recognizes the existence of judges of probate[31] and of justices of the peace.[32] Thus, the Supreme Court and the superior court are constitutional courts, and the judges of those courts, the judges of probate and justices of the peace are constitutional judicial officers.

The municipal courts and the district courts are statutory courts[33] and are entitled to only such tenure as the Legislature chooses to grant them. In addition, article 4 of part II provides that "the general court (except as otherwise provided by article 72-A, part 2) shall forever have full power and authority to erect and constitute judicial courts of record or other courts . . . ." This language clearly permits the Legislature to establish judges and courts inferior to the Supreme Court and to invest them with any subject matter jurisdiction not already granted by that document to a constitutional court.[34]

Library References

CJS Courts § 28

---

30 Reid, John Phillip, *Chief Justice: The Judicial World of Charles Doe* (Cambridge, Mass., 1967) pgs. 17–18, 25.

31 Pt. 2, arts. 76, 78, 80, 81, 82, and 94.

32 Pt. 2, arts. 75, 77, 79, 93, and 94.

33 See RSA 502 and 502-A.

34 See RSA 502 and 502-A. This authority has frequently been exercised in the past, and is the constitutional basis for the creation and abolition of the municipal courts and the establishment of the district courts in their place.

§ 1.09. Constitutional Courts and Judicial Officers—Justices of the Peace

The Constitution recognizes the existence of justices of the peace and limits them to a five-year term of office.[35]

Library References

CJS Justices of the Peace § 1

§ 1.10. —The Supreme Court

The Constitution does not set the number of Supreme Court Justices but leaves the matter instead to the Legislature's discretion. RSA 490:1 provides for a court of five members, consisting of a Chief Justice and four Associate Justices. The Court is required to have three Justices in attendance at any session, but may determine a case in such a session by any members who are not disqualified from hearing the case.[36] With the exception of finding facts upon the court's direction, a single Justice of the Court has no authority to act in the absence of a quorum.[37] Each calendar year constitutes one court term. The Court hears oral arguments in Concord during the week that includes the first Tuesday in each month throughout the year.[38] The Court announces its decisions in written opinions filed with the Clerk.[39]

Library References

CJS Courts § 423

§ 1.11. —The Superior Court

The Constitution does not set the number of justices of the superior court or provide for their organization.[40] RSA 491:1 provides that the superior court consist of a chief justice and twenty-eight associate justices.[41] The

---

35 Pt. 2, art. 75. See also RSA 455-A:1.

36 RSA 490:7.

37 RSA 490:8. But see Supreme Court R. 2.

38 RSA 490:6; Supreme Court R. 1; Belmain, Carol, *Filing an Appeal in New Hampshire: A Short Guide* (Concord, N.H., 1982) p. 11.

39 Supreme Court R. 20. The Clerk thereupon sends a copy of the opinion and notice of the resulting order to the parties or their counsel. The Court's order is not "valid and binding" until such a written opinion has been filed.

40 Pt. 2, art. 87 does require that a writ bear the test of the "chief, first or senior justice" of the court from which it issues, but no other reference to the chief justice of the superior court is contained in the Constitution.

41 There have been 28 associate justices since 1992. A justice who is retired from active service due to permanent disability is no longer considered a member of the court. RSA 491:1.

court does not sit en banc for any purpose; each justice acts alone for the whole court.[42] The court holds regular sessions in the county seat[43] of every county at least twice a year. Court terms begin on the first Tuesday of January, February, March, April, May, September, and November of each calendar year. Justices of the superior court have traditionally been assigned to different counties each year, with the result that no justice sits continuously in one location.

Library References

CJS Courts § 276

§ 1.12.   —Judges of Probate and Their Courts

There is one judge of probate for each county, and he or she holds regular sessions in the probate court at the county seat.[44] There are no associate or

---

42 The wording of amendments to RSA 491:1 has unnecessarily placed a cloud over this power. From the date of its enactment in 1901 until 1977, the statute prescribing the number and organization of the justices in the superior court stated that "each of the justices shall exercise the powers of the court unless otherwise provided." Since 1977 the amendments increasing the number of justices has replaced this clause with the statement that "said justices . . . shall exercise the powers of the court unless otherwise provided." The substitution of "said justices" for "each of the justices," might suggest an intention to require the court to act en banc, but as there is no other evidence to suggest either that the Legislature intended such a result or that the court has understood the statute to have that effect, such an interpretation will probably not be given effect.

43 RSA 496:1(I)(f) creates two judicial districts for Hillsborough County. The northern district shall hold its term in Manchester and will serve that city as well as the towns of Amherst, Antrim, Bedford, Bennington, Deering, Francestown, Goffstown, Greenfield, Hancock, Hillsborough, Lyndeborough, Mont Vernon, New Boston, Peterborough, Weare, and Windsor. The southern district shall hold its term in Nashua and will serve that city as well as the towns of Brookline, Greenville, Hollis, Hudson, Litchfield, Mason, Merrimack, Milford, New Ipswich, Pelham, Sharon, Temple, and Wilton. In Coos County, it has been customary to hold at least one session each year in Lancaster.

44 A person reading the Constitution, statutes, and Supreme Court opinions of New Hampshire might easily fall into considerable confusion as to whether jurisdiction over probate matters has been committed to the judges of probate or to their courts. The Constitution speaks both of the "judges of probate" and the "courts of probate," but also distinguishes between judges of court and judges of probate (see pt. 2, art. 78. But see pt. 2, art. 95, where the distinction could not have been meant to be applied) and omits mention of a "probate court" when outlining the structure of a judiciary (see pt. 2, art. 72-A). The statutes use the terms "judge of probate" and "probate court" interchangeably. RSA 547:2 refers to the "judge of probate to whom jurisdiction of the subject matter belongs," but it is not clear whether this section declares the Legislature's understanding that it is the judge, rather than his court, that holds jurisdiction over estates and administration, particularly because RSA 547:1 declares that "the court of probate is a court of record for all purposes." From the earliest date, the Supreme Court has used the terms interchangeably. See, e.g., Tebbetts v. Tilton, 24 N.H. 120 (1851); Morgan v. Dodge, 44 N.H. 255 (1862). In general, statutes passed within the last decade refer to the court, rather than the judge (see, e.g., RSA 170-B).

special judges of probate; one judge serves alone in each county. The judges of probate are appointed by the Governor and Council[45] for a term lasting during good behavior[46] until age seventy.[47]

The probate courts[48] have no clerks. Registers of probate, elected by the residents of each county every two years,[49] fulfill many of the functions of a clerk for the probate courts.[50] One or more deputy registers of probate may be appointed by the register to assist him or her.[51] The judges of probate may hold special sessions at any time and place as justice may require.[52] Judges

---

In fact, the apparently conflicting use of the terms "judge of probate" and "probate court" reflect differences of style, rather than of substance. To some minds, reference to the judge of probate seems to imply more dignity and deeper common law roots; to others, recognition of the "probate court" suggests a modern institution prepared to meet the expanded jurisdictional demands of the day. In either event, as Justice Young observed in Carr v. Corning, 73 N.H. 362, 62 A. 168 (1905), "it is a matter of common knowledge that, when a person attending to probate business or considering probate matters speaks of referring anything to the judge of probate, he usually intends the probate court, and not the person who exercises the function of that office." 73 N.H. at 365, 62 A. at 169.

45 Pt. 2, art. 46.

46 Pt. 2, art. 73. See Opinion of the Justices, 140 N.H. 297, 666 A.2d 523 (1995) (suspending the pay of a judge does not violate provisions of New Hampshire constitution covering tenure and permanent salaries of judges).

47 Pt. 2, art. 78.

48 The Constitution (pt. 2, art. 81), the Rules approved by the Supreme Court, and general practice all support the view that there are 10 separate probate courts. Although RSA 547:1 refers to "the court of probate" and some other statutes have followed the practice (see, e.g., RSA 170-B), the Supreme Court has frequently referred to the probate courts as separate entities. See, e.g., Wood v. Stone, 39 N.H. 572 (1859); Kimball v. Fisk, 39 N.H. 110 (1859); Morgan v. Dodge, 44 N.H. 255 (1862). Judge Treat seems to regard them as separate. See Treat, *Probate Law* (Orford, N.H., 1968), pp. 7–63.

49 RSA 653:1(V).

50 The register of probate must preserve and protect the probate court records and seal (RSA 548:3 and 6), organize and keep the records (RSA 548:4 and 5), provide forms and copies on request (RSA 548:9, 25 and 28), and give notices to certain parties, fiduciaries (RSA 548:5-a and 558:1), and public officials (RSA 7:29 548:7-a and 13). All communications must be addressed to the register, rather than the judge, with copies to counsel of record. Prob. Ct. R. 13.

51 RSA 548:14 and 548:14-a.

52 Pt. 2, art. 80, requires that the judges of probate "hold their courts at such a place or places on such fixed days as the convenience of the people may require; and the Legislature from time-to-time appoint." RSA 547:20 specifically allows the judge of probate to attend

at the dwelling-house or in the neighborhood of the residence of an administrator, guardian, trustee or other person who shall be unable by reason of sickness or other sufficient cause to attend the court of probate at the time of probate are prohibited from charging a fee to hold regular or special sessions.[53]

Whenever a judge of probate is "absent or unable to attend a session," a judge of probate from another county may be called in to take his or her place.[54] If a judge recuses himself or herself, he or she may refer the case to the judge of any other county.[55] If there is a vacancy in the office, any other judge of probate may be called in to act during the period of the vacancy.[56] Any judge of probate who is called upon to act because of the absence, inability to attend, or refusal of the judge of a county, or during a vacancy in the office, is referred to as an acting judge and is allowed a certain per diem compensation and expenses, in addition to regular salary.[57]

Any matter pending in a probate court may be transferred to another probate court upon a party's motion or petition and subject to the approval of the transferring and receiving courts. A change of venue must be based on "inconvenience, change of residence of a principal party to the proceeding, or other good cause shown." A change of venue requires that a petition or motion be filed in both the transferring and receiving courts. Once the

---

and place appointed by law, whenever the personal attendance of such person is required.

RSA 547:21 states simply that the court may be adjourned "for the transaction of any business to any convenient time and place." In Kimball v. Fisk, 39 N.H. 110 (1859), Justice Bell wrote at 121, that "for the convenience of the people, it would seem to have been intended that probate courts should be held on fixed days and at fixed places where all might conveniently attend, but it does not seem to have been necessary, for any purpose apparently in view, to divest the judge of his authority at all other times and places." The judge wears judicial robes at most proceedings he conducts. Prob. Ct. R. 47. Contested cases are only heard on regular term days when "time permits." Prob. Ct. R. 39.

53 RSA 547:24.

54 RSA 547:18-a. Full-time judges are called upon first for this assistance. See RSA 547:2-a.

55 RSA 547:15. Again, the preference for substitutes will go to the full-time judges. See RSA 547:2-a.

56 RSA 547:18.

57 See RSA 547:16, 547:18, and 547:18-a.

In two of the three situations in which an acting judge may be appointed (when the judge of the county recuses himself or herself or is absent or unable to attend), he or she is specifically granted the power to make all orders which the absent judge could make. See RSA 547:15 and 19. In the third situation (when the office is vacant), it must be assumed that the acting judge also possesses all the powers of the regular judge in the county. See RSA 547:18-a.

case has been approved for transfer, the transferring court will forward "authenticated" copies of all pertinent records to the receiving court.[58]

The court has discretion whether to allow any tape recordings of the proceedings.[59] However, official court reporters can make voice recordings to help discharge their official duties.[60] Normally, a stenographic record will be made at the expense of the party or parties requesting it, but the court has discretion to assess the costs differently, including requiring the state to pay the cost of making a stenographic record if a party cannot afford it or if other "good cause" appears.[61]

All proceedings brought into the probate court are begun by petition.[62] Each petition is addressed to the judge of probate and must "briefly [set] forth the ground of the application"[63] and contain the name of the attorney filing the same.[64] The judges of probate have approved a general petition form that can be used in all cases, and various special forms that may be used in particular matters.[65] Blank petitions and other forms can be obtained from the register of each county.[66] The judge of probate also has authority to begin a proceeding on his or her own motion by citation to a fiduciary "requiring such fiduciary to appear before him to inform the court concerning any matters relating to his trust over which the court has jurisdiction."[67]

Certain matters may be disposed of without notice to any party, other than the petitioner.[68] In all other cases, either a citation or an order of notice must

---

58 Prob. Ct. R. 21.
59 Prob. Ct. R. 15, which incorporates Super Ct. R. 78 regarding photographing, recording and broadcasting court proceedings.
60 Prob. Ct. R. 15.
61 RSA 547:31 and 32; Prob. Ct. R. 15.
62 RSA 550:1. See also Prob. Ct. R. 22.
63 RSA 550:1.
64 Prob. Ct. R. 3.
65 RSA 547:33; Prob. Ct. R. 22.
66 Prob. Ct. R. 22.
67 RSA 550:2.
68 These are set forth in RSA 550:4 as follows:

> (I) In the probate of wills in common form, (II) in the appointment of the person entitled to such trust or of the person by him appointed as administrator, (III) in the appointment of appraisers of estates, (IV) in licensing the sale of personal estates, (V) in licensing the sale of real estate whenever the heirs at law or devisees consent thereto in writing or it is of less than $500 in value, (VI) in the appointment of commissioners of insolvent estates, (VII) in the appointment of guardians of minors, (VIII) in granting allowances to widows, (IX) in the assignment of the homestead right, (X) in making orders

be issued, directing either the respondent or interested parties to appear at a hearing.[69] The requirements of service vary depending upon the nature of the citation or order. In the case of citations or orders requiring a person to perform a duty, service of a certified copy must be made in hand, or by leaving a copy at the respondent's abode, if he or she lives in New Hampshire.[70] A certified copy of all citations and orders of notice directed to persons residing out-of-state, or to widows, heirs, devisees, legatees, creditors, or persons interested in an estate, may be served in the same fashion or may be published.[71] Notice of the filing of any account and the date by which objections must be made is sent by registered or certified mail, return receipt requested to any person beneficially interested.[72]

The judge may also order such additional notice as "he shall deem proper in the case."[73] Whenever a party has filed an Appearance in a case, notice by regular mail, sent to the address in the Appearance, is sufficient.[74] Service by publication is usually made by publishing in a newspaper which circulates in the town or city where the decedent last resided,[75] but the judge may order that notice be published in some other fashion.[76] Notices are published in English language newspapers.[77] Publication must be at least once during each of two successive weeks, the last publication being at least fourteen

---

for suits upon probate bonds, (XI) in changing the names of persons, (XII) in the appointment of trustees named in wills, (XIII) in licensing the mortgage of real estate pursuant to RSA 554:30 35, (XIV) in allowing the payment of a sum not exceeding $500 for the perpetual care of a cemetery lot and the monuments thereon where the decedent is buried, and (XV) when an accounting is filed by a guardian who is a parent or a person standing *in loco parentis* to a minor having his home with such guardian.

69 RSA 550:5. See also Prob. Ct. R. 19 (personal service) and 9 (notice of motion hearings).

70 RSA 550:6.

71 RSA 550:7. See Prob. Ct. R. 19.

72 RSA 550:11. The term "person beneficially interested in an account" includes heirs or distributees of an estate, residuary legatees, wards, beneficiaries with a vested interest in a trust, and the Attorney General (in the case of a charitable trust). RSA 550:12.

73 RSA 550:8.

74 RSA 550:9; Prob. Ct. R. 4.

75 RSA 550:10; Prob. Ct. R. 19. The Rule has been changed to allow publication in a newspaper of general circulation "in the area" rather than "town or city" where the party last resided.

76 RSA 550:10; Prob. Ct. R. 19.

77 RSA 550:10. The statutes allow publication in a newspaper in another language so long as the same notice is simultaneously published in an English language paper.

days before the event.[78] Service by publication must be supported by registered or certified mail service on a "near relative" or "some friend" of the person to be notified.[79]

One notice may relate to more than one estate, but each separate subject matter must be separately set out. Notice by publication is arranged by the register in the register's name, but a party must pay the cost of publication in advance.[80] Any person may waive, in writing, the right to receive any citation or notice to which he or she is otherwise entitled.[81]

Notice of any decree in contested matters is sent by register to "all interested parties or their counsel."[82] The notice must contain a letter of transmittal and a copy of the decree.[83] The findings of the judge of probate are reviewable by the Supreme Court.[84]

Library References

CJS Courts §§ 298–310

§ 1.13. Statutory Courts—The Former Municipal Court System

The former municipal court system was created in 1915, and under the original system each town and city with a population of 2,000 or more was given a municipal court, and all other towns could establish one if they desired. This system left a number of smaller towns without their own courts and threw the burden for cases arising in those towns onto the larger towns and cities. Following a recommendation of the Judicial Council, the Legislature abandoned the municipal court system in favor of a new system of district courts.[85] This act abolished all municipal courts which were not

---

78   RSA 550:10; Prob. Ct. R. 19(4).

79   Prob. Ct. R. 19(4).

80   RSA 550:10. See also Prob. Ct. R. 19(4).

81   RSA 550:13; Prob. Ct. R. 9.

82   Prob. Ct. R. 40.

83   *Id.*

84   RSA 567-A:4 ("The findings of fact of the judge of probate are final unless they are so plainly erroneous that such findings could not be reasonably made."); In re Estate of Buttrick, 134 N.H. 675, 597 A.2d 74 (1991) (the Supreme Court will review the judge's findings to see if they could be reasonably made given the testimony).

85   Chapter 331, Laws of 1963. In recommending the abolition of existing municipal courts in favor of a system of district courts, the Judicial Council pointed to "constant criticism of the municipal courts . . . from parties to both criminal and civil proceedings" stemming from the lack of legal training of many judges (two-thirds were not lawyers in 1956), poor court organization, lack of uniformity in sentencing, "ineptness of individual justices and the occasional failure to observe the high standards which should

either converted to district courts under the legislation, or continued by a vote of the town at or prior to the 1964 annual town meeting.[86] The act provided that any municipal court that continued would be abolished upon the occurrence of a vacancy in the office of the justice.[87]

The municipal courts, like the district courts, were courts of record, and unlike the superior court, which is regarded as a single court even though its justices sit separately and simultaneously in ten counties, the various municipal courts were regarded as separate tribunals. For some purposes, the municipal courts and the district courts were interchangeable forums.

Originally, each municipal court was authorized to have a justice and a special justice[88] to act in the "absence, inability or disqualification of the Justice."[89] Each municipal court had to have a clerk.[90] The clerk was appointed by and served at the pleasure of the justice.[91] In the absence of the clerk, the justice, or in his absence, the special justice, acted as clerk.[92] Juvenile services officers[93] and adult probation and parole officers[94] were assigned to geographical regions and judicial districts within the state consistent with the workload formula established for the respective positions.

---

govern the performance of judicial duties," lack of suitable courtrooms, and the large number of courts. N.H. Judicial Council, 6th Report (1956), p. 16. The Judicial Council concluded that the "numerous courts under the system impaired rather than improved the administration of justice at the local level" and that "improvement can be had through fewer and better organized courts." N.H. Judicial Council, 6th Report (1956), pp. 16 and 17.

86 Chapter 331:1, Laws of 1963, now set forth in RSA 502-A:35, abolished all municipal courts absent an affirmative vote of the town. The same Act also terminated the terms of all special justices sitting as of June 30, 1964, unless the town voted to continue the court, in which case the terms of justices were to last as long as the courts.

87 RSA 502-A:35(III) provided that each municipal court would be abolished upon a vacancy of a justice who was sitting as of June 30, 1964. However, RSA 502:1 was, for some reason, left in place. That section authorizes the Governor and Council to appoint a special justice.

88 RSA 502:1, 502:5, and 502:6.

89 RSA 502:5.

90 RSA 502:10. The duties of the clerk are set forth in RSA 502:14.

91 RSA 502:10.

92 RSA 502:5 and 502:10.

93 RSA 170-G:15. The powers and duties of juvenile services officers are set forth in RSA 170-G:16.

94 RSA 504-A:11. The powers and duties of adult probation and parole officers are set forth in RSA 504-A:12.

All municipal courts met every week,[95] and all were required to hold a session for the trial of civil cases at least once a month.[96] Although the municipal courts were customarily held in the towns in which they served, the presiding justice could hold a session in any place in the county when he believed justice required it.[97] No record was made of hearings in the municipal courts unless one of the parties employed a stenographer.[98] Municipal courts had "the powers of the Justice of the Peace and quorum" throughout the state.[99]

The Greenville Municipal Court remains a vestige of the past, the final court in the municipal court system. Justice Taft is the justice of the Greenville Municipal Court, and if he serves until the constitutional limitation has been reached, the court will be abolished on May 19, 2000. Until abolished, the Greenville Municipal Court will continue to share its jurisdiction with the district court for the district in which it sits.

The Greenville Municipal Court meets weekly,[100] and is required to hold a session for the trial of civil cases at least once a month.[101] Sessions are customarily held in Greenville; however, Justice Taft may hold a session at any place in the county if justice requires.[102]

Library References

CJS Courts § 276

§ 1.14. —The District Court System

The district court system is a more comprehensive scheme of lower level courts of record than was the municipal court system. Under this plan the

---

95 This was the practice until Dist. and Mun. Ct. R. 1.12 was changed to provide that sessions would be scheduled "pursuant to guidelines promulgated by the Supreme Court."

96 RSA 502:29; Dist. and Mun. Ct. R. 3.12(A).

97 RSA 502:31.

98 Dist. and Mun. Ct. R. 1.18. See Super. Ct. R. 93-B; Dist. and Mun. Ct. R. 1.19 (requiring transcripts if sound recordings are to be used as evidence in appeals to the superior court).

99 RSA 502:18.

100 RSA 502:29; Dist. and Mun. Ct. R. 3.12(A).

101 RSA 502:29.

102 RSA 502:31.

state has been divided into "districts" and each district has been given its own court.[103] Each town, city, and unincorporated place falls within the

---

103 Auburn District Court, Berlin-Gorham District Court, Claremont-Newport District Court, Colebrook District Court, Concord District Court, Derry District Court, Dover-Sommersworth-Durham District Court, Franklin District Court, Goffstown District Court, Hampton-Exeter District Court, Hanover-Lebanon District Court, Haverhill District Court, Henniker-Hillsborough District Court, Hooksett District Court, Jaffrey-Peterborough District Court, Keene District Court, Laconia District Court, Lancaster District Court, Littleton District Court, Manchester District Court, Merrimack District Court, Milford District Court, Nashua District Court, New London District Court, District Court for Northern Carroll County, Pittsfield District Court, Plaistow District Court, Plymouth-Lincoln District Court, Portsmouth District Court, Rochester District Court, Salem District Court, and the District Court for Southern Carroll County.

The establishment of the district court system in 1963 was supposed to consolidate the hodgepodge of municipal courts into a "comprehensive system of judicial districts," each with its own court. But no sooner had the ink dried on the bill, than the towns left without a home court began lobbying to have one. Bills proposing the establishment of a district court in Hooksett, Epping, Rye, and Seabrook were introduced in the 1965 session. See H.B. 461 (1965 Journal of the House 329); H.B. 441 and 442 (1965 Journal of the House 306); H.B. 559 (1965 Journal of the House 481). In 1967, Epping tried again, and bills to create district courts in Bristol, New London, and Meredith were also introduced. See S.B. 41 (1967 Journal of the Senate 39 and Journal of the House 854); H.B. 400 (1967 Journal of the House 336); H.B. 545 (1967 Journal of the House 542); H.B. 384 (1967 Journal of the House 324). None of these efforts succeeded.

The pressure increased in 1969, when a total of nine bills were introduced, proposing the formation of district courts in New London, Seabrook, Rye, Meredith, Sunapee, Bristol, Lincoln, and Farmington. See S.B. 49 (1969 Journal of the Senate 40); H.B. 69 (1969 Journal of the House 48); H.B. 138 (1969 Journal of the House 55); H.B. 491 (1969 Journal of the House 497); H.B. 174 (1969 Journal of the House 75); S.B. 175 (1969 Journal of the Senate 324); S.B. 313 (1969 Journal of the Senate 768); H.B. 294 (1969 Journal of the House 224); S.B. 276 (1969 Journal of the Senate 584). Two of these efforts succeeded, and the New London District Court and Lincoln District Court were established in the summer of that year. See Chapters 110 and 167, Laws of 1969.

In 1971, proposals for seven additional District Courts were introduced leading the Judicial Council to remark that "this proliferation of district courts in the absence of a compelling reason for their establishment is a backwards step which will result in an emasculation of the system as originally conceived." N.H. Judicial Council, 13th Report, 1970, p. 25. The Judicial Council suggested, as an alternative, that RSA 502-A be amended to require certain existing district courts to hold regular weekly sessions in additional towns within their districts. The proposal was intended to confirm "the feeling of the council that the purpose of the establishment of the district court system is to provide the minimum number of courts which will adequately serve the convenience of the public, both transient and permanent residents of the State of New Hampshire." N.H. Judicial Council, 13th Report, p. 27. The Legislature adopted most of the Judicial Council's proposal (see RSA 502-A:2), relenting just enough to create two more district courts in Hooksett and Merrimack (see RSA 502:1(XIII), (XX)). At the same time, it imposed restraints upon its ability to create new district courts in the future. Under a new provision, no new District Court can be established unless: (1) the proposal has been referred by one regular session to the Judicial Council and the Judicial Council has reported its approval to the next regular session; and (2) the proposed courtrooms have been rated "accredited-excellent" by the court accreditation commission. RSA 502-A:1-a. Since the enactment of this provision, the Pittsfield District Court

territorial limits of a specific court. There are presently thirty-four district courts in operation in New Hampshire.[104]

Each district court has a justice, a special justice[105] and a clerk.[106] The Manchester, Keene, Nashua, and Concord District Courts also have an associate justice,[107] and all district courts may have a deputy clerk[108] and may appoint juvenile intake officers.[109] Juvenile services officers[110] and adult probation and parole officers[111] are assigned to each judicial district consistent with the workload formula established for the respective positions. The

---

has been created, a further regular session in Epping has been required of the Exeter District Court in 1975 (see chapter 248, Laws of 1975) and Madbury has been moved from the Dover to the Durham District in 1983. Chapter 82, Laws of 1983.

In 1985, the requirement of a regular session in Epping was repealed. Chapter 315, Laws of 1985. In 1987, RSA 502-A:2 was amended to allow a discontinuation of regular sessions in other towns, "if, upon a written request by the town following the mandate of the local legislative body and written agreement between the court and the governing body of the town, it is determined that such sessions are no longer required for the effective administration of justice." In 1991, the requirement of regular sessions in Auburn and Northwood was repealed.

104 RSA 502-A:1. Many of the original district courts were comprised of former municipal courts sitting in the same town or city.

105 RSA 502-A:3. There has been a freeze on district court appointments since 1993. RSA 502-A:3.

106 RSA 502-A:7. The duties of the clerk are also set forth in Dist. and Mun. Ct. R. 1.16, 1.17, 3.5, 3.21, and 3.23.

107 RSA 502-A:3-a. Chapter 253, Laws of 1992, which combines several judicial districts, provides that justices and special justices of the preexisting courts shall continue to serve as justices or special justices of the newly created district. A presiding justice shall be designated. If there is a full-time justice, that justice shall serve as the presiding justice. Otherwise, the senior justice shall serve as the presiding justice. RSA 502-A:3-b. Upon retirement, resignation, disability, or removal of a justice or special justice, the position is eliminated until there is one justice and special justice remaining in each district. RSA 502-A:3-b. The districts affected are: Berlin-Gorham, Claremont-Newport, Dover-Sommersworth-Durham, Hampton-Exeter, Hanover-Lebanon, Henniker-Hillsborough, Jaffrey-Peterborough, Plymouth-Lincoln, and the District Court for Southern Carroll County.

108 RSA 502-A:7-b and 502-A:8.

109 RSA 502-A:8-a. "The juvenile intake officer shall schedule and attend juvenile proceedings, maintain juvenile court records, collect fines, monitor temporary and final orders to insure compliance, and perform such other tasks as the court may require." RSA 502-A:8-b.

110 RSA 170-G:15. The powers and duties of juvenile services officers are set forth in RSA 170-G:16.

111 RSA 504-A:11. The powers and duties of adult probation and parole officers are set forth in RSA 504-A:12.

associate justices "have the same . . . powers as . . . the justice"[112] and sit on a case in place of the justice and in preference to the special justice. The special justice acts in the "absence, inability or disqualification" of the justice and the associate justice, if any.[113] If the justice, associate justice and special justice are all unable to sit, the justice may request in writing that "a member of the Bar of New Hampshire who is a disinterested justice of the peace" residing in the district, or a "disinterested justice or special justice from another district court"[114] act in his stead. The special justice performs the duties of the clerk if the offices of both clerk and deputy clerk are vacant.[115]

The Supreme Court, after due consideration of all relevant factors such as judicial economy and efficiency and convenience to the public, is author-ized to designate one or more district courts to be regional jury trial courts to hear and to determine civil cases.[116] If jurisdictional requirements are met and if a timely request for a jury trial is made, the case shall be transferred to the regional jury trial district court and heard as if originally entered there. Questions of law are appealed directly to the Supreme Court.[117]

Each district court is located in the town or city from which it derives its name and holds a regular daytime session in that town or city at least once a week.[118] District courts in the larger cities and towns are in session every weekday except holidays.[119] Although the district courts must hold at least one civil session each month,[120] few courts regularly devote one day solely to the trial of civil actions.[121] As a matter of practice, civil actions in most district courts are scheduled as frequently as the caseload requires.

---

112 RSA 502-A:3-a.

113 RSA 502-A:4.

114 RSA 502:4 and 502-A:5. The Supreme Court may also designate the full-time justice of another district court to sit. RSA 502-A:21-a.

115 RSA 502-A:4 and 502-A:7.

116 RSA 502-A:15(II) and 502-A:12-a.

117 RSA 502-A:15(II).

118 While this has been the consistent practice for several years, Dist. and Mun. Ct. R. 1.12 has been changed to allow scheduling "pursuant to guidelines promulgated by the Supreme Court." The Jaffrey-Peterborough District Court holds regular sessions in both Jaffrey and Peterborough. RSA 502-A:1(XXII) and (XXV).

119 RSA 502-A:22.

120 RSA 502-A:22; Dist. and Mun. Ct. R. 3.12(A).

121 Hampton District Court sets aside the first Tuesday of each month. Haverhill reserves each Monday.

Each district court must hold regular sessions in the town for which it is named.[122] All district courts may hold special sessions in any place within the district where justice and convenience of the communities would be served,[123] or "where justice and the convenience of the parties may so require."[124] All justices of the district courts must wear judicial robes.[125] The court has the discretion to permit, upon petition, the proceedings to be recorded by use of any device. However, the recordings shall be made at the expense of the party requesting the recordings,[126] and a party must employ a stenographer if one is desired.[127] The district courts also have "the powers of a justice of the peace and the quorum throughout the State."[128]

---

122 See RSA 502-A:l. They may also hold regular night sessions so long as those sessions start by 7:30 PM and conclude by 11 PM Dist. and Mun. Ct. R. 1.12.

123 RSA 502-A:1(VII) (town of Durham) and 502-A:2.

124 RSA 502-A:1 and 502-A:2.

125 RSA 502-A:23.

126 RSA 502-A:27-d.

127 Dist. and Mun. Ct. R. 1.18. But see RSA 503:10 (sound recording in Small Claims Actions) and Super. Ct. R. 93-B and Dist. and Mun. Ct. R. 1.19 (requiring transcripts if sound recordings are to be used as evidence in appeals to the superior court). In the absence of a record, however, the Supreme Court will "assume that the evidence supported the trial court's findings . . . and . . . limit . . . review to legal errors apparent on the face of the record [it has]." Perron v. Aranosian, 128 N.H. 92, 94, 508 A.2d 1087, 1089 (1986); Korpi v. Town of Peterborough, 135 N.H. 37, 599 A.2d 130 (1991).

128 RSA 502-A:11.

Part II

JURISDICTION AND VENUE

CHAPTER 2. PRINCIPLES OF JURISDICTION

§ 2.01. In Personam Jurisdiction—Defined

In personam, or personal, jurisdiction is the attachment of the court's full legal and equitable powers upon the body and property of a person involved in an action. When a New Hampshire court has personal jurisdiction over a party, it may make orders, within the limit of its subject matter jurisdiction and its inherent and statutory powers,[1] that are binding on the party both within and without the state,[2] and on his property within the state.

Library References

In personam jurisdiction under long-arm statute of nonresident banking institution. 9 ALR4th 661.

In personam jurisdiction, in libel and slander action, over nonresident who mailed allegedly defamatory letter from outside state. 83 ALR4th 1006.

CJS Courts § 73

---

1 There is a distinction between the power to act with respect to the parties and subject matter in a case, and the power to enter a wide range of orders resolving the case. Where a statute requires dismissal upon the finding of certain facts, the court has "jurisdiction" over the parties and the subject matter of the dispute, but lacks "jurisdiction" to enter any order other than dismissal. In re Doe, 126 N.H. 719, 495 A.2d 1293 (1985).

2 See Bartlett v. Dumaine, 128 N.H. 497, 523 A.2d 1 (1986) (when a court has personal jurisdiction over the parties, it may require them to take action respecting property existing outside the jurisdiction of the court).

§ 2.02. —Over Persons Resident or Found in New Hampshire

(a) *By Service in Hand.* Personal jurisdiction may be obtained over any person, regardless of where that person resides, by service in hand within the territorial limits of the State of New Hampshire.[3]

(b) *By Abode Service.* Jurisdiction over a person who is domiciled in New Hampshire may also be obtained by leaving an attested copy of the writ or other initial pleading at his abode.[4]

§ 2.03. —Over Persons Not Resident or Found in New Hampshire

(a) *By Long-Arm Statute.* "In the absence of personal service within this State, jurisdiction over a nonresident can only be obtained if the legislature has provided another method of service of process."[5] New Hampshire courts may exercise in personam jurisdiction over nondomiciliaries[6] who cannot be found in the state by service under the Long-Arm Statute.[7] The statute provides:

> Any person who is not an inhabitant of this state and who, in person or through an agent, transacts any business within this state,

---

3 RSA 510:2; Libbey v. Hodgdon, 9 N.H. 394, 396 (1838) ("If a citizen of another state is found here, and process is served on him personally, that gives the court jurisdiction."); M.H. Parsons & Sons Lumber Co. v. Southwick, 101 N.H. 258, 139 A.2d 883 (1958); Rosenblum v. Judson Engineering Corp., 99 N.H. 267, 109 A.2d 558 (1954). But persons who enter New Hampshire for the purpose of being witnesses are exempt from service while going to, attending or returning from a trial. Martin v. Whitney, 74 N.H. 505 (1908).

4 RSA 510:2. See Stankunas v. Stankunas, 133 N.H. 643, 582 A.2d 280 (1990) (citing RSA 458:5: New Hampshire can exercise jurisdiction over the parties where the plaintiff was domiciled in state for one year immediately preceding the filing of the action; RSA 458:6 (jurisdiction concerning divorces)); South Down Recreation Ass'n v. Moran, 141 N.H. 484, 686 A.2d 314 (1996) (abode service for nonresident defendant not proper where writ served an out-of-state abode).

5 Hutchins v. Del Rosso, 116 N.H. 421, 423, 365 A.2d 127, 129 (1976); South Down Recreation Ass'n v. Moran, 141 N.H. 484, 686 A.2d 314 (1996) (Long-Arm Statute did not provide for abode service on non-resident defendants at their abode out-of-state).

6 The question of whether the defendant is a nondomiciliary and may therefore be subjected to a long-arm service is determined as of the date of service, not as of the date of the acts complained of. Kinchla v. Baummer, 114 N.H. 818, 330 A.2d 112 (1974); Bouchard v. Klepacki, 116 N.H. 257, 357 A.2d 463 (1976).

7 RSA 510:4. The Long-Arm Statute applies to causes of action in general. Jurisdiction may also be obtained in specific cases by compliance with special Long-Arm Statutes which apply to the subject matter of the suit (RSA 264:1 (motor vehicle accidents; service on the Director of the Division of Motor Vehicles)) or to particular groups of defendants (RSA 5-A (the so-called "Interpleader Compact"); RSA 458-A (the Uniform Child Custody Jurisdiction Act); RSA 293-A:15.10 (foreign corporation); RSA 402-C:4 (insurance receivership); Mattleman v. Bandler, 123 N.H. 368, 461 A.2d 566 (1983)).

commits a tortious act within this state, or has the ownership, use, or possession of any real or personal property situated in this state submits himself, or his personal representative, to the jurisdiction of the courts of this state as to any cause of action arising from or growing out of the acts enumerated above.[8]

The Long-Arm Statute applies to both equity and law actions.[9] It is a remedial statute and is to "be construed in the broadest legal sense to encompass personal, private and commercial transactions."[10] Under the Long-Arm Statute, "jurisdiction over nonresidents [is] exercised to the full constitutional limit."[11] "This limit is met if the exercise of jurisdiction is reasonable from the standpoint of New Hampshire's interest in the litigation and is consistent with the principles of fair play and substantial justice."[12]

---

8 RSA 510:4(I). See also RSA 293-A:15.10 (service on foreign corporation); RSA 304-C:70 (service on registered foreign limited liability companies); RSA 356-A:19 (service on attorney general under Land Sales Full Disclosure Act); RSA 402-C:4 (jurisdiction over persons served in an action brought by the receiver of a domestic insurer or alien insurer domiciled in New Hampshire); RSA 406-A:5 (service upon unauthorized insurer); RSA 421-B:30, VII–IX (service on secretary of state under securities act).

9 Hutchings v. Lee, 119 N.H. 85, 398 A.2d 68 (1979).

10 Leeper v. Leeper, 114 N.H. 294, 297, 319 A.2d 626, 628 (1974); Hall, Morse, Gallagher & Anderson v. Koch & Koch, 119 N.H. 639, 406 A.2d 962 (1979). Phelps v. Kingston, 130 N.H. 166, 536 A.2d 740 (1987) (stating that the legislature's purpose in enacting the statute was to provide resident plaintiffs a convenient forum in which to sue for injuries attributable to foreign defendants).

11 Leeper v. Leeper, 114 N.H. 294, 296, 319 A.2d 626, 627 (1974). See also Roy v. North America Newspaper Alliance, Inc., 106 N.H. 92, 205 A.2d 844 (1964); Roy v. Transairco, Inc., 112 N.H. 171, 291 A.2d 605 (1972); Hutchings v. Lee, 119 N.H. 85, 398 A.2d 68 (1979); Estabrook v. Wetmore, 129 N.H. 520, 529 A.2d 956 (1987); Phelps v. Kingston, 130 N.H. 166, 536 A. 2d 740 (1987). A determination of the appropriateness of exercising jurisdiction under the Long-Arm Statute requires, first, that the court ascertain that the requirements of the statute have been met and, second, that the court find that exercise of jurisdiction in the case satisfies the constitutional requirements of minimal contact. See Tavoularis v. Womer, 123 N.H. 423, 462 A.2d 110 (1983); Weld Power Industries, Inc. v. C.S.I. Technologies, Inc., 124 N.H. 121, 467 A.2d 568 (1983); Altshuler Genealogical Service v. Farris, 128 N.H. 98, 508 A.2d 1091 (1986); Brother Records Inc. v. Harper Collins Publishers, 141 N.H. 322, 682 A.2d 714 (1996).

12 Engineering Associates of New England, Inc. v. B & L Liquidating Corporation, 115 N.H. 508, 511, 345 A.2d 900, 902 (1975); Altshuler Genealogical Service v. Farris, 128 N.H. 98, 508 A.2d 1091 (1986); Phelps v. Kingston, 130 N.H. 166, 536 A.2d 740 (1987).

    With regard to torts,

        RSA 510:4 subjects a non-resident defendant, whose out-of-state conduct has allegedly resulted in a tort in New Hampshire, to the jurisdiction of the New Hampshire courts when the impact in New Hampshire of the out-of-state conduct was more than fortuitous, so that the defendant knew or should

In applying this two-part test, the Supreme Court has determined that the following facts are significant:[13]

(1) New Hampshire's interest in the litigation:

(A) "Whether the defendant is a resident of a State which would take jurisdiction if the roles of plaintiff and defendant were reversed."[14]

(B) "Whether the statute of limitations has expired in all other forums."[15]

(C) "Whether another forum exists."[16]

(D) "Avoidance of dual trials."[17]

(E) Whether the defendant's residence or place of business lies at a great distance from the New Hampshire court.[18]

(F) Whether New Hampshire has a "significant interest in affording . . . a forum in which to litigate the question" involved in the case.[19]

---

have known his conduct could injure a person here. When a non-resident defendant performs allegedly tortious acts in New Hampshire, little doubt clouds a finding that New Hampshire has jurisdiction.

Estabrook v. Wetmore, 129 N.H. 520, 529 A.2d 956 (1987).

The standard of RSA 510:4 with regard to transacting business in the state is met when "the entire business enterprise was dependent upon the assistance of New Hampshire law." Town of Haverhill v. City Bank & Trust Co., 119 N.H. 409, 412–13, 402 A.2d 185, 188 (1979). That test is, in turn, satisfied if the defendant "purposely avails itself of the privilege of conducting activities" in New Hampshire as, for example, when it seeks and finds a market for its products in the state or when the plaintiff's activities are limited to New Hampshire and the case may most conveniently be tried here. Roy v. Transairco, Inc., 112 N.H. 171, 177, 291 A.2d 605, 608 (1972). The test of convenience is the same as applied in considering motions to dismiss on the ground of forum non conveniens. Phelps v. Kingston, 130 N.H. 166, 536 A.2d 740 (1987) (suggesting that courts may look to "the burden on the defendant," "the forum State's interest in adjudicating the dispute, " "the plaintiff's interest in obtaining convenient and effective relief," "the interstate judicial system's interest in obtaining the most efficient resolution of controversies," and "the shared interest of the several States in furthering fundamental substantive social policies." 130 N.H. at 172, 536 A.2d at 743). But see Kibby v. Anthony Industries, Inc., 123 N.H. 272, 459 A.2d 293 (1983) (the action must arise from the same facts as the exercise of personal jurisdiction).

13 For a summary of these aspects of the test, see Pono v. Brock, 119 N.H. 814, 816–17, 408 A.2d 419, 420–21 (1979). See also Phelps v. Kingston, 130 N.H. 166, 536 A.2d 740 (1987).

14 See Camire v. Scieszka, 116 N.H. 281, 358 A.2d 397 (1976); Forbes v. Boynton, 113 N.H. 617, 313 A.2d 129 (1973).

15 See Rocca v. Kenney, 117 N.H. 1057, 381 A.2d 330 (1977); Camire v. Scieszka, 116 N.H. 281, 358 A.2d 397 (1976).

16 See Camire v. Scieszka, 116 N.H. 281, 358 A.2d 397 (1976).

17 See Camire v. Scieszka, 116 N.H. 281, 358 A.2d 397 (1976); Phelps v. Kingston, 130 N.H. 166, 536 A.2d 740 (1987).

18 Phelps v. Kingston, 130 N.H. 166, 536 A.2d 740 (1987) (defendant's office was in Eliot, Maine, and the action was to be tried in Exeter, New Hampshire).

19 Phelps v. Kingston, 130 N.H. 166, 536 A.2d 740 (1987) (recovery for personal injuries resulting from medical malpractice).

(2) Defendant's minimum contacts with the state:[20]

(A) "Whether the defendant has ever 'set foot' in the state."[21]

(B) "Whether the defendant has ever committed an act the consequences of which would foreseeably injure a resident of New Hampshire."[22]

(C) "Whether defendant has ever invoked the benefits and protections of the State."[23]

(D) Whether the defendant "has 'purposely directed' the activities which are involved in the litigation at residents" of the state.[24]

(E) Whether the defendant has directed "substantial" contacts at residents of the state, even though the litigation in question "does not 'arise out of or relate to'" those contacts.[25]

20

> [T]he United States Supreme Court has frequently stated that the minimum contacts inquiry is best informed by asking whether the defendant's "conduct and connection with the forum State are such that he should reasonably anticipate being haled into court there." (World-Wide Volkswagen Corp. v. Woodson, 44 U.S. 286, 297 (1980)). The Supreme Court has further elucidated this inquiry by stating that, where the litigation in question arises out of or relates to the defendant's forum contacts, the minimum contacts requirement is satisfied provided the defendant "has 'purposefully directed' his activities at residents of the forum." . . . (Burger King v. Rudzewicz, 471 U.S. 462, 472 (1985)). However, even where the litigation does not "arise out of or relate to" forum contacts, those contacts directed at New Hampshire citizens may satisfy due process for jurisdictional purposes provided they are substantial.

Phelps v. Kingston, 130 N.H. 166, 171, 536 A.2d 740, 743 (1987).

21 See Rocca v. Kenney, 117 N.H. 1057, 381 A.2d 330 (1977); Camire v. Scieszka, 116 N.H. 281, 358 A.2d 397 (1976).

22 See Hall, Morse, Gallagher & Anderson v. Koch & Koch, 119 N.H. 639, 406 A.2d 962 (1979); Phelps v. Kingston, 130 N.H. 166, 536 A.2d 740 (1987) ("Many courts have held that in personam jurisdiction over a foreign defendant in tort suits does not offend due process merely because the injury alone occurred in the forum State. Due process concerns may be satisfied provided that it was reasonably foreseeable that the consequences of the defendant's out-of-state activities would manifest themselves in the forum." 130 N.H. at 173, 536 A.2d at 743). See also Tavoularis v. Womer, 123 N.H. 423, 462 A.2d 110 (1983).

23 Hall, Morse, Gallagher & Anderson v. Koch & Koch, 119 N.H. 639, 406 A.2d 962 (1979). See Altshuler Genealogical Service v. Farris, 128 N.H. 98, 508 A.2d 1091 (1986).

24 Phelps v. Kingston, 130 N.H. 166, 536 A.2d 740 (1987) ("[W]here litigation relates to the defendant's activities purposely directed at the forum State, the sufficiency of these activities or contacts reasonably to forewarn him of the possibility of suit in the forum, weighed in combination with other factors relevant to affording substantial justice, will determine whether the State may constitutionally exercise personal jurisdiction over the defendant." 130 N.H. at 172, 536 A.2d at 743).

25 Phelps v. Kingston, 130 N.H. 166, 536 A.2d 740 (1987).

Applying this two-part test, the Supreme Court has upheld the assertion of jurisdiction over nonresident corporations, which neither had an office nor were registered to do business in New Hampshire, but which: had made sales representation agreements for the solicitation of business in New Hampshire;[26] had sold copyrighted columns to a newspaper in-state;[27] or had entered into escrow agreements outside of New Hampshire which were to be performed in part in New Hampshire.[28] The Court has also sustained the exercise of jurisdiction over nonresident individuals[29] who had maintained property in and regularly visited the state,[30] who had personally engaged in tortious acts in whole[31] or in part[32] within the state,[33] and who had responsibility for the content of an allegedly libelous book sold within the state.[34]

---

26 Engineering Associates of New England, Inc., v. B&L Liquidating Corporation, 115 N.H. 508, 345 A.2d 900 (1975).

27 Roy v. North American Newspaper Alliance, 106 N.H. 92, 205 A.2d 844 (1964).

28 Town of Haverhill v. City Bank & Trust Co., 119 N.H. 409, 402 A.2d 185 (1979) ("The applicability of RSA 300:14 does not depend upon performance on the part of the defendant in this State, but may rest upon performance in New Hampshire by any party to the contract." 119 N.H. at 411, 402 A.2d at 187). See also Cove-Craft Industries, Inc. v. B. L. Armstrong Co., Ltd., 120 N.H. 195, 412 A.2d 1028 (1980). But see Benson v. Brattleboro Retreat, 103 N.H. 28, 164 A.2d 560 (1960), where the court declined to exercise jurisdiction over a foreign corporation on a tort claim arising out of state when the foreign corporation's only contacts with the state were the sale of a tract of land before the tort occurred and the convening of three meetings of its board of directors in state. The Court characterized these contacts as "tenuous at best." 103 N.H. at 29, 164 A.2d at 561.

29 Leeper v. Leeper, 114 N.H. 294, 319 A.2d 626 (1974). Long-arm jurisdiction extends to natural persons as well as to corporations.

30 Williams v. Williams, 121 N.H. 728, 433 A.2d 1316 (1981). See also Duford v. Duford, 119 N.H. 115, 403 A.2d 431 (1979).

31 Property Owner's Association at Suissevale, Inc. v. Sholley, 111 N.H. 363, 284 A.2d 915 (1971); Hutchings v. Lee, 119 N.H. 85, 398 A.2d 68 (1979); Leeper v. Leeper, 114 N.H. 294, 319 A.2d 626 (1974).

32 Hall, Morse, Gallagher & Anderson v. Koch & Koch, 119 N.H. 639, 406 A.2d 962 (1979); Tavoularis v. Womer, 123 N.H. 423, 462 A.2d 110 (1983); Phelps v. Kingston, 130 N.H. 166, 536 A.2d 740 (1987) (acts of medical malpractice occurred in Maine, but the effects of that malpractice developed and were felt in New Hampshire).

33 Estabrook v. Wetmore, 129 N.H. 520, 529 A.2d 956 (1987) (Allowing the exercise of long-arm jurisdiction to compel a nonresident officer of a nonresident corporation to respond personally in a co-employee suit under the Workers' Compensation Law, when the officer's "own acts for the corporation are the alleged cause of the injury . . . so long as the pleadings show that the officer knew or should have known his conduct could have a direct, substantial effect in New Hampshire." 129 N.H. at 526, 529 A.2d at 960).

34 Brother Records, Inc. v. Harper Collins Publishers, 141 N.H. 322, 682 A.2d 714 (1996).

CJS Courts §§ 73–79

In personam jurisdiction over nonresident manufacturer or seller under "long-arm" statutes. 19 ALR3d 13.

In personam jurisdiction over nonresident director of foreign corporation under "long-arm" statutes. 100 ALR3d 1108.

In personam jurisdiction over nonresident based on ownership, use, possession, or sale of real property. 4 ALR4th 1176.

Religious activities as doing or transaction of business under "long-arm" statutes or rules of court. 26 ALR4th 1176.

Place where claim or cause of action "arose" under state statute. 53 ALR4th 1104.

Execution, outside of forum, of guaranty of obligations under contract to be performed within forum state as conferring jurisdiction over nonresident guarantors under "long-arm" statute or rule of forum. 28 ALR5th 664.

§ 2.04. Quasi in Rem Jurisdiction—Defined

Quasi in rem jurisdiction gives the court power to determine the personal rights and obligations of a party, but limits satisfaction of the resulting judgment to a particular piece of property or right to payment[35] which is subject to the court's control. Although it is possible to obtain quasi in rem jurisdiction in a case in which personal jurisdiction could also be obtained, there is rarely any reason to do so because a judgment based on in personam jurisdiction is preferable to that limited to one asset and the absence of a defendant from the state is a common ground for permitting the attachment of his property at the beginning of an action in personam.

CJS Courts §§ 23, 43

§ 2.05. —Standards for Quasi in Rem Jurisdiction

(a) *In General.*   The test for exercising quasi in rem jurisdiction is in all respects the same as for acquiring personal jurisdiction under the Long-Arm Statute.[36] However, a decision that in personam jurisdiction cannot be

---

35 Obligations to defend and pay under liability insurance policies (see Forbes v. Boynton, 113 N.H. 617, 313 A.2d 129 (1973); Camire v. Scieszka, 116 N.H. 281, 358 A.2d 397 (1976); Ahern v. Hough, 116 N.H. 302, 358 A.2d 394 (1976); Rocca v. Kenney, 117 N.H. 1057, 381 A.2d 330 (1977); Pono v. Brock, 119 N.H. 814, 408 A.2d 419 (1979)) and the right to receive payment of a contingent fee from an out-of-court settlement of a case brought in New Hampshire (Hall, Morse, Gallagher & Anderson v. Koch & Koch, 119 N.H. 639, 406 A.2d 962 (1979)) have been held to be attachable property upon which the exercise of quasi in rem jurisdiction may be based.

36 Camire v. Scieszka, 116 N.H. 281, 358 A.2d 397 (1976) ("The *quasi in rem* jurisdiction is best analyzed in terms of the two-pronged test this court has applied in the context of *in personam* jurisdiction. 'First, the exercise of jurisdiction has to be reasonable from the standpoint of New Hampshire's interest in the litigation. Second, it has to be

asserted does not preclude a later finding that quasi in rem jurisdiction can be, if the case was begun by attachment,[37] because attachment of property in the state may form an additional basis for concluding that the "minimum contacts" test has been met.[38] Because the personal rights and obligations of the out-of-state defendant are being litigated in both situations, the fact that in one case the satisfaction of the judgment is limited to specified property should not affect whether it is reasonable and fair for a New Hampshire court to determine the claim.

(b) *Of Insurance Policies.* Perhaps the most common basis for the assertion of quasi in rem jurisdiction is the attachment of the obligations of defense and payment arising to the defendant under a liability insurance policy issued by a company doing business and maintaining an office in New Hampshire where the incident giving rise to liability occurred in another state, and the defendant is not a New Hampshire resident. "[T]he underlying test in allowing the attachment of automobile insurance policies as a basis for *quasi in rem* jurisdiction [is] that of providing a forum for resident plaintiffs injured in out-of-state accidents."[39] The attachment of the

---

consistent with the principles of fair play and substantial justice.' " 116 N.H. at 281, 358 A. 2d at 399); Shaffer v. Heitner, 433 U.S. 186 (1977); Pono v. Brock, 119 N.H. 814, 408 A.2d 419 (1979); Hall, Morse, Gallagher & Anderson v. Koch & Koch, 119 N.H. 639, 406 A.2d 962 (1979) ("It is 'the relationship among the defendant, the forum, and the litigation' that controls whether a State can assert jurisdiction over a nonresident. . . . In evaluating that relationship, we examine this State's interest in providing a forum for the resolution of the dispute . . ., and a review of the nonresidents' 'forum-related activities as they relate to the specific cause of action.' " 119 N.H. at 645, 406 A.2d at 965). See also Altshuler Genealogical Service v. Farris, 128 N.H. 98, 508 A.2d 1091 (1986).

37 Hall, Morse, Gallagher & Anderson v. Koch & Koch, 119 N.H. 639, 406 A.2d 962 (1979). Every action against a nondomiciliary should begin, if possible, with an attachment, because the attachment, if allowed, will support the claim for personal jurisdiction. As RSA 511-A:8(II) permits an ex parte attachment when the plaintiff can establish his probable right to recovery and when it is "necessary to vest quasi in rem jurisdiction of the court," in theory at least, it should be possible to commence every action against a nondomiciliary with an ex parte attachment of any property, including rights under a liability insurance policy, which he holds in New Hampshire. But see Travelers Indemnity Co. v. Abreem Corp., 122 N.H. 583, 449 A.2d 1200 (1982) (where quasi in rem jurisdiction was denied when both parties were nonresidents and the sole contact with New Hampshire was the location of the property attached); Altshuler Genealogical Service v. Farris, 128 N.H. 98, 508 A.2d 1091 (1986).

38 "However, there must also be sufficient contacts between the defendant and the forum State to satisfy the requirements of due process. . . . The attachable res itself is not enough to constitute minimum contacts." Altshuler Genealogical Service v. Farris, 128 N.H. 98, 101, 508 A.2d 1091, 1094 (1986).

39 Pono v. Brock, 119 N.H. 814, 816, 408 A.2d 419, 420 (1979); Forbes v. Boynton, 113 N.H. 617, 313 A.2d 129 (1973).

insurance policy "provides at least one contact between the defendant and the forum State,"[40] but it is not, in itself, sufficient to justify the exercise of jurisdiction.[41] The Supreme Court has refused to allow the exercise of quasi in rem jurisdiction when the defendant has never been to New Hampshire and has no other property in or business contacts with the state,[42] or when the defendant resides in the state where the accident occurred, making that state the preferable forum for a full trial of the issues.[43] The Court has not yet decided whether application of the *Seider* rule[44] by defendant's home state is a prerequisite for the exercise of quasi in rem jurisdiction based on attachment of his insurance policy here,[45] or whether the insurance company issuing the policy which is attached must not only be registered to do business here but also have an office in New Hampshire or write policies in New Hampshire.[46]

Library References

CJS Courts §§ 23, 43
Potential liability of insurer under liability policy as subject of attachment. 33 ALR3d 992.
Extraterritorial application of statute permitting injured person to maintain direct action against tortfeasor's automobile liability insurer. 83 ALR3d 338.

§ 2.06. —Method of Obtaining Quasi in Rem Jurisdiction

Quasi in rem jurisdiction is obtained by attachment of property or a right to payment in New Hampshire. Obligations arising under a liability insurance policy issued by a non–New Hampshire company which is registered to do business but which maintains no office or employees in New Hamp-

---

40 Pono v. Brock, 119 N.H. 814, 817, 408 A.2d 419, 421 (1979).

41 Pono v. Brock, 119 N.H. 814, 817–18, 408 A.2d 419, 421–22 (1979) ("The principles of fair play and substantial justice dictate that when, as here, the defendant has no contacts with the forum other than an insurance policy attachable in New Hampshire, there is insufficient basis for the exercise of *quasi in rem* jurisdiction over the defendant.").

42 Camire v. Scieszka, 116 N.H. 281, 358 A.2d 397 (1976); Pono v. Brock, 119 N.H. 814, 408 A.2d 419 (1979).

43 Ahern v. Hough, 116 N.H. 302, 358 A.2d 394 (1976); Rocca v. Kenney, 117 N.H. 1057, 381 A.2d 330 (1977).

44 Seider v. Roth, 17 N.Y.2d 111 (1966).

45 However, the Court has strongly suggested that it is. See Forbes v. Boynton, 113 N.H. 617, 313 A.2d 129 (1973); Pono v. Brock, 119 N.H. 814, 408 A.2d 419 (1979).

46 In Rocca v. Kenney, 117 N.H. 1057, 381 A.2d 330 (1977), the Court implied, but did not decide, that it must.

shire may be attached by service on the Insurance Commissioner.[47] Attachments that are "necessary to vest *quasi in rem* jurisdiction" may be obtained ex parte if the plaintiff can satisfy the court that the plaintiff will probably be entitled to a verdict or decree in his or her favor after trial.[48]

Library References

CJS Courts §§ 80, 89

§ 2.07. In Rem Jurisdiction—Defined

In rem jurisdiction is the power to determine the rights of claimants in particular property which is subject to the court's control. The personal rights and obligations of the claimants are not subject to the court's power in such a case.[49]

Library References

Suits that may be regarded as in rem or quasi in rem jurisdiction that may rest upon constructive service. 126 ALR 664.
CJS Courts §§ 43, 84

§ 2.08. —Property Subject to the Exercise of in Rem Jurisdiction

Any interest in real,[50] personal,[51] or other property[52] that is recognized in law or equity may be the subject of the exercise of the court's in rem jurisdiction. The residency of the claimants in the property is irrelevant to the existence of the court's power to make decrees respecting title to it.[53] The adjudication of New Hampshire courts "as to all property within the

---

47 RSA 405:10. See Pono v. Brock, 119 N.H. 814, 408 A.2d 419 (1979).

48 RSA 511-A:8(II).

49 See Eastman v. Dearborn, 63 N.H. 364 (1885).

50 Bancroft v. Conant, 64 N.H. 151, 5 A. 836 (1886) (petition to quiet title).

51 Downer v. Shaw, 22 N.H. 277, 280 (1851): "A State may assert jurisdiction over personal property, situated within its territorial limits, though the person or the owner is not within the jurisdiction of the Court which renders the judgment."

52 Minot v. Tilton, 64 N.H. 371, 374, 10 A. 682, 685 (1887) (for assets in a trust) ("By virtue of its jurisdiction over property of nonresidents, within its limits, the state through its tribunals may inquire into the nonresident's obligations to its own citizens to the extent of controlling the disposition of the property, if necessary, the action being in the nature of a proceeding *in rem* when there is no appearance and no service of process on the nonresident."); Robinson v. Carroll, 87 N.H. 114, 174 A. 772 (1934) (a debt is located wherever the creditor has his domicile).

53 Kidd v. New Hampshire Traction Co., 72 N.H. 273, 56 A. 465 (1903); Camire v. Scieszka, 116 N.H. 281, 358 A.2d 397 (1976).

state is final and conclusive upon nonresidents as well as residents, upon such notice as the statutes of the state require."[54]

Library References

Jurisdiction of suit involving trust as affected by location of res, resident of parties to trust, service, and appearance. 15 ALR2d 610.
CJS Courts §§ 84, 89

§ 2.09. —Method of Obtaining in Rem Jurisdiction

Attachment or payment into court is not necessary to the acquisition of in rem jurisdiction.[55] It may, however, be desirable either to assure the continued presence of the property in New Hampshire until judgment is rendered or to establish the plaintiff's priority over other claimants.

Library References

CJS Courts §§ 84, 89

§ 2.10. Conferring Jurisdiction by Consent or Waiver

The parties to an action may, either expressly[56] or by implication,[57] consent to the exercise of personal jurisdiction over them by a court or administrative agency,[58] or to the exercise of quasi in rem or in rem jurisdiction over their property. The parties have no ability, by their consent, to confer jurisdiction over the subject matter of a dispute[59] when that

---

54 Kidd v. New Hampshire Traction Co., 72 N.H. 273, 56 A. 465 (1903).

55 *Id.*

56 Parties who file a General Appearance or a counterclaim (Bartlett v. Dumaine, 128 N.H. 497, 523 A.2d 1 (1986)), who concede in open court (Downer v. Shaw, 22 N.H. 277 (1851)), or who include a choice of forum provision in a contract are considered to have expressly consented to jurisdiction. RSA 508-A. A New Hampshire court will enforce a choice of forum provision if the court possesses subject matter jurisdiction, the contractual term was fairly obtained, the doctrine of forum non conveniens does not apply, and the defendant was served in a manner provided by statute. RSA 508-A:2(I). See also RSA 508-A:3(III), (IV) and (V).

57 By filing a motion to dismiss within 30 days of filing a Special Appearance or by taking some action which converts the Special Appearance to a General Appearance, parties impliedly submit to the jurisdiction of the court. (Merrill v. Houghton, 51 N.H. 61 (1871); Patten v. Patten, 79 N.H. 388 (1920); Lachapelle v. Town of Goffstown, 134 N.H. 478, 593 A.2d 1152 (1991) (filing a motion for late entry of appearance and a motion to strike default is a voluntary submission to the jurisdiction of the court); Barton v. Hayes, 141 N.H. 118, 677 A.2d 694 (1996) (defendant waived personal jurisdiction challenge when she made a general appearance moving to strike default).

58 Jackson & Sons v. Lumbermen's Mutual Casualty Co., 86 N.H. 341, 168 A. 895 (1933).

59 Keenan v. Tonry, 91 N.H. 220, 16 A.2d 705 (1941); Burgess v. Burgess, 71 N.H. 293, 51 A. 1074 (1902); Pokigo v. Local No. 719, International Brotherhood of Electrical

jurisdiction is not otherwise committed to the court or administrative agency.

Library References

Litigant's participation on merits, after objection to jurisdiction made under special appearance or the like has been overruled, as waiver of objection. 62 ALR2d 937.
CJS Courts § 85

§ 2.11. Determining Issues of Jurisdiction—By the Court or Agency

Whether the court or administrative agency has jurisdiction over the parties or property and over the subject matter of the case before it is the first question the court examines in the case.[60] In determining this issue, the well-pleaded allegations of fact in the plaintiff's pleading will be taken as true and construed most favorably to the plaintiff.[61] If it appears that the exercise of jurisdiction in the case is lawful, the court or agency will proceed, unless the defendant raises an objection not previously observed.

Library References

CJS Courts §§ 34, 112

§ 2.12. —Time To Object

An objection to subject matter jurisdiction may be raised at any time[62] and, when raised, interrupts the case and takes precedence over any other

Workers, 106 N.H. 384, 213 A.2d 689 (1965); Hartnett v. Hartnett, 93 N.H. 406, 43 A.2d 153 (1945); Jackson & Sons v. Lumbermen's Mutual Casualty Co., 86 N.H. 341, 168 A. 895 (1933); LaBonte v. City of Berlin, 85 N.H. 89, 154 A. 89 (1931); Burleigh v. Wong Sun Leen, 83 N.H. 115, 139 A. 184 (1927); Manchester Dairy System, Inc. v. Hayward, 82 N.H. 193, 132 A. 12 (1926).

60 Morel v. Marable, 120 N.H. 192, 412 A.2d 747 (1980). The court has a duty to satisfy itself of its power to act in the case, regardless of whether a party objects, and it must, accordingly, examine the issue of jurisdiction on its own motion. See Appeal of Matheisel, 107 N.H. 479, 224 A.2d 832 (1966).

61 Kibby v. Anthony Industries, Inc., 123 N.H. 272, 459 A.2d 293 (1983).

62 Jackson & Sons v. Lumbermen's Mutual Casualty Co., 86 N.H. 341, 168 A. 895 (1933); Boston & Maine Railroad v. State, 77 N.H. 437, 93 A. 306 (1915); State v. Town of Richmond, 26 N.H. 232 (1853).

business.[63] Any other objection to the exercise of jurisdiction is waived if not raised at the earliest possible moment after its discovery.[64]

Library References

Objection before judgment to jurisdiction of court over subject matter as constituting general appearance. 25 ALR2d 833.

Stipulation extending time to answer or otherwise proceed as waiver of objection to jurisdiction for lack of personal service: state cases. 77 ALR3d 841.

CJS Courts §§ 107–111

§ 2.13. —Presumptions

The court or agency's jurisdiction over the subject matter, persons and property involved in the action or proceeding must affirmatively appear and will not be supplied by presumptions.[65] The plaintiff has the burden of

---

63 Patten's Petition, 16 N.H. 277 (1844); Jackson & Sons v. Lumbermen's Mutual Casualty Co., 86 N.H. 341, 168 A. 895 (1933); Morel v. Marable, 120 N.H. 192, 412 A.2d 747 (1980). Just as jurisdiction over subject matter cannot be conferred by consent, so "the right to object to the want of it cannot be lost by acquiescence or neglect." Mansfield v. Holton, 74 N.H. 417, 421, 68 A. 541, 542 (1907). See also Wright v. Cobleigh, 21 N.H. 339 (1850); State v. Richmond, 26 N.H. 232 (1853) ("If private individuals assume to act without any legal authority, or if authorized tribunals or officers proceed to act in cases to which their authority does not extend . . . their proceedings would be merely and absolutely void. Their want of legal authority cannot be supplied. No act or assent of the parties in such a case can confer any jurisdiction . . . . And the exception cannot be waived." 26 N.H. at 239–40); Tebbetts v. Tilton, 31 N.H. 273 (1855); State v. Ricciardi, 81 N.H. 223, 123 A. 606 (1924); LaBonte v. Berlin, 85 N.H. 89, 154 A. 89 (1931); Jackson & Sons v. Lumbermen's Mutual Casualty Co., 86 N.H. 341, 168 A. 895 (1933).

64 Gilmanton v. Ham, 38 N.H. 108 (1859); Warren v. Glynn, 37 N.H. 340 (1858); State v. Richmond, 26 N.H. 232 (1853) ("The party, who has not been duly summoned or notified, is always and everywhere understood to waive his exception, if he appears and suffers a general continuance, or pleads in bar of the action, or in any way submits his case to the judgment of the court, without at once making his objection at the earliest opportunity." 26 N.H. at 242). See Morel v. Marable, 120 N.H. 192, 412 A.2d 747 (1980).

65 Perhaps the sole exception to this rule is that the subject matter jurisdiction of the superior and Supreme Courts is presumed to encompass all rights and claims cognizable in a court of law or equity and, in those cases where it does not appear that special jurisdiction over a case has been conferred on any other tribunal, it will be presumed that the superior and Supreme Courts may hear it. See Wingate v. Haywood, 40 N.H. 437 (1860) ("The jurisdiction of a superior court of common law is to be presumed, unless the contrary appear; and nothing shall be intended to be out of its jurisdiction but that which specially appears to be so"); Flanders v. Atkinson, 18 N.H. 167 (1846); Ellsworth v. Health, 140 N.H. 833, 833, 678 A.2d 138, 140 (1996) (because the right of the parent to custody is protected by the state constitution, "the Superior Court as the court of general jurisdiction has subject matter jurisdiction to determine custody issues between unwed parents, even though the probate court has exclusive jurisdiction to entertain grandparent's petition for custody").

satisfying the court or agency that it has power to act in the premises, and, if the court or agency cannot affirmatively determine that it has such power, it may either require the plaintiff to supply evidence of its power or dismiss the case.[66]

Library References

CJS Courts §§ 96–100

---

[66] This presumption must also be modified somewhat by the recognition that several areas of jurisdiction are now committed, at least in the first instance, to administrative agencies. A court of general jurisdiction may no longer assume that a matter is within its jurisdiction but must examine and determine the question in each case. For instance, the Legislature has vested the Public Employees Labor Relations Board with the subject matter jurisdiction to define the terms of law of public employee's labor relations and its findings of fact are deemed "prima facie lawful and reasonable." Appeal of East Derry Fire Precinct, 137 N.H. 607, 609, 631 A.2d 918, 919 (1993).

CHAPTER 3. SUBJECT MATTER JURISDICTION OF THE NEW HAMPSHIRE COURTS

A. JUSTICES OF THE PEACE, THE SUPREME AND SUPERIOR COURTS

A. *Justices of the Peace, the Supreme and Superior Courts*

§ 3.01. Justices of the Peace

While the Constitution recognizes the existence of justices of the peace, it grants them no specific civil jurisdiction, going no further than to limit the subject matter jurisdiction which the Legislature may give them to jurisdiction over "civil causes, when the damages demanded shall not

35

exceed $100 and title of real estate is not concerned."[1] Civil jurisdiction of justices of the peace was terminated on September 23, 1957.[2] However, in 1986 the Legislature conferred jurisdiction on justices of the peace to examine complaints seeking involuntary admission to or revocation of conditional discharge from mental health facilities and to order compulsory mental examinations.[3]

§ 3.02. The Supreme Court

The Constitution does not grant any particular subject matter jurisdiction to the Supreme Court.[4] However, by recognizing its position at the head of the judiciary, the Constitution implicitly grants it ultimate authority over all the rights and powers which must appertain to the Judicial Branch of state government.[5] Specific subject matter jurisdiction is conferred on the Supreme Court by several statutes. The most general is RSA 490:4, which provides:

> The supreme court shall have general superintendence of all courts of inferior jurisdiction to prevent and correct errors and abuses, including the authority to approve rules of court and prescribe and administer canons of ethics with respect to such courts, shall have exclusive authority to issue writs of error, and may issue writs of certiorari, prohibition, habeas corpus, and all other writs and processes to other courts, to corporations and to individuals, and shall do and perform all the duties reasonably requisite and necessary to be done by a court of final jurisdiction of questions of law and general superintendence of inferior courts.

RSA 490:5 also confers on the Supreme Court the "jurisdiction of all other proceedings and matters to be entered or heard therein by special provisions of law." Following this general grant of authority, the Legislature

---

1 Pt. 2, art. 77. See also RSA 455-A:3.

2 Laws of 1957, ch. 244.

3 RSA 135-C:28(II) and 135-C:51.

4 The duty of the Chief Justice to preside at the trial of impeachment of the Governor (pt. 2, art. 40) and of the Justices of the Court to give their opinion to either house of the Legislature or to the Governor and Council (pt. 2, art. 74) are not actions by the court and thus do not involve the Court's jurisdiction.

5 Pt. 2, art. 72-a. While the Legislature has enacted statutes conferring these powers on the court, they merely confirm the existence of the court's constitutional powers and their repeal would have no effect on the court's jurisdiction.

has established jurisdiction in the Court over a number of appeals,[6] certified questions of law,[7] and administrative functions.[8] In addition, the Legislature has established a procedure for review of many state administrative agency decisions—often referred to as "statutory certiorari"—under RSA ch. 541 and has specifically provided for review under that chapter for a number of cases.[9]

Library References

CJS Courts § 423

Cross References

Appellate review, see Part XVI *infra*.

§ 3.03. The Superior Court

The Constitution states that the superior court shall be "a trial court of general jurisdiction"[10] and further provides that "all causes of marriage, divorce and alimony; and all appeals from the respective judges of probate shall be heard and tried by the superior court until the legislature shall by law make other provision."[11] Subject matter jurisdiction is granted to the superior court by a number of statutes, the most important of which, RSA 491:7, provides:

> The superior court shall take cognizance of civil actions and pleas, real, personal and mixed, according to the course of the common law, except such actions as are required to be brought in the district

---

6 RSA 79-A:9(VI) (appeal from the Board of Tax and Land Appeals under the Current Use Law); 281:37 (appeal from an order of the Superior Court relative to an order of the Labor Commissioner under the Workmen's Compensation Law); 282:5(G) (appeal from an order of the Superior Court relating to an order respecting benefits under the Unemployment Compensation Law).

7 RSA 77:35 (questions of law certified by the Board of Tax and Land Appeals); 78-A:2(III) (questions of law certified by the Commissioner of the Department of Revenue Administration).

8 RSA 71-B:2 (appointment of the members of the Board of Tax and Land Appeals); 292:1-a (approval of the Organization of the Legal Aid Corporation).

9 For a discussion of the procedure to be followed under RSA ch. 541, see Part XVI.

10 Pt. 2, art. 72-a.

11 Pt. 2, art. 76. In 1975, the Legislature did "make other provision" with respect to probate matters, abolishing appeals to the superior court after December 31, 1975, and providing instead for Supreme Court review. See RSA ch. 567-A. If that chapter is ever repealed without provision for a different route of appeal, jurisdiction over appeals from the judges of probate will revert to the superior court.

courts under RSA 502-A[12] or the probate courts under RSA 547; of writs of mandamus and quo warranto and of proceedings in relation thereto; of actions for support for children of unwed parents;[13] of petition and appeals relating to highways and property taken therefor[14] and for other public use; of actions commenced in the probate or district courts where a right to jury trial is guaranteed by the constitution; of actions commenced in a district court which are transferable by statute to the superior court;[15] of suits in equity under RSA 498:1; of petitions of divorce, nullity of marriage, alimony, custody of children and allowance to wife from husband's property for support of herself and children;[16] of petitions for new trials; of petitions for redemption[17] and foreclosure of mortgages;[18] of all other proceedings and matters to be entered in, or heard at, said court by special provisions of law;[19] and of all other proceedings and matters cognizable therein for which other special provision is made.

Other sections of chapter 491 grant the superior court jurisdiction over actions of contract against the state,[20] petitions to enforce subpoenas of state

---

12 The district courts share with the municipal courts original and exclusive jurisdiction over all "civil cases in which damages claimed do not exceed $1,500, the title to real estate is not involved and the plaintiff or defendant resides within" either the district or town. RSA 502-A:14(I) and 503:3-a. The district courts do not possess exclusive jurisdiction over actions for the possession of real estate; a common law action for ejectment may be brought in the superior court. Cooperman v. MacNeil, 123 N.H. 696, 465 A.2d 879 (1983).

13 RSA 546-A:4.

14 RSA 231:34.

15 RSA 502-A:14(III).

16 RSA ch. 458 and 458-C (establishing a uniform system for the determination of child support obligations). After granting a divorce and entering support and custody orders, the superior court retains jurisdiction to modify those orders in light of changed circumstances. RSA 458:14; McSherry v. McSherry, 135 N.H. 451 (1992). Decrees of property division are not subject to modification by the superior court, however, as they are final distributions, and not continuing orders. Id. (citing Stebbins v. Stebbins, 121 N.H. 1060, 1063, 438 A.2d 295, 297 (1981), and Dubois v. Dubois, 121 N.H. 664, 669, 433 A.2d 1277, 1280 (1981)).

17 RSA 479:10 and 479:14.

18 RSA 479:22.

19 See, e.g., RSA 506:7 (concurrent jurisdiction with the probate courts over proceedings regarding powers of attorney); RSA 304-B:45 and 46 (judicial dissolution of a limited partnership).

20 RSA 491:8.

and local administrative agencies,[21] application for naturalization of aliens[22] and petitions for declaratory judgment.[23] The Supreme Court has also held that the superior court "as an instrumentality of the State" possesses "*parens patriae* power" which it may use to "decide whether the welfare of [a minor] child warrants court-ordered visitation with grandparents to whom close personal attachments have been made."[24]

Library References

CJS Courts § 276

Cross References

Declaratory judgment, see Part IX *infra*.
Trials and final hearings, see Part XII *infra*.

B. The District and Municipal Courts

§ 3.04. The Municipal Courts—Generally

While both the district and the municipal courts possess a limited subject matter jurisdiction and are interchangeable for some purposes, their subject matter jurisdiction is not the same. Municipal courts are limited to small claims and the entry of miscellaneous orders.

Library References

CJS Courts § 276

Cross References

Executions, see Part XV, *infra*.

§ 3.05. —Small Claims

Municipal courts have no jurisdiction to try writs seeking the collection of a debt or money damages. Subject matter jurisdiction in civil causes to recover money is limited to actions under the Small Claims Act.[25] A "small

---

21 RSA 491:19.

22 RSA 491:21.

23 RSA 491:22.

24 Roberts v. Ward, 126 N.H. 388, 392, 493 A.2d 478, 481 (1985). The Court did not cite any authority for the creation or existence of this "power," but did suggest that it is separate and distinct from the superior court's equity jurisdiction.

25 RSA ch. 503. See also RSA 507:8-f (authorizing actions by merchants for damages resulting from shoplifting to be "brought in small claims court if the total damages do not exceed the jurisdictional limit of such courts").

now $5,000

claim" is "any right of action not involving the title to real estate in which the debt or damages, exclusive of interest and costs, does not exceed $2,500."[26] The small claims procedure may not be used, however, for claims exceeding $1,500 if either party desires trial by jury.[27] The small claims procedure is an "alternative and not exclusive" means of collecting debts or damages of this amount[28] and differs from the usual procedure in civil actions in twelve ways:

(1) The action is begun by the filing of a statement of the claim on a form prescribed by the rules, setting forth "a statement of the claim,[29] including the names of the parties involved,[30] the residence of each party,[31] the basis of the claim, and the amount alleged to be due."[32]

(2) The entry fee is only $25 plus $5 postage for each defendant.[33]

---

26 RSA 503:1; Dist. and Mun. Ct. R. 4.2. Any claim exceeding this amount must either be waived at the time the small claims action is begun (Dist. and Mun. Ct. R. 4.2), or tried in the district court (if the total does not exceed $25,000), or in the superior court. But the small claims procedure may not be used by a city or town to collect parking fines. City of Portsmouth v. Karosis, 126 N.H. 717, 498 A.2d 291 (1985).

27 RSA 503:1(II) and (III). If the defendant elects trial by jury, he must file a written request within five business days of the commencement of the action (RSA 503:1(III)) and the case will be transferred to the superior court. Within 10 days thereafter, either the party requesting trial by jury or the person required by statute to do so must pay the superior court transfer fee to the district or municipal court. Upon receipt of the fee, the case is "immediately" transferred to the superior court. Dist. and Mun. Ct. R. 4.26.

28 RSA 503:2.

29 A statement of the nature of the claim must include "the amount of the money claimed and a simple and short explanation of what happened and why the plaintiff is suing." Dist. and Mun. Ct. R. 4.6.

30 Identification of the parties includes their names, addresses and mailing addresses, if different. In the case of an unincorporated business, the tradename and address should be given. (Dist. and Mun. Ct. R. 4.3(a)) and in the case of a corporation, the name and address (Dist. and Mun. Ct. R. 4.4 and 4.5).

31 The residence and mailing addresses of both parties must be included. Dist. and Mun. Ct. R. 4.3(a).

32 RSA 503:3.

33 Dist. and Mun. Ct. R. 3.3. The court has power to waive payment of the entry fee or any other fee "for good cause shown." Dist. and Mun. Ct. R. 4.28.

(3) Service may be accomplished by certified mail[34] which is sent out by the court.[35] When there is more than one defendant, each must be separately served.[36]

(4) The defendant need not file any responsive pleading other than an indication in writing of the desire to be heard.[37] If the defendant responds that he or she wishes to be heard, a hearing will be scheduled no sooner than fourteen days later.[38]

(5) The defendant must respond within thirty days of receipt of the notice. Upon the defendant's failure to respond within that time, "judgment will be entered in favor of the plaintiff."[39]

(6) No interrogatories may be posed or depositions taken in preparation for trial.[40]

(7) The procedure at the hearing is informal and the technical rules of evidence do not apply. In addition, "the judge may freely ask such questions of parties and litigants as he believes necessary to resolve the issue,"[41] and

---

34 RSA 503:6; Dist. and Mun. Ct. R. 4.8. "Return receipt showing that defendant has received the statement shall constitute an essential part of the service." RSA 503:6. See Hudson v. Musor, 128 N.H. 804, 519 A.2d 319 (1986) (receipt signed by person not shown to be an agent of the defendant was inadequate).

35 RSA 503:6 requires the justice to send the notice; Dist. and Mun. Ct. R. 4.8 delegates the responsibility to the clerk. If service cannot be accomplished by mail, "the court may direct that service on the defendant be completed as in all other actions at law." RSA 503:6. The rules provide that in such a case, the court "will provide further instructions . . . concerning personal service." Dist. and Mun. Ct. R. 4.8.

36 Dist. and Mun. Ct. R. 4.5.

37 Dist. and Mun. Ct. R. 4.8.

38 Dist. and Mun. Ct. R. 4.9.

39 Dist. and Mun. Ct. R. 4.8. The rules and Chapter 503 are unclear on these time deadlines. RSA 503:6 requires only that the notice direct the defendant to appear at the time and place of hearing. Dist. and Mun. Ct. R. 4.8 provides that the defendant will be "requested to indicate in writing within thirty days his desire to be heard." Presumably, the 30-day period begins to run on receipt, rather than upon the mailing of the notice. Even so, Rule 4.8 does not state that the plaintiff will be entitled to judgment on the 31st day after the date of receipt, but rather speaks vaguely of judgment being entered upon the defendant's failure to respond. To be consistent with the generally relaxed procedure in small claims actions, it must be assumed that a late response will preserve the defendant's rights if judgment has not yet been entered. Failure to appear at the hearing results in judgment for the other party. Dist. and Mun. Ct. R. 4.14 and RSA 503:7. A party to a small claims action that has gone to judgment may seek appellate review in the supreme court "within 30 days of the notice of judgment date." RSA 503:10(II).

40 Dist. and Mun. Ct. R. 4.21.

41 Dist. and Mun. Ct. R. 4.12. See also Young v. Clogston, 127 N.H. 340, 499 A.2d 1007 (1985).

the parties may ask each other questions with the court's permission.[42] A sound recording may be made, so long as the party seeking the recording makes the request at least five business days before trial and pays all the costs of recording and any necessary transcription.[43]

(8) No formal pleading need be filed upon settlement of a claim. The plaintiff is only required to "notify the clerk's office so that the hearing may be properly cancelled."[44]

(9) Only the plaintiff is entitled to receive costs and interest if he or she prevails.[45]

(10) Executions are returnable within ninety days.[46]

(11) Scire facias for an amount greater than $2,500 can only be issued by the superior court.[47]

---

[42] Dist. and Mun. Ct. R. 4.12.

[43] RSA 503.10; Dist. and Mun. Ct. R. 4.27(I).

[44] Dist. and Mun. Ct. R. 4.13.

[45] RSA 503:7.

[46] RSA 527:5. The plaintiff may request a new writ within two years of the expiration of the prior writ. Dist. and Mun. Ct. R. 4.20.

[47] The municipal court has power to enter a judgment for $2,500 plus costs and interest and to issue writs of execution to collect the full amount as provided in RSA ch. 527. However, RSA 491:12 provides that only the superior court can issue a scire facias "when the amount of the judgment or other demand claimed, including *costs* and *interests*, exceeds the jurisdiction of said municipal court. . . ." On its face, the language of RSA 491:12 makes no sense, because the extent of the municipal court's jurisdiction is not measured by the demand plus costs and interest, but only by the demand, and because a judgment entered by a municipal court beyond its jurisdictional limit would be a nullity. The only sensible way to read RSA 491:12 is to substitute the figure $2,500 for the term "the jurisdiction of said municipal court" and to construe the statute as divesting the municipal court of power to issue a scire facias for any amount greater than $2,500. Of course, there is no reason to allow a municipal court to issue a scire facias on some of its judgments and not others, and RSA 491:12 should be amended to eliminate this inconsistency. The problem is not presented in small claims actions in district courts.

Two statutes impose conflicting requirements on writs of execution issued by municipal courts. RSA 502:32 provides that execution will not be issued on judgments rendered in municipal courts until 24 hours after judgment, and shall be returnable within 60 days of the date of issue. RSA 527:5 also formerly provided for return of executions in 60 days but was amended in 1975 to provide for return in 90 days. (Ch. 404, Laws of 1975). The two statutes do not conflict on the requirement for a 24-hour delay before issuing a writ of execution. But the conflict on the latest possible return day can only be resolved by assuming that the 1975 amendment expressed the Legislature's intention for all executions and that the legislature simply overlooked RSA 502:32 when making the change. This appears to have been the conclusion of the Supreme Court when it approved Dist. and Mun. Ct. R. 4.20.

(12) Small claims actions will be dismissed without further motion if no judgment is entered within two years of filing.[48]

The district and municipal courts will provide persons interested in commencing small claims actions; with a Small Claims Form and a copy of Section 4 of the District and Municipal Court Rules.

An attorney appearing in a small claims action must file an appearance to all opposing parties at least seven days prior to the hearing date. The court must give notice of the appearance requirement to all parties in small claims actions. If timely notice is not received, the party may request a continuance.[49]

Forms

Instructions to Plaintiff for Serving Orders of Notice—Small Claims Actions, see Appendix.
　　Notice of Decision—Small Claims Action (District Court), see Appendix.
　　Small Claims Action, see Appendix.

§ 3.06. —Miscellaneous Subject Matter Jurisdiction

The municipal court also has jurisdiction to enter the following orders: (1) to appoint inspectors of elections upon the petition of six qualified voters in the town or ward;[50] (2) to hear and determine actions for the enforcement of town or city orders to repair or remove a hazardous building;[51] and (3) to enforce obedience of a subpoena issued by the Labor Commissioner under RSA 275:51.[52]

§ 3.07. The District Courts—Concurrent Jurisdiction With the Municipal Courts

The district courts have all the "jurisdiction, powers and duties conferred upon municipal courts by the revised statutes annotated and amendments thereto."[53] Thus, every action that may be commenced in a municipal court may also be brought in the district court for that district.

Library References

CJS Courts § 488

---

48 Dist. and Mun. Ct. R. 4.7a.
49 RSA 503:2-a.
50 RSA 658:6.
51 RSA ch. 155-B.
52 RSA 275:51(IV).
53 RSA 502-A:34.

§ 3.08. —Actions for Damages

District courts have jurisdiction over civil actions for damages where the claimed damages are $25,000 or less, title to real estate is not in issue, and either the plaintiff or the defendant resides in the district.[54] The district court's jurisdiction is exclusive in all cases not handled under the small claims procedure where the damages claimed are $1,500 or less.[55] In other cases, the district court shares subject matter jurisdiction with the superior court.

Actions begun in the district court may be transferred to the superior court for that county if (1) an action "arising out of the same transaction or situation" is pending in the superior court;[56] (2) the defendant alleges a claim "arising out of the same transaction or situation" which exceeds $1,500;[57] or (3) the defendant wishes a jury trial in a case where the damages claimed exceed $1,500 or title to real estate is involved.[58]

If the defendant wishes to transfer the case to the superior court, he or she must file a "brief statement with an affidavit under oath," supporting the factual basis for the transfer.[59] Additionally, if the defendant wishes a jury

---

54 RSA 502-A:14. In addition, RSA 502-A:14(II-a) authorizes the Supreme Court to expand the jurisdiction of selected district courts to $50,000 "after consultation with the individual district courts." See Mountain Springs Water Co., Inc. v. Godston, 121 N.H. 408, 430 A.2d 180 (1981) (where the Court held that a mechanic's lien is not an interest in land, does not affect title to real estate, and thus comes within the jurisdiction of the district courts while efforts to collect a charge for water, which the defendant's deed required him to pay, did involve title to real estate and could not be brought in the district court).

55 RSA 502-A:14(I) and (II) present an apparent anomaly. The statute states that district courts have "exclusive jurisdiction of civil cases in which the damages claimed do not exceed $1,500." RSA 503:1 defines a "small claim" as "any right of action not involving the title to real estate in which the debt or damages, exclusive of interest and costs, does not exceed $2,500," and RSA 503:3, which authorizes a small claims action to be commenced in a municipal court. These sections can be read consistently only by adopting a definition of the term "civil cases" which requires their commencement by a writ. Thus, the subject matter jurisdiction of district courts is exclusive only of the superior court as to amount and of the municipal court only as to amount and form of process.

56 RSA 502-A:14(III)(a).

57 RSA 502-A:14(III)(b).

58 RSA 502-A:15. See Campton Crossroads, Inc. v. Wise, 131 N.H. 193, 551 A.2d 517 (1988) (trial court may extend the time to claim the right to jury trial up to the return day).

59 RSA 502-A:14(III)(c). This so-called "brief statement" is also called a "petition to remove" (RSA 502-A:14(III)(c)) and in fact, is more appropriately thought of under the latter title since Brief Statements contain no allegations of fact.

trial in a case where the damages exceed $1,500, he or she may file a written request.[60] Pursuant to legislation enacted in 1992, the Supreme Court is authorized to establish regional jury trial courts for regions to be determined by the Court. Questions of law therefrom are to be appealed directly to the Supreme Court.[61]

§ 3.09. —Juvenile Petitions and Domestic Violence Petitions

(a) *Juvenile Petitions.*   Municipal court jurisdiction over juvenile petitions was repealed in 1979 and reassigned to the district courts.[62] A petition regarding any child who is delinquent,[63] abandoned or abused,[64] or in need of services,[65] verified by affidavit,[66] may be filed in a district court by "any person."[67] The petition should show all the facts necessary to a finding that the child is delinquent, abandoned, abused, or in need of services.[68]

The judge or clerk must issue a notice requiring the person "having custody or control of the minor or with whom the minor may be" to appear with the child at a trial to be held between twenty-four hours and seven days after service of the notice.[69] The notice must include a copy of the petition[70] and a notice that the cost of placement and other services ordered by the court may be charged to the parents or other persons responsible for the child's support.[71] The notice must be served in hand on the person having

---

60 RSA 502-A:15. Upon a timely request for a transfer, the cause shall be heard in either the regional jury trial court for the region in which the district court is located, if such a jury trial court has been established, or the superior court for the county in which the district court is located. RSA 502-A:15.

61 RSA 502-A:12-a and 15.

62 Laws of 1979, Chapter 361. See RSA 169-B:2(I), 169-C:3(IX), and 169-D:2(III).

63 For a definition of "delinquent," see RSA 169-B:2(II).

64 For a definition of the terms "abandoned" and "abused" child, see RSA 169-C:3(I) and (II).

65 For a definition of the term "child in need of services," see RSA 169-D:2(IV).

66 RSA 169-B:6(I), 169-C:7 (Statutory Requirements and Guidelines for the Processing and Disposition of Abuse and Neglect Cases in the District Courts (hereinafter, "Guidelines"), 20), and 169-D:5.

67 City of Claremont v. Truell, 126 N.H. 30, 489 A.2d 581 (1985).

68 RSA 169-B:6(II), 169-C:7(III) (Guidelines, 20), and 169-D:5(II). See also In re Russell C., 120 N.H. 260, 414 A.2d 934 (1980).

69 RSA 169-B:7, 169-C:8(I) (Guidelines, 22 and 23), and 169-D:6(I).

70 RSA 169-B:7(II), 169-C:8(II) (Guidelines, 22(b)), and 169-D:6(II).

71 RSA 169-D:7(III), 169-C:8(III) (Guidelines, 22(b)), and 169-D:6(III). See also City of Claremont v. Truell, 126 N.H. 30, 489 A.2d 581 (1985) (notice constitutionally required).

custody or control of the child or with whom the child is or be left at that person's usual place of abode.[72] The child's parent or guardian, if he is not the person served, must also be notified if the child's residence is known.[73] If the child's residence is not known, any relative whose whereabouts are known can be notified.[74] The judge can also appoint counsel, a guardian ad litem,[75] or a surrogate parent[76] to act on behalf of the child.

The failure to appear in response to the notice constitutes contempt of court.[77] If the notice cannot be served, is not obeyed or will be ineffectual, the court may issue a warrant against "anyone having custody or control of the minor" requiring him to produce the child.[78] The preliminary hearing is generally limited to determining whether there is a legal and factual basis for the petition, what needs to be done immediately to protect the child, and whether the case can be settled.[79] If the court finds that there is a legal and factual basis for the petition, the case will be continued for investigation and reports by social service agencies.[80] Pending final disposition of the case, the court may make certain limited orders with respect to the child's custody.[81] Hearings are formal, with due regard for the due process rights of the parties,[82] and held separately from and in different rooms from those used for criminal cases.[83] Hearings are not open to the public, and the court may exclude anyone except a parent, party, witness, their counsel, prosecuting attorneys, and "representatives of the agencies present to perform

---

72　RSA 169-B:7(I), 169-C:8(I), and 169-D:6(I).

73　*Id.* Guidelines, 22(c).

74　*Id.*

75　RSA 169-B:12(I), 169-C:10 (Guidelines, 10–13 and 24(b) and (c)), and 169-D:12. See In re Lisa G., 127 N.H. 585, 504 A.2d 1 (1986) (holding that the district courts may appoint both defense counsel and a guardian ad litem for juveniles in CHINS proceedings).

76　RSA 186-C:14(IV).

77　RSA 169-B:8(I), 169-C:9(I), and 169-D:7(I).

78　RSA 169-B:8(II), 169-C:9(II), and 169-D:7(II).

79　RSA 169-B:13, 169-C:15 (Guidelines, 24–27), and 169-D:11. In superior court juvenile services reports will include financial information and must be kept in a sealed envelope and examined only upon the court's approval (Super. Ct. Admin. R. 8-1 and 8-2) and the same or stricter rules pertain in the district court. See RSA 169-C:25.

80　RSA 169-B:20, 21, and 23, 169-C:18 (Guidelines, 14), and 169-D:14(III).

81　RSA 169-B:14 and 15, 169-C:6 (Guidelines, 17–19 and 25), and 16 and 169-D:8.

82　RSA 169-B:16(II), 169-C:18(II) and (III) (Guidelines, 29), and 169-D:14(II). See In re Eric C., 124 N.H. 222, 469 A.2d 1305 (1983) (statutory time limits will be strictly enforced).

83　RSA 169-B:16(I) and 34, 169-C:18(I) (Guidelines, 29(a)), and 169-D:14(I).

their official duties."[84] If the court finds that the child is delinquent, abused, abandoned, or in need of services, it may make further limited orders for the child's commitment and treatment.[85]

Any order or decision of the district court may be appealed to the superior court within thirty days of entry of the order.[86] All appeals are entitled to priority in the superior court's calendar.[87]

(b) *Domestic Violence Petitions.* Any person who has been physically or sexually abused or placed in fear of bodily injury by a person with whom he or she lives or has lived may file a petition in the superior court for the county or the district court in the town or city where either the plaintiff or the defendant resides.[88] The clerks for all courts have forms for such petition, which may be filed and served without charge.[89] The court may enter temporary orders ex parte upon a showing of "immediate and present danger of abuse."[90] It may also, after the hearing, enter orders for a period of up to one year for the physical protection of the petitioner, award "the exclusive right of use and possession" of jointly held property, apportion custody and visitation, and order support.[91]

(c) *Involuntary Emergency Admission to Mental Health Facility.* The district courts have jurisdiction to determine whether there is "probable cause" to continue holding a person who has been temporarily admitted to

---

84 Evidence of "juvenile adjudications" is not "generally admissible" in other proceedings. NHRE 609(d).

85 See RSA 169-B:19 and 22, 169-C:19 and 21 (Guidelines, 30–38); and 169-D:17 and 18. See City of Claremont v. Truell, 126 N.H. 30, 489 A.2d 581 (1985); In re Adam E., 125 N.H. 368, 480 A.2d 160 (1984) (holding that a final order which allows custody to someone other than the parent must include a "statement of conditions on which the parent may regain custody and a plan of services to help the parent and child." 125 N.H. at 368, 480 A.2d at 160); In re Larry B., 125 N.H. 376, 480 A.2d 166 (1984) (holding that jurisdiction of the district court over "children in need of services," and accordingly the effect of those courts' dispositional orders in such cases, terminates on the children's 18th birthdays). See also In re Todd P., 127 N.H 792, 509 A.2d 140 (1986) (holding that the district court has authority to order a school district to review a juvenile's Individual Education Plan but not to review that Plan itself and enter orders based on its evaluation).

86 RSA 169-B:29, 169-C:28, and 169-D:20.

87 *Id.*

88 RSA 173-B:1 and 2. The mailing address of the petitioner does not have to be included in the petition. Dist. and Mun. Ct. R. 3.2(A).

89 RSA 173-B:3 (II) and (III).

90 RSA 173-B:6.

91 The Rules of Evidence do not apply to domestic violence proceedings. N.H.R.E. 1101(d)(3).

a mental health facility on an involuntary emergency basis[92] or to revoke a conditional discharge from such a facility.[93]

Forms

Domestic Violence Petition (District Court), see Appendix.
Temporary Orders and Notice of Hearing (District Court), see Appendix.

§ 3.10. —Landlord and Tenant Actions

The district courts have subject matter jurisdiction over actions for possession of real estate under RSA 540:12 by an owner, lessor, or purchaser at a mortgage foreclosure sale against the lessee, occupant, mortgagor, or other person in possession holding without right. Before the action is commenced, the plaintiff must serve in hand or leave at the tenant's "last and usual place of abode"[94] a Notice to Quit or demand for rent. A Landlord and Tenant Writ must "set forth in substance that the plaintiff is entitled to possession of the demanded premises and that the defendant is in possession thereof without right, after notice in writing to quit the same. . . ."[95] The writ cannot contain a claim for money damages,[96] and must be served at least seven days before the return day.[97] The writ must contain a notice in the form prescribed by statute.[98] No answer is required. If the defendant wishes to contest the eviction, he or she must file an appearance in the district court no later than the return day appearing on the writ.[99] If the tenant files an appearance, notice of the hearing shall be mailed to the parties no less than seven days prior to the hearing.[100] The matter will then be set for trial no later than fifteen days from the return date. Both parties will have a right to engage in discovery prior to the hearing on the merits.[101] If the tenant fails to file an appearance or fails to appear at the hearing on the merits, the court

---

92 RSA 135-C:31.

93 RSA 135-C:51.

94 RSA 540:5.

95 RSA 540:13.

96 Dist. and Mun. Ct. R. 5.6. But it can claim a right to collect charges against the property not specifically referred to in the lease. See Dow Associates Inc. v. Gulf Oil Corp., 114 N.H. 381, 321 A.2d 579 (1974).

97 RSA 540:13(II). Return days are only days when the court is in regular session. Compare RSA 502:30 and Dist. and Mun. Ct. R. 5.1. No trial of Landlord and Tenant actions is held on the return day. Dist. and Mun. Ct. R. 5.1.

98 RSA 540:13(II).

99 Id.

100 RSA 540:13(V).

101 RSA 540:13(IV).

shall mail a notice of default to the address set forth on the summons at least three days prior to the issuance of the writ of possession.[102] The writ of possession will not be issued until twenty-four hours have expired since judgment was entered.[103] The court may delay dispossession for up to three months from the date of judgment if justice requires the stay[104] and the defendant pays the rent in advance each week throughout the period of the stay.[105] In the case of nonpayment of rent, the parties may nonetheless agree that, the judgment notwithstanding, the writ of possession shall not be issued if the defendant makes payments in accordance with an agreed schedule.[106] Upon entry of judgment for the plaintiff, or in the case of a stay or a postjudgment agreement, breach of the condition to pay rent as specified, the court will issue writ of possession.[107] If the plaintiff "neglects to enter his action, or fails to support it," the defendant will be given judgment for costs.[108] Significantly, legislation enacted by the 1992 Legislature removes the right to a de novo jury trial in the superior court. Instead, appeals will be made directly to the Supreme Court.[109] After entry of judgment by the court,[110] either party may file a notice of intent to appeal to the Supreme Court.[111] The appeal must be filed in accordance with the Supreme Court Rule.[112] The rent shall be paid, as the court directs, to either the court or the plaintiff.[113] If the defendant wins on appeal, he or she may recover compen-

---

[102] RSA 540:13(V).

[103] Dist. and Mun. Ct. R. 5.2 and 5.4.

[104] The court's determination that justice requires the stay is supposed to be "based on the reasonableness and good faith of the parties in their respective reports, complaints, demands and evidence." RSA 540:13-c.

[105] RSA 540:13-c and 14.

[106] RSA 540:13-c(II).

[107] RSA 540:13-c and 14. The Rules require that the writ of possession not issue for at least 24 hours after judgment. Dist. and Mun. Ct. R. 5.2. Whether the 24-hour delay also applies to writs issued for failure to pay rent during the period of the stay is unclear. "An eviction order is merely 'a summary proceeding to recover possession of real estate,' . . . and not a permanent injunction barring visitation." Johnston v. Flatley Realty Investors, 125 N.H. 133, 136, 480 A.2d 55, 57 (1984).

[108] RSA 540:15; Dist. and Mun. Ct. R. 5.5.

[109] RSA 540:20.

[110] Judgment includes a stay of dispossession under RSA 540:13-c.

[111] RSA 540:20.

[112] Id.

[113] RSA 540:25.

satory and exemplary damages and have a writ of execution to recover them.[114]

Library References

Waiver of statutory demand-for-rent due or of notice-to-quit prerequisite of summary eviction of lessee for nonpayment of rent—modern cases. 31 ALR4th 1254.

Forms

Landlord and Tenant Writ, see Appendix.

§ 3.11. —Enforcement of Local Ordinances

The district courts have concurrent subject matter jurisdiction over proceedings to enforce local ordinances, codes, and regulations and to assess civil penalties for violation of those enactments up to the limit of their concurrent jurisdiction to award money damages.[115] The district courts also have concurrent jurisdiction over violations of local ordinances that are enforceable through cease and desist orders pursuant to RSA 676:17-a.[116]

§ 3.12. —Miscellaneous Subject Matter Jurisdiction

The district courts possess the same miscellaneous subject matter jurisdiction as municipal courts. The district courts do not share civil jurisdiction with the superior court in any areas, except in actions for damages or civil penalties for violation of a local ordinance, code, or regulation[117] between $1,500 and $25,000 and Domestic Violence Petitions.

C. The Probate Courts

§ 3.13. Subject Matter Jurisdiction

One of the most difficult problems in New Hampshire civil procedure is a definition and description of the limits of the subject matter jurisdiction of the judges of probate. The two thorniest issues in this difficult area are whether the probate courts possess any powers not specifically assigned by statute and how the jurisdiction of the probate court and the superior court are to be divided. It would not be accurate to say that the Supreme Court's approach to these questions has matured over time. Rather, it seems to have shifted from one period to the next in accordance with the institutional needs of the judicial branch.

---

114 RSA 540:23.
115 RSA 502-A:11-a(I)(b).
116 RSA 502-A:11-a(I)(c).
117 RSA 502-A:11-a(I)(b).

It has never been doubted that the probate courts are entrusted with jurisdiction over only a limited number of specific subjects, but there has been an extensive debate over the nature of its jurisdiction within the specific subject areas granted to it. On the one hand, it has been argued that probate courts have a specific and limited jurisdiction and are possessed only of the powers explicitly conferred by statute. On the other hand, it has been asserted that, when dealing with issues arising in the specific areas committed to them by statute, the probate courts have all the powers of courts of general jurisdiction.

Library References

CJS Courts §§ 298, 310

§ 3.14. Probate Courts v. The Superior Court—History of the Debate

The debate appears to have begun in 1859. Two opinions announced in that year attempted for the first time to delineate the general nature of probate jurisdiction. In the first, *Kimball v. Fisk*,[118] an action of trover was met by the claim that the defendant had taken the goods sought while acting as the plaintiff's guardian. Justice Bell, writing for the Court, made the following observations on the nature of probate court jurisdiction:

> In the argument, it has been suggested that the courts of probate are courts of merely statutory special and limited jurisdiction, and this view is expressed in some books to which we are accustomed to look as authority; but we are much inclined to question the soundness of the opinion. Powers of courts of probate were conferred in Massachusetts on the county courts, and in some cases, on special commissioners while New Hampshire was subject to that colony, but they were conferred as a body of well-known principles and rules; a settled and general jurisdiction then existing at common law in the ordinary or ecclesiastical courts. The statutes of the colony did not attempt to define or prescribe the powers of those courts in general otherwise than by reference to the existing law of the land. The like state of things has continued from that day to the present.

* * *

> They are not to be regarded as courts of special and limited jurisdiction but as courts of general jurisdiction on these subjects,

---

118   39 N.H. 110 (1859).

51

and entitled to all the presumptions in favor of their proceedings which are allowed in the case of other tribunals of general jurisdiction, more especially as they are now made by statute courts of record.[119]

However, in the second case, *Wood v. Stone*,[120] a judge of probate had decreed distribution to an heir's assignee after examining and upholding the validity of his assignment. By the time the decree was entered, the heir had died, and his representative objected that the judge had lacked jurisdiction to determine the validity of the assignment and, under applicable statutes, could not order distribution to anyone but the heir or his representative. Justice Fowler agreed with the heir's representative, writing:

> Courts of probate are of limited and special jurisdiction, restricted, unless enlarged by statute, to the probate of wills, to the administration of estates and the distribution thereof among the heirs and legatees and other like administrative and ministerial acts. They have no juries and the proceedings in them are not according to the course of the common law. Originally their powers were almost entirely administrative and ministerial, and in none of the statutes conferring additional and increased jurisdiction upon them, so far as our examination has extended, do the legislature seem to ever have contemplated investing them with general common-law powers as judicial tribunals.[121]

While the results in *Kimball* and *Wood* may be reconciled, their reasoning about the nature of probate court jurisdiction may not. These opinions have become the roots of two conflicting theories of probate jurisdiction.

The line of cases beginning with *Kimball* adopts the view that the probate courts are not possessed "of merely statutory and special limited jurisdiction," but rather enjoy a "general jurisdiction on the subjects" defined by "a settled and general jurisdiction existing in common law in the ordinary and ecclesiastical courts." Three years after the *Kimball* opinion was announced, its author, now Chief Justice Bell, wrote the Court's opinion in *Morgan v. Dodge*.[122] The question in that case was whether a probate court could correct its own error and revoke letters testamentary six years after they had been granted, upon the ground that the executrix had not originally met the

---

119   39 N.H. at 120.

120   39 N.H. 572 (1859). See also In re Estate of O'Dwyer, 135 N.H. 323 (1992).

121   39 N.H. at 575. See also In re Estate of O'Dwyer, 135 N.H. 323 (1992).

122   44 N.H. 255 (1862).

requirements for appointment, or whether the error could not be corrected after the time for taking an appeal had expired. In holding that a probate court could correct its own error, the Court announced a broad view of the inherent powers of the probate courts, as follows:

> [Courts of probate] exercise many powers solely by virtue of the provisions of our statutes; but they have a very extensive jurisdiction not conferred by statute, but by a general reference to the existing law of the land, that is, to that branch of the common law known and acted upon for ages, the probate or ecclesiastical law, ... An unusual number of the most necessary and useful rules of the common law in relation to the estates of persons deceased have been embodied in our statutes; but by no means the main body of the common law on this subject. And the courts of probate have an extensive jurisdiction of which the statutes take no particular notice. This jurisdiction is conferred and recognized by the Constitution (pt. 2, sec. 80) and by the revised statutes (ch. 152, sec. 3). . . .

* * *

> [A]ll the authority known to our laws in relation to the subject in question belongs in the first instance to the courts of probate, perhaps with the exception of some cases of equitable jurisdiction.[123]

This last point—that the probate courts possess no inherent equity jurisdiction—has proved to be one of the most frequent excuses for limiting the probate courts' jurisdiction and has caused a significant amount of confusion over the boundary between the subject matter jurisdiction of the probate courts and the superior court.[124]

---

123 44 N.H. at 258.

124 The effect of this confusion can be seen in attempting to apply a statute like RSA 506:7. That statute grants concurrent jurisdiction to the probate courts and the superior court to hear matters regarding powers of attorney and states that "[t]he court may . . . make orders and decrees, and take other actions necessary or proper to make determinations on matters presented. . . . " RSA 506:7(IV). This clause seems to imply equitable powers and is unexceptional as applied to the superior court. But when applied to the probate courts, it raises the question whether the Legislature truly intended to grant a new and broader jurisdiction by statute in one limited area or intended rather that the probate courts act, even on matters relating to powers of attorney, only within the range of powers they have traditionally enjoyed. In the absence of a clear indication of legislative intent to expand the powers of the probate courts, a reference to the two conflicting lines of decisions of the Supreme Court suggests that the probate courts

In 1868, the issue arose again in *Hayes v. Hayes*[125] when the Court was asked to decide whether a probate court had jurisdiction to advise trustees of a testamentary trust on the distribution of trust income. In his opinion for the Court, Chief Justice Perley adopted the theories of both *Kimball* and *Wood*. In order to find the "extent and limitation" of the probate court's jurisdiction, he wrote, the Court must "resort to ecclesiastical law." He continued:

> Where our statutes have not introduced change, the ecclesiastical law may be resorted to as a safe guide for the interpretation of our probate laws. The substance of our system is borrowed from that law and the methods and remedies in our courts of probate, except where others are provided by statute follow the general course of procedure in the ecclesiastical courts.[126]

But Chief Justice Perley went on to say that jurisdiction of equity matters relating to trusts was specifically committed by statute to the Supreme Judicial Court and that there was no reason to believe that the Legislature had intended that probate courts exercise a similar jurisdiction. He concluded his opinion with what has become a classic statement of the theory of limited jurisdiction in the probate courts:

> The general policy of the law in this state has been to confine the contentious jurisdiction of the probate courts within narrow limits leaving the practice there to be simple and generally free from such difficulty as would require the attendance of counsel and the expense of protracted trials. Questions relating to the interpretation of wills creating trusts, frequently involve difficult points of law and complicated matters of fact such as are not usually investigated in the courts of probate and such as cannot be well examined by the methods and machinery of those courts.[127]

When it is remembered that the ecclesiastical courts themselves had a limited subject matter jurisdiction, it is not difficult to understand how the Court could have seen a consistency in holding that the probate courts have

---

may exercise a limited, quasi-equitable power in the area of discovery (see also Prob. Ct. R. 10 and 11), orders to produce, and declaratory or advisory rulings, but should not attempt to issue injunctions or to fashion new forms of relief.

125 48 N.H. 219 (1868).

126 48 N.H. at 226.

127 48 N.H. at 229–30.

a limited jurisdiction, much of which was, nevertheless, expressed in specific legislative enactments and that when the Legislature had acted, it had generally sought to restrict the probate court's jurisdiction and to confer authority over the more complicated matters on the Supreme Judicial Court. And it is not necessarily inconsistent with this theory to hold that the probate courts could authorize a guardian to take possession of the ward's property and could revoke an order entered by mistake, but that it could not pass on the validity of an heir's assignment or advise trustees on the proper administration of their trusts. But as consistent as these holdings may have been, they failed to state a coherent theory for either the jurisdiction of the probate courts or the separation of that jurisdiction from the authority of the general trial court.

The issue arose only three more times in the nineteenth century, and in each case the Court favored the broader theory of jurisdiction.[128] In *Judge of Probate v. Lane*,[129] the Supreme Court said that the probate courts have "authority to try all questions of fraud arising in the settlement of estates."[130] In *Stearns v. Wright*,[131] Justice Sargent said:

> In one view, our courts of probate are of limited and special jurisdiction, viz., in that they have no jury and their proceedings are not according to the course of the common law. . . . Yet, they are to be regarded as courts of general jurisdiction on the subjects to which they relate, and are entitled to all the presumptions in favor of their proceedings which are allowed in the case of other tribunals of general jurisdiction,—more especially as they are now made by statute courts of record.[132]

And in *Reed v. Prescott*,[133] the Court held that the proper remedy for fraud in the allowance of claims and the acceptance of a commissioner's report by a probate court was not a bill in equity to enjoin the administrator from acting, but a petition filed with the probate court to vacate or modify the decree. Following the general tenor of the Doe Court's analysis on other questions of procedure, Justice Parsons wrote that, if the probate court finds

---

128 Interestingly enough, Chief Justice Stone never wrote an opinion on this subject.

129 51 N.H. 342 (1871).

130 51 N.H. at 348.

131 51 N.H. 600 (1872).

132 51 N.H. at 609.

133 70 N.H. 88, 46 A. 457 (1899).

fraud or error in its proceedings, it can "do justice in appropriate proceedings."[134]

However, the theory of general jurisdiction has found little support since the creation of the superior courts in 1901. Two cases decided in 1915 identify the two points of view, but clearly favor the *Wood* theory of limited jurisdiction. In *Crosby v. Charlestown*,[135] the Court again recognized the existence of implied powers in the probate courts, saying that "power to provide for the administration of an estate necessarily involves power to protect and preserve the estate until the administration[136] can be affected." But, in *Appeal of Henry W. Woodbury*,[137] the Court stated emphatically that "the power of the state over the probate courts is exclusive and they have such powers and only such as the legislature gives them."[138]

During the next twenty years, the Court, with only an occasional lapse, preferred the theory of limited jurisdiction, filling the void created by the decline of the implied powers theory of probate court jurisdiction with an expanded resort to the equity jurisdiction of the superior court. In *Patten v. Patten*,[139] the Court was presented with a bill in equity filed by one co-executor claiming that another co-executor owed money to the estate and seeking an accounting. The two co-executors were the only persons who still had any interest in the estate, and the respondent moved to dismiss the action on the ground that only the probate court had jurisdiction over the claim. Justice Peasley began his opinion by noting that, although part 2, article 80 of the Constitution "conferred exclusive jurisdiction substantially in accord with the English practice"[140] on the probate courts, under the earlier English practice a bill in equity could be brought by one co-executor against another for an accounting. While some statutes in the nineteenth century had attempted to grant exclusive jurisdiction to the probate courts over all matters relating to the settlement of estates, the Court pointed out that a more recent statute (now RSA 556:22) specifically allowed an action of assumpsit by one joint administrator against another who refused to account. The Court held that the effect of this statute was to restrict the jurisdiction of the probate courts to proceedings between executors and

---

134 70 N.H. at 89, 46 A. at 458.

135 78 N.H. 39, 95 A. 1043 (1915).

136 78 N.H. at 45, 95 A. at 1046.

137 78 N.H. 50, 96 A. 299 (1915).

138 78 N.H. at 53, 96 A. at 301.

139 79 N.H. 388, 109 A. 415 (1920).

140 79 N.H. at 390, 109 A. at 416.

persons interested in an estate to settle an estate, and to preclude them from entertaining actions by one co-executor to force an accounting by another. In his opinion, Justice Peasley drew a distinction between actions which are incidental to administration of the estate, and therefore within the jurisdiction of the superior court and actions involving a settlement of the estate, over which the probate court has exclusive jurisdiction. The distinction has become the cornerstone of the modern theory of probate jurisdiction.

In 1931, now Chief Justice Peasley attempted to define once and for all the limits of the probate courts' jurisdiction. *Rockwell v. Dow*,[141] began as a bill in equity filed by one of the trustees of a testamentary trust charging the other trustees with maladministration and refusing to consult. The superior court found that the will creating the trust required unanimous consent of the trustees and that the respondent trustees had, without the consent of the petitioner, made questionable investments and improper distributions. On the basis of these findings, the superior court entered a temporary order requiring that all future actions by the trustees be by unanimous consent and announced its intention to remove all the trustees and appoint a successor. By their bill of exceptions, the respondents raised the question of the superior court's jurisdiction over the case. Chief Justice Peasley began his opinion by noting the early roots of the superior court's equity jurisdiction over trusts. While he conceded that some parts of that jurisdiction had been shifted by statute to the probate courts, he went on to say that the *Hayes* case had established that those statutes had merely shifted the "business or administrative powers" over the estates in trust to the probate courts, leaving the superior court's general equity jurisdiction intact. After reviewing a number of conflicting cases, Chief Justice Peasley asserted:

> The general line separating probate jurisdiction from that of the superior court is not difficult of ascertainment. The distinction is that between things which are "incident to the business of conducting an administration" and "a settlement with the judge of probate" concerning administration already had.[142]

The Chief Justice was obliged to admit, however, that "this common-law test does not . . . solve every problem for the legislature has from time to time conferred additional powers upon the probate court . . ."[143] and that the

---

141 85 N.H. 58, 154 A. 229 (1931).
142 85 N.H. at 66, 154 A. at 233.
143 85 N.H. at 66, 154 A. at 233.

probate courts have jurisdiction to construe wills and deeds of trust as an incident to passing on their accounts and to decree distribution.[144] In the end, Chief Justice Peasley concluded that the superior court did not have jurisdiction to remove the trustees and appoint new ones and that the power belonged instead to the probate court.

Rockwell v. Dow represents an attempt, if not to define the full extent of probate jurisdiction, at least to draw the main distinction between equity jurisdiction in the superior court and probate court jurisdiction. The *Rockwell* case cannot, however, be regarded as successful. For one thing, the test it proposes for the separation of equity and probate jurisdiction is neither easy to apply nor consistent with the holdings in *Morgan v. Dodge* and *Reed v. Prescott*. In both those cases, the Supreme Court had held that the probate courts possessed inherent common law powers to "correct errors" and "do justice" even though the proceedings in which the errors had occurred were already closed. For another thing, it is difficult to square the results in *Patten* and *Rockwell* with each other. In *Patten*, Justice Peasley wrote that the probate courts had no jurisdiction to compel one co-executor to render an accounting during an administration of an estate. In *Rockwell*, he allowed the probate court to appoint trustees in a testamentary trust. *Rockwell* is, thus, an unreliable guide to determining the subject matter jurisdiction of the probate court.

The years since the announcement of the *Rockwell* decision have not seen a marked clarification in this area. In *Wentworth v. Waldron*,[145] the issue was whether the superior court had jurisdiction to nullify a waiver of a will filed by a widow's guardian and to enjoin the guardian from acting in reliance on the waiver. In deciding that the superior court did have that power, the Supreme Court held that "a guardian is a fiduciary whose conduct is subject to regulation by a court of equity in cases where the remedy at law is inadequate."[146] When it considered the remedies available against guardians in the probate court, it found that:

> It cannot be said that the remedies available against guardians in the probate courts are completely adequate. The jurisdiction of such courts is limited . . . and they have not been clothed with general equitable powers even with reference to these fiduciaries who are appointed by them. Matters affecting the conduct of

---

144 *Id.* Compare Hayes v. Hayes, 48 N.H. 219, 229–30 (1868).

145 86 N.H. 559, 172 A. 247 (1934).

146 86 N.H. at 561, 172 A. at 249.

fiduciaries which have not been placed by statute within the exclusive jurisdiction of probate courts, are still cognizable in equity.[147]

The *Wentworth* holding is obviously at odds with *Reed v. Prescott*, in which the Court held that if the probate court found fraud or error in any proceedings before it, it had ample power "to do justice in appropriate proceedings."[148] In the same year, the Court confirmed its adherence to the theory of limited jurisdiction when it held that a probate court can grant administration even though the only estate is a potential claim for coverage under an automobile insurance policy. The Court pointed out, however, that under the *Rockwell* test, the probate court could not, either directly or indirectly, try the merits of the claim.

The issue of probate court jurisdiction was not specifically addressed again for nearly thirty years. Finally, in a 1963 dissent, Chief Justice Kenison referred again to the theory of limited jurisdiction and identified its true roots in the *Wood* case. In his dissent to *State v. Moquin*,[149] the Chief Justice stated his understanding that the probate courts have no inherent power to punish for contempt because they "have limited and special jurisdiction only so far as granted by the legislature."[150]

The Court's attitude has become even more uncertain. In 1977, the Court announced its opinion in *In re Estate of Page*,[151] a case involving a petition by an estranged wife of a man under conservatorship for an order from the probate court requiring the conservator to pay support and the college expenses of the children. In its opinion, the Court recited the theory of limited jurisdiction, but went on to decide that the probate court had jurisdiction to enforce the conservator's duty to make payments for the support of his ward's family. While the result is sensible, it seems to be inconsistent with the holdings of *Appeal of Woodbury* and *Wentworth v. Waldron*.

It is interesting to note that the *Page* case relies in part upon *Hayes v. Hayes*, the Court's earliest attempt to reconcile the divergent theories of jurisdiction which had been separately identified by *Kimball* and *Wood*. This might seem to foreshadow a more liberal approach to probate court juris-

---

147 *Id.*

148 Reed v. Prescott, 70 N.H. 88, 46 A. 457 (1899).

149 105 N.H. 9, 191 A.2d 541 (1963).

150 105 N.H. at 13, 191 A.2d at 544.

151 117 N.H. 734, 378 A.2d 750 (1977).

diction but for the Court's opinion in the case of *In re Estate of Borkowski*.[152] In *Borkowski*, the probate court had authorized an administrator to offset the outstanding principal balance of an installment note held by the estate against the amount of the debtor's inheritance and to assign parts of the balance due to other heirs. The administrator argued that the powers granted to the probate court under RSA 554:10 to order the administrator to transfer "evidences of debt to the heirs," granted the probate court "broad discretion to exercise its equity powers over the distribution of assets to heirs."[153] Although this argument raised the question whether the probate courts had any equity powers to exercise, the Court did not speak directly to that point. Instead, the Court merely held that the statute does not allow the probate courts to authorize the setoff of an heir's unmatured debt against his inheritance, saying that the interpretation of RSA 554:10 which the administrator sought "would greatly expand the scope of the statute in contravention of the court's authority."[154]

It is difficult to reconcile the holding in *Page* that the probate court has power to order a conservator to make payments to support his ward's family, with the suggestion in *Borkowski* that the probate court had no discretion to exercise an equitable jurisdiction in formulating its decree of distribution. In neither case does it appear that a statute speaks directly to the point and in both it seems that the recognition of such power in the probate courts could only facilitate the purposes for which they were established. It cannot be doubted that the decision in *Borkowski* was reasonable—an installment note should not be converted to a demand note or a nonassignable note be assigned simply because a creditor dies—but a better basis for that decision might have been a recognition of the probate court's authority to do equity within its subject area and a decision that, in *Borkowski*, the probate court had simply abused its discretion.

The *Page* and *Borkowski* cases gave no clear signal of the Supreme Court's real preference between the two theories of probate jurisdiction, but they emphasized the need for a final clear statement on the subject. Looking at the development of case law since 1859, it is interesting to note that the liberal view of jurisdiction attained its greatest popularity at a time when the Supreme Court's case load was growing so onerous that the Chief Justice threatened to resign. Only after the superior court was established in 1901 did an expanding role for equity jurisdiction in the superior court begin to

---

152   120 N.H. 54, 410 A.2d 1121 (1980).
153   120 N.H. at 56, 410 A.2d at 1122.
154   120 N.H. at 57, 410 A.2d at 1122.

take the place of a wider jurisdiction in probate. By 1991, the increased case loads in both the superior court and the probate courts made more urgent a clear statement of the probate court's general jurisdiction, and there were indications that suggested the adoption of a more liberal view.[155] In 1992, the debate over the jurisdiction of the probate court may have finally been resolved as a result of separate actions by the Supreme Court and the Legislature. In *In re Estate of O'Dwyer*,[156] the issue before the probate court was the effect of the divorce of the decedent on the joint tenancy under which he owned the marital domicile with his former wife. The Court again recited the theory of limited jurisdiction, quoting from *Wood v. Stone*, and noted that RSA 547:3 did not contain a specific grant of jurisdiction to determine title to real estate. The Court therefore concluded that the probate court had neither statutory authority nor common law jurisdiction to decide a dispute over the title to the property in question.[157]

Although the Court's holding seemed to cut back on the jurisdiction of the probate court, the practical effect of this holding on the powers of the probate courts may have been undercut by the changes made to RSA 547:3 by the Legislature in the same year as part of an omnibus bill implementing the recommendations of the Supreme Court's Long-Range Planning Task Force Regarding the Judicial Branch. The changes to RSA 547:3 expanding the jurisdiction of the probate courts included the following: jurisdiction to the administration of all matters and things of probate jurisdiction relating to the composition of estates of deceased persons; jurisdiction over claims against the executor or administrator for services related to the prior care and maintenance of the decedent; jurisdiction over the administration of insolvent estates; jurisdiction of petitions for partition and to quiet title to real estate pursuant to RSA 547-C; jurisdiction of declaratory judgment actions pursuant to RSA 547:11-b; and jurisdiction relating to durable power of attorney for health care under RSA 137-J.

In addition to these changes, the Legislature inserted new sections in RSA 547 that dealt with the probate court's power to resolve factual disputes and exercise equity jurisdiction. RSA 547:3-a gives the probate court the jurisdiction to try issues of material fact that are in dispute in a proceeding before

---

155 Some indication of the Court's thinking may be found in the Probate Court Rules (eff. Sept. 1, 1987), which generally adopt the procedures of the superior and the district and municipal courts and for the first time provide for pretrial discovery, a pretrial procedure and standing pretrial orders, and motions practice.

156 135 N.H. 323 (1992).

157 135 N.H. at 324.

it once due notice has been given to all the interested parties. RSA 547:3- b grants the probate courts the powers of a court of equity "in cases in which there is not a plain, adequate and complete remedy at law involving partition, guardianships, conservatorships and the probate of an estate and in all other like cases cognizable in a court of equity arising under RSA 347, RSA 347-C and RSA 552:7." This section also gives the probate courts concurrent jurisdiction with the superior court in cases involving charitable uses and trusts other than express trusts. Finally, the probate courts were given the power to grant writs of injunction whenever they are necessary to "prevent fraud or injustice."

These changes will give the probate courts a greater ability to handle matters in which they were formerly powerless. However, the uncertainties regarding the precise limits of probate court jurisdiction will likely persist and the Supreme Court will undoubtedly rejoin the debate.

§ 3.15. —Common Areas of Conflict

The great majority of the cases that have addressed the question whether a person dissatisfied with the order he has received or apprehensive about the result he may receive from a probate court may seek the aid of equity for his protection have arisen during the twentieth century, when the Supreme Court has favored limiting the jurisdiction of probate courts to a narrow scope and replacing what might earlier have been recognized as the inherent powers of the probate courts with the equity jurisdiction of the superior court.

In *Rockwell v. Dow*, Chief Justice Peasley expressed the view that, in the area of estates of deceased persons, the superior court has jurisdiction of all things " 'incident to the business of conducting administration,' " while the probate courts are limited to matters arising in " 'a settlement with the judge of probate concerning administration already had.' " The *Rockwell* test, separating a wide range of issues that may arise during a fiduciary's administration from his or her narrow duty to account to the probate court, has been generally applied during this century to narrow the jurisdiction of probate and expand the equity jurisdiction of the superior court.

The three subject areas in which disputes most often arise regarding the dividing line between the jurisdiction of the superior court and the probate courts are custody and protection of minors, construction of testamentary instruments, and declarations of rights in a decedent's property.

Library References

CJS Courts § 490

§ 3.16. —Custody and Protection of Minors

Parents are by statute the legal guardians of their unmarried children under eighteen years of age.[158] The probate courts have exclusive jurisdiction to remove parents as guardians and to appoint new guardians for their children upon either the unfitness or death of both parents.[159] But the superior court also has authority in certain circumstances to regulate the custodial rights of the parents.[160] Under RSA 458:35, the superior court may "make such order as to the custody . . . of the children as justice may require" when the parents are living apart but have not obtained a legal separation or filed a libel for divorce.[161] While a divorce libel is pending, the court may make "such orders respecting the custody . . . of the minor children of the parties as shall be deemed expedient for the benefit of the children."[162] When a legal separation or a divorce has been obtained, the court can make an order relating to child custody that will "be most conducive to [the children's] benefit."[163] The superior court also has jurisdiction at common law to consider custodial rights in the context of a petition for writ of habeas corpus based on a claim that a child is being improperly held.[164] And the superior court can use its statutory equity powers to enjoin one person from interfering with another's custodial rights. Thus, although it is often said that the

---

158 RSA 463:4 and 21:44.

159 RSA ch. 463. See RSA 463:6-a (authorizing the appointment of either the Office of the Director of the Division of Children and Youth Services, the Child and Family Service of New Hampshire, or New Hampshire Catholic Charities, Inc., to be appointed guardian of a minor). See also Place v. Place, 129 N.H. 252, 525 A.2d 704 (1987) (noting the probate court's power to appoint a nonparent as guardian for a minor when both parents are found to be unfit). Leclerc v. Leclerc, 85 N.H. 121, 123, 155 A. 249, 251 (1931). The dicta in State v. Richardson, 40 N.H. 272, 273 (1860), and Prime v. Foote, 63 N.H. 52, 53 (1884), to the effect that a court of chancery in New Hampshire could remove a parent as guardian and appoint a new guardian in his place was implicitly overruled on the former point in Brown v. Jewell, 86 N.H. 190, 192, 165 A. 713, 714 (1933) ("Except when resort may be had to habeas corpus proceedings, and aside from cases where the child has property, a surviving parent can be removed from his statutory guardianship only on proof of his unfitness in a trial of a petition for the probate court's appointment of a guardian"), and expressly overruled on the latter point in Leclerc v. Leclerc, 85 N.H. 121, 124, 155 A. 249, 251 (1931).

160 White v. White, 77 N.H. 26, 86 A. 353 (1913).

161 RSA 458:35.

162 RSA 458:16.

163 RSA 458:17 and 27. While the various sections may seem to impose different standards upon custody orders depending upon the stage of proceedings at which they are entered, the Supreme Court has frequently held that only one standard can be applied: the welfare of the minor.

164 State v. Richardson, 40 N.H. 272 (1860).

superior court's jurisdiction over custodial rights is entirely a creature of statute and that the superior court has no independent equity jurisdiction over the custody of minors,[165] the superior court's jurisdiction is broad and flexible,[166] although confined to the custodial aspects of guardianship.

How far the superior court's jurisdiction extends is hard to determine. In *Carpenter v. Carpenter*,[167] the Court considered but did not decide whether a probate court could appoint a guardian while a petition for legal separation and custody was pending in the superior court. At that time, probate appeals were heard in the superior court, and the Supreme Court thought that the possibilities for a conflict in jurisdiction were unlikely because the probate court would probably appoint the same person as a guardian that the superior court would name as a custodian and because, if there was an objection to the probate court's action, the superior court could resolve it on appeal.[168]

In *Brown v. Jewell*,[169] a child's maternal aunt had petitioned the probate court for appointment as his guardian after the child's mother died. The child's father later filed his own petition for appointment, but the probate court appointed the aunt. The father appealed the denial of his petition to the superior court, where, although he was found to be a suitable custodian,

---

165 See, e.g., Trow v. Trow, 95 N.H. 529, 68 A.2d 538 (1949); Stetson v. Stetson, 103 N.H. 290, 171 A.2d 28 (1961).

166 See, e.g., Sheehy v. Sheehy, 88 N.H. 223, 186 A. 1 (1936), where the Supreme Court held that the superior court's jurisdiction over a petition for a writ of habeas corpus included power to decree temporary custody while the action was pending. But see Leclerc v. Leclerc, 85 N.H. 121, 155 A. 249 (1931), where the Court stated that habeas corpus proceedings could at most result in a temporary award pending final action by the probate court. In the recent case of Brauch v. Shaw, 121 N.H. 562, 432 A.2d 1 (1981), the Court has drawn the line more clearly, holding that the superior court cannot create custodial rights, either by the appointment of a guardian or custodian, but it can regulate the exercise of rights held jointly by two or more persons. The superior court has broad discretion in originating, modifying, or refusing to modify support orders to allocate responsibility for the educational expenses of adult children. Azzi v. Azzi, 118 N.H. 653, 392 A.2d 148, 151 (1978) (within court's discretion to order parties to jointly contribute toward reasonable college expenses of their children); Merrifield v. Merrifield, 122 N.H. 372, 374–75, 445 A.2d 1087, 1088 (1982) (no abuse of discretion when court declined to order divorced parent to contribute toward college costs of adult child); Kayle v. Kayle, 132 N.H. 402, 404–05, 565 A.2d 1069, 1071–72 (1989) (court did not err, under circumstances of the case, in ordering divorced parent to pay reasonable college expenses of adult child); Gnirk v. Gnirk, 134 N.H. 199, 203–06, 589 A.2d 1008, 1011–13 (1991) (no abuse of discretion when superior court ordered divorced father to contribute toward adult child's college expenses, despite lack of educational support provision in original support order); French v. French, 117 N.H. 696, 699, 378 A.2d 1127, 1128–29 (1977); LeClair v. LeClair, 137 N.H. 213 (1993).

167 78 N.H. 440, 101 A. 628 (1917).

168 78 N.H. at 456, 101 A. at 635.

169 86 N.H. 190, 165 A. 713 (1933).

his petition was dismissed on the ground that a guardian had already been appointed. The aunt then filed a bill in equity in the superior court seeking to enjoin the father from interfering with her custodial rights. After the superior court issued the injunction, the father objected that the order was beyond its jurisdiction. The Supreme Court agreed with the father, pointing out that the superior court had no independent equity jurisdiction in custody matters and could not therefore enjoin his interference with the plaintiff's custody. In addition, the Court held that the father, being the legal guardian by statute, could not be replaced by the aunt until found unfit. But the most interesting aspect of the case is its statement about probate court jurisdiction over custody. The aunt had objected that probate court jurisdiction could not be exclusive in the area of guardianship and custody of minors because it was not customary in probate court guardianship proceedings to consider the wide range of issues usually raised in custody hearings in the superior court. Justice Allen, writing for the Court, replied that "[a]ny matter which may be properly considered may be brought up in the probate proceeding"[170] and observed that "[a]ny view that the court may not inquire and receive evidence in full measure and as widely as in a proceeding in equity tends to defeat a proper appointment."[171] Finally, in *Leclerc v. Leclerc*[172] the Supreme Court was faced with the question whether the superior court may order that custody of two minor children which it had previously awarded to the father as part of a divorce decree be granted to another person after the father's death. The father had died slightly over six months after entry of the divorce decree which had split custody of the four children between the parents, and the father's sister had successfully petitioned the Supreme Court to have custody of the two children in his care awarded to her. The Supreme Court held, however, that the superior court's jurisdiction over custody was limited by statute and that its jurisdiction over divorce proceedings, including custody orders associated with those proceedings, terminated upon the death of one of the parties. Thus, at the father's death, custody of the two children in his care reverted to their sole living guardian, the mother, who could thereafter be displaced only by a finding in the probate court that she was unfit.

The *Brown* and *Leclerc* cases are even more interesting when it is recalled that at the time they were decided in the early 1950s the Supreme Court was at the height of its efforts to restrict the jurisdiction of the probate court to

---

170 86 N.H. at 191, 165 A. at 713.

171 *Id.*

172 85 N.H. 121, 155 A. 249 (1931).

those matters specifically assigned to it by statute and to refer issues of uncertain jurisdiction to the superior court. These cases therefore make clear, by contrast, the Court's desire to protect the integrity of the probate court's jurisdiction over guardianships.[173] In 1992, the Legislature amended the probate courts' jurisdictional statute to provide for "jurisdiction in relation to the appointment and removal of . . . the guardians of minors."[174]

Library References

CJS Courts § 490
CJS Divorce §§ 303, 305
CJS Guardian & Ward §§ 11, 176

§ 3.17. —Construction of Testamentary Instruments

The probate courts have "the exclusive jurisdiction to interpret and construct wills and to interpret, modify and terminate testamentary and express trusts."[175] Further, Chapter 284:50 of the Laws of 1992, now set forth as RSA 547:3-a h, authorizes probate court jurisdiction with the superior courts[176] with regard to deviation from the terms of trust,[177] cy pres actions,[178] and termination of charitable trusts.[179] In cases where there has been a change of circumstances that would substantially impair the accomplishment of the purposes of the trust, or where such a change is reasonably foreseeable, the probate court has jurisdiction, upon a filing of a bill in equity by a trustee, to enter a decree permitting the trustee to deviate from the terms of the trust.[180] Similarly, probate courts are now statutorily authorized, upon petition of a trustee or attorney general, to order distribution of property in a charitable trust when its purpose or application has become impossible, impracticable, illegal, obsolete, ineffective, or prejudicial to the public interest.[181]

---

173 This desire has recently been confirmed by In re Penny N., 120 N.H. 269, 414 A.2d 541 (1980) (holding that the probate court could authorize a guardian it appointed to consent to sterilization of a minor ward).

174 RSA 547:3.

175 RSA 547:3. See also RSA 491:7. The probate court is granted concurrent jurisdiction with the superior court in cases involving charitable uses and trusts other than express trusts. RSA 547:3; 547:3-b.

176 See RSA 498:4-4(e).

177 RSA 547:3-c.

178 RSA 547:3-d.

179 RSA 547:3-h.

180 RSA 547:3-c. See also RSA 547:3-g.

181 RSA 547:3-d. See also RSA 547:3-e.

The Legislature also provided that in any probate court proceedings, the courts "shall have jurisdiction to try such factual issues to court after due notice to all interested parties."[182]

The 1992 legislation is a significant step toward clarifying the ambiguities created by several decades of case law with regard to the jurisdictional lines between the superior court and probate courts.

Library References

CJS Courts § 490

§ 3.18. —Declarations of Rights in a Decedent's Property

The probate courts have original and exclusive jurisdiction to decree a distribution of personal property and any residuary property of an estate,[183] and the superior court has the power to determine contested claims to all other kinds of property.[184] In general, the probate courts have exclusive jurisdiction to determine to whom property in the estate of a decedent belongs, while the superior court has the exclusive power to decide whether property belongs to the estate in the first place. In an interesting variation on these general principles, the Court in *Barrett v. Cady*[185] reversed an attempt by the superior court to decide which of two *estates* owned a bank account. Because the account belonged in either event to an estate, it was clearly property over which the probate court had jurisdiction and only the probate court could therefore decide the identity of its owner. The superior court had certified its decision to the probate court "for its guidance in . . . formulating its decree of distribution,"[186] but, in his opinion for the Court, Chief Justice Parsons wrote:

> By the constitution and the statute, the probate court has exclusive, original jurisdiction of the settlement and distribution of the estates of deceased persons. . . . While the court may upon request advise the administrator as to the execution of his trust in a proper case, it has no power to advise or direct in advance the action of the probate court, or to interfere with due administration therein. While the procedure invented by the decree may be convenient,

---

182 RSA 547:3-a.

183 Pt. 2, art. 80; RSA 547:3, 561:7 and 7-a.

184 RSA 491:7.

185 78 N.H. 60, 96 A. 325 (1915).

186 78 N.H. at 62, 96 A. at 327.

existing constitutional limitations preclude its adoption. So much
of the decree as assumes to advise and direct the probate court is
set aside.[187]

While it is undisputed that only the probate court can enter a decree
establishing title to an asset of an estate in a particular person, a great deal
of litigation has resulted from uncertainty over how the probate court is to
make its decision. The previous subsection discussed the conflict between
the superior court's jurisdiction to give advice and instructions to a fiduciary
and the probate court's power to construe wills and trust instruments in
approving decrees and accounts. As a general matter, the probate court's
authority to construe wills and trust instruments is a necessary but limited
adjunct to its express statutory jurisdiction to perform certain acts, while the
superior court has a general jurisdiction in equity to give binding instructions
to fiduciaries to protect them from acting in future dealings at their peril.
More difficult questions arise when the superior court is asked not to
determine whether the decedent owned a particular piece of property but to
decide how that property should be distributed by the administrator or
executor after his death. At first, the Supreme Court was inclined to take the
view that decisions of this sort were decisions within the exclusive province
of the probate courts and that petitions for advice and instruction by
executors and administrators would not lie in the superior court to determine
who was entitled to a bequest. Thus, in *Cobleigh v. Spring*,[188] when an
administrator of a murdered woman's estate asked the superior court to
advise him whether the estate of the husband who murdered her was entitled
to share in her estate, the Court declined to give the advice, saying in a per
curiam opinion:

> The bill cannot be maintained. It is the duty of the probate court
> to make the decree of distribution. . . . "The Superior Court cannot

---

187 78 N.H. at 64, 96 A. at 328. It is interesting to compare Barrett v. Cady to In re Bunker
Estate, 110 N.H. 285, 266 A.2d 114 (1970). In *Bunker*, the Court refused to declare, as
an executor had requested, that a bank account established by the decedent 48 years
before in the name of a daughter who vanished in the next year belonged to his estate.
The decedent had retained possession of the bank book until his death, with the
exception of a few months when the depository bank had had it. But the Court felt that
there was a question of title which could be tried between the daughter, the bank and
the estate and held that only the superior court had jurisdiction to determine it. Both
Barrett and *Bunker* turn on the unstated premise that probate court jurisdiction over
estates of deceased persons is in rem and of necessity limited to items which are
included in an estate. While a probate court can choose an owner from among estates,
it cannot declare that property is part of an estate if a third party claims it.

188 85 N.H. 560, 157 A. 886 (1932).

interfere with the exercise of that jurisdiction. . . ." The decree of the probate court will fully protect the plaintiff and consequently he cannot invoke the direction of the Superior Court.[189]

And in *Podrasnik v. Rochester Trust Co.*,[190] the Court dismissed an executrix's petition to have a will construed, distribution decided, and, should part of the estate go to her as a trustee, instructions given relating to her fiduciary duties. Repeating that "[o]riginal jurisdiction to decree the distribution is by statute vested in the probate court,"[191] the Court said, again in a per curiam opinion, that the executrix must file her account in the probate court along with a petition for a decree of distribution of the estate in her possession. The Court went on to say that only a fiduciary thereafter receiving an appointment from the probate court could petition the superior court for advice.

However, in 1950, the Court abruptly changed direction and held that the superior court could advise an administrator on the proper distribution of property under a will. In *Duncan v. Bigelow*,[192] the Court was asked to determine whether a bank account containing proceeds from the sale of real estate and the contents of a house, which sale was conducted by the decedent's guardian after she was declared insane, should, after her death, pass under a clause in her will specifically bequeathing bank deposits or should instead pass as the real estate and house contents would have passed had they not been sold. The superior court reserved and transferred the question to the Supreme Court. In his opinion for the Court, Chief Justice Johnston said:

> While the Probate Court has exclusive, original jurisdiction of decrees of distribution . . . this does not prevent the Superior Court from giving advice to a fiduciary concerning his future handling of an estate. So far as the *Podrasnik* case holds otherwise, it is overruled.[193]

The Court then proceeded to advise the administrator to distribute the proceeds of the sale as he would have distributed the items sold, rather than as he distributed the bank accounts. In the next month the Court gave

---

189 85 N.H. at 560, 157 A. at 886.
190 92 N.H. 65, 24 A.2d 493 (1942).
191 *Id.*
192 96 N.H. 216, 72 A.2d 497 (1950).
193 96 N.H. at 218, 72 A.2d at 498.

instructions on distribution of an estate to an executor, saying: "The procedural remedy of a petition for instructions in the Superior Court by an
executor for advice as to the construction of a will is not improper in advance
of a decree of distribution by the probate court."[194]

It is difficult to distinguish the harm sought to be avoided in *Barrett v.
Cady* from that created by *Duncan v. Bigelow*. The reversal of *Podrasnik*
suddenly put the probate courts and the superior court in a constant danger
of conflicting decisions relating to distribution under a will. It soon appeared
that the most practical way of avoiding unnecessary conflicts would be for
the probate courts, prior to entering a decree of distribution, to certify
questions of law relating to construction of a will to the Supreme Court
under what is now RSA 547:8. Chief Justice Johnston had even hinted at
this procedure in his opinion in *Duncan v. Bigelow*, saying that it "in certain
cases may be more expeditious for ascertaining requested instructions."[195]
But when it came to applying the device during the Court's next term, the
Chief Justice was disturbed that rather than leading to an increased resort
to the superior court's equity jurisdiction, the *Duncan* case had prompted
the filing of petitions for advice and instruction in the probate courts and
the subsequent certification of the questions they raised to the Supreme
Court. In *Estate of Gay*,[196] Chief Justice Johnston tried to cut off his new
practice by refusing to answer questions propounded to the probate court
by an administrator, and holding that only the superior court could entertain
petitions for advice and instruction. But Justice Kenison dissented, saying
that the Court's construction of the statute was "stricter than required by its
express terms, more limited than its apparent policy and purpose . . . and
inconsistent with the action actually taken by this court under the same
statute in . . . *Amoskeag Trust Co. v. Haskell*."[197] Within four months, Justice
Kenison had won over a majority of the Justices to this point of view and,
in *In re Harrington Estate*,[198] was able to write an opinion for the Court
holding that a probate court *could* certify questions of law presented by a
petition for instructions filed by an administrator or executor. Chief Justice

---

194 Roberts v. Tamworth, 96 N.H. 223, 227, 73 A.2d 119, 123 (1950).

195 96 N.H. at 219, 73 A.2d at 499. In fact, the Court had given advice to an executor by
answering questions transferred under that statute three months before its decision in
Duncan v. Bigelow in the case of Amoskeag Trust Company v. Haskell, 96 N.H. 89, 70
A.2d 210 (1950).

196 97 N.H. 102, 81 A.2d 841 (1951).

197 97 N.H. at 106, 81 A.2d at 843.

198 97 N.H. 184, 84 A.2d 173 (1951).

Johnston remained true to his rationale in *Gay* and dissented on the ground that a probate court "has no jurisdiction to entertain a petition for advice and instructions. . . ."[199] Thus, the *Podrasnik* balance was again struck, if not in law, at least in practice, and the probate courts, rather than the superior court, again became the courts of most likely first resort on questions concerning the distribution of a decedent's property. During the following term, in *Tate v. Hooper*,[200] the Court reaffirmed the jurisdiction of the superior court under *Duncan* and *Roberts* to advise an administrator on the proper distribution under a will. Justice Duncan dissented from the decision on the ground that the case overruled *Podrasnik*,[201] but, of course, that horse was already out of the barn.

One year later, the Court put a finer point on its holding in *Harrington* and suggested in *In re Byrne Estate*[202] that, because the predecessor to RSA 547:8 only allowed the transfer of questions so that the probate court might make a "proper decision of matters duly before it in proceedings coming within its statutory jurisdiction,"[203] only petitions for instructions which sought advice on the settlement and final distribution of estates of deceased persons and the distribution of the personal estate bequeathed by a testator could be entertained by the probate court.[204] With Chief Justice Johnston in retirement, a unanimous Court also took the occasion to overrule expressly that portion of *In re Gay Estate* which forbade the filing of petitions for instructions in the probate court.[205] A decade later, the Court honed the point even finer by saying in *In re Peterson Estate*[206] that the questions presented by a petition for instructions can only be certified under RSA 547:30 if both the probate court and the fiduciary are in "justifiable doubt" concerning the proper construction of a will.[207] And in *In re Bliss Estate*,[208] the Court refused to answer questions posed by an executor and certified by a probate court where no party in interest took a position different from that adopted by the executor and all parties agreed that the Court's advice was not necessary to the distribution or administration of the estate.

---

199 97 N.H. at 187, 84 A.2d at 175.

200 97 N.H. 432, 89 A.2d 915 (1952).

201 97 N.H. at 434, 89 A.2d at 917.

202 98 N.H. 300, 100 A.2d 157 (1953).

203 RSA 547:30.

204 98 N.H. at 302, 100 A.2d at 159.

205 *Id.*

206 104 N.H. 508, 190 A.2d 418 (1963).

207 104 N.H. at 510, 190 A.2d at 419.

208 117 N.H. 914, 379 A.2d 839 (1977).

None of these cases, however, speaks to the problem that Chief Justice Johnston foresaw: that the probate courts might not transfer questions presented by a petition for instructions, but would instead sit as a court of equity and make a decision which, because no appeal was taken, would become final. Although it is difficult to see any functional difference between the probate court undertaking such an inquiry when examining a final account and examining the question upon a formal petition before the account is presented for its approval, there is the very practical difference that the ability to file such a petition in the probate court before filing an account detracts considerably from the attractiveness of filing a similar petition in the superior court. Before the superior court lost its jurisdiction over probate appeals in 1975,[209] the latter procedure still had the advantage of providing an interpretation which would be unchanged by appeal. But since 1975, appeals on issues of law from the probate courts have gone to the Supreme Court[210] and the only justification now for seeking the opinion of the superior court, rather than the probate court, is the hope that the former will, for some reason, decide the question in a way more favored by the petitioner.

Thus, while the probate court still has original and exclusive jurisdiction to enter a decree of distribution, it no longer has the sole power to decide how that decree will be worded. After *Duncan*, *Roberts*, and *Tate*, the superior court has a concurrent jurisdiction to instruct an administrator or executor as to the distribution he is to make, and under *Harrington*, *Byrne*, *Peterson*, and *Bliss*, the probate courts can entertain petitions for advice relating to distribution prior to being obliged to pass upon a decree of distribution. The concern expressed in *Barrett v. Cady* that the superior court will direct the process in the probate courts has already come to pass. And, although, in theory there is little likelihood of the superior court and a probate court entering conflicting decrees, since the fiduciary must be the petitioner in each proceeding, the utility of such a concurrent jurisdiction is far from obvious. It would be simpler to commit exclusive jurisdiction to the probate courts to entertain petitions for advice relating to distribution under a will, and to give the superior court the sole power to advise fiduciaries in the execution of their trusts after the settlement of an estate.

Library References

CJS Courts § 490

---

209 See Laws of 1975, Chapter 395.
210 RSA 567-A:1.

§ 3.19. Specific Areas of Subject Matter Jurisdiction

(a) *Settlement and Distribution of Estates of Deceased Persons.*　The probate courts enjoy a constitutional,[211] statutory,[212] and common law[213] jurisdiction over the settlement and distribution of estates.[214]

(b) *Accounting by Trustees and Other Fiduciaries.*　The probate courts have exclusive jurisdiction by statute and at common law to compel a trustee or other fiduciary appointed by them to account for the administration of their trust.[215]

(c) *Appointment and Removal of Trustees.*　The probate courts have exclusive jurisdiction by statute and at common law to appoint testamentary trustees[216] and to remove them.[217]

(d) *Appointment and Removal of Guardians.*　The probate courts have exclusive jurisdiction by statute to appoint guardians of the person, guardians of the estate, guardians of the person and estate, and temporary guardians.[218] The probate courts have the same statutory jurisdiction as other courts to appoint a guardian ad litem to represent the interests of a person or persons who are incompetent or not present in a particular proceeding.[219] And the probate courts can remove guardians they appoint.[220]

(e) *Appointment of Conservators and Termination of Conservatorship.* The probate courts have exclusive statutory jurisdiction to appoint conservators[221] and to terminate conservatorships.[222]

211　Pt. 2, art. 80.

212　RSA 547:3.

213　Kimball v. Fisk, 39 N.H. 110 (1859).

214　See Prob. Ct. R. 23 (decedent dies testate but with no estate).

215　RSA 564:19; Lisbon Savings Bank and Trust Co. v. Estate of Moulton, 91 N.H. 477, 22 A.2d 331 (1941). See also RSA 564:1 and 548:5-a.

216　RSA 564:2-a and 10; Rockwell v. Dow, 85 N.H. 58, 154 A. 229 (1931); Leclerc v. Leclerc, 85 N.H. 121, 155 A. 249 (1931); Petition of Straw, 78 N.H. 506, 102 A. 628 (1917); Carr v. Corning, 73 N.H. 362, 62 A. 168 (1905); In re Borthwick Estate, 102 N.H. 344, 156 A.2d 759 (1959).

217　RSA 564:9.

218　RSA 464-A:9 and 12.

219　RSA 464-A:41. In light of the definition of the term "court" set forth in RSA 464-A:2(IV), there is at least some doubt whether this section applies to any courts besides the probate courts. But the section seems to have been intended as a successor to RSA 462:1 and the use of the defined term "court" should probably be regarded as an oversight.

220　RSA 464-A:39.

221　RSA 464-A:13.

222　RSA 464-A:16 and 547:4.

(f) *Adoption.*   The probate courts have exclusive statutory jurisdiction over the adoption of any person.[223]

(g) *Partition of Real Estate.*   The probate courts may decree a partition of real estate in cases where there is no dispute as to title.[224]

(h) *Changes of Name.*   The probate courts have exclusive statutory jurisdiction to enter a decree changing a natural person's name,[225] except in cases of divorce, where the power lies with the superior court.[226]

(i) *Termination of Parental Rights.*   The probate courts have exclusive statutory jurisdiction to terminate the parent-child relationship.[227]

(j) *Power To Revise Its Orders, Re-open Decrees, Preserve the Status Quo, and Punish for Contempt.*   The probate courts have no common law powers to punish for contempt or to enter orders to preserve the status quo, but they do have statutory power to enforce all orders and punish contempt in the same manner as the superior court might,[228] to revise or revoke their orders,[229] and to impound books, records, and assets, enjoin withdrawal of money or deposits or transfers of securities, or require the temporary investment or deposit of assets.[230]

(k) *Involuntary Admission to State Hospital.*   The probate court in the county where a person resides or is detained has jurisdiction to order his involuntary admission to a mental health facility in nonemergency cases.[231] Unless the committing judge retains jurisdiction over the case, the probate

---

223 RSA 170-B:11. See Prob. Ct. R. 38. See also Smith v. Consul General of Spain, 110 N.H. 62, 260 A.2d 95 (1969); In re Adoption of Baby C., 125 N.H. 216, 480 A.2d 101 (1984) (hearing to withdraw consent to adoption).

224 RSA 547:3.

225 RSA 547:7 and 170-B:21.

226 RSA 458:24.

227 RSA 170-C:3. See also Statutory Requirements and Guidelines for the Processing and Disposition of Termination of Parental Rights Cases in the Probate Courts and In re Noah W., 131 N.H. 53, 549 A.2d 1210 (1988).

228 RSA 547:11.

229 See Conservatorship of Bradlee, 120 N.H. 430, 415 A.2d 1144 (1980).

230 *Id.*

231 See In re Sanborn, 130 N.H. 430, 545 A.2d 726 (1988) ("[M]ental illness and dangerousness, as predicates for civil commitment, . . . may . . . be demonstrated by clear and convincing evidence." 130 N.H. at 431, 545 A.2d at 727. See also In re Fasi a/k/a Cass, 132 N.H. 478, 567 A.2d 178 (1989) (quoting In re Sanborn, 130 N.H. 430, 446, 545 A.2d 726, 736 (1988)); In re Perley, Jr., 137 N.H. 209 (1993).

court for the county in which the facility to which a person has been admitted is located has jurisdiction to order his release from that facility.[232]

(l) *Powers of Attorney.* The probate courts have concurrent statutory jurisdiction with the superior court to determine the status of a power of attorney, to review the acts of an agent acting under a power of attorney, and to order a termination of the power of attorney.[233]

Library References

CJS Courts §§ 298, 304

---

232 RSA 135-C:20(II). See also In re Petition for Admission of Demers, 130 N.H. 31, 533 A.2d 380 (1987) (probate court has no authority to impose conditions on the subsequent release of a person involuntarily admitted to a mental health facility). The jurisdiction of the probate courts "over persons civilly committed is entirely statutory." In re Petition for Admission of Demers, 130 N.H. at 34, 533 A.2d at 383.

233 RSA 506:7. The statute is unusual for the probate courts in a number of respects. First, it permits almost any person to file the petition. RSA 506:7(I) and (II). Second, it allows the probate court to give advice to the fiduciary and to issue declaratory judgments on such matters as the status of the power of attorney and the permissibility of proposed actions. Third, it grants the probate courts the power to "make orders and decrees, and take other actions necessary or proper to make determinations. . . ." While the language is broad enough to include a wide range of equitable relief, it must be remembered that the statute is attempting to address actions in both the probate courts and the superior court, and it is unlikely that the probate courts could sustain a claim to injunctive or other broad equitable powers under the section. But, the statute probably is sufficient to justify orders for discovery and production. See Prob. Ct. R. 10 and 11.

CHAPTER 4. VENUE

A. PRINCIPLES OF VENUE

A. Principles of Venue

Library References

Validity of contractual provision limiting place or court in which action may be brought.
31 ALR4th 404.

77

§ 4.01. Definition

Venue is the locality in which a court having jurisdiction over a case will require it to be entered and tried. For the purposes of determining venue, there is no difference between actions at law and petitions or bills in equity.[1]

Library References

CJS Venue § 1

§ 4.02. Venue v. Exclusive Jurisdiction

Venue and exclusive jurisdiction are frequently designated in similar ways by New Hampshire statutes, but there is a fundamental difference between them. While venue is the location of the court in which an action or proceeding should be initiated or tried, exclusive jurisdiction is the grant to a specific court of sole power to determine that case or proceeding. As a general matter, exclusive jurisdiction cannot be waived or cured by a transfer from one court to another; a mistake of venue can always be waived or cured by transfer. Jurisdictional defects, unlike matters of venue, must be noticed and cured by the court sua sponte; questions of venue, because they do not relate to the power of the court or the enforceability of its judgment, are generally ignored by the court unless raised by one of the parties.

Library References

CJS Courts § 15

§ 4.03. Venue v. Forum Non Conveniens

The concept of venue must also be distinguished from the doctrine of forum non conveniens. While the former refers to the appropriate forum within a state for the entry and trial of an action, the latter addresses the question whether the case or proceeding should be tried in that state at all. Like questions of improper venue, the doctrine of forum non conveniens is not usually considered by the court unless raised by one of the parties. But unlike objections to venue, the effect of which can only be to transfer the case to another location within the state, the effect of requesting the application of the doctrine of forum non conveniens may be to terminate the case completely.

Library References

CJS Courts § 77

---

1 Bay State Iron Company v. Goodall, 39 N.H. 223, 232 (1859).

Cross References

Forum non conveniens, Chapter 5.

§ 4.04. Considerations of Venue

Although venue may be questioned at any stage of the proceedings,[2] considerations of venue usually focus on one of two issues: (1) the location or locations in which the action must be entered (hereinafter referred to as "original venue") and (2) the location in which an action ought to be tried (hereinafter referred to as "proper venue").

B. Original Venue

§ 4.05. Definition

"Original venue" is the location (or, more often, locations) in which an action must be commenced. Original venue is most often dictated by statute, but in many cases it may be determined by reference to the common law. In courts of limited jurisdiction—the municipal, district, and probate courts—original venue is almost entirely prescribed by statute. In the superior court, it is more frequently established by reference to the common law.

§ 4.06. Municipal Courts—History

From 1915 until 1963, the municipal courts in New Hampshire possessed concurrent jurisdiction with the superior court over certain civil actions involving less than $500, in which title to real estate was not involved and the defendant resided in the county.[3] The municipal courts also had civil jurisdiction over landlord and tenant actions, petitions involving neglected or delinquent children (after 1937), and small claims actions (after 1939). During this period, one statute prescribed original venue for claims for damages and other statutes set forth original venue provisions for landlord and tenant, small claims, and juvenile actions. As a result, different require-

---

2 Langdell v. Eastern Basket & Veneer Company, 78 N.H. 243, 99 A. 90 (1916).

3 From 1915 until 1931, the municipal courts had concurrent jurisdiction with the superior court over civil actions in which title to real estate was not involved and the defendant lived in the county. Municipal courts in towns or cities with a population of less than 50,000 could entertain such actions only if the amount in controversy was $100 or less. Municipal courts in other towns or cities could hear such cases if the amount in controversy did not exceed $500. Laws of 1915, Chapter 30:5. In 1931, the population limit was reduced from 50,000 to 1,500 persons. Laws of 1931, Chapter 164:1 and 2. In 1963, the municipal court system was abolished. Laws of 1963, Chapter 331:1. The municipal courts have never had any exclusive civil jurisdiction.

ments for original venue were applicable to each type of action over which the municipal courts had jurisdiction.

In 1963, the Legislature phased out the municipal courts and a new system of district courts was established to take its place.[4] As part of this reorganization, the municipal courts were stripped of all jurisdiction over claims for damages except in small claims actions.[5] But the original venue requirements that had previously applied to those damage actions were left in the statute and now appear in RSA 502:26, as follows:

> Actions shall be returnable to the municipal court in the town or city where either the plaintiff or defendant resides; if neither the plaintiff nor defendant resides in a town or city wherein a municipal court is located, then the action may be returnable to any municipal court in the county.[6]

Because the civil jurisdiction of the municipal courts is now limited, there is at present no situation in which this original venue statute can be used, and it remains only as an historical anomaly.

§ 4.07. —Landlord and Tenant Actions

RSA 502-A:6 provides that actions against tenants may be commenced in the district court of the judicial district where either the plaintiff or the defendant live or the district in which the premises are located.[7] The

---

4 See RSA 502-A:34 and 35. Laws of 1963, Chapter 331:1.

5 See RSA 502-A:34 and 35. Laws of 1963, Chapter 331:6 and 8.

6 Presumably this refers to the county in which either the plaintiff or the defendant resides.

7 This is consistent with RSA 540:13, which provides that an action by a plaintiff for possession of his premises may be brought in a district court.

RSA 502:26 states that an action may be brought in the municipal court for the town or city in which either party lives. Originally, a justice of the peace was authorized to hear any action arising in his county, including actions for possession. See Revised Statutes (1842), ch. 175, § 1 and ch. 209, § 8. In 1852, towns were authorized to establish police courts to hear any civil case that any justice of the peace in the county could hear, and justices were thereafter forbidden to hear an action over which they would otherwise have had jurisdiction if a police court had been established in their town. Laws of 1852, Chapter 1282. Although the statute granted police courts "original jurisdiction . . . of all suits and actions which may . . . be heard, tried, and determined before any justice of the peace in the county" (Revised Statutes (1842) ch. 209, § 3), it does not appear to have been construed to deprive all justices of the peace in a county of any civil jurisdiction once a police court had been established in a town in the county. Justice Page considered that the statute merely allowed police courts "to assume some of the jurisdiction of justices of the peace." Smith v. Tallman, 87 N.H. 176, 178, 175 A. 857, 858 (1934). This view seems also to have been adopted by the commissioners responsible for compiling the General Statutes in 1865–67 (see G.S., ch. 196, § 5), the

Supreme Court shares concurrent jurisdiction with the district court for actions arising under RSA 540-A:2 (concerning the right to quiet enjoyment and damage of property) and RSA 540-A:3 (prohibited acts of both landlord and tenant).

§ 4.08. —Small Claims Actions

RSA 503:3-a and 3-b set forth what appear to be inconsistent original venue requirements for small claims actions. Section 3-a requires that the action be filed in the municipal court where either the plaintiff or defendant resides or, if neither resides in a town with a municipal court, in the district court for the district where either resides. Section 3-b requires that the action be commenced in the municipal court in the town where the *defendant* resides or, if the defendant does not live in a town with a municipal court, in the district court in the defendant's district. Section 3-b goes on to provide that when the defendant is not a resident of New Hampshire, the claim may be filed in "the Court of any town or district" where the defendant does business, makes a contract with a resident, commits a tort, or owns, uses, or possesses property. It must be assumed that this latter reference to a court of any town or district permits filing the action in *either* a municipal or a district court. However, Section 3-b refers solely to the place of *defendant's* residence or conduct. Because Section 3-b became effective three days after the 1975 amendments to Section 3-a, it might be argued that one effect of Section 3-b was to repeal the permission given by the 1975 amendments to Section 3-a to commence a small claims action where the *plaintiff* resides. But a look at the legislative history of these two amendments suggests a contrary conclusion.[8] The two sections should be read together as follows:

General laws in 1877–78 (see G.L., ch. 215, § 5) and the Public Statutes in 1900 (see P.S., ch. 211, § 5). Thus, from 1852 until 1911, it appears to have been permissible to bring an action for possession before any police court or, if there was no police court in a town, before any justice of the peace in the county. In 1911, the Legislature gave towns without a police court the option of having a trial justice with all the jurisdiction of a justice of the peace and provided that actions which would otherwise be returnable to a justice of the peace in the town must thereafter be filed with the trial justice. Laws of 1911, Chapter 169. Then in 1915, the municipal court system replaced the police courts and assumed all their jurisdiction, the municipal court inherited the same jurisdiction that the justices of the peace and police courts once had to hear a landlord and tenant action arising anywhere in the county. Laws of 1915, Chapter 30; Smith v. Tallman, 87 N.H. 176, 175 A. 857 (1934).

8 Section 3-b appeared in the 1975 Session as SB 142 and, although second to take effect, it was the first of the amendments to be passed in that year. In his favorable report for the Senate Committee on Judiciary, Senator Bradley said:

(1) *When both parties reside in the state:*   The action may be filed in the municipal court in the town or city where either resides, or, if neither party resides in a town or city with a municipal court, in the district court for the district in which either resides.[9]

(2) *When the defendant alone resides in the state:*   The action may be filed in the municipal court in the town or city where he resides, or, if there is none, in the district court for the district in which he resides.

(3) *When the plaintiff alone resides in the state:*   The action may be filed in the municipal or district court for the town, city, or district in which the defendant does business, makes a contract with a resident, commits a tort, or owns, uses, or possesses property.

(4) *When neither party resides in the state:*   The action may be filed in the municipal or district court for the town, city, or district in which the defendant does business, commits a tort, or owns, uses, or possesses property.[10]

Mr. President, this bill makes it clear that the courts handling small claims have so-called long-arm jurisdiction over out of state defendants. The present law says that you sue a person in the town that he resides. The difficulty with that is that many of the defendants are out of state. As a matter of custom, most courts allow you to sue the out of state person on the theory that an out of state defendant does reside where he's doing business. All this bill would do is make it clear that you can sue a nonresident defendant in the district where the defendant transacts any business or maker, a contract with a resident of the town or district, commits a tortious act or owns, uses or possesses any real or personal property.

Apparently, the sole purpose of SB 142 was to establish original venue in small claims actions against out-of-state defendants. About a month after Senator Bradley's report, HB 592 (eventually enacted as Section 3-a) made its way to the Senate floor. This time Senator Bossie presented the favorable report of the Committee on Judiciary, saying in part, "This bill would just add in a district court system when one brings a small claim action, that it may be where either the plaintiff or the defendant resides. As we know, now it is only where the defendant resides." Obviously, HB 592 was designed to expand the choice of forums to include the town of the plaintiff's residence. The purposes of SB 142 and HB 592 are not inconsistent and, had they taken effect in reverse order, there would be little question today that the effect of HB 592 would be to amend SB 142 to provide a forum in the town where the plaintiff resided. There is no reason to believe that their effective dates were arranged by the Legislature to cause the repeal of HB 592 three days after it had taken effect.

9   The 1975 amendments to section 3-a demonstrate the Legislature's desire to expand the number of small claims cases which may be filed in the municipal rather than the district court. Section 3-a should therefore be read as requiring a plaintiff who does not live in a town with a municipal court to file in the municipal court in the defendant's town if there is one.

10   It is assumed that the reference in section 3-b to the place where the defendant "makes a contract with the resident of the town or district" is designed to restrict original venue for such a claim to the actual resident with whom the defendant contracts.

RSA 502:26 adds nothing to these choices of venue. As Sections 3-a and 3-b already authorize original venue at the residence of either the plaintiff or the defendant, the permission in RSA 502:26 to choose a municipal court in the county is contrary to both the requirements of Section 3-a that the case go to the district court if both parties are residents of New Hampshire and the requirement of Section 3-b that the case follow the defendant's activities if he is a nonresident.

§ 4.09. District Courts—In General

Under the municipal court system that existed from 1915 until 1963, each town or city with a population of 2,000 or more and any other town which had so voted was entitled to establish and operate a court having limited civil jurisdiction. This system left a number of smaller towns without their own courts and threw the burden for cases arising in those towns on the larger towns and cities.

When the Legislature abolished the municipal court system, it divided the state into thirty-seven districts; at present there are thirty-four.[11] Each town and city within the state is located within a district, and each district has its own court of limited civil jurisdiction.[12] The requirements for original venue are set forth in RSA 502-A:16, as follows:

---

11 RSA 502-A:1.

12 The nature of that jurisdiction has changed considerably over the past 30 years, as the old municipal courts have terminated and the jurisdiction of the district courts has expanded. Those changes may be summarized as follows:

Concurrent Jurisdiction

From 1963 until 1965, all district courts had concurrent jurisdiction with the superior court over civil actions for damages in which the defendant resided in the *county* and the damages claimed did not exceed $1,500. Laws of 1963, Chapter 331:1. From 1965 until 1969, the district courts possessed the same concurrent jurisdiction if the defendant resided within the *district*. Laws of 1965, Chapter 327:2. From 1969 until 1972, the district courts had the same concurrent jurisdiction if the title to real estate was not involved and either the plaintiff or defendant resided within the district. Laws of 1969, Chapter 234:4. In 1972, the concurrent jurisdiction of the district courts was expanded to include cases in which the damages claimed did not exceed $3,000, title to real estate was not involved and either the plaintiff or the defendant lived within the district. Laws of 1972, Chapter 13.1. In 1979 the concurrent jurisdiction of the district courts was expanded to include claims not in excess of $5,000, with the same restrictions. Laws of 1979, Chapter 273:1. In 1983, it was again expanded to encompass claims of up to $10,000 in all courts, and $20,000 in courts selected by the Supreme Court. Laws of 1983, Chapter 382. It was last expanded in 1992, and at present, the concurrent jurisdiction of the district court includes claims of up to $25,000 in which the title to real estate is not involved and either the plaintiff or the defendant live within the district. The Supreme Court now has the authority to increase the concurrent jurisdiction of the district courts up to $50,000. Laws of 1992, Chapter 284:37.

Actions shall be returnable to the district court of the judicial district where either plaintiff or defendant resides; except that actions arising under RSA 540, relative to actions against tenants, may also be returnable in the judicial district in which the real property in question is located. For the purposes of this section, a partnership or a corporation shall be deemed to reside in any judicial district in which it maintains an office or place of business.

Thus, any civil cause for damages over which the district court has jurisdiction may presently be commenced in the district of either the plaintiff's or the defendant's residence.

At present, the district courts have exclusive jurisdiction over claims for damages not exceeding $1,500, if the title to real estate is not involved and the plaintiff or defendant lives within the district. District courts share concurrent jurisdiction with the superior courts over claims for damages between $1,500 and $25,000, with the same restrictions. The Supreme Court has the authority to increase the jurisdictional amount to $50,000.

But the district courts also have jurisdiction over numerous other matters, including small claims when there is no municipal court in the town where either party resides,[13] and juvenile petitions.[14] In each such case, the statute creating the cause of action has its own original venue section which must be followed.[15]

Exclusive Jurisdiction.
   When the district courts were established in 1963, those in which the salary of the justice exceeded $10,000 per year were given original and exclusive jurisdiction over civil cases in which *all parties* lived within the *district*, the title to real estate was not involved and damages did not exceed $500. Laws of 1963, Chapter 331:1. In 1965, the same jurisdiction was given to four specific district courts (Keene, Nashua, Manchester, and Concord) and was expanded to cases where only the defendant lived within the *district*. Laws of 1965, Chapter 327:1. In 1967, this jurisdiction was given to four more district courts (Laconia, Hampton, Portsmouth, and Dover). Laws of 1967, Chapter 438:2. In 1969, the jurisdiction was given to six more district courts (Goffstown, Milford, Peterborough, Exeter, Derry, and Salem) and was expanded further to include cases where *either* the plaintiff or defendant lived in the *district*. Laws of 1969, Chapter 234:3. In 1972, the jurisdiction was extended to all district courts. Laws of 1972, Chapter 13:1. In 1991, exclusive jurisdiction was expanded to cover civil cases in which the damages claimed do not exceed $1,500, no title to real estate is involved, and either party lives within the district. Laws of 1991, Chapter 47.

13 See RSA 503:3-a and 3-b. A small claim is defined as any action not involving the title to real estate in which the damages do not exceed $2,500. RSA 503:1.

14 See RSA 169-B:5, 169-C:5, and 169-D:4.

15 See, e.g., RSA 540:13 and 502-A:16.

§ 4.10. —Juvenile Petitions

RSA 169-B:5, 169-C:5, and 169-D:4 permit juvenile petitions to be filed in any district court serving a district in which "the minor is found or resides." This is a much wider original venue provision than RSA 502-A:16 or 502:26, as it allows the action to be commenced wherever a party happens to be.

§ 4.11. Superior Courts—Generally

In the superior court, original venue is frequently specified by statute, but more often than not depends upon the application of common law tests which determine whether the action is "local" or "transitory."

§ 4.12. —Statutory Causes of Action

Over seventy-five statutes refer to a specific original venue in setting forth a procedure for their enforcement.[16] Most of these statutes set forth a mandatory and exclusive venue,[17] but a few create an additional venue to

---

16 Statutes which set forth specific original venue must be distinguished from statutes which assign exclusive subject matter jurisdiction to the court in one location. See, e.g., RSA 51:7 (a dispute between towns concerning the proper boundary between them must be heard by the superior court for the county in which the older town or the town paying the higher proportion of public taxes is located). The distinction between mandatory original venue and exclusive subject matter jurisdiction arises from the wording of the various statutes and is probably more often the result of legislative inadvertence than of legislative intent. The distinction is important, however, because a failure to comply with even mandatory original venue has no effect on the court's power to decide the case and can always be cured, while noncompliance with the requirements of exclusive subject-matter jurisdiction deprives the court of power to make a binding judgment.

17 See, e.g., RSA 35-A:15(IV) (suit by a trustee to enforce the rights of bondholders in the New Hampshire Municipal Bond Bank must be brought in Merrimack County); RSA 78-A:20(II) (action to collect Meals and Rooms Tax must be brought in the defendant's county of residence, or, if not a resident, in Merrimack County); RSA 120:2 (appeal from a condemnation award by selectmen on behalf of the United States government must be brought in the county where the land is located); RSA 161-C:14 (action to foreclose a support lien on real or personal property must be brought in the county where the property was located when the lien was filed); RSA 168-A:9 (paternity suit must be filed in the county where either the father or mother resides or where property of the father is located); RSA 471-C:30(I) (escheat proceeding must be filed in the Merrimack County Superior Court). However, the wording and context of each of these statutes must be closely examined. Some statutes which use permissive language in fact create a mandatory and exclusive venue. See, e.g., RSA 471-C:28 ("A person aggrieved . . . may bring an action to establish the claim in the Merrimack county superior court. . . ."). RSA 471-C:36 formerly stated that, "The administrator may bring an action in the Superior Court for Merrimack County," but has been expanded to include ". . . or in any federal court with jurisdiction."

that already available at common law.[18] When a statute does not specify any venue for the commencement of an action, reference must be made to general common law principles which determine whether the action is "local" or "transitory."

§ 4.13. —Common Law Principles

At common law, a "local" action could only be commenced in the county in which it arose, while a "transitory" action could be brought wherever the plaintiff or defendant could be found. The distinction between "transitory" and "local" actions was explained by the Supreme Court in *The Educational Society of the Denomination Called Christians v. Varney*,[19] as follows:

> Whatever cause of action arises out of a local subject, or is a violation of a local right or interest, is local. . . . Such are all real and mixed actions—actions of ejectment, trespass quare clausum, trespass on the case for disturbance of a right of way, obstruction or diversion of watercourses, and whatever is founded upon privity of estate, even though pecuniary damages only, and not a right or interest in land, may be recoverable. Such an action can only arise in a particular place, and the venue must be laid there.
>
> Transitory actions are those personal actions which might have arisen in any county—actions in assumpsit or of contract, actions which seek nothing more than the recovery of money, or personal chattels, whether they sound in contract or tort . . . because actions of this kind are generally founded on the violation of rights which, in contemplation of law, have no locality. Such are actions of assumpsit and contract, whenever the assumpsit or contract is not involved in privity of estate.[20]

While the principle seems clear enough, it has sometimes been difficult to apply. For example, in *Varney* the Court classified an action to recover personal property as "transitory." Yet only four years earlier, in *Sleeper v. Osgood*,[21] the Court had held that replevin was a local action and must be commenced in the county where the goods had been unlawfully taken.[22]

---

18 See, e.g., RSA 1:17 (civil matters arising in New Hampshire's marine territory may be filed in Rockingham county).

19 54 N.H. 376 (1847).

20 54 N.H. at 377–78.

21 50 N.H. 331 (1870).

22 This principle has since been modified by statute. See RSA 536-A. On the face of that statute, it would appear that a statutory writ of replevin may now be obtained from any

Over the years, the nature of several types of actions have been determined by the Supreme Court, as follows:

Local

(a) Scire facias (the writ is founded upon the court's record which is located in one place).[23]

(b) Damages to real estate.[24]

(c) Breach of duty by public officers (perhaps on the theory that public officers derive their authority and duties from the locality from which they are elected or for which they are appointed).[25]

(d) Waste.[26]

(e) Ejectment.[27]

(f) Quaere impedit.[28]

(g) Nuisance, trespass, and other damages to real property.[29]

(h) Foreclosure of a mortgage on real property.[30]

---

superior court or district court in the state (subject only to jurisdictional limits determined by the value of the property) regardless of the residence of the parties or location of the property. RSA 536-A:1. The only remaining vestige of its common law nature as a "local" action is the requirement that the writ be directed to the "sheriff, constable, or police officer within whose jurisdiction the property is located." RSA 536-A:8.

Similarly, a prejudgment attachment may be obtained from the court in which the underlying action is filed (see RSA 511-A) and the Court's order "may be filed with the register of deeds, town or city clerk, secretary of state or wherever notice is required to perfect attachments." RSA 511-A:5. Although it had been decided that the necessity to seek a prejudgment attachment from a court in the county where the property was located did not affect the original venue of the underlying action (Thayer v. Padelford, 69 N.H. 301, 302, 41 A. 447 (1897)), the problem has been eliminated by the new procedures under RSA 511-A.

23 Parsons v. Pearson, 1 N.H. 336 (1818).

24 State v. Kinne, 39 N.H. 129 (1859).

25 White v. Sanborn, 6 N.H. 220 (1833).

26 Worster v. Winnipiseogee Lake Co., 25 N.H. 525 (1852).

27 *Id.*

28 *Id.*

29 *Id.* See RSA 544:4 (a petition to abate a nuisance as defined in RSA 544:1 to be brought in the superior court for the county or judicial district in which the property on which the nuisance occurs is located).

30 Tucker v. Lake, 67 N.H. 193, 29A. 406 (1892). This is apparently still a local action. RSA 479:25, as amended in 1977, requires that a petition to enjoin a foreclosure sale be filed in the superior court for the county in which the mortgaged premises are situated.

(i) Breach of warranty covenants in a deed (based only upon privity of estate).[31]

(j) Action against a town for defects in a highway.[32]

Transitory

(a) Based on privity of contract.[33]

(b) Action for damages resulting from injury to a chattel.[34]

For the purposes of original venue, all proceedings incident to an action possess the same character as the underlying action itself.[35] It has also been suggested that where a plaintiff bases his claim on two causes of action, one local and the other transitory, he is entitled to a venue justified by either.[36]

At common law, a transitory action could be brought in any county. In New Hampshire, this common law rule has been altered by RSA 507:9, which provides that a "transitory" action may be brought in the county or judicial district where either party resides (if one or both parties are inhabitants of the state) or, if no party is an inhabitant, in any county or judicial district. For the purposes of RSA 507:9, a domestic corporation is an inhabitant of the county or judicial district where it has its principal place

---

31 Holyoke v. Clark, 54 N.H. 578 (1874).

32 Bartlett v. Lee, 60 N.H. 168 (1880). See also RSA 231:110 which prescribes original venue for actions for damages against any person other than a municipal corporation based upon injury caused by an "obstruction, defect, insufficiency, or want of repair" in a highway resulting from "negligence or carelessness."

33 White v. Sanborn, 6 N.H. 220 (1833).

34 Ford v. Burleigh, 62 N.H. 388 (1882).

35 See, e.g., Bartlett v. Lee, 60 N.H. 168 (1880) (petition for leave to file a claim against a town for damages caused by a defective highway was "local" because the claim itself was "local" and should be filed in the county where the highway is located); RSA 507:10 (an action by or against an administrator or executor must be filed in the same county or judicial district as the decedent could have filed in at the date of death).

36 See Holyoke v. Clark, 54 N.H. 578 (1874). The Court has suggested that where two theories of original venue may be applied to one cause of action, the plaintiff may take advantage of the theory which gives him the greater choice of forums. In *Holyoke*, the Court held that an action for breach of covenants in a deed, between the original parties to the transaction, could be brought where either of the parties resided (on a theory of privity of contract) as well as where the land was located (on a theory of privity of estate). This approach is certainly reasonable, consistent with the purpose of original venue in distributing judicial work while providing plaintiff with a choice of forums, and in keeping with the Court's liberal interpretation of statutes which specify original venue. There is no reason to think that this principle, already suggested for cases where one claim may be supported by two theories, could not also be applied to cases in which more than one claim is made.

of business,[37] but a foreign corporation, even one that has qualified to do business in New Hampshire, is not a resident of New Hampshire for the purposes of venue regardless of where it maintains offices.[38] The state is an inhabitant of the county in which its capitol is located.[39]

After it has been established that an action is "local" in character, it is necessary to determine where that locality lies.[40]

Library References

CJS Venue §§ 2, 7

§ 4.14. Original Venue Selection

Principles of original venue were once rigidly applied to cut short a case and decline jurisdiction, but today the doctrine's primary function is to distribute the judicial workload among the various towns, cities, and counties where the courts are located.[41] Original venue accomplishes this goal in most cases by tying the determination of venue in each case to some attribute of the parties or the subject matter.

Where more than one forum is available for the commencement of an action, the plaintiff may choose the one he prefers. There is a strong

---

37　Record v. Manchester Traction, Light, and Power Co., 79 N.H. 495, 111 A. 629 (1920).

38　Blanchette v. New England Telephone and Telegraph Co., 90 N.H. 207, 6 A.2d 161 (1939); The Educational Society of the Denomination Called Christians v. Varney, 54 N.H. 376 (1847); Bishop v. The Silver Lake Mining Co., 62 N.H. 455 (1883). No cases on this issue have been decided since RSA 293-A, the Revised Business Corporation Act, became effective January 1, 1993.

39　State v. Cote, 95 N.H. 108, 58 A.2d 749 (1948).

40　See, e.g., Connecticut Valley Lumber Company v. Maine Central Railroad, 78 N.H. 553, 103 A. 263 (1918) (cause of action for damages to a bridge between Canada and the United States lay partly in Canada and partly in New Hampshire); Worster v. Winnipiseogee Lake Co., 25 N.H. 525 (1852) (cause of action for flooding land in Carroll County by building a dam in Belknap County arose in Carroll County, where the damages were done).

41　This function was recognized at an early date. In Cochecho Railroad v. Farrington, 26 N.H. 428, 445 (1853), Justice Eastman pointed out that a transfer of the venue of actions solely for the convenience of the parties or witnesses "would oftentimes derange the dockets of the counties, and impose upon small counties burdens which would not fairly belong to them, and which would in some instances be extremely onerous." Mr. Justice Jackson referred to the same point in his opinion in Gulf Oil Corporation v. Gilbert, 330 U.S. 501, 508–09 (1947), when he said:

　　Administrative difficulties follow for courts when litigation is piled up in congested centers instead of being handled at its origin. Jury duty is a burden that ought not to be imposed upon the people of a community which has no relation to the litigation. In cases which touch the affairs of many persons, there is reason for holding the trial in their view and reach rather than in remote parts of the county where they can learn of it by report only.

89

preference for the plaintiff's choice of forum[42] so long as he chooses one which is available to him.[43] The best procedure for making this determination is as follows:

FIRST: Determine whether each cause of action on which plaintiff's claim is based was created by statute or exists at common law:

(a) If created by statute, check for that statute's section on original venue.

   (1) If such a section exists, determine whether it prescribes a mandatory and exclusive venue (in which case the inquiry is concluded), or merely allows an additional forum (in which case a search for other venue may continue).

   (2) If there is no venue section, or if the section is merely permissive, determine whether the cause of action is "local" or "transitory" in nature.

(b) If the cause of action is not created by statute, try to determine whether the cause of action is "local" or "transitory" in nature.

SECOND: If the cause of action is "local," determine the locality in which it must be brought.

THIRD: If the cause of action is "transitory," consult RSA 507:9.

Plaintiff's choice from among the available forums may be based upon any consideration and need not be explained. Plaintiff's reasons for choosing a forum are irrelevant to the question of whether the case should be transferred for trial.

Library References

CJS Venue § 6–8

§ 4.15. Pleading Venue

Once the plaintiff has filed his action, his choice of venue is subject to the court's examination and the defendant's objection. At the beginning of the last century, Justice Smith wondered whether the precedents require "a venue to be alleged."[44] He concluded that they did and noted that the

---

42 Indeed, because the doctrine of forum non conveniens is a lineal descendant of stricter common law principles of original venue, it might be suggested that the preference for plaintiff's choice of forum was derived directly from the early history of original venue.

43 The plaintiff cannot expand his choice of forums by assignments to straw men (Parsons v. Brown, 50 N.H. 484 (1871)), or other actions undertaken solely for the purpose of litigation.

44 See Hale v. Vesper, Smith's Report 283 (1809).

plaintiff's failure to do so could be the subject of a special demurrer.[45] But Justice Smith's belief that original venue should be specifically alleged did not survive scrutiny by subsequent generations of the Court. In *Berry v. Osborn*,[46] the Court held that a special demurrer would not lie for failure to allege venue where the basis of venue was clear from the other facts alleged in the writ and was correct. And in *Bartlett v. Lee*,[47] the Court, led by Justice Doe, went a step further and held that a writ should not be dismissed upon an objection to original venue, even when, from the facts alleged in the writ, it was clear that the venue was wrong, so long as it was also apparent where the venue should lie. The trial court, said Justice Doe, could simply transfer the case to the forum in which it ought to have been commenced.[48]

It is unfortunate that the rule has survived until today, when insufficient original venue no longer has any bearing on whether an action may continue,

---

45 Apparently, Justice Smith did not find this view of the matter inconsistent with the Court's decision in the case of Griffin v. Huse, 10 *Manuscript Reports* 305 (1808), in which the writ, although stating a transitory cause of action and reciting that the parties were both residents of Rockingham County, failed to allege the venue specifically and was met with a general demurrer. The Court held the demurrer bad, saying that because it was clear from the face of the writ that the case could only have been brought in Rockingham County, "[t]he venue . . . is a mere matter of form" and "[i]ts omission can only be taken advantage of by special demurrer."

46 28 N.H. 279 (1854).

47 60 N.H. 168 (1880).

48 Chief Justice Doe suggested in his opinion in Bartlett v. Lee, 60 N.H. 168 (1880), that the decision was required by General Laws, ch. 75, § 14 (a predecessor to RSA 514:8):

> If the Legislature had intended that a writ, declaration, return, process, judgment, or other proceeding should be defeated by an error or mistake of venue, it is to be presumed they would have said "except an error or mistake of venue," or used other words distinctly manifesting their intention to make such an extraordinary exception to the general rule. So unjust an exception cannot be interpolated, by construction, in a statute so explicit and comprehensive in terms, and so equitable and beneficent in design.

But the statute from which General Laws, ch. 75, § 14 was derived had in fact been in existence at the time Justice Smith gave his opinion in Hale v. Vesper, Smith's Report 283 (1809), and had been published in a compilation of New Hampshire statutes only five years before. See New Hampshire Laws (1805), p. 87. It is not likely that Justice Smith was unaware of this statute when he expressed his opinion that venue ought to be pleaded. Rather, the opposite reactions of the two Chief Justices at a span of 70 years illustrates the profound change in philosophy on matters of form and procedure which occurred during that century.

Recalling that incorrect original venue was originally a ground for dismissing a writ and terminating an action, it is not surprising to find the Doe Court applying to a question of original venue the same general standard (i.e., whether the parties may be rightly understood) which has since been developed by the federal courts as a test of whether a pleading states a claim upon which relief may be granted.

but applies only to where the action may continue. Because the principle purpose of original venue today is the distribution of cases among the various counties in some fashion related to the number of persons residing and the amount of business transacted in each, a rule which allows plaintiffs not to specify venue and requires instead that, when venue is challenged, the court must hunt through the writ or petition to find some factual basis for the chosen venue, is unnecessarily wasteful of court time. The Superior Court Rules should instead require that the theory and factual basis of venue be specifically and separately alleged in the beginning of any writ or petition and that before the writ or petition is accepted for filing, the clerk examine that statement to determine that the theory relied upon is a recognized one and that the facts are sufficient to support it. Such a rule would not only assure the enforcement of original venue requirements, but prevent the court or the parties from wasting their time challenging and examining the facts alleged as a basis for venue.[49]

Library References

CJS Pleading §§ 25, 67, 104
CJS Venue §§ 6–8
Lien as estate or interest in land within venue statute. 2 ALR2d 1261.
Relationship between "residence" and "domicil" under venue statutes. 12 ALR2d 757.
What is an action for damages to personal property within venue statute. 29 ALR2d 1270.
Retroactive operation and effect of venue statute. 41 ALR2d 798.
Venue of action for slander. 70 ALR2d 1340.
Venue of damage action for breach of real-estate sales contract. 8 ALR3d 489.
Venue of civil libel action against newspaper or periodical. 15 ALR3d 1249.
Venue in action for malicious prosecution. 12 ALR4th 1278.
Pleading tactics as to venue. 3 Am Jur Trials, pp. 681–797.
Venue in actions for or against decedent's estates, 19 Am Jur Trials, pp. 1–122.

§ 4.16. Objection to Plaintiff's Choice of Forum—Before a General Appearance or Plea to the Merits

If a case is filed in a forum which the defendant thinks is incorrect, either from the facts on the face of the pleadings or from additional facts known to him, he may file a Motion to Transfer the case to a correct venue. The defendant is not *required* to object to an incorrect venue in order to assure the power of the court to act; unlike a lack of jurisdiction, incorrect original

---

49 It would also prevent the county from incurring the expense of a trial which does not belong there. Under RSA 507:13, the transferor county must pay the transferee county the latter's costs for the trial by jury of any case transferred on account of venue. If the clerk refuses to accept a writ or petition without proof of correct venue, he will avoid incurring this cost in all cases except those later changed on motion in order to obtain a fair trial.

venue has no effect on the power of the court to try the facts and enter a binding decree.[50] But if the defendant wishes to object, he should do so immediately.

In theory, incorrect original venue can be cured at any stage of the proceedings,[51] but in practice the test of the defendant's motion will be different if it is made after he has filed a General Appearance or has pleaded to the merits. Before he has filed a General Appearance, the defendant has an absolute right to obtain a correction of original venue.[52] In many cases, the rules of original venue prescribe only one forum in which an action may be brought (e.g., all local actions and transitory actions in which only one party is a resident), and it is as much the defendant's as it is the plaintiff's right to have the case tried in the prescribed forum. In other cases, where more than one forum is possible, the defendant still has a right not to have the case tried elsewhere. Thus, although the defendant is not allowed to choose in the first instance, he can, prior to an Appearance or plea to the merits, enforce adherence to the rules when the plaintiff attempts to file in an impermissible location, and the court, in most cases, will grant his Motion to Transfer the case. When the plaintiff has chosen an inappropriate forum, the defendant should be allowed his preference from among the forums which are available to the plaintiff. Plaintiff's failure to choose from among the forums to which he is entitled may be regarded either as an admission that he has no preference or as a waiver of his right to choose. In either event, allowing the defendant to choose when the plaintiff has not chosen to do so is a suitable penalty to the plaintiff for either a negligent or an intentional attempt to obtain a forum to which he is not entitled.

---

50 But extreme care must be taken to distinguish between original venue and exclusive jurisdiction. See, e.g., Leary v. McSwiney, 103 N.H. 85, 166 A.2d 118 (1960), where the Court held that former RSA 110-A:77(I), which allowed recovery against the National Guard "by petition brought in the superior court for the county wherein such person resides or where the injury was suffered," was a venue statute additional to RSA 507:9 and 11 and did not impose a limitation on subject matter jurisdiction. See, e.g., RSA 195:16-b (a petition by a cooperative school board for the acquisition of land to be filed in the county where the land is located); former RSA 185:12 (proceedings on a bond are to be brought in any county where any patron of a bulk purchasing licensee resides).

51 Langdell v. Eastern Basket and Veneer Company, 78 N.H. 243, 99 A. 90 (1916).

52 Obviously, this will not always be a right which the defendant will wish to enforce. But where, for example, a Massachusetts corporation is sued by a resident of Hillsborough County on a theory of breach of warranty on equipment sold and operated only in Hillsborough County, the defendant will no doubt prefer to have the case heard in Manchester or Nashua rather than in Lancaster.

Library References

CJS Venue §§ 71–78

§ 4.17. —After a General Appearance or Plea to the Merits

Whatever may be his rights beforehand, the defendant waives his right to have the venue changed once he enters a General Appearance or pleads to the merits.[53] Thereafter, any request for a change of venue based solely on a failure to comply with original venue requirements will be denied.[54]

§ 4.18. How To Object

The defendant's challenge to the plaintiff's choice of forum may follow one of several routes. If the writ or petition discloses no facts from which any original venue can be inferred, it may well be that the pleadings are so deficient that a Motion to Dismiss for failure to state a claim would be appropriate. Or, if the pleadings do state a claim but give no reasonable indication of what the correct original venue is, the defendant can file a Motion for More Particular Statement.[55] Upon receipt of the Motion, the court should require the plaintiff to specify a basis for venue within ten days.[56] Once the plaintiff has done so, if the facts on the writ or petition disclose that the forum is incorrect, the defendant will have a basis to file a Motion to Transfer the case to an appropriate forum. Alternatively, if the

---

53 Bishop v. The Silver Lake Mining Co., 62 N.H. 455 (1883).

54 Both Record v. Manchester Traction, Light & Power Co., 79 N.H. 495, 111 A. 629 (1920), and Whitcher v. Union Grange Fair Association, 77 N.H. 405, 92 A. 735 (1914), were cases involving motions for a change of venue made during trial after witnesses had testified to facts tending to show that the correct original venue lay in another county. The Court in each case denied the motion, based not upon a decision of whether the rules of original venue had been complied with, but upon a consideration of whether justice required the transfer at that point in the proceedings. The *Record* and *Whitcher* cases suggest that defects of original venue will be corrected only if they are raised prior to joining the general issue. After that point, the only proper question is whether a fair trial can be had in the forum.

55 Because one of the purposes of original venue is the limitation of choices, it might be thought that where the nature of the action is unclear, the narrower choice of forums should be adopted. However, at least with regard to statutory prescriptions of original venue, the Supreme Court has made it clear that a technical construction is not favored and that it will liberally construe venue restrictions to allow the widest possible choice of forums. State v. Cote, 95 N.H. 108, 110, 58 A.2d 749, 751 (1948).

56 Super. Ct. R. 29. The plaintiff has the burden of establishing that the Court has obtained jurisdiction, and he should also carry the burden of establishing that the original venue which he has claimed is correct. The defendant should not be obliged to require a more particular statement of the cause of action before objecting to original venue, but should be able to take the pleadings as he finds them.

defendant knows of facts sufficient to show that the wrong forum has been chosen, he can file a Motion To Transfer with supporting affidavits.

A Motion to Transfer should state the appropriate basis for venue, recite the facts which support that venue, and suggest one or more forums to which the court may refer the case. Where the motion is founded upon facts which are not set forth in the writ or petition, it must be supported by affidavit.[57] If the defendant's motion is successful, he will be awarded his costs through the date of transfer.[58]

§ 4.19. Miscellaneous Effects

Incorrect original venue has no other effect than to present the basis for a transfer and an award of costs; it does not give the defendant the benefit of the statute of limitations[59] and it presents no issue for reversal if the defendant fails to object prior to the entry of a General Appearance or a plea to the merits. Moreover, a change of venue has no effect on any liens or attachments obtained before the transfer.[60]

---

57 Wheeler and Wilson Manufacturing Co. v. Whitcomb, 62 N.H. 411 (1882). Originally, an objection to the choice of venue (rather than to the method of pleading it) could only be made by filing a plea in abatement. In Eames v. Carlisle, 3 N.H. 130 (1824), the Court quashed a writ on motion and without a plea in abatement when it was clear from the face of the writ that the venue was improper. And in Little v. Dickinson, 29 N.H. 56, 61–62 (1854), the Court even expressed the opinion that a court had no power to transfer an action to cure improper original venue. But in the case of Bartlett v. Lee, 60 N.H. 168 (1880), and *Wheeler & Wilson*, the Court held that, despite the filing of a plea in abatement, actions were to be transferred and not abated if the correct original venue could be determined from the writ. In Whitcher v. Union Grange Fair Association, 77 N.H. 405, 92 A. 735 (1914), the Court held that a request for change of venue could be raised directly by a motion to that effect, saying that since the defendant had no chance of obtaining a dismissal for incorrect original venue anyway, there was no reason why we should be required to file a plea in abatement asking for it simply to accomplish a removal of the case to a correct forum. But the Bar continued to file pleas in abatement even after the *Whitcher* case, and the superior court was apparently put in a position of having to treat such pleas as something they were not. In Blanchette v. New England Telephone and Telegraph Co., 90 N.H. 207, 6 A.2d 161 (1939), the Supreme Court approved as "entirely proper" the superior court's decision to treat a defendant's plea in abatement as a motion to transfer and to order a change of venue based upon that plea. But for 80 years, the appropriate method of presenting objections to original venue has been by a Motion to Transfer, and this is the procedure which should be followed today.

58 Super. Ct. R. 57.

59 Hayes v. Rochester, 64 N.H. 41, 6 A. 274 (1886).

60 See RSA 507:12.

Library References

CJS Venue § 201
Venue of civil libel action against newspaper or periodical. 15 ALR3d 1249.
Change of venue as justified by fact that large number of inhabitants of local jurisdiction have interest adverse to party to state civil actions. 10 ALR 4th 1046.

C. Proper Venue

§ 4.20. Definition

"Proper venue" is the location in which a case *ought* to be tried. Determination of proper venue is made according to the same principles in all courts—municipal, district, probate, and superior—and all courts have the same powers to assure that a trial is fair to all parties.

§ 4.21. Original Venue v. Proper Venue

The terms "original" and "proper" venue represent two different concepts in the choice of a forum. Original venue, although originally a jurisdictional prerequisite, survives today primarily as a basis for distributing the judicial workload. Proper venue remains today what it has always been: a means of assuring that the accident of location will not prevent the delivery of justice.[61]

§ 4.22. Principles of Proper Venue

The earliest case which considered a change of venue for the purposes of obtaining a fair trial was *Cochecho Railroad v. Farrington*,[62] an action in assumpsit to recover assessments upon shares for which the defendant had subscribed in the plaintiffs railroad. The case was brought in Strafford

---

61 For example, in State v. Cote, 95 N.H. 108, 58 A.2d 749 (1948), the Court said: "The statute and decisions make it clear that venue is based on what 'justice or convenience requires' (RL, ch. 384, S. 3) and a technical interpretation is not favored." This statement was made in connection with a decision that the state could be regarded as a resident of the county in which its capitol is located for the purposes of bringing a transitory action—a proposition unexceptionable in itself but in the formulation of which "justice" would appear to have taken little part. Again, in Tucker v. Lake, 67 N.H. 193, 29 A. 406 (1892), the question was whether a bill in equity to foreclose a mortgage on land in Merrimack County could be brought in Rockingham County. Holding that the action was "local" and should have been brought in Merrimack County, the Court affirmed the trial court's decision to cure the error by transfer. But, for no apparent reason, the Court added: "Whether justice required the order to be made, was a question of fact that was decided affirmatively at the trial term, and the decision is not reviewable here." 67 N.H. at 194, 29 A. at 407. These statements by the *Tucker* and *Cote* Courts are inconsistent with the mass of New Hampshire case law on the subject of venue.

62 26 N.H. 428 (1853).

County, where the defendant lived, but the defendant sought a transfer to Merrimack County upon the ground that he could not obtain a fair trial there. In support of this motion, the defendant produced affidavits tending to show that his case had been discussed in the plaintiff's railroad cars and in each of the four towns in Strafford County through which the railroad passed. But the trial court refused to transfer the case, and the Supreme Court affirmed, saying that the purpose of a change of venue in such a situation is to secure a fair and impartial trial and that the motion will only be granted when the defendant shows *conclusively* that an impartial trial cannot be had where the action was commenced.[63] The Court rejected the notion that the convenience of the parties or witnesses was an adequate ground for a change of venue,[64] saying:

> [H]owever expedient and necessary this practice may be in large states, in this State . . . it is not probable that any motion of the kind would be granted. To transfer actions from one county to another for this reason only would oftentimes derange the dockets of the counties, and impose upon small counties burdens which would not fairly belong to them and which would in some instances be extremely onerous.[65]

The rather severe approach of *Cochecho* was softened nearly a quarter of a century later by *Hilliard v. Beattie*.[66] In that case, a request for a change of venue had been denied by the trial court, relying upon *Cochecho*, because the defendant had failed to show "conclusively" that he could not get a fair

---

63 The Court was also of the opinion that the trial court could reasonably find that a fair trial had not been prevented by talk in four towns, where the residents of the other nine towns in the county appeared to be generally ignorant of the case. The Court also commented that there was no reason to believe that the general issue had not been as freely and widely discussed in Merrimack as in Rockingham County.

64 But see RSA 507:11 (superior court may change venue when justice or convenience requires it).

65 26 N.H. at 446. But see Thistle v. Halstead, 95 N.H. 87, 58 A.2d 503 (1948), where, after refusing to invoke the doctrine of forum non conveniens to dismiss a case brought against a Massachusetts resident by another Massachusetts resident in New Hampshire, the Court commented that the venue might nevertheless be changed to suit the convenience of the parties. This is the only case in which the Court has suggested, despite the authority of RSA 507:11, that it would approve a change of venue based upon convenience alone. Indeed, it would seem that the rationale of the *Cochecho* case is, if anything, more persuasive today than it was 140 years ago when the court thought it not unduly inconvenient to travel for a whole day just to get from one part of the county to the county seat.

66 58 N.H. 112 (1877).

and impartial trial in the forum in which the case was begun. However, the Supreme Court overruled *Cochecho's* requirement of "conclusive" proof and remanded, saying:

> To give full force and effect to the language of the Court in [*Cochecho*] would be practically saying that in no case should there ever be a change of venue. We are compelled to dissent from this view. It is to facilitate the ends of justice that courts change the venue.[67]

The Court went on to remark that the "true rule" in transitory actions was that the court should change the venue whenever it appears that there is "probable ground to believe that a fair and impartial trial or at least a satisfactory trial cannot be had in the county where the action was brought."[68] The Court concluded:

> Not only is it essential to the preservation of the rights of all that there shall be an impartial administration of justice, and that those rights shall be determined by tribunals as impartial as the lot of humanity will admit, but it is also of almost if not quite equal importance that every person shall feel that he has had such a trial. That he will not so feel when probable ground exists to believe the contrary is beyond dispute.[69]

The *Hilliard* case has remained the standard to the present day.[70]

The question of whether a fair trial can be obtained in the original forum is a question of fact to be determined by the trial court. The trial court has discretion either to order a transfer or not, as it thinks necessary, and the exercise of that discretion will not be reversed except for "a plain abuse of judicial discretion; that is [a complete lack of] evidence to justify the conclusion arrived at."[71] However, once the issue has been called to the court's attention, the court is required to investigate and satisfy itself that a fair and impartial trial can be had.[72]

---

67 58 N.H. at 112.

68 58 N.H. at 112–13.

69 *Id.*

70 See Baer v. Rosenblatt, 106 N.H. 26, 203 A.2d 773 (1964).

71 Whitcher v. Union Grange Fair Association, 77 N.H. 405, 92 A. 735 (1914); Baer v. Rosenblatt, 106 N.H. 26, 203 A.2d 773 (1964).

72 Hopley v. Chronicle & Gazette Publishing Co., 94 N.H. 171, 174, 49 A.2d 637, 639 (1946). It is interesting to compare the facts of the *Hopley* and *Cochecho* cases. In

A Motion to Transfer may be filed at any time by either the plaintiff or the defendant.[73] Of course, no use can be made by the other party of the fact that such a motion has been filed or granted. In what must have been one of the most interesting cases of the last century, the plaintiff's counsel in *Hilliard v. Beattie*[74] used the defendant's request for a change of venue as a key point of his argument to the jury. The reporter summarized the events as follows:

> The action was originally commenced in the county of Coos, and on the defendant's motion the venue was changed to the eastern district of the county of Grafton. In opening the case to the jury, the plaintiff's counsel said that the suit was brought in Coos county, nearly a hundred miles north, and after it had been pending

---

Cochecho, the defendant objected that passengers on the train and people in all four towns that the railroad passed through had discussed his case, but the Court thought that an impartial panel could be obtained from the towns through which the railroad did not pass. In *Hopley*, the plaintiff sued for libel, as the *Portsmouth Herald* had published an article questioning his integrity and, after a jury had been picked and the trial was about to begin, the *Herald* published two more articles commenting upon the plaintiff's plea of nolo contendere to a criminal charge, falsely reporting that he had been fired, and hinting that more unpleasant news would come out about him in the course of the trial. The plaintiff asked for a change of venue. The superior court offered the plaintiff the opportunity to file another suit or to amend his declaration to include the subsequent potential libel actions. The plaintiff declined, and the superior court ruled that the plaintiff could have a fair trial without a change of venue. The Supreme Court, without apparently considering from what parts of the county the jurors had come, stated that it was "[i]nconceivable that some of the jurors . . . were unaware of the publications," (94 N.H. at 173, 49 A.2d at 639) and that it was entirely possible that, in light of the publications, the plaintiff could not have found a panel of jurors in all of Rockingham County that would be able to give him a fair trial. The two cases reflect the Court's recognition that information spreads more rapidly and more completely now than it did a century ago and suggest that the Court will be more easily convinced of prejudice now than it was at the time of *Cochecho*, particularly if a party has been the subject of newspaper publicity.

It is interesting to note that technological progress has had opposite effects upon original and proper venue: with regard to the former, it has no doubt made it more difficult for a defendant to change the venue based upon convenience, but in respect to the latter it has made it more likely that a change will be ordered to obtain a fair trial.

73 Cochecho Railroad v. Farrington, 26 N.H. 428 (1853); Hilliard v. Beattie, 58 N.H. 112 (1877) (defendants filed their motion before preparation for trial had begun); Whitcher v. Union Grange Fair Association, 77 N.H. 405, 92 A. 735 (1914); Record v. Manchester Traction, Light & Power Co., 79 N.H. 495, 111 A. 629 (1920) (defendant filed his motion during a trial before a jury); Vidal v. Errol, 86 N.H. 585, 172 A. 437 (1934) (plaintiff filed his motion after two jury trials); Baer v. Rosenblatt, 106 N.H. 26, 203 A.2d 773 (1964); Hopley v. Chronicle & Gazette Publishing Co., 94 N.H. 171, 49 A. 2d 637 (1946) (plaintiff filed his motion a few days before trial).

74 58 N.H. 112 (1877).

there nine years, because it was said the defendant could not get a fair trial among his acquaintances, "I am not saying for what reason"—the defendant's counsel, interrupting, objected to these remarks. The plaintiff's counsel replied "it is important to know why we are here," and complained of the increased expense of trial caused by the change of venue. In his argument the defendant's counsel made some observations in justification of the defendant's application for a change of venue to a county where a trial might be had before a jury uninfluenced by local excitement or prejudice. The plaintiff's counsel, in his closing address to the jury, argued that it was the defendant's assault that created a feeling against him in Coos county, where the public were familiar with the transaction, and that if a state of feeling existed in that county unfavorably to the defendant, it was simply because his case was that kind that no civilized being could help being prejudiced against it. To this the defendant objected.[75]

Not surprisingly, the jury gave its verdict for the plaintiff. On appeal, the Supreme Court said the issue was "whether the plaintiff can compel an abandonment of all effort to secure a fair trial."[76] In reversing and remanding the case for a new trial, the Court said, "To sustain this verdict would be to hold that the change of venue was rightfully used to prevent the fair trial it was made to secure, and that a change of venue is always legal cause for turning justice aside by influences which the change is intended to avoid."[77]

Library References

CJS Venue §§ 130, 142, 150
Choice of venue to which transfer is to be had, where change is sought because of local prejudice. 50 ALR3d 760.

---

75 58 N.H. at 463–64.
76 58 N.H. at 466.
77 Id.

CHAPTER 5. THE DOCTRINE OF FORUM NON CONVENIENS

Library References

CJS Courts § 77

Discretion of court to refuse to entertain action for nonstatutory tort occurring in another state or country. 48 ALR2d 800.

Power of court, in action under foreign wrongful death statute, to decline jurisdiction on ground of inconvenience of forum. 48 ALR2d 850.

Assumption or denial of jurisdiction in action between nonresident individuals based upon tort occurring within forum state. 92 ALR3d 797.

Forum non conveniens in products liability cases. 46 ALR4th 22.

§ 5.01. Definition

Even when a New Hampshire court[1] has jurisdiction over the parties and the subject matter of an action, one of the parties may prefer to try the case in another state or country and will ask the New Hampshire court to decline jurisdiction and to dismiss the suit.

§ 5.02. History

During the nineteenth and early twentieth century, pleadings to this end were customarily cast in terms of the principles of venue.[2] But in 1933, the

---

1 The principles of the doctrine of forum non conveniens would seem to be the same in all courts of the state. However, there are no reported cases in which the doctrine had been raised in the municipal, district, or probate courts.

2 For example, in the case of White v. Sanborn, 6 N.H. 220 (1833), the issue involved real estate located in Vermont which the plaintiff White had purchased from one Bohanon, who in turn had received it from defendant Abraham Sanborn by a deed with warranty covenants. Unfortunately, defendant Abraham Sanborn had previously sold the same property to Reuben Sanborn. Once plaintiff White took possession, Reuben Sanborn brought an action in Vermont to eject him and won. White then came across the river to New Hampshire and sued defendant Abraham Sanborn for breach of the warranty covenants in his deed to Bohanon. The defendant demurred, asserting that because the action was founded on privity of estate rather than on privity of contract, it was "local" and that the action could only be brought in the county in Vermont where the land was located. The New Hampshire trial court agreed and dismissed the action. On appeal, the Supreme Court affirmed. But it is interesting to examine the arguments raised by each side before the Supreme Court. Although cast in terms of venue,

Court was faced with the case of *Jackson & Sons v. Lumbermen's Mutual Casualty Co.,*[3] an action brought by an Ohio corporation against an Illinois insurance corporation claiming negligent defense of a lawsuit in Ohio. The plaintiff had previously asserted the same claim in Ohio, but the case had been dismissed. New Hampshire's sole connection with any of the parties or with the claim was that the defendant insurance corporation had been authorized to do business in the state. The defendant moved to dismiss "because the court ought not to take jurisdiction of the cause,"[4] and the issue was reserved and transferred before trial. The Supreme Court decided that the superior court should decline jurisdiction, saying:

> The question whether the courts of a state will take jurisdiction of a controversy between two non-residents is often largely one of fact. Convenience of the parties, nature of the matter to be litigated, state of the local demands upon the court and kindred topics are all considered relevant to the issue . . . [The underlying general principle] is that where in a broad sense the ends of justice strongly

---

defendant's argument stressed that the transaction occurred in Vermont, the property involved was located in Vermont, all parties were resident in Vermont, and the action would presumably involve witnesses living in Vermont and an application of the law of that state. By way of response, plaintiff raised the argument that an action for breach of covenants, although founded on privity of estate, was only a local action if the case was brought in Vermont, but was a transitory action elsewhere and could be brought in New Hampshire. This was an early attempt to separate concepts of venue from considerations of whether a state court should exercise jurisdiction at all, and the case may mark the earliest appearance of the doctrine of forum non conveniens in New Hampshire law. Few cases involving out-of-state parties came to the Supreme Court during the one hundred years following the decision in White v. Sanborn.

Fifty years later, in Bishop v. The Silver Lake Mining Co., 62 N.H. 455 (1883), the Court was faced with a case for money furnished under a contract. The case was commenced in New Hampshire by a resident of Massachusetts against a New York corporation. The defendant had a place of business in New Hampshire, but there was no indication of where the money was paid or contract made. Had the defendant objected before trial to trying the case in New Hampshire, an issue which we would now regard as forum non conveniens might have been presented, but the defendant instead filed a general appearance and tried the case without objecting to the place of trial. At the close of his evidence, however, the defendant sought a dismissal based upon improper original venue, saying that the case should have been brought in Carroll County where it had a place of business rather than in Rockingham County. The court denied the motion, first upon the ground that the action was transitory and could have been brought in any county since both the plaintiff and the defendant were nonresidents and second upon the theory that the defendant had waived his objections to original venue by proceeding with a trial on merits.

3 86 N.H. 341, 168 A. 895 (1933).

4 86 N.H. at 341, 168 A. at 896.

indicate that the controversy may be more suitably tried elsewhere, then jurisdiction should be declined.[5]

Fifteen years after *Jackson*, in *Thistle v. Halstead*,[6] a Massachusetts attorney sued a Massachusetts client for unpaid fees, and the action was begun by attaching real estate in New Hampshire that belonged to the defendant. As the defendant was not served personally in New Hampshire, jurisdiction was acknowledged to be quasi in rem. The defendant then moved to dismiss the action because neither she nor the plaintiff resided in New Hampshire, the cause of action had not accrued in New Hampshire, and the cause of action had not accrued in relation to property located in New Hampshire. The superior court granted the motion. Reaffirming the principles of *Jackson*, the Supreme Court reversed, noting that the doctrine of forum non conveniens is a device meant to limit the plaintiff's choice of forums only to prevent hardship to the defendant, not one designed to permit the defendant to evade or to minimize her obligations. The Court stated that the plaintiff's choice of forum should not be disturbed unless the balance of hardship is strongly in favor of the defendant,[7] and that the defendant here made no showing that witnesses would be difficult to obtain or that issues of foreign law were involved. The only reasons that the defendant asserted as a justification for the Court to decline jurisdiction were her age and ill health, that she lived 100 miles from the Court, and that both she and the plaintiff resided in Massachusetts. The Court determined that those reasons were not significant enough to bar the plaintiff from New Hampshire's courts, particularly because the Massachusetts statute of limitations had run and the plaintiff was without any alternative forum.

This last point was expanded upon in *Van Dam v. Smit*,[8] an action for money lent by the plaintiff and transferred to the defendant for safekeeping which the defendant did not return. The plaintiff resided in the Netherlands;

---

5 86 N.H. at 343, 168 A. at 896.

6 95 N.H. 87, 58 A.2d 503 (1948).

7 Bearing in mind that the doctrine of forum non conveniens is a descendant of more generalized common law principles of venue, it is interesting to compare this test with the early *Cochecho* holding that plaintiff's choice of forum will not be disturbed on a motion for change of venue without a *conclusive* showing that a fair and impartial trial cannot be had where the action was brought. Cochecho Railroad v. Farrington, 26 N.H. 428 (1853). See Section 4.14, fn. 41.

8 101 N.H. 508, 148 A.2d 289 (1959).

the defendant in New Hampshire.[9] The defendant appeared specially and filed a motion to dismiss plaintiff's claim based on the doctrine of forum non conveniens. The trial court denied the motion and the defendant appealed. The Supreme Court began its opinion by remarking that it was unusual for a New Hampshire resident to argue that maintenance of a suit in his home state and county was "oppressive or vexatious" and commented that this circumstance alone made a "weak case" for declining jurisdiction. The Court then reaffirmed the principle of *Jackson* that the plaintiff's choice of forum should be disturbed only for "weighty reasons" and confirmed what the *Thistle* case had implied—that a New Hampshire court would, in any case, not decline to exercise jurisdiction unless there was an alternative forum available to the plaintiff. As the Court said:

> [T]he suit will be entertained, no matter how inappropriate the forum may be, if the defendant cannot be subjected to jurisdiction in other states. The same will be true if plaintiff's cause of action would elsewhere be barred by the statute of limitations, unless the court is willing to accept the defendant's stipulation that he will not raise this defense in the second state.[10]

While the Court agreed with the defendant that the application of the doctrine of forum non conveniens is within its discretion and that its application will depend upon the facts of the case, they found that, even if there were no other forum available to the plaintiff, the court would be justified in denying the motion "as a matter of law."[11]

The plaintiff in *Leeper v. Leeper*[12] was a New Hampshire resident and the former wife of defendant. The plaintiff and the defendant had obtained a divorce in Argentina, where the defendant still lived. The plaintiff subsequently filed an action in New Hampshire charging her former husband with misappropriating for his own use and without an accounting, certain

---

9 For reasons not apparent in the opinion, the courts of other jurisdictions where the defendant had assets (the Netherlands and the former West Germany) were not available to the plaintiff for the litigation of his claim.

10 101 N.H. at 509, 148 A.2d at 291.

11 The same principle was later applied to retain jurisdiction over a petition to modify a child custody order when the plaintiff-father lived in New Hampshire and the defendant-mother lived in California, and the child resided with an aunt in Luxemburg. Potter v. Rosas, 111 N.H. 169, 276 A.2d 922 (1971). But the decision in that case seems also to have been influenced by the fact that a New Hampshire court had granted the divorce and issued the original custody order.

12 116 N.H. 116, 354 A.2d 137 (1976).

stocks, bonds, bank accounts, and savings certificates from a New Hampshire bank.[13]

First, the defendant appeared specially and moved to dismiss for lack of subject matter and personal jurisdiction. The denial of that motion was affirmed.[14] Next, based on the doctrine of forum non conveniens, the defendant asked the court to decline jurisdiction in favor of a tribunal in Argentina. The trial court refused, the defendant appealed, and the Supreme Court affirmed, reciting the familiar principle that the plaintiff's choice of forum will be disturbed only rarely and for "weighty reasons" and never unless there is an alternative forum available. The Court went on to say that it would be considerably less likely to dismiss based on forum non conveniens if the effect would be to relegate a United States citizen to a forum in another country. In such an instance, the Court said, the trial court should require "positive evidence of unusually extreme circumstances and should be thoroughly convinced that material injustice is manifest"[15] before denying a citizen access to U.S. courts.

The Court in *Leeper* listed considerations relevant to the application of the doctrines of forum non conveniens originally set forth by the U.S. Supreme Court in *Gulf Oil v. Gilbert*.[16] The court should compare New Hampshire and the suggested alternative forum with respect to: (a) the private interest of the litigants; (b) the relative ease of access to sources of proof; (c) the availability of compulsory process; and (d) the cost of obtaining the attendance of willing witnesses. The court should consider: (e) the possibility that a view will be required; (f) the question of the enforceability of a judgment from the alternative forum; and (g) other concerns of public interest.[17] The Court then weighed all of the reasons the defendant set forth to justify declining jurisdiction—that Argentinian witnesses and sources of proof might be required, that Argentina law might apply, and that New Hampshire was an inconvenient forum for him—and they determined that

---

13 The bank filed a bill of interpleader regarding one of the savings certificates.

14 Leeper v. Leeper, 116 N.H. 116, 854 A.2d 137 (1976).

15 Leeper v. Leeper, 116 N.H. 116, 118, 854 A.2d 137, 139 (1976) (quoting Burt v. Isthmus Development Company, 218 F.2d 353, 357 (5th Cir. 1955)).

16 330 U.S. 501, 508 (1947).

17 The *Leeper* test has been affirmed in Atherton's Furniture v. Halperin, 122 N.H. 1000, 453 A.2d 1268 (1982), Vazifdar v. Vazifdar, 130 N.H. 694, 547 A.2d 249 (1988) (declining to dismiss in favor of matrimonial court in India), and Digital Equipment Corp. v. International Digital Systems Corp., 130 N.H. 362, 540 A.2d 1230 (1988) (error to grant defendant's motion to dismiss based on forum non conveniens where forum selected by plaintiff was defendant's home state).

the circumstances were not sufficient to justify a dismissal in favor of the courts of another country, or even in favor of the courts of another state.

§ 5.03. Basic Principles of the Doctrine

The eight basic principles governing the doctrine of forum non conveniens in New Hampshire practice are as follows:

(1) The doctrine cannot be invoked until the court's jurisdiction has been established.

(2) The decision whether to invoke the doctrine is *generally* within the discretion of the trial court[18] and is to be based upon the individual facts of the case.[19] But the court has *no* discretion to invoke the doctrine when it appears that the plaintiff has no other court to which the plaintiff can appeal for relief.[20]

(3) The doctrine will not ordinarily be applied in favor of a defendant who resides in New Hampshire.[21]

(4) The plaintiff's choice of forum enjoys a presumption of appropriateness.[22]

(5) If neither the parties nor the case has any connection with New Hampshire, the plaintiff will have the burden of justifying his or her choice of forum. The plaintiff can meet this burden by showing that there is no other forum available, even if the plaintiff has allowed the statutes of limitation to run in other possible jurisdictions. The defendant then has the

---

18 Digital Equipment Corp. v. International Digital Systems Corp., 130 N.H. 362, 540 A.2d 1230 (1988); Stankunas v. Stankunas, 133 N.H. 643, 582 A.2d 280 (1990); Van Dam v. Smit, 101 N.H. 508, 510, 148 A.2d 289 (1959).

19 See Digital Equipment Corp. v. International Digital Systems Corp., 130 N.H 362, 540 A.2d 1230 (1988); Vazifdar v. Vazifdar, 130 N.H. 694, 547 A.2d 249 (1988).

20 Smith v. Smith, 125 N.H. 336, 480 A.2d 158 (1984); Stankunas v. Stankunas 133 N.H. 643, 582 A.2d 280 (1990) (husband's active participation in Massachusetts divorce proceedings is a sufficiently "weighty reason" to dismiss due to forum non conveniens even though he had no forum other than New Hampshire in which to file his case). There is also a statutory basis for application of the doctrine in cases brought pursuant to contractual choice of forum provisions. See RSA 508-A:3(II) and (III).

21 Digital Equipment Corp. v. International Digital Systems, Corp., 130 N.H. 362, 540 A.2d 1230 (1988) (abuse of discretion to dismiss based on forum non conveniens plaintiff's contract where defendant was a New Hampshire corporation).

22 Digital Equipment Corp. v. International Digital Systems Corp., 130 N.H. 362, 540 A.2d 1230 (1988); Vazifdar v. Vazifdar, 130 N.H. 694, 547 A.2d 249 (1988) ("Subject to the due process considerations expressed in *International Shoe*, 326 U.S. 310 (1945), plaintiff's choice of forum enjoys a favorable presumption which will not be disturbed except for weighty reasons or in the event that defendant will suffer a gross injustice." 130 N.H. at 697, 547 A.2d at 252).

burden of convincing the court by strong evidence that: (a) another specific forum with at least equal procedural advantages is available to the plaintiff for the trial for the action; and (b) the trial of the case in New Hampshire will be significantly less conducive to a just resolution of the dispute than the trial in another *specific* forum.[23]

(6) The Court will not invoke the doctrine solely because: (a) both parties or their witnesses reside outside of New Hampshire or the United States; (b) any of the parties or their witnesses are in ill health or find travel difficult; (c) the law of another jurisdiction may apply to the controversy; (d) important sources of proof are located outside of New Hampshire; (e) the cause of action arose elsewhere; or (f) an action for the same cause has already been commenced in the court of another jurisdiction, especially if the plaintiff seeks provisional relief which only a New Hampshire court can give.[24]

(7) The doctrine will not be applied in favor of a forum in another country, in the absence of unusually extreme circumstances, when it cannot be doubted that material injustice will otherwise result.[25]

(8) The Court may invoke the doctrine if:[26] (a) neither the parties nor the cause of action has any connection with New Hampshire or, in balancing the interests of New Hampshire and another state, it is clear that another state has a more significant connection to the parties or the issue being tried,[27] *and* there is another forum available; (b) the issue has already been commenced and dismissed on the merits in a more appropriate forum or another forum has already taken jurisdiction over related matters;[28] (c) it

---

23 See also Stankunas v. Stankunas, 133 N.H. 643, 582 A.2d 280 (1990) (doctrine of forum non conveniens successfully invoked by defendant where plaintiff had participated in Massachusetts divorce action and divorce decree recognized as a matter of comity).

24 Digital Equipment Corp. v. International Digital Systems Corp., 130 N.H. 362, 540 A.2d 1230 (1988) (defendant had commenced action in federal court in Massachusetts, but only a New Hampshire court could attach defendant's properties).

25 See, e.g., Vazifdar v. Vazifdar, 130 N.H. 694, 547 A.2d 249 (1988) (declining to dismiss in favor of the matrimonial court of India where defendant resided).

26 But see RSA 468:6 and 468:22; Brauch v. Shaw, 121 N.H. 562, 432 A.2d 1 (1981) (no error to retain jurisdiction over the action despite the pending of a prior action in England).

27 See Bartlett v. Dumaine, 128 N.H. 497, 523 A.2d 1 (1986).

28 See Bartlett v. Dumaine, 128 N.H. 497, 523 A.2d 1 (1986) (Massachusetts courts had already heard some issues related to the trust for which an accounting was now sought in New Hampshire); Stankunas v. Stankunas, 133 N.H. 643, 582 A.2d 280 (1990) (court dismissed based on forum non conveniens plaintiff's divorce action where he had participated in divorce proceedings in Massachusetts).

will be impossible or significantly more difficult to compel the production of important evidence in New Hampshire than in another specific forum which is available; (d) a view will be required in a jurisdiction whose courts are available; (e) a judgment issued by a specific alternative forum will be more enforceable or more likely to be enforced with effect;[29] (f) the cost of trying the case in New Hampshire is significantly higher than the cost of trying it in a specific alternative forum which is available and there is no compensating benefit to be derived from trying it here; or (g) the public interest requires it.[30]

Library References

Assumption or denial of jurisdiction of contract action involving foreign elements. 90 ALR2d 1109.

Assumption or denial of jurisdiction of action involving matrimonial disputes. 9 ALR3d 545.

Forum non conveniens doctrine in state court as affected by availability of alternative forum. 57 ALR4th 973.

§ 5.04. Application of the Doctrine

The doctrine of forum non conveniens is applied on the same terms regardless of the type of cases.[31] It may be invoked by the defendant against the plaintiff's case-in-chief, by the plaintiff against counterclaim, and by either party against a Petition to Intervene. There is no reported case in which the doctrine was applied when both parties were residents of New Hampshire, or in which it appeared that a party either took up residence in New Hampshire for the purpose of bringing the suit, or assigned his claim to a New Hampshire resident before bringing the action. And, although *Van Dam* spoke of dismissing upon the defendant's "Stipulation" not to raise the

---

29 See, e.g., Bartlett v. Dumaine, 128 N.H. 497, 523 A.2d 1 (1986) (proceeding dismissed because of doubt that the decree would be accorded "full faith and credit" in another state).

30 The public interest involved may be a due regard for the interest another state has in administering its protective laws. In Bartlett v. Dumaine, 128 N.H. 497, 523 A.2d 1 (1986), a New Hampshire court had jurisdiction over the parties, and the case could easily have been tried in the state. But because the case turned on a determination of the duties of trustees to beneficiaries under Massachusetts trust law, the Court felt that it should defer to the courts of Massachusetts.

31 The requirements and application of the doctrine may be different where a statute establishes a standard for dismissal or inconvenient forum to be applied in specific cases. See RSA 458-A; Cartelli v. Martin, 121 N.H. 296, 428 A.2d 1243 (1981); Brauch v. Shaw, 121 N.H. 562, 432 A.2d 1 (1981); Clarke v. Clarke, 126 N.H. 753, 496 A.2d 361 (1985).

statute of limitations in an alternative forum, no court appears to have considered granting a stay, rather than dismissing the case, as a means of assuring that the plaintiff would always have the available New Hampshire forum.

§ 5.05. Procedure To Invoke the Doctrine

A Motion to Dismiss for forum non conveniens should be made after the issue of jurisdiction has been admitted or resolved against the defendant. Such a motion, if made when jurisdiction is in doubt, amounts to a waiver of the defendant's objections to jurisdiction and converts a Special into a General Appearance. The motion follows the form of any other motion to dismiss, and it should state the specific facts from which the court can determine that an alternative forum has more substantial contacts with the case and is available to the plaintiff. The motion must be supported by affidavit.

The plaintiff may file an Objection to the Motion within ten days specifying New Hampshire's contacts with the case and the prejudice he would suffer by being required to file the case in the forum suggested by the defendant. The court will then hold a hearing on the motion.

Part III

PARTIES

CHAPTER 6.   PARTIES

A. INTRODUCTION

111

G. MISNOMER AND MISDESIGNATION

H. INTERVENTION

I. SUBSTITUTION OF PARTIES

J. DEATH OF A PARTY

K. THIRD-PARTY PRACTICE

A. Introduction

§ 6.01. Definition

A party is a person who is directly interested in some part of the subject matter of a court or administrative proceeding, who may produce evidence and cross-examine witnesses, and who can seek appellate review.[1] A party is bound by the judgment and by all decisions of fact and law upon which it is based.[2]

Library References

CJS Parties §§ 2, 3

§ 6.02. Classification of Parties

Parties are usually designated according to their respective positions in a case (e.g., plaintiff, defendant, petitioner, respondent, etc.), but they may also be grouped by their relationship to the subject matter of the dispute. Thus, "nominal parties" are persons in whose name an action is commenced but whose personal rights or obligations are not really at stake in the controversy. "Real parties in interest" are persons directly concerned with the outcome of the case.[3] "Necessary parties" are persons whose presence

---

1 Wheeler v. Towns, 43 N.H. 56 (1861).

2 Sanborn Seminary v. Newton, 73 N.H. 109, 59 A. 614 (1904). A number of court rules refer, in addition, to "opposing parties" and "adverse parties." These terms are not defined either in the Superior Court Rules or in the Supreme Court opinions, and their meaning apparently varies with the circumstances. For example, an "opposing party" is entitled to receive copies of all pleadings and communications addressed to the court (Super. Ct. R. 21) and to be informed regarding certain types of proof which may be offered or required at trial (Super. Ct. R. 68 and 89). Clearly, a co- plaintiff, co-defendant, or third party may, under some circumstances, be regarded as "an opposing party" to a person who, for most other purposes, is on the same side of the case. An "adverse party," on the other hand, may limit rights to amend as to form by pointing out the deficiency (Super. Ct. R. 25), may receive a detailed statement or pleading upon the court's order (Super. Ct. R. 29), is entitled to notice of depositions (Super. Ct. R. 38 and 43) and notice that a deposition has been filed (Super. Ct. R. 43), can agree to accept an affidavit as evidence (Super. Ct. R. 46), is entitled to notice of documents sought to be admitted without dispute (Super. Ct. R. 54), and must be notified of interlocutory orders and requests for preliminary injunctions (Super. Ct. R. 141 and 161). While it is dangerous to place too much reliance on the literal language of court rules, the distinction between an "adverse party" and an "opposing party" seems to be that the former is on the other side of the whole case, while the latter is on the other side only with respect to some issues in the case.

3 A real party in interest always has the right to control his part of the case. A vestige of the nineteenth century practice of bringing actions in the name of nominal parties survives today in the following proceedings:

on the record is essential to a final and binding resolution of the issue. "Permissible parties" are additional persons who have a direct interest in the subject matter or property involved in the action but whose presence in the case is not necessary to the rendition of a valid judgment. "Parties of record" are persons whose names appear on the docket. Nominal, necessary, and permissible parties are parties of record; real parties in interest may or may not be listed on the docket.

Library References

CJS Parties §§ 2–6, 18

§ 6.03. Importance of the Distinction Between Parties and Nonparties

The distinction between persons who are parties and persons who are not is more than a matter of form. Parties enjoy several privileges and are subject to a number of duties under the rules of court from which nonparties are excluded.[4] Nonparties are only expressly permitted to obtain a copy of any

---

1. Actions on a bond (See RSA 27:10, 565:6 and 8 and Judge of Probate v. Merrill, 6 N.H. 256 (1833)), which must be brought in the name of the officer or public agency in whose name the bond is posted.

2. Quo warranto proceedings to test the right to a public office where the Attorney General brings the action in his own name but appears on the relation of a private citizen. The relator, however, is often the person who claims the office and, under the modern practice, is most likely to present the case in court.

3. Actions to collect on bonds posted by regulated companies to secure their compliance with the orders of administrative agencies. See RSA 434:52.

4. Defense by insurance companies of claims against their insureds where the companies have a contractual right to control the litigation. Although the companies do not generally appear as parties of record and their participation can be barred if the insured is willing to forego coverage, they are regarded as the real parties in interest to the extent of coverage.

With these exceptions, however, a party with a recognized legal or equitable interest involved in the case is today permitted to appear or be called upon to respond in his own name. If his connection with the subject matter of the case is not apparent from the other parts of the record, it may be recited in the pleading which names him as a party.

4 See Super. Ct. R. 1 (party entitled to a blank writ), 2 (mail address of parties must be on pleadings), 10 (clerk to enter names of parties on the docket), 13 (parties may request that a case be placed on the trial calendar), 20 (parties are to be notified by the clerk of their attorneys' withdrawal), 21 (copies of papers go to opposing party), 24 (defendant is entitled to notice of intention to amend after default), 25 (plaintiff can amend as to matters of form as of right unless "adverse party" first shows the defect), 27 (third party may be brought in), 29 (court may order party to plead and file detailed statement for "adverse party"), 35 (parties may obtain discovery and have certain duties to supplement responses), 36 (parties may pose interrogatories to other parties), 38 ("adverse party" is entitled to notice of depositions), 40 (notice of deposition to "real party in

statements they have made regarding the action,[5] to apply for a protective order concerning discovery,[6] to file a petition to intervene,[7] and to be provided certain securities.[8]

B. Capacity To Sue and Be Sued

§ 6.04. Persons Who May Commence an Action or Proceeding

Any person with a legal or equitable right who is not specially disqualified by the terms of a statute[9] may bring an action in the appropriate court or

---

interest" if his identity is disclosed on the writ or docket), 43 (party may file deposition and notify "adverse party"), 46 ("adverse party" can agree to accept affidavit as evidence), 51 (clerk can notify "parties of record" if informed that case is settled), 52 (affidavit of party required if order of notice not filed), 53 (defendant may dispute authenticity of documents), 54 (any party may seek admission of documents, sending copies to the "adverse party"), 55 (parties file papers to make record complete), 57 (the motion may be heard if the facts are agreed to by the parties), 58 ("party" must object to a motion within ten days), 59 (court may assess costs against any party), 62 (pretrial stipulations by parties), 63 (parties to submit certain information before trial), 68 (party to give "opposing party" copy of criminal record to be used against a witness), 74 (parties may seek appellate review), 80 (parties to pay costs), 82 (parties may be nonsuited for failure to appear before auditors), 83 (parties may make requests regarding auditor's instructions), 85 (parties may request that auditors set out facts on an issue), 86 (trustees are allowed costs as a party until their liability is determined if they enter an appearance), 89 (party to notify "opposing party" that proof of a public highway will be required), 113 (notice of a motion to consolidate must be given "to all parties in all such actions"), 118 (bills and petitions in equity must contain the names, places of abode and proper description of all parties), 124 (a party filing a bill or petition has an election on return day), 141 (interlocutory orders require notice to the "adverse party"), 142 (parties may be arrested), 150 (parties must sign stipulations in marital cases), 155 (a petition for modification must be served on "opposing party"), 158 (parties must file affidavits in marital proceedings), 160 (temporary restraining order may be issued without notice to the "adverse party"), 161 (parties may consent to extension of the time limit on temporary restraining orders, preliminary injunctions may be issued only after notice to the "adverse party," security must be posted for the benefit of "any party," and an injunction is binding upon parties and those with knowledge of it who act in concert with them), 163 (an injunction ordered without notice to the "adverse party" requires a bond), and 166 (notice of a petition for dissolution of a business corporation to all "interested parties").

5 Super. Ct. R. 35(b)(2).

6 Super. Ct. R. 35(c).

7 Super. Ct. R. 139.

8 Super. Ct. R. 165.

9 See RSA 304-B:54(I) ("A foreign limited partnership transacting business in this state may not maintain any action, suit, or proceeding in any court of this state until it has registered in this state").

agency to enforce, determine, or protect it.[10] The plaintiff must bring the action in the capacity in which he holds his or her right. Most statutes which

---

10   See Arlington Trust Co. v. Estate of Wood, 123 N.H. 765, 465 A.2d 917 (1983) (bank which was to receive and hold payment on a life insurance policy as trustee for settlor's children could not sue settlor's estate for failure to maintain the policy). In the early part of the last century, it was generally held that an action at law could only be brought in the name of the person with legal title to the interest being enforced. Underhill v. Gibson, 2 N.H. 352 (1821); Moore v. Chesley, 17 N.H. 151 (1845); Woodbury v. Woodbury, 47 N.H. 11 (1866).

Under this doctrine, it was permissible to assign a note to a third person for the sole purpose of bringing suit in his name, so long as the procedure did not "render it less easy for the defendant to make his defense." Edgerton v. Brackett, 11 N.H. 218, 221 (1840). See also Gray v. Johnson, 14 N.H. 414 (1843); Berry v. Gillis, 17 N.H. 9 (1845). It is interesting, however, that even in those days of strict common law pleading, requirements of form were not permitted to defeat the ends of justice when a person with an equitable right but no legal title sought to enforce his claim. In such a case, he could bring an action in the name of the legal holder, so long as he indemnified the legal holder against the costs of the action. The rule was summarized by Justice Eastman in Pike v. Pike, 24 N.H. 384, 394 (1852), as follows:

> [P]ersons having equitable rights which can be enforced in courts of law only in the names of the parties in whom the legal title is vested, may prosecute and defend those rights in the names of the persons in whom the legal title exists. It is, of course, to be understood that in such cases, a full indemnity for costs must be furnished if required.

See also Bank of Newbury v. Rand, 38 N.H. 166 (1859).

After the Civil War, the Doe Court completely reversed the prior requirement that an action be brought only in the name of the person with legal title and established the modern rule that an action may be brought in the name of a person with any interest. In Boyd v. Webster, 58 N.H. 336 (1878), the Court allowed a partner to sue in his own name on a note to a partnership which he had taken in settlement of the partnership's affairs. In Towle v. Rowe, 58 N.H. 394 (1878), and Ramsey v. Fellows, 58 N.H. 607 (1879), the Court allowed a bankrupt to maintain a suit on a note given before bankruptcy and to bring suit on a cause of action accruing before bankruptcy when the assignee in bankruptcy declined to do so. In Folsom v. Orient Fire Insurance Company, 59 N.H. 54 (1879), the Court allowed the owner of an equitable interest in a house to sue in his own name for the benefit of the holder of the legal title in order to recover under a fire insurance policy after the house had been destroyed, and in Boudreau v. Eastman, 59 N.H. 467 (1879), the Court saw no objection to an agent suing for deceit by another agent where, even though the plaintiff did not own the property taken from him by the defendant's deceit, he was required to pay damages to its owner. The cases did not, however, eliminate the need to show some legal or equitable right in order to bring an action. See Contoocook Fire Precinct v. Hopkinton, 71 N.H. 574, 53 A. 797 (1902). This principle was reaffirmed in Henderson v. Sherwood Motor Hotel, 105 N.H. 443, 201 A.2d 891 (1964), where the Court held that the ex-husband of a decedent who was subject to the Workmen's Compensation statute could not sue under that statute as administrator of her estate, but was required to bring the action in her role as guardian of the decedent's minor child.

Under the modern rule, an action may be brought in the name of a person with any interest. However, in recent decisions involving the procedure for enforcement by an insurer of its rights under a subrogation clause, the Court has held that a payor of health insurance benefits may bring an action "in the patient's name" against a tortfeasor who

define causes of action or set forth the jurisdiction of administrative agencies specify the class of person who may commence or intervene in the actions they create.[11] The Supreme Court has recognized the capacity of a taxpayer to commence an action to recover moneys due the state so long as the taxpayer does so with the prior written permission of the Attorney General and submits that consent with the writ.[12] Presumably the same principles would apply to a taxpayer suit on behalf of a unit of local government.

Library References

CJS Actions §§ 28, 29
CJS Parties §§ 8–12
Joint venture's capacity to sue. 56 ALR4th 1234.

§ 6.05. Persons Who May Be Sued

Any person who violates the plaintiff's right, or whose rights may be foreclosed by a judgment in the action, may be required to respond. The defendant must be sued in the capacity in which his obligation arises or his interests are held.[13]

---

has caused injuries to a child for which health insurance benefits have been paid if neither the parents nor the tortfeasor agrees to repay the company and the parents fail to bring suit. Blue Cross/Blue Shield v. St. Cyr, 123 N.H. 137, 143 44, 459 A.2d 226, 229 (1983) (citing Montello Shoe Co. v. Suncook Industries, Inc., 92 N.H. 161, 26 A.2d 676 (1942)). See also Vachon v. Halford, 125 N.H. 577, 579 80, 484 A.2d 1127, 1129 (1984) and RSA 304-B:56–58 (a limited partner may sue in the name of the limited partnership).

11 See RSA 304-B:45 (the superior court may order a dissolution of a limited partnership "[o]n application by or for a partner."); RSA 304-B:46 (the superior court may "wind up" a limited partnership "upon application of any partner, his legal representative, or assignee"); RSA 304-B:55 (the Attorney General may commence a proceeding for injunction against an unregistered foreign limited partnership); RSA 506:7(I) and (II) (specified persons or "any other interested party" who has satisfied the statutory requirements may petition the superior court or probate court to take certain actions relating to powers of attorney).

12 Sununu v. Clamshell Alliance, 122 N.H. 668, 438 A.2d 431 (1982). Cf. RSA 471-C:37(V) (authorizing the state administrator to permit another party to bring an action in his name in another state to recover property escheated to the state).

13 Scamman v. Sondheim, 97 N.H. 280, 86 A.2d 329 (1952). The executor or administrator of an estate, rather than the heirs or legatees, is the proper defendant in an action against an estate. But the person need not be sued in each capacity in which he has acted; it is enough that the action is brought against him in the capacity in which his obligation arose. See Bartlett v. Dumaine, 128 N.H. 497, 523 A.2d 1 (1986) (trustees who accepted positions as officers and directors of a corporation controlled by their trust could be required to respond to the beneficiaries of the trust regarding their actions as corporate officers and directors on a petition for accounting brought against them solely in their capacities as trustees; it was not necessary that they also be named as directors and shareholders or that a proceeding be commenced against the corporation). In Shortlidge

Library References

CJS Actions §§ 28, 30
CJS Parties §§ 41–45

C. Joint or Separate Actions

§ 6.06. Potential for Joinder

When the rights or interests of more than one person are affected by the same set of facts, the question arises whether they should sue or be sued together. The resolution of this question depends upon whether the parties' interests are capable of being tried and settled separately.

§ 6.07. Plaintiffs

A person may always maintain an action in his name alone to enforce a right or to protect an interest which he holds separately from all others.[14] When a right is held jointly or in common with others, he should try to bring his action jointly with those others,[15] but if he cannot, he may still maintain the proceeding for the protection of his rights alone.[16] In some cases, where

---

v. Gutoski, 125 N.H. 510, 484 A.2d 1083 (1984), the Court held that, while the members of an unincorporated association may be held personally liable for the debts of the association to which they have given their assent (absent an agreement by the creditor to look solely to the association's assets for payment), action by the creditor against the association, rather than against the individual members, to collect that debt will constitute an election to satisfy any resulting judgment only out of the association's assets.

14 Farmer v. Stewart, 2 N.H. 97 (1819) (separate parcels of land); Appeal of Town of Plymouth, 125 N.H. 141, 479 A.2d 1388 (1984) (individual owner of undivided 15.81% interest in the common area of a condominium may seek an abatement of the real estate tax assessed on that interest without joining all other owners of percentage interests in the common area).

15 Kenniston v. Ham, 29 N.H. 501 (1854):

The general principle of law to be deduced from the authorities undoubtedly is that where there is a contract and the legal interest therein is joint in several, they should all join in one action, in form *ex contractu*, for a breach of it; but when the legal interest is several in each, the action should, in general, be several. 29 N.H. at 509.

See also Pearson v. Parker, 3 N.H. 366 (1826); Willoughby v. Willoughby, 5 N.H. 244 (1830); Smith v. Smith, 11 N.H. 469 (1841); Wilson v. Gamble, 9 N.H. 74 (1837) (in personal actions, but not in actions on real property); Pickering v. Pickering, 11 N.H. 141 (1840); Campbell v. Wallace, 12 N.H. 362 (1841); Stevenson v. Cofferin, 20 N.H. 150 (1849); Blake v. Milliken, 14 N.H. 213 (1843); Webber v. Merrill, 34 N.H. 202 (1856); Moulton v. Robinson, 27 N.H. 564 (1853); Reid v. Spadone Machine Co., 119 N.H. 198, 200, 400 A.2d 54, 55 (1979) (joinder "does not depend upon consent"); Brooks v. Howison, 63 N.H. 382 (1885).

16 Gray v. Johnson, 14 N.H. 414, 418 (1843):

two or more plaintiffs have separate rights or interests which depend on the same or similar facts and issues of law, the court may permit them to bring their actions together[17] or to consolidate their separate actions for trial.[18] Plaintiffs with separate interests which do not share a common basis in fact or law, other than the identity of the person against whom they wish to assert those rights, may not bring their actions together in the first instance[19] and will only be permitted to consolidate their separate actions for trial if the court's jurisdiction is in rem or if extraordinary circumstances exist which make it clear that justice will only be served by a joint trial.

Library References

CJS Parties §§ 33–40
Joinder of tort actions between spouses with proceeding for dissolution of marriage. 4 ALR5th 972.

§ 6.08. Defendants

Any person may be called upon to respond separately to an action if, in his own right, he owes a duty to the plaintiff. If more than one person is liable to the plaintiff on the facts alleged, the action may be brought against them all regardless of whether their liability is joint or several. If their liability is joint, the plaintiff should try to bring his action against all,[20] but if he is unable to do so the action may still be maintained against those he can find.[21] Any person whose rights will be concluded by the case or against

---

> The rule is well settled by the decisions, that though a man covenant with two or more jointly, yet if the interest and cause of action of the covenantees be several, the covenant shall be taken to be several, and each of the covenantees may bring an action for his particular damage, notwithstanding the words of the covenant be joint. 14 N.H. at 418.

17 See Sections 6.18–6.20.

18 See Chapter 42, Consolidation or Separation of Cases or Proceedings for Trial.

19 Woodward v. Sherman, 52 N.H. 131 (1872).

20 During the nineteenth century, the rule was settled that all persons jointly liable on a contract had to be named in an action to enforce rights arising under the contract (see Martin v. Fales, 24 N.H. 242 (1851) and Ela v. Rand, 4 N.H. 307 (1828)); but once having named them, if the plaintiff was unable to prove liability against all at trial, he could have judgment against those whose liability had been proven. Flanders v. White Mountain Bank, 43 N.H. 383 (1861); Protective Check Writer Company, Inc. v. Collins, 92 N.H. 27, 23 A.2d 770 (1942).

21 Auclair v. Bancroft, 121 N.H. 393, 430 A.2d 169 (1981).

whom the court's order must run if the plaintiff is to have complete relief is a necessary party defendant and must be named.[22]

Library References

CJS Parties §§ 43–55

D. Objecting to Nonjoinder

§ 6.09. Time To Object

Objections to nonjoinder must be made within the time set forth for filing a Motion to Dismiss for matters in abatement.

Library References

CJS Parties §§ 139–152
Order sustaining demurrer, or its equivalent, to complaint on ground of misjoinder or nonjoinder of parties. 56 ALR2d 1238.

§ 6.10. Procedure

Since 1833, New Hampshire has provided by statute that the failure to join a defendant or plaintiff will not abate the writ, but, if pleaded, may be cured by adding the omitted party. The statute is presently set forth in RSA 514:10 as follows:

> No action shall be abated by the plea that there are other plaintiffs or defendants who ought to be joined therein, but such persons may be made parties to the action upon such terms as the court shall order, and may be summoned by scire facias, or notified by publication, as the court may order and the action shall thereafter proceed as if their names were inserted in the original writ.[23]

With respect to real actions, RSA 514:11 also provides that "the writ shall not abate because all the tenants are not named in it, but those on whom it is served shall answer for such part of the premises demanded as they claim, and may disclaim for the residue." These statutes allow a case to continue

---

22 Woodstock Soapstone v. Carleton, 133 N.H. 809, 585 A.2d 312 (1991) (party whose rights would not be concluded by a judgment in the case is not a necessary party and need not be joined). But see Storch Engineers v. D&K Land Developers, 134 N.H. 414, 596 A.2d 131 (1991) (judgment against a partnership will not support an execution against the individual property of general partners in respect to whom the trial court has not yet entered judgment).

23 The substance of the original statute has not been changed since 1833. See Revised Statutes 186:18; Compiled Statutes 198:18; General Statutes 207:16; General Laws 226:16; Public Statutes 222:11; Public Laws 334:10; Revised Laws 395:10.

despite nonjoinder, either by adding the necessary parties in a personal action or by limiting the res in real actions.

The defendant may object that a necessary or proper[24] party has not been joined by filing either a Motion to Dismiss for Nonjoinder[25] or a Motion to Join the missing party. The motion should state the names of the person or persons who have not joined, the capacity in which they should be joined,[26] and the facts upon the basis of which the court may conclude that joinder is either necessary or appropriate to a just resolution of the case. The motion should also allege that the proposed additional parties are alive and within the jurisdiction of the court.[27] When the motion raises facts not apparent from the record, it must be supported by affidavits. A copy of the motion must be sent to the plaintiff, and when the defendant moves to join, an attested copy of the plaintiff's pleading and the Motion to Join must be served on the proposed additional party.

The plaintiff and the proposed new party, if any, may object within ten days of receipt of the motion. When the defendant has filed a Motion to Dismiss, the plaintiff may respond by moving to amend the pleading to add the additional party.[28] An attested copy of his initial pleading, the Motion to Dismiss, and the Motion to Amend must then be served on the proposed new party, who may thereafter respond within the time limits allowed for response to the initial pleading. The court will hold a hearing on the defendant's motion and the plaintiff's and any third party's response. In most cases, the action will not be dismissed unless it is clear that necessary parties have not and cannot be joined.

---

24 Merrill v. Coggill, 12 N.H. 97 (1841).

25 Merrill v. Coggill, 12 N.H. 97, 100 (1841); Pitkin v. Roby, 43 N.H. 138 (1861); Kenniston v. Ham, 29 N.H. 501 (1854); Shortlidge v. Gutoski, 125 N.H. 510, 484 A.2d 1083 (1984) (an individual member of an unincorporated association, when sued alone for the association's debts, could file a plea in abatement to compel the plaintiff to join the other members of the association).

26 Ela v. Rand, 3 N.H. 95 (1824).

27 Merrill v. Coggill, 12 N.H. 97, 100 (1841); Pitkin v. Roby, 43 N.H. 138 (1861).

28 Pitkin v. Roby, 43 N.H. 138 (1861). The purpose of RSA 514:10 was "to give the plaintiff the right to amend his declaration by adding new plaintiffs or defendants whenever his action would fail or be liable to fail for the want of them, in whatever way the objection of nonjoinder might be liable to be made." 43 N.H. at 141. But the plaintiff will not be allowed to amend as of right by adding new defendants if the time when the defendant could have objected to the nonjoinder has passed without any objection being filed. Gove v. Lawrence, 24 N.H. 128 (1851). Because the rule is established for the defendant's benefit, he can waive it by not objecting in a timely fashion. Pickering v. Pickering, 11 N.H. 141, 144 (1840); Nealley v. Moulton, 12 N.H. 485 (1842).

§ 6.11. Effect of Failing To Object

The defendant's failure to object that persons who are jointly liable with him for the debt or damages have not been joined subjects the defendant, on verdict, to the full liability asserted by the plaintiff.[29] However, the defendant's failure to plead in abatement that other persons should have been joined as plaintiffs does not prevent an apportionment of damages at trial.[30]

§ 6.12. Persons Who May Object to Nonjoinder

Any real defendant in interest may object that necessary or proper parties have not been joined. Nominal parties may not make the objection.[31]

E. Objecting to Joinder (Misjoinder)

§ 6.13. Procedure—By the Defendant

Just as he may object that necessary parties have not been joined, so the defendant may also object that persons with no interest in the case have been joined.[32] The defendant should raise his objection by a Motion to Dismiss either the action or the misjoined party. The motion must identify the misjoined party and state the facts upon the basis of which it may be concluded that the party has no interest in the case.[33] If the motion relies on facts not apparent from the record, it must be supported by affidavit. A copy must be sent to all parties, and any party may object within ten days.

The plaintiff may respond by moving to amend to delete a misjoined defendant but one plaintiff may not move to drop a co-plaintiff. If the

---

29 Pitkin v. Roby, 43 N.H. 138 (1861). See also Shortlidge v. Gutoski, 125 N.H. 510, 484 A.2d 1083 (1984).

30 Wilson v. Gamble, 9 N.H. 74 (1837). But see Smith v. Smith, 11 N.H. 459, 464 (1841) (apportionment may not be appropriate when the persons who would be co-plaintiffs are merely co-administrators of one estate).

31 Pike v. Pike, 24 N.H. 384 (1852).

32 In Murray v. Webster, 5 N.H. 391 (1831), the Court held that an action could not be maintained which joined a plaintiff who had no cause of action and a plaintiff who had one. This result would undoubtedly not be enforced today. While the principle is the same that persons without a claim should not be parties to an action by one with a claim, the Superior Court today would simply sever the actions and dismiss the former while letting the latter continue. But in Hills v. Doe, 6 N.H. 328 (1833), the Court also held that parties properly joined when the action was begun would not be subject to a motion for misjoinder if their status later changed.

33 It is important to distinguish between an objection that a party has no proper interest in the case (misjoinder) and an objection that two claims should not be tried together (sever).

allegedly misjoined party does not object and the plaintiff moves to delete him, no hearing will be necessary and the court will enter an order in accordance with the parties' agreement. Otherwise, the court will hold a hearing. The court will generally dismiss a party for misjoinder only if he raises no objection and it does not appear that he has any interest in the case. Where it appears that the party objected to has an interest and desires to remain in the case, the court will instead consider whether the defendant's objection justifies an order severing the claims for trial.

Library References

CJS Parties §§ 153–167
Order sustaining demurrer, or its equivalent, to complaint on ground of misjoinder or nonjoinder of parties. 56 ALR2d 1238.
Joinder of tort actions between spouses with proceeding for dissolution of marriage. 4 ALR5th 972.

§ 6.14. —By the Plaintiff

RSA 514:13 also permits the plaintiff to raise misjoinder. That statute provides as follows:

> In all civil proceedings when two or more are joined as plaintiffs or defendants, the writ or other process may be amended before the evidence is closed or the case is submitted, by striking out the name of any plaintiff or of any defendant on paying his costs to that time.[34]

§ 6.15. —By the Misjoined Party

A party who has no interest or obligation in a case may move to dismiss the case as to him for misjoinder.[35] The motion must show that there is no

---

34 The statute is derived from an Act of July 4, 1834, which provided that a writ would not abate because one or more defendants had been improperly joined, but that the case would proceed after discharge of the improperly joined defendants. In that form, the statute was construed by Chief Justice Parker in Blake v. Ladd, 10 N.H. at 190 (1839), as follows:

> The statute was intended for the benefit of plaintiffs who were before subjected to the loss of suits, founded on contracts, where they failed to sustain the action against all the defendants, notwithstanding good cause of action might be shown against one or more of them. It enables the court in actions founded on contract as well as those founded on torts, to render judgment against one or more of the defendants, notwithstanding the action cannot be maintained against others. 10 N.H. at 192.

The statute was amended in 1872 to allow discharge of improperly joined plaintiffs as well. This is the form in which it exists today.

35 A party's motion to dismiss for misjoinder of himself must be distinguished from a disclaimer of any interest in a res or the assertion of an affirmative defense to liability

set of facts provable on the plaintiff's pleading which could give rise to any liability or obligation on the part of the objecting party and that the objecting party's presence in the case is not necessary to give effect to any requested court order. A copy of the motion must go to all parties, who may object within ten days. If there is no objection, the court will grant the motion without hearing. If an objection is filed, the court will hold a hearing and will keep the objecting party in the case if there is any possibility that his rights or obligations could be affected by the case or his presence is necessary to make the court's order effective. The plaintiff may move to amend at any time before the case is submitted to the jury.[36] Once the amendment has been made, the defendant can replead as though the action had been begun in its new form.[37]

Library References

CJS Parties §§ 160–161

§ 6.16. Effect of Failing To Object

The defendant's failure to object in a timely fashion is a waiver of the misjoinder. The plaintiff's failure to amend before the case is submitted results simply in a directed verdict for the misjoined party.

Library References

CJS Parties §§ 156, 159

§ 6.17. Time To Object

Objections to misjoinder must be raised by the misjoined party no later than the return day. Other parties must object within the time set for filing a Motion to Dismiss for matters in abatement. Plaintiffs may move to amend for misjoinder any time before the case is submitted to the jury.

Library References

CJS Parties §§ 155, 158

(e.g., release). In neither of the latter two situations will the defendant be entitled to a dismissal since the plaintiff's assertion of interest is proved by the plea and his presence on the record is necessary to determine or conclude his interest.

36 See Griffin v. Simpson, 45 N.H. 18 (1863) (plaintiff not permitted to amend after judgment based on failure to prove a joint promise by eliminating all defendants except the one against whom the promise was proven).

37 Hartshorn v. Schoff, 51 N.H. 316, 321 (1871).

F. Class Actions and Representative Suits

§ 6.18. The Difference Between Class Actions and Representative Suits

Class actions are proceedings in which a number of plaintiffs are permitted to bring only one action against a common opponent. The plaintiffs in class actions join in one writ or petition claims that are identical in substance. While in consolidated actions several writs are joined to make one. In representative suits, the claims of several are prosecuted by a smaller number of plaintiffs who are to fairly represent the interests of all.

Actions on behalf of a class of unnamed persons are considered both class actions and representative suits. In fact, there is no significant difference in principle or in purpose between class actions and representative suits and the two are often referred to today by the single term "class actions."[38]

Library References

CJS Parties §§ 21–32

Maintainability in state court of class action for relief against air or water pollution. 47 ALR3d 769.

Consumer class actions based on fraud or misrepresentations. 53 ALR3d 534.

Appealability of order denying right to proceed in form of class action—state cases. 54 ALR3d 595.

Right to private action under state consumer protection act. 62 ALR3d 169.

Propriety of class action in state courts to assert tenants' rights against landlord. 73 ALR3d 852.

Inverse condemnation state court class actions. 49 ALR4th 618.

Absent or unnamed class members in class action in state court as subject to discovery. 28 ALR4th 986.

Class actions in state mass tort suits. 53 ALR4th 1220.

Propriety of attorney acting as both counsel and class member or representative. 37 ALR4th 751.

§ 6.19. Statutory Authority for Class Actions

There is no general statute in New Hampshire authorizing class actions or representative suits.[39] RSA 358-A:10-a authorizes class actions, but only for violations of the Unfair Trade Practices and Consumer Protection Act and related statutes.

---

38 See Super. Ct. R. 27-A.

39 Such legislation has, in fact, been proposed and rejected by the Legislature.

§ 6.20. Class Actions

(a) *Common Law Authority.*

(1) *Plaintiff Class:*   Class actions have been authorized by the common law of New Hampshire since the end of the nineteenth century. In *Smith v. Bank of New England*,[40] the court was presented with a bill in equity on behalf of the plaintiff and "all others of like interest" stating that the plaintiffs owned certificates of deposit issued by the Union Trust Company and that the Bank of New England had been negligent in obtaining security for the certificates from the issuer. The bill stated the names and addresses of 78 persons other than the plaintiffs who held certificates of deposit which differed from the plaintiffs' only in their face amounts. The petition sought an order, among other things, requiring that all persons with similar interests either join the action as plaintiffs or be barred from sharing in the decree. The defendant demurred, arguing that the plaintiff had no right to object to a multiplicity of suits if the defendant was willing to suffer them. But the Supreme Court allowed the action to proceed, noting "that the matters in dispute can be more conveniently, economically and expeditiously adjusted from one suit."[41] An order was allowed which forever barred nonappearing security holders from sharing in the trust res or other damages and from ever bringing a different suit on the same claim.

Almost sixty years later, in *Textile Workers Union v. Textron, Inc.*,[42] the Supreme Court allowed a union's director to sue for unpaid wages on behalf of 2,700 unnamed employees. The Court noted that no question had been raised regarding the plaintiff's authority to act as the agent of 2,700 employees and that there was sufficient reason to believe that he would adequately represent their interests. The Court concluded that "evidence may be presented of the names of the members involved, the amounts due each, and, if judgment be in the plaintiff's favor, an order may be entered insuring payment to the proper persons."[43] Thus actions may be brought on behalf of either named or unnamed plaintiff class so long as notice is given to all members of the class and the members sharing in the award are specifically named in the decree. More recently, in *State Employees' Association of New Hampshire v. Belknap County*,[44] the Court recognized class actions for use in cases where four prerequisites are met:

---

40   69 N.H. 254, 45 A. 1082 (1898).

41   *Id.*

42   99 N.H. 385, 111 A.2d 823 (1955).

43   99 N.H. at 387, 111 A.2d at 824.

44   122 N.H. 614, 448 A.2d 969 (1982).

First, there must be a definable class which is so numerous that joinder of all members would be impracticable. Second, the representative parties must have claims or defenses which typify the claims or defenses of all members of the class, and the representatives must fairly and adequately protect the interests of the class. Third, questions of law or fact common to the class must predominate over questions affecting individual members. Finally, the class action must be superior to all other available means for adjudicating the dispute.[45]

Since the decision in *State Employees' Association*, the superior court has promulgated Rule 27-A which authorizes class actions when the four criteria set forth in the Supreme Court's opinion have been met, and it can be reasonably assumed that "the attorney for the representative parties will adequately represent the interests of the class." An action begun as a class action may later be broken into separate actions if the court finds that, during the pendency of the case, any of those criteria cease to be met.[46]

(2) *Defendant Class:*　The reasoning of *Smith v. Bank of New England* could support an action against a defendant as well as a plaintiff class. In *Monitor Publishing Company v. Hill*,[47] a group of taxpayers filed a bill in equity against the Comptroller and Treasurer of the State of New Hampshire, challenging the constitutionality of a statute that increased mileage reimbursement for members of the General Court. The President of the Senate and the Speaker of the House petitioned to intervene as defendants, in both their individual and official capacities. While holding the statute unconstitutional, the Supreme Court also decided that it was not necessary for all members of the Legislature to be joined as parties to the action, since the President of the Senate and the Speaker of the House, both in their individual and official capacities, "could and fairly did represent the interests of all legislators in the mileage payments proposed under the . . . statute."[48]

(b) *Procedure Under Superior Court Rule 27-A.*

(1) *Approval of the Class Action:*　Where one or more persons seeks to enforce a claim for or against a class, they must identify in the caption of their initial pleading at least one representative of that class and state what

---

45　122 N.H. at 623–24, 448 A.2d at 974. See also Petition of State Employees' Association, 127 N.H. 89, 90, 497 A.2d 860, 861 (1985) (the same principles that support the use of class actions in court "highly commend the use of class actions in administrative proceedings. . . .").

46　Super. Ct. R. 27-A(b).

47　103 N.H. 397, 173 A.2d 725 (1961).

48　103 N.H. at 402, 173 A.2d at 727.

class he or she is supposed to represent. They must also recite in their pleading facts which will support a finding that the criteria of Rule 27-A have been met.[49] A class action may not be maintained without the court's permission,[50] and the plaintiff must therefore include in the initial pleading a request that the court allow the maintenance of the action on behalf of a named class and permit notice to the members of the class by means of a specified procedure. As in the case of other preliminary orders, the plaintiff will be best advised to draft the desired form of an order in advance and to file it with his initial pleading.

(2) *Defining the Class:* Rule 27-A permits either a plaintiff or a defendant class,[51] or both. The class may include persons who have not specifically been identified[52] and may bind all persons within the described class who do not elect against the joint trial of their claims by a certain date.[53]

(3) *Notice to the Class:* The court must approve the form of notice to be given to the class when it allows the device to be used.[54] Notice must, in any event, be "the best practicable under the circumstances" with respect to each individual member, and at least inform the members of the class that they may elect to be excluded by a certain date, that they will be bound by the judgment if they do not so elect, and that they may have individual counsel even though they remain in the class.[55] A person may not, however, choose to be excluded from a defendant class.[56] The plaintiff should prepare a proposed form and method of notice for the members of the class, with supporting lists of names and addresses, from which the court can determine at the time of filing how best to provide notice. The representatives of either a plaintiff or defendant class must advance the costs of notice to members of their class and see that notice is given in accordance with the court's order.[57]

---

49 The parties may stipulate to facts which they could otherwise contest and which are necessary to the maintenance of a class action, but they may not stipulate, and the court may not approve their stipulation, that a class action should be maintained. Private Truck Council of America v. State, 128 N.H. 466, 517 A.2d 1150 (1986).

50 Super. Ct. R. 27-A(b).

51 Super. Ct. R. 27-A(a).

52 Super. Ct. R. 27-A(i).

53 Super. Ct. R. 27-A(d), (e), and (f). See also Palmer v. U.S. Savings Bank of America, 131 N.H. 433, 553 A.2d 781 (1989) (citing Super. Ct. R. 27-A(a)(4)).

54 Super. Ct. R. 27-A(e).

55 *Id.* See also NH Rules of Professional Conduct, Rule 7.3(d).

56 Super. Ct. R. 27-A(f).

57 Super. Ct. R. 27-A(e).

(4) *Interlocutory Orders:* During the pendency of a class action, the court may enter further orders designed to protect the members of the class at large from their representatives or otherwise to assure that the procedure produces at least as just a result as could have been expected from a number of separate actions. The court may order special notices advising members of the class of various stages in the proceeding and of their rights at those stages, solicit their views on the adequacy of their representation or on the merits of the claim,[58] and even require that the class action cease and that the individual members of the class pursue or be pursued separately.[59] The court may also adopt special rules for the preparation and trial of the case designed to assure a fair, complete, but expeditious resolution on the merits.[60]

(5) *Partial Class Actions:* Individual issues in a case may alone be handled as class actions and subgroups of a class may be treated separately in the preparation and trial of the case, if the court orders.[61]

(6) *Discontinuance:* Once an action has been begun as a class action, neither the whole nor any part of it may be settled, nonsuited, or dismissed without notice to the class and an order from the court.[62]

(7) *Judgment:* A judgment in an action maintained as a class action must identify or describe all members of the class who are to be bound by it.[63] If a plaintiff class prevails, the court may require that damages be paid into court and that the members of the class apply to the court for payment, or may issue other orders to assure the orderly and prompt satisfaction thereof.[64]

(8) *Courts in Which a Class Action May Be Maintained:* Rule 27-A applies, of course, only to the superior court. As subsection (c) of that rule allows the individual claims of the members of a class to be combined in order to satisfy the jurisdictional limit, it is unlikely that a class action could be devised which could not be brought in the superior court. However, *State Employees' Association*, and the cases that preceded it, recognized the device without limiting its availability to the court of general jurisdiction, and there is no reason to believe that a class action could not be brought in

---

58 Super. Ct. R. 27-A(j)(2).
59 Super. Ct. R. 27-A(b).
60 Super. Ct. R. 27-A(j)(1) and (3).
61 Super. Ct. R. 27-A(i).
62 Super. Ct. R. 27-A(k).
63 Super. Ct. R. 27-A(g).
64 Super. Ct. R. 27-A(h).

an appropriate case in the district court *if* the total claims of the plaintiff did not exceed the court's jurisdictional limit, title to real estate was not involved, and no party elected a jury trial. The requirements of the district court's venue statute might, however, pose a problem if there were unidentified members on both sides and it could not be affirmatively determined that all unidentified members of the classes would themselves be amenable to involuntary process in that district court.

(c) *Class Actions in Administrative Proceedings.* In the absence of a statute which settles the point, administrative agencies are neither prohibited from allowing nor compelled to permit class actions in matters pending before them.[65]

Library References

Absent or unnamed class members in class action in state court as subject to discovery. 28 ALR4th 986.

Propriety of attorney acting as both counsel and class member or representative. 37 ALR4th 751.

Class actions in state mass tort suits. 53 ALR4th 1220.

G. Misnomer and Misdesignation

§ 6.21. The Difference Between Misnomer and Misdesignation

A "misnomer" occurs when the plaintiff identifies the correct person as his defendant but misspells his name. A "misdesignation" occurs when the wrong person is named as the defendant.

Library References

CJS Parties § 165

Effect of misnomer of landowner or delinquent taxpayer in notice, advertisement, etc., of tax foreclosure or sale. 43 ALR2d 967.

§ 6.22. Correction of Misnomers and Misdesignations

(a) *Misnomers.* A misnomer may be corrected upon either party's motion at any stage of the proceedings. The failure of either party to correct a misnomer will not affect the validity of any resulting judgment.[66]

---

65 Petition of State Employees' Association, 127 N.H. 89, 497 A.2d 860 (1985).

66 Where the defendant is correctly named but may be incorrectly described, the court will not order an amendment. In Bourget v. New England Telephone and Telegraph Company, 97 N.H. 193, 84 A.2d 830 (1951), the Court refused to order the plaintiff to change his description of the defendant from a New Hampshire corporation to a New York corporation, saying that this was a question of fact for the trial court.

(b) *Misdesignation.* If the wrong person is named as a defendant, the defendant so named may file a Motion to Dismiss within thirty days of entry. Where there is no connection between the intended and the designated defendant, the court will dismiss upon receiving evidence by affidavit of the mistake. If, as more often happens, the intended and the designated defendants are related, and the intended defendant receives notice and understands that he is intended to be charged, the court will simply treat the error as a misnomer and order an amendment without further service.[67]

From the earliest date, New Hampshire courts have consistently held that the plaintiff's error in naming a party can be cured by amendment if the effect of the amendment is to change the name and not the identity of the party concerned. In *Tibbetts v. Kiah*,[68] the defendant pleaded in abatement that he was known and called by the name "Currier," not "Kiah," and the plaintiff replied that he was known and called by both. The Supreme Court said that the issue was not how the defendant spelled his name, but whether he was the one intended to be called to answer the writ. In *Elliot v. Clark*,[69] the plaintiff moved to amend by changing his own name as stated in the writ from "Lafayette Elliot" to "Benjamin F. Elliot." Chief Justice Parker stated the Supreme Court's conclusion as follows:

> We are of opinion that the power to amend depends not upon the question whether the amendment changes the name, but whether or not it really changes the party. If it only cures a mistake in the name of a party in fact prosecuting the writ, it may be made; but if it introduces a different party, . . . it is inadmissible.[70]

In *Ballou v. Tilton*,[71] the Court allowed an amendment before trial changing the name of the plaintiff from the "administrator of Jonathan Ballou" to the "executor of Jonathan Ballou, Jr." The testator had commonly been called "Jonathan Ballou" but had signed his will "Jonathan Ballou, Jr.," and there was no doubt that the identity of the plaintiff was unchanged by the amendment. In *Burnham v. The President and Trustees of The Savings Bank for the County of Strafford*,[72] a new trial was sought by the defendants on

---

67 Dupuis v. Smith Properties, Inc., 114 N.H. 625, 325 A.2d 781 (1974). But see Rowe v. John Deere, 130 N.H. 18, 533 A.2d 375 (1987).

68 2 N.H. 557 (1823).

69 18 N.H. 421 (1846).

70 18 N.H. at 422.

71 52 N.H. 605 (1873).

72 5 N.H. 446 (1831).

the ground that evidence relating to the Bank's obligations was received against the president and trustees. The court reviewed the cases, noting "a distinction . . . between a variance in words and syllables only, and a variance in substance,"[73] and said that a new trial should be granted because the President and Trustees were not the same thing as the corporation and could not be charged for its debts.[74] And in *Wheeler v. Contoocook Mills Corporation*,[75] the plaintiff was allowed to change the designation of the defendant, after a Motion to Dismiss, from "Contoocook Mills Company" to "Contoocook Mills Corporation" on the ground that the Contoocook Mills Company had been dissolved, the case was brought under the Workmen's Compensation statute, and there was no doubt that the employee had simply named the wrong entity as her employer. Justice Peasley regarded it as "the ordinary case of a not very important mistake in the name of the corporation, curable by amendment in any event."[76]

Library References

CJS Parties § 172

Relation back of amended pleading substituting true name of defendant for fictitious name used in earlier pleading so as to avoid bar of limitations. 85 ALR3d 130.

H. Intervention

§ 6.23. Definition

Intervention is the admission of a person as a party to a case for the purpose of protecting his interest in the subject matter of the case. Once a

---

73 5 N.H. at 449. See also Burnham v. The Savings Bank for the County of Strafford, 5 N.H. 573 (1832).

74 The plaintiff subsequently amended his writ by dropping the words "the President and Trustees of . . ." from the defendant's name. See also Proprietors of Sunapee v. Eastman, 32 N.H. 470 (1855); State of New Hampshire v. Hollis, 59 N.H. 390 (1879).

75 77 N.H. 551, 94 A. 265 (1915).

76 77 N.H. at 553, 94 A. at 266. See also Remick v. J. Spaulding and Sons Company, Inc., 82 N.H. 182, 131 A. 608 (1926) (where the plaintiff-employee was allowed to amend during the second trial to name a corporation rather than a partnership of the same name as her employer); Worcester North Savings Institution v. Somerville Milling Company, 101 N.H. 307, 141 A.2d 885 (1958) (where the plaintiff was permitted to amend his designation of the defendant from "Somerville Milling Co." to "Somerville Milling Co. Inc." when both organizations existed and the defendant's lawyer was an organizer of both).

person has been allowed to intervene, as a party, he has all the rights of a party in the case as it then exists and thereafter develops.[77]

Library References

CJS Parties § 68

Right of insurer issuing "uninsured motorist" coverage to intervene in action by insured against uninsured motorist. 35 ALR4th 757.

Right of health or accident insurer to intervene in worker's compensation proceeding to recover benefits previously paid to claimant or beneficiary. 38 ALR4th 355.

§ 6.24. Historical Development of the Procedure

Common law practice resisted expansion of an action to include issues or parties which had not originally been brought into the suit. Early rules required dismissal of an action commenced by or against a person in an improper capacity or by a wrong name, but these were gradually relaxed during the nineteenth century to allow the change to be made by amendment. Persons were also allowed to be substituted for parties to whose rights they had succeeded after the commencement of the proceedings. Claims which arose separately could eventually be joined in an action by one plaintiff against the same defendant. Finally, even actions at law and bills in equity could be joined in an action between two parties. But changes of name, substitution of parties, and joinder of claims all left unaffected the essential notion that the progress of a case, once begun, should be directed towards a narrowing and elimination, rather than an expansion, of issues. Intervention, with the opportunity it provides to a third person to raise issues which the original parties would not have brought up, has been a late development in the civil practice of New Hampshire.

The progenitor of modern intervention was the rule allowing subsequently attaching creditors to appear and defend in an action by another creditor against their common debtor. This procedure was recognized early in New Hampshire practice[78] and went through extensive refinements during the nineteenth and early twentieth centuries.[79] It allowed any creditor who

---

77 See In re Petition for Admission of Demers, 130 N.H. 31, 533 A.2d 380 (1987) (the Superintendent of the State Hospital petitioned to intervene in an involuntary commitment proceeding after the entry of an order of commitment imposing special conditions on him; the Supreme Court recognized that the Superintendent became a party to the proceeding after being allowed to intervene and was thereby authorized to pursue a direct appeal of the order and of the court's refusal to reconsider it).

78 Buckman v. Buckman, 4 N.H. 319 (1828).

79 *Id.*; Webster v. Harper, 7 N.H. 594 (1835); Blaisdell v. Ladd, 14 N.H. 129 (1843); Dunbar v. Starkey, 19 N.H. 160 (1848); Reynolds v. Damrell, 19 N.H. 394 (1849); Pike v. Pike, 24 N.H. 384 (1852); Carlton v. Patterson, 29 N.H. 580 (1854); Holland v.

obtained an attachment on a particular piece of property belonging to the debtor to challenge the validity of a prior attachment on the same property and thus protect the debtor's property from diversion from the claims of his honest creditors.[80] The purpose of the procedure was to allow for the resolution of all creditors' claims against a piece of property in a single action. While the procedure did open the door to an expansion of issues, it also prevented a multiplicity of actions. Permission for subsequently attaching creditors to appear and defend was liberally granted in the nineteenth century and became a popular device for protecting creditors in the days before modern federal bankruptcy procedures. Although all the opinions in cases involving subsequently attaching creditors concerned efforts to defeat a prior attachment in a specific piece of property or other assets, the cases customarily stated that "any party who can satisfy the court that he has any right involved in the trial of a case may be admitted to prosecute or defend the action."[81]

The Supreme Court also decided at an early date that, after admission of a new party, the case "remains the action of the original plaintiff against the original defendant, and . . . still proceeds and is to be tried upon the same rules and principles as it would do if no third person had interfered."[82] Thus, while the language of these cases encouraged the presentation of a number

---

Seaver, 21 N.H. 386 (1850); Swamscot Machine Company v. Walker, 22 N.H. 457 (1851); Boscawen v. Canterbury, 23 N.H. 188 (1851); Bryant's Case, 24 N.H. 156 (1851); Barker v. Barker, 39 N.H. 408 (1859); Winship v. Conner, 43 N.H. 167 (1861); Child v. The Eureka Powder Works, 45 N.H. 547 (1864); Woodbury v. Woodbury, 47 N.H. 11 (1866); Parsons v. Eureka Powder Works, 48 N.H. 66 (1868); Kidder v. Tufts, 48 N.H. 121 (1868); Parker v. Perkins, 53 N.H. 607 (1873); Davis v. Fogg, 58 N.H. 159 (1877); Webster v. Farnum, 60 N.H. 288 (1880); Shaw v. Shaw, 60 N.H. 565 (1881); Clough v. Curtis, 62 N.H. 409 (1882); Levy v. Woodcock, 63 N.H. 413 (1885); Martin v. Wiggin, 67 N.H. 196, 29 A. 450 (1892); Commonwealth Trust Co. v. Salem Light, Heat and Power Co., 77 N.H. 146, 89 A. 452 (1914); Langdell v. Eastern Basket & Veneer Co., 78 N.H. 243, 99 A. 90 (1916).

80   Kidder v. Tufts, 48 N.H. 121, 124 (1868).

81   Carlton v. Patterson, 29 N.H. 580, 584 (1854).

82   Carlton v. Patterson, 29 N.H. 580, 584 (1854). See also Shaw v. Shaw, 60 N.H. 565, 566 (1881). The Court's review of relevant cases in Winship v. Conner, 43 N.H. 167 (1861), showed the distinction which was recognized in 1861 between statutory rights of intervention and the common law appearance to defend in the name of another. Two cases arising 15 years later illustrate the tension that was building between these two concepts. Dorr v. Leach, 58 N.H. 18 (1876), was an action to foreclose a mortgage on real property given by the defendant Leach to the plaintiff Dorr. One Plumer had been admitted to defend the action and offered to prove that he had title to the premises involved which was not derived from either the plaintiff or the defendant. The Supreme Court held that Plumer should not have been allowed to enter the case because "[t]here

of claims by different persons once an action had commenced, their holdings required that the person admitted stand in the shoes of the original parties and be limited to issues which could have been raised between them.

Resistance to allowing a person to intervene for the purpose of raising his own claims against an original party began to crumble in the 1880s. In *Chauncy v. German American Insurance Co.*,[83] the Supreme Court held that, in a suit by the owner of real estate against an insurance company to collect on his fire insurance policy, the owner's grantor/mortgagee could be joined as a plaintiff by amendment and have judgment for the amount of his mortgage without costs. While the case did not involve an attachment, it did involve a res and thus stands somewhere between contests over attachments and what might be referred to as modern intervention. Three years later, in *Cole v. Gilford,*[84] a suit by the owner of land against the town for damages caused by the discharge of water from a street drain, the Court held that the person having the use of the land and the right to take crops from it could be joined as a plaintiff by amendment and have judgment for his damages without costs. Although the Court cited *Chauncy* as authority for the procedure, *Cole* actually involved no res and is the earliest case in which a third person was admitted to assert an independent claim to an unliquidated amount of damages arising out of the subject matter of the suit.

§ 6.25. Modern Intervention—Statutory Basis

Some New Hampshire statutes allow intervention by certain classes of persons in limited situations. For example, RSA 512:26 provides that any third person claiming property attached in the hands of a trustee "shall, on motion and upon such terms as the court may order, be admitted to defend

---

is no way in which he will be prejudiced, or his rights affected, by the judgment." 58 N.H. at 18. A similar conclusion was reached in Parker v. Moore, 63 N.H. 196 (1884). On the other hand, in Riddle v. George, 58 N.H. 158 (1877), the defendant's grantor was allowed to appear and moved to recommit to a referee an issue affecting title to land which he had conveyed to the defendant after the referee had reported in favor of the plaintiff. The Court noted that the defendant's grantor would have been liable to the defendant on his warranty of title if the referee's report had remained unchallenged.

While the Dorr and Riddle cases are technically consistent in their reliance on the principle that a third person must be directly affected by the issue in a case to be allowed to appear and defend, they are uneven in the degree to which they allow a person who will be affected by the decision in the case to present his interest to the court before his rights are affected.

83   60 N.H. 429 (1881).

84   63 N.H. 60 (1884).

his right . . . ."[85] And there are apparently some occasions when a right will be recognized in heirs or legatees to intervene in proceedings begun or defended by their decedent or his executor or administrator.[86]

Library References

CJS Parties § 69
Sufficiency, as to content, of notice of garnishment required to be served upon garnishee. 20 ALR5th 229.

§ 6.26. —Common Law Basis

The preeminent case on modern intervention in New Hampshire is *Scamman v. Sondheim.*[87] In that case the guardian of minor legatees of the defendant's testator sought to take over the defense of an action for the recovery of a deposit by a person who had contracted with the testator for the purchase of real estate. Technically, the guardian was not so much seeking to intervene to try the legatees' separate interests as he was attempting to take over the defense of the case, and the Supreme Court held that his request was properly denied since "[i]n the absence of special circumstance, it is the general rule that an executor or administrator is the only proper patty to bring or defend an action relating to the personal estate of the deceased."[88] But Justice Kenison took the opportunity presented by the case to state the general principles of intervention, as follows:

> The right of a party to intervene in pending litigation in this state has been rather freely allowed as a matter of practice without the aid of a statute permitting it . . . . As early as 1828 practical intervention was accomplished in *Buckman v. Buckman*, 4 N.H.

---

85 Although the statute speaks in terms of a person whose interest becomes apparent from "the depositions," it was held a century ago that the statute "was not intended to limit or restrict the rights of claimants" and "[w]henever it appears, from the disclosure or otherwise that the property in the hands of the trustee is claimed by a third person, such claimant is allowed to appear and maintain his claim upon such terms as the court may order upon the same principle that a subsequent attaching creditor is allowed to appear and contest the claim of a prior attaching creditor." Webster v. Farnum, 60 N.H. 288, 289, 291 (1880).

86 See Scamman v. Sondheim, 97 N.H. 280, 86 A.2d 329 (1952) (the heirs or legatees might be entitled to intervene if they could show "special circumstances" such as neglect, fraud, collusion, or conflict of interest).

87 97 N.H. 280, 86 A.2d 329 (1952).

88 97 N.H. at 281, 86 A.2d at 330.

319. . . . However, the right to intervene has been usually determined as a matter of discretion by the Trial Court.[89]

Following *Scamman*, a person who seeks to intervene in a case must have a right involved in the trial[90] and his interest must be "direct and apparent; such as would suffer if not indeed be sacrificed were the court to deny the privilege."[91] The *Scamman* case has been consistently reaffirmed and, together with its successors, establishes that intervention will be permitted by a person with a direct and apparent interest in the subject matter of a case and on a petition by the interested party or by motion to amend filed by a party already in the case, but will not be allowed as a means of raising issues not related to the subject matter of the case. Because the right to intervene is a matter of discretion by the Trial Court, the Supreme Court has held that a decision regarding intervention would be overturned only if the Trial Court abused its discretion.[92]

Library References

CJS Parties §§ 71, 72, 77, 78

§ 6.27. —Survival of the Appearance To Defend

Although the line of cases beginning with *Buckman v. Buckman*[93] involving subsequently attaching creditors ends around the time of the First World War, the theory apparently still has some vitality, at least with respect to

---

89 *Id.* It is interesting that Justice Kenison relied on the *Buckman, Carlton*, and *Parsons* cases in setting his standard for modern intervention because those cases were the lynchpins for a line of cases that actually resisted the expansion of claims beyond the four corners of the original pleadings. Nevertheless, his reliance on those cases has had the effect of transmuting the former test for admission to defend into the modern test for intervention.

90 Carlton v. Patterson, 29 N.H. 580, 587 (1854).

91 Pike v. Pike, 24 N.H. 384, 394 (1852), Sklar Realty, Inc. v. Town of Merrimack, 125 N.H. 321, 480 A.2d 149 (1984); Blue Cross/Blue Shield v. St. Cyr, 123 N.H. 137, 141, 459 A.2d 226, 229 (1983) (holding that a health insurance company that has paid benefits for injuries to a minor child caused by an automobile accident "has the right to intervene . . . to protect its interest" in a suit brought by the parents against the tortfeasor, if the parents refuse to agree to protect the company's interests). See also Manchester Airport Authority v. Romano, 120 N.H. 166, 412 A.2d 1020 (1980); Vachon v. Halford, 125 N.H. 577, 484 A.2d 1127 (1984).

92 Snyder v. N.H. Savings Bank, 134 N.H. 32, 592 A.2d 506 (1991) (denial of motion to intervene upheld).

93 4 N.H. 319 (1828).

cases contesting the validity of mechanics' liens.[94] Whether the full range of limitations that were imposed on subsequently attaching creditors will today be enforced is uncertain.

§ 6.28. —Unresolved Questions

(a) *Ability To Raise Defenses.* The reliance in *Scamman* on the *Buckman, Carlton,* and *Parsons* cases has created some uncertainties regarding the degree to which the Supreme Court will require that the procedural limitations previously imposed on subsequently attaching creditors also be applied to intervenors. For example, one fundamental doctrine of the subsequently attaching creditor cases was the inability of a creditor, once admitted, to raise all the defenses which the debtor could have raised at the beginning of the case.[95] The Supreme Court has not decided how an intervenor is to be treated in this respect. Because an intervenor will in most cases be able to control the timing of his entry, there are substantial arguments in favor of his taking the case as he finds it, even on those occasions when a late entry is the result of excusable misfortune. But in those cases in which the intervenor finds himself entering late due to another's motion or where he wishes to raise new claims relating to the subject matter of the case, the case must be regarded as just beginning with respect to him, and he should be permitted to plead accordingly.

(b) *Adding Claims After Intervention.* It is unclear whether an intervenor may add a claim to the issues for which he was admitted or whether an original party may assert a new claim or a counterclaim against the intervenor once he is in the suit. There is no apparent reason why such additional claims should not be allowed as a general matter, although care must be taken to prevent an intervention from creating unnecessary expense or delay to the original parties.

(c) *Tolling Deadlines and Verified Petition.* Similarly, it is unclear whether the filing of a Petition to Intervene tolls time deadlines which would otherwise apply and whether a Petition to Intervene, due to its substantial

---

94 See Diamond Match Co. v. Joseph O. Hobbs Trust, 98 N.H. 97, 95 A.2d 142 (1953); Bader Company, Inc. v. Concord Electric Company, 109 N.H. 487, 256 A.2d 145 (1969).

95 This doctrine is to be distinguished from the doctrine that a person compelled to join an action may raise all defenses as though the suit had just begun. The difference between the two doctrines is based upon the difference in the situations of the parties. In the former the creditor comes in on his own volition and must take the case as he finds it; he cannot be allowed by his own delay in coming in to put the original parties to a procedural disadvantage. In the latter case the person joined is compelled to come in and in fairness should have the right to all defenses and objections which he would have had if the case had just been begun.

138

capacity for interrupting and delaying a case, should be verified. It would seem that the answer to both questions should be in the affirmative.

Library References

CJS Parties §§ 78, 86

§ 6.29. Procedure To Intervene

A person desiring to intervene in a pending action, where no statute prescribes the procedure,[96] should file a Petition to Intervene setting forth facts sufficient to show the nature of his interest in the subject matter of the suit, that the interest is direct and will either suffer or be sacrificed if he is not allowed to intervene, the issues he proposes to raise, and the parties against whom he wishes to raise them. The petition must be filed with the court and be served with orders of notice on the original parties. A copy should also be mailed to the attorneys who have appeared in the case. As with other initial pleadings, a Petition to Intervene must be the subject of a responsive pleading filed within the time limits which would pertain if the case had been begun by the Petition. The court will grant the Petition without hearing if no objection is made. If any party objects, the court will hold a hearing and will require that the petitioner show that actual prejudice to his legal or equitable rights will occur if he is not allowed to intervene. If the court permits the intervention, it may do so on terms, including an order to post security for costs incurred by the original parties as a result of the interference.[97]

---

96 Statutes occasionally prescribe their own procedures for intervention. RSA 512:26–28, for example, provides for an original party as well as a claimant to move admission of the intervenor, permits service by publication and an order that the claim will be barred unless he appears and allows the intervenor to claim the right to jury trial at whatever stage he appears.

97 See Buckman v. Buckman, 4 N.H. 319 (1828). Four cases referring to intervention have been decided since *Scamman* but two involved claims of subcontractors to enforce mechanics' liens and thus have more in common with cases involving subsequently attaching creditors than with cases on intervention. In Diamond Match Co. v. Joseph O. Hobbs Trust, 98 N.H. 97, 95 A.2d 142 (1953), two subcontractors were allowed to appear in an action by another subcontractor to enforce a mechanics lien after they alleged a financial interest in the property subject to lien. Although the case refers to the creditors as intervenors, they were admitted only to raise claims against the prior lien and not for the purpose of litigating their entire claim against the original parties. It is interesting to note, however, that, somewhat like Riddle v. George, 58 N.H. 158 (1877), the intervention was permitted after allowance of the lien and in order to facilitate an appeal.

In Bader Co., Inc. v. Concord Electric Company, 109 N.H. 487, 256 A.2d 145 (1969), the Court was again faced with disputes over a mechanics' lien and permitted a trustee in bankruptcy to appear and defend on behalf of his bankrupt against a claim by a

§ 6.30. Time To Intervene

A Petition to Intervene may be filed at any time before verdict or decree. However, a Petition to Intervene will be less likely to be granted the later in the case it is filed.

I. Substitution of Parties

§ 6.31. Introduction

One or more persons may replace either a nominal or a real party in interest after the commencement of an action if justice requires and the other parties to the action will not be prejudiced by the change.[98]

---

subcontractor for retainage. Again, the Court referred to the trustee as an intervenor, and cited *Scamman.* However, the case involved only a dispute over a particular asset and has more in common with the subsequently attaching creditor cases than with intervention.

Two other cases tend more to follow the line of Cole v. Gilford, 63 N.H. 60 (1884). Sibson v. Robert's Express, Inc., 104 N.H. 192, 182 A.2d 449 (1962), involved an attempt by an insurance company to collect advances to its insured for property damage by means of a suit after its insured had obtained judgment for personal injuries resulting from the accident. The insurance company had paid its insured and had obtained an assignment of his claims arising from the loss prior to the insured's suit. The Court held that the rule against splitting a cause of action precluded the insurance company from bringing a separate suit for property damage and limited it to the right to intervene in a suit begun by its insured.

And in Rye v. Ciborowski, 111 N.H. 77, 276 A.2d 482 (1971), the Court affirmed the refusal of the trial court to allow the Aviation Association of New Hampshire to intervene in an action by the Town of Rye to enjoin use of a private air strip. Because the issue was whether the use being made of the air strip exceeded that permitted by a variance, the Court saw no reason to allow a third party with no claim against either the owner or the town to introduce evidence on the need for air strips in the area.

98 The statutory basis for substitution may be found in RSA 514:9. See also Dupuis v. Smith Properties, Inc. d/b/a R.H. Smith Company, 114 N.H. 625, 628, 325 A.2d 781, 783 (1974).

CJS Parties § 56

§ 6.32. Differences Between Substitution, Misnomer, and Joinder

Substitution is the replacement of one or more persons for one or more others as parties to an action. The correction of a misnomer, on the other hand, involves changing the name which the pleadings give to a person who has already been made a party.[99] Joinder is the addition of a party to an action.

In addition to these theoretical distinctions, there are very practical differences between substitution, misnomer, and joinder. In the first place, the changes effected by both substitution and the correction of a misnomer relate back to the beginning of the action.[100] A joinder is effective only from the date it is granted.[101] In addition, regardless of when he is joined, a new party has all the rights which he would have had if the action had just been begun, including the right to raise formal and technical objections and the right to take the usual period to answer. A new party brought in by substitution has no such rights, but may be able to obtain equivalent protections upon a showing of necessity. Second, substitution and the correction of a misnomer can, in most cases, be accomplished by motion without further service.[102] Joinder requires service unless the new party has already submitted itself to the jurisdiction of the court. Third, the test for the correction of a misnomer is simply whether the parties suing or sued have been given a wrong name.[103] The court makes no particular inquiry to determine whether justice will actually be promoted or other parties prejudiced by the correction of the error. However, neither substitution nor joinder will be allowed unless it appears that the change is necessary to perfect the rights being enforced or defended in the action and will not deprive another party of a substantive defense or claim.

---

99 Dupuis v. Smith Properties, Inc. d/b/a R.H. Smith Company, 114 N.H. 625, 325 A.2d 781 (1974).

100 With regard to substitution, see State ex rel. Thorndike v. Collins, 68 N.H. 46, 36 A. 550 (1894); Whittier v. Varney, 10 N.H. 291 (1839); Ghilain v. Couture, 84 N.H. 48, 146 A. 395 (1929); Roy v. Roy, 101 N.H. 88, 133 A.2d 492 (1957); Edgewood Civic Club v. Blaisdell, 95 N.H. 244, 61 A.2d 517 (1948); Strong v. New Hampshire Box Company, 82 N.H. 221, 131 A. 688 (1926).

101 See, e.g., Lewis v. Hines, 81 N.H. 24, 120 A. 728 (1923).

102 But see Superior Court Rule 24, which requires service of a Motion to Amend by Substitution after default.

103 See Sections 6.21 and 6.22.

§ 6.33. Purpose of Substitution

The purpose of a substitution is always to make more perfect a legal process which has already been properly begun. Thus, the capacity in which a plaintiff sues may be changed by substitution;[104] another person may be substituted for the original plaintiff as a nominal plaintiff;[105] a next friend may be substituted for a plaintiff who is a minor[106] or one next friend may be substituted for another;[107] a person attaining majority may substitute himself for his next friend as plaintiff;[108] plaintiffs with standing may be substituted for plaintiffs with no standing;[109] and one person may be substituted for another when the effect is to make clearer the nature of the cause of action relied upon.[110]

§ 6.34. Standards for Substitution—Generally

The court considers two questions when deciding whether to permit a substitution: (a) whether the change will promote the interests of justice and (b) whether it will prejudice the rights of another party to the action.

§ 6.35. —Promoting the Interests of Justice

The overriding concern of the court when faced with a request for substitution is whether the interests of justice will be furthered by the change. If the court concludes that they will, it will find a way to avoid

---

104 Mann v. Marshall, 76 N.H. 162, 80 A. 336 (1911); Owen v. Owen, 109 N.H. 534, 257 A.2d 24 (1969); Henderson v. Sherwood Motor Hotel, 105 N.H. 443, 201 A.2d 891 (1964).

105 Judge of Probate v. Jackson, 58 N.H. 458 (1878); Prescott v. Farmer, 59 N.H. 90 (1879); Contoocook Fire Precinct v. Hopkinton, 71 N.H. 574, 53 A. 797 (1902).

106 Young v. Young, 3 N.H. 345 (1826).

107 Strong v. New Hampshire Box Company, 82 N.H. 221, 131 A. 688 (1926).

108 Paju v. Paju, 110 N.H. 310, 266 A.2d 836 (1970).

109 Edgewood Civic Club v. Blaisdell, 95 N.H. 244, 61 A.2d 517 (1948); State ex rel. Thorndike v. Collins, 68 N.H. 46, 36 A. 550 (1894); National Marine Underwriter's Inc. v. McCormack, 138 N.H. 6, 634 A.2d 1008 (1993) (substitution of plaintiff with one who has standing to sue is allowed when required to prevent injustice if not prejudicial to defendant).

110 Bagley v. Small, 92 N.H. 107, 26 A.2d 23 (1942).

prejudice to the other parties.[111] Prejudice to the defendant which is suffi-cient to prevent a substitution must be so great that the defendant is

---

111 This principle is illustrated by the case of Remick v. J. Spaulding & Sons Co., 82 N.H. 182, 131 A. 608 (1926), where the plaintiff had been injured on the job while attempting to fix a machine and brought suit at common law against J. Spaulding & Sons Company, a partnership. Her first trial ended in a nonsuit when the court decided that she had failed to exercise due care in trying to fix the machine. Later, the Supreme Court sustained the plaintiff's exception to that ruling (Sevigny v. J. Spaulding & Sons Company, 81 N.H. 311, 125 A. 262 (1924)) and a second trial was ordered. At the beginning of the second trial, counsel for "the Spaulding interests" disclosed on questioning by the Court that the partnership had been dissolved prior to Mrs. Remick's accident and that a corporation of the same name had succeeded to its interests and was operating the plant when Mrs. Remick was injured. The court suggested that the plaintiff substitute the corporation for the partnership as defendant, but the plaintiff delayed doing so until she could investigate the matter. The trial proceeded while the plaintiff made her investigation. After investigating the issue and before her case had been fully presented, the plaintiff moved the court to permit the substitution, and the court granted the motion at the conclusion of the plaintiff's case. The corporation then entered a Special Appearance and filed a Motion to Continue. When the continuance was denied, the corporation filed a General Appearance stating its intention to proceed "with said general defense under protest." 82 N.H. at 184. After the presentation of the defendant's case, the jury returned a verdict for the plaintiff.

Upon appeal, the corporation argued that the trial court had exceeded its authority when it ordered the substitution without a new service on the corporation and at such a late stage in the proceedings. The Supreme Court, however, upheld the trial court, asserting that the substitution was "hardly more than the correction of an unimportant misnomer." In support of this conclusion Justice Marble listed a number of similarities between the partnership and the corporation. Both had, at one time or another, employed the plaintiff at the same site in the same job, both had been organized and managed by the same persons, both were insured by the same company under the same policies and both had been defended at trial by the same counsel. Justice Marble stressed that the corporation had received notice of the suit and " 'understood fully' the plaintiff's claim," 82 N.H. at 185, 131 A. at 610. He also mentioned a few clerical errors by court officers and personnel which had involved the corporation's name in the proceedings from an early date. But most significant was Justice Marble's statement of the parties' intentions and understandings:

> It was very obviously the intention of the plaintiff to sue her employer. She had worked for the partnership for many years and neither she nor any of her colaborers had ever been notified of any change in the business organiza-tion. . . . [The vice president of the corporation] was informed that the suit had been brought and "understood fully" the plaintiff's claim. If he had read the writ he could not have failed to realize that the plaintiff was "acting under a misapprehension" as to the legal status of her employer. (82 N.H. at 184–185, 131 A. at 610).

And in Dupuis v. Smith Properties, Inc., 114 N.H. 625, 325 A.2d 781 (1974), an action for damages resulting from a gas explosion on September 4, 1966. When the suit was begun on August 4, 1972, the plaintiff named as the defendant "Smith Properties, Inc." a corporation which had originally been named "R. H. Smith Company, Inc." and which the New Hampshire Secretary of State's office had informed the plaintiff to be the user of the trade name "R.H. Smith Company" in New Hampshire. Unfortunately, the intended defendant was really a different corporation named "Ralph H. Smith

prevented from raising a valid defense on the merits. Mere procedural prejudice will not be considered.[112]

In addition, the plaintiff must have acted expeditiously to remedy the error once it was discovered.[113]

A New Hampshire court will allow almost any substitution if it perceives that the case involves a meritorious claim and that the defendant has no substantial defense to the claim.[114] The interests of justice which the court

---

Corporation" which had registered the trade name "R. H. Smith Company" after Ralph H. Smith Corporation had changed its name. Perhaps out of an excess of caution, the plaintiff designated the defendant as "Smith Properties, Inc. d/b/a R. H. Smith Company," thus including both the defendant's known trade name and its believed corporate name. The plaintiff did not learn of his mistake until a pretrial conference held after the statute of limitations had expired. Although he immediately moved to amend his writ and declaration to show the correct corporate name, his motions were denied. As it happened, the clerk and agent for service of process for both corporations was the same person, and, at the time of service, the clerk of Smith Properties, Inc. was also clerk, assistant treasurer and office manager for Ralph H. Smith Corporation, the intended defendant. On the day of service, she told the corporation's owner about the writ and the substance of the claim, and "he assumed as of the date of service of process that his company was the real object of plaintiff's suit." 114 N.H. at 627, 325 A.2d at 782.

Chief Justice Kenison felt that the critical issue in this case was whether the intended defendant knew before the statute of limitations had run that it was the intended defendant. If it did, the purpose of the statute of limitations "that defendants receive timely notice of actions against them" (114 N.H. at 629, 325 A.2d at 783) was fulfilled, the intended defendant could not be prejudiced by being required to pick up the defense, and the motion to amend should have been granted. Summarizing this point, Chief Justice Kenison wrote:

> If plaintiff is not permitted to amend, an entirely new cause of action against the intended corporate defendant will be barred by the statute of limitations. Such a result seems unjust in light of the fact that the intended defendant received actual notice of the action against it prior to the expiration of the statute of limitations. (114 N.H. at 628, 325 A.2d at 782).

By taking as his guide the question whether the intended defendant had actual notice of the action, regardless of whether he understood that he was the intended defendant, Chief Justice Kenison adopted a standard which is objectively determinable. See also Buckminster v. Wright, 59 N.H. 153 (1879); Willoughby v. Holderness, 62 N.H. 661 (1883); Pacific & Atlantic Shippers v. Schier, 109 N.H. 551, 258 A.2d 351 (1969). But see Lewis v. Hines, 81 N.H. 24, 120 A. 728 (1923); Parsons v. New Hampshire Southern Hydroelectric Corp., 85 N.H. 76, 153 A. 821 (1931); Rowe v. John Deere, 130 N.H. 18, 533 A.2d 375 (1987) (court did not inquire into the knowledge of the intended defendant at the time the original action was commenced, but simply affirmed a summary judgment on the ground that the wrong defendant was originally named and the statute of limitations had since expired).

112   Remick v. J. Spaulding & Sons Co., Inc., 82 N.H. 182, 131 A. 608 (1926).

113   Lewis v. Hines, 81 N.H. 24, 120 A. 728 (1923).

114   In National Marine Underwriter's Inc. v. McCormack, 138 N.H. 6, 634 A.2d 1008 (1993), a passenger on defendant's boat was injured in a boating accident. The passenger sued the defendant, who had been insured by North American Specialty

will consider when asked to permit a substitution are not simply those of the plaintiff before it, but include the wider interests of justice which are implicit in the underlying cause of action.[115]

§ 6.36. —Prejudice to the Defendant

If the court concludes that justice will be furthered by the substitution, it will inquire whether any party will be prejudiced by the change. A New Hampshire court will not allow a substitution that will deprive the defendant of a substantial defense on the merits,[116] but the loss of a merely technical defense will not be regarded as sufficiently prejudicial to prevent a substitution. In determining whether the parties will be prejudiced by the substitution, the court will consider six additional issues:

(a) *Clarifying the Issues To Be Tried.* In *Bagley v. Small*,[117] an administrator sued for negligently causing the death of his decedent. Two years later, he filed a Motion to Substitute his decedent's widow for himself as plaintiff,

---

Insurance Co., for which National Marine was the managing general agent. It was National Marine that collected the premiums and paid the claims, and who was the only named plaintiff in all of the pleadings. While being deposed, McCormack disclosed that he had failed to reveal on his liability insurance application that he had previously been involved in an alcohol-related offense. National Marine filed a petition for declaratory judgment seeking rescission of the insurance policy. McCormack asserted that National Marine was not the proper plaintiff, and the trial court denied National Marine's motion to amend to add North American as plaintiff. The Supreme Court determined that National Marine's motion was essentially one that requested substitution of one party plaintiff with another and that denial of the motion held potential for significant injustice and prejudice to the plaintiff, as North American might be barred by the statute of limitation from bringing a declaratory judgment action. The Court held further that the substitution did not introduce an entirely new cause of action, it did not call for substantially different evidence on the part of either the defendant or the plaintiff, and it caused no surprise to the defendant as the defense against North American would be identical to the defense against National Marine.

115 Willoughby v. Holderness, 62 N.H. 661 (1883). In King v. Nedovich, 118 N.H. 161, 384 A.2d 134 (1978), the Supreme Court allowed the plaintiff's insurance company to be substituted on its own motion for the original plaintiffs in an action against a mason and a former owner of a house for damages resulting when the house burned as a result of a faulty fireplace. In support of its motion, the company showed that the original plaintiffs had left for parts unknown after receiving nearly $7,000 under their homeowners policy and that they had failed to cooperate with the company or to respond to a subpoena. King is the first case in which the Court has allowed a person to substitute itself for the plaintiff in an action where the plaintiff's claim had not been disallowed. See Willoughby v. Holderness, 62 N.H. 661 (1883) (new plaintiff was admitted after it became clear that the original plaintiff had no claim, and he had not consented to the substitution).

116 Lewis v. Hines, 81 N.H. 24, 120 A. 728 (1923).

117 92 N.H. 107, 26 A.2d 23 (1942).

and the trial court allowed the substitution over the objection of the defendant that a new cause of action was thereby introduced. The Supreme Court agreed with the trial court's decision, saying that the plaintiff's original declaration had been ambiguous and the effect of the substitution was to clarify the statement of his claim.

(b) *Eliminating a Technical or Procedural Defense.* The Supreme Court has frequently pointed out that the elimination of a technical or procedural defense does not amount to sufficient prejudice to prevent a substitution which will otherwise further the interests of justice. As Chief Justice Kenison observed in *Dupuis v. Smith Properties, Inc.,*[118] "The approach to allowing amendments in this state is a liberal one which reflects the desire not to permit procedural error or omission to frustrate the maintenance of a valid action."[119]

Some decisions have allowed the case to continue after the person appearing as plaintiff has changed the capacity in which he appears.[120] Other cases have allowed a real party in interest to continue with a case after substituting another person as the nominal plaintiff.[121] There is also a line of cases in which original plaintiffs who had no standing at law to maintain

---

118　114 N.H. 625, 325 A.2d 781 (1974).

119　114 N.H. at 628, 325 A.2d at 782. This was one of the earliest points established in the law of substitution. In Young v. Young, 3 N.H. at 345, a writ of entry was begun by a minor and the defendant filed a plea in abatement raising the plaintiff's disability. The Court held that the case could proceed after substitution of a next friend as plaintiff.

120　In Owen v. Owen, 109 N.H. 534, 257 A.2d 24 (1969), the Court held that a person who began an action for wrongful death as a voluntary administrator could substitute himself as administrator if later appointed. In Mann v. Marshall, 76 N.H. 162 (1911), a widow who had obtained a note payable to herself after her husband's death from her husband's employer was allowed to maintain a suit on that note after changing the capacity in which she sued from herself personally to herself as administratrix of her husband's estate. And in Henderson v. Sherwood Motor Hotel, 105 N.H. 443, 201 A.2d 891 (1964), an ex-husband of a deceased employee was allowed to maintain an action under the Workmen's Compensation statute against his former wife's employer after substituting himself as guardian of his ex-wife's minor child for himself as administrator of his ex-wife's estate.

121　In Judge of Probate v. Jackson, 58 N.H. 458 (1878), a beneficiary of a trust was allowed to substitute the present trustee as nominal plaintiff in an action against the former trustee to recover income withheld from the beneficiary. In Merrill v. Woodbury, 61 N.H. 504 (1881), a widow brought suit as administratrix without appointment under a statute on a note given to her husband. Thereafter, another person was appointed administrator and declined to endorse the writ as required by the statute, and, on the defendant's motion, the action was dismissed. The widow then moved to substitute the administrator's name for her own as nominal plaintiff, while indemnifying him for costs, and the Court allowed the substitution.

the action were replaced by others who did.[122] And the Supreme Court has allowed an entirely new plaintiff to be substituted for the original plaintiff when it became clear from the defendant's objection that the original plaintiff had no right to recover.[123]

(c) *Permitting Trial of the Case After Substitution To Extinguish All Claims.* In *Pacific and Atlantic Shippers v. Shier*,[124] the Supreme Court allowed the owner of an unincorporated subcontracting trucking firm to be substituted as plaintiff in an action to recover damages for conversion from a retailer to whom the manufacturer's goods had been delivered, holding

---

In Smith v. Hadley, 64 N.H. 97, 5 A. 717 (1886), a beneficiary of an estate was substituted for the administrator as petitioner on a bill in equity to allow the sale of real estate by an estate, and in Prescott v. Farmer, 59 N.H. 90 (1879), a residuary legatee who was not paid by the executor and was later only partly satisfied from the executor's insolvent estate, was allowed to continue with an action against a surety on the executor's probate bond after he had substituted the judge of probate for himself as nominal plaintiff.

122   In State ex rel. Thorndike v. Collins, 68 N.H. 46, 50, 36 A. 550, 551 (1894), for example, the Court allowed two qualified voters to be substituted for two original plaintiffs before a hearing where the statute on which subject matter jurisdiction was founded required that the action be commenced by 20 qualified voters. In Edgewood Civic Club v. Blaisdell, 95 N.H. 244, 61 A.2d 517 (1948), 40 members of the plaintiff club were substituted for the club in an appeal to the superior court from the city's zoning derision after the city objected that the club was not a duly organized voluntary corporation. See also National Marine Underwriter's Inc. v. McCormack, 138 N.H. 6, 634 A.2d 1008 (1993).

123   In Willoughby v. Holderness, 62 N.H. 661 (1883), the Court permitted a suit on a note to be prosecuted by an entirely new plaintiff for an entirely different note. In Coburn v. Dyke, 103 N.H. 159, 167 A.2d 223 (1961), a foreign administrator brought suit against a New Hampshire resident on a promissory note secured by a mortgage on personal property which the defendant had given to the administrator's decedent. At a pretrial conference the defendant moved to dismiss the action on the grounds that a foreign administrator could not maintain an action in a New Hampshire court. The court permitted the plaintiff 10 days to submit authorities in support of his right to prosecute the action but indicated that, in the absence of such authorities, it would grant the defendant's motion. Before the expiration of 10 days, the plaintiff assigned the note and mortgage to the heirs of his decedent, obtained probate court approval for the assignment in his home state, and moved to substitute the heirs/assignees as plaintiffs in the action. The court granted the motion to substitute and denied the defendant's motion to dismiss.

Finally, in State ex rel. Hyde v. Lynch, 72 N.H. 185, 55 A. 553 (1903), the Court allowed a civil prosecution by the state to continue despite the attempts of the prosecuting police superintendent in Lebanon to withdraw the petition. When the county solicitor opposed the withdrawal and sought leave to appear in place of the police superintendent, the Supreme Court said that the change could be allowed if it was necessary in order to maintain the proceeding. See also National Marine Underwriter's Inc. v. McCormack, 138 N.H. 6, 634 A.2d 1008 (1993).

124   109 N.H. 551, 258 A.2d 351 (1969).

that the defendant would suffer no prejudice from the substitution since recovery by the substituted plaintiff "would extinguish all claims [under the cause of action] against the defendant."[125]

(d) *Substitution After Verdict.*

(1) To Preserve the Result: In *Boudreau v. Eastman*,[126] the Court allowed the substitution of an undisclosed principal for his agent after the entry of a verdict when the verdict would not be changed by the substitution.

(2) To Protect a Just Result Already Achieved: In *Hazen v. Quimby*,[127] the defendant defaulted in an action begun by trustee process. Later, a third person claimed the trusteed funds, and, in order to defeat the third person's claim, the plaintiff and defendant agreed to amend the writ by substituting the name of another person for the plaintiff. The trial court approved the substitution, and the trustee and the third party claimant appealed. However, the Supreme Court affirmed, saying simply that "justice may require the amendment . . . . [T]he case presents no question of law."[128]

(e) *Necessary To Reflect Changes in the Circumstances of the Parties Which Have Occurred Since the Commencement of the Action.* The Supreme Court has required minors who have themselves commenced an action to substitute a next friend as plaintiff and have compelled persons who have attained their majority during the pendency of an action to substitute themselves for the next friend who began the action.[129]

Library References

CJS Parties §§ 58, 59
See Sections 7.33–7.40, *infra.*

---

125   109 N.H. at 554, 258 A.2d at 354.

126   59 N.H. 467 (1879).

127   61 N.H. 76 (1881).

128   61 N.H. at 76.

129   In Strong v. New Hampshire Box Company, 82 N.H. 221, 131 A. 688 (1926), the trial court itself raised the issue and required the substitution of a next friend for the minor plaintiff. In Roy v. Roy, 101 N.H. 88, 133 A.2d 492 (1957), a person who had attained his majority was allowed to substitute himself for his next friend even though 16 years had passed since the action was begun. And in Paju v. Ricker, 110 N.H. 310, 266 A.2d 836 (1970), the case was dismissed when a plaintiff who had attained her majority refused to take the court's suggestion that she move to substitute herself for her next friend. The Supreme Court noted in affirming the decision that the action could be reinstated if the woman later filed a motion so long as no prejudice would result to the defendant.

§ 6.37. Procedure for Substitution

Substitution is accomplished by filing a Motion to Amend by Substitution. The issues raised by the Motion are matters of form within the meaning of RSA 514:8 and Superior Court Rules 24 and 25 and are addressed to the court's discretion.[130] The motion can be made at any time, and, if granted, relates back to the date of the writ, bill, petition or other pleading which is amended.[131] After a default, no substitution will be made until a further notice to show cause why the intended substitution should not be made has been served on the defendant.[132] Where the necessity of a substitution is pointed out by the pleadings of another party, the court may enter an order allowing costs to the party who points out the error.[133]

Library References

CJS Parties § 62
Appealability of order granting or denying substitution of parties. 16 ALR2d 1057.

§ 6.38. Responding to a Motion To Amend by Substitution

An objection to a Motion To Amend by Substitution is made in the same manner as an objection to any other motion. The objection must set forth the grounds and supporting facts relied upon, along with a request for a hearing, and be filed within ten days of the filing of the motion.[134]

Whether justice requires a substitution and whether another party will be prejudiced by the change are questions of fact to be resolved by the trial court.[135] The Supreme Court has, at various times, stated either that the resolution of these questions "presents no question of law"[136] for the Court or that the trial court's decision will not be reversed except for an abuse of discretion.[137] As a matter of practice, however, it must be expected that the Court will overturn the trial court's decision in only the most compelling case. The attitude of New Hampshire courts has traditionally been to favor a substitution which promotes the resolution of a cause. A party faced with

---

130 Super. Ct. R. 25. See also Dist. and Mun. Ct. R. 3.8(B); Prob. Ct. R. 8.

131 Whittier v. Varney, 10 N.H. 291 (1839); Ghilain v. Couture, 84 N.H. 48, 146 A. 395 (1929).

132 Super. Ct. R. 24.

133 Super. Ct. R. 25 and 59.

134 Super. Ct. R. 58; Prob. Ct. R. 9.

135 State ex rel. Hyde v. Lynch, 72 N.H. 185, 55 A. 553 (1903).

136 Hazen v. Quimby, 61 N.H. 76 (1881).

137 Roy v. Roy, 101 N.H. 88, 133 A.2d 492 (1957).

a Motion to Amend by Substitution should therefore carefully consider before he objects whether he has any substantial interest in preventing the change. As the loss of a procedural advantage will not justify an objection, the opponent must determine whether the substitution will require him to face a claim which is otherwise barred or will deprive him of a substantive defense or claim. If the answer on either of these points is in the affirmative, he may object.

Library References

CJS Parties §§ 162–164

J. Death of a Party

§ 6.39. Before the Action Is Commenced

(a) *Plaintiff.* Most rights of action, except those for the collection of penalties and forfeitures under penal bonds, actions for slander and libel or statutes which existed at the date of death,[138] survive a person's death and may be prosecuted by the administrator of the estate. The administrator may commence a proceeding to enforce the right, as follows:

(1) Tort for Physical Injuries to the Person: within three years of the tort.[139]

---

138 RSA 556:15. Perutsakos v. Tarmey, 107 N.H. 51, 53, 217 A.2d 177, 179 (1966) ("[s]ection 11 permits suits within a designated period after the decedent's death on all claims not already barred at the time of such death by the general statute of limitations"); Coffey v. Bresnahan, 127 N.H. 687, 506 A.2d 310 (1986).

139 RSA 556:11 and 508:4. RSA 556:11 provides that an administrator may bring a new cause of action within six years of the death of the party "subject to the provisions of RSA 508:4." But the limitations period for RSA 508:4 ("new causes of action") has been changed from six years to three years. The Court has only recently addressed the time limitation that will apply to new causes of action brought by administrators. In Cheever v. Southern New Hampshire Medical Center, 141 N.H. 589, 688 A.2d 565 (1997) the mother of decedent, acting as administrator of the estate, brought a wrongful death action against the hospital where decedent had been born and where he died several hours after birth. The writ was filed five years and 11 months after the death. The plaintiff asserted that the six-year limitation period provided by RSA 556:11 applied, and not the three-year period under RSA 508:4. But the Supreme Court held otherwise, stating that, "[T]he 'plain meaning' of the phrase 'subject to' indicates that the six year period set forth is subservient to or governed by the provisions [of the three year limitation period] of RSA 508:4." 141 N.H. at 591, 688 A. 2d at 690. The Court indicated that the three-year period would apply to other actions as well, stating that "there is no indication that the legislature intended to distinguish between survival and wrongful death actions for purposes of determining the length of the statute of limitations period." 141 N.H. at 591, 688 A. 2d at 691.

(2) All Other Actions: Within the later of the expiration of the statute of limitations or one year from the grant of administration.[140]

(b) *Defendant.* A claim which is due may be asserted against the administrator[141] of a deceased person when the estate is solvent[142] only as follows:

(1) The claim must be presented to the administrator,[143] even if it is contingent[144] or its amount is not yet liquidated,[145] within six months of the grant of administration.[146]

---

140 RSA 556:7; Atwood v. Bursch, 107 N.H. 189, 190, 219 A.2d 285, 287 (1966). (The statute " 'was enacted to extend the time within which suits may be brought which would otherwise be barred, and not to limit the time of bringing actions against which the general statute has not run.' "). See also Morse v. Whitcher, 64 N.H. 591, 15 A. 207 (1888); Frye v. Hubbell, 74 N.H. 358, 68 A. 325 (1907).

141 Actions to enforce claims by and against a deceased person are brought by or against the administrator or executor, not the estate. Scamman v. Sondheim, 97 N.H. 280, 86 A.2d 329 (1952). Persons interested in the estate are not permitted to intervene absent "special circumstances," such as neglect in bringing or defending the action, fraud or collusion, or conflict of interest. See Bean v. Bean, 71 N.H. 538, 53 A. 907 (1902), 74 N.H. 404, 68 A. 409 (1907).

142 The claimant against an insolvent estate presents and has his claims allowed under RSA 557 and is not subject to the six-month presentation rule. RSA 556:4.

143 RSA 556:1. See also Coffey v. Bresnahan, 127 N.H. 687, 506 A.2d 310 (1986). The demand may be "presented in any form which brings to the notice of the executor or administrator the nature and amount of the claim, and the purpose of presenting it." Lunderville v. Morse, 112 N.H. 6, 7, 287 A.2d 612, 613 (1972). See also Little v. Little, 36 N.H. 224 (1858); Dewey v. Noyes, 76 N.H. 493, 84 A. 935 (1912) (oral notice is satisfactory); Frost v. Frost, 100 N.H. 326, 125 A.2d 656 (1956); Watson v. Carvelle, 82 N.H. 453, 136 A. 126 (1926); Davis v. Cray, 109 N.H. 181, 246 A.2d 97 (1968) (administrator may request clarification). RSA 556:2 provides that a "notice sent to the administrator or his agent by registered mail, setting forth the nature and amount of the claim and a demand for payment, shall be deemed a sufficient exhibition and demand." This is, however, but one means of giving notice. Davis v. Cray, 109 N.H. 181, 246 A.2d 97 (1968); Frost v. Frost, 100 N.H. 326, 125 A.2d 656 (1956). The plaintiff must prove notice as part of his case (Lunderville v. Morse, 112 N.H. 6, 287 A.2d 612 (1972); Watson v. Carvelle, 82 N.H. 453, 136 A. 126 (1926); Amoskeag Manufacturing Company v. Barnes, 48 N.H. 25 (1868); Clough v. McDaniel, 58 N.H. 201 (1877); Libby v. Hutchinson, 72 N.H. 190, 55 A. 547 (1903); Mathes v. Jackson, 6 N.H. 105 (1833)), but need not plead it. Hurd v. Varney, 83 N.H. 467, 144 A. 266 (1929); Kittredge v. Folsom, 8 N.H. 98 (1835); Ayer v. Chadwick, 66 N.H. 385, 23 A. 428 (1890); Mathes v. Jackson, 7 N.H. 259 (1834); Tebbetts v. Tilton, 31 N.H. 273 (1855) (copy of note sufficient).

144 Walker v. Cheever, 39 N.H. 420 (1859).

145 W.A. Emerson's Sons, Inc. v. Cloutman, 88 N.H. 59, 184 A. 609 (1936).

146 RSA 556:3. The time limit is tolled during periods when administration is suspended (RSA 556:3 and Cummings v. Farnham, 75 N.H. 135, 71 A. 632 (1908)) or when the administrator or executor is absent from the state. (Walker v. Cheever, 39 N.H. 420 (1859)). See Skrizowski v. Chandler, 133 N.H. 502, 577 A.2d 1234 (1990); Coffey v. Bresnahan, 127 N.H. 687, 506 A.2d 310 (1986).

(2) The claimant must demand payment,[147] unless the administrator expressly or by implication waives demand.[148]

(3) The claimant must bring his action to collect no sooner than six months[149] and no later than one year from the grant of administration.[150] When a claim is not yet due, the claimant must file it with the Judge of Probate and request that the administrator be required to set aside a sufficient sum to pay it.[151] When the estate is insolvent, no tort action may be brought and the claim must be presented to the commissioner no sooner than three and no later than six months after his appointment.[152]

Library References

CJS Executors and Administrators §§ 394, 436, 688 et seq.

Effect of delay in appointing administrator or other representative on cause of action accruing at or after death of person in whose favor it would have accrued. 28 ALR3d 1141.

§ 6.40. While the Action Is Pending

(a) *Plaintiff.*

(1) Tort for Physical Injuries to the Person: When the plaintiff in a tort action for personal injuries dies after bringing suit, any party or attorney may notify the court, and, upon receipt of such notice, the court will continue the case for at least two terms. If the administrator appears and assumes the

---

147 RSA 556:1.

148 Frost v. Frost, 100 N.H. 326, 125 A.2d 656 (1956); Dewey v. Noyes, 76 N.H. 493, 76 A. 642 (1912); Jaffrey v. Smith, 76 N.H. 168, 80 A. 504 (1911).

149 RSA 556:1. The six-month delay period, being for the protection and convenience of the administrator, may be waived by him. American Policyholder's Insurance Company v. Baker, 119 N.H. 958, 409 A.2d 1346 (1979); Saurman v. Liberty, 116 N.H. 73, 354 A.2d 132 (1976).

150 RSA 556:5. The one-year period is tolled by suspension of administration (RSA 556:5; Cummings v. Farnham, 75 N.H. 135, 71 A. 632 (1908); Preston v. Cutter, 64 N.H. 461, 13 A. 874 (1887); Brewster v. Brewster, 52 N.H. 52 (1872)). The administrator has no power to waive the statute of limitations (Amoskeag Manufacturing Company v. Barnes, 48 N.H. 25 (1868); Hall v. Woodman, 49 N.H. 295 (1870); Preston v. Cutter, 64 N.H. 461, 13 A. 874 (1887)), either by promise or otherwise. Judge of Probate v. Ellis, 63 N.H. 366 (1885). See Skrizowski v. Chandler, 133 N.H. 502, 577 A.2d 1234 (1990). See also Coffey v. Bresnahan, 127 N.H. 687, 506 A.2d 310 (1986).

151 RSA 556:6.

152 RSA 557:7. The sole exception to this rule is the case where the defendant was insured. In such a case, the action may be brought but the judgment may not exceed coverage. RSA 556:8.

prosecution within one year[153] of death, the case will continue. If not, the court will dismiss it with prejudice.[154]

(2) All Other Actions: Any other action except the following, including appeals and reviews,[155] will survive[156] and the administrator may be substituted for the plaintiff upon motion:[157]

(A) Actions for penalties and forfeitures under a penal bond or statute.[158]

(B) Actions for possession of land which descends to heirs or vests in a joint tenant at death.[159]

(C) Actions in which the only issues remaining at death relate to an assessment of costs.[160]

(D) Actions for divorce where no property rights are involved.[161]

(b) *Defendant.*

(1) Tort for Physical Injuries to the Person: If the defendant dies while the action is pending, either the plaintiff or the defendant's administrator may notify the court. The plaintiff must file a Motion for Scire Facias, within one year[162] of the notice[163] from the administrator to the plaintiff or his

---

153 The requirement in RSA 556:10 that the administrator appear and prosecute by the end of the second term after the term in which the plaintiff died was declared unconstitutional in Belkner v. Preston, 115 N.H. 15, 332 A.2d 168 (1975), and replaced by the flat term of one year after death.

154 RSA 556:10 and Costoras v. Noel, 101 N.H. 71, 133 A.2d 495 (1957).

155 RSA 556:18.

156 RSA 556:15. See Kelley v. Volkswagenwerk, 110 N.H. 369, 268 A.2d 837 (1970).

157 Pettingill v. Butterfield, 45 N.H. 195 (1864).

158 See RSA 358-A:10(I) (exemplary damages); Coulombe v. Eastman, 77 N.H. 368, 92 A. 168 (1914).

159 Pierce v. Jaquith, 48 N.H. 231 (1868). In cases of insolvency, land does not descend (but will vest in a joint tenant). This limitation also does not apply to actions relating to real estate other than for possession (RSA 556:17), and the administrator may continue the action. RSA 556:16.

160 Farnsworth v. Page, 17 N.H. 334 (1845).

161 Leclerc v. Leclerc, 85 N.H. 121, 155 A. 249 (1931); Hazen v. Hazen, 122 N.H. 836, 451 A.2d 398 (1982); Coulter v. Coulter, 131 N.H. 98, 100, 550 A.2d 112, 114 (1988) ("Since the principle object of a suit for divorce is the dissolution of the marriage, there is no reason to render a divorce decree once the marital relation [is] already ended by death.").

162 Although Belkner v. Preston, 115 N.H. 15, 332 A.2d 168 (1975), dealt only with situations where the decedent was a plaintiff, the same rationale would presumably apply to cases in which he is a defendant.

163 Notice must be by registered mail and the administrator must file an affidavit with the judge of probate that he or she has given such notice. RSA 556:10.

attorney that administration has been granted.[164] The scire facias must be served upon the administrator before the end of the second term[165] and a return made to the court in which the action is pending.[166] If the plaintiff fails to obtain and serve a scire facias, the case will be dismissed with prejudice.[167] If he does obtain and serve the scire facias but the administrator fails to appear, judgment may be entered against the estate on default.[168]

(2) All Other Actions: In all other actions except the following, including appeals and reviews,[169] when the defendant dies, the action continues,[170] and the administrator may be substituted for the decedent on motion:

(A) Actions for penalties and forfeitures under a penal bond or statute.[171]

(B) Actions for possession of land which descends to heirs or vests in a joint tenant at death.[172]

(C) Actions in which the only issues remaining at death relate to an assessment of costs.[173]

In tort cases,[174] if the decedent's estate is insolvent, the administrator should notify the court of that fact and move to dismiss. Upon receiving notice that a petition for settlement in the insolvent course has been filed, the court will continue the action until the petition has been decided.[175] The court will only let the action proceed if it appears that the facts thereby

---

164 RSA 556:10. The period within which the surviving party must act is commenced at different times depending upon whether the decedent was a plaintiff or defendant. In the former case, it begins at death; in the latter, upon notice of the grant of administration.

165 RSA 556:10.

166 See Shea v. Starr, 76 N.H. 538, 85 A. 788 (1913) (delay in making return after good service not a bar to maintenance of the suit).

167 RSA 556:10.

168 RSA 556:23.

169 RSA 556:18.

170 RSA 556:15.

171 RSA 556:15. See Jaffrey v. Smith, 76 N.H. 168, 80 A. 504 (1911) (action by town to collect a penalty).

172 See Pierce v. Jaquith, 48 N.H. 231 (1868). In cases of insolvency, land does not descend (but will vest in a joint tenant). This limitation also does not apply to actions relating to real estate other than for possession (RSA 556:17), and the administrator may continue the action. RSA 556:16.

173 See Farnsworth v. Page, 17 N.H. 334 (1845).

174 See Simpson v. Gafney, 66 N.H. 261, 20 A. 931 (1890).

175 Fairfield v. Day, 72 N.H. 160, 55 A. 219 (1903).

established may be expected to result in payment by an insurer or to increase the assets available to satisfy claims.[176] If the court decides to let the action continue, it may substitute the administrator for the decedent, and any resulting judgment against the administrator will be certified to the judge of probate and become a claim against the estate.[177] If the trial court refuses to let the action continue, the plaintiff must submit the claim to the commissioner.[178]

Library References

CJS Abatement and Revival §§ 125–126

§ 6.41. After Judgment

If a party dies after the entry of final judgment, his estate is chargeable with the judgment debt and execution may be levied against it at any time.[179]

Library References

Right to maintain action or to recover damages for death of unborn child. 84 ALR3d 411.
Judgment in favor of, or adverse to, person injured as barring action for his death. 26 ALR4th 1264.
Amendment of pleading after limitation has run, so as to set up subsequent appointment as executor or administrator of plaintiff who professed to bring the action in that capacity without previous valid appointment. 27 ALR4th 198.
Time of discovery as affecting statute of limitations in wrongful death action. 49 ALR4th 972.

§ 6.42. Late Filings

If a person fails to commence an action against the administrator of a solvent[180] estate within the time allowed, he may file a Petition for Late Filing and Determination of Claim in the superior court.[181] However, he must still file before the statute of limitations expires on the claim. The Petition

---

176 See Brown v. Brockway, 87 N.H. 342, 179 A. 411 (1935) (action would establish breach of duty which would, in turn, support action on the defendant's bond); RSA 556:8.

177 RSA 556:8.

178 See RSA 557:7; Clark v. Robinson, 37 N.H. 579 (1859).

179 RSA 556:25. If, due to his fault, the administrator no longer has any goods or estate to satisfy the judgment, a suit may be brought on his bond, with the permission of the judge of probate. RSA 556:26; Patten v. Patten, 79 N.H. 388, 109 A. 415 (1920).

180 Late filing may only be allowed against a solvent estate. Judge of Probate v. Couch, 59 N.H. 506 (1880); Parsons v. Parsons, 67 N.H. 419, 29 A. 999 (1892).

181 RSA 556:28. See Vanni v. Cloutier, 100 N.H. 272, 124 A.2d 204 (1956); W.A. Emerson's Sons, Inc. v. Cloutman, 88 N.H. 59, 184 A. 609 (1936); Libby v. Hutchinson, 72 N.H. 190, 55 A. 547 (1903); Coffey v. Bresnahan, 127 N.H. 687, 506 A.2d 310 (1986); Cass v. Ray, 131 N.H. 550, 552, 556 (1989); Stewart v. Farrell, 131 N.H. 458, 461 (1989); Skrizowski v. Chandler, 133 N.H. 502, 577 A.2d 1234 (1990).

should state the facts of the claim[182] and show that the petitioner's failure to file within the time normally allowed was not due to "culpable neglect."[183] The clerk will issue orders of notice, and an attested copy must be served on the intended defendant's administrator. The administrator may thereafter file a Motion to Dismiss, based on the expiration of the time limit for filing, the lack of a substantial claim, or the petitioner's delay in commencing the action. Whether the administrator objects or not, the court will hold a hearing to determine whether the claim is substantial and whether the petitioner had delayed without excuse.[184] If it finds that the claim has merit and has not been delayed by neglect, it will permit the case to proceed as though filed within the time normally allowed.[185] If it finds "culpable neglect"[186] or a lack of substance to the claim,[187] it will not.

---

182 Sullivan v. Indian Head National Bank, 99 N.H. 226, 108 A.2d 553 (1954).

183 RSA 556:28; W.A. Emerson's Sons, Inc. v. Cloutman, 88 N.H. 59, 184 A. 609 (1936). See also Coffey v. Bresnahan, 127 N.H. 687, 693, 506 A.2d 310, 314 (1986) ("Culpable neglect has been interpreted as follows: " 'It is less than gross carelessness, but more than the failure to use ordinary care, it is a culpable want of watchfulness and diligence, the unreasonable inattention and inactivity of 'creditors who slumber on their rights.' " . . . It exists '[i]f no good reason, according to the standards of ordinary conduct, for the dormancy of the claim is found. . .' "); Stewart v. Farrell, 131 N.H. 458 (1989); Cass v. Ray, 131 N.H. 550, 556 A.2d 1180 (1989).

184 The administrator cannot waive noncompliance with the statute of limitations even by failing to object, and the court can only allow the late filing if it finds that "justice and equity require it, and that the claimant is not chargeable with culpable neglect in not bringing his suit within the time limited by law." The court's decision will not be set aside if supported by any evidence. Sullivan v. Indian Head National Bank, 99 N.H. 226, 108 A.2d 553 (1954); Jaques v. Chandler, 73 N.H. 376, 62 A. 713 (1905).

185 Without, however, any affect on payments made before the petition was filed. RSA 556:28. See American University v. Forbes, 88 N.H. 17, 183 A. 860 (1936) (estate's assets distributed).

186 "Culpable neglect has been defined to be that which is censorious, faulty or blamable. . . . It signifies a lack of due diligence. . . . . 'It is less than gross carelessness, but more than the failure to use ordinary care, it is a culpable want of watchfulness and diligence, the unreasonable inattention and inactivity of "creditors who slumber on their rights." ' " Mitchell v. Smith, 90 N.H. 36, 38, 4 A.2d 355, 357 (1939). See also Sullivan v. Marshall, 93 N.H. 456, 44 A.2d 433 (1945). Culpable neglect will not be found where the petitioner has delayed due to a mistake of fact or law or due to wrongdoing on the part of the administrator or the decedent. W.A. Emerson's Sons, Inc. v. Cloutman, 88 N.H. 59, 184 A. 609 (1936); Follett v. Ramsey, 101 N.H. 347, 143 A.2d 675 (1958); Webster v. Webster, 58 N.H. 247 (1878); Lisbon Savings Bank & Trust Company v. Moulton's Estate, 91 N.H. 477, 22 A.2d 331 (1941); Koziell v. Fairbanks, 115 N.H. 679, 348 A.2d 358 (1975); Coffey v. Bresnahan, 127 N.H. 687, 693 (1986); Cass v. Ray, 131 N.H. 550, 556 A.2d 1180 (1989).

187 "If no good reason, according to the standards of ordinary conduct, for the dormancy of the claim is found, the claim must be disallowed, although otherwise 'justice and equity' sustain it." Mitchell v. Smith, 90 N.H. 36, 38, 4 A.2d 355, 357 (1939).

Whether conduct in a particular case constitutes culpable neglect is a question of fact for the trial court.[188] Thus, as with other findings of fact, a finding as to culpable neglect can be set aside on appeal only if it is unsupported by the evidence or erroneous as a matter of law.[189]

§ 6.43. Settlements After Death

Any settlement of a case continued or begun after the death of a party should be approved by the judge of probate having jurisdiction over the decedent's estate.[190] Whenever the estate involves a charitable bequest, the Director of Charitable Trusts must join in the settlement.[191]

§ 6.44. Death of the Administrator

If an administrator dies after becoming a party to an action, his successor may be substituted for him in the case. The successor administrator may either appear voluntarily and move to be substituted, or, if he refuses, his opponent may file a Motion for Scire Facias, which will be granted as a matter of course. The opponent must then serve the successor administrator with the writ and make return to the court.[192]

Library References

CJS Abatement and Revival § 120
CJS Executors and Administrators § 81

§ 6.45. Actions by a Voluntary Administrator

Any action or proceeding which could be commenced by a duly appointed administrator may also be commenced in his place by anyone interested in the estate. If a duly appointed administrator moves to substitute himself for the voluntary administrator by the end of the second term of court following the term in which the action is begun, the case will continue

---

188 Cass v. Ray, 131 N.H. 550, 556 A.2d 1180 (1989) (citing Sullivan v. Bank, 99 N.H. 226, 228 (1954); W.A. Emerson's Sons, Inc. v. Cloutman, 88 N.H. 59, 62 (1936)).

189 Cass v. Ray, 131 N.H. 550, 556 A.2d 1180 (1989) (citing Concord Steam Corp. v. City of Concord, 128 N.H. 724, 727 (1986)).

190 RSA 556:27. Although approval is not required where the settlement is fair (Burtman v. Burtman, 94 N.H. 412, 54 A.2d 367 (1947)), it is required where the handling of assets in the estate is involved (Phinney v. Cheshire County Savings Bank, 91 N.H. 184, 16 A.2d 363 (1940)) and should be obtained as matter of prudence in all cases. See Protective Check Writer v. Collins, 92 N.H. 27, 23 A.2d 770 (1942).

191 RSA 556:27.

192 RSA 556:20.

as if originally commenced by him.[193] If not, the case will be dismissed with prejudice on the defendant's motion.[194]

K. Third-Party Practice

§ 6.46. Against a Person Who May Be Liable to the Defendant (Impleader)

(a) *In General*. Superior Court Rule 27 and District and Municipal Court Rule 3.9(A) provide that a party against whom a claim for affirmative relief is asserted may, in turn, bring an action against any other person who will be liable to him should his opponent prove any part of his claim.[195] Third-party pleadings follow the same form as initial pleadings, but recite the facts upon which it appears that the third party's liability may arise. They may also include claims not raised by the underlying action.[196] The third-party proceeding must be commenced in the superior court within sixty days of the return day of the writ when it is filed by the defendant or third party and within sixty days of the filing of the counterclaim when filed by the plaintiff, unless the deadline is extended "for good cause shown to prevent injustice." The time period is shortened to thirty days when the action is pending in the district or municipal courts.[197] The claim against the third party will automatically be consolidated with the original case or cases, but any party may move to sever the claims for trial. In all other respects, the third-party proceeding follows the same rules as any other action or proceeding to assert the claim it embodies.

---

193 RSA 556:19. See Owen v. Owen, 109 N.H. 534, 257 A.2d 24 (1969). If justice requires it, the voluntary administrator may be permitted to amend, after a duly appointed administrator has refused to come in, to insert the duly appointed administrator as nominal plaintiff yet continue to prosecute by himself upon indemnifying the administrator for costs. Merrill v. Woodbury, 61 N.H. 504 (1881).

194 Tanner v. King, 102 N.H. 401, 157 A.2d 643 (1960).

195 This procedure is called "impleader" in New Hampshire. (Sears, Roebuck and Company v. Philip, 112 N.H. 282, 294 A.2d 211 (1972)), but is to be distinguished from that form of proceeding which is recognized as "impleader" in other jurisdictions, where the third party is called in on a new writ to determine his liability to the original plaintiff, rather than to the original defendant. That type of proceeding was recognized by Chief Justice Doe in Owen v. Weston, 63 N.H. 599 (1885), but is today handled by the simple expedient of a motion to join a third party as a party defendant. Alternatively, the party against whom a claim is made may move that a third party be made a party to the action "for the purpose of being bound by the determination of any common issues." This, of course, could be done without the benefit of Rule 27. Sears Roebuck and Company v. Philip, 112 N.H. 282, 294 A.2d 211 (1972).

196 Morrissette v. Sears, Roebuck & Company, 114 N.H. 384, 322 A.2d 7 (1974).

197 Dist. & Mun. Ct. R. 3.9(A) and (B).

The procedure authorized by Superior Court Rule 27 and District and Municipal Court Rule 3.9(A) merely simplifies the consolidation of related cases and requires that related claims be asserted at an early date. It is not meant to create or to modify substantive rights[198] or to effect other common law procedures by which persons may be required to join.[199] And the rule may not be used by a defendant to substitute another defendant for himself in the underlying action.[200]

(b) *Contribution Among Joint Tortfeasors.*   If the plaintiff in a tort action consents, a defendant may commence an action at law[201] against another person who is "jointly and severally liable upon the same indivisible claim, or otherwise liable for the same injury, death or harm,"[202] and move that the two actions be consolidated for discovery and trial.[203] When the plaintiff receives a verdict in his favor, the court will enter judgment separately against each defendant for his proportionate share of the damages.[204]

Library References

CJS Parties §§ 95 100, 104
Right of municipal corporation or abutting property owner or occupant sued in tort action based on condition of sidewalk or highway to implead another. 15 ALR2d 1303.
Impleading minor child as party defendant in tort action by parent against third party. 60 ALR2d 1291.
Right of employer sued for tort of employee to implead the latter. 5 ALR3d 871.

§ 6.47. Against A Person Who May Be Liable to the Plaintiff (Joinder)

Any party to an action may, at any stage of the proceedings, move that third parties as to whom the claim has not been barred[205] be joined, either as plaintiffs or defendants, for the determination of their rights or obligations in the underlying claim. The motion must identify the party and show how his rights or obligations are involved in the proceeding. An attested copy of the motion must be served on the third party, and the third party may object.

---

198 Morrissette v. Sears, Roebuck & Company, 114 N.H. 384, 322 A.2d 7 (1974).

199 Super. Ct. R. 27; Dist. & Mun. Ct. R. 3.9(C).

200 Super. Ct. R. 27; Dist. & Mun. Ct. R. 3.9(D).

201 RSA 507:7-g(IV)(c).

202 RSA 507:7-f(I).

203 RSA 507:7-g(IV)(c).

204 RSA 507:7-e(III). ("The Act . . . adopts the rule of contribution among tortfeasors and allows apportionment of damages"). Jaswell Drill Corp. v. General Motors Corp., 129 N.H. 341, 343, 529 A.2d 875, 876 (1987).

205 Peabody v. O'Leary, 102 N.H. 496, 161 A.2d 167 (1960).

The court has discretion to permit the joinder, and usually will do so if the procedure may be expected to avoid a multiplicity of suits.[206] The new parties have the same procedural rights upon joinder that they would have if the suit had just been begun.[207]

Library References

CJS Parties §§ 92–94
Right to join principal debtor and guarantor as parties defendant. 53 ALR2d 522.

---

206 Remick v. J. Spaulding & Sons Company, Inc., 82 N.H. 182, 131 A. 608 (1926); Lawson v. Kimball, 68 N.H. 549, 38 A. 380 (1896); Roberts v. Claremont Power Company, 78 N.H. 491, 102 A. 537 (1917); Waumbec Mills, Inc. v. Bahnson Service Company, 103 N.H. 461, 174 A.2d 839 (1961).

207 Atwood v. Berry, 87 N.H. 331, 179 A. 412 (1935); Peabody v. O'Leary, 102 N.H. 496, 161 A.2d 167 (1960).

Part IV

PLEADINGS AND MOTIONS

CHAPTER 7. POLICIES AND RULES REGULATING PLEADINGS

A. NATURE OF PLEADINGS

A. *Nature of Pleadings*

§ 7.01. Introduction

Nothing has proved so important to the development of New Hampshire's traditionally "liberal practice" as the decline of strict rules of pleading and the attendant rise of a liberal policy of amendment and pretrial discovery.[1] "Our time," said Chief Justice Doe, "is too much needed for the consideration of subjects of some importance, to be properly occupied with the unnecessary . . . question of pleading."[2]

When Chief Justice Doe ascended the bench in 1859, pleadings in an action were taken to be a more serious limitation on an action or defense than they are today. During his tenure, Chief Justice Doe sought to reduce the importance of pleadings. That Doe accomplished his purpose is demon-

---

1 Reid, John, "From Common Sense to Common Law to Charles Doe—The Evolution of Pleading in New Hampshire," 1 N.H.B.J. 27 (1959); Reid, John, Chief Justice: *The World of Charles Doe* (Cambridge, Mass. 1967), pp. 93–108.

2 Reid, John, Chief Justice: *The World of Charles Doe* (Cambridge, Mass. 1967), p. 96.

strated by the following excerpt from an opinion by Justice Kenison in *Hackett v. Railroad*:[3]

> With statutory exceptions not material here, it has been long established in this state that one's rights will be protected by some remedy . . . . [P]rocedure and form will yield to substance and emphasis will be placed on the simple merits of the controversy rather than the form of the pleadings in which they may be presented . . . . [W]hatever plaintiff's rights may be, she is entitled to her day in court . . . .[4]

Unfortunately, Chief Justice Doe's intentions have been widely misunderstood by twentieth century practitioners. Professor Reid points out that Doe's work was a reaction to the equally successful efforts of Justice Jeremiah Smith and his successors to construct a rigid system of procedure to replace New Hampshire's previously anarchic civil practice.[5] Chief Justice Doe chose to correct an overemphasis on form by overstating the case for unrestrained discretion. Although the Chief Justice acted in a specific, historical context, his decisions have been taken out of that context and have been made to stand for generalizations that it is doubtful that any experienced jurist could have intended. In this century, Doe's memory has frequently been invoked to justify an ignorance of all rules of practice and pleading, and by the 1970s, cases too frequently proceeded to judgment along a tortuous and markless track of loose pleadings and oral amendments. Yet rules of pleading in New Hampshire are simple and logical; and, when followed, those rules can greatly assist in the orderly resolution of disputes.

§ 7.02. Pleadings—Defined

A pleading is any document addressed to the court or administrative agency by a party or a potential party that either addresses the merits of the controversy, or that requests that action be taken on some aspect of the case. Writs, bills, petitions, answers, appearances, motions, pretrial statements,[6]

---

3 95 N.H. 45, 57 A.2d 266 (1948).

4 95 N.H. at 46–47, 57 A.2d at 267.

5 Reid, John, "From Common Sense to Common Law to Charles Doe—The Evolution of Pleading in New Hampshire," 1 N.H.B.J. 27 (1959). Professor Reid separates the history of New Hampshire civil practice from 1776 to 1900 into three stages: (1) Common Sense Period (1776 to 1805); (2) Era of Common Law (1805 to 1859); and (3) Age of Pleadings as Procedure (1879 to 1900).

6 Chellman v. Saab-Scania, 138 N.H. 73, 78–79, 637 A.2d 148, 151 (1993) (parties are bound by the claims and defenses made therein).

Notices of Appeal, and Interlocutory Appeal Statements are all "pleadings." Returns of service, orders of the court, memoranda of law, documentary evidence, depositions, agreements between parties that are not presented for the court's approval, and extrajudicial notices upon which jurisdiction is based are not "pleadings." The distinguishing characteristic of pleadings is that they ask the court to take action. By making such a request, pleadings, of necessity, address discrete issues and either state specific facts or claims or ask for identifiable relief. Thus, it is in the nature of pleadings to define the issues, to narrow the dispute, and to direct the case toward a conclusion.

Library References

CJS Pleading §§ 1, 4

§ 7.03. —Purposes

The primary purpose of any pleading is to advance the action toward a just conclusion. One treatise has identified the "classical objectives" which every pleading seeks to accomplish as: issue formulation; notice to the adversary and the court of the claimant's position; and recordation of that claim and position for the purposes of appellate review.[7] Under today's practice, pleadings also:

(1) Invoke the jurisdiction of the court or tribunal;

(2) Establish both a timetable within which an adversary's rights must be exercised or lost and a date when the dispute must be concluded;

(3) Notify the parties of the claims, demands, and cross-demands of their adversaries, and induce reliance on that notification;[8]

(4) Make the parties' dispute a matter of public record;[9]

(5) State facts and claims clearly enough that an adversary may plead responsively;

(6) Sufficiently identify issues to allow separate resolution, to permit the adversary to enter a plea of res judicata or to avoid a plea of duplication,[10] to allow the elimination of groundless claims or defenses without trial, to separate issues of fact from issues of law, and to establish the basis for appellate review;

---

7 Weinstein and Distler, "Drafting Pleading Rules," 57 Colum. L. Rev. 518 (1957). See also Bernier v. Bernier, 125 N.H. 517, 484 A.2d 1088 (1984).

8 Before a party may introduce evidence on an issue, he must show reliance on that issue in his pleadings. Brann v. Exeter Clinic, Inc., 127 N.H. 155, 498 A.2d 334 (1985).

9 Public statement of positions has become a more important purpose in recent years due to increasing resort to courts by persons with purely political claims and the increasing interest of journalists in those cases.

10 See RSA 508:10.

(7) Facilitate preparation for trial by separating significant from insignificant issues, and by setting a background against which the relevance of requested discovery may be judged;

(8) Allow a proper assignment of trial method by showing the nature of the claim, define and limit the proof at trial, and shift presumptions and the burden of proof;[11] and

(9) Serve as a formal basis for judgment.[12]

Library References

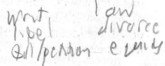

CJS Pleading § 1

B. General Rules of Pleading

§ 7.04. Sufficient Detail; The *Morency* Rule

It is axiomatic that a writ and declaration must state a claim recognized by the law, that a libel must state a statutory basis for divorce, and that a bill or petition must show a basis for the exercise of equitable jurisdiction or they will be dismissed upon the defendant's motion.[13] How detailed a pleading must be in order to survive a Motion To Dismiss is, however, sometimes difficult to determine.

The preeminent modern case on the amount of detail required in pleadings is *Morency v. Plourde*.[14] That case involved an action at law for damages caused by a landlord in shutting off the plaintiff's water, heat, and electricity and a subsequent bill in equity to enjoin further interruption of utility service. The declaration set forth twenty-three counts, alleged several causes of action, and seemed to involve persons who had not even been named as parties. The defendant demurred to the declaration, and the trial court sustained the demurrer on the ground that the declaration was so confused that it was not possible to ascertain either the nature of the action or the ground on which the plaintiff was proceeding. In his opinion for the Court, Justice Kenison set forth what has since become the standard for pleading in New Hampshire:

> Pleadings ought to be simple, concise and indicate the theory on
> which the plaintiff has proceeded so that the opposing party can

---

11 See RSA 511-A:6; 507-C:2.

12 See generally Rosenberg, Weinstein, and Smit, *Elements of Civil Procedure* (Mineola, New York 1970), p. 469.

13 See Cassidy v. Richardson, 74 N.H. 221, 66 A. 641 (1907).

14 96 N.H. 344, 76 A.2d 791 (1950).

adequately defend. The defendant is entitled to be informed of the theory on which the plaintiffs are proceeding, and the redress that they claim as a result of the defendant's actions. Under the liberal practice developed by Chief Justice Doe, "emphasis will be placed on the simple merits of the controversy rather than the form of the pleadings in which they may be presented". . . . It is probably no exaggeration to say that in no state is pleading treated more liberally and regarded as less of a game than in this jurisdiction. Here pleading is considered as only a means to an end. The end is accomplished if counsel can understand the dispute and the court can decide the controversy on its merits.[15]

---

15 96 N.H. at 345–46, 76 A.2d at 792. Tinkham v. Railroad, 77 N.H. 111, 88 A. 709 (1913). See also Owen v. Owen, 109 N.H. 534, 257 A.2d 24 (1969); Massachusetts Bonding Company v. Keefe, 100 N.H. 361–63, 127 A.2d 266 (1956); Porter v. Rosas, 111 N.H. 169, 276 A.2d 922 (1971); Berlinguette v. Stanton, 120 N.H. 760, 423 A.2d 289 (1980); Sexton Motors, Inc. v. Renault Northeast, Inc., 121 N.H. 460, 431 A.2d 116 (1981); Robbins v. Seekamp, 122 N.H. 318, 444 A.2d 537 (1982); Gleason v. Ebthal Realty Trust, 122 N.H. 411, 445 A.2d 1104 (1982); Brann v. Exeter Clinic, Inc., 127 N.H. 155, 498 A.2d 334 (1985). In a dissent in another case decided in the same year as *Morency*, Justice Kenison also said, "It is a well established rule in this state in considering written instruments and pleadings that their expressed intent will be enforced even though inarticulately worded." Gagnon v. Pronovost, 96 N.H. 154, 158, 71 A.2d 747, 750 (1950). By contrast, one commentator has said that "specificity is the real criterion" and that there should be a "general requirement that pleadings be sufficiently detailed to give the parties and court notice of the particular transactions relied upon and of the rule of law being invoked." See Weinstein and Distler "Drafting Pleading Rules," 57 Colum. L. Rev. 518 (1957). The Supreme Court seems to have leaned more toward the Weinstein and Distler view than Chief Justice Kenison's view in Jay Edwards, Inc. v. Baker, 130 N.H. 41, 534 A.2d 706 (1987). In *Jay Edwards*, the Court upheld the dismissal of a complaint which claimed four causes of action in relation to a particular transaction involving the lease and sale of a parcel of land but failed to allege sufficient facts, which, if proved, would support the causes of action at trial. The essence of the dispute and the nature of the plaintiff's claims were set out in the complaint and the factual details could presumably have been fleshed out by an amendment or during pretrial discovery, but the Court declined to authorize those remedies and instead agreed that the case should be dismissed. The Court commented that "when reduced to its essence, the plaintiff's petition is simply a collection of accusatory and argumentative statements." 130 N.H. at 48, 534 A.2d at 710. While the holding of the case does not contradict the holding of *Morency* or any of the other leading cases on pleading, its intolerance for brief and conclusory pleading and the lack of interest it expresses in looking behind inadequate pleadings to the substance of the dispute do seem a departure from Justice Kenison's general approach in *Morency* and *Gagnon* and may mark a shift in the court's attitude in favor of a requirement that pleadings be exact and detailed when filed if they are to survive a motion to dismiss. See also Williams v. O'Brien, 140 N.H. 595, 669 A.2d 810 (1995) (quoting Jay Edwards Inc., 130 N.H. 41, 130 N.H. 41, 44–45, 534 A.2d 706, 708 (1987)) (The court " 'must rigorously scrutinize the complaint to determine whether, on its face, it asserts a cause of action.' ").

Although *Morency v. Plourde* dealt with the sufficiency of a writ, the principles set forth in Justice Kenison's opinion apply with equal force to all types of pleadings.[16]

The *Morency* rule—that pleadings must be simple and concise, must inform the opponent of the theory and relief sought,[17] and must allow the court to decide the issue presented on its merits—captures the essence of Chief Justice Doe's attitude toward civil procedure. While not restricting the form of a pleading, the rule nevertheless requires that pleadings either meet a certain substantive standard and serve the purpose of advancing the litigation, or that they be dismissed.[18] The *Morency* rule has been repeatedly

---

16 In the remainder of this section, the discussion will focus on pleadings which begin litigation. But the principles which apply to initial pleadings apply as well to responsive and subsequent pleadings, and the discussion which follows should be viewed as relating to all types of pleadings. See, e.g., Terzis v. Estate of Whalen, 126 N.H. 88, 489 A.2d 608 (1985).

17 Perron v. Aranosian, 128 N.H. 92, 508 A.2d 1087 (1986) (plaintiff in action to revoke acceptance of motor vehicle and recover consideration paid plus damages could not raise further claim for restitution to prevent unjust enrichment for first time in his requests for rulings of law).

18 Just how much of a threat this is depends in practice on the desire of the trial judge to pursue the purposes of notice and issue formulation by the sanction of dismissal. With regard to pleadings that are too brief, the Court in Porter v. Dziura, 104 N.H. 89, 179 A.2d 281 (1962), stated that the defendant who points out deficiencies in pleadings is not himself entitled to a dismissal, but that the court can require, presumably on threat of a dismissal, that the plaintiff amend his pleadings to an acceptable form. The Court in J. Dunn and Sons, Inc. v. Paragon Homes of New England, Inc., 110 N.H. 215, 265 A.2d 5 (1970), pointed out that in some cases where the pleadings are lacking in detailed allegations, the additional information required by the defendant may also be obtained by pretrial discovery. Presumably, the trial court has the option, on a motion for a more definite statement, to decline to compel plaintiffs to amend and to require the defendant to seek the information by discovery. How a plaintiff could thereafter object to the breadth of discovery is an unsettled question. Later, in Green v. Shaw, 114 N.H. 289, 319 A.2d 284 (1974), the Court held that in the case of prolix and inconsistent pleadings, the sanction of dismissal should be applied only to those parts of a pleading which state no claim. And, in Sleeper v. World of Mirth Show, Inc., 100 N.H. 158, 121 A.2d 799 (1956), the Court held that notice of a theory set forth only in the pretrial statement was satisfactory. Thus, only the court, not a party, has a right to invoke the sanction of dismissal to correct pleadings, and it must exercise that power only to the extent necessary to reform the pleadings to an acceptable standard of clarity and notice. See also Bagley v. Controlled Env't Corp., 127 N.H. 556, 562, 503 A.2d 823, 827 (1986) ("While the courts and parties can reasonably demand more specific pleading than this, under our traditional practice the remedy for undue generality at this stage of a case is normally an order requiring a more definite statement rather than an order of dismissal"); Cilley v. New Hampshire Ball Bearings, Inc., 128 N.H. 401, 514 A.2d 818 (1986) (purely conclusory pleadings will survive Motion for Summary Judgment when they are supplemented by affidavit setting forth sufficient disputed facts to make out cause of action). But see Jay Edwards, Inc. v. Baker, 130 N.H. 41, 534 A.2d 706 (1987)

affirmed over the years. In *Kotarba v. Kotarba*,[19] the issue was whether the trial court had erred in refusing to dismiss a libel for divorce on the ground that, although the libel stated a general ground for divorce, it failed to set forth the specific facts on which the charge of wrongful conduct was based. The Supreme Court agreed that the libel did not meet the requirements of the Superior Court Rules and was not as specific as prior case law required.[20] But the Court's attitude toward the libelee's objection was colored by the fact that he had failed to object to these deficiencies until just prior to the divorce hearing. Had the libelee brought up the objection before answering, said the Court, he might have been entitled either to a more particular statement or a dismissal. But by waiting for such a lengthy period, he had changed the dispositive issue from the sufficiency of the pleadings to the likelihood of prejudice to his opponent. On the latter point, the Court noted that the libelee had in fact filed an answer and that, after denying the Motion To Dismiss, the Court was able to proceed to try the case. Thus, while the pleadings may not have informed the libelee of the precise theory and relief sought, they did tell him enough about "the nature of the dispute" to allow him to answer and to permit the court to decide the case on its merits.[21]

(upholding dismissal of complaint which asserted insufficient facts to support its legal conclusions); ERG, Inc., v. Barnes, 137 N.H. 186, 190, 624 A.2d 555, 558 (1993) ("The Court will not . . . assume the truth or accuracy of any allegations which are not well-pleaded, including the statement of conclusions of fact and principles of law.").

19 97 N.H. 252, 85 A.2d 377 (1952).

20 Prior case law required that divorce libels meet essentially the same standard as laid down by *Morency*. In K v. K, 43 N.H. 164 (1861), the Court had held that a libel which simply stated the ground for divorce without alleging the facts "with such particularity of time, place and circumstances as to give the libelee notice, not only of the general charge against him, but of the main facts upon which that charge is to be maintained" was insufficient and had to be amended. In Geers v. Geers, 95 N.H. 316, 63 A.2d 244 (1949), Justice Kenison cited the *K v. K* standard as a suitable basis for a libelee's motion to compel an amendment or to dismiss. The standard was again affirmed in Buck v. Buck, 97 N.H. 178, 83 A.2d 922 (1951).

21 This method of analysis had been previously employed in *Buck*, where the Court held that a libel which recited the ground of divorce (action to seriously endanger health) and the type of action supporting it (forced housework, declaration of dislike, etc.) without also stating the specific acts and dates on which the types of actions had occurred, was insufficient but that the libel did state "the gist of the cause of divorce" and that when the libelee had failed to raise the objection until trial, the court was not obliged to dismiss or require an amendment but could hear the evidence and grant a divorce. See also Lester v. Lester, 109 N.H. 359, 252 A.2d 429 (1969), in which the sufficiency of pleadings was reviewed more than six years after the decree of divorce was entered.

In *Porter v. Dziura*,[22] the Court was confronted with a writ to which a special declaration had been attached setting forth six claims arising out of an affair between the defendant and the wife of plaintiff's decedent. Some of the listed claims stated no separate cause of action. The defendant filed a plea in abatement for improper and confusing form of pleading. The Court refused the defendant's invitation to abate the writ for an unusual form (demonstrating once again the continuing vitality of Chief Justice Doe's work), but it did find that the declaration failed to meet the *Morency* test by not being concise or clear and that it did not allow the defendant to understand the plaintiff's theory. The Court held that the plaintiff should be required to amend and state with greater precision the grounds for relief.

In *Sleeper v. World of Mirth Show, Inc.*,[23] however, the Court held that the defendant did receive adequate notice of the plaintiff's claim for negligence, even though the writ stated only a strict liability theory and notice of an additional claim of simple negligence was not given to the defendant until the pretrial, and then only orally. And in *Milne v. Burlington Homes, Inc.*,[24] the plaintiff had sent the defendant a check for $13,500 as payment for a modular home that the defendant was to hold until further instructions had been received from the plaintiff. The defendant instead shipped the modular home to a dealer who encumbered it. The plaintiff sued in trespass on the case and assumpsit, alleging negligence by the dealer and breach of contract for the sale of goods, and seeking to have the defendant made a trustee of funds received from the plaintiff in other transactions. The trial court decreed that the defendant held the $13,500 in this transaction under a constructive trust and that it had breached that trust by sending the funds to its dealer. Before the Court, the defendant argued that the trial court had exceeded its authority when it entered an order based on a theory that was not pleaded by the plaintiff, because the defendant was entitled to be informed of the nature of the action against him. The Supreme Court disagreed, saying in part:

> We hold that plaintiff's declaration possessed the necessary elements to notify defendant that plaintiff claimed that he was entitled to the money given to it by plaintiff. Allegations of pleadings are sufficiently clear if they are understandable by the court and counsel .... There can be no argument that counsel for the defen-

---

22 104 N.H. 89, 179 A.2d 281 (1962).
23 100 N.H. 158, 121 A.2d 799 (1956).
24 117 N.H. 813, 379 A.2d 198 (1977).

dant understood that the control and disposition of $13,500 was the point in issue.[25]

The Court's decision in *Milne* is sound on the facts of that case, but the opinion goes too far to be generally applied. In some cases, the facts are so few and clear that their mere recitation suggests only a single or a limited range of theories of recovery. But, as a general rule, a defendant ought to be informed of more than that the plaintiff claims "he is entitled to the money."

More recently, the Court in *Morancy v. Morancy*[26] held that the trial court erred in finding the defendant liable for invasion of privacy when the same court had granted defendant's motion to dismiss the privacy claim before the trial had begun. The Court cited *Morency v. Plourde* and stated that: "Contestants in a law suit must be bound by rules, and the most basic of these rules is that the rules cannot be changed in the middle of the contest."[27] It found that allowing the claim would be "grossly unfair to the defendant."[28]

Morency v. Plourde still presents the best rule for judging the sufficiency of pleadings, and a defendant should be entitled to object to pleadings which fail to meet the standard of *Morency*, by filing either a Motion To Dismiss or a Motion for a More Particular Statement.

Library References

CJS Pleading § 6

§ 7.05. Sufficient Form

A pleading must adequately communicate the plaintiff's theory and requested relief, and provide enough information to allow the court to decide the case. Although deficiencies of form will not defeat the parties' substantive claims, they may unnecessarily delay the progress of a case and should be avoided. Suggested forms of pleadings discussed in this treatise are set forth in the Appendix, but some general rules are worth reviewing here.

With the exception of small claims actions,[29] the initial pleading in all cases brought in the trial courts in New Hampshire is either a writ, bill,

---

25   117 N.H. at 815, 379 A.2d at 199. See also Druding v. Allen, 122 N.H. 823, 451 A.2d 390 (1982); Terzis v. Estate of Whalen, 126 N.H. 88, 489 A.2d 608 (1985).

26   134 N.H. 493, 593 A.2d 1158 (1991).

27   124 N.H. at 497, 593 A.2d at 1160.

28   *Id.*

29   See RSA 503.

wrt
petition
Bill or libel

petition, or libel. Writs are preprinted with the name and seal of each court and a facsimile of the signature of the Chief Justice and the clerk. Preprinted writs may be obtained from the clerks,[30] and the blank spaces on the writ form must be filled in and the writ signed by a resident attorney. When the plaintiff represents himself, he must complete and endorse the writ if he is a resident, or have a resident do so if he is not.[31] Bills, petitions, and libels are not preprinted and must be individually typed.

C. How To Draft Pleadings

§ 7.06. Language

All pleadings must be stated in the English language.[32] Where exhibits or affidavits in a foreign language are attached to pleadings, a certified translation in English should be annexed.

§ 7.07. No Plea by Letter

The old practice of making requests or entering objections by letter addressed to the clerk of court is now forbidden by Superior Court Rule 4. All requests for action by the court must be set forth in a pleading format.[33]

§ 7.08. Size of Pleadings

"All pleadings and forms" must be set out on 8½" x 11" paper.[34] When documents of a different size are declared upon or filed, they should be duplicated by a process which converts them to 8½" x 11" size. If such a duplication cannot be done or the original must be filed, the clerk should be consulted for advice.

§ 7.09. Name of Court

The name of the court and, in the case of the probate court and the superior court, the county in which the action is to be filed must be stated at the top of the first page.[35]

---

30 Super. Ct. R. 1; RSA 509:2.

31 RSA 509:8.

32 RSA 509:1.

33 It goes without saying that no pleading may be addressed directly to a judge of the superior court, the probate courts, the municipal courts, or the district courts. See Super. Ct. R. 6.

34 Super. Ct. R. 4.

35 Super. Ct. R. 117 and 118.

§ 7.10. Names of Parties; Caption

In the caption, each party's name should be listed on a separate line, and, where a person is sued or is suing in an official capacity, or as a representative of someone else, the capacity in which he sues, or is sued, should be stated after the name.[36] Unless noted to the contrary, the statement in the caption of an individual natural person's name without some title or indication of capacity will make that person a party in his individual capacity. Where a business name is used, the nature of the organization (e.g., corporation, partnership, real estate trust, etc.) should be indicated.[37] In the case of partnerships, trusts, and other organizations that cannot themselves be parties to an action, the partner, trustee, or other person who can become a party should be named. The caption should not be cluttered with names which do not represent entities that can become parties. Where the name of the defendant is not known, a fictitious name may be used.[38]

§ 7.11. Titles of Pleadings

In bills, petitions, and libels, the pleading must be titled in capital letters under the caption. The title should be descriptive of the nature of the pleading.

§ 7.12. Introductory Paragraph

Many practitioners still follow the archaic form of introducing their bills, petitions, and libels with the phrase "NOW COMES plaintiff . . . ." But the superior court does not favor the form[39] and a straight-forward declarative form should be followed.

§ 7.13. Names and Addresses of Parties

The plaintiff is required to include his mailing address in the writ, petition, bill, or libel[40] and he should include the defendant's[41] as well, if he knows

---

36   Low v. Tilton, 19 N.H. 271 (1848).

37   If a corporate status is not alleged, the name will be assumed to refer to an individual or association. Winnipiseogee Lake Co. v. Young, 40 N.H. 420, 428 (1860).

38   RSA 509:7; Super. Ct. R. 117.

39   Super. Ct. R. 118; Appendix of Forms to the Superior Court Rules.

40   Super. Ct. R. 2, 119, and 144.

41   Super. Ct. R. 144 requires that the residence and address of the libelee be stated and R. 146 provides that when the libelee's residence is unknown "the libel shall state the libelee's last known post-office address, and the name and post-office address of some near relative of the libelee, if any is known to the libelant, and otherwise the name and

it. When drawing a bill, petition or libel, it is preferable to refer to each party in a separate paragraph and to state that party's full name, mailing address, residence or place of business (if different from the mailing address), capacity in which he is made a party, and relationship to other parties (if important to the action).[42] Parties should always be introduced before other points are stated.

All changes of address, of the parties or their attorneys, should be filed with the clerk if the action is pending.[43]

§ 7.14. Jurisdiction

Unless it is clear from the other allegations, the basis for the exercise of the court's jurisdiction over the subject matter and the parties must be specifically stated. Setting forth the basis of jurisdiction at the beginning of a pleading will assist the court in meeting its obligation to determine whether it has jurisdiction over the subject matter of the proceeding, and will compel the defendant either to admit or to contest subject matter jurisdiction at an early stage of the proceedings.[44]

§ 7.15. Venue

The writ, bill, petition, or libel should show, by allegations of specific facts, that venue is properly laid where the pleading is filed. If a Motion to Transfer is filed by the defendant based on a claim of improper venue, the facts justifying plaintiff's choice will have to be filed, and setting them forth as a matter of course when the action is begun may avoid needless motion.

§ 7.16. Statement of the Claim—General Principles

The Supreme Court long ago sanctioned the "kitchen sink" theory of pleading, by saying:

> A party may rightfully state . . . as many facts as constituting part
> of his cause of action as he supposes may in any event be useful
> to him, and upon the trial he may prove as many of them as he is

---

post-office address of some friend of the libelee, such facts to be verified by the libelant's personal affidavit filed with the libel."

42 Super. Ct. R. 118.

43 Super. Ct. R. 2; Prob. Ct. R. 3.

44 See Hodge v. Allstate Insurance Co., 130 N.H. 743, 546 A.2d 1078 (1988) (where defendant's admission in its Answer that proceeding was commenced under Declaratory Judgment Act was sufficient to foreclose defendant from objecting later that issue which the plaintiff sought to raise was not covered by that statute).

able; and he may well recover if he proves one good cause though he fail as to the others.[45]

But the Court has also approved pleading just enough facts to meet the minimum requirements of a statute, even though the writ fails to inform the defendant of the facts which bring the plaintiff under the statute.[46] Justice Kenison has even remarked that "it is a well-established rule in this state in considering written instruments in pleadings that their expressed intent will be enforced even though inarticulately worded."[47] Obviously, neither prolixity nor undue brevity represents a model form of pleading, and it is unwise to expect a court to make sense of pleadings that the pleader himself is unable to make sensible. A careful draftsman will always strive to allege enough facts and only enough facts to inform his opponent and the court fully of why and how he happens to be in the court and the basis of his claim.

Whether the claim is legal, equitable or a combination of the two, the statement of the claim should be simple, concise,[48] and informative. The plaintiff need not set forth every fact that he will be able to prove nor show the means by which he plans to prove the facts he alleges. He must at least say enough to show the court that he is entitled to maintain the action[49] and to allow his opponent to know the factual and legal basis of his claim. In order to accomplish these ends, the following practical rules should be followed:

(a) State the facts in chronological order;

(b) State the facts first, then the conclusions of fact and law which can be drawn from them;

(c) Use simple sentences. The time-honored practice of stating an entire claim in a writ in one run-on sentence should be avoided. In bills, petitions,

---

45 Littleton v. Richardson, 34 N.H. 179, 190 (1856). See also Hewes v. Roby, 135 N.H. 476, 477, 606 A.2d 810, 811 (1992), where the Court held that forcing plaintiffs to elect between common law negligence claim and statutory claim deprived them of opportunity to present all claims in a single proceeding. The Court also noted that the "clear rule in New Hampshire is that '[a] plaintiff may seek to recover on alternative legal grounds,' [as long as] the causes of action are [not] mutually exclusive . . . or mutually inconsistent," quoting Burley v. Kenneth Hudson, Inc., 122 N.H. 560, 563, 448 A.2d 375, 376 (1982).

46 Bodge v. Hughes, 53 N.H. 614 (1873).

47 Gagnon v. Pronovost, 96 N.H. 154, 158, 71 A.2d 747, 750 (1950).

48 Super. Ct. R. 120.

49 See Cassidy v. Richardson, 74 N.H. 221, 66 A. 641 (1907). In divorce proceedings, the libelant should set forth "the specific acts and dates relied upon to constitute a cause or causes for divorce, except as otherwise required by statute." Super. Ct. R. 144.

and libels, each different event or topic should be set forth in a separate paragraph;[50] and

(d) Number the counts and paragraphs consecutively.[51] In some lengthy bills and petitions, it is also helpful to label groups of paragraphs with the subject each group addresses (for example "Parties," "Jurisdiction and Venue," "Factual Background," and "Violations Alleged").

§ 7.17. —Separate Counts

A cause of action is one event or series of events which gives a person a right to seek the assistance of a court.[52] In any cause of action, there may be several grounds upon which relief may be granted. Each of these grounds of relief is called a "claim" or "count," and each claim or count must be set forth separately in a declaration, petition, bill, or libel. In addition, all claims or counts which the party wishes at any time to assert as a ground for recovery on the basis of the underlying facts and that can be joined in one case and every desired form of relief that can be joined in one case must be set forth in the declaration, petition, bill, or libel.[53] This practice allows each ground of relief to be separately tested by the pleadings before trial and by the proof at trial.[54]

---

50 Super. Ct. R. 121 and 122.

51 Super. Ct. R. 121.

52 See Eastern Marine Const. Corp. v. First Southern Leasing, Ltd., 129 N.H. 270, 274, 525 A.2d 709, 712 (1987) ("[T]he term 'cause of action' means the right to recover, regardless of the theory of recovery. . . . We . . . reject the view that the term is synonymous with the particular legal theory in which a party's claim for relief is framed. . . . [We] define cause of action collectively to refer to all theories on which relief could be claimed on the basis of the factual transaction in question. . . ." But see Aubert v. Aubert, 129 N.H. 422, 529 A.2d 909 (1987) (action for damages caused by wife firing gun in her husband's face not barred by prior proceeding for divorce on ground of extreme cruelty, based on same incident, because two actions are "fundamentally different," involve "entirely distinct" issues, have different purposes, and allow for different types of relief).

53 Eastern Marine Const. Corp. v. First Southern Leasing, Ltd., 129 N.H. 270, 525 A.2d 709 (1987) (any claim that could have been asserted and any form of relief that could have been awarded on basis of factual transaction alleged will be barred by judgment under doctrine of res judicata). But see Aubert v. Aubert, 129 N.H. 422, 529 A.2d 909 (1987) (second action will not be barred if it seeks relief which could not have been obtained, even if asked for, in context of the prior action).

54 New Hampshire still recognizes, for the purposes of form only, the common law counts (assumpsit, case, debt, trover, detinue, contract, covenant, and trespass) and each count in a writ must be labelled with one of these theories. However, a declaration which states sufficient facts to make out a common law count but fails to name it, may stand (Leeper v. Leeper, 114 N.H. 294, 319 A.2d 626 (1974)), and the determination of

Any number of counts may be set forth in a writ, bill, petition, or libel. Counts based on different forms of action may be joined in one declaration.[55] Counts may be inconsistent.[56] However, each count must state a distinct and separate claim,[57] and, regardless of the number of counts, only one cause of action may be the basis of each pleading.[58]

When setting forth more than one count, it is permissible to incorporate facts previously alleged by reference in the second and subsequent counts.[59] This is commonly done by inserting a sentence or paragraph at the beginning of the subsequent counts saying, for example, "The facts alleged in Paragraphs 3–10 are incorporated in this Count II by reference as if fully set forth herein."

---

whether a declaration alleges a common law count depends on the substance of the allegations, not their label. J. Dunn & Sons, Inc. v. Paragon Homes of New England, Inc., 110 N.H. 215, 265 A.2d 5 (1970); Kantor v. The Norwood Group, 127 N.H. 831, 508 A.2d 1078 (1986).

55 See generally Hutt v. Hickey, 67 N.H. 411, 29 A. 456 (1892) (a count in assumpsit may be joined with a count in tort); Rutherford v. Whitcher, 60 N.H. 110 (1880) (a count in assumpsit may be joined with a count in tort); Peaslee v. Dudley, 63 N.H. 220 (1884); Crawford v. Parsons, 63 N.H 438 (1885); Broadhurst v. Morgan, 66 N.H. 480, 29 A. 553 (1891); Owen v. Weston, 63 N.H. 599 (1885) (a count in contract may be joined with a count in tort); Crawford v. Parson, 63 N.H. 438 (1885) (a count in covenant may be joined with a count in case); Whitaker v. Warren, 60 N.H. 20 (1880) (counts in debt and case may be joined); Hewes v. Roby, 135 N.H. 476, 606 A.2d 810 (1992) (plaintiffs can plead both their statutory and common law claims).

56 Larry v. Herrick, 58 N.H. 40 (1876); Burley v. Kenneth Hudson, Inc., 122 N.H. 560, 448 A.2d 375 (1982). But see Hewes v. Roby, 135 N.H. 476, 606 A.2d 810 (1992) (while acknowledging that plaintiff could plead in the alternative, the Court noted that there was an exception where causes of action were mutually exclusive, or mutually inconsistent).

57 Hitchcock v. Munger, 15 N.H. 97 (1844).

58 Farnum v. Concord Land and Water Power Company, 69 N.H. 231, 45 A. 745 (1897) (a cause for negligent failure to maintain a spring cover which resulted in injury to a cow could not be joined with a cause for the value of water used from the spring); Pratt v. Magunson, 87 N.H. 486, 179 A. 355 (1935) (two counts of negligence causing an automobile accident were improperly joined with one count charging malicious conduct in causing the plaintiff's license to be suspended until a bond was posted). Although the general holding of these cases is still effective, the earlier Courts' view of what constituted a "cause of action" was much narrower than today's. In Eastern Marine Const. Corp. v. First Southern Leasing, Ltd., 129 N.H. 270, 274, 525 A.2d 709, 712 (1987), the Court adopted the modern view and defined the term "cause of action" as "the right to recover, regardless of the theory of recovery." But see Aubert v. Aubert, 129 N.H. 422, 529 A.2d 909 (1987) (when it would not be possible to obtain type of relief in one action, judgment in that action will not bar maintenance of second action based on same facts to obtain missing relief).

59 Hitchcock v. Munger, 15 N.H. 97 (1844).

Library References

CJS Pleading §§ 87–91

§ 7.18. —Setting Forth the Material Elements

A "material element" of a claim is some fact or set of facts which must be proven to establish the plaintiff's right to relief. It is not enough to set forth a cause in general or conclusory terms; all facts necessary to establish the material elements of a claim must be alleged in the writ, bill, petition, or libel.[60] It has been held that, when a claim is based on a statute, the plaintiff can either refer to the statute and not state all the facts that give him a right to sue upon it,[61] or recite all the facts giving him a right under the statute and not refer to the statute.[62] But it is unquestionably the better practice to set forth specifically the statutory basis for an action and all the facts that make out the plaintiff's right to proceed under it.[63]

Library References

CJS Pleading § 69

§ 7.19. —References to Documents

Superior Court Rule 120 provides in part: "No deed, will, agreement or other writing shall be set forth at length or annexed to any bill or answer, but only so much as may be material." The purpose of the rule is to reduce the volume of pleadings, while still assuring adequate notice of the substance of a plaintiff's claim. In general, it is best to quote from a lengthy document rather than to annex it to the pleadings. Nevertheless, complete copies of documents should still be attached to a plaintiff's pleadings whenever the existence of a particular document may be disputed or dispositive of the whole or a major portion of the case.

---

60 Proctor v. Bank of New Hampshire, 123 N.H. 395, 464 A.2d 263 (1983).

61 Eaton v. Miner, 5 N.H. 542 (1831).

62 Littleton v. Richardson, 34 N.H. 179 (1856); Gould v. Kelley, 16 N.H. 551 (1845); Smith v. Woodman, 28 N.H. 520 (1854); Henniker v. Contoocook, 29 N.H. 146 (1854); Crippen v. Laighton, 69 N.H. 540, 44 A. 538 (1899). Where the facts alleged could support an action under either common law right or a statute, if the plaintiff fails to allege specifically that the action is brought under the statute, the court will assume it to be brought under the common law right and the plaintiff will thus lose rights under the statute. Fasekis v. J.J. Newbury Company, 93 N.H. 468, 44 A.2d 817 (1945). See also Gilman v. County of Cheshire, 126 N.H. 445, 493 A.2d 485 (1985).

63 See In re DeLucca, 121 N.H. 71, 426 A.2d 32 (1981). If a person bases his claim on the statute of another jurisdiction, he must either specifically allege that fact or state facts from which it may be clearly discerned. Crippen v. Laighton, 69 N.H. 540, 44 A. 538 (1899).

Library References

CJS Pleading § 33

§ 7.20. —Jurisdictional Prerequisites

Because the court has an obligation to satisfy itself, even without objection, that it has jurisdiction over the subject matter of a dispute, carefully drawn pleadings should set forth the basis for jurisdiction. Where some specific action must be taken by the plaintiff prior to bringing suit, the accomplishment of that action should be stated.[64] Even though the plaintiff is not required to show the absence of an affirmative defense or of negative facts that the defendant has the burden of establishing,[65] when the proceeding is based on a statute and the statute states a qualification or exception, the pleadings should allege facts sufficient to bring the case within the qualification or put it outside the exception.[66]

Library References

CJS Pleading § 76

§ 7.21. —Specification of Damages

Where the plaintiff has suffered damages that are not readily apparent from the facts alleged, those damages should be specifically stated.[67]

Library References

CJS Damages §§ 129–140
CJS Pleading §§ 83, 95

§ 7.22. Relief Sought

Three rules apply to requests for relief. First, requests for relief should be as specific as possible. A party seeking an injunction, for example, should

---

64 Hicks v. Burns, 38 N.H. 141 (1859); Hillsborough County v. Londonderry, 43 N.H. 451 (1862). See RSA 507-C:5 (Notice of Intent to Sue); 540:3 (Notice to Quit); 498-A:4 (Notice to Offer to Purchase); 541:4 (Motion for Rehearing). However, where the action would be barred but for an excuse, the plaintiff must allege it or be vulnerable to a demurrer. See RSA 508:8 and 4-b. The plaintiff ought to negate any affirmative defenses when he seeks a temporary restraining order or other unusual preliminary relief (see RSA 508-A:3), or if he seeks a summary judgment.

65 Gould v. Kelley, 16 N.H. 551 (1845).

66 Gould v. Kelley, 16 N.H. 551 (1845); Clough v. Shepard, 31 N.H. 490 (1855).

67 See Woodbury v. Jones, 44 N.H. 206 (1862). But see RSA 508:4-c (in personal actions, the plaintiff may not state certain sum but must "instead, state that the damages claimed are within any minimum or maximum jurisdictional limits of the court.").

set forth the type of injunction that is needed and exactly what the injunction should say.[68]

Second, requests for relief should be complete. Any relief, whether requested or not, that could be granted based on the factual transaction alleged, will be barred by the judgment as a result of the doctrine of res judicata.[69]

Third, requests for relief should always leave room for a surprise. In bills, petitions, and libels, it is customary to conclude the list of requested relief with the phrase "and for such other relief as may be just,"[70] as this phrase at least puts an opponent on notice to consider other forms of relief the pleading party may later request and to prepare for it.[71] In personal actions, including those for medical injury,[72] the writ should not specify or allege the amount of damages claimed, but should set forth that the damages claimed are within the appropriate minimum or maximum jurisdictional limits.[73]

Library References

CJS Equity § 138
CJS Pleading § 95

§ 7.23. Signature

If the plaintiff is a resident of the state, his writ, petition, bill, or libel must be endorsed, before service, either by the plaintiff, plaintiff's attorney[74] or by an agent on the plaintiff's behalf. If plaintiff is not a resident, it must be

---

68 Super. Ct. R. 118, 161, and 162.

69 Eastern Marine Const. Corp. v. First Southern Leasing, Ltd., 129 N.H. 270, 275, 525 A.2d 709, 712 (1987) ("[A] subsequent suit based upon the same cause of action as a prior suit is barred 'even though the plaintiff is prepared in the second action (1) to present evidence or grounds or theories of the case not presented in the first action, or (2) to seek remedies or forms of relief not demanded in the first action.' "). But see Aubert v. Aubert, 129 N.H. 422, 529 A.2d 909 (1987) (relief that could not have been granted in prior proceeding may be sought in second action).

70 Super. Ct. R. 118. But see Eastern Marine Const. Corp. v. First Southern Leasing, Ltd., 129 N.H. 270, 525 A.2d 709 (1987) (rejecting appellant's argument that he did not seek and could not have obtained damages in prior proceeding that sought primarily injunctive relief by pointing out that in that prior proceeding, appellant's pleadings had included catch-all prayer for "such relief as [is] just and fair").

71 Cf. Milne v. Burlington Homes, Inc., 117 N.H. 813, 379 A.2d 198 (1977).

72 RSA 507-C:6 (eliminating requirement for ad damnum in actions for medical injury).

73 RSA 508:4-c (eliminating requirement for ad damnum in personal actions).

74 Signing the writ does not make the attorney a surety for his client in violation of Super. Ct. R. 22.

endorsed "by some responsible person" who is a resident.[75] The purpose of the requirement is to assure that a defendant who prevails can recover his costs.[76]

All petitions and bills must be signed by the plaintiff or his attorney.[77] Libels for divorce and some other pleadings[78] must be signed by the libellant if of sound mind and of legal age or, if not, by the parent, guardian, or next friend.[79]

It is customary to conclude bills and petitions with "Respectfully Submitted," followed by the name of the plaintiff, the name and address of the lawyer or firm representing him, and the signature of the attorney who prepared the pleadings or who will represent the plaintiff at trial.

Library References

CJS Equity § 180
CJS Pleading §§ 339–342

§ 7.24. Choice of Trier

If the plaintiff desires a trial by jury, he must claim it by checking the box next to the word "Jury" on the writ before it is entered, or by stating his claim in the bill or petition. If the defendant wants a jury trial, he must claim it by checking a similar box on the Appearance slip.[80] If neither party claims a jury trial in this manner, the case will be tried by the court.[81]

---

75 RSA 509:8.

76 Farley v. Day, 26 N.H. 527 (1853); RSA 509:9.

77 Super. Ct. R. 15 provides, in part:

> The signature of an attorney to a pleading constitutes a certification by him that he has read the pleading; that to the best of his knowledge, information and belief there is a good ground to support it; and that it is not interposed for delay. If a pleading is not signed, or is signed with an intent to defeat the purpose of this rule, it may be stricken and the action may proceed as though the action had not been filed.

78 See RSA 498-A:5(II).

79 RSA 458:10.

80 Note that checking the jury trial box on the appearance form may constitute a waiver of objection to jurisdiction and should not be done on an Appearance form used to give notice of only a Special Appearance. In such a case the claim for jury trial should be made by filing a second Appearance card after the objections to jurisdiction have been waived or overruled. If the case is begun in a district court and seeks more than $1,500, the right must be claimed within five days of entry of the action. RSA 502-A:15. But see Compton Crossroads, Inc. v. Wise, 131 N.H. 193, 551 A.2d 517 (1988) (failure of Writ of Summons to notify defendant that he must claim jury trial within five days of entry of writ constitutes "good cause" as matter of law for court to grant additional time "up to, and including, the return date" in which to claim right).

81 Super. Ct. R. 8.

§ 7.25. Date

All pleadings should be dated.

§ 7.26. Certification of Service

Writs, bills, petitions, and libels must be served by the sheriff, or by some other means approved by the court. All other pleadings may be mailed, postage prepaid, or hand-delivered to the opposing party, and must contain a certificate that such mailing or delivery has been accomplished.[82]

Library References

CJS Pleading §§ 407–417

D. Bars to Further Action

§ 7.27. Splitting a Cause of Action

A party must bring his entire claim against a single person arising out of the same transaction in one proceeding. He may sue separate defendants and may assert separate causes of action[83] in separate proceedings, but he may not assert one part of his claim against a single defendant in one proceeding, and another part in a second. All aspects of his claim will be foreclosed by the judgment in the first action, whether they were specifically raised or not.[84]

The defense that a plaintiff has split his cause of action and is bringing, in a second action, part of the claim that should have been litigated in the first, may be raised by a Motion to Dismiss filed within thirty days of the return date.[85]

---

82 Super. Ct. R. 21; Prob. Ct. R. 3 and 4.

83 See Reid v. Spadone, 119 N.H. 198, 400 A.2d 54 (1979) (wife's action against her husband's employer for loss of consortium was not barred by judgment in his prior action for personal injuries). But see RSA 507-B:3 (all actions for bodily injury, personal injury, and property damage to one person to be litigated in one proceeding). See also Eastern Marine Const. Corp. v. First Southern Leasing, Ltd., 129 N.H. 270, 274, 525 A.2d 709, 712 (1987) (defining "cause of action" as "the right to recover, regardless of the theory of recovery") and Aubert v. Aubert, 129 N.H. 422, 426, 529 A.2d 909, 911–12 (1987) (proceeding for divorce on ground of extreme cruelty and subsequent action for tort to recover damages for same cruelty are "fundamentally different" types of proceedings, with different purposes, distinct issues, and different types of relief available, and thus do not involve same "cause of action").

84 See Boucher v. Bailey, 117 N.H. 590, 375 A.2d 1160 (1977); Eastern Marine Const. Corp. v. First Southern Leasing, Ltd., 129 N.H. 270, 525 A.2d 709 (1987).

85 Super. Ct. R. 28.

Library References

Pleading §§ 219, 400
CJS Actions §§ 102–106
CJS Pleading §§ 266, 563
Waiver of, by failing to promptly raise, objection to splitting cause of action. 40 ALR3d 108.

§ 7.28. The Doctrine of Election of Remedies

The doctrine of election of remedies requires that a person recover only once for the same wrong. Where he has an equal right to select either of two inconsistent[86] avenues of redress,[87] he must choose between them.[88] Once his choice has been made, he is bound by the result. If he loses on his chosen theory, he may not commence a second action to enforce the conflicting remedy which he at first rejected.[89]

The doctrine of election of remedies is modified somewhat by the rule that if a party initially mistakes his remedy, he may, upon discovering the error, apply for the relief to which he was originally entitled.[90] The doctrine bars only the use of two remedies for the same wrong, and does not prohibit an application for supplemental remedies, thereby making the remedy chosen more complete.[91]

In New Hampshire, the doctrine of election of remedies is limited "to avoid injustice" and is "confined to cases where the plaintiff may be unjustly enriched or the defendant has actually been misled by the plaintiff's conduct

---

86 "It is the inconsistency of the demands that makes the election of one remedial right an estoppel against the assertion of the other, and not the fact that the forms of action are different." Gehlen v. Patterson, 88 N.H. 328, 331, 141 A. 914, 915–16 (1928). See McQua v. Michou, 85 N.H. 299, 157 A. 881 (1932) (malpractice not inconsistent with breach of contract to cure); Noyes v. Edgerly, 71 N.H. 500, 53 A. 311 (1902); McNamara v. Chapman, 81 N.H. 169, 123 A. 229 (1923) (inconsistent to sue first on master-servant theory and later on theory that defendant was not servant); Judge of Probate v. Webster, 46 N.H. 518 (1866).

87 Gordon v. Amoskeag Mfg. Co., 83 N.H. 221, 140 A. 704 (1928).

88 Lessard v. Darker, 94 N.H. 209, 49 A.2d 814 (1946); Daniels v. Barker, 89 N.H. 416, 200 A. 410 (1938).

89 Todd v. Duncklee, 94 N.H. 226, 52 A.2d 285 (1946).

90 Bolger v. Boston & Maine Railroad, 82 N.H. 372, 134 A. 524 (1926); Gould v. Blodgett, 61 N.H. 115 (1881); Kittredge v. Holt, 58 N.H. 191 (1877).

91 State v. Cote, 95 N.H. 248, 61 A.2d 710 (1948) (plaintiff no longer required to elect between law and equity where the two together may provide more complete relief than either alone). See also In re Estate of Ward, 129 N.H. 4, 523 A.2d 28 (1986) (administrator could simultaneously seek order from probate court that his decedent's attorney repay misappropriated funds and attachment from superior court to secure same obligation to repay). Cf. Eastman v. Amoskeag Mfg. Co., 47 N.H. 71 (1866) (setting forth old rule to the contrary).

or the result is otherwise inequitable or res judicata can be applied."[92] Election of remedies is a bar to the maintenance of a second action and must be raised by a Motion to Dismiss filed within thirty days after the return date.[93]

Library References

Pleading § 369(1)–(6)
CJS Election of Remedies §§ 1 et seq.
CJS Pleading §§ 483–494
Commencement of action, or its prosecution short of judgment on the merits, as a conclusive election. 6 ALR2d 10.
Pleading of election of remedies. 99 ALR2d 1315.

E. Special Rules and Proceedings

§ 7.29. Special Rules—Proceedings in Equity

In actions begun by petition or bill, separate points must be stated in separate paragraphs.[94] Individual paragraphs may consist of more than one sentence, but each paragraph should deal with a discrete subject.[95]

§ 7.30. —Marital Proceedings

When adultery is alleged in marital proceedings: (1) the name and address of the person who is alleged to have engaged in adultery with the spouse or a statement that the name or address is not known must be included in the libel;[96] and (2) any fact that excuses personal service on the co-respondent under RSA 458:11 must be set forth.[97]

§ 7.31. —Petitions To Dissolve Business Corporations

Under the revised New Hampshire Business Corporation Act[98] in effect since 1993, the superior court has jurisdiction to dissolve a New Hampshire

---

92 Ricker v. Mathews, 94 N.H. 313, 317–18, 53 A.2d 196, 199 (1947); In re Estate of Ward, 129 N.H. 4, 523 A.2d 28 (1986).

93 Super. Ct. R. 28.

94 Super. Ct. R. 121.

95 Petitions to remove clouds from titles to real estate should include "a separate paragraph setting forth specifically the clouds sought to be removed and the legal basis relied upon on their removal." Super. Ct. R. 122. Petitions for special school district or town meetings must allege specific facts showing an emergency and include the text of specific articles that the petitioners desire to have inserted in the warrant. Super. Ct. R. 123.

96 Super. Ct. R. 153.

97 *Id.*

98 RSA 293.

corporation upon petition of the Attorney General if there was fraud in the incorporation, or if the corporation has abused its authority.[99] The superior court may also dissolve a corporation upon petition of a shareholder when the directors or shareholders are so divided that they cannot direct the corporation's affairs,[100] or if the directors or those in control of the corporation have acted illegally or fraudulently.[101]

If the corporation is insolvent, the superior court has authority, either upon petition from a creditor[102] or upon petition by the corporation itself if the corporation desires court supervision, to dissolve the corporation.[103]

Furthermore, the Secretary of State may dissolve a corporation if he determines that it has failed to pay taxes on time for two consecutive years, failed to file an annual report on time for two consecutive years, or if it has failed to have a registered agent in the state.[104] The Secretary of State may also dissolve a corporation if it has failed to prevent the period of duration in the corporation's articles of incorporation from expiring.[105]

Although Superior Court Rule 166, prescribing the contents of petitions by corporations or shareholders for the dissolution of a domestic corporation, no longer has any application, its general requirements that a petition set forth the interest of the parties with specific reference to their percentage of stock ownership and that the petition identify the factual and statutory basis for the action are still sound.

§ 7.32. —Paternity Cases

Under RSA ch. 168-A, paternity may be established upon filing a petition to the superior court by the mother, child, or public authority chargeable by law with the support of the child, or by filing an affidavit of paternity with the clerk of the town where the birth of the child occurred.[106]

---

99 RSA 293-A:14.30(a).

100 RSA 293-A:14.30(b)(i) and (ii).

101 RSA 293-A:14.30(b)(iii).

102 RSA 293-A:14.30(c)(i) and (ii).

103 RSA 293-A:14.30(d).

104 RSA 293-A:14.20(1), (2) and (3).

105 RSA 293-A:14.20(5).

106 Super. Ct. Admin. R. 6-3.

F. Amendments

§ 7.33. Basis for the Practice in Statutes and the Common Law

The statutory basis for New Hampshire's traditionally liberal amendment policy was set forth in New Hampshire Gen. Stat., c. 207, Sections 8 and 9, the modern versions of which are RSA 514:8 and 9, and which read as follows:

> 514:8. Abatement. No writ, declaration, return, process, judgment or other proceeding in the courts or course of justice shall be abated, quashed or reversed for any error or mistake, where the person or case may be rightly understood by the court, nor through defect or want of form or addition only; and courts and justices may, on motion, order amendment in any such case.
>
> 514:9. Amendments. Amendments in matters of substance may be permitted in any action in any stage of the proceedings, upon such terms as the court shall deem just and reasonable, when it shall appear to the court that it is necessary for the prevention of injustice; but the rights of third persons shall not be affected thereby.[107]

The policy behind these statutes is confirmed by Superior Court Rule 25 and District and Municipal Court Rule 3.8(B), which provide:

> Amendments in matters of form will be allowed or ordered, as of course, on motion; but, if the defect or want of form be shown by the adverse party by demurrer, plea, or motion, the order to amend will be made on such terms as justice may require.

Superior Court Rule 26 and District and Municipal Court Rule 3.8(C) also state:

> Amendments in matters of substance may be made on such terms as justice may require.

Probate Court Rule 8 combines the significant points of both these rules, as follows:

> Amendments in matters of form will be allowed or ordered on motion; however, amendments in matters of substance may be made only upon such terms as justice may require.

---

[107] To the same effect, see Super. Ct. R. 25 and 26. Super. Ct. R. 24 prohibits an amendment of substance after default without special notice of the intended amendment to the defendant.

It has been said that the case that firmly established the doctrine of liberal amendment is *Stebbins v. Lancashire Insurance Company.*[108] In *Stebbins*, decided in 1879, the trial court had refused to permit the plaintiff to change the form of his action from assumpsit to covenant. Relying upon the statutory predecessors to RSA 514:8 and 9, the Court held, in an opinion written by Justice Stanley, that the amendment should have been allowed: "Taking these two sections together, it is not apparent how it ever could have been held that it was not within the power of the court to allow any amendment called for by the necessities and justice of the case, whether it be of form or substance, and in whatever stage of the proceedings it may be asked for."[109]

Six years later, in *Owen v. Weston,*[110] Chief Justice Doe set forth what he conceived to be the common law basis of his liberal policy of amendment: "Statutes allowing amendments of form and substance in any stage of the proceedings, are reenactments of the common law right of litigants, compelling judges to do their common law duty."[111]

Library References

CJS Pleading §§ 275 et seq.

Amendment of pleading before trial with respect to amount or nature of relief sought as ground for continuance. 56 ALR2d 650.

Amendment of pleading as to parties or their capacity as ground for continuance. 67 ALR2d 477.

Amendment to show giving of requisite notice or presenting of claim to municipality or other public body. 83 ALR2d 1208.

Amendment of pleading after limitation has run, so as to set up subsequent appointment as executor or administrator of plaintiff who professed to bring the action in that capacity without previous valid appointment. 27 ALR4th 198.

§ 7.34. The Traditional Liberal Doctrine of
Amendments—Amendments Allowed

After the end of the Doe era in 1896, New Hampshire continued to follow the policy of liberally allowing amendments of both form and substance. Amendments were allowed before trial that added and deleted allegations,[112]

---

108 59 N.H. 143 (1879); Reid, John, "From Common Sense to Common Law to Charles Doe—The Evolution of Pleading in New Hampshire," 1 N.H.B.J. 34 (1959).

109 59 N.H. at 145. See also Brann v. Exeter Clinic, Inc., 127 N.H. 155, 498 A.2d 334 (1985).

110 63 N.H. 599 (1885).

111 63 N.H. at 600. The opinion in *Owen v. Owen* sets forth several cases in which the Court had previously allowed amendments. See 63 N.H. at 603–04.

112 Mansfield v. Federal Services Finance Corporation, 99 N.H. 352, 111 A.2d 322 (1955) (adding a new element of damage which accrued after the action began); Brown v.

made allegations more specific[113] and that changed the form of action[114] or the type of relief sought.[115] Amendments were also allowed that changed the names of the parties,[116] that added new parties,[117] changed a replication,[118]

Brockway, 87 N.H. 342, 179 A. 411 (1935) (adding a count in negligene after the statute of limitations had run); Arcadia Knitting Mills, Inc. v. Elliot Manufacturing Company, 89 N.H. 188, 195 A. 681 (1937) (adding a claim for interest on bills declared on); Prentiss v. New England Box Co., 75 N.H. 605, 75 A. 984 (1910); Staltare v. Granite State Insurance Company, 107 N.H. 6, 216 A. 2d 793 (1966).

113 Green v. Merrill, 76 N.H. 50, 79 A. 122 (1911); Blanchard & Son Co. v. American Realty Company, 79 N.H. 295, 108 A. 291 (1919); Masterson v. Berlin Street Railway, 83 N.H. 190, 139 A. 753 (1927) (after settlement with one of two defendants); Beard v. Henniker and Hillsborough, 69 N.H. 279, 39 A. 1016 (1897) (after the defendant sought to confess judgment on one alternative claim).

114 Hub Construction Company v. New England Breeders' Club, 74 N.H. 282, 67 A. 574 (1907); Community Oil Company v. Welch, 105 N.H. 320, 199 A.2d 107 (1964) (defendant was allowed to amend response to motion for summary judgment to show existence of a genuine issue of material fact).

115 *From Law to Equity*: Hanford v. Clancy, 87 N.H. 458, 183 A. 271 (1936); Milne v. Burlington Homes, Inc., 117 N.H. 813, 379 A.2d 198 (1977). *From Equity to Law*: Lambert v. Lambert, 96 N.H. 376, 77 A.2d 34 (1950) (from specific performance to replevin or trover); Davison v. Davison, 71 N.H. 180, 51 A. 905 (1901) (after the defendant demurred on the ground that plaintiff had an adequate remedy at law); Claremont v. Rand, 76 N.H. 116, 79 A. 689 (1911) (where there was no showing that equity provided a better remedy than law). *Adding Equity to Law*: Dondero v. Ferranti, 90 N.H. 554, 3 A. 831 (1939) (tort for embezzling funds and securities amended by bill in equity for an accounting). *From Trustee Process to Equity*: Lombard v. Maguire-Penniman Company, 78 N.H. 110, 97 A. 892 (1916). *From One Common Law Court to Another*: Perreault v. Hall, 94 N.H. 191, 49 A.2d 812 (1946) (changing "plea of the case" and "based upon contract" to "special assumpsit"); Brunel v. The Nashua Building and Loan Association, 95 N.H. 391, 64 A.2d 315 (1949) (from breach of contract for the sale of land to negligent performance of an undertaking to protect plaintiff's interest); Lambert v. Lambert, 96 N.H. 376, 77 A.2d 34 (1950) (plaintiff could change from specific performance of contract to other equitable relief); Beard v. Henniker and Hillsborough, 69 N.H. 279, 39 A. 1016 (1897) (plaintiff dropped one alternative request for relief when defendant sought to admit judgment on that request).

116 *Changing Plaintiff's Name*: Wheeler v. Contoocook Mills Corporation, 77 N.H. 551, 94 A. 265 (1915) (before trial); Remick v. J. Spaulding & Sons Co., Inc., 82 N.H. 182, 131 A. 608 (1926) (at trial). *Changing Defendant's Name*: Dupuis v. Smith Properties, Inc., 114 N.H. 625, 325 A.2d 781 (1974) (after the statute of limitations had run).

117 Edgewood Civic Club v. Blaisdell, 95 N.H. 244, 61 A.2d (1948) (adding 40 individual club members after the time for appeal had expired and defendant had objected to the club's standing to sue).

118 Gehlen v. Patterson, 83 N.H. 328, 141 A. 914 (1928).

added[119] or changed[120] allegations at trial, raised new claims[121] or defenses[122] that had been established by the evidence at trial, increased the ad damnum during trial[123] and after verdict,[124] and that even added a claim after a dismissal had been affirmed on appeal.[125]

---

119 Hall v. Wentworth's Location, 84 N.H. 236, 141 A. 136 (1930) (adding a claim of dangerous embankment to faulty culvert in highway damage case); Bacon v. Thompson, 87 N.H. 270, 177 A. 548 (1935) (second count added at trial).

120 Davidson v. Maine and New Hampshire Granite Corporation, 89 N.H. 535, 3 A.2d 106 (1938) (changing the date of injury).

121 Gosselin v. Lemay, 85 N.H. 13, 153 A. 716 (1931) (after trial on a broader theory than set forth in the pleadings, amendment to the declaration allowed "to avoid an unseemly record"); Mayhew v. New England Teamsters and Trucking Industry Pension Fund, 115 N.H. 581, 347 A.2d 610 (1975).

122 Lyman v. Brown, 73 N.H. 411, 62 A. 650 (1905) (to meet special pleading requirements for issue actually tried); McCrillis v. American Heel Company, 85 N.H. 165, 155 A. 410 (1931) (to meet proof that contract was within the statute of frauds); LePage v. St. Johnsbury Trucking Company, Inc., 97 N.H. 46, 80 A.2d 148 (1951) (to meet evidence at trial that injury was caused in self-defense).

123 Jackson v. Leu-Pierre, 112 N.H. 406, 296 A.2d 902 (1972) (from $13,500 to $40,000 on the second day of trial, where a demand of $25,000 had been made one year before trial, there was no claim that the new ad damnum exceeded the policy limits and the defendant did not ask for a continuance or allege to the trial court that he was prejudiced by the change). This is no longer necessary in personal actions. See RSA 508:4-c, which prohibits ad damnum in a "declaration or other affirmative pleading" in personal actions), and RSA 507-c:6, eliminating the requirement for ad damnum in actions for medical injury.

124 Derby v. Public Service Company of New Hampshire, 100 N.H. 53, 119 A.2d 335 (1955) (increasing from $10,000 to $11,000 to meet the jury's verdict where the defendant would have presented the same defense if the amendment had been made before trial); Simon v. Lambert, 115 N.H. 242, 340 A.2d 101 (1975) (increasing by the amount of the plaintiff's prior recovery against a co-defendant and allowing a setoff for the same amount where the increase did not exceed insurance coverage); Heath v. Joyce, 114 N.H. 620, 326 A.2d 260 (1974) (allowing an increase from $20,000 to $50,000 to meet the jury's verdict of $40,000 in spite of the defendant's claim that he would have taken the case more seriously if the amendment had been made before trial, where the original ad damnum already exceeded the insurance coverage by $10,000 and should have provided "sufficient incentive for self-protection").

125 Barry v. Bank of New Hampshire, 113 N.H. 158, 304 A.2d 879 (1973) (where the dismissal had been based on a holding that the Uniform Commerical Code applied and the plaintiff, appearing pro se, added a claim of violation of the Uniform Commercial Code); Morphy v. Morphy, 112 N.H. 507, 298 A.2d 580 (1972) (where petitioner could amend to seek renewal of her support order after the Supreme Court had held that the order had expired and that her husband had been improperly found in contempt for discontinuing payments). See also Phinney v. Levine, 117 N.H. 968, 381 A.2d 735 (1977). But see Tapley v. Tapley, 122 N.H. 727, 449 A.2d 1218 (1982) (where the Court announced that such amendments will only be allowed in the future "in exceptional instances." 122 N.H. at 731, 449 A.2d at 1220).

§ 7.35 —Amendments Denied

Despite the Court's preference for amendments, they were not granted in every case. As the Court said in *Lewis v. Hines*:[126] "While the rule that all amendments essential to the promotion of justice ought to be allowed has been applied to the fullest extent in this jurisdiction, it does not follow that every proposed amendment is to be allowed as a matter of course."[127] Motions to amend were denied when the amendment had no apparent purpose,[128] when they prejudiced the defendant by surprise,[129] and when it was beyond the ability of the Court to compensate the party with other relief.[130]

Amendments were also denied that sought: to force the plaintiff to change his description of the defendant;[131] to add a defendant after the statute of limitations had run;[132] to change the defense after most of the plaintiff's case had been presented;[133] and to increase the ad damnum after verdict beyond the amount of the insurance coverage.[134] Denials of motions to amend were set aside only if unsupported by the record.[135]

---

126 81 N.H. 24, 120 A. 728 (1923).

127 81 N.H. at 26, 120 A. at 730. See also Valliere v. Filfalt, 110 N.H. 331, 333–34, 266 A.2d 843, 845 (1970) ("Our practice relating to the allowance of such motions even after verdict is a liberal one . . . but it is not without some restrictions.").

128 See R.C. Hazelton Co. v. Southwick Constr. Co., 105 N.H. 25, 192 A.2d 610 (1963) (pleading defense that was not likely to bar recovery).

129 Steeves v. New England Tel. and Tel. Co., 92 N.H. 52, 24 A.2d 606 (1942) (plaintiff could not add allegation on the first day of trial that her accident was caused by a hump in the floor to her prior claim that it resulted from a highly polished surface).

130 Valliere v. Filfalt, 110 N.H. 331, 266 A.2d 843 (1970) (plaintiff sought to increase ad damnum after verdict beyond policy limits).

131 Bourget v. New England Telephone and Telegraph Co., 97 N.H. 193, 84 A.2d 830 (1951) (defendant sought to change its description in the pleadings from a corporation duly organized "under law" to one organized under the laws of New York, in order to assist its efforts to remove the case to the federal court).

132 Lewis v. Hines, 81 N.H. 24, 120 A. 728 (1923).

133 R.C. Hazelton v. Southwick Construction Company, 105 N.H. 25, 192 A.2d 610 (1963) (could not plead defense of breach of warranties in action for replevin of a bulldozer).

134 Valliere v. Filfalt, 110 N.H. 331, 266 A.2d 843 (1970) (the original ad damnum equalled the insurance coverage and the defendant had no reason to protect his interests against a higher claim).

135 LePage v. St. Johnsbury Trucking Company, Inc., 97 N.H. 46, 80 A.2d 148 (1951).

§ 7.36. Amendments in the Trial Court

Whether an amendment should be made is a question of fact for the trial judge.[136] Amendments may be made on motion of a party or by the court sua sponte and will be given retroactive effect when necessary.[137]

In deciding whether to permit an amendment, the court is guided by "what justice and convenience require,"[138] and in determining this issue, the court will balance the injustice that the moving party will suffer if the amendment is not allowed against the prejudice that his opponent will suffer if it is.[139] When the proposed amendment will do nothing more than correct an error of form upon which no party has relied to his detriment, the amendment should be ordered as a matter of course.[140] When the amendment has a substantive effect on the progress of the case, however, the court will scrutinize the amendment more closely.

Under New Hampshire's traditional liberal doctrine of amendment, the preference for amendments, in practice, shifted the burden of persuasion from the proponent of the motion to his adversary, and even required that the opponent of the motion carry the burden of showing that he would suffer an overriding prejudice which could not be corrected by other orders of the court if the amendment was allowed. This can no longer be said to be true.

§ 7.37. Restrictions in the Doctrine: *V.S.H. Realty* and *Merchants Manual*

The Court began to restrict significantly the use of amendments in New Hampshire practice with *V.S.H. Realty, Inc. v. City of Rochester*,[141] decided almost twenty years ago. In that case, the plaintiff, a developer, submitted to the Rochester Planning Board its plan to build a store on a plot of land in the city in February 1977. Four months later, the city amended its zoning ordinance to bar the development. Plaintiff then brought an action for declaratory judgment, seeking a determination that the zoning amendments

---

136 Community Oil v. Welch, 105 N.H. 320, 322–23, 199 A.2d 107, 109 (1964).

137 Morphy v. Morphy, 112 N.H. 507, 511, 298 A.2d 580, 582 (1972); Dupuis v. Smith Properties, Inc., 114 N.H. 625, 325 A.2d 781 (1974).

138 Brunel v. The Nashua Building and Loan Association, 95 N.H. 391, 393, 64 A.2d 315, 317 (1949).

139 Dupuis v. Smith Properties, Inc., 114 N.H. 625, 325 A.2d 781 (1974); Sanborn v. Boston and Me. R.R., 76 N.H. 65, 79 A. 642 (1911).

140 Prentiss v. New England Box Co., 75 N.H. 605, 75 A. 984 (1910) ("[W]hen an alleged defect can be cured by an amendment of the pleadings, the amendment is ordered without considering whether it is necessary.").

141 118 N.H. 778, 394 A.2d 317 (1978).

did not apply to its project. On November 16, 1977, the superior court made that declaration and found that the city had no valid reason not to issue a building permit for the store. Later that day, the plaintiff's attorney was advised by the city's building inspector that the city might take the position that the proposed site was located in a residential zone. The plaintiff immediately filed a motion to amend his prior petition to state the most recent occurrences and to ask for an order that a building permit be issued. On December 12, 1977, after a brief nonevidentiary hearing, the superior court granted the motion to amend and issued an injunction that, in effect, ordered the city to issue the building permit.

On appeal, however, the Court with Justice Brock writing, reversed and remanded, in part because the city had been given inadequate notice of the purpose of the December 12 meeting and had too little time to prepare to meet the new claim. But the Court went one step further, stating that the motion to amend should not have been granted, because it "was not intended merely to cure a technical defect in the pleadings."[142] The Court saw that the plaintiff, in the proposed amendments, was attempting to introduce a new and independent cause of action based on new facts and new issues, and that he was seeking broader relief than was originally requested. "The general rule allowing liberal amendment of pleadings," Justice Brock wrote, "applies only if the amendment does not change the cause of action or call for substantially different evidence."[143] The Court held that the plaintiff could not amend the petition.[144]

Justice Grimes, who took no part in the *V.S.H. Realty* decision, authored the following year the opinion for *MacLeod v. Chalet Susse International, Inc.*,[145] in which a unanimous Court upheld the decision of the trial court to allow defendant to amend his answer to state an alternative theory of defense four years after the case was commenced.[146] But just four days later, in *Merchants Mutual Ins. Co. v. Bean*,[147] Justice Brock, writing again for the Court, sustained the trial court's refusal to allow an amendment to a petition for declaratory judgment that sought a determination of whether a family was entitled to compensation under their own uninsured motorist coverage

---

142 118 N.H. at 781, 394 A.2d at 319.

143 *Id.*

144 *Id.*

145 119 N.H. 238, 401 A.2d 205 (1979).

146 119 N.H. at 244, 401 A.2d at 205. Justice Grimes wrote: "This State takes a liberal view toward amendment of pleadings."

147 119 N.H. 562, 406 A.2d 457 (1979).

for an auto accident in which their son, a pedestrian, was injured. The trial court had based its decision on the proponent's failure to raise the issue in the pleadings. The Court could have upheld the trial court's refusal to amend because of the possibility of prejudice to the opponent insurance company caused by the delay in bringing the amendment and because the proponent was still free to bring a second action. But, instead, the Court used the same language as it had in *V.S.H. Realty*, finding that the proponent had attempted to make "an amendment of substance, adding a new issue,"[148] and held that the amendment was not "necessary for the prevention of injustice."[149]

§ 7.38. The Modern Liberal Doctrine of Amendments

The Court has recently reiterated that New Hampshire's "modern rules of pleading incorporate a liberal doctrine of amendment, which was originated by Chief Justice Doe."[150] Though the practice in New Hampshire is still to allow amendments liberally, especially in comparison to other jurisdictions, the modern trend has been to limit significantly amendments to pleadings.

§ 7.39. —Amendments Allowed

Since *V.S.H. Realty* and *Merchants Mutual* were decided, the Court has allowed, on average, one amendment for every two that it has denied, a marked departure from past practice. Whereas the Court previously focused on justice to the proponent of the motion to determine whether to allow an amendment, the Court today appears to have shifted its focus to the prevention of injustice to the opponent of the motion to amend.

Plaintiff landowners in *Burrows v. City of Keene*[151] originally brought an action to review city denial of subdivision approval, and later amended their petition to include a constitutional claim that inclusion of their land in a conservation zone amounted to an inverse condemnation. The Court upheld the decision of the trial court allowing the amendment. Although the Court acknowledged that the constitutional claim was "a new and different issue,"[152] it noted that it was one that plaintiffs could have raised any time prior to the statute of limitations expiring, and that the defendant city had had sufficient time to prepare to meet it.

---

148 119 N.H. at 567, 406 A.2d at 460.

149 *Id.*

150 In re Proposed New Hampshire Rules of Civil Procedure, 139 N.H. 512, 516, 659 A.2d 420, 422 (1995).

151 121 N.H. 590, 432 A.2d 15 (1981).

152 121 N.H. at 595, 432 A.2d at 18.

In *Burley v. Hudson*,[153] the Court held that it was not error for the trial court to allow the plaintiff, a pedestrian who was hit by a vehicle operated and owned by the defendant driver, to amend his complaint for negligence in order to add a theory of negligent entrustment. The Court noted that the plaintiff had derived the information he used as a basis for the amendment from the defendant's answers to interrogatories and that any surprise resulting to the defendant had come from his own delay.

Plaintiff in *Carrols Equities Corp. v. Della Jacova*[154] was allowed to add an amendment for deficiency to a claim for recovery of mortgage payments four years after the suit had commenced. Defendant argued that, under the rule of *V.S.H. Realty*, the deficiency claim was different from that for recovery, and that it should not be allowed. The Court disagreed, holding that the two claims were part of one continuing cause of action, the defendant's failure to pay, and that because the amendment neither stated a new cause of action, called for substantially different evidence from the original claim, nor prejudiced the defendant, it could be added.

In the latest three cases in which amendments have been allowed, the Court has also overturned the decisions of the lower court. In *Iacomini v. Liberty Mutual*,[155] the Court held that the trial court abused its discretion in not allowing plaintiff, an auto mechanic who had performed work on a vehicle that was stolen and that was owned by defendant, to make a timely specification that his claim included unjust enrichment.

In *Lavoie v. Hollinracke*,[156] the Court overturned the trial court's refusal to allow the plaintiff to increase the ad damnum after the trial from $250,000 to $260,000 to meet the verdict, holding that the defendant had had a full and fair opportunity to litigate his liability regarding the damages issue and that the amount of the excess was not so large that the Court could assume that, with notice of the amendment before trial, the defendant would have retained separate counsel from that provided by his insurance company.[157]

---

153 122 N.H. 560, 448 A.2d 375 (1982).

154 126 N.H. 116, 489 A.2d 116 (1985).

155 127 N.H. 73, 497 A.2d 854 (1985).

156 127 N.H. 764, 513 A.2d 316 (1986).

157 But see Drop Anchor Realty v. Hartford Fire Insurance Co., 126 N.H. 674, 496 A.2d 399 (1985) (denial of amendment to increase ad damnum from $75,000 to $100,000 based on additional evidence presented at trial upheld as jury verdict was only for $14,000). The requirement for ad damnum in personal actions has been eliminated by RSA 508:4-c, and RSA 507-C:6 has eliminated the requirement for ad damnum in actions for medical injury. The declaration should no longer include a specific statement of amount, but should instead state that damages claimed are within the appropriate jurisdictional minimum and maximum.

And finally, in *National Marine Underwriters, Inc. v. McCormack*,[158] Justice Brock, who had written the opinions for *V.S.H. Realty* and *Merchants Mutual*, wrote again for the Court, holding that the trial court had abused its discretion in denying a motion to amend to substitute one plaintiff with another who had standing to sue. The Court found in this instance that the amendment did not introduce a new cause of action, that it did not call for substantially different evidence, that there was no surprise to the defendant, and that it was necessary to prevent injustice.

§ 7.40. —Amendments Denied

The Court in *Moore v. Aksten*[159] focused on injustice to the opponent of the motion in upholding the trial court's denial of the defendants' motion to amend to assert that his assault of plaintiff was justified. The Court noted that the defendant had waited until the day the jury was selected to file the motion and that the pleadings did not support the amendment.[160]

In *Kenneth E. Curran, Inc. v. Auclair Transportation*,[161] the Court upheld the trial court's refusal to permit the plaintiff, a transportation company, to amend its pleadings where the amendment, challenging extensions of a contract by the state to another transportation company, did not fall within the subject of the original claim which charged illegality of the state's acceptance of bids. The Court held that the amendment introduced an entirely new subject of litigation, therefore constituting a new cause of action as the term was used in *V.S.H. Realty*. Subsequently, in *Real Estate Planners v. Newmarket*,[162] the Court held that the trial court had discretion to deny the plaintiff's motion to amend his petition for declaratory judgment where the original petition challenged a zoning ordinance and the plaintiff sought by amendment to add a count for equitable relief which would have extended to persons who were not originally parties to the action.

---

158   138 N.H. 6, 634 A.2d 1008 (1993).

159   123 N.H. 220, 459 A.2d 266 (1983).

160   The Court in Clinical Labs v. Martina, 121 N.H. 989, 437 A.2d 285 (1981), had found that it was error for a trial court to award damages on a claim not presented by the pleadings and not otherwise referred to by either party. See also Numerica Savings Bank v. Mountain Lodge Inn, 134 N.H. 505, 596 A.2d 131 (1991) (plaintiff not allowed to amend to include entitlement as third party beneficiary where amendment was unsupported by facts).

161   128 N.H. 743, 519 A.2d 280 (1986).

162   134 N.H. 696, 597 A.2d 78 (1991).

In *Laroche v. Doe*,[163] the plaintiff's son had been killed by a motorcyclist who had obtained alcoholic beverages at a state liquor store. The plaintiff had originally filed his action against "Jane Doe," an unidentified defendant who was said by plaintiff to be one of four state liquor store employees who could have sold the alcohol. The plaintiff later moved to amend his complaint to include the names of the four employees and to plead the res ipsa doctrine. The trial court did not allow the amendment, and the Court affirmed, holding that the amendment would have set forth a new cause of action and would have required the trial court to hear substantially new evidence on new issues.

In *Belcher v. Paine*,[164] day care operators whose indictments for sexual assault had been nol prossed, sought to amend their writ against the prosecutor for negligence and malicious prosecution in order to clarify that the damages resulted from the prosecutor's investigation, the only action for which he did not have absolute immunity. The Court upheld the trial court's denial of the motion to amend, holding that prosecutorial immunity is "absolute when functionally related to the initiation of criminal process or to the prosecution of criminal charges,"[165] and that any injury even as alleged in the proposed amendment was related directly to initiation of the criminal proceeding.

In *Gould v. George Brox*,[166] the Court held that it was within the discretion of the trial court to deny a motion to amend where the amendment could not have caused defects in the writ and only incorporated facts of the original complaint and alleged conclusions of law.[167]

---

[163] 134 N.H. 562, 594 A.2d 1297 (1991).

[164] 136 N.H. 137, 612 A.2d 1318 (1992).

[165] 136 N.H. at 146, 612 A.2d at 1325.

[166] 137 N.H. 85, 623 A.2d 1325 (1993).

[167] See also Rahaim v. Psaros, 122 N.H. 613, 448 A.2d 401 (1982) (statute pleaded did not apply to facts of case); Kennedy v. Titcomb, 131 N.H. 399, 553 A.2d 1322 (1989) (denial of motion to amend writ upheld where amendments stated no cognizable cause of action); Attorney General v. Morgan, 132 N.H. 406, 565 A.2d 1072 (1989) (denial of defendant's motion to amend answer upheld where defendant made no challenge to the ruling of the trial court that the original answer presented no issues of fact or law requiring adjudication). Several months later in ERG v. Barnes, 137 N.H. 186, 189, 624 A.2d 555, 557–58 (1993), the Court stated: "Once leave to amend has been given, a second action will be precluded where the plaintiff fails to amend or the amendment fails to cure the deficiency."

And in 1995, in *Arsenault v. Scanlon*,[168] the Court held that it was not error for the trial court to have refused to allow plaintiffs to amend their writ where the motion to amend was not filed until after the order of dismissal had become final. The Court ruled that the trial court's power to allow the amendment to the writ had ceased when judgment was entered on the dismissal.

---

[168] 139 N.H. 592, 660 A.2d 1110 (1995).

CHAPTER 8.   MOTIONS GENERALLY

§ 8.01. Definition

A motion is a formal request, made while a case is pending, that a court or administrative agency take a specific action at a particular stage of the proceedings.[1]

Library References

CJS Motions and Orders § 1
CJS Pleading §§ 421, 422

§ 8.02. When Motions May Be Made

Motions can be made at any time after an action has been commenced. As a general rule, a motion should be filed as soon as possible after the moving party is aware that he has grounds for making it. Late motions are more frequently decided by inquiring whether the moving party will be prejudiced by *not* receiving the requested relief than by determining whether he had a right to relief in the first place. Late motions should always set forth a reason for the moving party's delay in seeking relief.

Library References

CJS Motions and Orders § 8
CJS Pleading § 497

---

1 See Dist. and Mun. Ct. R. 1.8.

§ 8.03. The Nature and Purpose of Motions

Most motions are interlocutory in nature,[2] and all ask the court to exercise its discretion.[3] Motions that have been decided once may be reconsidered at any time before the final judgment.[4]

Motions serve many of the purposes of other pleadings. They record a party's allegations and position, require his opponent to respond, separate the many factual and legal issues in a case and refine them toward judgment, and they record a party's position and objections for appellate review.[5]

Library References

CJS Motions and Orders § 3

§ 8.04. Form of Motions

Generally all motions, except those made during trial or hearing, must be made in writing.[6] Motions or requests relating to the motion made in letter form will not be accepted by the clerk.[7]

---

2 Germain v. Germain, 137 N.H. 82, 623 A.2d 760 (1993) (order which does not conclude proceedings before the court is interlocutory).

3 Even motions that seek the court's determination of an issue of law involve an exercise of discretion in determining when they shall be heard and decided. Compare Chase v. Mary Hitchcock Memorial Hosp., 140 N.H. 509, 668 A.2d 80 (1995) (review by trial court of prior interlocutory rulings takes place at discretion of trial judge) with Nashua School District v. State, 140 N.H. 457, 667 A.2d 1036 (1995) (determination of a motion is one of law). The failure of the court to rule on a motion may be an abuse of discretion. Granite State Minerals, Inc. v. City of Portsmouth, 134 N.H. 408, 593 A.2d 1142 (1991) (stating that trial court's denial of motion for summary judgment will not be overturned unless it is "unsupported by the evidence or is erroneous as a matter of law"); Real Estate Planners, Inc. v. Town of Newmarket, 134 N.H. 696, 597 A.2d 78 (1991) (noting that while motions to amend are liberally allowed, trial court has discretion to deny them, and that such denials will be overturned only for abuse of discretion); LaRoche v. Doe, 134 N.H. 562, 594 A.2d 1297 (1991) ("[t]he trial court has discretion to dismiss a case upon its own motion."); Richelson v. Richelson, 130 N.H. 137, 536 A.2d 176 (1987).

4 N.E. Redlon Co. v. Franklin Square Corp., 91 N.H. 502, 505, 23 A.2d 370, 373 (1941) ("By the weight of common-law authority and upon the better reasoning, the Superior Court's discretionary powers are continuous. They may be exercised, and prior exercise may be corrected, as sound discretion may require, at any time prior to final judgment.").

5 An issue not raised by motion in the trial court will rarely be considered on review; filing the motion without also noting an exception to its denial will not preserve the issue for appellate review. See Rockingham Bank v. Claggett, 29 N.H. 292 (1854).

6 See Dist. and Mun. Ct. R. 1.8.

7 Super. Ct. R. 4.

There are essentially two forms of motions, one supported by the previous record in the case, and the other based on new material introduced by affidavit[8] or stipulation when the motion is filed.

An oral motion, made in the presence of the court, will always be based on the prior record in the case, and the moving party will specifically refer to the parts of that record which support his motion at the time he makes it. A written motion may or may not be based on the prior record; however, it must specifically refer to the parts of the record or new material submitted with it supporting the conclusions on which it is based and on which relief is requested.

Motions made in writing begin, like all pleadings, with the caption of the case. Every motion should bear a title which indicates both its character as a motion and the nature of the action it requests the court to take. When a motion is specifically authorized by a rule of court, regulation, or statute, the preamble to the motion should invoke the authority of that rule, regulation, or statute. All written motions must be submitted on 8½" x 11" paper.[9]

The substantive portion of a motion consists of a statement of the relief requested, allegation of facts apparent in the record or shown by supporting affidavit that support the request, and a recitation of the grounds upon which the court is justified in granting that relief.[10] The statement of relief sought should be so precise that it is possible for the court to draw its order or decree directly from the wording of the motion.[11] When it is impossible to state the relief requested succinctly, a draft order should be attached to the motion as an appendix, and the motion should request that the court enter the order so drafted.

A recitation of the grounds upon which a motion is based should be equally concise and exact. When the motion is specifically authorized by a rule of court, regulation, or statute, the statement of grounds should satisfy all material elements of that rule, regulation, or statute. The motion should

---

8 Manchenton v. Auto Leasing Corp., 135 N.H. 298, 301, 605 A.2d 208, 211 (1992) (defined affidavit as "a written statement, under oath, sworn to or affirmed by the person making it before some person who has authority to administer oath or affirmation").

9 Super. Ct. R. 4.

10 See Dist. and Mun. Ct. R. 1.8. For purposes of clarity, motions may list elements of requested relief in paragraphs designed by Arabic numerals and grounds for relief in paragraphs labeled with capital letters.

11 The practice of simply entering the notation "motion granted" on the docket is founded on this principle and cannot be followed when a motion is so unartfully or imprecisely drafted as to leave the parties in doubt as to the effect of such an order.

fully state all grounds relied upon.[12] Where the facts upon which a motion is based are not admitted or are not apparent from the record, they must be set forth by affidavits filed with the motion.[13]

Every motion filed in superior court,[14] "except . . . dispositive motions, motions for contempt or sanctions or comparable motions where it can be reasonably assumed that the [moving] party or [his] counsel will be unable to obtain concurrence,"[15] must also contain a certification that a "good faith attempt"[16] has been made to obtain the consent of the other parties[17] to the motion.[18]

A motion is always concluded with a prayer for "such other relief as may be just," a closing "Respectfully submitted," the name of the party for whom it is filed, and the name and address of the party or attorney who has prepared the motion. All motions should bear the date of their filing, must contain a

---

12 See Dist. and Mun. Ct. R. 1.8. The grounds for a motion are not always the same thing as the factual circumstances giving rise to its filing. A recitation of grounds for a motion is a list of conclusions to which the moving party has arrived, based upon his research into either the facts or the law, that justifies the grant of relief. In some cases, the conclusions may follow so closely upon the facts as to be indistinguishable from them; in others, conclusions may require a consideration of several facts.

13 Super. Ct. R. 57; Dist. and Mun. Ct. R. 1.8; Prob. Ct. R. 9; Ossipee Auto Parts v. Ossipee Planning Bd., 134 N.H. 401, 403, 593 A.2d 241, 242 (1991) (citing Super. Ct. R. 57) ("The trial court will not consider any facts relied on in a motion or objection unless they are verified by an accompanying affidavit or are apparent from the record."). Affidavits may, however, be submitted as late as the hearing. Manchenton v. Auto Leasing Corp., 135 N.H. 298, 605 A.2d 208 (1992) (because court held that deposition satisfied affidavit requirement of summary judgment motion, presumably deposition could support affidavit requirement of other motions as well); Goodwin v. Blanchard, 73 N.H. 550, 64 A. 22 (1906).

14 The requirement to attempt to obtain concurrence in the relief sought by a motion does not yet apply to motions filed in the district, municipal, or probate courts or the Supreme Court, but the principal is a good one and there is no reason why a party should not make the attempt and report the result in any motion he files in court.

15 Super. Ct. R. 57-A.

16 *Id.* A "good faith attempt" will, in many cases, require more than a mere telephonic request for concurrence. It may require negotiations and concessions on both sides to further the rule's purpose of advancement of the case with a minimal use of court time.

17 Super. Ct. R. 57-A. The rule does not limit the obligation to obtain concurrence only to opposing parties in the case, although it may be a fair inference that it only intends to refer to obtaining the consent of parties who might be expected to oppose the motion. The best approach is to seek the concurrence of all other parties.

18 Super. Ct. R. 57-A. Note, also, that a party need not choose between consenting to the motion or objecting. He may also neither consent nor object, and this position may frequently be an appropriate means of preserving a position without wasting the court's time on a contested hearing or the consideration of merely formal objections.

certification that copies have been simultaneously furnished to all other counsel or parties,[19] and must be submitted to the clerk.[20]

Library References

CJS Motions and Orders §§ 10, 22 et seq.

§ 8.05. Rejection by the Clerk

A motion that is defective in form may be rejected by the clerk. The filing party may then either recast the motion in a form acceptable to the clerk or object to the rejection and file a second motion seeking a determination of the motion's sufficiency by the court.[21]

§ 8.06. Responses to Motions—Objections

Unless a party files an objection and requests a hearing within ten days of the filing of a motion, his right to a hearing will be waived.[22] It is no longer possible to object to a motion and to request a hearing by merely sending a letter to the clerk of court. An objection to a motion must now be set forth in a pleading of the same name which identifies the motion or part thereof objected to, and which states the grounds for the objection.[23] The same principles apply to a statement of the grounds and factual basis for an objection as apply to the statement of the grounds for a motion.[24] Objections follow the same form of conclusion as motions, and they must carry a certification that copies have been provided to other parties or counsel.[25]

---

19   Super. Ct. R. 21; Prob. Ct. R. 3 and 31.

20   Super. Ct. R. 6; Prob. Ct. R. 3.

21   Super. Ct. R. 5; Prob. Ct. R. 3.

22   Super. Ct. R. 58; Dist. and Mun. Ct. R. 3.11(B); Prob. Ct. R. 9. By failing to object the opponent merely waives his right to a hearing; the failure to object does not automatically result in the motion being granted. McGann v. Steenstra, 130 N.H. 411, 412, 543 A.2d 406, 406–07 (1988) ("Rule 58 does not provide that a motion to which no objection is filed within ten days may be ministerially granted. . . . We construe the language in Rule 58 as requiring that a trial judge decide whether or not to grant the motion only after the judge has considered the law and the pleadings before the court."). The court then has the choice of granting the motion without holding a hearing at which the plaintiff may be permitted to present his case for the relief requested by the motion. Chabot v. Chabot, 126 N.H. 793, 497 A.2d 851 (1985). The court does not, however, have the choice of ignoring the motion completely. See Richelson v. Richelson, 130 N.H. 137, 536 A.2d 176 (1987).

23   Super. Ct. R. 58; Prob. Ct. R. 9; Ross v. Eichman, 130 N.H. 556, 543 A.2d 427 (1988) (objecting party has obligation to make his theory clear to court).

24   Super. Ct. R. 57 and 58; Prob. Ct. R. 9.

25   Super. Ct. R. 21; Prob. Ct. R. 3.

Of course, if a party has no objection to a motion, he should inform the clerk by letter immediately upon receipt of the motion.

References

CJS Motions and Orders §§ 33–35

§ 8.07. Hearings on Motions

It is not always necessary or advisable to request a hearing on a motion.[26] If the moving party wants a hearing, he should so state in his motion. If the objecting party desires a hearing, he must request it in his objection, and he must file his objection within ten days after the motion was filed.[27] The court may grant a motion without a hearing, if there is no objection, but the court may not deny a motion without a hearing[28] and usually will not grant a motion without a hearing if the opponent objects in a timely fashion. Nevertheless, the motion, objection, and supporting affidavits and memoranda should be complete enough to allow the court to decide the matter without a hearing.[29] If the court decides to hold a hearing on a motion, the clerk will mail a notice to each party informing them of the time and place of the hearing and the issues to be heard.[30]

Each court carries motions on a list separate from other issues, and calls that list separately on the first day of each term or new session of court. As the court usually hears a number of motions in a short period of time, parties

---

26 See Chemical Bank v. Rinden Professional Ass'n, 126 N.H. 688, 498 A.2d 708 (1985) (attorney fees assessed for requesting unnecessary hearing).

27 Super. Ct. R. 58; Prob. Ct. R. 9. Although the Rules do not set forth a time limit for filing objections to a motion, the general practice is to assume that a party has no objection to a motion if he has not filed an objection within the 10 days allowed for requesting a hearing.

28 See also Richelson v. Richelson, 130 N.H. 137, 536 A.2d 176 (1987) (failure to rule on motion may be abuse of discretion); Chabot v. Chabot, 126 N.H. 793, 497 A.2d 851 (1985); State v. Sefton, 125 N.H. 533, 537, 485 A.2d 284, 286 (1984) (construing *Yancy* to apply only when denial "is a final response on the merits," but not as prohibiting court from reversing earlier decision to grant motion and deferring final decision on motion until trial); Yancy v. Yancy, 119 N.H. 197, 399 A.2d 975 (1979).

29 Super. Ct. R. 58. Failure to request a hearing in the objection is a waiver of any right to a hearing and permits the court to decide the motion on the basis of the pleadings.

30 Prob. Ct. R. 9. "Notices furnished by our courts to counsel and parties should make clear what is to be heard or considered." V.S.H. Realty, Inc. v. City of Rochester, 118 N.H. 778, 781, 394 A.2d 317, 319 (1978). See also Merrill v. City of Manchester, 124 N.H. 8, 466 A.2d 923 (1983); Reardon v. Lemoyne, 122 N.H. 1042, 454 A.2d 428 (1982); Carrols Equity Corporation v. Jacova, 126 N.H. 116, 489 A.2d 116, (1985) (amended pleading that did not state a new cause of action and that did not call for substantially different evidence than the original claim was properly allowed).

should limit their oral presentation and take only the time necessary to highlight and flesh out their pleadings.

Hearings may be held in the courtroom but often they are convened in the judge's chambers where the attorneys and judge can discuss the issues in a less formal atmosphere.

A record may be made of a motion hearing, whether it is held in the courtroom or in chambers. In the usual case, however, no record is made because the parties are obligated to state fully the grounds for their motion and objection in written form, and the court has wide discretion in deciding whether to grant or to deny the relief sought.

§ 8.08. Conduct of Hearings

"The conduct of hearings on motions," wrote Justice Bingham in 1906, "is largely within the judicial discretion of the trial judge."[31] A motion hearing is normally not an evidentiary hearing and, in most cases, neither witnesses nor documentary evidence is presented.[32] However, a party may offer, and should always be prepared to produce, evidence at the hearing if required. The court may call for such evidence on its own motion.[33]

Procedure at motions hearings can follow any suitable form and, unless a party objects at the time, any irregularity of the procedure will be waived and provide no basis for appellate review.[34] Although motions based on facts

---

31 Goodwin v. Blanchard, 73 N.H. 550, 64 A. 22 (1906).

32 *Id.* at 551, 64 A. at 23 ("He may require a motion involving an issue of fact to be heard upon affidavits only, and his ruling will not be set aside unless it is clear that in the particular case he abused his discretion."). The Court concluded that "the practice . . . of only receiving affidavits, should not be departed from unless it be in exceptional cases and to avoid a miscarriage of justice." *Id.*

33 *Id.* ("[The judge] may require the moving party to present his whole case at once, and decline to receive affidavits or other proof in rebuttal of counter-affidavits . . . . He may cause persons who have made ex parte affidavits in support of a motion to be brought before him and examined orally with respect to statements made in their affidavits, and how they came to give them, for the purposes of testing their knowledge and credibility . . . . But it is not within his power to require persons who have made ex parte affidavits, either in support of or in opposition to a motion, to give additional affidavits."). See also Farris v. Daigle, 139 N.H. 453, 656 A.2d 825 (1995) (whether to receive further evidence on motion for reconsideration rests in sound discretion of the trial court).

34 Chasan v. Village Dist. of Eastman, 128 N.H. 807, 523 A.2d 16 (1986); Sanborn v. Johnson, 100 N.H. 428, 129 A.2d 194 (1957); Poisson v. Manchester, 101 N.H. 72, 133 A.2d 533 (1957); Windele v. Interstate Passenger Serv., Inc., 99 N.H. 449, 114 A.2d 670 (1955); Rosenblum v. Judson Engineering Corp., 99 N.H. 267, 109 A.2d 558 (1954); Saykaly v. Manchester, 97 N.H. 4, 79 A.2d 625 (1951) (noting that it is not uncommon to have no request for findings of fact and no records of fact or statements

are required to be supported by affidavit,[35] the court may hear a motion which is not so verified,[36] or may decide the motion by reference to documents submitted with the pleadings.[37] If the parties do not object to the proceedings, the court may even decide motions without affidavits, testimony or documentary evidence and in reliance solely on the statements of counsel.[38]

---

of counsel at hearing on motions); Kusky v. Laderbush, 96 N.H. 286, 74 A.2d 546 (1950); Morrill v. Amoskeag Savings Bank, 90 N.H. 358, 359 9 A.2d 519, 522 (1939) ("It has for many years been the rule in this state that, in the absence of a statute, the test of the validity of a form of procedure is not the date of invention . . . but whether or not it is what justice and convenience require."); Perreault v. Allen Oil Company, 87 N.H. 306, 179 A. 365 (1935); Vidal v. Errol, 86 N.H. 585, 172 A. 437 (1934); Carpenter v. Carpenter, 78 N.H. 440, 101 A. 628 (1917).

35 Super. Ct. R. 57; Prob. Ct. R. 9; Manchenton v. Auto Leasing Corp., 135 N.H. 298 (1992) (because Court held that deposition was sufficient to fulfill affidavit requirement of summary judgment motion, presumably Court may find depositions to be sufficient for other motions as well).

36 See Muder v. Bentley, 109 N.H. 71, 242 A.2d 396 (1968); Theriault v. Theriault, 104 N.H. 326, 184 A.2d 459 (1962).

37 Chasan v. Village District of Eastman, 128 N.H. 807, 523 A.2d 16 (1986).

38 Theriault v. Theriault, 104 N.H. 326, 184 A.2d 459 (1962). See also Town of Gilmanton v. Champagne, 116 N.H. 507, 509, 363 A.2d 411, 412 (1976) ("The practice of submitting motions on the statements of counsel is well established in this state."); Salmonsen v. Rindge, 113 N.H. 46, 299 A.2d 926 (1973). The court can even rely on the disputed statements of a party's counsel "if the parties [have elected] to rest upon such method of proof." Vidal v. Errol, 86 N.H. 585, 586, 172 A. 437 (1934); Manchenton v. Auto Leasing Corp., 135 N.H. 298, 605 A.2d 208 (1992); Topjian Plumbing and Heating, Inc. v. Bruce Topjian, Inc., 129 N.H. 481, 529 A.2d 391 (1987) (holding that trial court did not err in discharging prejudgment attachment after offer of proof hearing in which defendants' counsel merely presented statements and arguments, and not testimony or affidavits, since plaintiff's counsel made no objection to evidence proffered by defendants' counsel or to proceedings themselves); Russell v. Philip D. Moran, Inc., 122 N.H. 708, 449 A.2d 1208 (1982) (reversing trial court's decision to dismiss all actions, where decision had been based, in part, on representations by defendant's attorney at motion hearing); Town of Bedford v. Brooks, 121 N.H. 262, 428 A.2d 897 (1981) (holding that trial court cannot decide motion solely on basis of statements of counsel if one side objects and requests opportunity to present evidence); Johnson v. Nash, 131 N.H. 731, 559 A.2d 842 (1989) (citing Town of Bedford v. Brooks, 121 N.H. 262, 265, 428 A.2d 897, 899–900 (1981); Lortie v. Bois, 119 N.H. 72, 398 A.2d 540 (1979) (where court relied on representations of plaintiff's counsel submitted in affidavit to counter motion for summary judgment where representation concerned defendant's deposition and other pre-trial discovery.); Cushing v. Thomson, 118 N.H. 292, 386 A.2d 805 (1978); Paju v. Ricker, 110 N.H. 310, 266 A.2d 836 (1970); Stiles v. Dube, 106 N.H. 339, 211 A.2d 402 (1965); Fowler v. Taylor, 99 N.H. 64, 104 A.2d 746 (1954) (procedure where court based its findings on statements of counsel deemed "entirely valid"); NH Rules of Professional Conduct, Rule 3.3 (lawyer has obligation of candor to court).

§ 8.09. Offers of Proof

New Hampshire has a tradition of reliance on the truthfulness of an attorney's representations in open court. They are regarded as being at all times under oath.[39] From the earliest days, New Hampshire courts have conducted motion hearings based solely on the representations of the attorneys appearing in the case. These representations are referred to loosely as "offers of proof," and are regarded as being so reliable that a court may accept such offers in lieu of both testimony and documentary evidence. The court may even decide a motion based solely on such offers.[40]

§ 8.10. Memoranda of Law

If difficult issues of law are raised by a motion, the court will sometimes ask for memoranda to aid it in deciding such issues. The court may either ask both parties to submit memoranda by a certain date, or may require one party to file first and to allow his opponent a certain number of days to respond. A party is always free to submit a memorandum of law with his motion or objection, during or after the hearing but before a decision has been announced if it will aid the court in deciding the issues involved.

The court will frequently take the case under advisement at the conclusion of the hearing and will announce its decision at a later date. Written opinions are not required but may be issued by the court, particularly in deciding motions which dispose of the case. In the case of other motions, the clerk usually just informs each party or his counsel in writing that the court has granted or denied the motion.

§ 8.11. Motions for Reconsideration

Motions, although decided, may be reconsidered prior to final judgment.[41] When the court has decided a motion against a party without a hearing, it may grant him a hearing on a Motion for Reconsideration which raises a new matter, or an issue not previously perceived.[42] Otherwise, any party in

---

39 See N.H. Rules of Professional Conduct, Rule 3.3 (obligation of candor to court).

40 *Id.*

41 N.E. Redlon Co. v. Franklin Square Corp., 91 N.H. 502, 23 A.2d 370 (1941); State v. Thomson, 110 N.H. 190, 263 A.2d 675 (1970); Town of Nottingham v. Bonser, 131 N.H. 120, 135, 552 A.2d 58, 67 (1988) ("The superior court's consideration of rehearing motions is not mandated, but is discretionary with the court.").

42 Cagan's, Inc. v. New Hampshire Dep. of Revenue Admin., 128 N.H. 180, 512 A.2d 411 (1986) (denial of Motion for Reconsideration was error where Motion raised issue of surprise and disclosed new matter that was relevant but that was not submitted prior to decision complained of).

the superior court may file a Motion for Reconsideration "within 10 days of the date of the Clerk's written notice of decision."[43] The Motion must "state, with particular clarity, points of law or fact that the court has overlooked or misapprehended."[44] A supporting memorandum of law may not be filed, but the Motion itself must "contain such argument in support of the motion as the movant desires to present."[45] The Motion, with supporting argument, may not be longer than ten pages.[46] The filing of a Motion for Reconsideration does not stay any order of the court unless the court has, upon specific written request, ordered such a stay.[47] No response or objection to a Motion for Reconsideration need be filed unless the court requests it by special notice from the clerk.[48] If a response or objection is submitted, it must be filed within ten days of a party's receipt of a copy of the Motion.[49] No party is entitled to a hearing on the Motion, but the court may hold one if requested, or may do so on its own motion.[50] The court will not permit a party to renew a Motion for Reconsideration once it has been decided without a change of circumstances,[51] or an excuse for failing to present the facts at an earlier date.[52]

Library References

CJS Motions and Orders §§ 37(1)–(6), 38–40, 44 et seq.
Prejudicial effect of judge's disclosure to jury of motions or proceedings in chambers in civil case. 77 ALR2d 1253.

---

43 Super. Ct. R. 59-A(1).

44 *Id.*

45 *Id.*

46 *Id.*

47 Super. Ct. R. 59-A(4).

48 Super. Ct. R. 59-A(2).

49 *Id.*

50 Super. Ct. R. 59-A(1). If the court denies a request for reconsideration, the court is required to make the basis for denial of Motion for Reconsideration clear. Palazzi Corp. v. Stickney, 136 N.H. 290, 619 A.2d 1001 (1992).

51 N.E. Redlon Co. v. Franklin Square Corp., 91 N.H. 502, 23 A.2d 370 (1941); Simonds v. Hayden and Lucas, 64 N.H. 152, 5 A. 717 (1886).

52 N.E. Redlon Co. v. Franklin Square Corp., 91 N.H. 502, 23 A.2d 370 (1941); Town of Gilmanton v. Champagne, 116 N.H. 507, 363 A.2d 411 (1976). Notice that Super. Ct. R. 59 and Prob. Ct. R. 9 permit the court to assess costs and attorney fees against any party "whose frivolous or unreasonable conduct makes necessary the filing of or hearing on any motion." But see Contra Chemical Bank v. Rinden Professional Ass'n, 126 N.H. 688, 498 A.2d 708 (1985) (attorney fees assessed for requesting unnecessary hearing); Perley v. Roberts, 92 N.H. 135, 26 A.2d 365 (1942) (holding that costs may not be taxed as penalty simply for exercising procedural rights).

Forms

Motion—Court Form (Superior Court), see Appendix.
Motion—Generally, see Appendix.
Motion for Summary Judgment (Superior Court), see Appendix.
Motion for Weekly Payments, see Appendix.

§ 8.12. Frivolous Motions or Responses

If any person files a motion for the purpose of delay[53] or harassment or without a good faith and reasonable purpose, or requests a hearing on his motion when the matter has either already been disposed of or can more easily be disposed of at trial,[54] the court may award costs and attorney fees to the innocent party.[55] Similarly, the court may award costs and attorney fees if a party's actions require an appeal for the court's assistance in a situation where the reasonable or accepted practice is clear and the party has no justification for departing from it. The court may also require the offending party's counsel to pay costs and attorney fees personally.

Library References

CJS Motions and Orders § 37(5)

---

53 See N.H. Rules of Professional Conduct, Rule 3.2 ("A lawyer shall make reasonable efforts to expedite litigation consistent with the interests of the client.").

54 Chemical Bank v. Rinden Professional Ass'n, 126 N.H. 688, 498 A.2d 708 (1985).

55 Super. Ct. R. 59; Prob. Ct. R. 9. See also N.H. Rules of Professional Conduct, Rule 3.1 ("A lawyer shall not bring or defend a proceeding, or assert or controvert an issue therein, unless there is a basis for doing so that is not frivolous."); Rule 3.4(d) (unprofessional conduct to "fail to make reasonably diligent effort to comply with a legally proper discovery request by an opposing party").

CHAPTER 9.   RESPONSIVE PLEADINGS

A. ANSWER

A. Answer

§ 9.01. Definition

An answer is a responsive pleading in which the defendant replies in substance to the plaintiff's allegations of fact. It narrows the controversy at an early stage by establishing the issues that are in dispute, and limits discovery of the defendant's case.

Library References

CJS Pleading § 99

§ 9.02. Law v. Equity

Under New Hampshire practice, an answer is not filed in response to a writ.[1] If a defendant disputes some or all of the facts on which the plaintiff's action is based, he need only file a general appearance to put them in issue.[2] A general appearance, without more, is regarded as a denial of every well-pleaded fact which the plaintiff must establish in order to prevail. If the defendant has an affirmative defense, he may file a brief statement setting it out. If he wishes to take advantage of some matter in bar of the maintenance of the action or of a procedural or jurisdictional defect in the case, he must file a Motion to Dismiss. And when he wishes to assert a claim against the plaintiff, he may file a counterclaim.[3]

In equity and in other proceedings not begun by writ, where the defendant does not plan to challenge jurisdiction or the sufficiency of the pleadings by a Motion to Dismiss, he must file an answer.[4] The Supreme Court of New Hampshire has rejected the argument that a plaintiff can transform a suit from an action at law into an action in equity merely by filing a bill of particulars, thus forcing the defendant to file an answer.[5]

§ 9.03. Requirements of the Answer—Form

An answer is individually typed, bears the caption of the case, and is entitled "Answer of X."[6] Each separately numbered paragraph in the plaintiff's petition, bill, libel, or other pleading must be responded to in a correspondingly numbered paragraph in the answer. If the defendant wishes to set forth affirmative defenses, allegations of mitigating facts, or a counterclaim, he should do so in separately lettered paragraphs after responding to the plaintiff's allegations of fact.

The answer may, but need not, conclude with a prayer for relief. Typically, this prayer will ask the court to dismiss the plaintiff's petition, bill, libel, or

---

1 See Blaisdell v. Raab, 132 N.H. 711, 715, 571 A.2d 261, 264 (1990).

2 *Id.*

3 The plaintiff files an answer to the counterclaim in the form of a replication. See Super. Ct. R. 137.

4 Super. Ct. R. 133; Brady v. Mullen, 139 N.H. 67, 69, 649 A.2d 47 (1994); Blaisdell v. Rabb, 132 N.H. 711, 715, 571 A.2d 261 (1990); Weeks v. Weeks, 124 N.H. 252, 254–55, 469 A.2d 1313 (1983) (appearance without answer admits evidentiary facts but is sufficient to contest issues of irremedial breakdown of marriage and property division); Bernier v. Bernier, 125 N.H. 517, 519, 484 A.2d 1088 (1984) (in a divorce action, general appearance, without further pleading, entitles the defendant to contest only the grounds for divorce and the division of property).

5 See Blaisdell v. Raab, 132 N.H. 711, 716, 571 A.2d 261 (1990).

6 Super. Ct. R. 132.

other pleading with prejudice and to grant the defendant specific relief plus "such other and further relief as may be just and proper." The answer must conclude like a motion and contain a certification that a copy has been forwarded to the plaintiff or to his attorney,[7] but the answer need not be signed and sworn to by the defendant personally in lieu thereof.

Forms

Answer—Equity Proceeding (Superior Court), see Appendix.

§ 9.04. —Substance

The defendant is required to answer the allegations of fact in the plaintiff's petition, bill, libel, or other pleading "fully and specifically."[8] Rule 133 requires that the defendant not answer "evasively" but instead, "answer . . . every material allegation . . . and set out his defense to each claim."[9] This rule imposes on the defendant an obligation of good faith, candor, and forthrightness in responding to the plaintiff's claims.

The defendant, however, is not required to go beyond the facts which are well-pleaded in the plaintiff's petition, bill, libel, or other pleading. He need respond only to the specific facts as they are alleged. If any allegation is ambiguous, he need not attempt to construe it but may state that it cannot be understood and he may decline to respond until it is clarified by the plaintiff in an amendment. If the plaintiff has made an allegation in a scandalous form, the defendant may refuse to respond. Statements of extraneous matter that are unrelated to the plaintiff's claim, conclusions, or legal positions also require no response other than for the defendant to note that they are of that character and that he therefore declines to answer. Allegations of fact that inquire into privileged matters need not be answered in substance, but the privilege must be claimed.

With regard to the plaintiff's substantive allegations, the defendant may make one of the following four responses:

(a) *A Substantive Answer.* The defendant may state that he either admits or denies each and every allegation in a paragraph of the petition, bill, libel, or other pleading. Alternatively, he may state that he admits some parts and denies others.

---

7 Super. Ct. R. 136.

8 Super. Ct. R. 133; Bernier v. Bernier, 125 N.H. 517, 484 A.2d 1088 (1984); Weeks v. Weeks, 124 N.H. 252, 469 A.2d 1313 (1983).

9 Super. Ct. R. 133.

(b) *Lack of Knowledge.* The defendant may state that he has insufficient knowledge on which to base a conclusion as to the truth or falsity of the matter alleged. Such a response is treated as a denial and puts the plaintiff to his proof.[10]

(c) *Refusal To Admit or Deny.* It is customary for a defendant to state that he neither admits nor denies some allegations in a petition, bill, libel, or other pleading and puts the plaintiff to his proof. The practice is an adoption into equity of the plea of the general issue which has been allowed in law actions for more than 160 years. Although it has the authority of long custom, the practice runs contrary to the requirement of Rule 133 that the defendant not answer "evasively but . . . fully and specifically," and is treated as an admission.[11] As long as the superior court continues to allow this practice, defendants who have no substantive defense but who wish to avoid a direct admission may do so in this manner.

(d) *Refusal To Respond.* A defendant must respond in some way to every separable and substantive allegation in the plaintiff's petition, bill, libel, or other pleading.[12] While the defendant may refuse to answer scandalous, conclusory, or ambiguous allegations of fact, conclusions of law, and any allegation of fact which inquires into a privileged matter, he must specifically state the reason for his refusal. He may not use an objection to one part of a paragraph containing several allegations to justify a general denial or blanket refusal to respond to the entire paragraph. What is considered a good ground for declining to answer one part of a paragraph in the plaintiff's petition, bill, libel, or other pleading is not a justification for refusing to answer the whole. The defendant must separate and identify those portions which he chooses not to answer, and he must respond fairly to each of the rest.

Library References

CJS Pleading §§ 103, 105–108

---

10 *Id.*

11 Super. Ct. R. 133. A refusal to admit or deny is thus the civil equivalent of a plea of nolo contendere.

12 Super. Ct. R. 133.

§ 9.05. Alleging New Matter

The defendant may allege new facts in his answer which explain, contradict, or establish an affirmative defense[13] to the plaintiff's assertions.[14] These may be set forth in his responses to the plaintiff's specific numbered paragraphs or in a separate section at the end of the answer. In addition, the defendant may assert a claim for affirmative relief against the plaintiff by way of a counterclaim.

Library References

CJS Pleading §§ 106, 166

§ 9.06. Multiple or Inconsistent Defenses

Although the defendant will be precluded from denying any admissions or statements of fact that he makes in his answer,[15] he may assert any number of defenses to the plaintiff's claims based upon those admissions and statements of fact, and whether consistent with each other or not,[16] he may rely upon them at trial.

Library References

CJS Pleading § 121

---

13 Brief statements are only filed in actions at law. If a defendant has an affirmative defense in other types of proceedings, he must set it forth by way of further answer to the plaintiff's pleading. An answer on brief statement which sets forth an affirmative defense will be construed according to the rules relating to pleadings generally, and will be regarded as a sufficient basis for the introduction of evidence at trial if it puts the plaintiff on notice of the general theory of the defense. See Terzis v. Estate of Whalen, 126 N.H. 88, 489 A.2d 608 (1985) (defense of lack of consideration in a proceeding to foreclose a mortgage gave plaintiff "sufficient notice of issue [of fairness in fee arrangement pursuant to which the mortgage was delivered] to prevent unfair surprise"); Bernier v. Bernier, 125 N.H. 517, 484 A.2d 1088 (1984) (suggesting that something like a brief statement may be filed to request alimony in a divorce proceeding).

14 Super. Ct. R. 133: "The defendant may allege any new or special matter in his answer with a prayer of relief."

15 See Hodge v. Allstate Ins. Co., 130 N.H. 743, 747, 546 A.2d 1078 (1988) (defendant's admission that proceeding had been brought pursuant to Declaratory Judgment Act foreclosed argument that Act did not apply).

16 See Super. Ct. R. 133 ("The answer of the defendant may state as many defenses as the defendant deems essential to his defense."). See also True v. Huntoon, 54 N.H. 121, 122 (1873) ("The fact that pleas are repugnant to each other is no objection when they are filed together.").

§ 9.07. Time for Filing

An answer must be filed within the time allowed in the order of notice. The usual period is thirty days.[17] Answers to amended petitions, bills, libels, and other pleadings must be filed within ten days of the date on the clerk's notice informing the defendant that the Motion to Amend has been granted.[18]

§ 9.08. Effect of the Answer

A plaintiff's petition, bill, libel, or other pleading aids in discovery and forces the defendant to state with particularity his position on each separable part of the plaintiff's claim, as a matter of record. The defendant will be bound by his admissions and statements in the answer,[19] in all other cases involving the same issue. "All facts well alleged in the bill, and not denied or explained in the answer, will be held to be admitted."[20]

If the defendant fails to answer all or part of the allegations in the plaintiff's petition, bill, libel, or other pleading, the unanswered portions

---

17 Super. Ct. R. 127.

18 Super. Ct. R. 136 provides that the defendant's answer to an amended petition, bill, libel, or other proceeding must be filed "within ten days after the amendment or amended bill is filed." The rule fails to take into account the possibility that the defendant will oppose the amendment or that the court will not grant it immediately upon filing. It seems more reasonable to adopt the rule which pertains in the entry of judgments (see Super. Ct. R. 74(a)) and allow the defendant 10 days from the date on the clerk's written notice of the court's action.

19 See Hodge v. Allstate Ins. Co., 130 N.H. 743, 546 A.2d 1078 (1988) (defendant's admission that proceeding had been brought pursuant to Declaratory Judgment Act foreclosed argument that Act did not apply).

20 Super. Ct. R. 133. See Super. Ct. R. 58-A (provides that a defendant cannot prevent his opponent from introducing evidence of the circumstances of an accident simply by admitting liability). Rule 58-A follows the holding in Rawson v. Bradshaw, 125 N.H. 94, 98, 480 A.2d 37 (1984), and requires that the parties either agree on a statement of facts "sufficient to explain the case (specifically the defendant's negligent conduct) to the jury and to place it in a proper context so that the jurors might more readily understand what they will be hearing in the remaining portion of the trial" or try the issues of liability and damages together. The rule gives too much power to the defendant, who is permitted to obtain a trial on the issue of liability after admitting it, solely by refusing to agree on a statement to be read to the jury. It might make more sense to hold the defendant to his admission and either permit the court to compose a statement for him or simply default the defendant on the issue of damages if he refused to agree to a reasonable statement of facts proposed by the plaintiff. Cf. Weeks v. Weeks, 124 N.H. 252, 469 A.2d 1313 (1983) (grounds for divorce and appropriate property division are not admitted by failing to file an answer).

will be taken as confessed[21] and, where they are sufficient to support an order, they may result in a judgment on default.[22]

The answer also joins the parties and issues in the contest and begins the pretrial process. Filing an answer at a date earlier than required may therefore shorten the period of pretrial preparation and provide a tactical advantage to the party who is better prepared.[23]

Library References

CJS Pleading § 155

§ 9.09. Amendments to the Answer

A defendant may move to amend his answer at any time. Whenever he discovers that the answer is incorrect, incomplete, or misleading, he must move to amend to make it more accurate, and the court will allow the amendment as a matter of course. When the defendant wishes to amend his answer or add affirmative defenses, a counterclaim or statements of miti-gating circumstances, he must set forth facts in his motion from which it may be determined that his failure to include these allegations at an earlier date was not the result of neglect and that allowance of the amendment will promote justice. The plaintiff may object to the motion on the ground that he will be prejudiced by allowing the new issue to be raised at such a late stage in the proceedings, and he may ask that, if the amendment is allowed, he be reimbursed for costs incurred in preparing to meet a different set of defenses. But the court will usually allow an amendment which is requested in time for the plaintiff to meet the defendant's changed position, and the

---

21 Super. Ct. R. 127, 131, 133 and 136. See Brady v. Mullen, 139 N.H. 67, 69, 649 A.2d 47 (1994); Blaisdell v. Raab, 132 N.H. 711, 571 A.2d 261 (1990) (citing Super. Ct. R. 131); Weeks v. Weeks, 124 N.H. 252, 469 A.2d 1313 (1983).

22 Super. Ct. R. 127, 131, and 136 are ambiguous on the question whether the defendant will suffer default if he answers but fails to deliver a copy to the plaintiff's attorney within the time allowed. As a matter of practice, if a copy of the answer is mailed by first class mail, postage prepaid, to the plaintiff or his attorney before the deadline, the defendant will not be defaulted. However, the answer must actually be received by the clerk before the deadline expires. See Blaisdell v. Raab, 132 N.H. 711, 571 A.2d 261 (1990) (citing Super. Ct. R. 131).

23 See Tenn v. 889 Associates, 127 N.H. 321, 500 A.2d 366 (1985) (The defendant filed an answer to the petition for injunction nearly a month before it was due, and the court scheduled a final hearing for three weeks later and a week before the original due date for the answer. The plaintiff then moved for a continuance of the hearing date on the ground that he could not obtain necessary expert testimony by that time, but the trial court refused. The Supreme Court held that the defendant's answer had joined the issues and that the plaintiff had had ample opportunity to prepare for the final hearing both before and after the petition had been filed).

court may impose terms upon the defendant, including the payment of costs, as a condition to allowing the amendment.[24]

Library References

CJS Pleading §§ 294 et seq.
Amendment raising defense of privilege in defamation action. 51 ALR2d 752.
Amendment of pleadings to assert statute of limitations. 59 ALR2d 169.
Amendment to correct failure to plead specially defense of assumption of risk. 59 ALR2d 253.

B. Brief Statement

§ 9.10. Introduction

The brief statement was created by an Act of July 2, 1931.[25] It is a form of pleading by which the defendant, in an action at law, notifies the court and the plaintiff of a special theory of defense upon which he proposes to rely at trial. Failure to file a brief statement does not result in a default being entered against the defendant, but it does allow the plaintiff to object at trial to the introduction of evidence which tends to prove a defense of which he should have received notice before trial.

Uncertainty about the effect of this early statute[26] was resolved by an amendment permitting the use of brief statements in actions before justices of the peace.[27] The authorization for a *plaintiff's* brief statement was removed before the end of the Civil War[28] and the statute was later amended from time to time to update its reference to the State's lowest court.[29] The statute is now set forth as RSA 515:3 and it provides:

Brief Statement. No special plea shall be required in a civil action, except a plea of title to real estate in actions in municipal courts; but any defense may be proved under the general issue, upon a brief statement thereof being filed, in such time as the court may order.

---

24 Super. Ct. R. 135.

25 "That in all civil actions the defendant may plead the general issue which shall be joined by the plaintiff, and either party may give in evidence any special matter in support or defense of the action upon filing in the court of a brief statement of such special matter either of law or of fact, within such time as the court order, of which statement the other party shall be entitled to a copy."

26 See Colby v. Stevens, 38 N.H. 191 (1859); Foster v. Leavitt, 8 N.H. 353 (1836); Flagg v. Gotham, 7 N.H. 266 (1834).

27 See Gen. Laws ch. 227 at 3.

28 See Gen. Stat. ch. 208 at 3.

29 See Pub. Stat. ch. 223 at 3; Rev. L. ch. 391 at 3; RSA 515:3.

By allowing the defendant to state briefly the nature of his special defense, the 1831 statute simplified the method, without sacrificing the usefulness by which pleadings narrow the issues for trial. In this respect, the Act was an early example of the liberal procedure that has become a hallmark of New Hampshire civil practice.

Library References

CJS Pleading § 143

§ 9.11.　Brief Statement—Requisites

A brief statement may be filed in any action at law under the general issue to raise any defense which could have been entered by means of a special plea at common law.[30] Although the brief statement is a creation of statute, the statute has been given a liberal construction to allow the inclusion of matters which would not originally have been permitted in a special plea filed with the general issue.[31] But a brief statement is still not available to raise matters in abatement of the writ[32] or any defense[33] prior to the general issue being joined.[34]

The brief statement must state the defendant's theory of defense, and it must include the essential facts upon which that theory relies.[35] "Precision and exactness are not necessary, but substance is essential."[36] The brief statement may set forth more than one defense and may even set forth inconsistent defenses.[37] It may state a defense either to the whole or to a part of the plaintiff's claim[38] but it must be concise.

The brief statement is only a notice and informs the plaintiff and the court of the defendant's present intentions, but does not obligate the defendant to rely upon the defenses it states at trial. The defendant is always free to

---

30　RSA 515:3; Foster v. Leavitt, 8 N.H. 353 (1836); Flagg v. Gotham, 7 N.H. 266, 271 (1834).

31　See Wisheart v. Legro & McDuffee, 33 N.H. 177, 182 (1856).

32　Cocheco Mfg. Co. v. Whittier, 10 N.H. 305 (1839). See also Super Ct. R. 30; Dist. and Mun. Ct. R. 3.10(c).

33　RSA 515:3.

34　See Super Ct. R. 31 (sole exception to this general rule is defense that contract declared on was not duly executed, and defense must be raised by a brief statement).

35　Noyes v. Edgerly, 71 N.H. 500, 53 A. 311 (1902); Pike v. Taylor, 49 N.H. 124 (1869); Clough v. Clough, 26 N.H. 24 (1852).

36　Folsom v. Brawn, 25 N.H. 114, 121 (1852).

37　Carter v. Piper, 57 N.H. 217 (1876).

38　McIntire v. Randolph, 50 N.H. 94 (1870); Pittsfield v. Barnstead, 38 N.H. 115 (1859).

abandon the brief statement if some other tactic later seems preferable.[39] Nothing set forth in the brief statement may be taken as an admission for use in proving the plaintiff's case in chief.[40]

§ 9.12. —Reasons to File

There is generally no reason not to file a brief statement if any reasonable chance exists that the defendant will want to assert a special defense at trial. But there is a very substantial disadvantage to not filing one: failure to file a brief statement within the time allowed by the Rules may foreclose the possibility of establishing that special defense at trial.[41]

The brief statement becomes important when the nature of the general issue is considered. Defense counsel will often file a general appearance and assume that he can take advantage at trial of any special defense shown by the evidence. He may even succeed on this assumption if plaintiff's counsel fails to object to the introduction of evidence on that special defense at trial. But a general appearance amounts only to a plea of the general issue, and a plea of the general issue is merely a denial of each fact that is well-pleaded in the declaration.[42] It "is not, in form or substance and does not include an affirmative allegation of any fact; it is a mere denial of every fact alleged in the declaration which is material to the plaintiff's case."[43] Thus, any facts tending to show the acts complained of, but offering an excuse or justification, are inadmissible under the general issue.[44] Unless a brief statement setting forth those facts and the theory of defense is filed within the time allowed by the Rules, the plaintiff can object to the offer of evidence on that defense at trial and will prevail.[45]

---

39 Cocheco Mfg. Co. v. Whittier, 10 N.H. 305 (1839).

40 Piper v. Boston and Maine R.R., 75 N.H. 435, 447, (1910); Solomons v. Chesley, 58 N.H. 238 (1878); Carter v. Piper, 57 N.H. 217 (1876); McIntire v. Randolph, 50 N.H. 94 (1870); Bartlett v. Prescott, 41 N.H. 493 (1860); Pittsfield v. Barnstead, 38 N.H. 115 (1859); Buzzell v. Snell, 25 N.H. 474, 480 (1852); Bump v. Smith, 11 N.H. 48, 50 (1840).

41 See Fortier v. Stone, 79 N.H. 235, 107 A. 342 (1919).

42 Cocheco Mfg. Co. v. Whittier, 10 N.H. 305 (1839).

43 Kendall v. Brownson, 47 N.H. 186, 197 (1866) (Doe, J., dissenting).

44 Fuller v. Rounceville, 29 N.H. 554, 561 (1854).

45 See Super. Ct. R. 28; Dist. and Mun. Ct. R. 3.10(A); Exeter Hospital v. Hall, 137 N.H. 397, 399, 629 A.2d 88, 90 (1993) (". . . it is the defendant's responsibility to raise [the statute of limitations] an affirmative defense . . . failure to do so . . . should be deemed a waiver"); Fothergill v. Seabreeze Condominiums, 141 N.H. 115, 677 A.2d 696 (1996) (statute of limitations defense may be raised in motion for summary judgment).

§ 9.13. —Form

The superior, district, and municipal courts have not established a preferred form for brief statements, but any form which is concise and which sets forth the nature of the defense and the facts on which it relies should be sufficient. Frequently, defense counsel file notice of special defenses within more lengthy pleadings or motions which also raise other issues. While this practice does give the plaintiff notice of the special defenses, it may tend to confuse, rather than to simplify, the issues, as it mixes pleadings to which a response is required with the brief statement. It will, therefore, generally be preferable to file a brief statement separately from those motions and special pleas which require a response.

§ 9.14. Special Problems in the Use of the Brief Statement—When a Special Appearance Is Filed

RSA 515:3 permits the brief statement to be used only under the general issue. This raises the question of how to use the brief statement when the defendant intends first to object to jurisdiction. The Rules of the superior, district, and municipal courts presently require that a brief statement be filed within thirty days of the return day or "the cause shall be tried upon the general issue."[46] A brief statement may not thereafter be filed except upon motion, "for good cause shown."[47] The Rules also require that unless a special plea or a Motion to Dismiss setting forth objections to jurisdiction is filed within thirty days of the return day, the defendant's special appearance "shall be deemed general."[48] Thus, a defendant who wishes to contest jurisdiction but who also wishes to present a special defense, if obliged to defend on the merits, is required to choose between waiving his objection to jurisdiction in order to raise the special defense or retaining his objection to jurisdiction and taking the chance that the court will allow him to file a late brief statement if his special appearance is later converted to a general appearance.

Because a brief statement cannot be filed until the general issue has been joined,[49] the effect of filing a brief statement while a special appearance is pending is to convert the special appearance to a general one. A defendant with any good ground for objecting to jurisdiction cannot take the chance

---

46 Super. Ct. R. 28; Dist. and Mun. Ct. R. 3.10(A).

47 *Id.*

48 Super. Ct. R. 14; Dist. and Mun. Ct. R. 3.6(A).

49 See RSA 515:3.

of filing a brief statement until he has finally lost on that objection. In the normal case, however, the defendant with a good objection to jurisdiction should be able to satisfy the court that he has "good cause" for filing a late brief statement if he applies for leave promptly upon being compelled to defend on the merits. But the court will not agree that "good cause" exists when the request for late filing has been necessitated by an intentional or negligent delay in bringing the matter forward once the general issue has been joined[50] or by the prior consideration of an objection to jurisdiction which has no reasonable basis or was so badly handled that it resulted in the inadvertent conversion of the defendant's special appearance.

In such cases, the court will balance the harm that would be suffered by the defendant from being denied the opportunity to present a defense, against the harm that the plaintiff would suffer if required to respond to it. This sort of analysis requires that the merits of the special defense sought to be pleaded be considered, and it may deprive a defendant of a special defense as to which he is unable, before discovery, to convince the court that a substantial basis exists in fact. Even if the defendant has a good faith defense, when the request for late filing is presented close to the trial date, the court may think that the plaintiff risks the more substantial harm by being compelled either to defend after surprise or to postpone his anticipated relief.

While nothing will excuse bad faith or neglect, the defendant who desires to challenge jurisdiction and raise a special defense if the merits are reached may be able to blunt the force of some of the plaintiff's objections to a late brief statement by preparing and delivering a brief statement to the plaintiff—but not to the court—within the time required by the Rules for filing under the general issue. As long as the defendant does not file the brief statement with the court, he will not have submitted an issue on the merits to the court and will not have waived his objection to jurisdiction.[51] Yet, weeks or months later, when the special appearance is converted, the plaintiff will hardly be able to claim surprise if the defendant requests leave to file a late brief statement in the form which was previously provided him and to present evidence on it at trial. Because the primary purpose of the brief statement is to notify the plaintiff of a claimed defense, the court should have no objection to the late filing and no reason to refuse the request for late filing if the defendant has otherwise acted diligently and in good faith.

---

50 See Lehigh Navigation Coal Co. v. Keene Coal Co., 89 N.H. 274, 197 A. 410 (1938).
51 See Beggs v. Reading Co., 103 N.H. 156, 167 A.2d 61 (1961).

§ 9.15. —When the Court Orders the Filing

The Rules also provide that the court may, "in all cases order either party to plead and also to file a statement in sufficient detail to give to the adverse party and to the court reasonable knowledge of the nature and grounds of the . . . defense."[52] No case has been found in which the court has used this rule as a basis for ordering a defendant to file a brief statement, but there is no reason to doubt that it could be so employed. Because a brief statement is only a notice an order that a brief statement be filed should not prejudice any good faith defense, requires no response from the plaintiff, cannot be used as an admission against the defendant, and a brief statement has no function in limiting or in shaping the defendant's case. It should only be of help in narrowing the issues before trial. In fact, more frequent use of the power granted by the Rule might eliminate the continued pendency of suits when the defendants have no apparent defense and seek only delay.

Of course, it should not be assumed that the court will make such an order without reason to believe that the defendant is without a defense, or that he relies solely upon a special defense. But once the order is made, the defendant must determine how best to respond to it. A defendant who fails to raise a particular defense in response to such an order and who later seeks to rely upon it at trial, will be forbidden the chance to present such evidence. Similarly, a defendant who does not raise a defense in response to such an order, and who later moves for permission to file a late brief statement, will bear a very heavy burden in convincing the court that he could not have discovered and pleaded the defense when ordered to do so. Thus, the best practice for a defendant who is faced with an order to file a brief statement is to check thoroughly all possible avenues of defense and to set forth all such theories, whether or not they seem at the moment to be strong.

§ 9.16. —Use of Brief Statement in Transfers From the District or Municipal Court

RSA 502-A:14(III) requires that a defendant's request for leave to transfer an action from the district or municipal court to the superior court be filed by brief statement within five days of entry of the action. As the brief statement required by this statute must be accompanied by an affidavit, it is closer in form to a special plea than to the pleading discussed in this chapter. But the defendant should take note of its special time limit.

---

[52] Super. Ct. R. 29; Dist. and Mun. Ct. R. 3.10(B).

§ 9.17. Responding to a Brief Statement

When a brief statement is filed, the plaintiff must decide whether to challenge it. Because the Brief Statement is only a notice of defenses, no responsive pleading is required.[53] But the plaintiff may wish to assert that it sets forth an impermissible theory of defense or to take the opportunity presented by the notice to resolve other points of law or fact in advance of trial.[54] When he thinks that an inadequate brief statement has been filed, the plaintiff must choose between filing a Motion to Reject a Brief Statement before trial and objecting to evidence offered under it at trial. If the plaintiff moves to reject the brief statement and the court finds it defective for not setting forth a defense, the court will order the defendant to put the brief statement in substantial and definite form. If the defendant is unable to do so, the brief statement will be stricken and the defendant will not thereafter be allowed to present any evidence under the proffered theory of defense at trial.[55] The Motion to Reject, therefore, has the effect of testing the sufficiency of a defendant's theory of defense and of limiting the range of the defendant's evidence at trial.[56]

A Motion to Reject a Brief Statement should be filed, within ten days of the date the plaintiff receives the brief statement. The plaintiff's decision on whether to move to reject a brief statement or instead to hold his objection and to protest the introduction of evidence under it at trial must, of course, be based on the particular tactical considerations important to his case. But a few points are worth considering in every instance. First, the Supreme Court has clearly expressed its preference for a Motion to Reject before trial, rather than an attempt to block evidence at trial, "as the parties will then go to trial without any uncertainty as to their positions."[57] Second, waiting to raise objections at trial, while calculated to unbalance the presentation of the defendant's case, may have the same effect on the plaintiff's case if the

---

53 Piper v. Boston and Maine R.R., 75 N.H. 435 (1910); Leslie v. Harlow, 18 N.H. 518 (1847).

54 See Piper v. Boston and Maine R.R., 75 N.H. 435, 447 (1910) (brief statement filed in response to an action for personal injuries was held not to state a defense when it pleaded terms of agreements between plaintiff and his employer and between his employer and defendant); Pallet v. Sargent, 36 N.H. 496 (1858) (brief statement filed in response to an action for slander was held not to state a defense when it relied upon proof that plaintiff had done other actions than ones which defendant had accused him of).

55 Folsom v. Brawn, 25 N.H. 114, 121 (1852).

56 See Piper v. Boston and Maine R.R., 75 N.H. 435, 447 (1910); Kezer v. Clifford, 59 N.H. 208 (1879).

57 Folsom v. Brawn, 25 N.H. 114, 121 (1852).

objection is rejected by the court. Third, the result of withholding objections and successfully asserting them at trial may be to require a new trial or a substantial continuance rather than to strip the defendant of his defenses. Not only will such a result only add to the plaintiff's expenses and delay his expected recovery, but, if his conduct in delaying the objection seems unreasonable, it could result in the assessment of costs.[58]

Of course, there may be compelling reasons in a particular case to await the trial to raise an objection to a brief statement. The brief statement may relate only to a small part of the case and the expense of moving to reject it may, on balance, not be justifiable. Or, the plaintiff may be satisfied that the court will see no merit in the defense when it is raised. But in the usual case, the best procedure will be to move to reject the brief statement before trial.

The plaintiff should always bear in mind, while preparing his Motion to Reject, that the objection is to the theory and the elements of the defense presented, and not to the form of the brief statement itself. Although particularly rambling and diffuse pleadings will be rejected on motion if the court is unable to ascertain the theory being put forward,[59] the objection even in such a case is to the substance, rather than to the form, and leave is freely given to amend.

The Supreme Court has commented that "[i]t is generally more difficult to ascertain whether there is any substance in a complicated and confused brief statement than to determine any ordinary question of special pleading."[60] The reason for this is that when a brief statement is challenged, the court is called upon to determine whether the defendant has given notice of the substance of an acceptable defense. The Supreme Court has not adopted a clear position on whether a brief statement will be rejected if it states the theory but fails to allege all material elements of an acceptable defense. As the brief statement was originally invented to relax the rigorous requirements of common law pleading, it would seem reasonable, in close cases, to let the pleading stand if it sets forth the major elements of a defense in a way which is sufficient to alert the plaintiff to the defendant's theory and to the primary facts on which it is based.

---

58 Super. Ct. R. 59.

59 See Morency v. Plourde, 96 N.H. 344, 346, 76 A.2d 791, 792 (1950); Morancy v. Morancy, 134 N.H. 493, 593 A.2d 1158 (1991) (trial court erred in grounding decision for plaintiffs in part on plaintiffs' invasion of privacy claim where plaintiffs did not assert it in original declaration, but only in response to motion for summary judgment).

60 Clough v. Clough, 26 N.H. 24, 31 (1852).

In fact, the Supreme Court has affirmed such an approach on a number of occasions.[61] But the court has also taken a stricter view, and rejected brief statements which omitted to state all of the particular facts along with the theory of defense which it was contended they would establish.[62] Most of the cases in which the Supreme Court has held a brief statement to be insufficient have either involved challenges to the pleadings *before* trial, or challenges after a trial which resulted in a verdict for the plaintiff. In either situation, the court's adoption of a strict rule could have been met by an amendment to the brief statement without any disadvantage to the defendant. In fact, the Supreme Court has sustained verdicts for defendants based on defenses which could not have been proved under the general issue, despite the inadequacy or even absence of a brief statement.[63]

These cases suggest that the Supreme Court favors, as a matter of theory, a strict standard of pleading for brief statements, but is reluctant to enforce that preference against a defendant who has passed the point of jeopardy in the trial of the case. Although the plaintiff can insist upon a brief statement of defense as a necessary prerequisite to the defendant's introducing evidence relating to that defense at trial, the plaintiff's failure to raise the objection when the evidence is offered will usually be regarded as a waiver of the objection. Once the trial has begun, the court will be less inclined to

---

61 See Taylor v. True, 27 N.H. 220 (1853) (brief statement in reply to writ of replevin alleging that property sought belonged to defendants was held acceptable as either "substantially a plea of property in Defendants" or a denial of plaintiffs' claim of ownership); Clough v. Clough, 26 N.H. 24 (1852) (brief statement alleging tender and payment into court but failing to state that defendant had been ready and willing to pay from date of tender was held acceptable).

62 See Noyes v. Edgerly, 71 N.H. 500 (1902) (brief statement in action for false imprisonment stating that, by a prior suit to recover a penalty for not accounting for prison wages, the plaintiff had admitted the correctness of his imprisonment and had made an election of remedies, was rejected because it did not cover the full period of detention and did not allege that the plaintiff was cognizant of his legal rights or of the facts necessary to make an intelligent decision when he made the claimed election of remedies.); Carter v. Piper, 57 N.H. 217 (1876) (brief statement in response to writ of replevin alleging three inconsistent theories of title to the property could have been rejected if it had set forth facts tending to admit the taking); Bartlett v. Prescott, 41 N.H. 493 (1860) (brief statement setting up right of way in response to an action for trespass to land was rejected because it did not state that right of way extended to defendant's servants).

63 Only one case has been found in which the Supreme Court overturned a verdict for the defendant based upon an inadequate brief statement, and there it appeared that the defendant had neither introduced evidence upon nor relied upon the ground of defense by which he prevailed. Fortier v. Stone, 79 N.H. 235, 107 A. 342 (1919). See also LePage v. St. Johnsbury Trucking Co., Inc., 97 N.H. 46, 80 A.2d 148 (1951); Bogrett v. Hromada, 91 N.H. 351, 19 A.2d 432 (1941); Lyons v. Child, 61 N.H. 72 (1881).

foreclose a theory of defense or method of proving it which, although objectionable, has been the basis for the defendant's preparation for months. If the plaintiff cannot succeed in his objections to the evidence at trial, and a defendant's verdict is returned, the plaintiff will probably not succeed in obtaining a new trial by pursuing his objections to the brief statement.[64] As the Court said in *H & B Construction Company v. Irwin & Sons*,[65] "[I]t is not our practice to spend time in the investigation of the accuracy of pleadings after the action has without objection been fully tried by the parties."[66]

Accordingly, the plaintiff's best strategy when faced with a brief statement which either omits key facts or presents an inadequate theory of law is to move to reject it before trial. Because the Supreme Court has indicated an inclination to impose stricter requirements on brief statements before the trial than after, a plaintiff who is successful in raising this issue early may obtain an order foreclosing a theory of defense or method of proving that defense which the defendant might otherwise be allowed to use at trial.

A Motion to Reject a Brief Statement, like any other motion, should set forth the precise manner in which the brief statement is inadequate. The superior, district, and municipal court Rules do not provide an approved form for such a motion nor state when it will be in order for hearing. But, because the purpose of a Motion to Reject will only be adequately served if the motion is heard well in advance of trial, the plaintiff should request an early hearing at the time the motion is filed.

C. Specification

§ 9.18. More Particular Statement—Specifications

The primary purpose of initial and responsive pleadings is to notify the opposing side and the court of the issues in dispute and the relief sought.[67] Although a party's pleadings will not be rejected or his case dismissed solely

---

64 Bogrett v. Hromada, 91 N.H. 351, 19 A.2d 432 (1941); Lyons v. Child, 61 N.H. 72 (1881).

65 105 N.H. 279, 198 A.2d 17 (1964).

66 *Id.* at 282, 198 A.2d at 19.

67 The plaintiff's pleadings must be "sufficiently full, clear, and distinct to give the defendant, the jury and the court reasonably complete and certain information concerning the [claim] on which the action is founded." Merritt v. American Woolen Co., 71 N.H. 493, 494, 53 A. 303, 304 (1902).

because his pleadings are ambiguous,[68] the opposing party and the court are entitled to know with some certainty before the case proceeds what claim is made.[69] In order to accomplish this purpose, the court may, either on its own or on a party's motion, order any party to file "a statement in sufficient detail to give to the adverse party and to the Court reasonable knowledge of the nature and grounds of the action or defense."[70] This statement is sometimes referred to as a "specification" of the plaintiff's claim.[71]

The court may enter the order at any time and at the request of any party. While the court will generally take care to allow the party to preserve his options for trial by stating a broad or multifaceted claim or defense,[72] it will also require that each part of the claim or defense be comprehensible to the other side in time for it to frame and prepare a response.[73] If an opponent neglects to move for a more definite statement when the pleadings are unclear, he may have difficulty claiming surprise at trial.[74]

If an opponent understands the nature of the claim or defense stated, even when stated broadly, but believes that part or all of it cannot be sustained by the evidence, he should move for summary judgment or, at trial, for a nonsuit or a directed verdict. If he understands the claim but believes it is insufficient as a matter of law, he should move to dismiss for failure to state a claim on which relief may be granted.

The court's decision on a Motion for More Particular Statement will never be revised.[75] If a party fails to comply with an order to file a more particular

---

68 RSA 514:8, 9. See Bagley v. Controlled Env't Corp., 127 N.H. 556, 503 A.2d 823 (1986).

69 Porter v. Dziura, 104 N.H. 89, 179 A.2d 281 (1962). See also McGranahan v. Dahar, 119 N.H. 758, 408 A.2d 121 (1979); J. Dunn & Sons, Inc. v. Paragon Homes of New England, Inc., 110 N.H. 215, 265 A.2d 5 (1970).

70 Super. Ct. R. 29; Dist. and Mun. Ct. R. 3.10(B); Prob. Ct. R. 7. But it may not require the specification of an amount of damages in a personal action. See RSA 508:4-c. This statement may either be an amendment or a supplement to the original pleadings, but it will be taken as a part thereof. See Dumas v. Hartford Accident & Indem. Co., 92 N.H. 140, 26 A.2d 361 (1942); Chesley v. Dunklee, 77 N.H. 263, 90 A. 965 (1914); Merritt v. American Woolen Co., 71 N.H. 493, 53 A. 303 (1902).

71 See Abbot v. Hayes, 92 N.H. 126, 26 A.2d 842 (1942); Dumas v. Hartford Accident & Indemnity Co., 92 N.H. 140, 26 A.2d 361 (1942); Prob. Ct. R. 7.

72 See Abbot v. Hayes, 92 N.H. 126, 26 A.2d 842 (1942) (specifications ended with "and such other act or acts of negligence on his part as evidence may develop in the course of trial," and defendant's motion to strike that ending was denied).

73 Brown v. Barnard, 91 N.H. 58, 13 A.2d 470 (1940).

74 Menard v. Cashman, 94 N.H. 428, 55 A.2d 156 (1947).

75 See State v. Cote, 95 N.H. 248, 252, 61 A.2d 710, 713 (1948); Abbot v. Hayes, 92 N.H. 126, 26 A.2d 842 (1942).

statement, the court may dismiss the case, in whole or in part, or it will enter a further order limiting the party's right to recover on the claim.[76]

Library References

CJS Pleading §§ 376 et seq.

---

[76] Super. Ct. R. 29; Dist. and Mun. Ct. R. 3.10(B).

CHAPTER 10. PRETRIAL DISPOSITIVE PLEADINGS

229

Cross References

Disposition Without Trial, see Part IX *infra*.

Library References

CJS Dismissal and Nonsuit §§ 45 et seq.
CJS Pleading §§ 450 et seq.

§ 10.01. Introduction

Prior to trial, the defendant may object to the continuation of the action for any one of three reasons: (1) the procedures by which the action was commenced were insufficient; (2) the plaintiff has not stated a claim upon which relief may be granted; or (3) the plaintiff is disqualified, as a matter of law, from recovering on the claim. The first reason involves matters in abatement, and at common law was raised by filing either a plea in abatement, a motion to quash, a motion to stay or a motion to dismiss. The second reason involves a dispute over the legal sufficiency of the pleadings, and was raised at common law by a demurrer. The third reason relies upon events outside the present case to defeat the plaintiffs right to recover and was raised at common law by either a plea in bar, a motion to dismiss, or a plea of discharge or confession and avoidance.

Under modern practice, all three types of objection are raised by a Motion To Dismiss. The motion may be based on facts apparent from the record or supplied by affidavit or stipulations of the parties.[1] However, the time within which the Motion To Dismiss must be filed and the form which the motion must take depend upon the nature of the objection being raised. Thus, any Motion To Dismiss that relies upon matters in abatement must be filed within thirty days of the entry of the writ,[2] while motions objecting to the sufficiency of the declaration or to the plaintiff's legal ability to recover may be filed at any time prior to the expiration of thirty days from the return day.[3]

A. *Motions To Dismiss*

§ 10.02. The Function of a Motion To Dismiss

Until the middle of the twentieth century, Motions To Dismiss were very infrequently used and had no unique or specific role in New Hampshire civil practice.[4] Occasionally, they were associated with motions to quash, and at some times a theoretical difference seems to have been recognized between abating or quashing a writ and dismissing an action from the court's docket.[5]

---

1 Super. Ct. R. 57; Prob. Ct. R. 9.

2 Super. Ct. R. 30.

3 Super. Ct. R. 28 and 127.

4 Motions To Dismiss (or for nonsuit) were occasionally filed in cases where pleas in abatement or motions to quash could have been filed. *See* Philbrick v. Hazen, 3 N.H. 120 (1824) (prematurely brought); Campbell v. Wallace, 12 N.H. 362 (1841) (misjoinder not apparent on the record); Kimball v. Wellington, 20 N.H. 439 (1846); Parsons v. Eureka Powder Works, 48 N.H. 66 (1868) (no such person as plaintiff); Bowman v. Brown, 51 N.H. 549 (1872) (nonjoinder); State v. Spirituous Liquors, 75 N.H. 273, 73 A. 169 (1909) (failure to make return); Martin v. Wiggin, 67 N.H. 196, 29 A. 450 (1892) (defect in service); Warren v. Glynn, 37 N.H. 340 (1858) (defect in writ).

Motions To Dismiss were also filed in place of pleas in bar. See Hoyt v. Massachusetts Bonding and Insurance Company, 80 N.H. 27, 113 A. 219 (1921).

5 See, e.g., Crawford v. Crawford, 44 N.H. 428 (1862) (where the defendant moved to quash the writ and dismiss the action).

But until recently, pleadings filed to terminate an action before trial carried different names depending upon the ground of termination relied upon.

After the adoption of the Federal Rules of Civil Procedure, the distinctions between different types of pretrial dispositive pleadings under New Hampshire practice began to blur, and it became increasingly common in New Hampshire to raise all types of objections to the further maintenance of an action under the rubric of a Motion To Dismiss.[6] The practice has become so far advanced that today pleas in abatement and pleas in bar are virtually unknown, and motions to quash and special demurrers are rarely seen. Whether this trend towards homogenization of form is beneficial to the practice or not, it is an accomplished fact and an element of modern practice which poses some pitfalls for the practitioner.

The major problem created for the plaintiff by today's Motion To Dismiss is an inability to determine easily the nature of the objection being raised. Only by examining the motion and analyzing the substance of its objections can the plaintiff draw any conclusions about whether its objections have been raised properly and in a timely fashion or about what must be done to meet them. For the defendant, today's Motion To Dismiss creates the danger that, by raising more than one ground of objection in a single pleading, the defendant will inadvertently waive objections upon which he or she intends to rely.

Although the form for raising objections has changed, the substantive law relating to the basis for those objections and the order, time, and manner in which they must be presented has not. It is important, therefore, for both the plaintiff and the defendant to determine whether a Motion To Dismiss is in the nature of a plea in abatement, motion to quash, plea in bar, special demurrer, or other special plea and to follow the rules which have long been established for the presentation and disposition of each.[7]

---

6 The Motion To Dismiss has become a vehicle for raising objections which previously required two or more separate pleas or motions. See, e.g., Nixon v. Bonenfant, 97 N.H. 230, 84 A.2d 841 (1951) (Motion To Dismiss raised nonjoinder and lack of equity). The Motion To Dismiss has also become a substitute form for special pleas and motions. See, e.g., Davis v. Cray, 109 N.H. 181, 246 A.2d 97 (1968) (Motion To Dismiss filed in place of a plea in abatement); Hall v. Brusseau, 100 N.H. 87, 119 A.2d 703 (1956) (Motion To Dismiss filed in place of plea in abatement or motion to quash on ground that action was begun prematurely); Paju v. Ricker, 110 N.H. 310, 266 A.2d 836 (1970) (Motion To Dismiss filed in place of plea in abatement for incapacity).

7 The sufficiency and timeliness of a Motion To Dismiss will be judged by the rules relating to the substance of the claim it raises. See Martin v. Whitney, 74 N.H. 505, 69 A. 888 (1908) (Motion To Dismiss treated like a plea in abatement).

Library References

Effect of nonsuit, dismissal or discontinuance of action on previous orders. 11 ALR2d 1407.

B. Motion To Dismiss for Matters in Abatement[8]

§ 10.03. Manner of Raising Matters in Abatement

A Motion To Dismiss with supporting affidavits was unknown to the common law, and pleas, rather than motions with affidavits, were used to add allegations of fact to the record. Thus, at common law, matters in abatement could be raised by a motion to quash or motion to dismiss if the facts supporting the abatement were apparent on the record but could only be raised by a plea in abatement if they were not.

The form of the plea in abatement was very strictly prescribed, and deviations from the allowed form frequently resulted in a refusal of the plea.[9] Under today's practice, the plea in abatement has been replaced by the Motion To Dismiss with supporting affidavits and the strict requirements of form are no longer so significant. Motions To Dismiss for matters apparent on the record require no supporting affidavits.

Library References

CJS Abatement and Revival §§ 104, 105, 187, 191

§ 10.04. Grounds of Abatement

At least twenty-two separate grounds of abatement have been recognized by the Supreme Court since 1819. These may be grouped into four categories, as follows:

(a) *Defects in Service.*

(1) *Improper Method of Service:* A defendant may plead in abatement that, on the date of service, he or she could not be served by the manner adopted.[10]

---

8 When a writ is abated, its legal force is terminated, and the claim which it seeks to assert may only be renewed by a second writ. A matter in abatement, therefore, is directed at the legal power of the writ and seeks to establish that something is lacking which must be present to give the writ its legal effect.

9 See, e.g., Reynolds v. Damrell, 19 N.H. 394 (1849); Pike v. Bagley, 4 N.H. 76 (1827); Goodall v. Durgin, 14 N.H. 576 (1844); Colby v. Dow, 18 N.H. 557 (1847); Dinsmore v. Pendexter, 28 N.H. 18 (1853); Parker v. McKean, 34 N.H. 375 (1857); Messer v. Smythe, 58 N.H. 312 (1878).

10 Tilton v. Parker, 4 N.H. 142 (1827).

(2) *Wrong Person Served:* Service on a person who is not a proper officer, director, or agent of a corporation for service of process may be pleaded in abatement.[11]

(3) *Wrong Paper Served:* A writ may be abated because the serving officer left a copy of the summons, rather than of the writ, at the defendant's abode.[12]

(4) *Service by the Wrong Person:* An action may be abated upon the defendant's objection that the writ or other process was served by an officer who was disqualified to serve it.[13]

(5) *Lack of Timely Notice:* Under some statutes, the plaintiff must give notice, as well as serve a designated agent. In those cases, a failure to give notice in a timely fashion may be pleaded in abatement of the action.[14]

(b) *Defects in the Writ or Summons.*

(1) *Defects of Form:* Generally speaking, defects in the form or completion of a writ or other process (e.g., teste of the wrong judge, lack of clerk's signature, lack of a seal, etc.) must be pleaded in abatement, if they are objected to at all.[15] In disposing of such objections, however, the court must resolve a conflict between statutes and an Article of the Constitution. On the one hand, RSA 509:2, 11, and 12 and part 2, article 87, of the Constitution require that writs include certain basic information. On the other hand, RSA 514:8 provides that "[n]o writ . . . in the courts . . . shall be abated, quashed or reversed for any error or mistake, where the person or case may be rightly understood by the court, nor through defect or want of form or addition only and the courts may, on motion order amendment in any such case." The Court has generally resolved these conflicts by holding that the requirements imposed by article 87 and chapter 509 are requirements of form, and, as such, make the process voidable but not void;[16] that a plaintiff's failure to comply with these requirements must be raised in abatement or be waived; and that such a plea in abatement will result in

---

11 Libbey v. Hodgdon, 9 N.H. 394 (1838).

12 Coughlin v. Angell, 68 N.H. 352, 44 A. 525 (1895).

13 Nichols v. Smith, 26 N.H. 298 (1853); Wood v. Carpenter, 9 N.H. 153 (1838); Ingraham v. Olcock, 14 N.H. 243 (1843) (service by a sheriff's deputy in an action in which the sheriff was a defendant); Barker v. Remick, 43 N.H. 235 (1861) (service by a deputy sheriff on former sheriff in suit for default of his deputy, now sheriff); State v. Walpole, 15 N.H. 26 (1844) (service by sheriff in suit against town of which he was an inhabitant).

14 Hoyt v. Nick, 113 N.H. 478, 309 A.2d 917 (1973).

15 Nichols v. Smith, 26 N.H. 298 (1853); Parsons v. Swett, 32 N.H. 87 (1855).

16 Carroll County Elderly Housing Assoc. v. Merrimac Tile Co., 127 N.H. 538, 503 A.2d 817 (1985) (typographical error in the statement of the return date). See, e.g., Parsons v. Swett, 32 N.H. 87 (1855).

an order requiring the plaintiff to amend his writ, rather than terminating the action. As the Court said in *Kelly v. Gilman*:[17]

> Defects of forms, in this State, are not grounds of demurrer or of pleas in abatement, where the person or case can be rightly understood, but the courts are to order amendment.[18]

Thus, in the early part of the nineteenth century, the Court held that any failure to comply with the statutory requirements for the form or completion of a writ was a good ground of abatement.[19] But later, in *Rogers v. Farnham*[20] the Court held that a writ would be abated only for deficiencies in matters "clearly required by the statute" or which result in a substantial failure of the process "to give the notice to the defendant that a suit has been commenced against him, returnable at a particular court, and at a certain time and place."[21] And in *Jenkins v. Sherburne*,[22] the Court applied the *Rogers* holding to overrule a plea in abatement which was based in part on the plaintiff's use of an old writ form bearing the wrong teste and court name where there was no reason to believe that the defendant had been misled by these mistakes.

In *Stone v. Sprague*,[23] the Court held that a writ might be abated for the sheriff's completion of the return in pencil, rather than in ink. Under today's rule allowing a sheriff to testify to the facts stated in his return, this defect could also be cured by amendment.

(2) *Defects of Substance:*   The writ must, however, fulfill its purpose of providing notice and correct information regarding the case, and, where important information has been left out of the writ, or each count taken separately does not state a cause of action although the counts taken together might,[24] or where the wrong or conflicting information has been inserted in the count,[25] the defendant may plead the error in abatement. In such a case,

---

17 29 N.H. 385 (1854).

18 29 N.H. at 389. See also Carroll County Elderly Housing Assoc. v. Merrimac Tile Co., 127 N.H. 538, 503 A.2d 817 (1985); Berry v. Osborn, 28 N.H. 279 (1854).

19 Putney v. Cram, 5 N.H. 174 (1830).

20 25 N.H. 511 (1852).

21 *Id.* at 513.

22 56 N.H. 17 (1875).

23 24 N.H. 309 (1851).

24 Kempton v. Sullivan Savings Institution, 53 N.H. 581 (1873).

25 In both Nelson v. Swett, 4 N.H. 256 (1827), and Keniston v. Chesley, 52 N.H. 564 (1873), the Court abated a writ upon the defendant's objection that the process stated two different return days.

In the mid–nineteenth century, defects of substance were frequently found in variances between the summons and the writ. In those days, the declaration was separate from the summons, and the sheriff served the summons with a copy of the writ. In cases of attachment, an 1829 statute specifically provided that the summons should "briefly give to the defendant the same information which the declaration gives more at large, and . . . contain the substance thereof" or the writ must abate. Compiled Statutes, ch. 194, § 4. As a result, it was common in the 1830s, 1840s, and 1850s for defendants to plead in abatement of writs in actions begun by attachment that some variance between the writ and the summons resulted in the summons failing to give the defendant the substance of the writ. Many of these cases made their way to the Supreme Court, and they are interesting, not only for what they show about the way law was practiced 125 years ago, but for what they disclose about the development of the Court's prejudice against pleas in abatement. Contrary to Mr. Reid's thesis in *Chief Justice: The Judicial World of Charles Doe*, the Supreme Court in the period from 1830–1860 was very concerned that litigants not subvert justice by reliance on the technical rules of pleading, and, on more than one occasion, the Court objected at length to what it regarded as the Legislature's wrong, but clearly expressed, desire to allow defendants to escape from a case otherwise properly begun simply because of a variance between the writ and summons.

Thus, in Wendell v. Moulton, 14 N.H. 573 (1844), Chief Justice Parker, relying on the statute, held that the writ must abate when the summons failed to include the writ of entry's allegation of seizin, but added:

> Whether this is a wise provision or not, it does not belong to us to determine. It is sufficient that the language of the statute is imperative; to which it might be added that the legislature have seen fit to adhere to the policy of it, notwithstanding an attempt to procure a change mitigating its rigor. (14 N.H. at 575.)

But in the companion case of Goodall v. Durgin, 14 N.H. 576 (1844), the Chief Justice unveiled the tactic which the Court planned to follow in order to vitiate the harmful effects of the statute. In *Goodall*, the defendant pleaded in abatement that the summons stated that the note sued on was for $10,500 rather than for $105 and that the note was payable "in one year now past" rather than "in one year from its date now past." The Court held that, while it was bound by the statute to abate the writ for a variance which was properly called to its attention, the defendant would be held to a strict standard of pleading and that any defect in his plea would result in the Court overruling his objection. The defendant in *Goodall* had omitted one word in copying over the summons, and his plea was accordingly denied.

Three years later, again in companion cases, the Court receded from the *Goodall* doctrine slightly and held that the defendant's copying error must be in that part of the summons on which his plea relies in order to justify a rejection of the plea. Baker v. Brown, 18 N.H. 551 (1847). The Court receded from the stricter standard because it had found that the *Goodall* holding, rather than diminishing the frequency of technical objections by encouraging plaintiffs to look for copying errors in defendants' pleas in abatement, had simply shifted the source of technical objections from the defendants to the plaintiffs. This problem reached its peak in Colby v. Dow, *supra*, when the plaintiff objected that the defendant, in copying the writ to support his plea, had corrected two misspellings that the plaintiff had made in the original writ. Justice Gilchrist, writing for the Court, said:

> It is often said that pleas in abatement are not to be favored—that they are merely dilatory. But whatever loose remarks may have been made at times, we have no right to say that such pleas are to be discountenanced, and that for that purpose a more strict and different rule is to be applied to the reading of them than that which is to be used in other cases. A rational view is to be

the court will apply the principles of RSA 514:9, rather than RSA 514:8, and permit an amendment only if necessary for the prevention of injustice, upon terms, and if third parties' rights will not be affected by it. Otherwise, the action will be terminated.

(3) *Lack of Endorsements.* If the defendant believes that the endorsement on the plaintiff's writ does not set forth the signer's true name or is made without authority, that the endorser is not an inhabitant of the state, that the endorsement is forged, or that the endorser is not responsible, he may raise the matter in abatement.[26] He or she may also object to a lack of any endorsement by pleading the defect in abatement.[27] Similarly, the lack of an adequate bond in replevin actions may be objected to in abatement.[28]

(c) *Problems With the Parties.*

(1) *Nonjoinder:*

(A) *Of Defendants.* If the plaintiff has failed to name all persons who are jointly liable, the defect may be pleaded in abatement.[29] But unless

---

taken of them, as of every other matter. We are not to be astute in finding means to prevent a party from making use of a defence which the statute allows. (18 N.H. at 558.)

The Court followed the *Baker/Colby* doctrine in Smith v. Butler, 25 N.H. 521 (1852) (holding that a failure of the summons to set forth two out of the four counts in the declaration was a "substantial" variance and that the defendant's use of the terms "vs." and "L.S." in his plea and his insertion of figures and letters in the body of the plea after saying in the preamble of the plea that he would use only "words" were not defects which justified a rejection of the plea) and in Pitman v. Perkins, 28 N.H. 90 (1853).

In mid-century, the requirement that a writ abate for a variance between the summons and writ was repealed. In Adams v. Wiggin, 42 N.H. 553 (1861), Justice Doe, writing for the Court, held that the repeal put variances on the same footing as other defects in pleadings, and that, where the variance was a defect of form only and not a substantial variance from the writ, it could not be used to abate the writ. However, the *Adams* holding only legitimized the approach which the Court had been taking for 14 years, and in Grant v. Durgin, 45 N.H. 167 (1863), and Keniston v. Chesley, 52 N.H. 564 (1873), the Court reaffirmed that the writ could be abated for variances of substance between the writ and summons. A similar ruling would not be expected today.

Under present practice, the writ and summons are part of the same form and the chances of conflicting or ambiguous statements of the plaintiff's claim are not as great as they were in the past. However, a defendant may still plead in abatement of the writ any variance between the declaration and the summons which is substantial enough to defeat the summons' purpose of informing the defendant of the nature of the claim and the time and place where he must respond to it.

26 Scruton & Hand v. Deming, 36 N.H. 432 (1858); Haverhill Insurance Company v. Prescott, 38 N.H. 398 (1859); Nichols v. Smith, 26 N.H. 298 (1853).

27 Pettingill v. McGregor, 12 N.H. 179 (1841).

28 Briggs v. Wiswell, 56 N.H. 319 (1876).

29 Powers v. Spear, 3 N.H. 35 (1823); Nealley v. Moulton, 12 N.H. 485 (1842); Moulton v. Robinson, 27 N.H. 550 (1853); Hartshorn v. Schoff, 51 N.H. 316 (1871); Judge of Probate v. Webster, 46 N.H. 518 (1866); Gove v. Lawrence, 24 N.H. 128 (1851);

the plaintiff's declaration or other pleading shows on its face that another person is jointly liable, the defendant must name the other persons who are jointly liable "and give the plaintiff a better writ."[30] He or she may not simply allege a joint liability and leave the plaintiff to discover the identity of the co-obligors. If the plaintiff has named but failed to serve all persons who are jointly liable, that defect, too, may be pleaded in abatement.[31] But in all cases of nonjoinder, unless the facts are admitted in the plaintiff's pleading, the defendant must plead that the omitted person is liable, that he is or she alive, and is subject to the jurisdiction of the court.[32]

(B) *Of Plaintiffs.* If the plaintiff has no right to sue alone and has failed to join another person who also has the right to charge the defendant, the defendant may take advantage of the defect by pleading it in abatement.[33] In actions founded on contract or dealing with rights in property, the defendant must plead the defect in abatement;[34] in tort actions, the defendant may either plead the defect in abatement or take advantage of it by an apportionment of damages at trial.[35] If the defendant fails to plead a nonjoinder of plaintiffs in abatement of the first action brought against him for a cause, he may not plead the defect in any subsequent action by persons who might have been joined in the first action.[36]

(2) *Misjoinder:* The inclusion of persons, as either plaintiffs[37] or defendants,[38] who are not proper parties to the action may be pleaded in abatement. The misjoinder may be cured by amendment.[39]

Shortlidge v. Gutoski, 125 N.H. 510, 484 A.2d 1083 (1984). The plaintiff himself may point out the defect and move to correct it by amendment at any time when the defendant might still plead it in abatement.

30 Ela v. Rand, 4 N.H. 307, 308 (1828).

31 Merrill v. Coggill, 12 N.H. 97 (1841); Curtis v. Baldwin, 42 N.H. 398 (1861); Bowman v. Brown, 51 N.H. 549 (1872).

32 Merrill v. Coggill, 12 N.H. 97 (1841); Nealley v. Moulton, 12 N.H. 485 (1842).

33 Jordan v. Cummings, 43 N.H. 134 (1861); Parker v. Way, 15 N.H. 45 (1844); White v. Brooks, 43 N.H. 402 (1861).

34 Pickering v. Pickering, 11 N.H. 141 (1840).

35 Wilson v. Gamble, 9 N.H. 74 (1837); True v. Congdon, 44 N.H. 48 (1862); Garvin v. Paul, 47 N.H. 158 (1866); Cooper v. Grand Trunk Railway, 49 N.H. 209 (1870); Pickering v. Pickering, 11 N.H. 141 (1840); Webber v. Merrill, 34 N.H. 202 (1856). The defendant may not be able to rely upon an apportionment of damages where both joint plaintiffs are fiduciaries who must account to a probate court. In such a case, an excessive award to one fiduciary would eventually be tendered to the fiduciary who was entitled to receive it but had not been joined. Smith v. Smith, 11 N.H. 459 (1841).

36 Garvin v. Paul, 47 N.H. 158 (1866).

37 Campbell v. Wallace, 12 N.H. 362 (1841); Demeritt v. Mills, 59 N.H. 18 (1879).

38 Demeritt v. Mills, 59 N.H. 18 (1879).

39 *Id.*

(3) *Misnomer:*

(A) *In General.* Designation of either the plaintiff or the defendant by an incorrect name may be pleaded in abatement.[40] The error may in all cases be cured by amendment.[41]

(B) *Spelling Errors, Misnomer, and Misdesignation.* There are three types of errors which may be committed in naming parties to a suit. The first and simplest is a misspelling or the inclusion or omission of a middle initial. Both errors, although presenting a technically incorrect name, leave no doubt about the identity of the person sought to be made a party to the action. Such errors have never been a ground for abating an action[42] or been thought serious enough to require the formality of an abatement.

The second type is a designation of a party by a name which, rather than being misspelled or omitting an initial, varies by words or syllables (including the addition or deletion of a middle name) from the intended party's true name. In this class of cases, the name given can be mistaken neither for the intended party's actual name nor for the name of anyone else, and it is clear who the correct party should be. This sort of error is called a misnomer and may be pleaded in abatement[43] and cured by amendment.[44]

Lastly, there is a class of cases in which the plaintiff simply names the wrong person but the named defendant has a name which is similar to the intended defendant's. As a general principle, this type of mistake has no effect on the intended defendant; the action is regarded as not being against

---

40 Burnham v. President & Trustees of the Savings Bank for the County of Strafford, 5 N.H. 446 (1831); School District No. 1 in Orange v. Blaisdell, 6 N.H. 197 (1833); The Proprietors of Sunapee v. Eastman, 32 N.H. 470 (1855).

41 Burnham v. Savings Bank for the County of Strafford, 5 N.H. 573 (1832); Belknap v. Clark, 58 N.H. 150 (1877); Wheeler v. Contoocook Mills Corporation, 77 N.H. 551, 94 A. 265 (1915).

42 Tibbetts v. Kiah, 2 N.H. 557 (1823) (name put in writ sounded the same, but was spelled differently from defendant's name); Hart v. Lindsey, 17 N.H. 235 (1845); Peck v. Wilson, 14 N.H. 587 (1844) (omission of a middle initial). In order to avoid the error, however, the plaintiff must show, in the case of a misspelling, that the name given in the writ sounds the same as the party's true name (idem sonans) and, in the case of an omission of a letter or of an initial, that the party is known as well with as without the initial.

43 Burnham v. President & Trustees of the Savings Bank for the County of Strafford, 5 N.H. 446 (1831); School District No. 1 in Orange v. Blaisdell, 6 N.H. 197 (1833); The Souhegan Nail, Cotton and Woolen Factory v. McConihe, 7 N.H. 309 (1834); The Proprietors of Sunapee v. Eastman, 32 N.H. 470 (1855); Hart v. Lindsey, 17 N.H. 235 (1845).

44 Burnham v. Savings Bank for the County of Strafford, 5 N.H. 573 (1832); Belknap v. Clark, 58 N.H. 150 (1877).

the party who should have been named. The error may be taken advantage of by pleading in abatement or under the general issue.[45]

(C) *Misdesignation of Corporate Defendants*. The application of these principles to corporations has undergone some evolution over the years as the law's attitude toward the powers and nature of corporations has changed. In the early part of the nineteenth century, when corporate existence and powers were tightly restricted, any substantial mistake in the naming of a corporate defendant was regarded as ineffective to bring the corporation into the suit, even when it was reasonably clear who the intended defendant was.[46] In the early part of the twentieth century, when corporate powers were broader and the need for protection against corporate avoidance of liability was more keenly appreciated, it was possible to bring an intended corporate defendant into court by naming its predecessor, even though the named defendant was an entirely different and dissolved corporation.[47]

In 1974, the Supreme Court held that a corporation could be validly summoned even when an entirely different and unassociated corporation was named in the writ, so long as there was a reasonable basis for the error, the person receiving the service for the named defendant was also an authorized agent for service on the intended defendant at the time of service, and, shortly after service, the intended defendant became aware that it was the intended defendant.[48] As a result, at least with regard to corporations,

---

45 Burnham v. President & Trustees of the Savings Bank for the County of Strafford, 5 N.H. 446 (1831).

46 Burnham v. President & Trustees of the Savings Bank for the County of Strafford, 5 N.H. 446 (1831) (deputy sheriff sued for his fees in the service of a writ on behalf of the bank but named as defendants the president and trustees of the bank; the Court regarded the error as substantial and as preventing the writ from running against the corporation); The Souhegan Nail, Cotton & Woolen Factory v. McConihe, 7 N.H. 309 (1834):

> When a corporation is sued, if the name of the corporation is mistaken materially and substantially, the corporation cannot be affected by the proceedings. There is in these cases a distinction made between a variance in words and syllables only, and a variance in substance. If a corporation be sued by a name varying only in words and syllables, and not in substance, from the true name, the misnomer must be pleaded in abatement, otherwise it will not be regarded. But if the name be mistaken in substance, the writ cannot be regarded as against the corporation. (7 N.H. at 319.)

47 Wheeler v. Contoocook Mills Corporation, 77 N.H. 551, 94 A. 265 (1915).

48 Dupuis v. Smith Properties, Inc., 114 N.H. 625, 325 A.2d 781 (1974). But see Rowe v. John Deere, 130 N.H. 18, 533 A.2d 375 (1987) (Plaintiff was injured by an allegedly defective John Deere manure spreader. He brought suit, three days before the statute of limitations expired, against John Deere Leasing Company. Several months later, the trial court granted the defendant's motion for summary judgment on the ground that

any error in naming the intended defendant may be corrected by amendment if the error has not prevented the intended defendant from being validly served and learning of the claims in a timely fashion.

(4) *No Such Person as Plaintiff:*   The defendant may plead in abatement that there is no such natural person or corporation as the plaintiff who is described in the writ.[49] If the plaintiff has misdescribed itself, the error may be corrected by amendment. If a fictitious person has been represented to the court as an actual plaintiff, the court may allow a substitution of an existing person if justice requires. If the plaintiff, in fact, no longer has any legal existence, the action must abate.

(5) *Defendant Sued in Wrong Capacity:*   A defendant may plead in abatement that suit has been brought in the wrong capacity.[50] The defect may be cured by amendment or, if the plaintiff insists on asserting liability in that capacity, the defendant may file a Brief Statement and take advantage of the error under the general issue.

(6) *Disability of Plaintiff To Sue:*   The defendant may plead in abatement that the plaintiff does not have legal capacity to bring the action. In the case of actual persons, the plaintiff's incapacity may arise from infancy,[51] mental deficiency,[52] or lack of authority.[53] In the case of foreign corporations,

---

the original named defendant had not manufactured the spreader. Thereafter, plaintiff began a new action against John Deere, John Deere Spreader Works c/o John Deere and Company, and John Deere Well and Works c/o John Deere, Ltd. The trial court dismissed the second action on the ground that the statute of limitations had expired, and the Supreme Court upheld the dismissal. The issues in the case were framed in terms of the statute of limitations for personal injury actions, principles of tolling, and the application of the saving statute (RSA 508:10), and, unlike *Dupuis v. Smith Properties, Inc., supra,* there was no showing that the actual and intended defendants were related, that the intended defendant had received notice within the period of limitations or that the plaintiff had moved to amend to name the correct defendant in the original action. But on its face, the *Rowe* case seems very similar to *Dupuis,* and it may be wondered whether it signals a change to a more conservative attitude towards errors in naming and serving corporate defendants.).

49 School District No. 1 in Orange v. Blaisdell, 6 N.H. 197 (1833); Nashua Fire Insurance Co. v. Moore, 55 N.H. 48 (1874); Parsons v. Eureka Powder Works, 48 N.H. 66 (1868).

50 Clements v. Swain, 2 N.H. 475 (1822) (administrator sued as executor de son tort).

51 Young v. Young, 3 N.H. 345 (1826); Paju v. Ricker, 110 N.H. 310, 266 A.2d 836 (1970). See Norton v. Patten, 125 N.H. 413, 480 A.2d 190 (1984) (Legislature has the power to change the age of majority with respect to causes of action which have already accrued).

52 Lang v. Whidden, 2 N.H. 435 (1822) (lunatics or idiots).

53 Mathewson v. Eureka Powder Works, 44 N.H. 289 (1862).

the deficiency may arise from a failure to obtain a certificate of authority to do business in New Hampshire.[54]

(7) *Wrong Defendant:*   There is some authority for the view that the fact that the wrong person has been sued may be pleaded in abatement of the action.[55] However, the defect may also be raised under the general issue, and this fact probably accounts for the lack of any body of case law on the point.

(8) *Defendant Exempt From Service:*   The defendant may plead in abatement of the action that the service was not lawful. The defendant's exemption may result from the fact that service was made on a Sunday or legal holiday[56] or that he or she is a nonresident and was, at the time of service, on the way to, in attendance upon, or returning from an appearance as a witness in another action then pending in this state.[57]

(9) *Defendant Temporarily Exempt From Suit:*   RSA 556:1 provides that "[n]o action shall be sustained against an administrator if begun within six months after the original grant of administration . . . ." If an administrator is sued within that period, he may plead the statute in abatement of the action.[58]

(d) *Problems With the Action.*

(1) *Prematurely Brought:*   If a plaintiff sues in a capacity which he or she does not yet, but may soon, enjoy or sue on the basis of events which expected to happen but which have not yet occurred, the defendant may object and plead the matter in abatement of the action.[59] If the expected events occur before a decision on the defendant's objection, the plaintiff may be allowed to amend on terms, and the case will proceed.

(2) *Remedy Is Misconceived:*   When a plaintiff brings an action at common law for an injury for which a statute provides a specific and exclusive remedy, the defendant may plead the error in abatement of the

---

54 R.C. Allen Business Machines v. Acres, 111 N.H. 269, 281 A.2d 162 (1971); Guyette v. C & K Development Co., 122 N.H. 913, 451 A.2d 1318 (1982).

55 Whidden v. Proctor, 17 N.H. 90 (1845); Marsh v. Smith, 18 N.H. 367 (1846) (involving pleas of special non tenure to writs of entry by mortgagees).

56 Hubbard v. Sanborn, 2 N.H. 468 (1822).

57 Ela v. Ela, 68 N.H. 312, 36 A. 15 (1895); Martin v. Whitney, 74 N.H. 505, 69 A. 888 (1908); Dickinson v. Farwell, 71 N.H. 213, 51 A. 624 (1902); Dolber v. Young, 81 N.H. 157, 123 A. 218 (1923).

58 Clements v. Swain, 2 N.H. 475 (1822); Kittredge v. Folsom, 8 N.H. 98 (1835); Amoskeag Manufacturing Company v. Barnes, 48 N.H. 25 (1868); Hall v. Brusseau, 100 N.H. 87, 119 A.2d 703 (1956).

59 Philbrick v. Hazen, 3 N.H. 120 (1824); Williams v. Walker, 95 N.H. 231, 61 A.2d 522 (1948).

action.[60] The plaintiff can amend if the requirements of the statute can thereby be met.

(3) *Prior Action Pending:*   No person should be subjected to two actions for the same cause at the same time, and, in general, an action will be abated upon the defendant's objection that a prior suit is pending for the same cause between the same parties in the U.S. District Court for the District of New Hampshire or in a New Hampshire court of at least equivalent jurisdiction.[61] The action will not be abated if the prior suit is for a different cause,[62] if it is not between precisely the same parties,[63] or if it is pending in an inferior court in New Hampshire, in a federal court outside of New Hampshire[64] or in the courts of another state, territory, or country.[65] In addition, the second suit will not be abated, even though it is between the same parties for the same cause and in the same court, if it is not clear that

60 Woods v. The Nashua Manufacturing Co., 4 N.H. 527 (1829).

61 Smith v. The Atlantic Mutual Fire Insurance Company, 22 N.H. 21 (1850); Parker v. Colcord, 2 N.H. 36 (1819); Davis v. Dunklee, 9 N.H. 545 (1838); Chase v. Strain, 15 N.H. 535 (1844); Yelverton v. Conant, 18 N.H. 123 (1846); Haselton v. Monroe, 18 N.H. 598 (1847); Clark v. Lisbon, 19 N.H. 286 (1848); Bennett v. Chase, 21 N.H. 570 (1850); Rogers v. Odell, 39 N.H. 417 (1859); Gamsby v. Ray, 52 N.H. 513 (1872).

62 Rogers v. Odell, 39 N.H. 417 (1859) ("What is meant by the same cause of action, is, where the same evidence will support both the actions, although the actions may happen to be grounded on different writs." 39 N.H. at 419–20); Sworoski v. Sworoski, 75 N.H. 1, 70 A. 119 (1908); Perham v. Lane, 76 N.H. 580, 83 A. 805 (1912); Hoyt v. Massachusetts Bonding & Insurance Co., 80 N.H. 27, 113 A. 219 (1921).

63 Bennett v. Chase, 21 N.H. 570 (1850) (plaintiffs must be the same except in cases for the assessment of a penalty); Barker v. Eastman, 76 N.H. 277, 82 A. 166 (1912) (parties must be the same on both sides).

64 Nixon v. Bonenfant, 97 N.H. 230, 84 A.2d 841 (1951) (pendency of petition for partition and accounts in probate court did not preclude the petitioner from bringing a bill in equity for accounting and to restrain conveyance); Pitman v. Thompson, 63 N.H. 73 (1884) (submission of claim to arbitrators did not preclude suit on the claim and attachment).

65 Weeks v. Pearson, 5 N.H. 324 (1831); Yelverton v. Conant, 18 N.H. 123 (1846) ("We have no doubt upon the general proposition, that the pendency of an action for the same cause in another state, is no cause for abating an action in our courts." 18 N.H. at 126); Moore v. Maryland Casualty Co., 74 N.H. 47, 64 A. 1099 (1906) (but a N.H. court may stay an action pending decision in the other state, rather than dismiss it); Sworoski v. Sworoski, 75 N.H. 1, 70 A. 119 (1908) (divorce action in Massachusetts on a different ground); Drake v. Drake, 76 N.H. 32, 78 A. 1071 (1911) (divorce action in Massachusetts resulted in decree nisi but no final judgment); Pacific & Atlantic Shippers, Inc. v. Schier, 106 N.H. 69, 205 A.2d 31 (1964) ("A prior action pending in a foreign jurisdiction is ordinarily no ground for abatement, since a court of this jurisdiction cannot assure full protection of the plaintiff's rights elsewhere." 106 N.H. at 70, 205 A.2d at 32).

the plaintiff can obtain full relief in the first action,[66] if abatement will not further "the best inventible procedure,"[67] or if abatement is not, on the whole, what justice requires.[68]

(4) *Venue Improper:* Objections to venue, including a claim that the real plaintiff in interest has conspired with the nominal plaintiff to assign the claim so that the case may be brought in a county in which it could not otherwise be prosecuted,[69] must be pleaded in abatement.[70]

(5) *Lack of Prosecution After Plaintiff's Death:* RSA 556:10 provides that, if an action of tort for physical injuries is pending at the time of the plaintiff's death, the action will be abated unless the administrator appears and prosecutes the action before the end of the second term after the plaintiff's decease. This statute has been construed to require one year to expire after the plaintiff's death.[71]

---

66 Tinkham v. Boston and Maine Railroad, 77 N.H. 111, 88 A. 709 (1913) (plaintiff brought common law action for negligence, then an action under FELA, and it was doubtful whether it could provide full relief).

67 Hoyt v. Massachusetts Bonding and Insurance Company, 80 N.H. 27, 113 A. 219 (1921) (at trial of the first action, the defendant moved for a nonsuit on the ground that the action had been prematurely brought; the court granted the motion and the plaintiff excepted. On the same day, the plaintiff brought the action again, but the defendant objected that the plaintiff's exceptions in the first suit kept it alive and required abatement of the second suit. The Supreme Court held that the plaintiff was entitled to a procedure that preserved his exceptions in the first case while not risking the termination of his claim by the statute of limitations); Adams v. Sullivan, 110 N.H. 101, 261 A.2d 273 (1970) ("Where it is doubtful whether plaintiff can secure his rights in the original suit, justice does not necessarily require abatement of the second suit for the same cause of action and by consolidation of suits or some other convenient procedure the rights of both parties may be protected and afford them an opportunity to litigate the merits of the controversy." 110 N.H. at 104, 261 A.2d at 276).

68 State v. Cote, 95 N.H. 248, 61 A.2d 710 (1948) (replevin to recover pipe need not be abated because a bill in equity is pending seeking relief from contracts under which the pipe was sold and remedies are complementary); Morency v. Plourde, 96 N.H. 344, 76 A.2d 791 (1950) (actions at law for damages pending bill in equity was brought to enjoin shutting off utilities); Pacific & Atlantic Shippers, Inc. v. Schier, 106 N.H. 69, 205 A.2d 31 (1964) (The issue is "whether justice requires that the second action stand; or that it be dismissed as vexatious." 106 N.H. at 70, 205 A.2d at 32).

69 Parsons v. Brown, 50 N.H. 484 (1871).

70 The Educational Society of the Denomination Called Christians v. Varney, 54 N.H. 376 (1874); Bishop v. Silver Lake Mining Co., 62 N.H. 455 (1883); Stiles v. Dube, 106 N.H. 339, 211 A.2d 402 (1965).

71 Belkner v. Preston, 115 N.H. 15, 332 A.2d 168 (1975).

Library References

CJS Abatement and Revival §§ 82 et seq.
Motion to dismiss on ground of obtaining personal service by fraud or trickery. 98 ALR2d 600.
Mistake or error in middle initial or middle name of party as vitiating or invalidating civil process, summons, or the like. 6 ALR3d 1179.

Cross References

Service of Process, see ch. 14 *infra*.
Parties, see ch. 6 *supra*.
Venue, see ch. 4 *supra*.

§ 10.05. No Ground for Abatement

During the last 150 years, the Supreme Court has announced that a few types of objection are so trivial or unrelated to the events of the action that they may not be raised either in abatement or by any other means as an impediment to the progress of the case. Those types of objections are:

(a) *Defendant's Name Is Misspelled.*   A minor variance, by misspelling or the inclusion or omission of a middle initial, is no ground for abatement if the name given in the writ sounds like the defendant's true name or if the defendant is as well known by that name as he is by his true name.[72]

(b) *Insubstantial Inconsistency Between the Writ and Summons.*   An insubstantial inconsistency between the writ and summons is no basis for abatement or amendment.[73]

(c) *Failure To Include Unnecessary Information in the Summons.*   A failure to include useful but unnecessary information in the summons is no ground of abatement.[74]

(d) *Serving Officer's Default.*   Generally speaking, errors or defects caused solely by the serving officer, when he or she is not legally disqualified to act, may not be used to defeat the action. If the parties suffer damage due to the serving officer's default, they must bring a separate action against him to recover. Thus, it has been held that the sheriff's failure to attest to the copy of the writ left at the defendant's abode,[75] failure to leave a true copy of the writ,[76] and failure to take the oath of office before making service,[77] may not

---

72 See §§ 6.21, 6.22, *supra*. See also Tibbetts v. Kiah, 2 N.H. 557 (1823); Hart v. Lindsey, 17 N.H. 235 (1845); Peck v. Wilson, 14 N.H. 587 (1844).

73 Bishop v. Lyman, 6 N.H. 268 (1833); Smith v. Butler, 25 N.H. 521 (1852); Grant v. Durgin, 45 N.H. 167 (1863); Rogers v. Farnham, 25 N.H. 511 (1852).

74 Stickney v. Stickney, 16 N.H. 163 (1844) (ad damnum in action of debt on a bond).

75 Davis v. Cray, 109 N.H. 181, 246 A.2d 97 (1968).

76 Bolles v. Bowen, 45 N.H. 124 (1863).

77 Merrill v. Palmer, 13 N.H. 184 (1842).

be pleaded in abatement of the writ or otherwise taken advantage of to defeat the plaintiff's action.

(e) *Defendant Is Plaintiff's Trustee in Prior Suit by Third Party.* Originally, it was held that a writ would be abated if, at the time it was brought, the defendant had been named as the plaintiff's trustee in another suit by a third party.[78] The rationale for this holding was that the defendant trustee should not be exposed to double payment of the debt.[79] But this doctrine was revised in *Drew v. Towle*,[80] and the pendency of a trustee suit is no longer a cause for abating a subseque nt action by the principal debtor against the trustee. If the trustee pays the debt as a consequence of the second action, the trustee can take advantage of that payment, after being charged as trustee, under the general issue in the second action.

Cross References

Service of Process, see ch. 14 *infra.*

§ 10.06. Persons Who May Raise Matters in Abatement—Principal Defendants

Any principal defendant may plead matters in abatement within the time allowed after entry of the writ. If a person is joined as a principal defendant without his consent after entry of the writ, he should have thirty days from notice of the joinder to raise any defects which either the original defendants or he could have pleaded in abatement of the action. If a person intervenes as a principal defendant, either after the time for pleading in abatement or too close to the deadline to be able to plead in time, that person should be allowed to plead in abatement only if he or she can satisfy the court that the delay in entering the suit and pleading was not intentional or due to inexcusable neglect.

Library References

CJS Abatement and Revival § 188

§ 10.07. —Plaintiffs

Although a plaintiff will generally be allowed to amend at any time and in any respect if the defendant and third parties are not prejudiced thereby,

---

78 Burnham v. Folsom, 5 N.H. 566 (1832); Haselton v. Monroe, 18 N.H. 598 (1847).

79 In line with this theory, it was also held that a trustee writ might be abated due to the pendency of an action between the principal defendant and trustee for the same debt. Burnham v. Folsom, 5 N.H. 566 (1832).

80 27 N.H. 412 (1853).

it has been held that a plaintiff may not amend after the deadline for raising matters in abatement in order to cure a defect which could only have been pleaded in abatement.[81] The purpose of this rule is obviously to avoid wasting the court's time on matters no longer in issue.

§ 10.08. —Subsequently Attaching Creditors

During the greater part of the nineteenth century, it was held that subsequently attaching creditors who were admitted to defend could raise matters in abatement, but only if they did so before the same deadlines which the principal defendant was required to meet.[82] However, at about the turn of the century, the Court took a different approach and announced that subsequently attaching creditors would no longer be permitted to raise any matter in abatement. Justice Chase noted that subsequently attaching creditors are granted leave to appear "to prevent an unjust diversion of property, or some other wrong . . . [and] not . . . to enable a party to abate an action for defective form, or for other cause of a dilatory nature."[83] This view was reaffirmed eleven years later in *Brown v. Ellsworth*[84] and has remained the law to the present day.

§ 10.09. When Matters in Abatement May Be Raised—In General

Superior Court Rule 30 and District and Municipal Court Rule 3.10(C) require that matters in abatement be raised by pleading and delivering a copy to the plaintiff within thirty days of the entry of the writ or other process,[85] or, when the right to plead in abatement arises during the pendency of the action, within thirty days of the event which gives rise to the objection.[86] In addition, matters in abatement must be pleaded at the earliest stage of the

---

81 Cf. Pitkin v. Roby, 43 N.H. 138 (1861).

82 Kimball v. Wellington, 20 N.H. 439 (1846); Reynolds v. Damrell, 19 N.H. 394 (1849); Child v. Eureka Powder Works, 45 N.H. 547 (1864); Garvin v. Legery, 61 N.H. 153 (1881).

83 Martin v. Wiggin, 67 N.H. 196, 29 A. 450 (1892).

84 72 N.H. 186, 55 A. 356 (1903).

85 Shortlidge v. Gutoski, 125 N.H. 510, 484 A.2d 1083 (1984). In Colby v. Knapp, 13 N.H. 175 (1842), the Court held that the deadline for filing pleas in abatement did not expire until the close of business on the last day of the filing period.

86 Hartshorn v. Schoff, 51 N.H. 316 (1871).

proceedings,[87] in the first court in which the defendant has the opportunity to raise them.[88]

Matters in abatement must be pleaded before trial,[89] and defects in jurisdiction, service, and notice must be raised before any other defects. In cases where the matter being pleaded in abatement is a defect of jurisdiction, service, or notice,[90] the defendant may file a Special Appearance,[91] but he may not do so when he pleads other grounds in abatement, because a Special Appearance is waived by submitting any question other than jurisdiction, service, or notice to the court.[92] Therefore, in cases where the defendant has objections both to jurisdiction and to other abatable defects, the defendant should raise jurisdictional objections first by a Motion To Dismiss with a

---

[87] Nichol v. Smith, 26 N.H. 298 (1853):

> Rules were made at a very early period requiring the party, who desired to take advantage of any defect in the proceedings by which he was brought into court, to make his exception by a plea in abatement, or a proper motion, at the earliest stage of the proceedings in court. And it was settled long since that if a party neglected to take his exception at that stage of the cause he was deemed to have waived it, and to have closed his own mouth against objecting afterwards. (26 N.H. at 301.)

See also Carroll County Elderly Housing Assoc. v. Merrimac Tile Co., 127 N.H. 538, 503 A.2d 817 (1985); Hanson v. Hoitt, 14 N.H. 56 (1843).

[88] Bedford v. Rice, 58 N.H. 227 (1877) ("A plea in abatement should be filed in the first court in which the defendant has an opportunity to file it, to avoid the cost of further litigation, if the plea is good." 58 N.H. at 228); Murphy v. Crain, 59 N.H. 244 (1879).

[89] Williams v. Walker, 95 N.H. 231, 61 A.2d 522 (1948); Jewett v. Jewett, 112 N.H. 341, 296 A.2d 11 (1972). In the early days of New Hampshire practice, it was also held that a plea in abatement had to be filed before pleading the general issue. Morse v. Calley, 5 N.H. 222 (1830) ("All defects in the service of a writ, which are not apparent on the face of the record, are cured by an appearance, unless exception is taken to the service by a regular plea in abatement." 5 N.H. at 223); School District No. 1 in Orange v. Blaisdell, 6 N.H. 197 (1833) ("The general issue is, in its nature, a plea in bar with full defence, and is a waiver of all exceptions to the person of the plaintiff." 6 N.H. at 197–98); Murphy v. Crain, 59 N.H. 244 (1879); Smith v. Whittier, 9 N.H. 464 (1838); Hanson v. Hoitt, 14 N.H. 56 (1843); Lyman v. Dodge, 13 N.H. 197 (1842); Tandy v. Rowell, 54 N.H. 384 (1874). But this was long before the Special Appearance was recognized or the filing of a General Appearance was regarded as raising the general issue. Prior to the recognition of the Special Appearance in 1858, it seems to have been the law that the mere filing of a plea in abatement was adequate to preserve the defendant's objections and that the entry of an Appearance at the same time did not amount to a plea of the general issue or a waiver of the defects raised by the plea. See Colby v. Knapp, 13 N.H. 175 (1842). Thus, it seems to have been customary prior to 1858 to file what would today be referred to as a General Appearance along with a plea in abatement.

[90] See §§ 2.01 et seq., *supra* and 14.01 et seq., *infra*.

[91] Dolber v. Young, 81 N.H. 157, 123 A. 218 (1923).

[92] *Id.*

Special Appearance and, if the defendant loses and decides to proceed with the action rather than seek appellate review, file a second Motion To Dismiss within thirty days of the court's order denying the motion.

Library References

CJS Abatement and Revival §§ 193 et seq.

§ 10.10. —Extension of Time To File

(a) *Implied From the Plaintiff's Defaults.* In the days when pleas in abatement had to be filed within the first four days of the term, regardless of when the plaintiff entered the writ, the Supreme Court held that the plaintiff's delay in entering the writ after service did not, by implication, extend the time for the defendant to file the plea.[93] The decision seems to have been based on a policy of restricting the period of time within which the plaintiff might raise matters in abatement and of measuring that pleading period from the date of actual notice of the defect. Although Superior Court Rule 30 has liberalized the practice by extending the time for pleading and by measuring it from the date the writ is entered, the principle that subsequent errors or defaults by the plaintiff will not toll the running of the period is still applied.

(b) *By Agreement of the Parties.* The rules that pleas in abatement are not favored and that filing time limits will be strictly enforced exist for the benefit of the plaintiff, not the court, and the plaintiff is always free to agree that a matter in abatement may be raised late.[94] The plaintiff may even consent that matters in abatement be raised by subsequently attaching creditors.[95]

(c) *By the Court.* The court will not ordinarily grant a motion for leave to raise matters in abatement after the deadline for filing such pleadings has passed.[96] However, the court does have the power to extend the time for filing in an appropriate case, for good cause shown.[97]

---

93 Seaver v. Allen, 48 N.H. 473 (1869).

94 Child v. Eureka Powder Works, 45 N.H. 547 (1864).

95 *Id.*

96 Wisheart v. Legro & McDuffee, 33 N.H. 177 (1856) ("It must be more than an ordinary case to induce the court to extend the time . . . to receive a plea in abatement." 33 N.H. at 180).

97 Tappan v. Tappan, 31 N.H. 41 (1855) (plea filed two years after entry and just before trial); Seaver v. Allen, 48 N.H. 473 (1869); Coughlin v. Angell, 68 N.H. 352, 44 A. 525 (1895).

§ 10.11. Effect of Raising Matters in Abatement—If Grounds for Abatement Exist

If the defendant convinces the court that grounds for abatement exist, the court will in most cases allow the plaintiff to cure the defect by amendment.[98] If the defect is of a type which cannot be cured by amendment (e.g., improper service) or if the plaintiff refuses to move to amend after being given the opportunity to do so,[99] the court will dismiss the action without prejudice.[100] In either event, the defendant will be entitled to costs.[101]

§ 10.12. —If Grounds for Abatement Do Not Exist

If the defendant does not convince the court that grounds for abatement exist, the court will overrule the plea and order him to plead further.[102] No costs will be allowed in such a case.[103]

§ 10.13. —If the Plea Is Defective

At an early date, the Supreme Court announced that, because a plea in abatement is dilatory in nature and disfavored, any defect in the form of the plea would cause it to be overruled without inquiry into its foundation and without an opportunity to correct the plea's defect by amendment.[104] This policy was at first applied with good effect to pleas in abatement based on insubstantial variances between the writ and summons,[105] but was later rescinded to some extent in that class of cases when it was observed that the

---

98 Young v. Young, 3 N.H. 345 (1826) (inserting name of plaintiff infant's next friend); Tilton v. Parker, 4 N.H. 142 (1827) (changing defendant's residence as stated in the writ); Burnham v. Savings Bank for the County of Strafford, 5 N.H. 573 (1832) (correcting misnomer); Carroll County Elderly Housing Assoc. v. Merrimac Tile Co., 127 N.H. 538, 503 A.2d 817 (1985).

99 In Paju v. Ricker, 110 N.H. 310, 266 A.2d 836 (1970), the Court dismissed an action for improper parties when the plaintiff refused to amend after being given the opportunity to do so.

100 In divorce proceedings, the court may dismiss one libel without affecting other libels. When a libel is dismissed "for insufficiency in the allegations or in the service," the court will state that cause in its order. Super. Ct. R. 149.

101 Eames v. Carlisle, 3 N.H. 130 (1824).

102 The common form of this order was *"respondeat ouster."*

103 Whitford v. Flanders, 14 N.H. 371 (1843); Trow v. Messer, 32 N.H. 361 (1855).

104 Pike v. Bagley, 4 N.H. 76 (1827) ("It is well settled that in these dilatory pleas the greatest precision is necessary and if they are found defective even in form they cannot be adjudged good." 4 N.H. at 76).

105 See Goodall v. Durgin, 14 N.H. 576 (1844).

policy had merely increased the number of trivial objections to form being raised by plaintiffs.[106]

The Court then reshaped its policy[107] to require that a plea in abatement for variance between the summons and writ be sufficient to place the defect clearly before the court but not to require that the plea be rejected for mere clerical or insubstantial defects of form.[108] Defects of form in Motions To Dismiss for matters of abatement may now be corrected by amendment.[109]

The Court has, however, continued to apply the stricter policy of rejecting a plea for any defect of form when the plea is filed by subsequently attaching creditors.[110] In such cases, the court is presented with a disfavored plea from a disfavored class of parties and presumably feels fewer compunctions about rejecting the defective plea.

Library References

CJS Abatement and Revival § 3
CJS Pleading § 135

§ 10.14. —With Respect to Other Parties

Pleas in abatement affect all parties on whose behalf they are filed. Thus, if several defendants join in pleading in abatement, and the plea is bad as to one, it is bad as to all.[111] And if one defendant successfully pleads in abatement a defect which is personal, the action will abate only as to that defendant.[112] Both situations are governed by the principle that pleas in abatement are disfavored pleadings and should be limited in effect. Whether a plea in abatement for a defect which is not personal would abate a writ as to all defendants if only one defendant had raised it has never been decided, but it probably would not. A defendant's failure to raise the defect on his or her own behalf, even when the defendant knew that a codefendant was raising the issue, would probably be regarded as a waiver of the objection.

---

106 See Colby v. Dow, 18 N.H. 557 (1847).

107 See Colby v. Dow, 18 N.H. 557 (1847); Dinsmore v. Pendexter, 28 N.H. 18 (1853); Parker v. McKean, 34 N.H. 375 (1857) (The defendant must state "by way of amendment what it is which he relies on to abate the writ." 34 N.H. at 376).

108 The policy was reaffirmed during Chief Justice Doe's Tenure in Messer v. Smythe, 58 N.H. 312 (1878).

109 Wheeler v. Bates, 21 N.H. 460 (1850).

110 Reynolds v. Damrell, 19 N.H. 394 (1849).

111 Marsh v. Smith, 18 N.H. 366 (1846).

112 Ingraham v. Olcock, 14 N.H. 243 (1843).

Library References

CJS Abatement and Revival § 188

§ 10.15. —Admissions and Trial of Issues of Fact

In some situations, it is not possible to plead a defect in abatement without simultaneously admitting either the whole or a material element of the plaintiff's claim.[113] Because matters in abatement must be raised before pleading to the merits, it is not possible to raise such matters and at the same time to deny the substance of the claim. The purpose of this rule is, of course, to limit the degree to which pleas in abatement may be used to avoid the resolution of substantial issues.

In some actions of assumpsit, the defendant must choose between pleading in abatement and contesting the merits of the claim. When the plaintiff sues in assumpsit on an account annexed, for example, and the defendant claims that the debt was incurred jointly with another, the defendant must plead the nonjoinder in abatement in order to prevent the judgment from running against the defendant alone for the full amount. But the Supreme Court has held that the entry of a plea in abatement for nonjoinder in such a case is an admission of all other well-pleaded facts and, upon the plea being disposed of, may form the basis for the entry of judgment against the defendant without a further hearing.[114] The same principle applies to actions of assumpsit for goods sold and delivered, except that, there being no allegation in such a writ of a fixed amount due, the issue of damages must still be tried.[115]

---

113 Two points must, however, be borne in mind. First, where a defect is apparent on the face of the plaintiff's pleadings, the defendant need not himself aver the facts which make it out. The defendant can then raise the defect in abatement without also admitting the truth of the facts on which it is based. Second, a plea in abatement which raises only an issue of law neither admits facts on which a judgment may be based nor permits the court to enter judgment without further proceedings. These two points may be illustrated by one example. If the plaintiff alleges a joint debt from two people who are still living and within the jurisdiction of the court, but sues only one of them, the defendant may plead the nonjoinder in abatement without filing any affidavits making any implied admissions, or raising any issue of fact. The only issue raised in such a case is an issue of law and, if the defendant fails to support the plea, the only order will be that he plead further. If, however, the plaintiff does not allege a joint debt but the defendant asserts that the debt is joint, he can only raise the defect in abatement with supporting affidavits. The effect of such a pleading is to admit the debt and to raise an issue of fact regarding the identity of the creditors. Once that issue of fact has been resolved, judgment may be entered for the amount of the debt.

114 Dodge v. Morse, 3 N.H. 232 (1825); Jewett v. Davis, 6 N.H. 518 (1834).

115 Chase v. Deming, 42 N.H. 275 (1860).

A plaintiff has the right to a jury trial on issues of fact raised by a plea in abatement.[116] However, in most cases, the plaintiff will not wish to go to the trouble and expense of such a procedure, especially where the plea in abatement does not imply sufficient admissions for the jury to assess damages upon their verdict. In most cases, the court will decide the factual issues raised by a plea in abatement on the basis of the affidavits submitted and any evidence or offers of proof adduced at a hearing.[117]

Library References

CJS Pleading § 138

§ 10.16. Effect of Not Raising Matters in Abatement

Any defect which must be pleaded in abatement to be raised at all is waived if not so pleaded within the time allowed. The defendant may also waive the defect by agreement or by pleading to the substance of the action.[118] Any defect which has not been pleaded in abatement may not be assigned as a ground of error in any appellate court[119] or raised in subsequent proceedings involving the same cause[120] or issues.[121]

Library References

CJS Abatement and Revival § 187

§ 10.17. Responses to Pleadings in Abatement

Matters in abatement of an action are raised by means of a Motion To Dismiss, which may be accompanied by supporting affidavits. The plaintiff may file an objection to the motion, either with or without affidavits, or a Replication and may request a hearing at any time within ten days of the filing.[122]

Cross References

Replication, see ch. 12 *infra.*

---

116 Scruton & Hand v. Deming, 36 N.H. 432 (1858).
117 Stiles v. Dube, 106 N.H. 339, 211 A.2d 402 (1965).
118 Kelly v. Gilman, 29 N.H. 385 (1854).
119 Merrill v. Coggill, 12 N.H. 97 (1841).
120 Garvin v. Paul, 47 N.H. 158 (1866).
121 Nichols v. Smith, 26 N.H. 298 (1853).
122 Super. Ct. R. 58 and 137.

C. Motion To Quash

§ 10.18. Motion To Quash

At common law, a Motion To Quash was a plea in abatement without the averment of new facts. Motions To Quash relied entirely on facts apparent on the face of the pleadings already filed or other records of the court, and any matter which could form the basis for a Motion To Quash could also be objected to by plea in abatement.[123] As a result, the principles which governed pleading matters in abatement generally[124] applied with equal force to Motions To Quash.

Today, Motions To Quash are no longer filed. If a party wishes to raise matters in abatement which appear on the record, he may simply file a Motion To Dismiss without supporting affidavits.[125] The motion must call the court's attention to specific defects on the face of the writ or process or in the records of the court which form the basis for abating the writ or process.

Since a Motion To Quash raises no issues of fact, the plaintiff is not entitled to a jury trial in the decision of any issues raised by the motion.[126]

Library References

CJS Pleading § 422

D. Motion To Dismiss for Matters in Bar

§ 10.19. Introduction

Matters in bar may exist at the beginning of an action or may arise during its course. When they arise at the commencement of the action, they are

---

123 The court will abate an action, on motion, "only when the abatable defects are apparent upon the writ itself." Haverhill Insurance Company v. Prescott, 38 N.H. 398, 399 (1859). See also Hibbard & Carpenter v. Clark, 54 N.H. 521 (1874); Jacobs v. Stevens, 57 N.H. 610 (1876); Crawford v. Crawford, 44 N.H. 428 (1862) ("Where the defect is not apparent upon the record, the court will not take notice of it, without plea . . . . " 44 N.H. at 431); R.C. Allen Business Machines, Inc. v. Acres, 111 N.H. 269, 281 A.2d 162 (1971).

124 See Section 10.03 *supra*.

125 Although it is common to speak of quashing writs and dismissing bills, there is no recognized procedural distinction between the judicial acts of quashing and dismissing. (See, e.g., the synonymous use of the terms by Justice Bellows in Crawford v. Crawford, 44 N.H. 428 (1862).) And the substance, rather than the title, of a pleading controls its effect.

126 Scruton & Hand v. Deming, 36 N.H. 432 (1858).

pleaded in bar of the action generally; when they appear later, they are pleaded in bar of the further maintenance of the suit.[127]

A plea in bar neither disputes the accrual of a cause of action nor quarrels with the manner of asserting it, but instead raises a reason why the claim can no longer be enforced.[128] While a matter in abatement merely defeats the writ or initial pleading, but leaves the plaintiff free to bring his claim again in a legally sufficient manner, a matter in bar, if successful, utterly defeats the action and prevents it from ever being recommenced. Motions To Dismiss or a Brief Statement which raise matters in bar of the action generally must be filed within thirty days of the return day.[129] Motions To Dismiss or a Brief Statement raising matters in bar of the further maintenance of the suit should be filed within thirty days of the date when the matter in bar arises. Since a Motion To Dismiss or a Brief Statement raising a matter in bar addresses the merits of the action, it acts as a waiver of objections to jurisdiction, service, notice, the parties, or any preexisting abatable defects.

Library References

CJS Pleading §§ 140 et seq.

§ 10.20. Raising Matters in Bar by Brief Statement or Motion To Dismiss

A plea in bar is a special plea and accordingly may be set forth in a Brief Statement.[130] It may also be raised by a Motion To Dismiss, either with or without affidavits. The choice of pleadings will depend upon whether the defendant can presently prove the facts upon which the defense relies and whether the defendant believes that the matter he or she pleads in bar is strong enough to allow disposal of the case without further proceedings.

§ 10.21. Requisites of the Plea

(a) *Supporting Affidavits.* The matter pleaded in bar may be apparent on the face of the plaintiff's pleadings or the records of the court, but, in most cases, it will have to be shown by additional averments from the defendant. When the defendant pleads matters in bar by means of a Brief Statement, the court is not required to take action on the new averments, and

---

127 Bailey v. March, 2 N.H. 522 (1823).

128 See Kempton v. Sullivan Savings Institution, 53 N.H. 581 (1873).

129 Super. Ct. R. 28.

130 See RSA 515:3; School District No. 3 in Lisbon v. Aldrich, 13 N.H. 139 (1842); Sullivan v. Marshall, 93 N.H. 456, 44 A.2d 433 (1945).

no supporting affidavits are required.[131] But when the defendant pleads matters in bar by means of a Motion To Dismiss, the defendant must support the new averments with affidavits or stipulations before the court will consider it.[132]

(b) *Specific Allegations of Fact.* Whether the defendant raises matters in bar by Brief Statement or Motion To Dismiss, he or she must set forth enough specific facts in support of the plea that the plaintiff will know exactly what is relied upon and that the court may judge whether the facts set forth in the plea, if proved, would be sufficient in law to bar the action.[133]

§ 10.22. Grounds for a Plea in Bar—Of the Action Generally

The following specific grounds for a plea in bar of the action generally have been recognized by the Supreme Court:

(a) *No Such Corporation.* This is the sole case of a matter which may be pleaded either in abatement or in bar.[134] The substance of the plea is that there is no such legal entity as the corporation which is named as the plaintiff in the action. This objection must be distinguished from misnomer (variation by words and syllables from a correct name) and misdesignation (correctly naming the wrong person), both of which defects may only be pleaded in abatement.[135]

(b) *Plaintiff Is Alien Enemy.* A citizen of a country which is presently at war with the United States has no right to claim the protection of its laws for the enforcement of a claim. If such a person commences an action in a New Hampshire court, the defendant may plead in bar that the plaintiff is an alien enemy.[136]

(c) *Statute of Limitations.* The expiration of the statute of limitations is a bar to an action generally,[137] but not to the further maintenance of an action which was begun before it expired.

(d) *Election of Remedies.* When the plaintiff sues at common law for injuries sustained in the course of employment, after having first claimed a

---

131　Super. Ct. R. 57.

132　*Id.*

133　Hearn v. Boston & Maine Railroad, 67 N.H. 320, 29 A. 970 (1892).

134　School District No. 1 in Orange v. Blaisdell, 6 N.H. 197 (1833); The Proprietors of Sunapee v. Eastman, 32 N.H. 470 (1855); School District No. 3 in Lisbon v. Aldrich, 13 N.H. 139 (1842); Nashua Fire Insurance Co. v. Moore, 55 N.H. 48 (1874).

135　*Id.*

136　Morrison v. Woolson, 23 N.H. 11 (1851).

137　Amoskeag Manufacturing Co. v. Barnes, 48 N.H. 25 (1868).

remedy under the Workmen's Compensation Statute, the defendant may plead an election of remedies in bar of the action at common law.[138]

(e) *General Release.*   Regardless of when a general release is given by the plaintiff, it may be pleaded in bar of the action generally.[139]

(f) *Payment.*   In actions for defaulted payments, the defendant may plead in bar of the action generally that the payments were made before commencement of the action.[140]

(g) *Prior Judgment for Same Cause (Res Judicata).*   If the plaintiff has recovered judgment for the same cause of action or has otherwise had the merits of the claim determined in a federal court or in a court in the State of New Hampshire or any other state, that judgment may be pleaded in bar of the action generally.[141]

§ 10.23.   —Of the Further Maintenance of the Action

The following specific grounds for a plea in bar of the further maintenance of the action have been recognized by the Supreme Court:

(a) *Tender.*   There is some authority for the proposition that the defendant can tender the amount demanded and plead the tender in bar of the further maintenance of the Suit.[142]

(b) *Payment.*   The defendant is always free to pay the amount due after the suit has been commenced and to plead the payment in bar of the further maintenance of the action.[143]

---

138 Dion v. Cheshire Mills, 92 N.H. 414, 32 A.2d 605, 37 A.2d 708 (1943).

139 Kimball v. Wilson, 3 N.H. 96 (1824); Pemigewasset Bank v. Brackett, 4 N.H. 557 (1829):

> The reason of this is, that when a general release is given, the costs of the suit, up to the time of the release, are presumed to have been adjusted, and cannot be made the subject of any contest in the cause. There is, therefore, no reason why the release should not be pleaded as a general bar . . . . But in such a case, the release must be pleaded according to the fact as given after the commencement of the action otherwise it cannot be admitted in evidence (4 N.H. at 559).

See also Wisheart v. Legro & McDuffee, 33 N.H. 177 (1856).

140 Russell v. Fabyan, 28 N.H. 543 (1854).

141 Weeks v. Pearson, 5 N.H. 324 (1831); Child v. Eureka Powder Works, 45 N.H. 547 (1864); Goodall v. Marshall, 14 N.H. 161 (1843) (plaintiff's claim denied in Vermont). But the judgment must have been validly obtained and be enforceable in this state. Whittier v. Wendell, 7 N.H. 257 (1834) (judgment obtained by default without personal jurisdiction); Jessiman v. The Haverhill & Franconia Iron Manufactory, 1 N.H. 68 (1817) (arbitrament and award).

142 Reynolds v. Libbey, Smith 197 (1808).

143 Pemigewasset Bank v. Brackett, 4 N.H. 557 (1829); Williams v. Tappan, 23 N.H. 385 (1851); Dana v. Sessions, 46 N.H. 509 (1866).

(c) *Judgment for the Same Cause.*   If the plaintiff recovers judgment or otherwise has the merits of the cause of action decided in another case by a federal court or a court in New Hampshire or in another state after the action is begun, that judgment may be pleaded in bar of the further maintenance of the suit.

(d) *Release After Suit Begun.*   If the plaintiff releases the defendant after suit is commenced and the defendant has not yet pleaded in the action, he or she may plead the release in bar of the action generally.[144]

(e) *Defendant Charged as Plaintiff's Trustee.*   If the defendant is charged and recovered against as the plaintiff's trustee in another suit by one of the plaintiff's creditors, the defendant may plead that payment in bar of the further maintenance of the whole or a portion of the suit.[145]

§ 10.24. No Grounds for Pleading in Bar

Generally speaking, a defect which may be pleaded in abatement may not be pleaded in bar. In addition, the following specific objections have been held not to support a plea in bar:

(a) *Judgments in Other Actions.*

(1) *Related Causes:*   While the preferred procedure is to join all causes of action arising out of the same transaction in one trial, the fact that one related cause has already been tried is no bar to the commencement of a suit for another.[146]

(2) *Different Causes:*   Judgment for one cause is no bar to suit for another unrelated and distinct cause.[147] Similarly, decision of an issue in one case is no bar to a second case in which the issue decided is not an element of the cause of action.[148]

(3) *Dismissed for Lack of Prosecution:*   A dismissal for lack of prosecution is no bar to a subsequent action for the same cause.[149]

(b) *Prior Judgment Without Jurisdiction.*   A prior judgment obtained without jurisdiction in this or another jurisdiction is no bar to the mainte-

---

144 See note 139 *supra*; True v. Huntoon, 54 N.H. 121 (1873).

145 Foster v. Dudley, 30 N.H. 463 (1855).

146 Reid v. Spadone Machine Company, 119 N.H. 198, 400 A.2d 54 (1979).

147 Webster and Atlas National Bank v. Fuller, 85 N.H. 186, 155 A. 697 (1931).

148 McQuaid v. Michou, 85 N.H. 299, 157 A. 881 (1932).

149 See Super. Ct. R. 168; Carveth v. Latham, 110 N.H. 232, 265 A.2d 1 (1970).

nance of an action for the same cause in New Hampshire so long as the prior judgment has not been satisfied.[150]

(c) *Recovery of Judgment by Administrator Appointed in Another State.* Since an administrator appointed in another state has no obligation to account to the courts of New Hampshire, recovery of a judgment in New Hampshire by such an administrator is no bar to an action for the same cause by an administrator appointed in New Hampshire if the judgment remains unsatisfied.[151]

§ 10.25. Persons Who May Plead in Bar

Any party who has a right to contest the merits of the plaintiff's claim may plead in bar. Pleas in bar are not dilatory pleas and, accordingly, subsequently attaching creditors may raise matters in bar after being granted leave to appear. Newly joined defendants will be given thirty days to plead in bar. Unless an intervenor can show that the delay in petitioning to join the action is not the result of neglect, the intervenor will be denied the privilege of entering a plea in bar after the time for filing has expired.

§ 10.26. When Pleas in Bar May Be Filed

Pleas in bar of the action generally must be filed within thirty days of the return day.[152] Pleas in bar of the further maintenance of the action should be filed within thirty days of the defendant's learning of the basis for the plea. The court may extend the time for filing "for good cause shown and upon such terms as justice may require."[153]

§ 10.27. Effect of Pleading in Bar

A plea in bar waives all defects which have or could have been pleaded in abatement of the action and admits the jurisdiction of the court.[154]

---

150 Whittier v. Wendell, 7 N.H. 257 (1834).

151 Taylor v. Barron, 35 N.H. 484 (1857).

152 Super. Ct. R. 28; Dist. & Mun. Ct. R. 3.10(A).

153 Super. Ct. R. 28; Dist. & Mun. Ct. R. 3.10(A). See, e.g., Braun v. Braun, 116 N.H. 714, 366 A.2d 484 (1976); Gagnon v. Croft Manufacturing & Rental Co., 108 N.H. 329, 235 A.2d 522 (1967); Blanchard v. Calderwood, 110 N.H. 29, 260 A.2d 118 (1969). However, the court will not extend the time for filing a plea based on the statute of limitations where there is a clear statutory mandate to limit the period (Torr v. Dover, 107 N.H. 501, 226 A.2d 96 (1967)), or where the failure to raise the plea results from neglect. Institute for Trend Research v. Griffin, 101 N.H. 255, 139 A.2d 628 (1958); Yeaton v. Skillings, 100 N.H. 316, 125 A.2d 923 (1956).

154 Nichols v. Smith, 26 N.H. 298 (1853).

§ 10.28. Effect of Not Pleading in Bar

Most matters in bar, such as no such corporation, alien enemy, statute of limitations, election of remedies, and prior judgment, must be pleaded as soon as they are discovered by the defendant or be deemed waived.[155] Some events, such as release, tender, payment, and charging as a trustee, may be relied upon under the general issue to limit the plaintiff's recovery even though they have not been pleaded in bar. In these cases, a failure to plead in bar does not amount to a waiver of the defendant's ability to rely on the defense.

§ 10.29. Responses to Pleas in Bar

At common law, pleas in bar could be met by Replications which averred new facts to counter the alleged bar or demurrers which tested the legal sufficiency of the plea. Under modern practice, matters pleaded in bar by Brief Statement or Motion To Dismiss may still be met by a Replication. If the plaintiff wishes to test the sufficiency of the pleading, however, he or she must now either move to reject the Brief Statement or file an objection to the Motion To Dismiss.

Cross References

Replication, see ch. 12 *infra*.

E. Motion To Stay Further Proceedings

§ 10.30. Introduction

The mere pendency in another jurisdiction of a prior action for the same cause between the same parties is no ground for abatement of an action in New Hampshire and, unless the defendant can show that New Hampshire "is a seriously inappropriate forum for the trial of the action"[156] due to the location of witnesses and other factors,[157] it is also no ground for dismissal of the action under the doctrine of forum non conveniens. But there is a class of cases in which, although New Hampshire is an appropriate forum for resolution of the dispute, it appears that the prior action may be concluded sooner than the action brought in New Hampshire and that a refusal to proceed with trial of the case here may either shorten or eliminate the need

---

155 Super. Ct. R. 28 provides, in part, that a failure to plead in bar results in the cause being "tried upon the general issue."

156 Leeper v. Leeper, 116 N.H. 116, 117, 354 A.2d 137, 138 (1976).

157 Leeper v. Leeper, 116 N.H. 116, 354 A.2d 137 (1976).

for a trial of the case in New Hampshire. In this class of cases, the Supreme Court has held that the defendant may make a Motion To Stay Proceedings and that the trial court may grant the motion if it believes that justice and judicial economy will be served.[158]

---

158 Whittier v. Wendell, 7 N.H. 257 (1834); Moore v. Maryland Casualty Co., 74 N.H. 47, 64 A. 1099 (1906); Glover v. Baker, 76 N.H. 393, 83 A. 916 (1912).

The procedure appears to have been first suggested by Justice Parker in Whittier v. Wendell, 7 N.H. 257 (1834). In that case, the defendants in an action on a promissory note had filed a Brief Statement in which they asserted that a default judgment had been entered against them for the same cause in an action by the same plaintiff in Maine. The defendants had resided in New Hampshire ever since making the note and had not been personally served in Maine. The Court held that the recovery of the Maine judgment was no bar to the action in New Hampshire since it did not appear that the Maine court had either personal or in rem jurisdiction in the case. But Justice Parker also suggested that, if the plaintiff had attached the defendants' property in Maine and had either obtained or might soon obtain a judgment there which could be enforced against that property, "this might furnish ground for an application to stay further proceedings here, until the proceedings there were closed, and the property applied in satisfaction of the debt" (7 N.H. at 258). According to Justice Parker's view, if part or all of the controversy would shortly be settled in another jurisdiction, even in a situation where New Hampshire had better access to the parties and more substantial contacts with the case, New Hampshire courts could wait to begin their work until it was clear what remained to be done.

For a while, a similar procedure was used where two cases were pending in New Hampshire courts, one to collect a debt from B to A and the other to collect a debt from A to C, with B served as trustee. In Wadleigh v. Pillsbury, 14 N.H. 373 (1843) (trustee suit begun first), and Foster v. Dudley, 30 N.H. 463 (1855) (trustee suit begun after the action to collect the debt), the Supreme Court held that the action between the principal defendant and the trustee could be stayed pending the outcome of the trustee suit. This view was later reversed, however, and the pendency of a trustee suit is presently no ground either for abating or staying the other action.

The procedure was recognized again in Moore v. Maryland Casualty Co., 74 N.H. 47, 64 A. 1099 (1906), where the Court continued a New Hampshire action "to await the final disposition" of the same action in Massachusetts. In *Moore*, the plaintiff-employee had recovered a judgment for job-related injuries against a Massachusetts streetcar company by means of an action in Massachusetts, but the streetcar company had later been declared insolvent and the judgment had not been collected. The plaintiff then brought a bill in equity in New Hampshire against the defendant's insurance company alleging that the insurance company was required to indemnify the streetcar company for the judgment and requesting that it be ordered to pay the plaintiff instead. The insurance company apparently was personally served in New Hampshire, but its codefendants, the streetcar company and the streetcar company's receiver, were not. The insurance company moved to dismiss "for want of jurisdiction," and the trial court granted the motion. On its first consideration of the case, the Supreme Court affirmed the dismissal, not on the grounds of lack of jurisdiction but for the reason that it would be inequitable to determine the issue of the insurance company's obligation to pay when all concerned parties were not before the court. The case was immediately retransferred by the superior court for an undisclosed reason, and, on its second consideration, the Supreme Court retained jurisdiction and continued the case until the insurance contract could be interpreted by a Massachusetts court. Although the case was at first handled in accordance with what modern practitioners would recognize as the doctrine of forum

Library References

CJS Actions §§ 131 et seq.
CJS Courts §§ 497, 540, 548
Stay of civil proceedings pending determination of action in another state or country. 19 ALR2d 301.

§ 10.31. Motion To Stay v. Forum Non Conveniens

In the early part of this century, it was easy to distinguish between Motions To Stay based on the pendency of another action and forum non conveniens, simply by observing that the former sought to retain the New Hampshire court's jurisdiction over the case while the latter attempted to terminate it. But some of the principles which have been applied to the development of Motions To Stay have found their way into the doctrine of forum non conveniens and, under present practice, a New Hampshire court confronted with a Motion To Dismiss for forum non conveniens may be just as inclined to stay the proceedings to await the outcome of the action in another jurisdiction as to terminate them. It is, therefore, no longer possible to distinguish these procedures by their remedies; the focus must instead be placed upon the situations in which they may be used.

Motions To Stay will be appropriate in cases where New Hampshire is the best forum available, due to contacts with the case or public policy considerations, for a resolution of the dispute or where another action pending in another state may be expected to eliminate some of the issues in the New Hampshire case in a manner consistent with New Hampshire law or public policy. The doctrine of forum non conveniens will be applied only when New Hampshire is not the best forum available. Both a Motion To

---

non conveniens, the Court changed its course for some reason and decided only to continue the action until the contract had been interpreted by a Massachusetts court and until that court had decided what relief to give the plaintiff. The procedure adopted in *Moore* follows Justice Parker's suggestion in *Whittier*. The case was cited six years later by Chief Justice Parsons in Glover v. Baker, 76 N.H. 393, 83 A. 916 (1912), when he remarked that the Court would not attempt to resolve an issue of law then pending before a Massachusetts Court in an action between the same parties "unless it were essential to the rights of the parties that it should do so without delay" (76 N.H. at 404, 83 A. at 924–25).

And, in Barker v. Eastman, 76 N.H. 277, 82 A. 166 (1912), the Court again considered the procedure and decided that it could not be employed in a case where the second action did not involve all the parties who were present before the New Hampshire court and where there was some question whether the other tribunal would ever proceed to act in the case at all. Finally, in Johns Manville Sales Corp. v. Barton, 118 N.H. 195, 385 A.2d 118 (1978), the Court similarly held that a motion to stay an action in New Hampshire for another case pending should be denied where the causes of action in the two cases were not the same.

Stay and a Motion To Dismiss for forum non conveniens are addressed to the discretion of the court.

Cross References

Forum Non Conveniens, see ch. 5 *supra*.

§ 10.32. Time To File a Motion To Stay

No rule of court sets deadlines for filing a Motion To Stay. Because the motion raises matters which are neither in abatement nor in bar, Superior Court Rules 28 and 30 do not apply. In addition, because a Motion To Stay may be based on an action brought either before[159] or after[160] the suit in which it is filed, it is apparent that no time deadline measured from the commencement of the action would be appropriate. Following the general guidelines of Rule 28, it would seem reasonable to require that the motion to be filed within thirty days of the return day for the other action on which it is based.

§ 10.33. Persons Who May File a Motion To Stay

Motions To Stay are not dilatory and are addressed to the discretion of the court. Accordingly, there is no reason why any party may not make the motion, subject to the general principles which apply to that party's obligations to meet time deadlines in the case.

§ 10.34. Requirements of a Motion To Stay

A Motion To Stay should follow the form of motions generally and be supported by proof, in the form of affidavits, certificates, or otherwise, of the pendency and status of the other case and the issues which it involves.[161]

§ 10.35. Response to a Motion To Stay

The plaintiff may either file an Objection or consent to the motion. In any case, the plaintiff may also either stipulate to the facts alleged in the motion and affidavits or dispute them with affidavits or certificates. The motion is addressed to the court's discretion. When the plaintiff objects, the court will hold a hearing on the motion.

Library References

Appealability of order staying, or refusing to stay, action because of pendency of another action. 18 ALR3d 400.

---

159 Whittier v. Wendell, 7 N.H. 257 (1834).

160 Moore v. Maryland Casualty Co., 74 N.H. 47, 64 A. 1099 (1906).

161 See Super. Ct. R. 57.

F. Motion To Dismiss (Demurrer)

§ 10.36. Introduction

At common law, a party who wished to raise a substantive defect apparent on the face of his opponent's pleading filed a demurrer. Under today's practice, he submits a Motion To Dismiss for failure to state a claim upon which relief may be granted or for lack of jurisdiction.[162]

Library References

CJS Dismissal and Nonsuit § 45
CJS Pleading § 211
    Demurrer on ground of noncompliance by plaintiff with statute as to doing business under an assumed or fictitious name or designation not showing the names of the persons interested. 42 ALR2d 565.
    Raising defense of statute of limitations by demurrer, equivalent motion to dismiss, or by motion for judgment on pleadings. 61 ALR2d 300.
    Demurrer for insufficiency of plaintiff's allegations in defamation action as to defendant's malice. 76 ALR2d 696.

§ 10.37. Persons Who May File a Motion To Dismiss

Any party who is required to respond to a request for affirmative relief may file a Motion To Dismiss which asserts that the claim for relief, as stated, is not recognized by law or equity. A defendant may file the motion in response to a writ, petition, libel, or other pleading, and a plaintiff may submit it against a Counterclaim. Third parties may also use it against pleadings which raise claims against their interests.

Library References

CJS Dismissal and Nonsuit §§ 48, 50, 51

§ 10.38. Actions in Which a Motion To Dismiss May Be Filed

A Motion To Dismiss may be filed in actions at law, proceedings in equity, and any other proceedings before any court or administrative agency. A Motion To Dismiss may be filed with respect to all or part of the case or on behalf of any number of the parties against whom separate claims are asserted.

§ 10.39. When a Motion To Dismiss May Be Filed

(a) *Failure to State a Claim.* The defendant must file a Motion To Dismiss for failure to state a claim upon which relief may be granted within

---

162 Adams v. Bradshaw, 134 N.H. 7 (1991) ("the proper remedy for . . . unartful pleading is a dismissal of the claim").

thirty days of the return day or by such other date as specified in the order of notice. Any other party must file the motion no later than the date by which a responsive pleading must be filed. When the motion is submitted in response to an amended pleading, it must be filed within the time set for filing an Answer to that amended pleading.

(b) *Lack of Personal Quasi In Rem or In Rem Jurisdiction.*   A Motion To Dismiss for lack of in personam, quasi in rem, or in rem jurisdiction must be filed within the same period as a Motion To Dismiss for failure to state a claim. A Motion To Dismiss for lack of in personam or quasi in rem jurisdiction may not be filed or maintained after the defendant has filed a General Appearance or submitted any other issue on the merits for the court's consideration.

(c) *Lack of Subject Matter Jurisdiction.*   The absence of subject matter jurisdiction cannot be supplied by agreement, consent, or acquiescence and may, therefore, be raised by Motion To Dismiss at any time.[163]

§ 10.40. Procedure for Filing a Motion To Dismiss—Form

A Motion To Dismiss for failure to state a claim on which relief may be granted or for lack of jurisdiction follows the form of motions generally. It must separately and briefly set forth the grounds for challenging the opponent's claim or the court's jurisdiction, citing appropriate authority without argument. If the issue is complex or requires extended discussion, the moving party should accompany the motion with a supporting memorandum of law. When the Motion To Dismiss requires proof of facts outside the record for its support, it should be accompanied by one or more affidavits.[164] When it relies on defects apparent on the face of the opponent's pleading, no supporting affidavit is required.

§ 10.41. Filing

A Motion To Dismiss, with supporting affidavits and memorandum, must be filed with the clerk of court and a copy sent to all other parties. Where the action is based on a lack of in personam or quasi in rem jurisdiction, it should be accompanied by a Special Appearance. In any other case, the motion must be filed with a General Appearance.

---

163 Gettler-Ryan, Inc. v. Kashulines, 130 N.H. 15, 534 A.2d 376 (1987).

164 A Motion To Dismiss, accompanied by affidavits, will be treated like a Motion for Summary Judgment. Chasan v. Village District of Eastman, 128 N.H. 807, 523 A.2d 16 (1986).

§ 10.42. Responses

Any other party may object to the Motion To Dismiss by filing an Objection within ten days.[165] The Objection should, whenever possible, specifically set forth the basis upon which the court may sustain the claim as stated or assert jurisdiction. Alternatively, the party seeking affirmative relief may move to amend his pleading to meet the moving party's objections.[166] That motion will usually be granted, unless the moving party can show prejudice.

§ 10.43. The Standard for Decision

(a) *For Failure To State a Claim.*[167]   In determining whether to grant a Motion To Dismiss for failure to state a claim upon which relief may be granted, the court will assume that all of the opponent's well-pleaded allegations of fact and the reasonable inferences to be drawn therefrom are true and can be proved,[168] will construe those allegations and inferences in

---

165 Ossipee Auto Parts v. Ossipee Planning Board, 134 N.H. 401 (1991) (citing Super. Ct. R. 58) (trial court could not consider facts raised in the plaintiff's objection to a motion to dismiss unless the plaintiffs filed an affidavit or other documentation in support of objection within 10 days of the defendant's motion to dismiss).

166 But see Morancy v. Morancy, 134 N.H. 493 (1991) (defendants could not raise a new defense in their response where they had not moved to amend their declarations).

167 The standard as articulated in this section has been reaffirmed by the New Hampshire Supreme Court. See Palmer v. U.S. Savings Bank of America, 131 N.H. 433, 553 A.2d 781 (1989) (citing R. WIEBUSCH, 4 NEW HAMPSHIRE PRACTICE § 353 at 247); Ossipee Auto Parts, Inc. v. Ossipee Planning Board, 134 N.H. 401 (1991); LaRoche v. Doe, 134 N.H. 562 (1991); Real Estate Planners, Inc. v. Town of Newmarket, 134 N.H. 696 (1991); Adams v. Bradshaw, 134 N.H. 7 (1991); Granite State Minerals, Inc. v. City of Portsmouth, 134 N.H. 408 (1991); Adkin Plumbing & Heating Co. v. Harwell, 135 N.H. 465 (1992).

168 Hartman v. Town of Hooksett, 125 N.H. 34, 480 A.2d 12 (1984); Hamilton v. Volkswagen of America, Inc., 125 N.H. 561, 484 A.2d 1116 (1984); Mountain Springs Water Co. v. Mountain Lakes Village District, 126 N.H. 199, 489 A.2d 647 (1985); Tilton v. Dougherty, 126 N.H. 294, 493 A.2d 442 (1985); Gould v. Concord Hospital, 126 N.H. 405, 493 A.2d 1193 (1985); Morin v. Berkshire Mutual Insurance Co., 126 N.H. 485, 493 A.2d 500 (1985); Collectramatic, Inc. v. Kentucky Fried Chicken Corp., 127 N.H. 318, 499 A.2d 999 (1985) (allegations of the plaintiff in an underlying action will also be assumed to be true and construed in favor of the opponent of the motion); Bagley v. Controlled Environment Corp., 127 N.H. 556, 503 A.2d 823 (1986); Morvay v. Hanover Insurance Cos., 127 N.H. 723, 506 A.2d 333 (1986); Kantor v. The Norwood Group, 127 N.H. 831, 508 A.2d 1078 (1986); Chasan v. Village District of Eastman, 128 N.H. 807, 523 A.2d 16 (1986); Jaswell Drill Corp. v. General Motors Corp., 129 N.H. 341, 529 A.2d 875 (1987); Jay Edwards, Inc. v. Baker, 130 N.H. 41, 534 A.2d 706 (1987); Rounds v. Standex International, 131 N.H. 71, 550 A.2d 98 (1988); Flags I, Inc. v. Kennedy, 131 N.H. 412, 553 A.2d 778 (1989) (citing Collectramatic, Inc. v. Kentucky Fried Chicken Corp., 127 N.H. 318, 320 (1985)); Ferreira v. Bedford School District, 133 N.H. 785, 584 A.2d 182 (1990) (citing Collectramatic, Inc. v. Kentucky Fried

the manner most favorable to the plaintiff,[169] and will deny the motion if "the plaintiff is entitled to judgment upon any state of facts findable under the

---

Chicken Corp., 127 N.H. 318, 320 (1985)) Numerica Savings Bank v. Mountain Lodge Inn, 134 N.H. 505 (1991); LaRoche v. Doe, 134 N.H. 562 (1991) (citing Collectramatic, Inc. v. Kentucky Fried Chicken Corp., 127 N.H. 318 (1985)) ("For review purposes, we accept the plaintiff's well-pleaded allegations of fact as true."); Adkin Plumbing & Heating Co. v. Harwell, 135 N.H. 465 (1992) (noting that for a motion to dismiss, the reviewing curt must accept the nonmoving party's version of the facts as true); ERG, Inc. v. Barnes, 137 N.H. ___ (Apr. 19, 1993); Sorenson v. City of Manchester, 136 N.H. 692, 621 A.2d 438 (1993); Bonte v. Bonte, 135 N.H. 286, 616 A.2d 464 (1992) (citing Collectramatic, Inc. v. Kentucky Fried Chicken Corp., 127 N.H. 318, 320, 499 A.2d 999, 1000 (1985)); Thompson v. Forest, 136 N.H. 215 (1992); Island Shores Estates Condo. Assoc. v. City of Concord, 136 N.H. 300, 302 (1992).

169 Hartman v. Town of Hooksett, 125 N.H. 34, 480 A.2d 12 (1984); Hamilton v. Volkswagen of America, Inc., 125 N.H. 561, 484 A.2d 1116 (1984); Mountain Springs Water Co. v. Mountain Lakes Village District, 126 N.H. 199, 489 A.2d 647 (1985); Tilton v. Dougherty, 126 N.H. 294, 493 A.2d 442 (1985); Collectramatic, Inc. v. Kentucky Fried Chicken Corp., 127 N.H. 318, 499 A.2d 999 (1985); Morvay v. Hanover Insurance Cos., 127 N.H. 723, 506 A.2d 333 (1986); Kantor v. The Norwood Group, 127 N.H. 831, 508 A.2d 1078 (1986); Chasan v. Village District of Eastman, 128 N.H. 807, 523 A.2d 16 (1986); Jaswell Drill Corp. v. General Motors Corp., 129 N.H. 341, 529 A.2d 875 (1987); Rounds v. Standex International, 131 N.H. 71, 550 A.2d 98 (1988); Ossipee Auto Parts v. Ossipee Planning Board, 134 N.H. 401 (1991) (holding that the court must "accept all facts pled by the plaintiff as true, construing them most favorably to the plaintiff"). But this does not mean that the court will assume the existence of nonpleaded facts necessary to support a pleaded conclusion of law. Jay Edwards, Inc. v. Baker, 130 N.H. 41, 534 A.2d 706 (1987); Ferreira v. Bedford School District, 133 N.H. 785, 584 A.2d 182 (1990) (citing Collectramatic, Inc. v. Kentucky Fried Chicken Corp., 127 N.H. 318, 320 (1985)); Provencal v. Vermont Mut. Ins. Co., 132 N.H. 742, 571 A.2d 276 (1990) (citing Collectramatic, Inc. v. Kentucky Fried Chicken Corp., 127 N.H. 318, 320 (1985)); Flags I, Inc. v. Kennedy, 131 N.H. 412, 553 A.2d 778 (1989) (citing Collectramatic, Inc, v. Kentucky Fried Chicken Corp., 127 N.H. 318, 320 (1985)); Numerica Savings Bank v. Mountain Lodge Inn, 134 N.H. 505 (1991); Renovest Co. v. Hodges Development Corp., 135 N.H. 72 (1991); Masse v. Commercial Union Insurance Co., 134 N.H. 523 (1991) (citing Collectramatic, Inc. v. Kentucky Fried Chicken Corp., 127 N.H. 318 (1985)) ("The trial court, upon consideration of the motion to dismiss, must determine whether the plaintiffs can prevail based on their allegations, which are to be taken as true and in the light most favorable to the plaintiffs."); Real Estate Planners, Inc. v. Town of Newmarket, 134 N.H. 696 (1991). But see Ossipee Auto Parts v. Ossipee Planning Board, 134 N.H. 401 (1991) (where motion to dismiss challenges the plaintiff's standing to sue, and not the sufficiency of the plaintiff's claim, "the trial court must look beyond the plaintiff's unsubstantiated allegations and determine, based on the facts, whether the plaintiff has sufficiently demonstrated his right to claim relief"); Sorenson v. City of Manchester, 136 N.H. 692, 621 A.2d 438 (1993); Bonte v. Bonte, 136 N.H. 286, 287 (1992); Island Shores Estates Condo. Assoc. v. City of Concord, 136 N.H. 300, 302 (1992); Thompson v. Forest, 136 N.H. 215 (1992).

pleadings"[170] or if those "facts and inferences so viewed 'would constitute a basis for legal relief.' "[171] The court will not, however, assume the truth or

---

170 Collectramatic, Inc. v. Kentucky Fried Chicken Corp., 127 N.H. 318, 499 A.2d 999 (1985); Jay Edwards, Inc. v. Baker, 130 N.H. 41, 534 A.2d 706 (1987) ("In ruling on a motion to dismiss, the court must determine whether the facts as pled are sufficient under the law to constitute a cause of action. . . . It must rigorously scrutinize the complaint to determine whether, *on its face*, it asserts a cause of action. What is involved is a pre-trial, threshold inquiry that tests the facts in the complaint against the applicable law." 130 N.H. at 45, 534 A.2d at 708). See also Rounds v. Standex International, 131 N.H. 71, 550 A.2d 98 (1988) (the inquiry is the same when the trial court's decision is challenged in the Supreme Court); Ferreira v. Bedford School District, 133 N.H. 785, 584 A.2d 182 (1990) (citing Jay Edwards, Inc. v. Baker, 130 N.H. 41, 44 (1986)) ("The issue thus becomes 'whether the facts as pled are sufficient under the law to constitute a cause of action.' "); Numerica Savings Bank v. Mountain Lodge Inn, 134 N.H. 505 (1991) ("the only issue raised is whether the allegations are reasonably susceptible of a construction that would permit recovery"); Granite State Minerals, Inc. v. City of Portsmouth, 134 N.H. 408 (1991) (the issue is "whether [the] pleadings contain facts which are sufficient to state a cause of action upon which relief may be granted"); Ossipee Auto Parts, Inc. v. Ossipee Planning Board, 134 N.H. 401 (1991) ("[I]n ruling upon a motion to dismiss, the trial court is required to determine whether the allegations contained in the . . . pleadings are sufficient to state a basis upon which relief may be granted."); Renovest Co. v. Hodges Development Corp., 135 N.H. 72 (1991); Real Estate Planners, Inc. v. Town of Newmarket, 134 N.H. 696 (1991) (quoting Collectramatic, Inc. v. Kentucky Fried Chicken Corp., 127 N.H. 318, 320 (1985)) ("[W]e must determine 'whether the allegations [in the pleadings] are reasonably susceptible of a construction that would permit recovery.' "); Ronayne v. State, 137 N.H. 281 (1993) (holding plaintiff's failure to draw sufficient causal connection between highway design and contamination of property by runoff pollutants justified dismissal); Bonte v. Bonte, 136 N.H. 286 (1992); Island Shores Estates Condo. Assoc. v. City of Concord, 136 N.H. 300 (1992); Thompson v. Forest, 136 N.H. 215 (1992).

171 Flags I, Inc. v. Kennedy, 131 N.H. 412, 553 A.2d 778 (1989) (citing Collectramatic, Inc. v. Kentucky Fried Chicken Corp., 127 N.H. 318, 320 (1985)); Kennedy v. Titcomb, 131 N.H. 399, 553 A.2d 1322 (1989) (citing Garabedian v. William Company, 106 N.H. 156, 157–58 (1965); Burgess v. Burgess, 71 N.H. 293 (1902)); Provencal v. Vermont Mut. Ins. Co., 132 N.H. 742, 571 A.2d 276 (1990) (citing Chasan v. Village District of Eastman, 128 N.H. 807, 814 (1986); Collectramatic, Inc. v. Kentucky Fried Chicken Corp., 127 N.H. 318 at 320 (1985)); LaRoche v. Doe, 134 N.H. 562 (1991) (citing Kennedy v. Titcomb, 134 N.H. 399 (1989) ("The trial court has discretion to dismiss a case upon it sown motion where the allegations contained in the writ do not state a claim upon which relief can be granted."); Collectramatic, Inc. v. Kentucky Fried Chicken Corp., 127 N.H. 318 (1985) ("The standard this court applies in reviewing a motion to dismiss is whether or not the plaintiff's allegations are reasonably susceptible of a construction that would permit recovery.")); Numerica Savings Bank v. Mountain Lodge Inn, 134 N.H. 505 (1991) ("If the facts as alleged would constitute a basis for legal relief, the motion to dismiss should be denied."); Sorenson v. City of Manchester, 136 N.H. 692, 621 A.2d 438 (1993); Bonte v. Bonte, 136 N.H. 286 (1992); Island Shores Estates Condo. Assoc. v. City of Concord, 136 N.H. 300 (1992).

accuracy of any allegations which are not well-pleaded, including the statement of conclusions of fact and principles of law.[172] Dismissal of a writ for failure to state a claim is considered on the merits.[173]

(b) *For Lack of Personal or Quasi in Rem Jurisdiction.* Where a court has jurisdiction over the subject matter of a case, it will indulge every presumption in favor of jurisdiction over the persons or property involved in it.[174] Unless it affirmatively appears that service was defective or that the exercise of jurisdiction over the personal rights and obligations of the intended defendant would be inconsistent with constitutional requirements of substantial justice and fair play, the court will deny the motion.

(c) *For Lack of Subject Matter Jurisdiction.* The defendant's burden on a Motion To Dismiss for lack of subject matter jurisdiction is much higher than on a Motion To Dismiss for failure to state a claim or for lack of in personam or quasi in rem jurisdiction. In the latter cases, the court will indulge all presumptions in favor of maintaining the action and will proceed if there is any ground upon which it may do so. But when a court's subject matter jurisdiction is challenged, the court must satisfy itself that it possesses the lawful power to act. If the court cannot affirmatively determine that it has such power, it must dismiss the action.

(d) *For Lack of Standing.* "In determining whether to grant a motion to dismiss for lack of standing, a court must look at all the relevant facts to determine whether the plaintiff will fairly and adequately represent other similarly situated shareholders. Presentation of some evidence that a plain-

---

172 Mountain Springs Water Co. v. Mountain Lakes Village District, 126 N.H. 199, 489 A.2d 647 (1985); Chasan v. Village District of Eastman, 128 N.H. 807, 523 A.2d 16 (1986); Jay Edwards, Inc. v. Baker, 130 N.H. 41, 534 A.2d 706 (1987) (trial court will not assume the existence of nonpleaded facts necessary to support a pleaded conclusion of law); Kennedy v. Titcomb, 131 N.H. 399, 553 A.2d 1322 (1990) (citing Jay Edwards, Inc. v. Baker, 130 N.H. 41, 45 (1987)); Provencal v. Vermont Mut. Ins. Co., 132 N.H. 742, 571 A.2d 276 (1990) (citing Mountain Springs Water Co. v. Mountain Lakes Village District, 126 N.H. 199, 201 (1985)).

173 Colebrook Water Co. v. Commissioner of Department of Public Works, 114 N.H. 392, 394–95, 324 A.2d 713, 715 (1974); ERG, Inc. v. Barnes, 137 N.H. 186 (1993).

174 Phelps v. Kingston, 130 N.H. 166, 536 A.2d 740 (1987) ("The plaintiff bears the burden of demonstrating facts sufficient to establish personal jurisdiction over the defendant. . . . In determining whether this burden has been met, the court will take facts that the plaintiff has properly pleaded as true and will construe reasonable inferences therefrom in the manner most favorable to the plaintiff." 130 N.H. at 170, 536 A.2d at 742). See also Weld Power Industries, Inc. v. C.S.I. Technologies, Inc., 124 N.H. 121, 467 A.2d 568 (1983).

tiff can fairly and adequately represent the other similarly situated . . . shareholders does not require a finding of fair representation."[175]

Library References

CJS Dismissal and Nonsuit §§ 60, 64
CJS Pleading §§ 457 et seq.

§ 10.44. Procedure for Decision

When a Motion To Dismiss is filed and the opposing party files no Objection, the court may grant the motion without hearing. When an Objection is filed, however, the court will hold a hearing.[176]

In the superior court, either party may request, either in the Motion or Objection or by letter to the clerk at any time, that a hearing be held on the Motion To Dismiss. Thereupon, the court will generally hold a hearing "as soon as practicable, but no later than thirty (30) days prior to the date scheduled for trial on the merits."[177]

District and Municipal Court Rule 3.11(E) provides that a Motion To Dismiss "will not be heard prior to the trial on the merits, unless counsel shall request a prior hearing, stating the grounds therefor."[178] Some judges have cited this rule as authority for declining to grant a pretrial hearing on a Motion To Dismiss for failure to state a claim or for lack of jurisdiction. Such an application of the rule can only be counterproductive, since a defendant who believes that his opponent has no right to relief will not participate in pretrial discovery or take any other steps to advance the case until his Objection is decided, and the court's refusal to schedule a special hearing on the motion will only have the effect of changing the forum in which the arguments are presented from a hearing on a Motion To Dismiss to a hearing on a motion to Compel Discovery.

---

175 Palmer v. U.S. Savings Bank of America, 131 N.H. 433, 553 A.2d 781 (1989) (citing Rothenberg v. Security Management Co., 667 F.2d 958, 961 (11th Cir. 1982); Hornreich v. Plant Industries, Inc., 535 F.2d 550 at 552 (9th Cir. 1976)).

176 Although a party may be entitled to a hearing, he is not necessarily entitled to introduce evidence at that hearing. The trial court has discretion to control the course of proceedings before it and may decide not to hear testimony or to review other evidence if it is convinced, on the basis of the party's offers of proof, that no evidence can be produced which would justify a different decision.

177 Super. Ct. R. 58. The Court is permitted in the exercise of its discretion to schedule the hearing at any other time, including at the trial on the merits. *Id.*

178 Prob. Ct. R. 9 is to a similar effect, as follows:

Motions to dismiss will not be heard prior to the hearing on the merits, unless the moving party shall request a prior hearing stating the grounds therefor, and the court grants such a request on good cause shown.

At the hearing, the court will hear arguments of counsel and receive any necessary evidence.[179] The court will usually issue its decision in writing after the hearing, but the court may decide to reserve decision until after presentation of some or all of the parties' cases at the trial or final hearing.

§ 10.45. Effect of a Decision on a Motion To Dismiss

A decision to deny a Motion To Dismiss may be the subject of an interlocutory appeal under Supreme Court Rule 8. An order dismissing the case, in whole or in part, is a final order on the merits and may be reviewed under Supreme Court Rule 7.

In reviewing the trial court's order of dismissal, the Supreme Court must "rigorously scrutinize the [plaintiff's] complaint to determine whether, on its face, it asserts a cause of action."[180] Upon appeal of a motion to dismiss, the court will consider "whether the allegations are reasonably susceptible of a construction that would permit recovery."[181]

Cross References

Interlocutory Appeal, see Part XVI *infra.*

G. Civil Suits Against Municipal Officials

§ 10.46. Preliminary Hearing

Whenever a municipal official or member of a municipal board or agency who is subject to good faith immunity under RSA 31:104 is sued personally for money damages and the plaintiff alleges injury or damage resulting from action taken in bad faith or with malice on the part of the official when acting in his official capacity, the superior court shall hold a preliminary hearing within ninety days of the return date of the action.[182] At the hearing, the

---

179 See Super. Ct. R. 58; Chasan v. Village District of Eastman, 128 N.H. 807, 523 A.2d 16 (1986); Difruscia v. Department of Public Works & Highways, 136 N.H. 202 (1992) (although court normally considers only the allegations in the pleadings, it will also consider any evidence submitted without objection).

180 Kennedy v. Titcomb, 131 N.H. 399, 553 A.2d 1322 (1989) (citing Jay Edwards, Inc. v. Baker, 130 N.H. 41, 44 (1987)).

181 Ferreira v. Bedford School District, 133 N.H. 785, 584 A.2d 182 (1990) (citing Collectramatic, Inc. v. Kentucky Fried Chicken Corp., 127 N.H. 318, 320 (1985)); Real Estate Planners, Inc. v. Town of Newmarket, 134 N.H. 696 (1991) (quoting Collectramatic, Inc. v. Kentucky Fried Chicken Corp., 127 N.H. 318, 320 (1985)) ("[W]e must determine 'whether the allegations [in the pleadings] are reasonably susceptible of a construction that would permit recovery.' ").

182 RSA 491:24.

plaintiff must demonstrate that the allegation is well grounded in fact and that there is a substantial likelihood that after discovery there will be an issue created for determination by a finder of fact.[183] If the court determines that the plaintiff has failed in its demonstration, the action will be dismissed. Furthermore, if the court finds that the action was frivolous or intended to harass or influence the official's actions, the court will order the plaintiff to pay the court costs and reasonable attorney fees of the defendant.[184]

---

183 *Id.*
184 *Id.*

CHAPTER 11. SET-OFFS, RECOUPMENTS, AND OTHER COUNTERCLAIMS

Library References

CJS Set-off and Counterclaim §§ 1, 2, 3, 6

Failure to assert matter as counterclaim as precluding assertion thereof in subsequent action, under federal rules or similar state rules or statutes. 22 ALR2d 621.

Dismissal of plaintiff's case for want of prosecution as affecting defendant's counterclaim, set-off, or recoupment, or intervenor's claim for affirmative relief. 48 ALR2d 748.

Set-offs, counterclaims, and the like as within operation of statute permitting new action after limitation period, upon failure of timely action. 79 ALR2d 1335.

Proceeding for summary judgment as affected by presentation of counterclaim. 8 ALR3d 1361.

Right in equity suit to jury trial of counterclaim involving legal issue. 17 ALR3d 1321.

Appealability of order dismissing counterclaim. 86 ALR3d 944.

§ 11.01. Introduction

It frequently happens that both parties to a proceeding have claims against the other and that the plaintiff is not so much the first person aggrieved, as the first to sue. At common law, the defendant in the first action was obliged to bring a separate writ to enforce his claim. If the defendant was unable to consolidate the cases for trial, he could set off his claim against the plaintiff's only by reducing it to a separate judgment and, if the judgments were entered in different courts, putting an execution for that judgment debt in the hands of the same sheriff or deputy sheriff to whom the plaintiff in the first action

273

had delivered his own execution.[1] This was obviously a cumbersome and wasteful procedure, and over time other procedures were developed to resolve the parties' claims against each other in one proceeding without the need of additional writs. These procedures are limited by the requirements that the mutual claims arise against the same parties in the same capacity, are within the subject matter jurisdiction of the court, and are not barred by the statute of limitations.

Counterclaims are today allowed to "avoid circuity of action, multiplicity of suits, inconvenience, expense, unwarranted consumption of the court's time, and injustice by resolving all controversies and granting full relief in one proceeding."[2]

§ 11.02. Distinctions Between Set-offs, Recoupments, and Other Counterclaims

Set-offs, recoupments, and other counterclaims are not defenses,[3] but in law or equity are claims for affirmative relief that the defendant asserts against the plaintiff. A "recoupment" is a claim arising from the same facts and circumstances as the plaintiff's claim, and diminishes it.[4]

A "set-off" is a debt or demand arising from different facts and circumstances but existing at the time the plaintiff's writ is filed.[5] Both recoupments and set-offs are types of counterclaims. The term "counterclaim" encompasses any claim that the defendant has at the time of answering which could form the basis of a separate suit. Although the procedures for recoupments, set-offs, and counterclaims developed separately and are conceptually distinguishable, all three are treated in the same fashion under modern practice and are referred to together as "counterclaims."

---

1 See Chandler v. Drew, 6 N.H. 469 (1834).

2 Zurback Steel Corporation v. Edgcomb, 120 N.H. 42, 45, 411 A.2d 153, 156 (1980); City of Concord v. 5,700 Square Feet of Land, 121 N.H. 170, 427 A.2d 46 (1981).

3 Chandler v. Drew, 6 N.H. 469 (1834); Leavitt v. Peabody, 62 N.H. 185 (1882).

4 "Recoupment has traditionally been viewed as the right of defendant to reduce or eliminate the plaintiff's demand either because the plaintiff has not complied with some cross obligation of the contract on which he sues or because he has violated some duty which the law imposes upon him in the making or performance of that contract." Zurback Steel Corporation v. Edgcomb, 120 N.H. 42, 44, 411 A.2d 153, 155 (1980). *Zurback* established that recoupment may be used offensively as well as defensively and may seek a greater amount than the plaintiff claims, or other affirmative relief. See also O'Connor v. Hancock, 135 N.H. 251, 604 A.2d 565 (1992).

5 See RSA 515:7 and 8.

§ 11.03. Matters That May Be Asserted by Way of Counterclaim—Recent Development of the Doctrine

The leading New Hampshire case on counterclaims is *Varney v. General Enolam, Inc.*[6] In that case, a building contractors' suit against the owner and the tenant of a commercial building for slightly more than $12,000 in labor and materials was met by the tenant's counterclaim for $100,000 for abuse of process. The plaintiffs moved to dismiss the counterclaim on the ground that it was not within the recognized boundaries of either a statutory set-off[7] (because it was not a claim existing at the time the plaintiff's writ was filed) or common law recoupment (because it did not arise out of the same contract) and that no other form of counterclaim was recognized under New Hampshire law. The trial court granted the motion, and the defendant sought review in the Supreme Court.

While conceding that the defendant's counterclaim for abuse of process was neither a recoupment nor a set-off, the Supreme Court held that New Hampshire law recognized a broader range of counterclaims than was defined by those two procedures. Justice Lampron, writing for the Court, said, "Counterclaim is broader than set-off or recoupment and consists in a cross demand existing in favor of the defendant against the plaintiff on which he could have sued the plaintiff and obtained a judgment."[8]

But the Court also went on to hold that any type of counter-claim—whether recoupment, set-off, or something else—could be rejected by the trial court if it either failed to find "special circumstances which in equity and justice require the allowance of any one of such pleas"[9] or concluded that "the allowance of [the counterclaim] would produce undue complexity and confusion of issues which might prejudice the rights of one or of both parties."[10] The Court thought that special circumstances justifying allowance of the counterclaim could include: (a) "Nonresidence of the plaintiff which would make it difficult for the defendant to enforce his claim otherwise"[11] or (b) insolvency or fraud by the plaintiff. In the end, the Supreme Court affirmed the trial court's decision to dismiss the counter-claim on the theory that the trial court had failed to find special circum-

---

6 109 N.H. 514, 257 A.2d 11 (1969).

7 See RSA 515:7 and 8.

8 109 N.H. at 516, 257 A.2d at 13.

9 *Id.*

10 *Id.*

11 *Id.*

stances (the plaintiffs and defendant were all New Hampshire residents) and had reasonably concluded that a joint trial of the action for labor and materials and the action for abuse of process might be too confusing for a jury and result in prejudice to both parties' claims. The *Varney* Court did not explain why rejection of the counterclaim altogether was preferable to allowing the counterclaim but severing the cases for trial.

The *Varney* case has been frequently relied upon and modified since its announcement in 1969. In *Kline v. Burns*,[12] the Supreme Court cited it as support for a counterclaim by a tenant for breach of the warranty of habitability filed in response to a landlord's action for rent. In *Westinghouse Electric Supply Company, Inc. v. Electromech, Inc.*,[13] the Court relied on *Varney* to support a reduction in a materialman's lien by the amount of a contractor's claim against his subcontractor. And in *City of Concord v. 5,700 Square Feet of Land*,[14] the Court used it to allow a condemnee to counterclaim for breach of contract to buy the subject land in a proceeding under RSA ch. 498-A.

In *Phinney v. Levine*,[15] the Court limited *Varney*, holding that a counterclaim could be asserted only for those claims the defendant could have asserted on the date the plaintiff's action was begun.[16] The *Phinney* holding

---

12 111 N.H. 87, 276 A.2d 248 (1971).

13 119 N.H. 833, 409 A.2d 1141 (1979).

14 121 N.H. 170, 427 A.2d 46 (1981).

15 117 N.H. 968, 381 A.2d 735 (1977).

16 It is possible that the language of the Court's decision went farther than the Court intended in its holding. In the *Phinney* case, a building contractor had given his customer a mortgage on his house as security for completion of the project. The builder died after the statute of limitations for contract actions had expired, without any claim by the customer having been made but before the customer had given a discharge of the mortgage. The builder's widow brought a petition to discharge the mortgage and, three years after her action was commenced, the customer filed a counterclaim for breach of contract. The Supreme Court based its affirmance of the trial court's dismissal of the counterclaim on RSA 515:8 which prohibits asserting as a set-off any claim which could not have been made at the time of the plaintiff's writ and held that "[t]he statutory requirements for set-off are applicable to counterclaims." 117 N.H. at 970, 381 A.2d at 736. The literal effect of this language was to overrule *Varney*'s holding that "[c]ounterclaim is broader than set-off" and encompassed any claim which the defendant had at the time of assertion against the plaintiff. But it appears that the real purpose of the Court's holding was to disqualify for revival by counterclaim any claim which had expired prior to the date of the plaintiff's action—to say, in effect, that a person may not lie by and let the statute of limitations expire on his claim but still hold it in reserve as a defense to an unexpired claim by his opponent. Taken in this light, the *Phinney* case is not nearly so destructive as it might otherwise seem and, in fact, introduces a very sensible clarification into the procedure.

was further refined in *Zurback Steel Corporation v. Edgcomb*,[17] when the Court held that a claim which was not barred by the statute of limitations on the date the plaintiff's action was begun could be asserted by counterclaim at any time before judgment if the trial court found that justice so required, even though the statute had expired after the case was brought and before the counterclaim was asserted.

In *Van Miller v. Hutchins*,[18] the Court held that the trial court had no discretion to dismiss a counterclaim for slander and libel occurring in New Hampshire, Virginia, and the District of Columbia which had been filed in response to an action to collect a judgment recovered in California. The Court found that the plaintiff's nonresidency and the defendant's consequent inability to bring an action against him in New Hampshire for the defamation occurring in Virginia and the District of Columbia were "special circumstances" which justified allowance of the counterclaim. Unfortunately, "the majority of the allegations" of defamation in *Van Miller* were barred by applicable statutes of limitation in the jurisdiction in which they had allegedly occurred, and the Supreme Court found that this circumstance, resulting in a complete absence of forums in which the defendant could assert his claim for defamation if the counterclaim were not allowed, "required as a matter of law" that the trial court allow the counterclaim in New Hampshire.

However, the *Van Miller* Court also decided that the mere fact that a counterclaim is allowed does not require a joint trial of all claims in a case, and that the trial court has power to sever the claims for trial if they would be too confusing to try together.[19] This part of the holding, in effect, reduced the importance of the second part of the *Varney* test and focused the decision on whether to allow counterclaims solely on the issue of "special circumstances."

Finally, in *In re Estate of Borkowski*,[20] the Court held that a debt that was not yet due could not be set off against the assertion of a debt that was due. To this extent, the holding merely confirmed the Court's prior decisions relating to set-offs under RSA 515:7 and, in light of *Varney* and its succes-

---

17 120 N.H. 42, 411 A.2d 153 (1980).

18 118 N.H. 204, 384 A.2d 791 (1978).

19 The Court recognized the following causes of confusion in the *Van Miller* case: (a) the issues in the main action and in the counterclaim were unrelated; (b) the counterclaim was asserted by only one of the two defendants; (c) the counterclaim would require out-of-state witnesses and depositions; and (d) the counterclaim sought much more extensive and complex types of relief than the action in chief.

20 120 N.H. 54, 410 A.2d 1121 (1980).

sors, must be regarded as applying to recoupments and other types of counterclaims as well. The Court went on to hold that the debt asserted by counterclaim must be due on the date it is asserted, not on the date the action is begun. This part of the Court's holding is directly contrary to its decision in *Zurback* that a claim which was due and could have been asserted on the date the writ was brought may thereafter form the basis of a counterclaim even if, by the time the counterclaim is filed, the statute of limitations has run.

§ 11.04. —The Rule

Although the development of the law of counterclaims since *Varney* has followed an uncertain course, the following rules may be said to constitute the law of counterclaims as it presently exists in New Hampshire:

(a) *Type of Claim.* Any claim may be asserted which:

(1) Could stand independently as the basis for an action at law or in equity;

(2) Has accrued on or before the date it is asserted; and

(3) Falls within the subject matter jurisdiction of the court.

(b) *Parties.*

(1) The claim must arise between some, but not necessarily all, of the same parties involved in the plaintiff's action;

(2) The claim may not require the joinder of other persons not already involved in the plaintiff's action unless the defendant can also show that those other persons should have been joined by the plaintiff originally; and

(3) The claim must arise between the parties in the same capacities in which they appear in the plaintiff's action.

(c) *Size of Claim.* The claim may be for an unliquidated amount or for an amount lesser or greater than that claimed by the plaintiff.

(d) *Right To File a Counterclaim.*

(1) The defendant has no right to file a counterclaim, but the court may allow it when no objection is filed or when, upon objection, the court finds "special circumstances" (relating to the defendant's difficulty in asserting the claim in another forum[21] or the plaintiff's wrongdoing) which justify allowance of the pleading; and

(2) In proceedings relating to special and limited subject areas (e.g., divorce, land condemnation, etc.), the court will limit the counterclaim to claims arising out of the same facts or relationships.

---

21 Nonresidence of the defendant is "recognized as a special circumstance which usually demands the application of the doctrine of equitable set-off." Van Miller v. Hutchins, 118 N.H. 204, 205, 384 A.2d 791, 792 (1978).

(e) *Obligation To File a Counterclaim (Compulsory Counterclaim).* There is no rule or statute in New Hampshire that specifically requires a defendant to raise any matters by way of counterclaim. However, the Supreme Court has recently supported the principle of a compulsory counterclaim in one case in which both sides sought equitable relief[22] and in another in which the rules of the forum where a prior case had been tried required it.[23] The theory of compulsory counterclaim, to the extent it is recognized in New Hampshire, rests entirely upon the doctrine of res judicata, which provides that a second action may not be commenced by either party to a former action to determine any matters which were actually litigated or which might have been litigated in the former action. Res judicata is applied only to that class of counterclaims which arise from the same facts that the plaintiff asserts as the basis for his cause of action. Although the Supreme Court has not extended the application of this doctrine to require that a counterclaim be asserted at the first opportunity or be lost, it is probably safest to raise by counterclaim, any claim which the defendant believes he has arising out of the same facts that the plaintiff relies upon.

(f) *Treatment After Filing.*   Even when a counterclaim is allowed, the court may order the claims severed for separate trials where they do not arise out of the same contract or transaction or would cause complexity, confusion, or prejudice if tried together.

(g) *Cases and Courts in Which a Counterclaim May Be Filed.*   A counterclaim may be asserted in any case at law or proceeding in equity pending in any court in New Hampshire. It may not be filed in proceedings before administrative agencies.

(h) *Types of Relief Which May Be Sought.*   A counterclaim may seek any relief which the court has jurisdiction to grant. A counterclaim in an action at law may seek equitable relief and vice versa.

§ 11.05. Procedure for Asserting a Counterclaim—Requirements of Pleading

Regardless of whether the action was begun by writ, petition, or other form of pleading, a counterclaim may be filed either as a part of the

---

22 Boucher v. Bailey, 117 N.H. 590, 375 A.2d 1160 (1977).

23 Scheele v. Village District of Eidelweiss, 122 N.H. 1015, 453 A.2d 1281 (1982).

defendant's answer or on an individually typed form styled like a motion.[24] The counterclaim must, however, be labelled as such[25] and must meet all the formal and substantive requirements which would apply if it were asserted as the basis for an independent action.[26] Even when it states a claim which might have formed the basis for an action at law, it should recite the separate allegations of fact in separate numbered paragraphs, rather than in a long, run-on sentence.[27] A counterclaim which is timely filed need not be accompanied by a motion for permission to file it.

§ 11.06. —Time for Filing

A counterclaim must be filed within thirty days of entry of the action, unless otherwise ordered by the court upon motion and for good cause shown.[28]

If a party wishes to file a late counterclaim, he should file his motion along with the counterclaim and send a copy of both to his opponent.[29] The plaintiff may object[30] to the motion for lack of subject matter jurisdiction, forum non conveniens, inconvenience or injustice resulting from joining the claims or from being obliged to meet the claim so late, expiration of the statute of limitations before the action was begun, lack of "special circumstances" requiring that the claims be joined, lack of maturity of the claim, or failure to show an excuse for late filing.

---

24 Even when the claim asserted by the counterclaim would, if brought separately, have to be alleged in a writ, it may be set forth as a counterclaim on an individually typed form.

25 Use of alternative or more particularized terms like set-off, recoupment, cross-demand, cross-libel, and so forth is not required and will probably prove counterproductive in many cases. See Zurback Steel Corporation v. Edgcomb, 120 N.H. 42, 411 A.2d 153 (1980).

26 The counterclaim must clearly state the relief requested and, where that relief includes an injunction, should set forth the terms of the proposed injunction. See RSA 508:4-c (in personal actions, the "declaration or other affirmative pleading" may not specify an amount of damages).

27 There is no purpose to be served by perpetuating a cumbersome and confusing style.

28 Super. Ct. R. 33; Dist. & Mun. Ct. R. 3.10(D). The late filing party will, at a minimum, be required to pay costs.

29 Dist. & Mun. Ct. R. 3.10(D). The counterclaim does not need to be separately served unless it seeks relief against someone who is not yet a party to the action or against a party in another capacity. In that case, both a Motion to Join and a Motion for Leave to File a Late Counterclaim must be filed and served.

30 A proposed new party may object to the joinder for lack of jurisdiction upon a special appearance but may not object to allowance of the counterclaim without filing a general appearance.

If the plaintiff objects, the court will hold a hearing. If not, the court will grant the motion unless the delay has been for too long a period[31] upon condition that the defendant pay any costs incurred by the plaintiff after the thirtieth day following entry in reliance on the defendant's apparent decision not to assert a counterclaim.[32]

Library References

CJS Pleading § 171

§ 11.07. Objections—To Allowance of the Counterclaim

In theory, no counterclaim may be entered without the court's permission upon a finding of "special circumstances" which require its inclusion in the action, but in practice usually any counterclaim, whether filed on time or not, which is not objected to will be allowed without hearing or findings by the court. Accordingly, if a plaintiff wishes to have the counterclaim disallowed, he must object, and his objection must be filed within ten days of the date he receives the counterclaim. The objection may be based on lack of subject matter jurisdiction, forum non conveniens, inconvenience or injustice resulting from joining the claims, lack of special circumstances requiring the joining of the claims, expiration of the statute of limitations prior to the commencement of the action, or lack of maturity of the claim. The court will usually hold a hearing on the objection.

§ 11.08. —To a Joint Trial

Whether or not the plaintiff objects to allowance of the counterclaim, he may object to a joint trial of the claims on the ground of complexity, confusion or prejudice. Because it requests affirmative relief from the court, the objection should be set forth in a separate Motion to Sever, rather than with other objections to allowance of the counterclaim. The defendant will have ten days from receipt of the Motion to Sever in which to object. If he does object, the court will hold a hearing on the motion. The court will generally be more inclined to grant a Motion to Sever or to make the order on its own motion in a jury case than in a trial to the court.

---

31 See Phinney v. Levine, 117 N.H. 968, 381 A.2d 735 (1977) (over three years).
32 Super. Ct. R. 33.

§ 11.09. Exercise of the Court's Discretion

"[W]hether to allow a counterclaim is within the discretion of the court."[33] The exercise of that discretion will only be revised when the defendant's rights to assert the claim have been permanently foreclosed by the order and it seems possible to permit the two claims, if both are proved, to be set off against each other.[34]

§ 11.10. Payment Into Court

If the counterclaim is for an amount less than the plaintiff asserts, the defendant can pay the balance due into court and thereby limit the plaintiff's right to recover future costs.[35]

§ 11.11. Subsequent Proceedings—In General

After a counterclaim has been allowed, the case proceeds in the normal course with expanded issues. None of the usual pretrial procedures are effected by the pendency of the counterclaim, and all apply with equal effect to both claims. When a procedural obligation or right accrues to a party in the normal course because he is the plaintiff in an action, that obligation or right will usually be accorded to the first to bring suit, but the court may change the burden, if appropriate, either on its own or on a party's motion.

§ 11.12. —Dispositive Motions

Any motion that could have been filed to defeat the claim if it had been brought as a separate action, including a Motion for Summary Judgment[36] or Motion to Dismiss, may be filed against it when brought as a counter-claim.

---

33 City of Concord v. 5,700 Square Feet of Land, 121 N.H. 170, 172, 427 A.2d 46, 48 (1981).

34 See Van Miller v. Hutchins, 118 N.H. 204, 384 A.2d 791 (1978) (plaintiff was a nonresident, physically disabled, and barred from asserting the claim where it arose).

35 Super. Ct. R. 61.

36 RSA 491:22-a.

CHAPTER 12.   REPLICATION

§ 12.01. Definition

A replication is a supplementary pleading the plaintiff uses to respond to special pleas, affirmative defenses,[1] and affirmative claims for relief set forth in the defendant's answer and responsive pleadings. It is the proper vehicle for the plaintiff to dispute any new matter of substance which the defendant introduces in response to the writ or petition.

Library References

CJS Pleading § 184

---

1 At common law and throughout the nineteenth century, a replication was used only to respond to special pleas and affirmative defenses. See, e.g., Williams v. Little, 11 N.H. 66 (1840); Great Falls Company v. Worster, 15 N.H. 412 (1844); Fowler v. Watkins, 1 N.H. 251 (1818). The former distinction between general and special replications and the special rules for use of de injuria replications are no longer followed. The principle that a defendant might assert any claim he had against the plaintiff arising out of the same or related transactions in response to the writ or petition was not well established. The general rule of pleading required that each side plead and replead in alternation until all of the material allegations that either side wished to make on the matters in issue had been replied to. In this context, the replication was one means by which the plaintiff could negate the defendant's response to his writ. Under today's practice, however, it is permissible, but not necessary, to respond to a defendant's claim of an affirmative or special defense (Barnard v. Elmer, 128 N.H. 386, 515 A.2d 1209 (1986)), and the replication finds a more frequent use in answering the defendant's claim for affirmative relief against the plaintiff.

§ 12.02. Cases in Which a Replication May Be Filed

A replication may be filed in any action at law, proceeding in equity,[2] administrative proceeding,[3] or other civil case.[4]

§ 12.03. Replication—Form

A replication is entitled by that name, but in all other respects follows the form of an answer.[5] The plaintiff may, but should not, file a separate replication to counter each special plea, affirmative defense, or request for affirmative relief asserted by the defendant.[6]

Library References

CJS Pleading §§ 194–201

§ 12.04. —Substance

A replication is in substance nothing but an answer, and in composing replication, the plaintiff follows the same rules of definiteness and responsiveness that apply when a defendant's claim is asserted by writ or petition.[7]

---

2 See Rogers v. Mitchell, 41 N.H. 154 (1860); Merrill v. Town of Plainfield, 45 N.H. 126 (1863).

3 If not forbidden by the agency's special rules of practice, a replication may be filed in an administrative proceeding.

4 E.g., State v. Olcott, 6 N.H. 74 (1832) (quo warranto); Moore v. Stevens, 42 N.H. 404 (1861) (replevin); and divorce.

5 Super. Ct. R. 137.

6 RSA 515:4 provides:

> When the defendant pleads one or more special pleas the plaintiff may reply thereto all such matters as may be material in answer to or avoidance of the matters alleged therein, and for that purpose may file as many separate replications as the case requires.

This statute was originally enacted in 1847 and amends the common law requirement that the plaintiff obtain permission of the court before filing more than one replication. Pickering v. Pickering, 19 N.H. 389 (1849). The common law rule rested on the principle that each replication should reply to only one substantive claim. Mooney v. Demerrit, 1 N.H. 187 (1818). This principle is no longer followed, and the preferred practice is to file only one replication setting forth all the plaintiff's responses to the defendant's special pleas, affirmative defenses, and claims for affirmative relief. See Wadleigh v. Pillsbury, 14 N.H. 373 (1843).

7 See Austin v. Walker, 26 N.H. 456 (1853). A replication is sufficient if it denies only one of several material facts asserted by the defendant when the fact denied is necessary to the maintenance of the defendant's defense or claim (Tebbets v. Tilton, 24 N.H. 120 (1851); Watriss v. Pierce, 36 N.H. 232 (1858); Austin v. Walker, 26 N.H. 456 (1853)), but under modern practice it should fully, fairly, and specifically answer each separate allegation of the defendant's pleading. See Austin v. Walker, 26 N.H. 456 (1853) (the

Although the plaintiff may assert inconsistent defenses to the defendant's claim for affirmative relief, the plaintiff may not make assertions in his replication contradicting the substance of the claims of his writ or petition.[8] If he does, they will be taken as admissions against his writ or petition.

§ 12.05. —When To File

A replication is filed only in response to a defendant's pleading and only when the defendant has asserted some new matter, either by way of affirmative defense or claim for affirmative relief, against the plaintiff. It may not be filed when the defendant defaults or pleads only the general issue. If the plaintiff wishes merely to expand his case in chief after an answer or appearance has been filed, he must instead file a Motion to Amend.[9]

As an alternative to filing a replication, the plaintiff may move to amend to avoid the defense which the defendant has raised.[10]

§ 12.06. —Procedure for Filing

A replication must be filed within ten days of the plaintiff's receipt of the defendant's answer[11] and, when filed within that time, will be received as a matter of right. The plaintiff must file the original in court and must mail a copy to the defendant and to any other parties. No service by the sheriff is required because the defendant has already submitted himself to the jurisdiction of the court by his answer. The replication must contain a certification that copies have been mailed or delivered to the other parties.

---

replication need not deny immaterial allegations); Thompson v. Fellows, 21 N.H. 425 (1850) (the replication must be responsive to the plea). Note, however, that even in a replication the plaintiff may not specify the amount of damages claimed in a personal action. See RSA 508:4-c.

8 Such an inconsistent allegation was called a "departure" at common law and formed the basis for judgment for the defendant on the pleadings. Moore v. Stevens, 42 N.H. 404 (1861); Breck v. Blanchard, 22 N.H. 303 (1851); Thompson v. Fellows, 21 N.H. 425 (1850); Tarleton v. Wells, 2 N.H. 306 (1820).

9 See Watriss v. Pierce, 36 N.H. 232 (1858). This was formerly accomplished by a special replication. Fowler v. Watkins, 1 N.H. 251 (1818).

10 See Palmer v. Tuttle, 39 N.H. 486 (1859).

11 Super. Ct. R. 137.

§ 12.07. The Defendant's Response

The defendant is neither required nor allowed to make any response to a replication that is proper in form and substance.[12] If the replication is defective either in form or substance,[13] or filed too late, the defendant may object to its receipt by the court and may move to have it rejected. If the plaintiff improperly includes a matter in amendment of his case in chief, the defendant may move to have that portion of the replication severed and retitled and may then file an answer to the amended pleading. The old common law rule that pleadings continue in alternation until every substantive allegation has been specifically met by a response is no longer followed in New Hampshire. The replication is the last initial pleading which either party is allowed to file against the other.

Library References

CJS Pleading § 207

§ 12.08. Amendment of Replications

A replication may be amended on the same terms as any other pleading.[14]

---

12 At common law, the defendant was allowed to file a rejoinder, either asserting new facts which rebutted the substance of the plaintiff's replication or simply denying it. The plaintiff could thereafter demur to the rejoinder. See Joy v. Simpson, 2 N.H. 179 (1820); Tarleton v. Wells, 2 N.H. 306 (1820); Cheever v. Mirrick, 2 N.H. 376 (1821); Great Falls Company v. Worster, 15 N.H. 412 (1844); Peck v. Jenness, 16 N.H. 516 (1845); Bowman v. Harper, 17 N.H. 571 (1845); Breck v. Blanchard, 20 N.H. 323 (1850); Judge of Probate v. Ordway, 23 N.H. 198 (1851); Bills v. Vose, 27 N.H. 212 (1853); Jordan v. Gillen, 44 N.H. 65 (1862); Judge of Probate v. Lane, 50 N.H. 556 (1871). Such extended pleading has come to be regarded as pointless and wasteful. It is now assumed that by continuing the case the parties dispute each other's claims of a defense, and that no time, therefore, need be spent on pleadings once the parties' affirmative claims and denials have been clearly stated.

13 See Cheshire Bank v. Robinson, 2 N.H. 126 (1819).

14 Gehlen v. Patterson, 83 N.H. 328, 141 A. 914 (1928).

Part V

COMMENCEMENT OF A CIVIL ACTION

Cross References

Pretrial Procedure, see Part VIII *infra*.

CHAPTER 13. FORMS, PREPARATION, AND FILING OF WRITS

A. FORMS AND PREPARATION

A. *Forms and Preparation*

§ 13.01. Actions at Law—Generally

Actions at law are begun and advanced at critical stages by filling out a writ.[1] At common law, writs were divided into three categories: (1) original writs, by which an action was commenced; (2) writs of mesne process, by

---

1 In general, a civil action is commenced when a writ of summons is prepared with the present intention to complete service. Arsenault v. Scanlon, 139 N.H. 592, 594, 660 A.2d 110, 112 (1995) (citing Hodgdon v. Weeks Memorial Hosp., 122 N.H. 425, 426, 445 A.2d 116, 117–18 (1982), appeal after remand, 128 N.H. 366, 515 A.2d 1199 (1986)); Berg v. Kelley, 134 N.H. 255, 258, 590 A.2d 621, 623 (1991) (citing Mason v. Cheney, 47 N.H. 24, 25 (1866)). See Sections 13.08 and 13.09.

which action was compelled while an action was pending; and (3) writs of final process, by which the judgment was made effective.[2]

Library References

CJS Process § 1

§ 13.02. —Forms of Writs

All writs are headed with the name of the state and bear the seal of the court, the original or facsimile of the signatures of the clerk, and the teste[3] of the first, chief, or senior justice or, if he is interested in the case, of any justice in the court.[4] All writs, except writs of attachment, from the superior and Supreme Courts are directed to "the sheriff of any county or his

---

2 *Black's Law Dictionary* (4th Ed.) Although at common law, a writ of summons was a writ of mesne process, because the action was actually begun by a common writ, the two have been combined in New Hampshire practice and the writ of summons is now, by statute, an original writ. RSA 509:4 and 6. The statute also refers to a writ of attachment as an original writ, but this view is inconsistent with the current attachment procedure and cannot be sustained. See RSA 511-A. Writs of attachment (including trustee process), replevin, and capias must be regarded as writs of mesne process under New Hampshire practice; writs of possession, writs of scire facias, and writs of execution are writs of final process.

3 The "teste" is the statement of authority by which the writ is issued. A writ bears the "teste" of the first, chief, or senior justice if, at its conclusion, the word "Witness" is followed by the justice's name. On blank writs, the teste is located in the lower left hand corner of the writ.

4 RSA 509:12 provides that where a municipal court has no clerk, the justice shall sign the writs. Although no similar provision is expressly made for district courts which lack clerks, there is no reason why the same procedure should not apply there as well. However, the occasions when RSA 509:12 might be used have been greatly reduced, if not eliminated, by the enactment of RSA 509:2-a, providing for a uniform writ. That section states that for the purposes of satisfying the constitutional and statutory requirements of form for writs in the district and municipal courts, the district and municipal courts are to be regarded as one court of which the "chief or first justice" is the chairman of the administrative committee, having a single seal; and that the clerk of any municipal or district court may sign a writ to be used in any other court. The constitutionality of RSA 509:2-a was confirmed by the Supreme Court in Opinion of the Justices, 119 N.H. 325, 401 A.2d 1084 (1979). Thus, RSA 509:12 is probably useful now only in a case where a recognized form of writ cannot be used, a new form must be devised under RSA 509:5, the court has no clerk, and there is not time to obtain the signature of a clerk of another court.

When a judge signs a writ because the court has no clerk, he is not obliged by RSA 509:2 and Art. 87 to sign it again as justice. Smith v. Tallman, 87 N.H. 176, 175 A. 857 (1934). When a judge directs another person to sign for him, which person thereupon, in his presence and pursuant to his direction, subscribes the judge's name to the writ, the act will be regarded as the signature of the judge. Hanson v. Rowe, 26 N.H. 327 (1853). But the signature will not take effect if the agent is not in the presence of the judge when he signs. Kidder v. Prescott, 24 N.H. 263 (1851).

deputy."[5] Writs of attachment are directed to "the sheriff, the plaintiff, his attorney or any other person."[6] Writs from the municipal courts and district courts are, in addition, directed to any constable of any town in the county where the district or municipal court sits,[7] unless the defendant has personal property liable to attachment in a county in which he does not reside. In that case, the writ may be directed to the constable of any town in which the defendant resides or has property.[8]

Seven types of writs[9] are recognized for use in civil actions in New Hampshire. They are the writs of summons, attachment,[10] replevin, capias,[11] possession, scire facias, and execution. The forms of these writs have traditionally been prescribed by statute.[12] Only the writ of summons may be

---

5 RSA 509:3. This section of the writ is called the "precept." Although the precept customarily contains directions for the sheriff or constable, the officer may also follow instructions placed elsewhere in the writ. Manchester Federal Savings & Loan Association v. Letendre, 103 N.H. 64, 164 A.2d 568 (1960). The serving officer's authority is limited by the instructions (Bryant v. Warren, 51 N.H. 213 (1871)), with the result that those instructions must be drafted to conform to the theory of the writ, but it has been held that if the officer properly serves within the scope of his authority and the theory of the writ (Rodd v. Titus Construction Co., 102 N.H. 264, 220 A.2d 768 (1966)), but beyond the scope of the instructions stated in the writ, the plaintiff will be allowed to amend the instructions to authorize the action. Parker v. Barker, 43 N.H. 35 (1861).

6 RSA 509:3.

7 RSA 509:11.

8 RSA 509:13.

9 "[B]y the term writ, as used in the constitution, is meant that class of writs of mesne process by which civil actions are commenced, and writs of execution by which the judgments of the court are executed." State v. Bradford, 57 N.H. 188, 198 (1876).

10 The function of the writ of trustee process is now fulfilled by the writ of attachment. See Rules and Procedures to Implement Attachment Law.

11 Although the form for a writ of capias and attachment was abolished in 1971 (Laws of 1971, 227:7), a capias writ may still be issued to compel attendance at court.

12 See former RSA 509:15 (attachment), 17 (summons), 18 (trustee process), 19 (replevin), 20 (scire facias), 527:12 (execution), and 527:13 (possession). These statutory writ forms were repealed by Laws of 1981, Chapter 328:3, but the Supreme Court immediately issued Administrative Order 81-1A providing: "[A]ll forms repealed pursuant to Chapter 328, of the Laws of 1981, shall also remain in effect pending further order of the Court." No such further order has yet been made. When a writ is needed but no suitable form is prescribed by statute, the court will follow the general form of the recognized writs "so far as the nature of the case will admit." RSA 509:5. In Manchester Federal Savings and Loan Association v. Letendre, 103 N.H. 64, 164 A.2d 568 (1960), the Court held that a writ of summons filed by a subcontractor against a prime contractor could be modified to require a mechanic's lien attachment of the real estate belonging to a third party on which the work was done and that setting forth the direction to the sheriff to make the attachment in the specification, rather than in the precept, met the requirements of RSA 509:5 and accomplished its purpose.

completed and served by the plaintiff's attorney without the permission of the court.

Library References

Omission of signature of issuing officer on civil process or summons as affecting jurisdiction of the person. 37 ALR2d 928.

Sufficiency of designation of court or place of appearance in original civil process. 93 ALR2d 376.

Forms

Writ of Summons (Superior Court), see Appendix.
Writ of Summons (District Court), see Appendix.
Landlord and Tenant Writ (District Court), see Appendix.
Writ of Attachment and Trustee Process (Superior Court), see Appendix.
Writ of Attachment and Trustee Process (District Court), see Appendix.
Writ of Attachment (District Court), see Appendix.
Writ of Replevin (Superior Court), see Appendix.
Writ of Replevin (District Court), see Appendix.

§ 13.03. —Blank Writs of Summons

The clerks of the superior court in each county and of each of the municipal courts and district courts maintain stocks of preprinted blank writs of summons to which the court seal and clerk's signature have been affixed[13] and to which place names have been added to make the forms particularly suited for each county or court. The Rules provide that the clerks may deliver blank writs of summons only to attorneys admitted to practice in New Hampshire or to a person who has stated in writing his intention to represent himself in a particular action or to be represented by a citizen of good character who is not an attorney[14] and with respect to whom he has

---

13 Former RSA 509:21 was repealed by Laws of 1981, Chapter 328:3, but the Supreme Court immediately issued Administrative Order 81-1A providing: "[A]ll forms repealed pursuant to Chapter 328, of the laws of 1981, shall also remain in effect pending further order of the court." In Dearborn v. Twist, 6 N.H. 44 (1832), the Court said:

> And we are inclined to think that no mesne process ought to be pronounced valid, in any court in this state, unless it is upon a blank writ, signed and sealed by the clerk, and which has been issued, by him, to be used as process in the court named in the blank, and which has not been used in the commencement of any other suit. This is a plain and simple rule, which will cure all irregularities on this subject, and which can never be inconvenient to those, who take due care to be always provided with a proper supply of blanks.

14 Super. Ct. R. 1; and New England Capital Corporation v. The Finlay Company, Inc., 137 N.H. 226, 624 A.2d 1358 (1993).

filed a power of attorney.[15] In the case of a person not wishing to be represented by an attorney, the clerks are directed to provide the prospective plaintiff with only one blank writ of summons after filling in the date and the name of the case in which it is to be used.[16] Use of the blank writ of summons for any other case is an abuse of process and a contempt of court.[17]

Forms are also available from registers of probate,[18] but there is no similar restriction on their distribution.[19]

§ 13.04. —Completing the Writ of Summons

To begin an action at law, the plaintiff or his attorney must fill in the writ of summons, setting forth the names and addresses of the parties,[20] a

---

15 Super. Ct. R. 14. In Stevens v. Fuller, 55 N.H. 443 (1875), Justice Smith wrote:

> It is objected that none but an attorney regularly admitted should be entrusted with a blank process for the purpose of commencing a suit; but I cannot see by what authority the court can deny to a party, or to such person as he may select to act as his attorney, the process of the court to enable him to commence his suit. Such prohibition would practically nullify the provisions of the statute . . . and would deprive one of the means of commencing or prosecuting his suit.

Super. Ct. R. 2 and Dist. and Mun. Ct. R. 3.11 apparently date from the *Stevens* case.

16 Super. Ct. R. 1; Dist. and Mun. Ct. R. 3.1.

17 Attorneys are instructed by the Superior Court Rules to prevent any blank writs given them by the clerks from being used by anyone but other licensed attorneys. Super. Ct. R. 1. The District and Municipal Court Rules are generally to the same effect (see Dist. and Mun. Ct. R. 3.1), with the exception that small claims forms may be delivered freely to anyone and that writs provided to persons not planning to use an attorney are to be numbered.

18 Prob. Ct. R. 22.

19 These rules illustrate the distinction in theory between writs and other forms of process. A blank writ is in fact a fully executed order of the Court. Blank writs are freely provided to licensed attorneys in reliance upon those portions of their oath which state that they "will not wittingly or willingly promote, sue, or procure to be sued any false or unlawful suit, nor consent to the same" and that they "will act in the office of the attorney . . . with all good fidelity . . . to the court." RSA 311:6. See also N.H. Rules of Professional Conduct, Rule 3.1 (lawyer not to assert frivolous case); Rule 3.3 (lawyer's obligation of honesty to the court). Having already been sworn to act honestly and with loyalty to the interests of the court, licensed attorneys are permitted to take and hold unlimited quantities of writs signed in blank, subject to the requirement that they keep them secure and only pass them on, in turn, to other attorneys. Persons who have not taken the attorney's oath (RSA 311:1), have a statutory right to represent themselves or to be represented by others who have also not taken the oath, but their access to these presigned court orders is restricted and a record is kept of each blank writ which is handed out.

20 Super. Ct. R. 2; Dist. and Mun. Ct. R. 3.2(A). A mail address is not required to be inserted in Domestic Violence petitions.

declaration of the claim,[21] the amount demanded,[22] and, in the superior court, whether trial by jury[23] is elected. He must also choose a return day.[24] In actions returnable to the district courts and to the superior court, the plaintiff may choose any return day more than fourteen days after service[25] and in the district courts within two months of the date of the writ.[26] No similar time limits are fixed for actions returnable to the municipal courts, because the only types of civil actions which may be heard by those courts require relatively short periods of notice. In the superior court, the first Tuesday of every month is a return day.[27] In the municipal courts, the return day for all actions except those for the removal of tenants is whichever day of the month is customarily set aside for the trial of civil cases.[28] Actions to remove tenants may be made returnable on any day.[29] In the district courts, the first Tuesday of each month, apparently even when it is a legal holiday, is the return day.[30]

Once the plaintiff has completed the writ of summons and obtained the necessary endorsement,[31] he may deliver it and a return copy for each defendant to the sheriff or constable for service.[32]

Cross References

Service of Process, see ch. 14 *infra*.

---

21 Super. Ct. R. 23; Dist. and Mun. Ct. R. 3.7.

22 But see RSA 508:4-c (in personal actions, the "declaration or other affirmative pleading" may not contain an ad damnum, but must "state that the damages claimed are within any minimum or maximum jurisdictional limits of the court.").

23 Super. Ct. R. 8.

24 The return day may be changed in the writ before service without applying to the clerk for a new seal or signature. Eastman v. Morrison, 46 N.H. 136 (1865); Dearborn v. Twist, 6 N.H. 44 (1832).

25 RSA 503:6.

26 RSA 502-A:26.

27 When the first Tuesday is a legal holiday, the first Wednesday is the return day for that month. See former RSA 496:2.

28 RSA 502:29 and 30; Dist. and Mun. Ct. R. 3.12(A). But see RSA 503:6 (small claims actions). However, where a municipal court has no clerk, the writ must specify the day, hour, and place for return. RSA 509:12.

29 RSA 502:30.

30 RSA 502-A:26. But see RSA 508:6 (small claims actions).

31 RSA 509:8. The plaintiff's attorney should also type his name and address on the return copy.

32 Addresses for delivery of civil process to the sheriffs are set forth in Volume 1 of New Hampshire Court Rules Annotated, Court Personnel and Terms, in the pages entitled "County Attorneys and Sheriffs."

see Practice volume

§ 13.05. Other Proceedings

In proceedings in equity, marital proceedings and actions authorized by remedial statutes, no preprinted process, signed in blank by the court, is available for use in commencing the action. Neither is there usually any form prescribed by statute or rule which must be used to begin the action. A party is, therefore, obliged to prepare his own form for each such proceeding and to file it with the court or administrative agency[33] before delivering it to the sheriff for service.

Upon receipt of the pleading, the court or administrative agency will issue an order of notice directing the petitioner to notify the respondent of the pendency of the action and to summon him to appear by a regular or special return day.[34] The respondent will be directed to file his response within thirty days of the return day.[35] The order of notice may also specify a date and time for hearing on requests for provisional remedies or make other special requirements. Until the petition, libel, or other pleading has been filed and an order of notice has been issued, no such proceeding has been commenced and even if he is served, the respondent is under no obligation to take any action in response.

Once the order of notice has been issued, the party commencing the action may deliver the pleadings, with the order of notice attached, to the sheriff for service.[36]

§ 13.06. Orders of Notice in Special Cases

Orders of notice are directed to the parties, not the sheriff, and may set forth special orders relating to service or provisional remedies. Thus, although orders of notice must be obtained as a matter of course in commencing proceedings in equity, divorce proceedings, and many statutory proceedings, they may also be required in actions at law where the usual means of service have failed but where jurisdiction can be obtained by some other means of service and when an action at law is joined with an equity,

NB

---

33 Bills and petitions addressed to courts and administrative agencies may be filed at any time. Super. Ct. R. 124.

34 In the superior court, the return day will be within three months of the date of filing. Super. Ct. R. 124; Blaisdell v. Raab, 133 N.H. 711, 571 A.2d 261 (1990) (citing Super. Ct. R. 124 and 127).

35 Blaisdell v. Raab, 133 N.H. 711, 571 A.2d 261 (1990) (citing Super. Ct. R. 124 and 127).

36 Addresses for delivery of civil process to the sheriffs are set forth in Volume 1 of New Hampshire Court Rules Annotated, Court Personnel and Terms, in the pages entitled "County Attorneys and Sheriffs."

divorce, or statutory proceeding.[37] In the former cases, the writ may be entered in court along with the sheriff's return of non est inventus[38] and the clerk will issue an order of notice prescribing "such notice . . . as the case requires."[39] The case will be "continued for notice" thereafter.[40] In the latter cases, the best procedure is to file with the clerk a petition and the writ together and obtain an order of notice for service and response to both.

Where the method of service specified in the order of notice varies from the method set forth in the preprinted writ, the party commencing the action should modify the precept accordingly.[41]

Forms

Instructions to Plaintiff for Serving Orders of Notice—Small Claims Actions, see Appendix.
Order of Notice—Equity Proceeding (Superior Court) see Appendix.
Order of Notice—Replevin Proceeding (Superior Court) see Appendix.
Order of Notice—Labor Proceeding (Superior Court) see Appendix.
Order of Notice—Contempt (District Court) see Appendix.

B. Filing

§ 13.07. Introduction

There are three dates of significance in the commencement of a civil action:

(1) *Commencement Date*—The date on the writ in actions at law[42] and the date when a libel or petition is filed with the clerk in other proceedings.

(2) *Entry Date*—The date when the writ in actions at law is filed in the clerk's office, either before or after service, and the date when a libel or petition is filed with the clerk *before* service in other proceedings.

(3) *Return Day*—The date by the end of which the sheriff's return of service must be filed in court.

---

37 See Super. Ct. R. 129.

38 "[He] is not to be found." *Black's Law Dictionary* (4th Ed.).

39 RSA 510:8; Therrien v. Scammon, 87 N.H. 214, 176 A. 116 (1935).

40 RSA 514:3.

41 RSA 509:5; Manchester Federal Savings & Loan Association v. Letendre, 103 N.H. 64, 164 A.2d 568 (1960).

42 Society for Propagating the Gospel v. Whitcomb, 2 N.H. 227 (1820); Maguire v. Merrimack Mutual Fire Insurance Co., 125 N.H. 269, 480 A.2d 112 (1984) ("Since 1820 it has been clear that an action begins when a plaintiff or his counsel completes a writ with the intention to cause it to be served on the defendant." 125 N.H. at 272, 480 A.2d at 113).

§ 13.08. Commencement Date—Generally

Any pleading may be filed with the clerk of court at any time. What is necessary to commence a procedure at law differs from that necessary to begin a proceeding in equity.

§ 13.09. —Law

An action at law is commenced when a plaintiff or his counsel completes a writ with the intent to cause it to be served on the defendant.[43] "That the date of the writ is the true time when the action is brought,"[44] is a rebuttable presumption,[45] to which there are three exceptions recognized by the court. If a writ is altered by plaintiff or his counsel prior to the writ being served, then the date of the alteration is the date the suit is considered commenced.[46] If the writ is completed, but plaintiff intends to wait until a future event to serve it, then the date of the writ is not considered the date of commencement.[47] And, ". . . if the writ 'cannot be served until some further act is done,' the suit commences when the act is done."[48]

Because commencement depends upon intent, whether commencement has occurred is an issue about which courts have differed. Recently, the Court in *DeSaulnier v. Manchester School Dist.*,[49] overturned a decision of the lower court that a plaintiff's lawsuit had not commenced. The plaintiff in *DeSaulnier* wished to file suit against the school district for injuries she allegedly suffered while cheerleading for her high school. Prior to the statute

---

43 Society for Propagating the Gospel v. Whitcomb, 2 N.H. 227, 230 (1820); Maguire v. Merrimack Mut. Fire Ins. Co., 125 N.H. 269, 272, 480 A.2d 112, 113 (1984). See Arsenault v. Scanlon, 139 N.H. 592, 660 A.2d 1110 (1995).

44 Society for Propagating the Gospel v. Whitcomb, 2 N.H. 227, 230 (1820).

45 *Id.*

46 *Id.*

47 Mason v. Cheney, 47 N.H. 24 (1866); Hodgen v. Weeks Memorial Hospital, 122 N.H. 424, 445 A.2d 1116 (1982), appeal after remand, 128 N.H. 366, 515 A.2d 1199 (1986). In *Hodgen*, plaintiff's decedent was in an accident, was taken to the hospital and died several weeks later. Plaintiff's counsel prepared writs prior to the statute of limitations expiring on the actions, but he did not serve the writs until two months after the statute expired, as he was involved in settlement negotiations with another defendant involved in the accident. Counsel acknowledged that he did not intend to serve the writs until after the settlement was negotiated. The Court held that because the settlement was a precondition of service, the suits were not considered commenced until after the settlement occurred, which was after the statue of limitations had expired.

48 Clark v. Slayton, 63 N.H. 402, 402, 1 A.113, 113 (1885), quoted in DeSaulnier v. Manchester School Dist., 140 N.H. 336, 339, 667 A.2d 1380, 1382 (1995).

49 140 N.H. 336, 660 A.2d 1380 (1995).

of limitations expiring, plaintiff's counsel completed and signed a writ naming the school district as defendant. Ten days later, counsel sent a copy to the school district asking if it would accept service. The city solicitor's office replied that the school district would not, and that the city was a better defendant. After the statute of limitations ran, the plaintiff served the city. The city then moved to dismiss based on the statute. The lower court ruled against the plaintiff, finding that the intent to serve the school district became conditional upon serving the city, and barred her claim because the statute of limitations had expired. But the Supreme Court reversed, holding that the action was commenced on the date that the original writ was *prepared* with the intent of having it served on the defendant and that none of the exceptions applied, noting that there was no future event or act preventing plaintiff's counsel from serving the writ.[50]

§ 13.10. Proceedings in Equity

A proceeding in equity is initiated upon filing the bill or petition with the clerk, but no pleading becomes effective to put matters in issue until the defendant has received notice of its filing and substance according to the procedures prescribed by law. Bills and petitions[51] in equity, libels for divorce, and other statutory proceedings must be filed in court before notice. Writs of summons are not customarily filed until after service has been completed, but nothing in the common law of New Hampshire appears to preclude an earlier filing when the plaintiff thinks it necessary,[52] and such is no doubt the better practice when an action at law is to be joined with another type of proceeding.[53]

---

[50] Justices Thayer and Horton dissented, Justice Thayer writing that the better rule would be to require an overt act by the plaintiff to qualify as commencement, and Justice Horton that plaintiff's intent to file against the school district was abandoned when she filed against the city.

[51] There is no difference in New Hampshire practice between a bill and a petition in equity. Mitchell v. Smith, 90 N.H. 36, 4 A.2d 355 (1939).

[52] In fact, filing prior to service may be a good precaution against the possibility of loss by the serving officer. Taylor v. Cobleigh, 16 N.H. 105 (1844). In the early days of the nineteenth century, it was apparently the practice for attorneys to retain possession of the writs until some proceeding in court made their production necessary. See Mattocks v. Bishop, 4 N.H. 439, 440 (1828). That practice is not followed today.

[53] However, the original writ cannot be left in the clerk's office but must be delivered to the sheriff or constable as his authority for service. As the Court held in Carroll County Bank v. Goodall, 41 N.H. 81, 83 (1860): "[U]ntil the writ is delivered to him, the office has no authority to make service in any way . . . his whole authority being derived from the precept."

§ 13.11. Entry Date

"[L]itigation is pending from its institution by service; . . . jurisdiction attaches from that time."[54] After service has been completed in any type of action and before the return day specified in the writ or orders of notice, or when the usual means of service have failed but jurisdiction can be obtained by substituted service,[55] the plaintiff files his original writ,[56] bill, petition, libel, or other process with the clerk of court along with the officer's certificate of service and the entry fee.[57] The clerk will then enter the action on the docket,[58] along with the names of the attorneys or parties conducting the action,[59] and the matter will thereafter be regarded as pending in court.

§ 13.12. Return Day

The return day[60] is theoretically the date by the close of which the party commencing an action must have completed all the tasks necessary to the entry of the action and have returned the writ or other process to the clerk. However, the Superior Court Rules allow the party commencing an action one additional day to file the process with the officer's return and fee[61] and permit the respondent seven additional days to file his Appearance without suffering default.[62]

---

54 Burleigh v. Leon, 83 N.H. 115, 117, 139 A. 184, 187 (1927).

55 See RSA 510:8.

56 When the original writ or other process has been lost, without the fault of the plaintiff, a copy may be filed (called a "pluries writ") by leave of the court if there is satisfactory proof (e.g., by means of a certified copy previously filed with a public officer) of the contents of the lost writ or other process. Taylor v. Cobleigh, 16 N.H. 105 (1844).

57 Writs in aid of a bill in equity, libel for divorce, or petition for legal separation may be entered without charge. Super. Ct. R. 129. Entry fees are not required when pleadings are filed by "a legal aid society, a federally funded legal services project, or counsel assigned in accordance with the rules of court" and will be waived on motion of any other person who is unable, by reason of poverty, to pay them. RSA 499:18-b. See Scully's Auto Marine Uphol. v. Peerless, 136 N.H. 65, 68, 611 A.2d 635, 637 (1992).

58 Super. Ct. R. 3 and 10; Dist. and Mun. Ct. R. 3.2(B) and 3.5(A); Prob. Ct. R. 3. The district and municipal court docket is referred to in the most recent rules by the term "court record."

59 Super. Ct. R. 14; Dist. and Mun. Ct. R. 3.6(A); Prob. Ct. R. 4.

60 " 'The Entry Date is not synonymous with the Return Date.' " Campton Crossroads, Inc. v. Wise, 131 N.H. 193, 195, 551 A.2d 517, 519 (1988).

61 Super. Ct. R. 3.

62 Super. Ct. R. 14. In addition, a change in statutory return days automatically changes the return days stated in outstanding writs and orders of notice. Woodward v. Peabody, 39 N.H. 189 (1859).

A writ or other process may be filed late only by agreement or upon the court's order, based upon a finding of accident, mistake, or misfortune,[63] and after filing an affidavit of defense "specifically setting forth the defense and the facts on which the defense is based,"[64] and giving notice to the other parties.[65] In *Brady v. Duran*,[66] the Court refused to allow a late filing, even though the writ had been served and the defendant had appeared within the time allowed, where the plaintiff's counsel did not seek permission for late filing until eighteen months after the return day and admitted that the failure to file on time had resulted from clerical error in his office.

---

63 Fome Associates v. Palmer, 122 N.H. 985, 453 A.2d 1274 (1982); Arsenault v. Scanlon, 139 N.H. 592, 594, 660 A.2d 1110, 1112 (1995).

64 Super. Ct. R. 14; Dist. and Mun. Ct. R. 3.6(A).

65 Super. Ct. R. 3. See also former RSA 496:2; Chadbourne v. Sumner, 16 N.H. 129 (1844); Langdell v. Eastern Basket and Veneer Company, 78 N.H. 243, 99 A. 90 (1916); Mattocks v. Bishop, 4 N.H. 439 (1828); Taylor v. Cobleigh, 16 N.H. 105 (1844).

66 117 N.H. 275, 372 A.2d 283 (1977). Later, in Brady v. Duran, 119 N.H. 467, 403 A.2d 416 (1979), the Court held that plaintiff was entitled to invoke RSA 508:10 which allowed plaintiff to bring a second suit within one year after the judgment was rendered against her and to litigate her claim on its merits.

CHAPTER 14. SERVICE OF PROCESS

§ 14.01. Purposes

Service of process accomplishes two purposes. First, it establishes the court's jurisdiction over the defendant or the res in connection with the action. Second, it informs the defendant of the pendency and the particulars of the proceeding. Although it is not necessary to accomplish both purposes by the same act or service, both must be achieved before any constitutionally sufficient proceedings can begin.[1]

Library References

CJS Process § 25

A. On Natural Persons

§ 14.02. Present or Residing in New Hampshire

Service may be made on any natural person by giving a copy[2] of the process to him or her at any place within the state ("in-hand service") or by leaving a copy of the process at his or her New Hampshire abode ("abode service").[3]

Library References

CJS Process §§ 26, 47

Necessity, in service by leaving process at place of abode, etc., of leaving a copy of summons for each party sought to be served. 8 ALR2d 343.

Place or manner of delivering or depositing papers, under statutes permitting service of process by leaving copy at usual place of abode or residence. 87 ALR2d 1163.

§ 14.03. What Constitutes an "Abode"

What constitutes a person's abode for the purposes of service of civil process is unclear. When the statute formerly required that a copy of the process be left at "the last and usual place of abode" of the defendant, it was held in *Bruce v. Cloutman*[4] that the defendant's dwelling house, "being his place of present abode," fell within the term. But the statute was amended shortly after *Cloutman*,[5] and has provided for over a century that the copy

---

1 See City of Claremont v. Truell, 126 N.H. 30, 35, 489 A.2d 581, 585 (1985) ("It is well settled that '[a]n elementary and fundamental requirement of due process . . . is notice reasonably calculated, under all the circumstances, to apprise interested parties of the pendency of the action and afford them an opportunity to present their objections.' The type of notice that is required in a given case depends upon the nature of the governmental interests and the private interests affected.").

2 Although RSA 510:2 requires service of an "attested copy," the Supreme Court held in Davis v. Cray, 109 N.H. 181, 246 A.2d 97 (1968), that service of a "true copy" was satisfactory.

3 RSA 510:2. Service of process may no longer be accomplished by reading the process to the defendant. See P.S., ch. 219, § 2; Laws 1893, ch. 67, § 6; Blake v. Smith, 67 N.H. 182, 38 A. 16 (1892) (service of a writ of attachment by reading when the statute authorized only in-hand or abode service was insufficient).

4 45 N.H. 37 (1863).

5 See G.L., ch. 223, § 2.

need only be left at the defendant's "abode." Combining that amendment with the strict construction usually applied to statutes providing for service of process,[6] it seems reasonable to construe the term as allowing process to be left at any place, known by the officer, where the defendant is currently residing.[7] The question is not resolved by the character of the premises or the length of time in which the defendant has been in residence, but by a consideration of whether the place where the process is left is the place where the defendant has been living and to which he or she may be expected to return in sufficient time to become apprised of the pendency of the action and to prepare a response.[8]

Library References

CJS Domicile § 1
Construction of phrase "usual place of abode," or similar terms referring to abode, residence, or domicil, as used in statutes relating to service of process. 32 ALR3d 112.

§ 14.04. The Distinction Between "Abode" and "Domicile"

The concepts of "abode" and "domicile" have sometimes been confused,[9] but are separate. The common law of New Hampshire has long recognized a distinction between the two for purposes of service.

In *Ward v. Cole*,[10] the Court said that "[a] person may not, by his absence, lose his domicile in the state, and he may have it for the purpose of voting and probably for other purposes, without having a usual place of abode, within the meaning of the statute, for the service of legal process."[11] In *Gilman v. Cutts*,[12] the Court held that a person who maintained a house in

---

6 In Rogers v. Buchanan, 58 N.H. 47 (1876), the Court said:

> The service of legal process is a power by means of which a person may be deprived of his estate. It is indispensable to the protection of his rights that no rule or regulation should be infringed which the law prescribes for securing to him notice of the claim and proceeding by which his estate is thus imperilled. (58 N.H. at 48.)

7 Thus, the defendant's abode may include his house, a hotel room, or a camping trailer.

8 See Duncan v. McDonough, 105 N.H. 308, 309, 199 A.2d 104, 106 (1964).

9 See, e.g., Bailey v. Bailey, 93 N.H. 259, 40 A.2d 581 (1945), where the Court seems to have upheld an abode service on the ground, not that the defendant was living in the apartment at the time or was expected to return, but that the statute allowed service on his "last abode" and he had, since leaving the apartment, not gained a domicile in another state.

10 32 N.H. 452 (1855).

11 32 N.H. at 457.

12 23 N.H. 376 (1851).

Exeter at which his wife and children lived but who was absent from the state for six months at a time in connection with his work, returning only on alternate weekends for one day, nevertheless retained both his domicile and his "usual place of abode" in Exeter and could be summoned by abode service left at the house. But in *Ward v. Cole*,[13] the Court held that a man who took his family on a whaling voyage that they expected would last for three years did not have a "usual place of abode" in the state during his absence, even though his house and farm were maintained in the expectation of his return. And in *Brown v. Rollins*,[14] the Court similarly held that a man had no abode within the state during an absence of twelve years, during which time he was in California, even though his wife and child remained on the family farm in New Hampshire throughout the period of his absence. In that case, the Court said that even if he had retained an intention to return to New Hampshire, "his legal domicile would have been here yet his actual place of abode in the meaning of the statute must be regarded as California."[15]

§ 14.05. Abode Service on a Person Who Is Not Domiciled in New Hampshire

While it is clear that a person who is both domiciled and maintains a place of abode in New Hampshire may be served by leaving a copy of the process at his or her abode, the Court has never addressed the question of whether a person who is not or has never been domiciled in New Hampshire, but who has an abode here, may be served in the same way. The question would appear to depend upon whether abode service is the constitutional equivalent of in-hand service. A century ago, Justice Ladd concluded that it was not,[16] but a different conclusion might be reached today. The issue rests on not how the defendant receives the process, but whether he or she receives the process while in the state. There is no reason why a defendant should be allowed to escape the exercise of a New Hampshire court's jurisdiction simply because a copy of the writ is found in his or her hotel room rather than receiving a copy in-hand by the sheriff.

In Justice Ladd's time, when a sheriff's return was conclusive and a holding that in-hand and abode service were equivalent could have pre-

---

13   32 N.H. 452 (1855).

14   44 N.H. 446 (1863).

15   44 N.H. at 448.

16   Lewis v. Whittemore, 5 N.H. 364 (1831).

vented the defendant from objecting that he or she had never seen a copy of the writ, there might have been justification for requiring that the defendant be domiciled in the state at the time the court's jurisdiction was made in order to attach by abode service. But because the sheriff's return is now subject to challenge,[17] there is no reason not to give abode service the same effect as in-hand service, at least until the defendant objects that he or she has not received a copy of the writ. In accordance with this principle, the question of whether the defendant has ever been domiciled in New Hampshire should have no bearing on the issue of abode service.

§ 14.06. Neither Present nor Residing in New Hampshire ("Long Arm")

If a natural person has no abode in New Hampshire and cannot be found within the state for the purpose of completing in-hand service, but nevertheless transacts business, commits a tort, or owns, uses, or possesses property in the state, he or she may be subject to the jurisdiction of the courts of the state for claims arising from that business, tort, or ownership, use, or possession of property.

Service of process in actions based on such claims must be made in part by the usual serving officer and in part by the plaintiff or the attorney. The serving officer leaves one copy of the process in the Secretary of State's Office, State House, Concord, with a fee of $10.00. At the same time, the plaintiff or the attorney must send a copy of the process by registered mail, postage prepaid, to the defendant at "the last known abode or place of business in the state or country in which the defendant resides."[18] In addition to the sheriff's return showing service on the Secretary of State, the plaintiff or the attorney must complete an affidavit stating that the plaintiff has forwarded process as required and file that affidavit, plus the registered mail return receipt, with the court.[19]

Library References

CJS Process §§ 73, 74

What amounts to doing business in a state within statute providing for service of process in action against nonresident natural person or persons doing business in state. 10 ALR2d 200.

---

17 Adams v. Sullivan, 110 N.H. 101, 261 A.2d 273 (1970).

18 RSA 510:4(II). South Down Recreation Ass'n v. Moran, 686 A. 2d 314 (N.H. 1996).

19 RSA 510:4(II). In addition, the Secretary of State keeps a record of the hour and date when service is completed on his office. RSA 510:4(III).

Validity of service of process on nonresident owner of watercraft, under state "long-arm" statutes. 99 ALR2d 287.

Airplane or other aircraft as "motor vehicle" or the like within statute providing for constructive or substituted service of process on nonresident motorist. 36 ALR3d 1387.

B. On Corporations

§ 14.07. Domestic Corporations

Effective in 1993, the Legislature revised the Business Corporation Act and added specific means by which a domestic corporation can be served. RSA 293-A:5.04 provides that a corporation's registered agent is the appropriate agent for service of process, notices, or demands on the corporation. Service may be made either in-hand or by leaving an attested copy at the abode of the agent. If a corporation has no registered agent, or if the agent cannot with reasonable diligence be served, the corporation may be served by registered or certified mail, return receipt requested, addressed to the secretary of the corporation at its principal office.[20] It is no longer required that service on a domestic corporation be perfected in the state; service can be mailed to the secretary where the corporation has its principal office, whether it be in-state or out-of-state. Service is considered perfected on the date the corporation receives the mail, the date shown on the receipt, or five days after its mailing, whichever is earliest.[21]

Additionally, prior methods of service still remain valid as the revised Act ". . . does not prescribe the only means, or necessarily the required means, of serving a corporation."[22] Service in-state, therefore, upon one of the directors, trustees, managers, clerks, treasurers or cashiers, remains valid.[23] Service can also be made on any principal member, stockholder, agent, overseer or person who has the care or charge of any property or business of the corporation.[24]

---

20 RSA 293-A:5.04(b).

21 RSA 293-A:5.04(b)(1)–(3).

22 RSA 293-A:5.04(c).

23 RSA 510:14. The phrase "one of the directors, trustees, managers" means a member of "the board of control of the corporation," however designated. Dinnin v. Hutchins, 75 N.H. 470, 76 A. 126 (1910).

24 RSA 510:14. The statute provides that service may be made upon these officers "if any in the state." The statute is not clear on and no case has determined the question of whether service may be made on the second tier of agents, when one or more of these officers, although in the state, cannot with reasonable diligence be found. However, there is no reason to believe that the Legislature intended to invalidate service in such a case or to provide the basis for a defendant corporation that has in fact received notice of the proceeding to move to dismiss the writ for improper service.

§ 14.08. Railroads and Manufacturing Corporations

There are special statutory provisions for service on railroads and manufacturing corporations. Under RSA 510:15, service may be made on a railroad corporation by giving an attested copy, in-hand, at any station to "any person doing the business of the corporation as ticket master for the sale of passenger tickets."[25] Under RSA 510:16, a "manufacturing corporation"[26] may be served "by leaving an attested copy of the writ at the office or counting room of the corporation." These provisions are, however, supplementary to the general procedure set forth in RSA 510:14.

Library References

CJS Process § 31
Who is "managing agent" of domestic corporation within statute providing for service of summons or process thereon. 71 ALR2d 178.

§ 14.09. Foreign Corporations

To conduct business in New Hampshire, a foreign corporation[27] must procure a certificate of authority from the Secretary of State, and it must appoint and maintain a registered agent.[28] The registered agent is the proper agent for service on the corporation.[29] If there is no registered agent, if the registered agent cannot with reasonable diligence be served, if the corporation has withdrawn from transacting business in New Hampshire, or if the corporation has had its certificate of authority revoked, service may be made by registered or certified mail, return receipt requested, to the secretary of the foreign corporation at its principal office.[30]

Service is considered perfected on the date the foreign corporation receives the mail, the date shown on the return receipt, or five days after

---

25 It would appear that service is to be made at the station and that abode service may not be employed against a ticket master.

26 The statutes do not define the term "manufacturing corporation," and it is unclear whether the mode of service authorized by RSA 510:16 may be employed against all corporations that manufacture anything anywhere or was intended to be restricted to corporations that turn out a product suitable for sale and that complete their production at a point within the state.

27 "Foreign corporations" include "Massachusetts trusts" or "business trusts." RSA 293-A:15.01.

28 RSA 293-A:15.01; 15.07.

29 RSA 293-A:15.10.

30 RSA 293-A:15.10(b).

service was mailed, whichever is earliest.[31] Methods of service under RSA 510:14 also remain valid.[32]

Library Rferences

Attorney representing foreign corporation in litigation as its agent for service of process in unconnected actions or proceedings. 9 ALR3d 738.

Who is "general" or "managing" agent of foreign corporation under statute authorizing service of process on such agent. 17 ALR3d 625.

C. On Government Officials and Agencies

§ 14.10. State Government—Generally

Some statutes that specifically authorize actions against officers, boards, commissions, and agencies of the state, quasi-corporate bodies, and the state itself specify the person to be served and the mode of service. No general statute, however, provides for service in cases not specifically authorized. Although many forms of action are still barred against the state by the doctrine of sovereign immunity, some general principles may be set forth for service of process in aid of those that are not.

Library References

CJS Process § 31

§ 14.11. —Employees v. Appointed or Elected Officials

A state officer or employee against whom relief is sought should be served at a time and place where he or she has legal authority to act on the subject of the suit.[33]

In the case of an employee in the classified service, it is at least arguable that the employee has no authority to act outside of the business hours that are customary for his or her job or at a place (such as the employee's home) where the business of the agency is not normally carried on. Such a person should be served in hand at the office during the normal working period.

A person holding a commission from the Governor and Council or an elected official may be regarded as bearing more authority and able to exercise his or her office at all times. Although it is preferable to serve such

---

31 RSA 293-A:10(c).

32 RSA 510:14; State v. Luv Pharmacy, Inc., 118 N.H. 398, 388 A.2d 190 (1978).

33 This situation is to be distinguished from the case where a claim against an official or employee based on official acts is joined with a claim against the same person based on action taken outside the scope of his employment or office. In the latter case, the defendant should be served separately on each claim.

a person in-hand at his or her office or the place where official duties are normally exercised, service may also be rendered in any manner that could be used on a natural person.[34] In the absence of specific statutory authorization, though, an officer or employee should not be served by leaving a copy of the process at his or her office.

§ 14.12. —Official v. Individual Capacities

In most cases, when a specific state official or employee is named defendant in an action, relief will be sought against him or her only in the employee's official capacity and service should be made as set forth above. However, in those cases in which an additional remedy is sought against the official or employee in the individual capacity, the defendant need not be served twice, but should be served in a manner that would be sufficient to obtain personal jurisdiction on the claim.

§ 14.13. —Agency, Board, or Commission

In the absence of a statute declaring otherwise, an agency, board, or commission of state government has no existence separate from the rest of the branch of government of which it forms a part and cannot be analogized to a corporation for the purpose of determining an appropriate method of service. When an agency is the named defendant, the chief executive officer of that agency should be served in-hand during the business hours of that agency and at a place where the agency is then performing official functions. When a board or commission is the defendant, every member of the board or commission and its secretary should be served, if possible, in the board or commission's office during working hours, but in any event in-hand at times and places where a member may be regarded as exercising his or her office.

§ 14.14. —The State as a Defendant

When the state, as a body politic and not acting through one of its boards, agencies, or commissions, is the intended defendant, in-hand service should be made on the Secretary of State in the State House in Concord. When specific relief is sought from the state as a body politic, service should also be made on the state officer who exercises the state's primary authority in that field.

---

34 Where a person sits on a board or commission, not by appointment from the Governor and Council but as an incident and part of his other employment by the state, he should be served as a state official or employee.

§ 14.15. —Accepting Service of Process

The Attorney General, his or her Deputy, and Assistants are the only officers of state government authorized to represent state officials, employees, agencies, boards, and commissions in court. In that capacity, they have the same authority as any private attorney to agree to accept service of process on behalf of their clients.

§ 14.16. County Government

When a county is a named defendant, service may be completed in-hand or abode on one of the county commissioners and in-hand service on the county treasurer at the court house.[35] Where there is no county commissioner or officer, service may be made instead on one of the "principal inhabitants" of the county.[36]

§ 14.17. City Government

Service may be completed against a city by in-hand or abode service on either the mayor or a member of the city council or board of aldermen and the city clerk.[37] Where there is no mayor, alderman, or councilman in office or where there is no person holding the office of city clerk, service that would have been made on that person may be made instead and in the same manner on any "principal inhabitant" of the city.[38] The city clerk may, alternatively, be served by leaving a copy at his or her office, if the office is not a home office.[39]

§ 14.18. Town Government

When a town is sued, service may be made by in-hand or by abode service on one of the selectmen and the town clerk.[40] When there is neither a selectman nor a town clerk in office, the service that would have been made on that person may be made instead on any "principal inhabitant" of the

---

[35] RSA 510:10.

[36] RSA 510:11.

[37] RSA 510:10.

[38] RSA 510:11.

[39] RSA 510:12.

[40] RSA 510:10. This requirement is not satisfied by service on the town clerk and the administrative assistant to the selectmen. Lachapelle v. Town of Goffstown, 134 N.H. 478 (1991).

town.[41] The town clerk may, alternatively, be served by leaving a copy at his or her office, if the office is not a home office.[42]

§ 14.19. School Districts

When a school district is the defendant, a member of the school board who is not the school district clerk and the school district clerk may be served in-hand or by abode service.[43] When there is neither school district clerk nor a member of the school board other than the clerk, service may be made on any "principal inhabitant" of the school district.[44]

§ 14.20. Village Districts

Village districts should be served by in-hand or by abode service on one of the commissioners and the clerk.[45] If there is no commissioner or clerk, the service that would have been made on that officer may instead be made on a "principal inhabitant" of the district.[46]

D. On Mutual Associations

§ 14.21. Organized or Existing in New Hampshire

Any "mutual association of persons" organized or conducting its activities in this state, other than a partnership with fewer than four general partners,[47] certain churches and religious societies,[48] and fraternal benefit societies,[49] may be served by in-hand or abode service on any officer of the association or, if there are no officers, on any two members.[50] The term

---

41 RSA 510:11.

42 RSA 510:12.

43 RSA 510:10.

44 RSA 510:11.

45 RSA 510:10.

46 RSA 510:11.

47 RSA 510:13 refers only to a "partnership having not more than four members." The term "members" must be construed to mean "general partners."

48 RSA ch. 306.

49 RSA 418:18.

50 RSA 510:13; Sununu v. Clamshell Alliance, 122 N.H. 668, 448 A.2d 431 (1982). "RSA 510:13 allows an individual, when bringing an action against an unincorporated association, to treat that association as an entity. . . . The statute relieves a plaintiff from the task of having to name and personally serve process on each and every member of the association. By suing an unincorporated association in this manner, however, a plaintiff limits his remedy. We conclude that 'the collection of any judgment obtained

"mutual association" includes, but is not limited to, unincorporated associations, joint stock companies, limited liability companies, syndicates, orders, and partnerships with fewer than four general partners.[51]

§ 14.22. Not Organized or Existing in New Hampshire

Mutual associations, which have been organized outside of New Hampshire, may be served under RSA 510:4 for claims arising from business done, torts committed or property owned, used, or possessed in New Hampshire.

E. On Partnerships

§ 14.23. Domestic General Partnerships

Any partnership organized or existing within the state and having more than four general partners may be served by in-hand or abode service on any officer, or if there are no officers, on any two members. A New Hampshire partnership with four or fewer general partners cannot be sued in the firm name,[52] and all general partners must be served by in-hand or abode service.

§ 14.24. Foreign General Partnerships

Any general partnership, regardless of the number of its general partners, organized outside New Hampshire but that does business in New Hampshire, must register under RSA 305-A:53 and must maintain a registered office and registered agent in the state.[54] Once a foreign general partnership has been registered, service may be made on the partnership in its own name by leaving an attested copy in the registered office of the registered agent during regular business hours.[55] If, after being registered, the foreign general

---

against such association must be satisfied out of its property alone and the property of its members is immune from seizure.' " Shortlidge v. Gutoski, 125 N.H. 510, 515–16, 484 A.2d 1083, 1087 (1984). But the Court in *Shortledge* held that nothing in RSA 510:13 precludes a plaintiff from suing the members of an unincorporated association individually.

51 RSA 510:13.

52 Rosenblum v. Judson Engineering Corporation, 99 N.H. 267, 109 A.2d 558 (1954); RSA 510:13.

53 RSA 305-A:1(I).

54 RSA 305-A:1(II).

55 RSA 305-A:6.

partnership fails to maintain a registered agent or loses its certificate of authority, service may be made instead on the Secretary of State,[56] by leaving one copy in the office of the Secretary of State or by serving the Secretary of State in-hand, and paying $25.00.[57] The same method of service may be used when the foreign general partnership has a registered agent who cannot, "with reasonable diligence and providence," be served.[58] Foreign general partnerships with any number of general partners that have never been registered may also be served in this manner.[59]

§ 14.25. Domestic Limited Partnerships

Any limited partnership organized or existing within the state is required to maintain an agent for service of process. Any domestic limited partnership having more than four general partners may be served by in-hand or abode service on any officer, or if there are no officers, on any two members. A limited partnership with fewer than four members may be served by in-hand or abode service to the registered agent or by in-hand or abode service, to all members of the limited partnership.

§ 14.26. Foreign Limited Partnerships

Every limited partnership organized under the laws of another jurisdiction and doing business in the state must register with the Secretary of State.[60] Upon registering, every foreign limited partnership is required to appoint an agent for service of process, and is also required to appoint the Secretary of State as agent for service of process if no agent has been appointed or if the agent cannot be found with the exercise of reasonable diligence.[61]

---

56 RSA 304-B:49(III) and (IV).

57 RSA 305-A:7.

58 RSA 305-A:6.

59 RSA 305-A:6 enumerates the occasions when service may be made on the Secretary of State, and RSA 305-A:7 provides the procedure for such service. Section 6 does not list, among the instances when the Secretary of State may be served, the situation where a foreign partnership is doing business in New Hampshire but has never been registered. However, Section 7, when setting forth the addresses to which copies of the process are to be mailed, states that the plaintiff shall provide the address for a partnership which has never been registered. This language suggests that the Legislature intended to allow service by this procedure on foreign partnerships that have never been registered. But, at least with respect to partnerships having four or fewer partners, such a construction conflicts with dicta in *Rosenblum v. Judson Engineering Corporation, supra*, and makes it easier to serve foreign than domestic partnerships.

60 RSA 304-B:49.

61 RSA 304-B:49(III) and (IV).

Service on the Secretary of State must be made on the office of the Secretary of State by leaving a copy with the Secretary of State along with the proper fee. If no agent exists or can be found with reasonable diligence, and service is not made on the Secretary of State, service may be made by registered or certified mail, return receipt requested, to its principal office.[62] Service is perfected on the date of receipt of the mail, the date shown on the receipt, or five days after mailing, whichever is earliest.

F. On Limited Liability Companies

§ 14.27. Limited Liability Companies

(a) *Domestic Limited Liability Companies.* Service on a domestic limited liability company may be made on the company's registered agent in-hand or at the agent's abode.[63] If the registered agent cannot with reasonable diligence be found, service may be made by registered or certified mail return receipt requested, addressed to the company at its principal office.[64] Service is considered perfected on the date the mail is received, the date of the return receipt, or five days after mailing, whichever occurs first.[65]

In-hand or abode service may also be made upon any officer, or if there is no officer, then upon any two members of the company.[66]

(b) *Foreign Limited Liability Companies.* Every limited liability company organized under the laws of another jurisdiction and doing business in the state must register with the Secretary of State, and at that time must appoint an agent in the state for service of process.[67] Service upon any registered foreign limited liability company can be made upon this registered agent.[68] If no registered agent exists, or if one cannot be found with the exercise of reasonable diligence, then service can be made by registered or certified mail, return receipt requested, to the company's principal office.[69] Any foreign limited liability company not registered under RSA

---

62 RSA 304-B:49(IV). See also RSA 293-A:15.10 (service of process on foreign corporation); RSA 304-B:54(IV) (Secretary of State appointed agent for service of process by foreign limited partnership's "transaction of business" without registration).

63 RSA 304-C:6(I).

64 RSA 304-C:6(II).

65 RSA 304-C:6(II)(a)–(c).

66 RSA 304-C:10.

67 RSA 304-C:64.

68 RSA 304-C:70(I).

69 RSA 304-C:70(II).

Chapter 304-C, doing business in New Hampshire, is deemed to have appointed the Secretary of State as agent for service of process.[70] Service can be made by leaving a copy in the hands of the Secretary of State along with $10.00.[71]

G. Other Service

§ 14.28. Alternative Methods

Many statutes prescribing methods of service specifically state that the means set forth are not exclusive and that other methods in other statutes may also be followed.[72] Thus, while the terms of statutes authorizing methods of service must be closely followed, there is frequently more than one way to serve a defendant.

§ 14.29. Scire Facias Against a Nonresident

A writ of scire facias, arising as it must from some action in which jurisdiction was obtained after sufficient service, may be served by giving or mailing a copy to the attorney[73] who represented the nonresident defendant at the conclusion of the underlying action, by giving a copy of the writ to the defendant at a place outside the state, or by leaving a copy at the abode outside the state.[74]

Library References

CJS Scire Facias § 10

§ 14.30. Substituted Service—Generally

In some circumstances, the plaintiff may request and the court may order service by some method other than the ones prescribed by statute. The most common methods of substituted service are registered mail and publication.

Library References

CJS Process §§ 43–53
Difference between date of affidavit for service by publication and date of filing or of order for publication as affecting validity of service. 46 ALR2d 1364.

---

70 RSA 304-C:71, 304-C:68(I)(d).

71 RSA 510:4,II.

72 See, e.g., RSA 510:2, 510:13, and 510:4(V).

73 Service may be made on an attorney by mailing or leaving a copy of the writ in his office.

74 RSA 510:6.

Sufficiency of affidavit made by attorney or other person on behalf of plaintiff for purpose of service by publication. 47 ALR2d 423.

Validity of substituted service of process upon liability insurer of unavailable tort-feasor. 17 ALR4th 918.

§ 14.31 —Nonresident

RSA 510:8 provides that when the defendant does not reside in New Hampshire and he or she either cannot be served in the manner prescribed or no method of service is set forth in any statute, the plaintiff may enter the writ and the court may order some other means of notice.[75] The statute does not expand the jurisdiction that the courts of this state will exercise over nonresident defendants,[76] and its main use is in providing for an alternative means of notice where the procedures set forth in RSA 510:4 ("Long Arm") and 510:6 (scire facias) cannot be satisfied.

§ 14.32. —Resident

(a) *In Personam Jurisdiction.* Substituted service can never be used to obtain jurisdiction over a person who is, in fact, a resident of the state, even though he or she cannot be served in-hand or the abode cannot be found.[77]

(b) *In Rem Jurisdiction.* Substituted service can be used to notify a resident defendant of the pendency of an action begun by attaching his or her property in state[78] or of an action involving property to which he or she may have a claim.[79] It has been held that such substituted service may even be employed in preference to the procedures set forth in the statute if it is just as likely to give actual notice and is more convenient to the plaintiff.[80]

(c) *Requisites of Publication.* Substituted service by publication must contain the title of the case, the name of the court, the time and place of

---

75 RSA 510:8. South Down Recreation Ass'n v. Moran, 686 A.2d 314 (N.H. 1996).

76 Rosenblum v. Judson Engineering Corporation, 99 N.H. 267, 109 A.2d 558 (1954). Indeed, it could not since the state has already chosen to exercise jurisdiction to the maximum constitutional limit. Downer v. Shaw, 22 N.H. 277 (1851).

77 It was formerly held that substituted service could be made on a person who was in fact a resident of New Hampshire if the sheriff first returned non est inventus as to the defendant. Burney v. Hodgdon, 66 N.H. 338, 29 A. 493 (1890). In the days when a sheriff's return was conclusive, a defendant was not allowed to invalidate that service by proving that he was in fact a resident of the county even though the sheriff couldn't find him. Clark v. Bradstreet, 99 N.H. 55, 104 A.2d 739 (1954). Now, however, since a sheriff's return can be challenged, there would appear to be no continuing vitality to these holdings.

78 Thompson v. Carroll, 36 N.H. 21 (1857); Kendrick v. Kimball, 33 N.H. 482 (1856).

79 This is the basis for service by publication in actions to quiet title to real estate.

80 Sampson v. Conlon, 100 N.H. 70, 119 A.2d 707 (1955).

return and any scheduled hearing, the place where the pleadings may be examined, and any other information that the court thinks necessary.[81]

H. Return of Service

§ 14.33 Return of Service

After the sheriff or constable has completed service, or has attempted to do so and concluded that he or she cannot make service, the sheriff will make return of that fact to the plaintiff's attorney. If the sheriff or constable has succeeded in making service, the return will state the day, time, and manner of service. If the sheriff or constable has not succeeded in making service, he or she will say that, despite diligent search, the defendant cannot be found within the precinct.[82] In either case, the return will be inscribed on the back of an attested copy of the writ, petition, libel, or other pleading that the sheriff had sought to serve and will be signed, but not sworn to, by the sheriff or constable making the return.

Upon receipt of a return reciting service, the plaintiff's attorney should do two things:

(1) Examine the return to make sure that it is complete, that it contains no typographical or other errors, and that the right person was served within the time allowed and in a lawful manner; and

(2) Make a copy of the return for his files and send the original to the clerk of court.

If the return shows an error in service, is incomplete, or contains a mistake, the plaintiff's attorney should immediately return it to the sheriff for a correction of the error.[83]

Upon receipt of the return reciting an inability to serve, the plaintiff's attorney must decide whether to try to effect service in another county or by the Long Arm statute (if appropriate) or to apply to the court for permission to make service by alternative means. Because the court's decision on the latter issue will frequently turn on the extent to which the plaintiff has exhausted conventional methods of service, the plaintiff will most often choose to try again to attempt service by the usual means.

---

81 RSA 510:9. See Sununu v. Clamshell Alliance, 122 N.H. 668, 448 A.2d 431 (1982).

82 This is the non est inventus return.

83 A "sheriff's return may be amended . . . to accord with the facts." Bissonnette v. Alpine, Inc., 96 N.H. 419, 420, 77 A.2d 586, 587 (1951); Goodwin v. Goldberg, 85 N.H. 548, 161 A. 375 (1932).

In some cases, someone associated with the plaintiff's attorney must execute a document as part of the return of service in court.[84] It is always wise for the plaintiff's attorney to avoid executing the affidavit if it is possible to have another person do it. This will avoid disqualifying the plaintiff's counsel from representation at trial should it be necessary to prove service.

Library References

CJS Process §§ 90–105

Failure to make return as affecting validity of service or court's jurisdiction. 82 ALR2d 668.

Sufficiency of affidavit as to due diligence in attempting to learn whereabouts of party to litigation, for the purpose of obtaining service by publication. 21 ALR2d 929.

Mistake or error in middle initial or middle name of party as vitiating or invalidating civil process, summons, or the like. 6 ALR3d 1179.

§ 14.34. Challenge to the Officer's Return

Throughout most of New Hampshire's history, a sheriff's return has been regarded as conclusive proof of the facts recited therein, and the parties have been prohibited from introducing evidence to contradict that return.[85] If the sheriff made return indicating that he or she had validly served a party when the party had not been served, the remedy was by an action against the sheriff for the resulting harm, not by proof of the inaccuracy in the proceeding in which service had been made.

After some weakening,[86] this ancient common law rule was finally put to rest in 1970 by the Court's holding in *Adams v. Sullivan*.[87] Chief Justice Kenison, writing for the court, said:

> The common-law rule that a sheriff's return in the service of process is conclusive and not controvertible has more history in its favor than it does either logic or common sense . . . . Time has eroded this common-law rule both here as well as in a majority of states and it is generally recognized today that the rule, which preferred fiction over fact, is inconsistent with modern procedure

---

84 See, e.g., RSA 510:4(II), which requires an "affidavit of the plaintiff or his attorney of compliance with the section." A similar requirement may be imposed on a party who is authorized to make service by publication.

85 See, e.g., Goodwin v. Goldberg, 85 N.H. 548, 161 A. 375 (1932); Bolles v. Bowen, 45 N.H. 124 (1863); Clough v. Monroe, 34 N.H. 381 (1857); Wendell v. Mugridge, 19 N.H. 109 (1848); Lewis v. Blair, 1 N.H. 68 (1817); Clark v. Bradstreet, 99 N.H. 55, 104 A.2d 739 (1954).

86 See Pike v. Scribner, 101 N.H. 314, 142 A.2d 154 (1958).

87 110 N.H. 101, 261 A.2d 273 (1970).

and practice . . . . The sheriff's return of service is entitled to a presumption of correctness which the contestant must overcome by evidence but it is not conclusive.[88]

The same principles apply to any part of a return made by the plaintiff, the attorney, or their agent.

I. Exemptions From Service

§ 14.35. Introduction

A person may be temporarily exempted from service of civil process because he or she is on his way to, returning from, or in attendance upon a hearing before a court or administrative agency of the state or federal government sitting in New Hampshire. The person can, however, waive the exemption.

§ 14.36. Historical Background

Exemptions from service of civil process in New Hampshire have their roots in English Common Law and were first applied in the days when civil actions were commonly begun by arrest under a Writ of Capias and Attachment. The common law of England that New Hampshire inherited after the Revolution had provided that certain people, because of the roles they fulfilled in society, should be exempt from interference while performing functions of great importance to society. Members of Parliament, ambassadors, judges, jurors, and other judicial officers, married women, soldiers, certificated bankrupts, and clerics were among those who were allowed exemptions from arrest in aid of civil process under English Law.[89] These exemptions were adopted into early New Hampshire law with certain modifications necessary to fit the new form of government.[90] Jurors, married women, ambassadors, soldiers, and certificated bankrupts were allowed a complete privilege by virtue of the roles they fulfilled in the life of the community. Members of the legislature, judges, and clerics were exempted

---

88 110 N.H. at 103, 261 A.2d at 275.

89 These privileges are briefly reviewed by Chief Justice Richardson in his opinion for the Court in Hubbard v. Sanborn, 2 N.H. 468 (1822), and by Justice Fowler in his opinion for the Court in Woods v. Davis, 34 N.H. 328 (1857).

90 The exemption for members of Parliament was converted into an exemption for members of the federal (art. 1, § 6, U.S. Const.) and state legislatures (pt. 2, art. 21, N.H. Const.) and for legal voters of a town attending town meeting (see Hubbard v. Sanborn, 2 N.H. 468 (1822); Woods v. Davis, 34 N.H. 328 (1857); Statute of June 23, 1813, § 5).

from arrest only while performing or on their way to or from the performance of their official duties. In addition, all persons were exempt from service of any process, including arrest, on Sunday.

Most of these exemptions remained in New Hampshire practice until the early twentieth century. But, as the practice of beginning a civil action by arrest was gradually discontinued and was then abolished, and as people's roles in society became more complex and their obligations to each other for the consequences of their actions came to be more widely recognized, some of these exemptions were abandoned and the New Hampshire Supreme Court adopted the view that the remaining exemptions from service should not be expanded "unless there [is] some compelling reason to do so."[91] Today, privileges from service of civil process are enjoyed only by parties and witnesses in cases pending before state and federal courts and administrative agencies and only while such parties and witnesses are on their way to, returning from, or in attendance at hearings relating to those cases.

§ 14.37. Parties and Witnesses

(a) *Residents of New Hampshire.* Although parties and their witnesses were originally exempt from service by arrest while going to, returning from, or in attendance at a trial,[92] the Supreme Court has never recognized a privilege against service by other means on such persons. In fact, as early as 1822, in *Hubbard v. Sanborn*,[93] Chief Justice Richardson suggested that service by other means might come outside the exemption.[94]

(b) *Nonresidents.* In *Dolber v. Young*,[95] Justice Snow stated the modern rule as follows:

> Nonresident parties and witnesses are privileged from service of process while in attendance upon, going to, or returning from the trial of a cause.[96]

91　Pitman v. Cunningham, 100 N.H. 49, 52, 118 A.2d 884, 885–86 (1955).

92　State v. Buck, 62 N.H. 670 (1883).

93　2 N.H. 468 (1822).

94　2 N.H. at 470. The same point was touched upon, but not decided, in Justice Chase's opinion in Dickinson v. Farwell, 71 N.H. 213, 220–21, 51 A. 624, 628 (1902).

95　81 N.H. 157, 123 A. 218 (1923).

96　81 N.H. at 158, 123 A. at 219. Justice Snow's statement of the rule was broader than Justice Bingham's earlier formulation in Martin v. Whitney, 74 N.H. 505, 506, 69 A. 888, 889 (1908), which had provided:

The rule was refined in *Forbes v. Boynton*[97] to protect a nonresident defendant in a quasi in rem action, founded on the attachment of an automobile liability insurance policy, from service of process "while attending any court proceeding relating thereto or coming or returning from the same."[98] The *Dolber* rule protects nonresident witnesses and parties only. Neither resident parties and witnesses nor nonresident relatives and friends attending the proceedings are exempt from service while in the state to attend hearings related to the case. Nonresident witnesses and parties, however, enjoy the privilege even though they come into the state voluntarily to attend the hearing. In addition, nonresident plaintiffs are privileged from service despite the fact that they have voluntarily come into the state to prosecute their claims.[99]

The rule protects persons who intend to testify or who intend to be available to testify at the hearing.[100] There is no requirement that the proposed witness be a necessary or a sole witness on a point or that the witness, in fact, testifies.[101] Although the point has never been decided, it is fair to assume that a witness would be exempt from service while attending a hearing at which testimony on which his testimony depended was to be given.

Library References

CJS Process § 80
Immunity of nonresident defendant in criminal case from service of process. 20 ALR2d 163.
Immunity from service of process as affected by relationship between subject matter of litigation in which process was issued, and litigation which nonresident served was attending. 84 ALR2d 421.

Nonresident witnesses and nonresident parties as witnesses are privileged from arrest or summons upon civil process while in attendance upon, going to or returning from the trial of a cause in the courts of this state . . . .

Since neither point of variance was in issue in the latter case, it is impossible to determine whether Justice Snow's statement of the rule was intended to expand the law or merely to state in brief a principle which the Court understood to have been settled some years before. Whatever the intention, the *Dolber* rule completed the evolution of a rule to protect nonresidents from service of process other than by arrest, which began with Justice Chase's opinion in Ela v. Ela, 68 N.H. 312, 36 A. 15 (1895).

97 113 N.H. 617, 313 A.2d 129 (1973).

98 113 N.H. at 624, 313 A.2d at 133.

99 Martin v. Whitney, 74 N.H. 505, 69 A. 888 (1908).

100 Ela v. Ela, 68 N.H. 312, 36 A. 15 (1895).

101 *Id.*

§ 14.38. Attorneys

Attorneys are not protected by any privilege against service of civil process, and a nonresident attorney who comes into the state to attend a hearing on behalf of a client is not exempt from service while travelling to or from or attending the hearing.[102] However, nonresident attorneys who attend hearings as witnesses, even though they do so voluntarily and may also act as attorneys for their clients at the hearing, are exempt from service while going to or from or attending the hearing in which they expect to act as a witness.[103] It is not required that the attorney actually testify at the hearing to be entitled to this exemption,[104] but whether he or she attends "in good faith as a witness" is a question of fact about which the trial court may inquire.[105]

§ 14.39. Judges, Jurors, Administrative Hearings Officers, and Other Court or Agency Personnel

The Supreme Court has repeatedly said that an exemption from service of civil process "was not established for the benefit of the persons privileged, but to protect the administration of justice."[106] Initially, the administration of justice was protected by assuring that witnesses and parties would not be deterred from attending court by fear of arrest.[107] More recently, the administration of justice has been interpreted to include the "proper and efficient administration" of the courts and protection of "the dignity and authority of the court and administrative agency or . . . the performance of their duties."[108] No statute or case expressly grants a privilege from service to persons who are engaged in performing judicial or quasi-judicial duties or in assisting those who are, and it is unlikely that a serving officer would interrupt such proceedings in order to make in-hand service. If such a service were made, however, it would appear to be consistent with the purpose of protecting the dignity and efficiency of the tribunal to hold the service improper.

---

102 Pitman v. Cunningham, 100 N.H. 49, 118 A.2d 884 (1955).

103 Ela v. Ela, 68 N.H. 312, 36 A. 15 (1895).

104 *Id.*

105 68 N.H. at 314, 36 A. at 16.

106 Dickinson v. Farwell, 71 N.H. 213, 214, 51 A. 624, 625 (1902). See also State v. Buck, 62 N.H. 670 (1883); Pitman v. Cunningham, 100 N.H. 49, 118 A.2d 884 (1955).

107 Ela v. Ela, 68 N.H. 312, 36 A. 15 (1895).

108 Pitman v. Cunningham, 100 N.H. 49, 52, 118 A.2d 884, 885 (1955).

Library References

CJS Process §§ 84, 86
Immunity from service of process of public officer while attending court in official capacity. 45 ALR2d 1100.

§ 14.40. Members of the State and Federal Legislatures

Although members of the General Court[109] and Congress[110] are, by constitutional provisions, exempt from arrest while going to, returning from, and attending upon sessions of their respective houses, the privilege has never been extended to a protection from service of civil process by other means.[111]

§ 14.41. Time Limits on the Privilege for Nonresidents

Nonresident parties and witnesses are allowed a "reasonable time" to travel to and from the hearing in New Hampshire without being subject to service.[112] What constitutes a "reasonable time" will depend upon the circumstances of the case, and as a general rule, a person will not be permitted to use the shield of exemption as a party or witness to take care of other matters for which personal presence in New Hampshire is required, but for which he or she would not otherwise be protected from service. But a party or witness should not be required to abstain from all other activities while in state simply to protect his exemption from service, and the performance of minor and peripheral functions should not be regarded as a waiver of the privilege.

Library References

CJS Process § 88

§ 14.42. Attendance at Court Proceedings

The privilege against service extends to nonresident witnesses and parties who are going to, returning from, or attending the "trial of an action."[113] This includes not only trials and hearings on the merits before judges only and

---

109 Part 2, art. 21, N.H. Const.
110 U.S. Const., art. 1, § 6.
111 Bartlett v. Blair, 68 N.H. 232, 38 A. 1004 (1894).
112 Dolber v. Young, 81 N.H. 157, 120 A. 884 (1923).
113 Dickinson v. Farwell, 71 N.H. 213, 214, 51 A. 624, 625 (1902).

juries,[114] but hearings before referees,[115] auditors,[116] and administrative agencies[117] as well.

Whether the privilege extends to other activities in the case is a more troublesome question. In *Forbes v. Boynton*,[118] Justice Lampron wrote that a nonresident defendant who came to New Hampshire to contest an action begun by trustee process on his automobile liability insurance carrier could not be served "while attending any court proceedings relating thereto or coming or returning from the same."[119] It is not clear whether Justice Lampron intended, by the use of the term "court proceedings," to expand the privilege, at least for this type of defendant, to proceedings other than the trial or hearing on the merits. It would seem that a party or witness should be exempted from service while attending preliminary and posttrial hearings, meetings, conferences, and other events at which both sides are present and which are convened for the purpose of advancing the case. Depositions, settlement negotiations, examinations of a scene, personal property or person, and other meetings are just as likely to advance the case and to require the presence of parties and witnesses as hearings before the court, and it would seem most consistent with the efficient administration of justice to grant an exemption from service to nonresident parties and witnesses while in attendance upon them.

Library References

CJS Process § 81
Immunity from service of process of nonresident witness appearing in other than strictly judicial proceedings. 35 ALR2d 1353.

§ 14.43. Remedies—Motion To Dismiss (Abatement)

A person who has been served with civil process when exempt from service may not ignore the service and treat it as a nullity, but must, if he or she objects to the suit, file a Special Appearance with a Motion To Dismiss.

---

114 Dolber v. Young, 81 N.H. 157, 123 A. 218 (1923); Ela v. Ela, 68 N.H. 312, 36 A. 15 (1895); State v. Buck, 62 N.H. 670 (1883).

115 Dickinson v. Farwell, 71 N.H. 213, 51 A. 624 (1902).

116 Martin v. Whitney, 74 N.H. 505, 69 A. 888 (1908).

117 Pitman v. Cunningham, 100 N.H. 49, 118 A.2d 884 (1955). Presumably, the implication in Chief Justice Kenison's opinion to the effect that administrative agency hearings are included within the group of hearings to which the exemption applies is meant to extend to all local, state, and federal administrative agencies.

118 113 N.H. 617, 313 A.2d 129 (1973).

119 113 N.H. at 624, 313 A.2d at 133.

It has been held repeatedly that a writ served on a person exempt from service may be abated on the defendant's motion.[120]

CJS Process § 89

§ 14.44. —Petition for Contempt

There is some authority for the view that service in a manner that interferes with a hearing in progress is a contempt of court and may be punished by a fine.[121] These cases, however, involved service by arrest, and it is unlikely that any court would consider service by other means on an exempt person a sufficient contempt to justify imposition of a fine unless the service was accomplished in such a manner or at such a time as to obstruct directly the workings of the court.

§ 14.45. —Continuance for Proper Service

There is a suggestion in the last part of Justice Bingham's opinion in *Martin v. Whitney*,[122] that, in some cases, an action improperly begun by service on a person when exempt may be continued for service by another means at a time when not exempt. The suggestion has never been expressly accepted or rejected by the Court. It probably arose from confusion over the exemptions that applied to residents and to nonresidents at the time the case was decided. When civil actions were begun by arrest, a resident was exempt from arrest when attending court but could be served by other means, such as abode service either while he was at court or afterwards. A nonresident, however, was exempt from service of all process while attending court and jurisdiction could not be obtained while the nonresident was in the state. While it might have been consistent with the purpose of the exemption to allow an action that had been improperly begun against a resident to be continued for notice, such a procedure against a nonresident would have completely eviscerated the exemption and avoided its purpose. It is doubtful that the Court would adopt Justice Bingham's suggestion today.

§ 14.46. —Actions Against the Serving Officer

The sheriff or other officer who serves a writ is neither required nor competent to judge whether the person served is entitled to an exemption

---

120 Hubbard v. Sanborn, 2 N.H. 468 (1822); Ela v. Ela, 68 N.H. 312, 36 A. 15 (1895); Martin v. Whitney, 74 N.H. 505, 69 A. 888 (1908); Dobler v. Young, 81 N.H. 157, 123 A. 218 (1923); Dickinson v. Farwell, 71 N.H. 213, 51 A. 624 (1902).

121 See State v. Buck, 62 N.H. 670 (1883); Ela v. Ela, 68 N.H. 312, 36 A. 15 (1895).

122 74 N.H. 505, 507, 69 A. 888, 889 (1908).

from service. The sheriff is simply required by the precept in the writ to serve the named defendant. Regardless of whether the defendant is exempt and states a claim to exemption, the sheriff or other serving officer is entitled to complete the service and cannot be held liable for doing so in an otherwise lawful manner.[123] If the service amounts to a contempt of court, the plaintiff, not the sheriff, will be the offending party so long as the sheriff acts in an otherwise proper manner.

Library References

Attack on personal service as having been obtained by fraud or trickery. 98 ALR2d 551.
Civil liability of one making false or fraudulent return of process. 31 ALR3d 1393.

§ 14.47. Waiver of Exemption

Although the Court has repeatedly stated that an exemption from service exists for the protection of the judicial system and not for the benefit of the defendant, it has also held that an exemption is a "personal privilege"[124] and can be waived.[125] The exemption protects the administration of justice by assuring certain persons that if they are served they will not have to answer. Where a particular person who is otherwise exempt is willing to waive the exemption and submit to the jurisdiction of the court, there is no reason to prevent him or her from doing so. If the circumstances of the service are such that the workings of the court are obstructed, punishment for contempt may be appropriate.

In some cases, a waiver may be implied from the circumstances, despite the lack of an express consent from the defendant. Filing a General Appearance or submitting any issues to the court beyond the defendant's objection to service will be regarded as a waiver of the exemption.[126] Justice Chase has also suggested that the defendant's failure to disclose the facts on which an exemption is based when served will be a waiver if the plaintiff is ignorant of those facts and the defendant knows that he or she is ignorant of them.[127] This seems to be a very hazardous rule, requiring inquiry by the defendant rather than the plaintiff and a communication with the plaintiff directly (because the sheriff is not required to take back the writ on a claim of

---

123 Woods v. Davis, 34 N.H. 328 (1857).

124 *Id.* at 334.

125 Dolber v. Young, 81 N.H. 157, 123 A. 218 (1923); Woods v. Davis, 34 N.H. 328 (1857); Dickinson v. Farwell, 71 N.H. 213, 51 A. 624 (1902); Lyman v. Littleton, 50 N.H. 42 (1870).

126 Dolber v. Young, 81 N.H. 157, 123 A. 218 (1923).

127 Dickinson v. Farwell, 71 N.H. 213, 51 A. 624 (1902).

exemption) with the hopeless goal of obtaining a voluntary discontinuance of the action without the necessity of filing a pleading. On the whole, it seems that the only reasonable occasion for implying a waiver is when the defendant submits issues sufficient to convert a Special to a General Appearance.

Library References

CJS Process § 88

CHAPTER 15. APPEARANCE

A. GENERAL APPEARANCE

B. SPECIAL APPEARANCE

C. WITHDRAWAL OF APPEARANCE

A. *General Appearance*

§ 15.01. Definition

A General Appearance is a party's submission to the exercise of the court's jurisdiction over him in a pending case.[1] When the action is in personam or quasi in rem, the General Appearance subjects the party to a determination by the court of his or her personal rights and obligations. When the action is in rem, it submits the party to a determination of title in the property in question.

Library References

CJS Appearances § 2
What amounts to "appearance" under statute or rule requiring notice, to party who has "appeared," of intention to take default judgment. 73 ALR3d 1250.

Cross References

In personam jurisdiction, see §§ 2.01, 2.02 *supra*.
In rem jurisdiction, see §§ 2.06–2.08 *supra*.
Quasi in rem jurisdiction, see §§ 2.03–2.05 *supra*.

§ 15.02. Form of a General Appearance

A General Appearance[2] is filed on a form prescribed by the court. It must contain the names of the parties as they appear in the caption, the name and docket number of the case, the name of the court in which the case is pending, the day by which an Appearance must be filed, the signature and typed name and address of the person making the Appearance,[3] and the name and mailing address[4] of the person for whom the Appearance is being filed.[5]

---

1 "In a broad sense, the term 'appearance' embraces the act of a party coming into court." Chenausky v. Chenausky, 128 N.H. 116, 509 A.2d 156 (1986).

2 Prob. Ct. R. 4 refers to both a "written appearance notice" and a "responding appearance notice." The distinction appears to be in the degree to which a party submits himself to the jurisdiction of the court and, in turn, has the ability to raise issues for decision. Any person filing a petition or other request for affirmative relief files a "written appearance notice" and subjects himself to the personal jurisdiction of the court for the purposes of that case. But any other person who wishes to contest the matter but only on a limited range of issues may file a "responding appearance notice" and specification of the issues contested, and thereby submit himself to the personal jurisdiction of the court not for all purposes connected with the case but only for those limited issues. Of course, a person can also file a "responding appearance notice" with a specification contesting all issues, and thereby submit himself to the personal jurisdiction of the court for all purposes in the case.

3 Super. Ct. R. 15 permits the attorney who will conduct the case ("the attorney of record") to have his or her "associate" sign the Appearance Form on his or her behalf.

4 Super. Ct. R. 15.

5 Super. Ct. R. 15 and Prob. Ct. R. 4.

Forms

Appearance/Withdrawal, general form, see Appendix.
Appearance (Superior Court), see Appendix.
Appearance/Withdrawal (District Court), see Appendix.

§ 15.03. Persons Who May Enter an Appearance—The Party

A party may appear on his own behalf (pro se) as a matter of right.[6] When a party intends to represent himself, he should file an Appearance Form giving his own name and address and stating that he appears pro se.

Library References

CJS Appearances § 9
Propriety and effect of corporation's appearance pro se, through agent who is not attorney.
19 ALR3d 1073.

§ 15.04. —The Party's Friend

A party may be represented by a person who is not a licensed attorney if that person is "of good character," does not engage in such representation as a common practice,[7] and has filed with the clerk a power of attorney signed by the party, witnessed and acknowledged, which specifically refers by caption to the pending case and appoints that person the party's attorney-in-fact for the purposes of the case.[8]

Library References

CJS Appearances § 9

§ 15.05. —An Attorney Licensed in New Hampshire

Any attorney licensed in New Hampshire may appear for any party in any court or before any agency or judge[9] in the state. His authority to appear and

---

6 See Super. Ct. R. 1; Prob. Ct. R. 4; Murano v. Murano, 122 N.H. 223, 442 A.2d 597 (1982). A corporation, a partnership, or an unincorporated association cannot appear pro se, but must be represented by a licensed attorney. State v. Settle, 129 N.H. 171, 523 A.2d 124 (1987) (noting, however, a possible exception to the rule in cases, such as small claims actions, where "a lawyer's skill is not required and could be unduly expensive." 129 N.H. at 179, 523 A.2d at 129).

7 Bilodeau v. Antal, 123 N.H. 39, 455 A.2d 1037 (1983); State v. Settle, 129 N.H. 171, 176, 523 A.2d 124, 127 (1987) (a person not licensed to practice law may not "appear with unrestricted frequency on behalf of an association [or corporation] of which he is an officer" even if he is of good character and the association or corporation authorizes him to do so).

8 Super. Ct. R. 1 and 14; Prob. Ct. R. 4.

9 See Prob. Ct. R. 4.

bind the party in the action[10] will be presumed unless a contrary fact appears as a matter of record.[11]

Library References

CJS Appearances § 9
CJS Attorney and Client § 197

§ 15.06. —An Attorney Not Licensed in New Hampshire

An attorney who is not licensed in New Hampshire may not file a General or Special Appearance for a party in an action pending here. He or she may participate in the trial or in a motion hearing only when associated with New Hampshire counsel who files an Appearance and upon approval of the court.[12]

Library References

CJS Attorney and Client § 28
Attorney's right to appear pro hac vice in state court. 20 ALR4th 855.

§ 15.07. Time for Filing an Appearance—Actions at Law

In actions at law, the defendant's Special or General Appearance must be filed no later than the seventh day after the return day specified in the writ.[13]

Library References

CJS Appearances §§ 15, 16

§ 15.08. —Equity and Other Proceedings

In proceedings in equity and other types of cases, the defendant's Appearance must be filed on or before the return day, if there is one,[14] or by the time when a responsive pleading must be filed, if no return day is specified.[15]

---

10 See Halstead v. Murray, 130 N.H. 560, 547 A.2d 202 (1988) (" '[A]ction taken in the conduct and disposition of civil litigation by an attorney within the scope of his authority is binding on his client.' " 130 N.H. at 565, 547 A.2d at 204).

11 See, e.g., Bock v. Lundstrom, 133 N.H. 161, 573 A.2d 882 (1990) ("If a settlement agreement has in fact been reached by counsel, the critical inquiry in determining its enforceability is whether the lawyer was authorized by the client to make the agreement.").

12 See Super. Ct. R. 19; Prob. Ct. R. 4.

13 Super. Ct. R. 14.

14 Super. Ct. R. 131.

15 In proceedings before administrative agencies, no return day exists, and the Appearance generally must be filed by the time an Answer is due.

§ 15.09. —After a Prior Attorney Withdraws

If a licensed attorney or an attorney-in-fact withdraws and no new attorney simultaneously appears, the clerk will set a date by which a new Appearance must be filed by an attorney or the party and will notify the party of that requirement in writing.[16]

Library References

CJS Appearances §§ 55, 57

§ 15.10. How a General Appearance May Be Entered

A General Appearance may be entered expressly or by implication.

When a party wishes to enter a General Appearance expressly, he or she completes an Appearance Form and files it with the clerk.[17] When a party has not filed an Appearance Form, the party may nevertheless appear generally if he or she submits to the court or participates in the contest of any issue on the merits.[18] The party may also appear generally if, having filed a Special Appearance, he or she thereafter submits any issue on the merits to the court for determination.[19]

A Special Appearance will automatically be converted to a General Appearance on the thirty-first day after it is filed if the defendant has not filed a Motion To Dismiss by the end of the thirtieth day.[20]

---

16 Super. Ct. R. 20; Prob. Ct. R. 5.

17 See Super. Ct. R. 14; Dist. and Mun. Ct. R. 3.6(A); and Prob. Ct. R. 4.

18 Although Super. Ct. R. 14 provides that a defendant will be defaulted if he fails to file an Appearance within seven days of the return day, it is not uncommon for defendants to neglect to file an Appearance and still participate in pretrial discovery and other procedures with the obvious intention of contesting the case on the merits and without any objection from the plaintiff. In such a case, the defendant will not be considered to have defaulted but will be regarded as having appeared generally and, if the defect is called to the court's attention, will be allowed to file an Appearance Form confirming that fact. Merrill v. Houghton, 51 N.H. 61 (1871); Sweeney v. McQuaid, 83 N.H. 585, 141 A. 307 (1928); Mauzy v. Mauzy, 97 N.H. 514, 92 A.2d 908 (1952); Clark v. Bradstreet, 99 N.H. 55, 104 A.2d 739 (1954).

19 Lyford v. Trustees of Berwick Academy, 97 N.H. 167, 83 A.2d 302 (1951); Beggs v. Reading Co., 103 N.H. 156, 167 A.2d 61 (1961); Sanborn v. Johnson, 100 N.H. 428, 129 A.2d 194 (1957); Jewett v. Jewett, 112 N.H. 341, 296 A.2d 11 (1972); Smith v. Smith, 125 N.H. 336, 480 A.2d 158 (1984) (cross-libel was a waiver of objections to personal jurisdiction under the original libel); Lachapelle v. Town of Goffstown, 134 N.H. 478 (1991) (motion for late entry of appearance resulted in voluntary submission to the personal jurisdiction of the court, despite defective service of process); Barton v. Hayes, 141 N.H. 115 (1996) (motion to strike default judgment submitted defendant to jurisdiction of the court). See also Brodowski v. Supowitz, 122 N.H. 694, 448 A.2d 430 (1982) (motion for leave to file a late Appearance was a waiver of objections to service).

20 Super. Ct. R. 14; Dist. and Mun. Ct. R. 3.6(A).

Library References

CJS Appearances §§ 18, 19, 21, 24

Objection before judgment to jurisdiction of court over subject matter as constituting general appearance. 25 ALR2d 833.

Motion to vacate judgment or order as constituting general appearance. 31 ALR2d 262.

Garnishee's pleading, answering interrogatories, or the like, as affecting his right to assert court's lack of jurisdiction. 41 ALR2d 1093.

Filing of bond to secure release or return of seized property as appearance. 57 ALR2d 1109.

Stipulation extending time to answer or otherwise proceed as waiver of objection to jurisdiction for lack of personal service: state cases. 77 ALR3d 841.

§ 15.11. Effect of a General Appearance

A General Appearance is a waiver of all objections to:

(1) The jurisdiction[21] of the court over the person or property involved in the case;[22]

(2) Defects in venue;[23]

(3) Deficiencies of form in the initial pleading;[24]

(4) Defects in service or notice, whether apparent in the record or not;[25]

(5) Improper entry of the writ or other process;[26] and

(6) Misnomer.[27]

A General Appearance prevents a default, whether entered with authority or not,[28] and entitles the appearing party to receive copies of all pleadings filed in the case and notice of and an opportunity for hearing on any

---

21 Woodbury v. Swan, 58 N.H. 380 (1878). It is not, however, a waiver of objections to subject matter jurisdiction. Pokigo v. Local No. 719 International Brotherhood of Electrical Workers, 106 N.H. 384, 213 A.2d 689 (1965). A motion for late entry of appearance also results in a waiver of objections to the personal jurisdiction of the court. Lachapelle v. Town of Goffstown, 134 N.H. 478, 593 A.2d 1152 (1991).

22 In the probate courts, however, a "responding appearance notice" must be followed within 10 days by a "written specification generally summarizing the cause, reason or occasion for [the party's] appearance" and "automatically expire[s] upon resolution of that contested issue or matter." Prob. Ct. R. 4. Apparently, it is not intended to operate as a general submission to the in personam jurisdiction of the court for all purposes connected with the case.

23 Bishop v. Silver Lake Mining Co., 62 N.H. 455 (1883).

24 Lovel v. Sabin, 15 N.H. 29 (1844) (lack of clerk's signature or court's seal on the writ).

25 White v. White, 60 N.H. 210 (1880); Kittredge v. Emerson, 15 N.H. 227 (1844); Smith v. Whittier, 9 N.H. 464 (1838); Morse v. Calley, 5 N.H. 222 (1830); Gagnon v. Croft Mfg. & Rental Co., 108 N.H. 329, 235 A.2d 522 (1967).

26 White v. White, 60 N.H. 210 (1880).

27 Wheeler v. Contoocook Mills Corp., 77 N.H. 551, 94 A. 265 (1915).

28 Bodge v. Butler, 57 N.H. 204 (1876).

dispositive motion or pleading.[29] Under modern practice, a General Appearance is a plea of the general issue and acts as a denial of every well-pleaded and material fact in the plaintiff's initial pleading.[30]

Library References

CJS Appearances §§ 35–49

Appearance as waiver of omission of signature of issuing officer on civil process or summons. 37 ALR2d 939.

General appearance as avoiding otherwise effective bar of statute of limitations. 82 ALR2d 1200.

Cross References

Jurisdiction, see chs. 2, 3 *supra.*
Misnomer, see §§ 6.21, 6.22 *supra.*
Service of Process, see ch. 14 *supra.*
Venue, see ch. 4 *supra.*

§ 15.12. Rejection of an Appearance

If an Appearance is defective in form and rejected by the clerk or by the court for that reason, it may be corrected and resubmitted upon the defendant's motion "for good cause shown."[31] When the time for filing has passed, the defendant should file a Motion To Allow a Late Appearance. The court will allow the motion, as a matter of course, if the delay has been short and it does not appear that prejudice will result to the opponent or third parties.

B. *Special Appearance*

§ 15.13. Introduction

A defendant may file a Special Appearance and a Motion To Dismiss based on deficiencies in service, notice, or personal or subject matter jurisdiction. A Special Appearance is not favored, and will automatically be waived and converted to a General Appearance if the defendant fails to file a Motion To Dismiss within thirty days after the return day,[32] if he participates in the case, or submits any issue other than jurisdiction, service, or notice to the court for consideration.

---

29 Mauzy v. Mauzy, 97 N.H. 514, 92 A.2d 908 (1952).

30 The denials implied by a General Appearance may be contradicted by specific responses in an Answer, Motion To Dismiss, or other responsive pleading, in which case the more specific statements in the responsive pleading will control. See Storch Engineers v. D&K Land Developers, 134 N.H. 414, 593 A.2d 245 (1991) (general appearance by defendant serves as a denial of the plaintiff's allegations concerning the defendant's individual liability).

31 Super. Ct. R. 2; Dist. & Mun. Ct. R. 1.1; Prob. Ct. R. 1.

32 Super Ct. R. 14; Asadorian v. Asadorian, 127 N.H. 388, 499 A.2d 1354 (1985).

CJS Appearances §§ 4, 5

Motion To Dismiss, see ch. 10 *supra*.

§ 15.14. History of the Procedure

The Special Appearance was unknown to the common law. Until the middle of the nineteenth century, New Hampshire practice recognized only one form of Appearance and accorded it no greater significance than a mere "notice of defense."[33] Objections to jurisdiction, service, or notice were presented by pleas in abatement, motions to quash, and, in some cases, under the general issue.[34]

The Supreme Court first recognized the concept of appearing "specially" in 1858 in the case of *Wright v. Boynton & Hayward*,[35] an action of debt partially founded on a default judgment recovered in Massachusetts. The defendant Boynton resided in New Hampshire and had not been personally served with the writ in the Massachusetts action. Prior to the entry of the default judgment in Massachusetts, Boynton filed a motion to dismiss reciting that he came into court "specially" for the purposes of the motion to raise a lack of personal jurisdiction. The Massachusetts court overruled the motion and entered judgment, but in the New Hampshire action to collect

---

33 Colby v. Knapp, 13 N.H. 175 (1842):

> The rules as to the entry of an appearance and as to pleadings are discon-
> nected. The entry of an appearance upon the docket does not restrict or limit
> the time or mode of pleading, or affect it in any manner. It is a mere notice
> of defence. It is no waiver of a special plea of any kind. (13 N.H. at 177.)

34 Morse v. Calley, 5 N.H. 222 (1830):

> All defects in the service of a writ, which are not apparent on the face of the
> record, are cured by an appearance, unless exception is taken to the service
> by a regular plea in abatement. (5 N.H. at 223.)

See also Colby v. Knapp, 13 N.H. 175 (1842) (defendant filed an appearance before filing a plea in abatement for defective service; the court rejected the plaintiff's argument that the appearance waived the defect so long as the plea was timely filed). Even in proceedings where the parties "appeared" in person for the first time at the hearing, it was not the appearance alone but the appearance followed by participation in the hearing without objection that amounted to a waiver of objection to service or notice. See Parish v. Gilmanton, 11 N.H. 293 (1840); Petition of Gilford, 25 N.H. 124 (1852). See also Candia and Hooksett v. Chandler, 58 N.H. 127 (1877), where the same principle is applied, but the case of Roberts v. Stark, 47 N.H. 223 (1866), is cited as authority for it. That inappropriate citation tends to confuse the old doctrine that appearance and defense together waived objection, with the new view that appearance alone was sufficient to do so.

35 37 N.H. 9 (1858).

the judgment debt, Boynton introduced evidence of the foregoing facts to show that the Massachusetts court had not had jurisdiction to enter a judgment against him. The New Hampshire Supreme Court noted that the Massachusetts court "had no jurisdiction of the person of Boynton . . . unless by a special appearance" and concluded:

> The question then arises, whether such a restricted appearance, for the purpose of objecting to the jurisdiction merely, will give to the court jurisdiction of the person, if they had none before; and we are of opinion, upon considerations of public policy and convenience, that such an appearance alone ought not to confer such jurisdiction. Such an appearance must be understood to be made upon application to the court, and leave granted without prejudice if the application is unsuccessful.[36]

The Court therefore concluded that the Massachusetts judgment was inoperative against Boynton.[37]

Two years later, in *March v. Eastern Railroad Company*,[38] the Court held for the first time that the mere appearance of a party "except when the party appears for the sole purpose of making objection to the authority of the court to proceed"[39] was sufficient to confer jurisdiction on a New Hampshire court.[40]

---

36 *Id.* at 19.

37 The first report of the use of a Special Appearance in a New Hampshire court may be found in Warren v. Glynn, 37 N.H. 340 (1858).

38 40 N.H. 548 (1860).

39 *Id.* at 583.

40 In the process, Justice Sargent revised history a bit, writing that "an appearance of the party has always been held to confer jurisdiction." As the preceding discussion points out, such a holding had never before been made.

    For later developments, see Robinson v. Potter, 43 N.H. 188 (1861) (holding that a general appearance could be inferred from an agreement to refer to arbitrators). In his opinion, Justice Nesmith noted that a party could object to jurisdiction by entering a "restricted appearance." Prior to this date, defendants were generally reported to have "appeared specially," but the appearance itself had not yet been separately named. See, e.g., Warren v. Glynn, 37 N.H. 340, 341 (1858); Parker v. Barker, 43 N.H. 35 (1861). See also Messer v. Smyth, 60 N.H. 436 (1881) (where the Court held that "appearance by the defendants for the manifest purpose of resistance, and [an] agreement to judgment" were equivalent to pleading the general issue. 60 N.H. at 439); Roberts v. Stark, 47 N.H. 223 (1866) ("An objection to service of notice is waived when a party, by general appearance or otherwise, submits any other questions, except the sufficiency of service or notice, to the court or other tribunal." 47 N.H. at 225); Merrill v. Houghton, 51 N.H. 61 (1871); White v. White, 60 N.H. 210 (1880) (holding that a defendant could not file a motion to dismiss based on improper service even within the time for filing pleas in abatement if he had previously filed a general appearance and motion to continue); Shea v. Starr, 76 N.H. 538, 85 A. 788 (1913) ("If to make any defence they were advised was wise the actual paper constituting the writ was essential, they could

Next, in *Patten v. Patten*,[41] the Court held that a Special Appearance and accompanying objection to personal jurisdiction were waived when objections to subject matter jurisdiction and to the sufficiency of the claim were included in the Motion To Dismiss. Justice Peaslee wrote:

> A special appearance for the purpose of objecting to want of jurisdiction over the defendant must be limited to that purpose. If it be extended so as to present other questions for decision by the court, this objection is waived and jurisdiction is conferred.[42]

Between the Wars, two cases arose involving the question whether a defendant could file a Special Appearance objecting to jurisdiction, then set forth his position on the merits along with a statement that he did not thereby waive his prior objection to jurisdiction. The Court held, in each case, that he could not. Any attempt, no matter how conditional, to obtain the court's protection on the merits of the case, will subject the defendant to the full range of the court's power over him personally.[43] In the first of the cases, *Dolber v. Young*,[44] the nonresident defendant was served in New Hampshire while returning within a reasonable time from a trial. Six months later, he filed a Special Appearance and objection to jurisdiction based on his exemption from service. Two days after that, he filed a plea in abatement based on the pendency of a prior action, and, within a month, filed an Answer. Both the plea in abatement and Answer stated that they were filed "without waiving" the defendant's prior objections. The Court held that, while the defendant had been entitled to have the writ dismissed because of his exemption from service, his submission of a plea of prior action pending and Answer constituted a waiver of that objection and submitted him to the in personam jurisdiction of the court. The attempted reservation of objections was ineffectual, the Court said, because it could "not modify the character of his acts in praying the consideration of the court in his plea in abatement and in his answer to the merits."[45] Justice Snow wrote: "Any act which recognizes the jurisdiction has some tendency to show that the actor

---

and should have appeared specially and moved that the same be placed on file or delivered to their counsel." 76 N.H. at 540, 85 A. at 789).

41 79 N.H. 388, 109 A. 415 (1920).

42 *Id.* at 389, 109 A. at 415.

43 However, the attempt to submit another issue must be made by the defendant to be charged with waiver, not by his codefendant in another part of a common brief. Rosenblum v. Judson Engineering Corporation, 99 N.H. 267, 109 A.2d 558 (1954).

44 81 N.H. 157, 123 A. 218 (1923).

45 *Id.* at 157, 123 A. at 220.

intends to submit to it . . . . He could not at the same time invoke the judgment of the court upon the merits of the case and deny its jurisdiction."[46]

The second case, *Maryland Casualty Co. v. Martin,*[47] involved the question whether the defendants, having restricted themselves to objections to jurisdiction in the trial court, could branch into other issues in their brief to the Supreme Court. The Court again held that they could not. Chief Justice Allen, writing for the Court, said:

> The fact that they have first contested the merits in this court is immaterial . . . . Having made their special appearance general by opposing the plaintiff as though they were duly in court, they abandoned their right to say they were not. Their attempt to obviate this result by request that no consideration be given to their brief on the merits if the jurisdictional issue was thereby prejudiced, is vain . . . . The issue of jurisdiction is not only separate but also preliminary, and reasonable procedure demands that it be finally decided before other issues of the litigation are reached . . . . The undertaking not to be in court and at the same time take part in the trial of the main issues is one of inconsistency, and technique of pleading or practice is of no avail to validate it.[48]

The Court's prejudice in favor of submission to jurisdiction found its most extreme expression in the holding of *Mauzy v. Mauzy,*[49] stating that a person who wrote to the clerk, before he was represented by counsel, and asked for a continuance thereby waived all objections to jurisdiction, service, and notice. "In effect," wrote Chief Justice Kenison, "he recognized the case as being in court, requested a continuance and thereby made a general appearance . . . . He had the statutory right to appear without counsel if he chose to do so."[50]

§ 15.15. Issues Which May Be Raised on a Special Appearance

A Motion To Dismiss filed with a Special Appearance may only challenge the court or tribunal's jurisdiction over the subject matter of the action,[51] the

---

46 *Id.*

47 88 N.H. 346, 189 A. 162 (1937).

48 *Id.* at 347–48, 189 A. at 163–64. See also Lyford v. Trustees of Berwick Academy, 97 N.H. 167, 83 A.2d 302 (1951).

49 97 N.H. 514, 92 A.2d 908 (1952).

50 *Id.* at 515, 92 A.2d at 909.

51 Objections to subject matter jurisdiction may also be raised with a General Appearance since such objections cannot be waived, by Appearance or otherwise.

person of the defendant, or, in quasi in rem and in rem actions, the property which is the focus of the action. The court's subject matter jurisdiction must be determined on the pleadings and the law. The challenge to jurisdiction over the property may be based on a faulty attachment or the absence of the property as a matter of fact or law from the territorial jurisdiction of the court or agency. An objection to jurisdiction over the person may be based on faulty service or the inapplicability of the Long Arm Statute.

Library References

CJS Appearances § 51

Cross References

Long Arm Statute, see ch. 2 *supra.*

§ 15.16. Persons Who May File a Special Appearance

Any person who is involuntarily called upon to respond in a New Hampshire court or before a judge or agency in New Hampshire may file a Special Appearance challenging the jurisdiction of the tribunal over his person or over the subject of the proceeding.

§ 15.17. When a Special Appearance May Be Filed

A Special Appearance may be filed at any time before the defendant has participated in the case or submitted any other issue to the court for decision. A Special Appearance must be filed by the date when a General Appearance would otherwise be due. When a Special Appearance has been filed, a Motion To Dismiss setting forth the basis for objecting to the tribunal's jurisdiction must be filed no later than thirty days after the return day.[52]

Library References

CJS Appearances § 15

§ 15.18. Requirements of the Special Appearance

A Special Appearance is filed on the same form as a General Appearance, with the exception that the word "Special" is added to the title. All information which is included in a General Appearance must be set forth in a Special Appearance.

§ 15.19. Requirements of the Motion To Dismiss

The Motion To Dismiss, filed with the Special Appearance, follows the same form as any other Motion To Dismiss and may be supported by

---

52 Super. Ct. R. 14.

affidavit.[53] It may raise as many objections to jurisdiction as the defendant has but must not raise any other issues. It must not be filed with any other pleading.

Cross References

Motion To Dismiss, see ch. 10 *supra*.

§ 15.20. Effect of Filing a Special Appearance and Motion To Dismiss

When a Special Appearance and Motion To Dismiss are filed within the required time limits, the running of all other time periods for responsive pleadings and pretrial procedures is tolled until the issue is decided.[54]

§ 15.21. Procedure Upon the Filing of a Special Appearance and Motion To Dismiss—Generally

The plaintiff is not required to respond to a Special Appearance. If he does nothing and a Motion to Dismiss is not filed within thirty days after the return day, the Special Appearance will automatically be converted into a General Appearance and the case will proceed on the general issue.[55]

If a Motion To Dismiss is filed within the thirty days, the plaintiff may file an objection within ten days which supports his claim to jurisdiction. The objection should be supported by affidavits, references to the return of service and other parts of the record, and, where there are difficult issues of law, a brief memorandum setting forth the plaintiff's position. The defendant may respond to the plaintiff's memorandum within ten days. The parties may employ the procedures of pretrial discovery to test the merits of the objection to jurisdiction, but any inquiry on discovery into the merits of the case will waive the objection.

Unless the defendant's Motion To Dismiss is completely without foundation, the court will not decide the issue on the pleadings but will hold a

---

53 The effect of a Special Appearance and Motion To Dismiss supported by affidavit is to require the plaintiff to demonstrate the facts giving rise to jurisdiction. Weld Power Indus., Inc. v. C.S.I., Inc., 124 N.H. 121, 467 A.2d 568 (1983).

54 In this respect, the effect of filing a Special Appearance and Motion To Dismiss is different from the effect of filing a General Appearance. See Colby v. Knapp, 13 N.H. 175 (1842).

55 The defendant who files nothing before the end of 30 days after the return day waives not only his objection to jurisdiction, but any other ground of abatement, demurrer or bar, any affirmative defense, and any right to recover on a Counterclaim. He may then only contest the truth of the plaintiff's well-pleaded facts and then only if he preserves these claims by filing a Motion To Dismiss, Brief Statement, or Counterclaim raising the issues within the 30 days. But he will thereby waive the Special Appearance by presenting an issue on the merits for the court's consideration.

hearing. It must decide the issue of jurisdiction before moving on to the merits of the case.[56] The hearing will rarely require the presentation of evidence, but in most cases will be confined to arguments of law on the admitted facts or offers of proof. If the defendant, even during this hearing, submits any argument or evidence directed at the case in chief, he will be deemed to have waived his objection and the issue will be decided.

> An objection to service or notice is waived when a party, by general appearance or otherwise, submits any other question, except the sufficiency of service or notice, to the court or other tribunal. He cannot take the chance of succeeding on any other objection to the case made against him, and at the same time reserve his exception to service or notice.[57]

The defendant must at all times refuse to raise or respond to any suggestions regarding the case in chief and, in fact, even decline to recognize its existence. He must treat his Motion To Dismiss and participation in the hearing on that motion as an overly prudent and courteous gesture which calls the court's attention to its lack of jurisdiction before further time is wasted on the case.

A Special Appearance may be used to challenge the court's jurisdiction in any respect. When the defendant asserts a lack of subject matter jurisdiction, the court will conduct its own inquiry, aided by the parties, and will not deny the motion unless it can be affirmatively satisfied that it has jurisdiction in the case. When the motion relies upon a lack of jurisdiction over the person or property involved in the suit, the court will look upon the motion with disfavor, indulge all presumptions in favor of the exercise of jurisdiction, and grant the motion only when forced to conclude that its jurisdiction has not attached to the person or property involved. In this latter class of cases, the court will use any procedural mistake it can find to justify the exercise of jurisdiction. The court's order will usually be announced in writing at some time after the hearing.

---

56 Maryland Casualty Company v. Martin, 88 N.H. 346, 189 A. 162 (1937).

57 Roberts v. Stark, 47 N.H. 223, 225 (1866). See also Merrill v. Houghton, 51 N.H. 61 (1871); White v. White, 60 N.H. 210 (1880); Patten v. Patten, 79 N.H. 388, 109 A. 415 (1920); Dolber v. Young, 81 N.H. 157, 159, 123 A. 218 (1923); Beggs v. Reading Company, 103 N.H. 156, 167 A.2d 61 (1961); Sanborn v. Johnson, 100 N.H. 428, 129 A.2d 194 (1957); Clark v. Bradstreet, 99 N.H. 55, 104 A.2d 739 (1954); Nelson v. Morse, 91 N.H. 177, 16 A.2d 61 (1940); Vezina v. Vezina, 95 N.H. 297, 62 A.2d 756 (1948).

Library References

CJS Appearances § 51

§ 15.22. —Denial of a Special Appearance and Motion To Dismiss

The filing of a Special Appearance and Motion To Dismiss in a timely fashion tolls the running of all other time periods. If the Motion To Dismiss is denied, the defendant has the same period of time after the date on the clerk's notice of that denial which he would have had after filing a General Appearance in which to file any other Motions To Dismiss, Counterclaims, or a Brief Statement.

If the defendant desires to seek review or even decides to default and take his chances that the court in which enforcement of the judgment is attempted will recognize his dispute of jurisdiction, he must take care not to participate in the case or submit any question on the merits to the court after denial of his Motion To Dismiss. Such an action will automatically concede the jurisdiction of the court and waive any exceptions to the denial of his Motion To Dismiss.[58] If the defendant decides to seek appellate review, he must do so within thirty days.[59] The timely filing of his Interlocutory Appeal Statement in the trial court for signature, and in the Supreme Court for review, will again toll the time periods for pleading and pretrial actions. After the tribunal has received notice of the Supreme Court's decision, it will inform the parties, and the time periods will begin to run again.

Library Reference

Litigant's participation on merits, after objection to jurisdiction of person made under special appearance or the like has been overruled, as waiver of objection. 62 ALR2d 937.

Cross References

Interlocutory Appeal, see Part XVI *infra*.

---

[58] Sweeney v. McQuaid, 83 N.H. 585, 141 A. 307 (1928); Jewett v. Jewett, 112 N.H. 341, 296 A.2d 11 (1972); Gagnon v. Croft Manufacturing and Rental Company, 108 N.H. 329, 235 A.2d 522 (1967); Lyford v. Trustees of Berwick Academy, 97 N.H. 167, 83 A.2d 302 (1951); Worthen v. Kingsbury, 84 N.H. 304, 149 A. 869 (1930):

> [M]ere physical presence in the court room or . . . participation in the proceedings for the sole purpose of raising the question of jurisdiction, does not constitute a waiver of [the defendant's] right to object to the authority of the tribunal to act. (84 N.H. at 808, 149 A. at 871.)

See also Smith v. Smith, 125 N.H. 336, 480 A.2d 158 (1984).

[59] See Super. Ct. R. 74; Dist. and Mun. Ct. R. 1.11. See also Prob. Ct. R. 14. This will be an Interlocutory Appeal from Ruling. See Super. Ct. R. 8. The period is 20 days when review is sought of administrative agency proceedings. RSA 541:3.

C. *Withdrawal of Appearance*

§ 15.23. Procedure for and Effect of Withdrawal

When an attorney is discharged or resigns his participation in a case in which he has already filed an Appearance, he must immediately file a Withdrawal[60] of that Appearance on a form approved by the court and send a copy of the Withdrawal to his client and the opposing attorney.[61] Regardless of the nature of his relationship with the client, an attorney continues to represent that client before the court until the court accepts the Withdrawal and releases him.[62] If the court refuses to accept the Withdrawal as filed, it will usually hold a hearing on the matter and require the client to attend. Generally, the court will accept an attorney's Withdrawal as a matter of course prior to assignment for trial unless the party involved has abused the privilege of changing attorneys and the court is concerned that the practice, unless stopped by a refusal to allow further changes, will hinder a resolution of the case, or the client will be prejudiced by the Withdrawal. After assignment for trial in the superior[63] and in the district and municipal courts,[64] and at any time in the probate courts,[65] an attorney may withdraw only on motion setting forth the reasons for the withdrawal and approved by the court.[66]

When the court accepts an attorney's Withdrawal, the clerk will signify the acceptance by notifying the client in writing of the Withdrawal. The

---

60 The Withdrawal must be "signed by the attorney of record or his associate" and have the attorney's name, address, and telephone number "typed or stamped" beneath the signature. Super. Ct. R. 15. The Rule also seems to permit a pro se party to file a Withdrawal, but there is no sense in such a practice because a party not represented by an attorney of record is not required to file an Appearance and an attempt to "withdraw" as a pro se party could have no effect on the status of the case.

61 Super. Ct. R. 15; Prob. Ct. R. 4. If he knows who will replace him as the client's attorney, the withdrawing attorney should try to coordinate his Withdrawal with the filing of the substitute attorney's Appearance. See also N.H. Rules of Professional Conduct, Rule 1.16(b)(4) (withdrawing lawyer must take "reasonable steps to avoid foreseeable prejudice to the rights of the client, including giving due notice to his client, [and] allowing time for employment of other counsel"); Rule 1.16(d).

62 See Super. Ct. R. 15; Dist. and Mun. Ct. R. 3.6; Prob. Ct. R. 4. In the probate court, the judge will release him as a matter of course upon a substitute attorney or the party pro se coming in. See also N.H. Rules of Professional Conduct, Rule 1.16(c) ("When ordered to do so by a tribunal, a lawyer shall continue representation notwithstanding good cause for terminating the representation.").

63 Super. Ct. R. 15.

64 Dist. and Mun. Ct. R. 1.3(I).

65 Prob. Ct. R. 5.

66 Super. Ct. R. 15 provides, in part:

clerk will also inform the client that he must obtain substitute counsel who will file an Appearance by a certain date or suffer a default or dismissal.[67] A copy of that notice will be sent to the withdrawing attorney. If substitute counsel files an Appearance shortly after the Withdrawal, no such notice will be sent and the court will signify its acceptance of the Withdrawal simply by allowing the new Appearance.

Library References

CJS Appearances §§ 55, 57
CJS Attorney and Client §§ 221, 222
Withdrawal or vacation of appearance. 64 ALR2d 1424.
Authority of trial judge to impose costs or other sanctions against attorney who fails to appear at, or proceed with, scheduled trial. 29 ALR4th 160.

Forms

Appearance/Withdrawal, general form, see Appendix.
Appearance/Withdrawal (District Court), see Appendix.
Withdrawal (Superior Court), see Appendix.

Cross References

Default upon withdrawal of attorney, see § 33.29 *infra*.

§ 15.24. Filing of Appearance by New Attorney

When the new attorney files his Appearance, he should send a copy to the withdrawing attorney. The name of the new attorney will be entered on the docket when his Appearance is filed.[68]

No attorney shall be permitted to withdraw his appearance in a case after the case has been assigned for trial or hearing except upon motion to permit such withdrawal granted by the Court for good cause shown, and on such terms as the Court may order.

Dist. and Mun. Ct. R. 1.3(I) imposes similar restrictions.

67 Super. Ct. R. 20; Dist. and Mun. Ct. R. 1.3(G) and (I); Prob. Ct. R. 5. Upon a failure to obtain new counsel to file an Appearance, "the action will be dismissed, nonsuited, discontinued or defaulted, as the case may be." See Cote v. Cote, 123 N.H. 376, 461 A.2d 566 (1983) (defendant could avoid dismissal by showing he had not received the Court's notice).

68 Super. Ct. R. 20; Dist. and Mun. Ct. R. 1.3(D); Prob. Ct. R. 4.

Part VI

PROVISIONAL REMEDIES

CHAPTER 16. IN GENERAL

§ 16.01. Introduction

Commencement of an action does not ensure that the plaintiff, even if victorious, will secure the objectives of the action: an enforceable judgment. Therefore, "provisional" remedies have been made available to maximize a plaintiff's opportunities for enforcing any judgment ultimately secured in the action. These remedies are, in effect, security devices which operate during the action to preserve the plaintiff's opportunities for an effective remedy. Provisional remedies generally available in New Hampshire, including attachment, trustee process, replevin, injunctions, appointment of receivers and guardians ad litem, and confession of a claim, are discussed in Chapters 17 to 21. Provisional remedies of a more limited application are discussed in this chapter.

The related matter of enforcement of judgments by execution is discussed in Chapter 60.

§ 16.02. Interlocutory Orders

Any order that the court has power to enter at the conclusion of the case may be entered at an earlier time, if justice requires.[1] Interlocutory orders are usually entered to preserve the status quo[2] while the case is pending, and

---

1 RSA 498:11 and RSA 498:12; Super. Ct. R. 141.

2 When libel for divorce or petition for legal separation is filed, the clerk may recommend, on the basis of the pleadings, that the court order the parties to consult an approved family service agency in the county while the case is pending. Super. Ct. Admin. R. 7-4. In addition, the parties may agree or the court may determine on its own motion that an order should be entered referring the case to the Probation Department or the Division of Welfare or both for investigation. No such order of referral to the Division

may be entered ex parte if sufficient evidence is presented, by affidavit or otherwise, for the court to conclude that there is insufficient time to notify the opponent before the order is issued, or that either property or rights would be endangered by notice prior to the entry of an order.

Library References

CJS Motions and Orders §§ 2, 51, 65
Reviewability, on appeal from final judgment, of interlocutory order, as affected by fact that order was separately appealable. 79 ALR2d 1352.

§ 16.03. Arrest

Civil arrest, a remedy commonly included in enumerations of provisional remedies, was available in New Hampshire until 1971, when RSA ch. 513 was repealed.

Library References

CJS Arrest §§ 73–111

§ 16.04. Sequestration

Sequestration is the setting aside of the property that is at the heart of the controversy from the possession of both parties until the conclusion of the litigation. It is a provisional remedy specifically provided for in RSA 401-B:9 III for actions involving insurance holding companies.

Library References

CJS Sequestration §§ 1–3
Power of equity to sequester, for seizure and sale, beneficial equitable interests in corporate stock shares. 42 ALR2d 920.
Recovery of damages for mental anguish, distress, suffering, or the like, in action for wrongful attachment, garnishment, sequestration, or execution. 83 ALR3d 598.

§ 16.05. Application of State Law Regarding Provisional Remedies in Actions in Federal District Court

Under Rule 64 of the Federal Rules of Civil Procedure, any remedy authorized by the law of New Hampshire that provides for the seizure of a person or property in order to satisfy a judgment is also available in an action in the United States District Court for the District of New Hampshire unless

---

of Welfare will be entered without a hearing. When the court refers the matter to the Probation Department or Division of Welfare, it will require that the parties pay part of the expense if they are able. The usual charge for the Probation Department is $200. The Division of Welfare may also be ordered to investigate the need for support, and in such a case the parties will be required to report financial information to the Division and file a copy of their last income tax returns. Super. Ct. Admin. R. 12-14(D).

a federal statute provides a remedy, in which instance the statute controls. If available, the remedy would be applied in the federal court "under the circumstances and in the manner provided by the law"[3] of New Hampshire. Arrest, attachment,[4] garnishment, replevin, sequestration, and other equivalent remedies are specifically referred to in Rule 64, and are available regardless of whether they can be obtained in the principal action or whether a separate action must be filed.

Library References

CJS Federal Civil Procedure §§ 233–241

---

3 Fed. R. Civ. P. 64.

4 Diane Holly Corp. v. Bruno and Stillman Yacht Co., Inc., 559 F. Supp. 559, 561 (1983) (in prejudgment attachment proceeding, New Hampshire law requires that plaintiff make showing beyond a reasonable doubt that he will ultimately prevail on the merits). See also Granny Goose Foods, Inc. v. Teamsters, 415 U.S. 423 (1974) (availability of prejudgment attachment in federal court is governed by the law of the state in which the district court sits).

CHAPTER 17.   ATTACHMENT AND TRUSTEE PROCESS

A. PREJUDGMENT ATTACHMENT

349

Forms

Petition for Ex Parte Attachment (Superior Court), see Appendix.
Petition for Ex Parte Attachment (District Court), see Appendix.
Petition to Attach With Notice (Superior Court), see Appendix.
Writ of Attachment and Trustee Process (Superior Court), see Appendix.
Writ of Attachment and Trustee Process (District Court), see Appendix.

Cross References

Default, see § 33.12 *infra*.

A. *Prejudgment Attachment*

§ 17.01. Definition

An attachment is a lien[1] created by judicial process on a defendant's property or right to receive property. Attachments serve as a basis for jurisdiction and provide security for payment of a plaintiff's claim. The power to attach is derived entirely from statute.[2]

---

1 Kittredge v. Warren, 14 N.H. 509 (1844); Lachance v. Dondero, 91 N.H. 157, 16 A.2d 59 (1940).

2 Rogers v. Elliott, 59 N.H. 201 (1879); New Hampshire Judicial Council Fourth Report (1952), p. 37.

Library References

CJS Attachment § 2

§ 17.02. Distinction Between Attachment and Trustee Process

Attachments of identifiable items of real and personal property in the defendant's possession are called "attachments." Attachments of a defendant's personal property in the hands of another or of a defendant's right to receive property from another are referred to as "trustee process."[3] Although both attachments and trustee process are obtained by means of the same procedures,[4] different rules apply to the two forms of attachment after they have been obtained. Both the superior court and the municipal and district courts may grant attachments. The Supreme Court could in theory grant attachments under its superintending jurisdiction,[5] but the probate courts have no power to grant attachments.[6]

Library References

CJS Attachment § 2

Cross References

Trustee process, see §§ 17.41 et seq. *infra*.

§ 17.03. 1973 Revisions to the Law of Attachments

Prior to July 1973, writs of attachment and writs of trustee process could be filled out, signed by a plaintiff's attorney, and served on the defendant or a holder of a defendant's property without any prior review or approval by a judge. New Hampshire law allowed plaintiffs a "broad power" of attachment which required no special circumstances for its use and was "practically unrestricted."[7] However, in 1973 the General Court enacted RSA ch. 511-A which required notice and a hearing before most attachments could be granted and court review and approval of all. RSA ch. 511-A took effect

---

3 "Trustee process" is referred to as "garnishment" in many jurisdictions. It was also called "foreign attachment" in early N.H. statutes and decisions. DeLellis v. Burke, 134 N.H. 607 (1991) ("Trustee process is a statutory procedure by which a judgment creditor, in order to satisfy a debt owed him by a debtor, may attach either property owned by the debtor that is presently held by a third party, or the debtor's right to receive property from a third party.").

4 See Rules and Procedures to Implement Attachment Law (RSA 511-A), "Writ Forms," and Dist. and Mun. Ct. R. 3.4(A).

5 The Supreme Court has the constitutional power to grant attachments, but in most cases will direct the lower court to enter the order rather than granting the remedy itself.

6 In re Estate of Ward, 129 N.H. 4, 523 A.2d 28 (1986).

7 Cnaeps v. Brown, 101 N.H. 116, 118, 135 A.2d 721, 723 (1957).

on July 2, 1973, and the Supreme Court approved rules to implement the new statute on August 15, 1973.[8] During the following year the Court held, in *Hampton National Bank v. Desjardins*,[9] that, in all but "extraordinary situations," the old method of prejudgment attachment without notice and hearing would violate a defendant's rights to due process under the Fourteenth Amendment to the United States Constitution. The Court's holding was applied only to cases begun on or after July 2, 1973. Thus, since July 2, 1973, all attachments have required prior court review and approval and most have been granted only after notice to the defendant and an opportunity for a hearing.

Library References

CJS Attachment § 5

§ 17.04. Persons Who May Attach

Any proponent of a legal or equitable claim may seek an attachment to secure satisfaction of his judgment in the event he prevails. However, a party who is merely defending and does not seek affirmative relief, other than an award of costs or dismissal of the action, may not seek an attachment and, if insecure, may only petition the court to require the plaintiff to post a bond or other security for the payment of costs should he prevail.[10]

Library References

CJS Attachment § 9

§ 17.05. Actions in Which Attachments May Be Made

Attachments of a defendant's interests in real and personal property may be obtained to secure a mechanic's or materialman's lien[11] or in any civil

---

8 See former Rules and Procedures to Implement New Attachment Law (RSA 511-A) and RSA 511-A:10.

9 114 N.H. 68, 314 A.2d 654 (1974).

10 Super. Ct. R. 140.

11 Prior to enactment of RSA ch. 511-A, it was permissible to secure a mechanic's or materialman's lien by filing a writ of attachment stating that purpose and without also completing and serving a writ of summons to recover damages for the nonpayment of the claim secured by the lien. See, e.g., Hale v. Brown, 58 N.H. 323 (1878); Manchester Federal Savings & Loan Ass'n v. Letendre, 103 N.H. 64, 164 A.2d 568 (1960). That practice may still be followed today by filing a Petition to Attach with Notice or Petition for Ex Parte Attachment. Pine Gravel, Inc. v. Cianchette, 128 N.H. 460, 514 A.2d 1282 (1986). In the Petition to Attach with Notice, the reference to an underlying suit or equity proceeding should be deleted. In both forms, the words "to secure a lien under RSA 447:10" should be inserted in the preamble. The plaintiff may also record a copy

action except replevin.[12] Attachments of a defendant's right to receive property from another (i.e., "trustee process") may only be made in personal actions.[13]

Library References

CJS Attachment §§ 12–22
Attachment in alienation of affections or criminal conversion case. 67 ALR2d 527.

§ 17.06. Property Which May Be Attached—Generally

The purpose of an attachment is to obtain security for the payment of a plaintiff's judgment should he prevail. Thus, any property which could be levied against and sold on execution may be attached prior to judgment.[14]

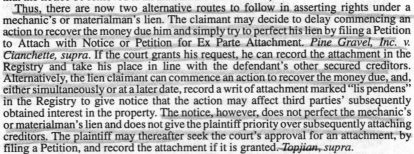

of a writ of attachment, either contemporaneously with the service of a writ of summons or thereafter, in the Registry of deeds " 'to give notice to third parties that any interest they may acquire in the property [of the named defendant] is subject to the outcome of the litigation.' " The writ, as recorded, must be marked "lis pendens," but no judicial approval is required before it may be recorded. Topjian Plumbing and Heating, Inc. v. Bruce Topjian, Inc., 129 N.H. 481, 484, 529 A.2d 391, 393 (1987). It is unclear whether recording the writ as a notice of lis pendens must be followed up by application to the court for an attachment with notice and, if so, what the effect of a refusal of such a request would be on the notice of lis pendens. See RSA 511-A:8(III) (which requires that the notice be limited "to the particular real estate described in the . . . return of attachment"); *Topjian Plumbing and Heating, Inc. v. Bruce Topjian, Inc., supra* (because the effect of the lis pendens is to give notice, but "not [to] create an attachment or perfect a lien," 129 N.H. at 484, 529 A.2d at 393, there might be no reason to require that the notice be removed if an attachment were denied).

Thus, there are now two alternative routes to follow in asserting rights under a mechanic's or materialman's lien. The claimant may decide to delay commencing an action to recover the money due him and simply try to perfect his lien by filing a Petition to Attach with Notice or Petition for Ex Parte Attachment. *Pine Gravel, Inc. v. Cianchette, supra.* If the court grants his request, he can record the attachment in the Registry and take his place in line with the defendant's other secured creditors. Alternatively, the lien claimant can commence an action to recover the money due, and, either simultaneously or at a later date, record a writ of attachment marked "lis pendens" in the Registry to give notice that the action may affect third parties' subsequently obtained interest in the property. The notice, however, does not perfect the mechanic's or materialman's lien and does not give the plaintiff priority over subsequently attaching creditors. The plaintiff may thereafter seek the court's approval for an attachment, by filing a Petition, and record the attachment if it is granted. *Topjian, supra.*

12 RSA 511-A:1 and 2, 503:3-c, and 498:16. The procedure is the same regardless of the nature of the underlying action. Dist. and Mun. Ct. R. 3.4. For the replevin procedure, see RSA ch. 536. See RSA 545-A:7(I)(6) (attachment to prevent a fraudulent conveyance or obligation).

13 RSA 512:1.

14 RSA 511:1 and 512:3; Dow v. Sayward, 14 N.H. 9 (1843); Treadwell v. Brown, 43 N.H. 290 (1861).

New Hampshire statutes provide only limited exemptions from attachment. An exemption need not be claimed to be preserved.[15]

Library References

CJS Attachment §§ 47–61

Retirement or pension proceeds or annuity payments under group insurance as subject to attachment or garnishment. 28 ALR2d 1213.

What sort of claim, obligation, or liability is within contemplation of statute providing for attachment, or giving right of action for indemnity, before a debt or liability is due. 58 ALR2d 1451.

Interest of spouse in estate by entireties as subject to attachment lien in satisfaction of his individual debt. 75 ALR2d 1172.

Joint bank account as subject to attachment, garnishment, or execution by creditor of the joint depositors. 11 ALR3d 1465.

Attachment and garnishment of funds in branch bank or main office of bank having branches. 12 ALR3d 1088.

Potential liability of insurer under liability policy as subject of attachment. 33 ALR3d 992.

Client's funds in hands of his attorney as subject of attachment or garnishment by client's creditor. 35 ALR3d 1094.

Special bank deposits as subject of attachment or garnishment to satisfy depositor's general obligations. 8 ALR4th 998.

§ 17.07. —Exemptions

During the last century, the Supreme Court recognized some common law exemptions from attachment. Bank bills[16] and railroad cars when not in use[17] could be attached, but standing grass could not be.[18] And goods belonging to a partnership could not be attached to secure the debts of an individual partner,[19] but that partner's interest in the property of the partnership could be.[20]

RSA 480:1 and 4 exempt $5,000 worth of the defendant's homestead from attachment in all cases except the enforcement of liens for debts created in constructing, repairing, or improving the homestead.[21]

---

15 Johnson v. Lang, 71 N.H. 251, 51 A. 908 (1902).

16 Spencer v. Blaisdell, 4 N.H. 198 (1827).

17 Boston, C & M Railway Company v. Gilmore, 37 N.H. 410 (1858); DeRochemont v. New York Central & Hudson River Railroad Company, 75 N.H. 158, 71 A. 868 (1909).

18 Rogers v. Elliott, 59 N.H. 201 (1879); Norris v. Watson, 22 N.H. 364 (1851).

19 Morrison v. Blodgett, 8 N.H. 238 (1836); Hill v. Wiggin, 31 N.H. 292 (1855).

20 Dow v. Sayward, 14 N.H. 9 (1843).

21 The exemption also does not apply in the case of tax liens and may be waived when giving a mortgage. RSA 480:4. The exemption does not prevent levy on execution but simply reserves the first $5,000 after sale to the defendant. RSA 480:4(IV). A homestead may be claimed in "any structure transportable in one or more sections, which,

New Hampshire statutes also exempt the following types of personal property from attachment:

(1) Clothes necessary for the use[22] of the debtor and his family.[23]

(2) Beds and bedding necessary for the debtor and his family.[24]

(3) Household furniture worth $2,000.[25]

(4) One cook stove, one heating stove, and one refrigerator and the necessary utensils belonging to them.[26]

(5) One sewing machine.[27]

(6) Provisions and fuel worth $400.[28]

(7) The uniform, arms, and equipment of every member of the National Guard.[29]

(8) Bibles, school books, and the library of a debtor which are used by the debtor and his family worth $800.[30]

(9) Tools of the debtor's occupation worth $1,200.[31]

---

in the traveling mode, is 8 body feet or more in width and 40 feet or more in length, or, when erected on site, is 320 square feet or more, and which is built on a permanent chassis and designed to be used as a dwelling with or without a permanent foundation when connected to required utilities, which include plumbing, heating and electrical systems contained therein" it is "owned and occupied as a dwelling by the same person" and in land of that person on which it is placed. RSA 480:1 and 674:31.

22 Where the exemption depends on use, whether the actual use of the property brings it within the exemption is a question of fact. Towne v. Marshall, 64 N.H. 460, 13 A. 648 (1887).

23 RSA 511:2(I). This exemption includes suitable apparel for labor plus an extra suit for religious worship and an overcoat for every season (see Peverly v. Sayles, 10 N.H. 356 (1839)), but does not include jewelry. Towns v. Pratt, 33 N.H. 345 (1856).

24 RSA 511:2(II).

25 RSA 511:2(III). "Household furniture" does not include a mahogany cabinet box or a traveling trunk. Towns v. Pratt, 33 N.H. 345 (1856). Valuations of these exemptions are presumably to be made on the basis of foreclosure auction prices.

26 RSA 511:2(IV).

27 RSA 511:2(V).

28 RSA 511:2(VI). The question whether a particular item of foodstuffs comes within the term "provisions" is for the jury. Plummer v. Currier, 52 N.H. 287 (1872) (unthreshed wheat and oats). Intoxicating liquor is not exempt. Gignoux v. Bilbruck, 63 N.H. 22 (1884).

29 RSA 511:2(VII).

30 RSA 511:2(VIII).

31 RSA 511:2(IX). What constitutes the tools of a debtor's occupation has been a matter of some dispute over the years. In Rice v. Wadsworth, 59 N.H. 100 (1879), the Court said that the question is a mixed one of law and of fact to be determined upon a consideration of his employment and the nature, character, and use of the chattels for which an exemption is claimed. See also Hall v. Nelson, 59 N.H. 573 (1880). A motor truck (Rosenblum v. Griffin, 89 N.H. 314, 197 A. 701 (1938)) and a wagon and harness

(10) One hog and one pig or the pork of the same if slaughtered.[32]

(11) Six sheep and their wool.[33]

(12) One cow, a yoke of oxen, or a horse (if required for farming or teaming) and four tons of hay.[34]

(13) Domestic fowls worth $300.[35]

(14) The debtor's interest in one pew in any meeting house in which he or his family usually worship.[36]

(15) The debtor's interest in a lot or right of burial in any cemetery.[37]

(16) One automobile worth $1,000.[38]

(17) Jewelry to the value of $500.[39]

The proceeds of insurance on exempt property are *not* exempt from attachment.[40] And an item which is not exempt may be attached even though it contains exempt articles, if the debtor is given a chance to remove the property that is exempt.[41]

---

used by a doctor in making house calls (Richards v. Hubbard, 59 N.H. 158 (1879)) have been held exempt under this provision, but a wagon used only for convenience or pleasure was held not to be exempt. Parshley v. Green, 58 N.H. 271 (1878). Tools belonging to a partnership are not exempt no matter what their use, and neither the partnership itself (Bateman v. Edgerly, 69 N.H. 244, 45 A. 95 (1897)) nor a partner (Peaslee v. Sanborn, 68 N.H. 262, 44 A. 384 (1895)) can claim the exemption. Tools are exempt, whether or not they are required for immediate use (Wilkinson v. Alley, 45 N.H. 551 (1864)), and if a debtor has two occupations, the tools he uses in both are exempt (Parshley v. Green, 58 N.H. 271 (1878)), but only to the combined value of $1,200.

32 RSA 511:2(X). The debtor is entitled to only two porcine animals, whether they are alive or dead. Parker v. Tirrell, 19 N.H. 201 (1848).

33 RSA 511:2(XI).

34 RSA 511:2(XII). If some of a debtor's animals in an exempt class are mortgaged, he must take one that is not. If all are mortgaged, he may take any of them. Hill v. Loomis, 6 N.H. 263 (1833); Greenleaf v. Sanborn, 44 N.H. 16 (1862); Richardson v. Chase, 64 N.H. 617 (1888). Whether a horse or yoke of oxen is required for use and thus is exempt is a question of fact. Cutting v. Tappan, 59 N.H. 562 (1880); George v. Fellows, 60 N.H. 398 (1880); Rice v. Wadsworth, 59 N.H. 100 (1879); Towne v. Marshall, 64 N.H. 460, 13 A. 648 (1887).

35 RSA 511:2(XIII).

36 RSA 511:2(XIV). A debtor's interest in a pew is personal property. RSA 511:21. The debtor's right of occupancy is, however, attachable. Holy Trinity Polish National Catholic Church v. O'Dowd, 86 N.H. 298, 167 A. 556 (1933).

37 RSA 511:2(XV).

38 RSA 511:2(XVI). The exemption does not extend to all "motor vehicles" but is limited to automobiles. Valuation will, as with other exemptions, be a question of fact.

39 RSA 511:2(XVII).

40 Wooster v. Page, 54 N.H. 125 (1873).

41 Towns v. Pratt, 33 N.H. 345 (1856) (locked trunk containing exempt clothing).

Social security benefits are also made exempt by 42 U.S.C. § 407(a).[42]

By these statutory exemptions, the Legislature at one time evidenced an intention to reserve to a debtor such items of clothing, furniture, food, tools, and equipment as might be necessary to allow him and his family to continue to live and remain self-sufficient and such books and access to a place of worship as would provide him with intellectual and spiritual relief should he fall on hard financial times. The purpose was an enlightened one but time has placed its attainment beyond the reach of this statute. The scope and nature of these exemptions are obviously unsatisfactory for a modern society which relies on a liberal extension of credit, and a wholesale revision of the statutory exemptions is long overdue.

The list set forth in RSA 511:2 contains those categories of property which are exempt from attachment. A further list of property rights which are exempt only from trustee process is set forth in RSA 512:21, as follows:

(1) Wages for labor performed by the debtor *after* service on the trustee.[43]

(2) Wages for labor performed by the debtor *before* service on the trustee except:

(A) When the action is debt on the judgment of a New Hampshire court or

(B) Any amount over fifty times the minimum hourly wage under federal law unless the defendant is a woman and the action is on a loan contract subject to RSA ch. 399-A on which her husband was the obligor.[44]

(3) Wages for the personal services and earnings of the debtor's wife and children.[45]

(4) Any unpaid pension or bounty money allowed by federal law.[46]

42　Todd v. Romano, 131 N.H. 96, 550 A.2d 111 (1988).

43　RSA 512:21(I). Only one wage attachment may be made; the plaintiff cannot reach wages earned after the first attachment, either by successive attachments or by discharging the first writ and making a new attachment. Cady v. Budd, 93 N.H. 243, 41 A.2d 88 (1944); Redington v. Dunn, 24 N.H. 162 (1851). But the exemption for wages earned after service on the trustee does not apply to money received as a result of work done before service (Steer v. Dow, 75 N.H. 95, 71 A. 217 (1908) (insurance renewal commissions)) or in cases where "wages" claimed to be exempt are so blended with money which is not exempt as to make it impossible to separate them. Robinns v. Rice, 18 N.H. 507 (1847); Gray v. Fife, 70 N.H. 89, 47 A. 541 (1899). "Wages" includes money received as an elected official. Robinson v. Aiken, 39 N.H. 211 (1859).

44　RSA 512:21(II) and (X).

45　RSA 512:21(III). Money due a wife from boarders is exempt. Hoyt v. White, 46 N.H. 45 (1865). Wages due to a child for her own use are also exempt. Johnson v. Silsbee, 49 N.H. 543 (1870).

46　RSA 512:21(IV).

(5) Funds held in the capacity of clerk, cashier, and employee of the debtor which were received in the ordinary course of employment.[47]

(6) Unpaid jury or witness fees.[48]

(7) Damages recovered for conversion of exempt property.[49]

(8) Sums due from an insurance company for loss of or damage to exempt property, *except* that when the building was a part of the homestead only the amount due that when added to the value of the building remaining equals $5,000[50] is exempt.[51]

(9) Up to $50 per week in wages for labor earned before service of the writ when the action is founded on any contract subject to RSA ch. 399-A.[52]

Library References

CJS Exemptions §§ 26 et seq.
CJS Homesteads §§ 52 et seq.
Family allowance from decedent's estate as exempt from attachment, garnishment, execution and foreclosure. 27 ALR3d 863.
What is "necessary" furniture entitled to exemption from seizure for debt. 41 ALR3d 607.
Employee retirement pension benefits as exempt from garnishment, attachment, levy, execution or similar proceedings. 93 ALR3d 711.

§ 17.08. When a Prejudgment Attachment May Be Made

A prejudgment attachment may be made at any time, either before[53] or after filing the writ of summons with the court. Prejudgment attachments can be ordered either ex parte or after notice and hearing.

Library References

CJS Attachment § 83

§ 17.09. Attachments With Notice—Preferred Method

RSA ch. 511-A favors attachments after notice over ex parte attachments. RSA 511-A:1 provides that "[i]n all civil actions, . . . a defendant shall be

---

47 RSA 512:21(V). Money collected by an attorney for his client is not exempted by this section. Narramore v. Clark, 63 N.H. 166 (1884).

48 RSA 512:21(VI).

49 RSA 512:21(VII).

50 RSA 512:21(VIII).

51 RSA 512:21(VIII).

52 RSA 512:21(IX).

53 An attachment may be obtained to secure a mechanic's or materialman's lien before a writ of summons is completed or even when no action at law is contemplated. Pine Gravel, Inc. v. Cianchette, 128 N.H. 460, 514 A.2d 1282 (1986).

given notice and an opportunity for a preliminary hearing before any prejudgment attachment . . . shall be made."

Library References

Inclusion or exclusion of first and last days in computing time for giving notice of attachment which must be given a certain number of days before a known future date. 98 ALR2d 1411.

§ 17.10. —Procedure for Filing and Service

When a plaintiff wishes to obtain an attachment prior to judgment he must fill out a Petition to Attach with Notice, serve that petition on the defendant and file it in court.[54] Where the plaintiff seeks an attachment at the beginning of an action at law, he must fasten the Petition to the face of the writ of summons,[55] deliver the original writ and Petition with service copies to the sheriff or other serving officer[56] for service, and enter the writ and Petition with the return of service in the court.[57] When the plaintiff seeks an attachment at the beginning of a proceeding in equity or a divorce proceeding, he must fasten the Petition to Attach to the face of the bill or libel, file the original with the court and obtain orders of notice, deliver the original and copies to the sheriff or other serving officer for service, and file the bill or libel and Petition to Attach with the return of service in court.[58]

Library References

Sufficiency of affidavit for attachment, respecting fraud or intent to defraud, as against objection that it is a merely legal conclusion. 8 ALR2d 578.

---

54 RSA 511-A:2. The procedural requirements of the statute and rules must be strictly obeyed. Manchester Federal Savings & Loan Association v. Letendre, 103 N.H. 64, 164 A.2d 568 (1960).

55 Rules and Procedures to Implement Attachment Law, "Attachment With Notice," paragraph 2 and Dist. and Mun. Ct. R. 3.4(B)(2).

56 *Id*. paragraph 3; Dist. and Mun. Ct. R. 3.4(B)(3).

57 *Id*. When the plaintiff seeks only to secure a mechanic's or materialman's lien and is not presently commencing a parallel action or proceeding to recover damages for breach of contract or other relief, he must note on the Petition that the attachment is sought to secure a lien under RSA 447:10, deliver the Petition with service copies to the sheriff or other serving officer, and enter the Petition with return of service in the court. See Pine Gravel, Inc. v. Cianchette, 128 N.H. 460, 514 A.2d 1282 (1986).

58 Rules and Procedures to Implement Attachment Law, "Attachment With Notice," paragraphs 2 and 3; "Attachments in Proceedings Other Than Actions at Law"; Dist. and Mun. Ct. R. 3.4(B)(2) and (3); RSA 498:17, 18, and 19.

§ 17.11. —Form of Petition

White

The form of a Petition to Attach with Notice is prescribed by the Superior Court Rules and the Rules of the District and Municipal Courts.[59] Those forms include a prominent notice to the defendant that the plaintiff is seeking an attachment, but that the defendant may object and have a hearing if he files his objection on or before the stated return day.[60] The notice requires that, if the defendant objects to the attachment, he must set forth his reasons for objecting in detail and in writing on or before the return day.[61] It also requires that the objecting defendant request a hearing,[62] notifies the defendant that his objections will be deemed waived if he fails to object on or before the return day, warns him not to transfer "any property after receiving this notice,"[63] and suggests that, even if he does not object to the attachment, he file an Appearance by the return date in order to avoid the entry of a default judgment.[64]

---

59 See N.H. Court Rules (1979). "Rules of the Superior Court," pp. 83 and 85; "Rules of the District and Municipal Courts," pp. 41 and 43. When an attachment is sought only to secure a mechanic's or materialman's lien and not in aid of an action at law or other proceeding, the form must be altered to reflect that fact. See Pine Gravel, Inc. v. Cianchette, 128 N.H. 460, 514 A.2d 1282 (1986).

60 See N.H. Court Rules (1979). "Rules of the Superior Court," pp. 83 and 85; "Rules of the District and Municipal Courts," pp. 41 and 43; RSA 511-A:2(I)–(III). In light of the remedial nature of this notice, if the return day stated in the writ is earlier than the return day set forth in the Petition to Attach, the latter should control.

61 See N.H. Court Rules (1979). "Rules of the Superior Court," p. 84. This requirement is not set forth in the statute. See RSA 511-A:2(III). Considering the remedial nature of the notice and the fact that the filing of an Objection shifts the burden to the plaintiff to show his right to an attachment, it is unlikely that an informal or general statement of reasons for objecting would be ignored by the court. At a minimum, such a response would be met by an order for a more definite statement of objection.

62 *Id.* at 84. Neither of these requirements is contained in the statute, but their inclusion in the form follows the practice established for motions in the Superior Court. See Super. Ct. R. 4 and 58.

63 This is much broader than RSA ch. 511-A would seem to require. RSA 511-A:6 was apparently intended to bring conveyances by defendants after notice within the scope of RSA 545:4. That section declares that a transfer or obligation is fraudulent as to a creditor if made or incurred "[w]ith actual intent to hinder, delay or defraud" the creditor and sets out, as one factor to be considered in determining the debtor's intent, whether "the debtor has been sued or threatened with suit" prior to the transfer being made or obligation incurred. RSA 545-A:4(I)(a) and (II)(d). However, proof that notice of suit was received is not conclusive of intent to hinder, delay, or defraud creditors and, in all other situations, a transfer is not fraudulent as to creditors if the debtor is not insolvent at the time and receives "a reasonably equivalent value in exchange for the transfer or obligation." RSA 545-A:5.

64 The forms of notice prescribed for the superior and for the district and municipal courts are the same.

RSA 511-A:3 provides that the plaintiff has the burden at any hearing on the attachment "to show that there is reasonable likelihood that the plaintiff will recover judgment including interest and costs on any amount equal to or greater than the amount of the attachment." Because the amount of the attachment can be amended at the hearing and interest and costs simply follow judgment, the plaintiff's burden is to show a "reasonable likelihood" that he will win. Under the statute he does *not* also have to show that the attachment is necessary. RSA 511-A:3 says simply that "[u]pon satisfying said burden, the plaintiff shall be entitled to the attachment . . . unless the defendant shall establish to the satisfaction of the court that his assets will be sufficient to satisfy such judgment with interest and costs if the plaintiff recovers same." Despite this clearly limited statutory burden of proof, the form of petition approved by the superior court requires the plaintiff to certify that there is a reasonable likelihood *both* that he will recover judgment *and*, based on detailed reasons, that the defendant's assets will be insufficient to satisfy judgment. The superior court, by its form, has thus placed the burden on the plaintiff to allege facts negating the defendant's affirmative defense. Although it is certainly within the superior court's discretion to refuse an attachment in any case where it would be unjust to grant it, including situations where the attachment is sought in order to harass the defendant rather than to protect a plaintiff's legitimate interests, there seems little justification for limiting the grant of all attachments to situations in which the plaintiff can certify that it is a necessary rather than a preferred means of protecting his judgment.

The Petition requires that the plaintiff specify the name of the defendant owning the property to be attached, the type (real estate or other) of attachment sought, and the amount of the attachment.[65] The caption, county

---

[65] Rules and Procedures to Implement Attachment Law, "Attachment With Notice," paragraph 1. But see RSA 508:4-c (prohibiting the specification, in an "affirmative pleading," of an amount of damages sought in a personal action).

See Gothic Metal Lathing v. Federal Deposit Insurance Corp., which states the three-part test that must be strictly complied with in order for a writ of attachment to be sufficient. The writ "must state the purpose for which the attachment is brought, describe the property to be attached with reasonable accuracy and specificity, and direct the officer to attach that specific property." 135 N.H. 262 (1992) (citing Ferns v. American Moore Peg Co., 81 N.H. 283, 283, 125 A. 434, 434 (1924), for three-part test and for principle that court requires strict compliance with test; Rodd v. Titus Construction Co., 107 N.H. 264, 266, 220 A.2d 768, 770 (1966); Wurm v. Reilly, 102 N.H. 558, 563, 163 A.2d 13, 17 (1960); Mathers v. Connelly, 95 N.H. 107, 107–08, 58 A.2d 510, 511 (1948)).

In *Gothic Metal*, the Court found that the writ of attachment was insufficient as it did not meet any of the three parts of the test. The court distinguished Manchester Federal Savings & Loan Association v. Letendre, 103 N.H. 64, 164 A.2d 568 (1960),

of venue, and return day must also be inserted in the space provided and, of course, must be the same as set forth on the writ of summons.[66]

The Petition must be executed by the plaintiff under oath.[67] Where the plaintiff is a corporation, partnership, or other artificial person, a duly authorized officer or partner must execute it under oath on the plaintiff's behalf.[68] The plaintiff or his attorney must also sign the notice of defendant's rights.[69]

Forms

Petition To Attach With Notice, see Appendix.

§ 17.12. —Hearing on the Petition

RSA 511-A:3 requires the court to hold a hearing within fourteen days of the date the court receives the defendant's objection.[70] The hearing may be held before a master, magistrate, or judge and is informal.[71] Even though the superior court petition form requires a plaintiff to certify under oath his belief that the defendant has no defense to the attachment, he is not required to prove that belief at the hearing. The statute states clearly that the plaintiff meets his burden if he shows a reasonable likelihood of recovering judgment and that the defendant must then satisfy the court that his assets will be sufficient to satisfy the judgment.

Library References

CJS Attachment § 114

§ 17.13. —The Court's Findings and Order

While the court should make a special finding after the hearing,[72] the petition form does not allow for it, and the plaintiff should be sure to request it.[73] Even if the court declines to grant the attachment, if its decision is based

---

as a case where the required elements were "physically too lengthy to fit on the writ, and this court allowed them to run onto a second page." 135 N.H. at 263.

66 See N.H. Court R., "Superior Court," p. 83.

67 Dist. and Mun. Ct. R. 3.4(B)(1).

68 N.H. Court R., "Superior Court," p. 83.

69 *Id.* at 84.

70 RSA 511-A:3. There is no requirement that the court hold a hearing within any particular period of time after service of the petition and writ or bill on the plaintiff.

71 RSA 511-A:3.

72 See RSA 511-A:4.

73 See Super. Ct. R. 72.

on findings that the plaintiff is likely to recover but that the defendant's assets will be sufficient to satisfy the judgment, the effect of the finding could be to subject any transfer of assets after the attachment is refused to the provisions of RSA ch. 545-A.

If the court grants the attachment it may limit or expand it beyond the scope requested by the plaintiff and may make other orders relating to its duration and the manner in which it is to be secured.[74] The court's order must be strictly obeyed. In *Maine National Bank v. Baker*,[75] the plaintiff bank obtained permission ex parte to make an attachment on defendant's car, but the order required that the defendant be served within ten days. The defendant was not served until twenty-four days had elapsed, and he thereupon moved to dissolve the attachment. The plaintiff met the defendant's motion to dissolve with a motion that the "writ be amended to make good service" (i.e., a motion to strike the requirement for service within ten days and to confirm the attachment). After hearing, the court granted the defendant's motion and dissolved the attachment. Thereafter the plaintiff filed motions to make a bulky article attachment under RSA 511:23, to require the defendant to produce the car for attachment, and for summary judgment, all of which motions were granted. In the Supreme Court, however, the plaintiff argued that the trial court had abused its discretion by dissolving the original attachment. The Supreme Court disagreed, saying, "The remedy of attachment is in derogation of the common law and failure to conform to prescribed procedures may invalidate the attachment."[76]

Library References

CJS Attachment § 115

§ 17.14. Ex Parte Attachments—Requirement for Exceptional Circumstances

Prior to 1973, New Hampshire law permitted a plaintiff, without notice to the defendant and prior to any hearing, to obtain an attachment "without the existence of special circumstances."[77] Under RSA ch. 511-A, however, it is impossible to obtain any attachment without the express permission of

---

74 RSA 511-A:4. The petition form provides room for only a duration limitation on the attachment, but further limits or expansions are certainly permissible under the statute.

75 116 N.H. 185, 355 A.2d 429 (1976).

76 116 N.H. 185, 186, 355 A.2d 429, 430.

77 Cnaeps v. Brown, 101 N.H. 116, 118, 135 A.2d 721, 723 (1957).

the court and an ex parte attachment can only be obtained upon a showing of special circumstances.[78]

RSA 511-A:8 authorizes the court "in exceptional circumstances" to grant an attachment without prior notice to the defendant. The plaintiff must establish two facts to the satisfaction of the court in order to be granted ex parte attachment: (1) that there is probable cause to believe that he will recover judgment, including interest and costs, in an amount equal to or greater than the amount of the attachment, and (2) that one of the following six types of special circumstances exists:

(1) There is a substantial danger that the property will be damaged, destroyed, concealed, or removed from the state and placed beyond the attachment jurisdiction of the court.[79]

(2) The attachment is necessary to vest quasi in rem jurisdiction in the court.[80]

(3) There is an imminent danger that a parcel of land or a unique chattel that is the subject of a petition for specific performance will be transferred to a bona fide third party.[81]

(4) The plaintiff is a creditor who has received notice of a bulk sale[82] and the ten-day notice period required in such transactions[83] will expire before the court can notify the defendant transferor and hold a hearing under RSA 511-A:3.[84]

(5) The attachment is "necessary to secure an important governmental or general public interest."[85]

(6) Other exceptional circumstances exist.[86]

---

78 RSA 511-A:8.

79 RSA 511-A:8(I).

80 RSA 511-A:8(II). Now that the minimum standards for quasi in rem jurisdiction are the same as for personal jurisdiction the only point of claiming quasi in rem jurisdiction may be to obtain an ex parte attachment as of right. See Section 2.04,—"Standards for Quasi in Rem Jurisdiction."

81 RSA 511-A:8(III).

82 RSA 382-A:6–104.

83 RSA 382-A:6–105.

84 RSA 511-A:8(IV).

85 RSA 511-A:8(V). This section presumably may only be used by government agencies, large plaintiff classes, and plaintiffs seeking a penalty or exemplary damages allowed by a remedial statute. See, e.g., RSA 358-A:10(I).

86 RSA 511-A:8(VI). This grant of general discretion to the court must be read in light of the consistent legislative statements during consideration of Senate Bill 268 (later RSA ch. 511-A) that the purpose of the bill was to require notice and a hearing before *any* attachments can be made. See 1973 Senate Journal 1555 and 1973 Journal of the House 1842.

Library References

CJS Attachment §§ 5, 114

Cross References

Quasi in rem jurisdiction, see §§ 2.03–2.05 *supra*.

§ 17.15. —Plaintiff's Burden of Proof

In order to obtain an ex parte attachment, a plaintiff must show probable cause, rather than a reasonable likelihood to believe, that he will recover judgment on his claim. He must, in short, show facts from which the court can determine *both* that he has a claim and that it is unlikely that his opponent can establish a defense.

§ 17.16. —Procedure for Filing and Service

A plaintiff who wishes to obtain an ex parte attachment must file a Petition for Ex Parte Attachment in the form prescribed by the Rules before filing or serving any other papers in the case. The Petition must be executed under oath by the plaintiff or by an authorized officer or partner of the plaintiff[87] and must set forth specific facts from which the court can determine *both* the probability that the plaintiff will succeed on his claim *and* the exceptional circumstances which justify the attachment. It is not enough simply to repeat the language of the statute in the Petition; the Petition must allege specific facts from which the court can conclude that the standard of the statute has been met.

In actions at law, a Petition for Ex Parte Attachment, with copies for service, must be filed with the court *prior* to the service or entry of any writ of summons or other pleading.[88] In equity and divorce proceedings, the Petition for Ex Parte Attachment is filed with the bill, petition for libel.[89] The petition form requires the plaintiff to certify facts that establish his right

---

87 Rules and Procedures to Implement Attachment Law (RSA ch. 511-A) *"Ex Parte Attachment,"* paragraph 1; "Petition for *Ex Parte* Attachment"; Dist. and Mun. Ct. R. 3.4(C)(1).

88 Rules and Procedures to Implement Attachment Law (RSA ch. 511-A) *"Ex Parte Attachment,"* paragraph 2; Dist. and Mun. Ct. R. 3.4(C)(2). When the plaintiff is seeking only to secure a mechanic's or materialman's lien and is not also commencing an action at law or other proceeding in aid of his claim, he need only file the Petition for Ex Parte Attachment. See Pine Gravel, Inc. v. Cianchette, 128 N.H. 460, 514 A.2d 1282 (1986); Topjian Plumbing and Heating, Inc. v. Bruce Topjian, Inc., 129 N.H. 481, 529 A.2d 391 (1987).

89 Rules and Procedures to Implement Attachment Law (RSA ch. 511-A) "Attachments in Proceedings Other than Actions at Law."

to recover[90] and facts that make out one or more of the special circumstances listed in the statute.[91] If the court grants the attachment, the plaintiff's attorney or, if the plaintiff is not represented by an attorney admitted in New Hampshire, the clerk of court, is authorized to fill out a Writ of Attachment,[92] fasten a certified copy of the Petition for Ex Parte Attachment to the Writ of Summons,[93] and deliver the original writs with service copies to the sheriff or other officer for service.[94] The Rules specifically require that the plaintiff's attorney instruct the sheriff to serve the Writ of Attachment *first* and within the time allowed by the court's order and to serve the Writ of Summons "immediately thereafter."[95] The sheriff's return must be filed with the court with the original writs "immediately after service has been completed."[96]

Forms

Petition for Ex Parte Attachment (Superior Court), see Appendix.
Petition for Ex Parte Attachment (District Court), see Appendix.

§ 17.17. —Hearing

The form for the Petition for Ex Parte Attachment contains a notice to the defendant informing him that the court has ordered the attachment, that the defendant may request a hearing by filing a written request within fourteen days of service which details his objections, and that his failure to request a hearing will amount to a waiver of his objections to the attachment.[97] The notice is signed by the clerk of the court.[98] RSA 511-A:8(V) further provides that the court must schedule a hearing "as promptly as possible" after the defendant's request.[99]

---

90 But see RSA 508:4-c (prohibiting the specification in an "affirmative pleading" of an amount of damages sought in a personal action).

91 See also N.H. Rules of Professional Conduct, Rule 3.3(d) ("In an *ex parte* proceeding, a lawyer shall inform the tribunal of all material facts known to the lawyer which will enable the tribunal to make an informed decision whether or not the facts are adverse.").

92 Rules and Procedures to Implement Attachment Law (RSA ch. 511-A) "*Ex Parte* Attachment," paragraph 4; Dist. and Mun. Ct. R. 3.4(C)(4).

93 *Id.* paragraph 5; Dist. and Mun. Ct. R. 3.4(C)(5).

94 *Id.* paragraph 6; Dist. and Mun. Ct. R. 3.4(C)(6).

95 *Id.*

96 *Id.*

97 Rules and Procedures to Implement Attachment Law (RSA ch. 511-A) "Petition for *Ex Parte* Attachment."

98 *Id.*

99 This requirement must be strictly observed. Maine National Bank v. Baker, 116 N.H. 185, 186, 355 A.2d 429, 430 (1976).

The requirement that the defendant detail his objections to the attachment is not set forth in the statutes and is wholly a creation of the Rule. A defendant served with a Petition to Attach with Notice is not required to do anything more than object and put the plaintiff to his proof. At first blush, it seems odd to require a person whose property has already been attached without a hearing to set forth reasons for objecting to the attachment, when a person whose property has not been attached need say nothing. But the rationale of the Rule is that, while the defendant has an automatic right to a hearing, he does not enjoy the presumption that he has a defense since the plaintiff, in order to get the ex parte attachment, has already shown that the defendant probably does not have one. Thus, although his right to a hearing is uncontestable, the defendant must plead and prove a defense to the claim and to the alleged special circumstances already shown by the plaintiff. Unlike the situation where the defendant objects before attachment, merely claiming the hearing after an ex parte attachment has been allowed does not shift the burden of proof back to the plaintiff.

Furthermore, the warning that the failure to object to the attachment, will be deemed a waiver of a right to hearing on the attachment, and thus of objections to the attachment, is not based upon the statute and should not be read too broadly.[100] It cannot, for example, be regarded as a limitation on a defendant's statutory right to apply to the superior court for reduction or discharge on the grounds that the attachment is excessive or "unreasonable."[101] The statute imposes no time limit on the making of such a motion and specifically provides that it is to be construed broadly to effect its "remedial" purpose.[102] Nor can the defendant's failure to object for fourteen days be regarded as a waiver of his right to petition the superior court for release of an attachment on real estate upon the substitution of a bond.[103] Certainly no failure to object within a fixed period can be taken as a waiver of the defendant's right to contest the attachment at a later date based on the plaintiff's fraud in obtaining it or to move for a reduction or release based on changed circumstances which make it no longer equitable to continue the attachment.

Library References

CJS Attachment § 114

---

100 RSA 511-A:10 cannot be read as statutory authority for the adoption of substantive rules which cut off other statutory rights.

101 RSA 511:53 and 54. See also RSA 511-A:9.

102 RSA 511:54.

103 RSA 511:48–52.

§ 17.18. —The Court's Findings and Order

If the defendant requests a hearing within the time allowed after being notified that his property has been attached ex parte, he may have a hearing.[104] The issue at the hearing will be whether the attachment should be continued. This is a different issue from that involved in a hearing on a Petition to Attach with Notice. In that case, the plaintiff must show that there is reasonable likelihood that he will recover a judgment at least equal to the amount of the attachment, and the defendant must then show that his assets will be sufficient to satisfy the judgment if plaintiff wins. By the time an ex parte attachment has been granted, the plaintiff has already convinced the court that he not only has a good claim, but that the defendant has no defense and that some special circumstance exists which makes the attachment necessary, regardless of the defendant's ability to pay damages out of his other assets at the conclusion of the case. While the defendant can attempt, at a hearing on the attachment, to show that he has a good defense to the plaintiff's claim, unless he also shows that the special circumstances making his net worth irrelevant and the attachment necessary do not exist, it is unlikely that the court will release the attachment. Thus, the primary issue at the hearing is the existence of special circumstances which require the attachment, and because the plaintiff has already shown the court, in order to get the attachment, probable cause to believe that such special circumstances exist, the burden of showing that they do not rests on the defendant at a hearing on his objection.

Upon the conclusion of the hearing, the court will enter an order either continuing,[105] modifying, or releasing the attachment. If the parties request specific findings of fact before the case is submitted,[106] the court will make them.

§ 17.19. —Procedure When Ex Parte Attachment Is Denied

Neither the statute nor the Rules and Procedures prescribe the actions to be followed if a Petition for Ex Parte Attachment is denied. To be sure,

---

104 An Objection after an attachment has been allowed ex parte pursuant to RSA 511-A:8 does not give rise to a hearing under RSA 511-A:3. Such hearings are still, however, not bound by the rules of evidence and may be conducted by masters, referees, or magistrates.

105 Technically, no order continuing the attachment is required since, unlike a temporary restraining order, an ex parte attachment has no expiration date and will continue in force until modified or released. However, where the plaintiff successfully defends the attachment at a hearing at which the defendant has appeared, the court's resulting order should reflect that fact and specifically authorize the continuation of the attachment.

106 Super. Ct. R. 72.

Paragraph 3 of the Ex Parte Attachment section of the Rules and Procedures and District and Municipal Court Rule 3.4(c)(3) do authorize the plaintiff to file a Petition to Attach with Notice, but they do not state whether the plaintiff may instead file a second Petition for Ex Parte Attachment. Nor do they provide any time deadline within which to file one or the other or specify whether a Petition for Ex Parte Attachment which has been denied must be given to the defendant. These questions arise because a Petition for Ex Parte Attachment is filed and acted on before any Writ of Summons is entered. If the petition is denied, no action is pending between the plaintiff and the defendant and no court order has been entered altering their rights. It is conceivable, therefore, that a plaintiff may be so discouraged by the denial of his Petition that he might never serve or enter a Writ of Summons or, alternatively, that he may be so intent on obtaining an order to the defendant's prejudice without his knowledge that he will keep trying until he succeeds. For these reasons, some limitation on the plaintiff's actions when an ex parte attachment has been refused are necessary.

Because there is no provision in the statutes or Rules for the withdrawal of a Petition for Ex Parte Attachment that has been denied or for the record of its filing to be expunged, once such a Petition has been filed the court will enter it on the docket and make it a matter of public record. Under these circumstances, it would be inequitable not to notify the defendant of its filing and the court's action thereon. Similarly, if special circumstances exist justifying an ex parte attachment, it would be unjust not to allow the plaintiff to cure defects in his Petition or proof and to resubmit the Petition before being required to notify the defendant that he has sought such an order.

The key element in each case is time: how long should the plaintiff have to do it correctly and how long may the defendant fairly be kept in the dark about matters directly affecting his property? Obviously the amount of time suitable to each case will be determined by the circumstances, but as a general rule it would not seem unreasonable to require a plaintiff to notify a defendant that he has filed an unsuccessful Petition within two business days of the filing. If he needs to amend his original Petition, he ought to be able to do so in a day and to have the court's decision in another day after that.[107] If he does not intend to amend the Petition, there is no reason not to tell the defendant what he has done immediately, whether or not he intends to continue with the suit. If he does intend to file a Petition to Attach with Notice, he can do so within the same amount of time it would take to amend

---

[107] The plaintiff should not be allowed more than two attempts at obtaining an ex parte attachment. If he cannot show a basis for it in two tries it is unlikely that the necessary probable cause exists.

his original Petition and can serve the old and new Petitions with the Writ of Summons.[108]

§ 17.20. Securing a Prejudgment Attachment—Generally

If the court grants the attachment, the plaintiff's attorney, or, when the plaintiff appears pro se, the clerk must fill out a Writ of Attachment and deliver the original and copies to the sheriff or other serving officer for service.[109] The attachment is then made in different ways, depending on the nature of the property attached. In no case, however, is it necessary to serve the defendant again with a Writ of Attachment.[110] The original service of the Writ of Summons and Petition to Attach with Notice is sufficient to obtain personal jurisdiction and to put the defendant on notice of the intended attachment. Nevertheless, the plaintiff must send a copy of the Writ of Attachment with sheriff's return to the defendant when he submits it to the court.[111]

Library References

CJS Attachment §§ 170 et seq.
Sheriffs negligent failure to attach property. 17 Am.Jur.POF2d, pp. 715–754.

Forms

Writ of Attachment and Trustee Process (Superior Court), see Appendix.
Writ of Attachment and Trustee Process (District Court), see Appendix.

§ 17.21. —Attachments of Real Estate

(a) *Service on the Register of Deeds.*   The sheriff makes an attachment on real estate by leaving an attested copy of the Writ of Attachment, along with the necessary recording fees,[112] at the office or dwelling house of the Register of Deeds for the county in which the land is located and thereafter making return of his attachment.[113] The sheriff is not required to serve the Register or any of his deputies personally.

---

108 There is no justification for serving only the Petition to Attach With Notice and not the Petition for Ex Parte Attachment. The defendant is entitled to know that the court has declined to find either probable cause to believe that the plaintiff will prevail or that exceptional circumstances exist.

109 Dist. and Mun. Ct. R. 3.4(B)(4) and 3.4(C)(4). Note that the Rules and Procedures to Implement Attachment Law (RSA ch. 511-A) paragraph 4 conflicts with RSA 511-A:5 and 511:13 in requiring that the sheriff, rather than the plaintiff or his attorney, make all filings or service of writs of attachment.

110 RSA 511-A:5-a.

111 Super. Ct. R. 21.

112 RSA 511:6.

113 RSA 511-A:3 and 511:5. See note 108 *supra*.

(b) *Indexing by the Register of Deeds.*   The sheriff must make return of the time when he left the writ at the Register's office or dwelling house, and the Register is required to certify on the writ the time when the copy was "received."[114] Although the Register may not actually become aware that a Writ of Attachment has been left at his dwelling house until hours after the sheriff has delivered it, the Register should adopt the date and time set forth in the sheriff's return as the date and time of receipt. This practice will assure that the protection of an attachment is not lost by the accident of a Register's personal absence from home or office at the time of service.

The Register is also required to maintain a separate index of attachments, arranged alphabetically by the names of defendants. The index must contain a record of the date and time when the writ was received, the name of the court to which the writ is returnable, and the names of the plaintiff and defendant.[115] The Register enters on the index the same time of receipt which he has already noted on the service copy of the writ. Once the fact of receipt of the writ has been entered on the index of attachments and the service copy has been filed in the Registry, the writ has been "recorded" and the attachment is good against any person.[116] At that point, there should be three separate but identical notations of the date and time of Register's receipt of the writ: the sheriff's return, the Register's receipt, and the index. In the case of a disagreement between these three notations, the sheriff's return should control.[117] As a matter of practice, when a Register receives a writ at his office, he immediately files it in the order received with all other documents which have not been indexed. A careful title examiner always checks this pile of unprocessed work before reaching conclusions about the state of title. Thus, for all practical purposes, any writ which is received by the Register at his office during business hours will be available for examination immediately upon receipt, and any writ which he receives at home during nonbusiness hours should be available in his office immediately upon the opening of the office on the following business day. Although a writ in the latter case may technically not be indexed for some hours, it is unlikely that bona fide purchasers for value could subsequently maintain a title superior to the attaching creditor's if they had failed to check to see whether the writ

---

114 RSA 511:4.

115 RSA 511:5.

116 RSA 511-A:5. This is a change from pre-1973 law. Under Manchester Federal Savings & Loan Association v. Letendre, 103 N.H. 64, 164 A.2d 568 (1960), the attachment was considered perfected and good against the world upon filing regardless of whether the Register properly indexed it.

117 RSA 511:4.

was in the unprocessed work at the Register's office. Similarly, it is common practice to close on the purchase or financing of real estate only after checking the Registry and then to make the closing conditional on an updated check as of the time of filing to be sure that no attachments or other encumbrances have lately arisen. It is unlikely that a bona fide purchaser for value who closed unconditionally at a time when the Registry was closed would be allowed to maintain a superior claim against an attachment which was obtained by service at the office or home of the Register outside business hours but before closing.

Thus, the only occasions when a delay between the time of receipt and the time of recording is likely to be of significance is when the writ is left at the Register's home during office hours. In such a case, the date and time of receipt will be of limited effect by themselves in establishing the priority of an attaching creditor's lien. The relative priority among prejudgment attachments is determined by the date and time of service of the Petition to Attach with Notice.[118] Furthermore, no attachment of real estate can be effective against a bona fide purchaser for value until it has been recorded[119] under the name of the *present* record holder of title[120] in all counties[121] in which the land is situated. Thus, the date and time of receipt by the Register, standing alone, is only effective to establish priorities among persons other than prejudgment attaching creditors and bona fide purchasers for value. The effect, then, of the Register being served at home during business hours may be to allow bona fide purchasers for value to obtain a superior title between the time of service and the time of recording. All these difficulties strongly suggest that a plaintiff should take care to instruct the sheriff in the manner of service and to check immediately to assure that his instructions have been followed.

§ 17.22. —Attachments of Personal Property

(a) *Generally.* An attachment on personal property is perfected by seizure and is continued thereafter by means of either actual or constructive possession.[122] However, RSA 511-A:5 also provides that the writ of attach-

---

118 RSA 511-A:5.

119 *Id.* Chagnon Lumber Co. v. Stone Mill Construction Corp., 124 N.H. 820, 474 A.2d 588 (1984).

120 Pittsburgh Plate Glass Company v. American Crystal, Inc., 91 N.H. 102, 13 A.2d 721 (1940).

121 RSA 511-A:5.

122 See, e.g., Dunklee v. Fales, 5 N.H. 527 (1831).

ment may be filed "wherever notice is required to perfect attachments" and that attachments of personal property "shall not be effective against bona fide purchasers for value until . . . [they] are filed with the town or city clerk, Secretary of State or wherever notice is required to perfect attachments." Only attachments of church pews are expressly required to be perfected by a public filing,[123] and the language quoted above makes little sense unless it is construed to allow filing wherever a filing would be necessary to perfect a *security interest* in the property attached. And while the first sentence of Section 5 indicates that the filing is permissive, the loss of priority over bona fide purchasers for value which results from not filing, as a practical matter, makes it mandatory.[124] The statute thus adds a further requirement of public record filing to the common law requirement of seizure to perfect an attachment of personal property.

(b) *Seizure.*   When the serving officer seizes personal property pursuant to a Writ of Attachment, he must take it into his possession or place it under his control.[125] He need not touch every separate article of property being attached, so long as the articles are accessible to him and under his control,[126] he manifests an intent to exercise control over them,[127] and he puts the property attached out of the debtor's control.[128] As the court said in *Treadwell v. Brown*:[129]

> As a general proposition it may be conceded that to constitute a valid attachment of personal property there must be an actual seizure or its equivalent but it is not necessary that the officer should actually touch every article or any of them. It is sufficient if they be brought within his power and he do some act significant of his purpose to attach them; as by entering a house or store and declaring that he attaches all the furniture or goods and then

---

123 RSA 511:21 (an attested copy of the writ and officer's return must be left with the town clerk of the town in which the church is located).

124 See, e.g., Carpenter v. Cummings, 40 N.H. 158 (1860) (bona fide mortgagee of personal property in possession of mortgagor holds as against prior attachment of which he had no notice).

125 Odiorne v. Colley, 2 N.H. 66 (1819).

126 Huntington v. Blaisdell, 2 N.H. 317 (1820). See Brown v. Davis, 9 N.H. 76 (1837); Souhegan Nail, Cotton & Woolen Factory v. McConihe, 7 N.H. 309, 324 (1834); Johnson v. Farr, 60 N.H. 426 (1880); Page Seed Company v. City Hardware Store, 96 N.H. 359, 77 A.2d 35 (1950); Dunklee v. Fales, 5 N.H. 527 (1831).

127 Morse v. Hurd, 17 N.H. 246 (1845).

128 Page Seed Company v. City Hardware Store, 96 N.H. 359, 77 A.2d 35 (1950).

129 43 N.H. 290 (1861).

proceeding to inventory them; or locking them up and taking the key or placing his servant in charge of them.[130]

The officer must make return of his attachment, being careful to identify with particularity the items he has attached.[131]

(c) *Preserving the Attachment by Continued Possession.* The serving officer must retain control over the property in order to preserve the attachment.[132] He may retain control over the items attached "by remaining present himself, by appointing an agent in his absence,[133] by taking a receiptor for the property,[134] by inventorying and marking them, or by a reasonable removal of them."[135] If the officer or his agent or receiptor allows the debtor to retake possession of, or to use the property without restriction,[136] the attachment will not be completely dissolved but will be dissolved

---

130 43 N.H. at 291. See also Morse v. Hurd, 17 N.H. 246, 249 (1845).

131 Clement v. Little, 42 N.H. 563 (1861) (return of bricks in a brickyard which had not been attached on a previous attachment was specific enough).

132 Dunklee v. Fales, 5 N.H. 527 (1831).

133 This agent is sometimes called a "keeper." Kivel v. Murray Cone Shoe Company, 73 N.H. 523, 63 A. 673 (1906).

134 It has long been a common practice for the sheriff to take in lieu of the property attached the written undertaking (receipt) of a third person (receiptor) in whom he has confidence that that third person will keep the attached property safe and deliver it to the sheriff free of expense upon his demand. As the Court said in Rowe v. Page, 54 N.H. 190 (1874):

> The receiptor is not regarded as the mere servant of the officer. His undertaking is a security for the debt to the extent of the property. So long as he retains possession of the property it may be reclaimed by the officer to satisfy the execution or to restore it to the debtor, or because he is not satisfied with the responsibility of the receiptor. The receiptor may, if he chooses, restore the property to the debtor, and suffer him to dispose of it, but he thereby deprives himself of the power of returning it to the officer, and the officer is entitled to recover its value of him upon a lawful demand. If the property is thus restored to the debtor and sold by him, the officer cannot then retake it by virtue of the attachment. (54 N.H. at 193.)

The sheriff may make his demand in person or when the receiptor is out of the county, by a writing left at the receiptor's abode. RSA 511:59. Such contracts, however, are not absolute. The receiptor can keep the attached property if he has a title superior to the attachment or can deliver it to someone else with a better title, or he can return it to the defendant if the plaintiff loses. Berry v. Flanders, 69 N.H. 626, 627, 45 A. 591, 596 (1899). In some cases the sheriff may even make a nominal attachment of property and take as his real security the receiptor's promise to pay money. See Morrison v. Blodgett, 8 N.H. 238 (1836); Berry v. Flanders, 69 N.H. 626, 45 A. 591 (1899).

135 Bryant v. Osgood, 52 N.H. 182 (1872); Chadbourne v. Sumner, 16 N.H. 129 (1844).

136 There is a statutory procedure for restoration of the attached property to the defendant (see RSA 511:35–39) if the defendant gives the sheriff a bond for the full value of the attached property conditioned to satisfy any judgment obtained in the pending or any

far enough either to allow a second attaching creditor without notice of the prior attachment and of the continued pendency of the action in which it was made to make an attachment superior to the first[137] or to permit a bona fide purchaser for value without notice to obtain clear title from the debtor.[138]

> What act, what species of possession, and what degree of vigi-
> lance, will constitute legal custody, is often a question of difficulty,
> depending on a variety of circumstances, having respect to the
> nature and situation of the property, and the purposes for which
> custody and vigilance are required; and especially, to the notice
> to other officers, and persons having conflicting claims.[139]

(d) *Attachments on Bulky Articles of Personal Property.* RSA 511:23 provides that an officer who has attached "any livestock or articles which by reason of their size, situation, fluidity, explosive or inflammable quality, including motor vehicles, trucks, trailers and tractors, are incapable of being taken into actual possession"[140] may substitute a public record filing for continued possession.[141] The purpose of the statute "is to relieve the officer and parties from the burden and expense of actual possession of property which, it is inconvenient to hold in possession while still giving the officer full rights to possession (sometimes loosely called constructive possession), thus preserving the lien as fully as if there were actual possession by the officer or his keeper."[142] The officer must first make his attachment[143] (i.e., he must put all the property under his actual control and put the defendant

---

> future suit for which the property may be attached. Under that procedure it would appear that the first attachment is not dissolved by the giving of a bond and restoration of the property to the defendant's possession and that subsequent attachments of the same property all of which are to be satisfied from the same bond may be made by the sheriff who originally attached it without again seizing the property. See RSA 511:38.

137 Houston v. Blake, 43 N.H. 115 (1861); Young v. Walker, 12 N.H. 502 (1842).

138 However, the purchaser must have no reason to suspect that the property has been attached "[w]hen a purchaser is put upon inquiry, he is to be charged with notice of all such facts as he would have learned by reasonable inquiry." Rowe v. Page, 54 N.H. 190, 194 (1874).

139 Young v. Walker, 12 N.H. 502, 507 (1842).

140 Stock certificates do not qualify for bulky article attachment. Dupont v. Moore, 86 N.H. 254, 166 A. 417 (1933).

141 The absence of similar permission in RSA 511-A:3 in the case of other items of personal property is further evidence that the filing requirement set forth in that section is cumulative rather than alternative to continued possession.

142 Claremont Gas Company v. Wooster, 91 N.H. 439, 440, 21 A.2d 171, 173 (1941).

143 Scott v. Manchester Print Works, 44 N.H. 507 (1863).

out of possession), then within forty-eight hours of making the attachment, leave an attested copy of the writ with his return of attachment thereon. Wherever filing is required to perfect the security interest under RSA 382-A:9–101 et seq., the officer must also make return of his attachment and filing to the court. The return which the officer files with the town clerk must "furnish a subsequent attaching creditor or a purchaser of the property from the debtor with substantially and practically the same information as would be derived from knowledge of the officer's retention of possession in common law."[144]

The decision to rely upon filing rather than continued possession as a means of preserving the attachment will be made by the sheriff alone, in the absence of specific instructions from the plaintiff. Filing is, of course, cheaper than appointing a keeper or otherwise retaining possession until a bond is poked or the case is decided. But the filing alone will not prevent the defendant from concealing, destroying or removing the goods.[145] And a filing which is defective in its description of the goods or in some other particular may be ineffective to protect the attachment against the claims of subsequently attaching creditors and bona fide purchasers.[146] As a result, the officer who chooses to file rather than retain possession runs a greater risk of incurring liability to the plaintiff for loss of the property or attachment than he would if he retained the property. On the other hand, the plaintiff will not be allowed to recover the cost of putting the property in the hands of a keeper or otherwise guarding it if the court later determines that such precautions were unnecessary, and the sheriff who chooses to retain possession where it is clearly not necessary for the protection of the property when the filing procedure under RSA 511:23 could be used may find himself liable to the plaintiff for incurring unnecessary expense. Thus, it is always in the sheriff's best interest to take advantage of the provisions of RSA 511:23 unless there is reason to believe that the property cannot be safely left in the place where it is attached. If the plaintiff, upon learning that the sheriff has chosen this method of preserving the attachment, feels that some greater precautions should be taken, he can instruct the sheriff to take them, but he will have to bear the expense of those precautions, most likely without

---

144 Bryant v. Osgood, 52 N.H. 182, 186 (1872).

145 It is, however, a misdemeanor to "waste, destroy, remove from the state or diminish the quantity of any property attached" under RSA 511:23.

146 Bryant v. Osgood, 62 N.H. 182 (1872); RSA 511-A:5.

hope of reimbursement.[147] In cases where the sheriff is in doubt concerning the safety of the goods, he can decide not to rely upon filing and, if he is right, the costs of preserving the goods will be allowed to the plaintiff.[148] If he is not, the costs may be chargeable to the sheriff for failing to use due care.

As a result of the uncertain position in which the sheriff is often placed in attaching bulky articles, it is not uncommon for the sheriff to ask for specific instructions from the plaintiff or his attorney concerning the method by which the plaintiff is to be preserved. On those occasions the plaintiff is obliged to balance the safety of the goods against the cost of holding them until trial. In cases where the defendant needs the goods but the plaintiff prefers not to incur the expense of holding and is also not satisfied that the goods will be safe, the plaintiff may best be able to protect himself by taking possession with the expectation that deprivation of the goods will force the defendant to post a bond for their return. This device will give the plaintiff better security than filing without much additional expense.

The sheriff's return must specifically state that the property was attached by him at a particular time and place, must sufficiently identify the property attached so that any subsequently attaching creditor or bona fide purchaser will have "substantially and practically the same information as would be derived from the knowledge of the officer's retention of possession at common law,"[149] must state that the officer found the items "incapable of being conveniently taken into possession" and why, and must recite when filing was made in the appropriate office.

Library References

Validity of attachment of chattels within store or building other than private dwelling, made without removing the goods or without making an entry. 22 ALR2d 1276.

§ 17.23. Effect of an Attachment—Generally

An attachment holds the property attached "as security for the judgment the plaintiff may recover."[150] But an attachment can give the creditor no

---

147 RSA 511:23. If the sheriff who is on the scene has determined that further precautions are unnecessary, the plaintiff will need independent knowledge of facts tending to show that the goods are in jeopardy if he is to recover the cost of protecting the property.

148 Kivel v. Murray Cone Shoe Co., 73 N.H. 523, 63 A. 673 (1906).

149 Bryant v. Osgood, 52 N.H. 182, 186 (1872).

150 RSA 511:1.

greater right than the debtor already has,[151] and an attachment of encumbered property holds that property subject to the prior mortgage, pledge, security interest, or lien.[152]

Library References

CJS Attachment § 191

§ 17.24. —Real Estate

An attachment of real estate holds "all the debtor's interest," except his homestead right,[153] in the real estate.[154] Whether that interest is a right of redemption or a right to receive a conveyance under a contract,[155] real estate which is subject to a mortgage or other lien may be attached without the requirement that the mortgage or other lien be immediately paid off and discharged. However, an attaching creditor may elect to discharge the mortgage or other lien.

Once a real estate attachment has been made, it cannot be defeated by any change in the nature of the debtor's rights in the real estate.[156] If the debtor's interest is conveyed or extinguished as between the debtor and a third party, the transaction is nevertheless ineffective to remove the attachment lien from the property, and the new state of ownership holds title subject to the attachment.[157] If the debtor or his grantee redeems the

---

151 Thompson v. Barber, 12 N.H. 563 (1842) (because it effects a partition, an attaching creditor can attach some, but not all, parcels of land in which the debtor has an interest as a cotenant).

152 Clement v. Little, 42 N.H. 563 (1861); Hill v. Wiggin, 31 N.H. 292 (1855). But the attachment is only subordinate to prior mortgages, security interests, pledges, and liens actually obtained in compliance with the law; the attaching creditor's lien is not subject to claims of which he may be aware which have not been validly secured or perfected. Hill v. Gilman, 39 N.H. 88 (1859).

153 See RSA 480:1; Beland v. Goss, 68 N.H. 257, 44 A. 387 (1894).

154 An attachment to secure a mechanic's or materialman's lien cannot be effective against real estate which the debtor has sold to a bona fide purchaser for value prior to recording of the writ. Chagnon Lumber Co. v. Stone Mill Construction Corp., 124 N.H. 820, 474 A.2d 588 (1984).

155 RSA 511:7. The attachment holds whatever interest the debtor has *in fact* regardless of what he may appear to have as a matter of record. Exeter Banking Co. v. Sleeper, 97 N.H. 321, 326, 327, 87 A.2d 151, 153, 154 (1952) (Justice Duncan dissenting on other grounds). Where the debtor is a joint tenant, the attachment holds his "proportionate share." Manchester Savings & Loan Association v. Emery-Waterhouse, 102 N.H. 233, 238, 153 A.2d 918, 921 (1959).

156 RSA 511:17.

157 This was the view of Justice Smith in Beland v. Goss, 68 N.H. 257, 44 A. 387 (1894), apparently relying on the first clause of the section only.

mortgage, receives a conveyance, or otherwise increases or makes more definite his interest in the real estate or its value, his entire new interest and increased value will be held by the attachment.[158] In addition, if the debtor or his grantee threatens to take any action with respect to the real estate attached which could diminish its value and thus defeat the attachment, the attaching creditor may obtain equitable relief against the threatened harm.[159]

Cross References

Homestead right, see § 17.07 *supra*.

§ 17.25. —Personal Property

An attachment of nonexempt personal property holds the debtor's interest in that property if the attaching creditor pays or tenders, to any prior mortgagee, pledgee, secured party,[160] or holder, the amount for which he holds the property.[161] The attaching creditor may discover how much to tender or pay by, either personally or through the attaching officer demanding that the mortgagee, pledgee, secured party, or holder give a written account under oath of the amount for which the property is held.[162] The

---

"[T]he debtor or other person in possession is not disturbed in his possession until the levy of the execution; but the attachment fastens itself, as a charge or incumbrance upon the land, from the time it is made, so that any subsequent purchaser, even before levy, can only take subject to the encumbrance of the attachment, nor can any other creditor, by a levy of an execution, avoid the operation of this charge or incumbrance." Kittredge v. Warren, 14 N.H. 509, 522 (1844).

158 See Beland v. Goss, 68 N.H. 257, 258, 44 A. 387, 387 (1894). "By the attachment, the creditor acquired a statutory lien upon the debtor's interest in the property, not only as it was at the time the attachment was made, but such additional interest as he might have at the time the property was taken on execution." See also Lachance v. Dondero, 91 N.H. 157, 16 A.2d 59 (1940), where a vacant lot was attached and the attachment properly recorded. Subsequently, the defendant sold the vacant lot without mentioning the attachment to Lachance, who built a house upon it and mortgaged it to a bank. Neither Lachance nor the bank had actual knowledge of the attachment. The plaintiff later recovered judgment in an amount greater than the value of the vacant lot but less than the value of the lot with house. The question presented was whether at the time of execution the attachment held just the value of the lot in the defendant's hands or the value of the lot and house, regardless of who owned it at the time its value was increased. The Court decided that the attachment followed the real estate and was effective to hold the entire value less any preexisting liens or mortgages at the time of the execution.

159 Moulton v. Stowell, 16 N.H. 221 (1844) (where the defendant cut off wood after the attachment). "Whatever would be waste as between mortgagor and mortgagee may be restrained if it impairs the security." 16 N.H. at 222.

160 A preexisting security interest takes priority over an attachment if it is perfected or if the attaching creditor has knowledge of it. RSA 382-A:9–301.

161 RSA 511:26.

162 RSA 511:27.

demand need not be served but is sufficient if actually communicated.[163] The officer may hold the property pending receipt of that account.[164] Where the prior mortgage is fraudulent, the attaching creditor may hold the goods attached without tendering or paying anything,[165] but he must be certain that the mortgage is fraudulent since he will be liable in trespass if it is not. The prior mortgagee, pledgee, secured party, or holder must deliver his account to the creditor or officer who made the demand within fifteen days of the demand.[166] Upon receipt of the account, unless the account is false, the attaching creditor must pay or tender the amount stated or lose his attachment.[167] If the mortgagee, pledgee, secured party, or holder either fails to give the account within fifteen days of receipt or gives a false account, he will lose not just the priority but the entire security of his mortgage, pledge, security interest, or other lien.

As might be expected in the case of such a severe penalty, there has been a good deal of litigation over what constitutes a satisfactory demand for an account and what constitutes a false account. In *Farr v. Dudley*,[168] the first case to consider the question of the sufficiency of the demand,[169] Justice Eastman laid down the standard that "the attaching creditor should be held to comply strictly with all the substantial requisitions of the statute."[170] This standard has been repeatedly affirmed.[171] In a series of cases decided since *Farr v. Dudley*, the Supreme Court has determined what constitutes strict compliance. In *Gilmore v. Gale*,[172] the Court allowed a demand to be made by words other than those set forth in the statute, saying that "a literal

---

163 See Gilmore v. Gale, 33 N.H. 410 (1856) (where the demand was mailed).

164 RSA 511:27.

165 Angier v. Ash, 26 N.H. 99 (1852); Pettee v. Dustin, 58 N.H. 309 (1878); Janvrin v. Fogg, 49 N.H. 340 (1870).

166 RSA 511:28.

167 RSA 511:26 and 28. The falsity of the account may result from the amount claimed or the fact that any amount is claimed at all. A fraudulent mortgage of personal property is no protection against a subsequent attachment. Pettee v. Dustin, 58 N.H. 309 (1878); Janvrin v. Fogg, 49 N.H. 340 (1870).

168 21 N.H. 372 (1850).

169 *Farr v. Dudley, supra*, dealt with the provisions allowing for removal of liens on real property. However, there is no substantive difference between the procedures involved, and, in Messer v. Bailey, 31 N.H. 2 (1855), the Court held that the same standards of compliance apply to both.

170 21 N.H. at 380.

171 Messer v. Bailey, 31 N.H. 2 (1855); Putnam v. Osgood, 51 N.H. 192 (1871); Gilmore v. Gale, 33 N.H. 410 (1856).

172 33 N.H. 410 (1856).

compliance is not to be exacted where substantially the same thing is done which the statutes requires."[173] However, the Court has required that the attaching creditor state, "with reasonable certainty and distinctness, that the mortgagee may see that he is bound by law to comply,"[174] his authority for making the demand and state that the account is to set forth the amount due as of the date of the demand rather than as of the date of the attachment.[175] Regardless of how many mortgages, security interests, pledges, or other liens may be on the property when attached, the attaching creditor need only make one demand of each prior creditor.[176] No matter how many attachments he makes on the same property, the attaching officer need only make one demand, and, regardless of whether the demand is answered, the officer is not required to demand again.[177] In short, the attaching creditor or officer's demand must state that an attachment has been made and ask for an accounting under oath of the amount which was due on the day and hour of the demand with respect to the debt which is secured by the prior mortgage, pledge, security interest, or lien.

No statute or case expressly requires that the demand be in writing.[178] But in light of the substantial rights which hang on the demand being correctly

---

173 33 N.H. at 418. The statute required a demand for "an account on oath of the amount due upon the debt or demand secured by the mortgage" and the attaching creditor demanded "an account under oath of the amount of the debt or debts, demand or demands, secured by said mortgage."

174 45 N.H. at 46. See also Farr v. Dudley, 21 N.H. 372 (1850); Ricker v. Blanchard, 45 N.H. 39 (1863); Eastman v. Batchelder and Wife, 36 N.H. 141 (1858). A statement that an attachment has been made is probably a sufficient statement of that authority. See *Ricker v. Blanchard, supra* (although Justice Bellows suggested in the *Ricker* case that a deputy sheriff should also state his residence, presumably to show his qualification to hold and exercise his office. The view has never been adopted and seems unnecessarily cumbersome). The demand need not specify the name of the attaching creditor (unless he, rather than the officer, is making the demand) or identify the action in which the attachment has been made, the nature of the claim, or the court granting the attachment. Kimball v. Morrison, 40 N.H. 117, 130 (1860).

175 Farr v. Dudley, 21 N.H. 372 (1850); Messer v. Bailey, 31 N.H. 2 (1855). The rationale for this requirement is that the attaching creditor needs to know the exact amount necessary to extinguish the indebtedness which is secured by the prior lien or mortgage and is therefore entitled to be informed if the indebtedness has been reduced or increased since the attachment. To be consistent, then, the demand should require an account as of the time of receipt or of tendering the account, but the cases only require that an account be demanded for the amount due as of the time of the demand.

176 Barton v. Chellis, 45 N.H. 135 (1863).

177 Kimball v. Morrison, 40 N.H. 117 (1860).

178 In Fife v. Ford, 67 N.H. 539, 41 A. 1051 (1893), the Court declined to resolve the question but held that even if a written demand were required the requirement could be waived.

made and on the time when it is made, there are likely to be very few situations in which it will be prudent to make the demand only in an oral form. Similarly, there is no requirement that the demand be served or even delivered in hand, and, although there has been some doubt expressed on the point,[179] it appears to be settled by long practice that the demand may be mailed. It is not even clear that the demand must actually be received by the prior mortgagee, pledgee, secured party, or holder. In *Gilmore v. Gale*,[180] the only case in which nonreceipt has arisen as an issue, the Court declined to consider whether a failure to give an account because of nonreceipt would nevertheless discharge the prior mortgage. Because RSA 511:29 allows a person to be relieved in equity from a failure to render an account because of accident or misfortune, it is unlikely that most defaults resulting from nonreceipt will result in the discharge of a prior mortgage, except, of course, where the prior creditor has intentionally avoided receiving the demand and therefore cannot show accident or misfortune. In most cases, it will be to the attaching creditor's advantage to assure that the prior mortgagee, pledgee, secured party, or holder actually receives the demand and, to that end, to hand-deliver the demand to him in written form on the same day that it is made.

When the prior creditor receives a demand for an account which is insufficient or which he believes to have been made without authority, he should not take the risk of failing to respond but instead should either immediately seek a clarification of the doubtful point or, if that seems unlikely to produce a result, petition the superior court for a determination of the demanding person's authority.[181]

In making his response, the prior mortgagee, pledgee, secured party, or holder is required to act "in perfect good faith and with all reasonable efforts to make it just and correct."[182] He must state the amount actually due or give sufficient facts on the face of the account from which the amount can be computed.[183] He may state that other sums are due which are not secured, if he is not thereby attempting to mislead the attaching creditor.[184] And he must

---

179 See Ricker v. Blanchard, 45 N.H. 39, 46 (1863).

180 33 N.H. 410 (1856).

181 See Farr v. Dudley, 21 N.H. 372 (1850).

182 Putnam v. Osgood, 51 N.H. 192, 208 (1871).

183 Sullivan Savings Institution v. Kelley, 59 N.H. 160 (1879); Duncklee v. Gay, 39 N.H. 292 (1859). Merely stating the amount claimed or identifying the underlying notes, rather than stating the amount due on the notes, is defective. *Sullivan Savings Institution v. Kelley, supra*; Page v. Ordway, 40 N.H. 253 (1860).

184 Belknap v. Wendell, 21 N.H. 175 (1850).

state the amount due to all persons besides himself for which the mortgage, pledge, security interest, or other lien serves as security.[185] But he is not required to state any extra details[186] or to explain points which may be easily determined by the attaching creditor through the "exercise of reasonable diligence" and by reference to public records.[187] The account is intended to give the attaching creditor more information than is apparent in the public record.[188] "The exact nature of the information required to be given by the mortgagee is apparent from the object and purpose for which that information is required, which is to enable the creditor or officer to make tender of *the exact sum* for which the goods are held under the mortgage, and thus to preserve his attachment."[189] However, a prior creditor does not waive any objections he may have to the attaching creditor's authority to demand an account simply by responding to the demand.[190]

An account will be defective if it is not submitted within fifteen days of the demand or is not signed and sworn to by the prior creditor.[191] It will also be defective if it is evasive[192] or states an incorrect amount due and the "error is willful or caused by bad faith or by culpable negligence or carelessness which would imply bad faith"[193] or if it fails to state the full amount due to all persons secured by the prior mortgage, pledge, security interest, or lien or fails to state sufficient facts on the face of the account from which that amount may be determined. An account which refers the attaching creditor to another person for further information[194] or which gives estimates of amounts due[195] is defective. However, an account will not be regarded as defective if it merely contains a plain error in computation[196] or misstates the amount due despite the exercise of good faith and all reasonable efforts

---

185 Putnam v. Osgood, 51 N.H. 192 (1871).

186 For example, that he holds other security for the same debt, Barton v. Chellis, 45 N.H. 135 (1863).

187 Barton v. Chellis, 45 N.H. 135 (1863) (prior creditor was not required to state that some property was subject to both a first and a second mortgage).

188 Page v. Ordway, 40 N.H. 253 (1860).

189 40 N.H. at 258.

190 Ricker v. Blanchard, 45 N.H. 39 (1863).

191 RSA 511:27–29.

192 Gilmore v. Gale, 33 N.H. 410 (1856).

193 Putnam v. Osgood, 51 N.H. 192, 208 (1871).

194 Duncklee v. Gay, 39 N.H. 292 (1859).

195 Currier v. Webster, 45 N.H. 226 (1864).

196 *Id.* (error in subtracting).

to make the account correct.[197] The prior creditor is not at liberty to be careless, but if "the error be unintentional and the result of pure accident or mistake and without culpable negligence" and if the creditor has used "reasonable diligence to make out a just and true account,"[198] his error will not cost him his security.[199]

Upon receipt of an account which is satisfactory in form, the attaching creditor must tender or pay the amount due to the mortgagee, pledgee, secured party, or holder.[200] The full amount secured by all prior mortgages, pledges, security interests, or liens must be tendered or paid; the attaching creditor is not free to pay only one or a few of the debts or to redeem less than all prior liens.[201] The statute does not prescribe a time limit within which that payment must be made, but it may be assumed that no delay longer than fifteen days, in the absence of special circumstances, will be regarded as reasonable. If the attaching creditor fails to pay or tender the amount due within a reasonable time, his attachment will be lost and the attaching officer will be obliged to release the property.[202]

If the attaching creditor receives the account late or in an improper form, he may ignore it and assume that the prior lien has been discharged as a matter of law.[203] To avoid a claim that he has waived the discharge by

---

197 Gibbs v. Parsons, 64 N.H. 66, 6 A. 93 (1886) (account stated too low); Putnam v. Osgood, 52 N.H. 148 (1872) (account stated too high).

198 "In determining whether the mortgagee had used reasonable diligence to make out a just and true account, all the circumstances of the case should be considered, including the extent of injury to the creditor to be caused by an erroneous account." Putnam v. Osgood, 51 N.H. 192, 208 (1871).

199 It may, however, cost him the difference between the amount actually due and an understatement of that amount in the account. In Duncklee v. Gay, 39 N.H. 292 (1859), Justice Doe wrote that, while an error in stating the amount due should not dissolve the security for the indebtedness, it should be regarded as a waiver of the amount actually due in excess of the amount stated. While this view is likely to have little effect so long as it is possible to be relieved from the consequences of the mistake under RSA 511:29, there may be some circumstances which would justify a court in treating an understatement as a waiver. If the account overstates the indebtedness and the attaching creditor pays the full amount stated, he may recover the excess. Putnam v. Osgood, 51 N.H. 192 (1871).

200 If the account contains a clear computation error, the attaching creditor need only pay the amount which a correct computation would have shown to be due. Currier v. Webster, 45 N.H. 226 (1864). If the account is itemized and includes some improper charges but the amount of the proper charges can be determined, the attaching creditor can pay the amount of the proper charges only. *Id.*

201 Barton v. Chellis, 45 N.H. 135 (1863).

202 See Sullivan Savings Institution v. Kelley, 59 N.H. 160 (1879).

203 RSA 511:28. See Gilmore v. Gale, 33 N.H. 410 (1856).

accepting a late or imperfect account, he should notify the prior creditor that he regards the lien as discharged. This will place the burden on the prior creditor to seek relief under RSA 511:29, and, if he fails to do so within a short time after receipt of the notice, he may be barred by the doctrine of laches. If the attaching creditor receives an account which is satisfactory in form but seems to contain a mistake or is inadequate in some way and the attaching creditor has no reason to think that the error was intended or the result of inexcusable neglect, he should immediately seek a clarification. No purpose will be served by forcing the prior creditor to convince a judge that he has acted in good faith when there is no reason to doubt that he has.

If the attaching creditor receives an account that is satisfactory in form but that he believes to be evasive, false, or intentionally inadequate, he may either ignore it and treat the prior lien as discharged or seek a court order compelling a truthful and complete disclosure. The first option places the burden on the prior creditor to bring the matter into court[204] but runs the risk that, if the court finds that the account was adequate, the attaching creditor's failure to tender or pay the amount due will be regarded as having discharged his lien. The latter route is more immediate but will result in additional expense at an early stage of the proceedings before the attaching creditor has any indication of whether he will prevail on this claim and runs the risk of providing a vehicle by which the prior creditor can amend his account in a timely fashion. The choice between these approaches will depend on the tactical considerations unique to each case. If the attaching creditor decides to bring the issue to the court himself, he should file a petition to require the prior mortgagee, pledgee, secured party, or holder to account. Such a petition can only be entertained by the superior court and its filing may require that proceedings in the district or municipal courts be temporarily stayed.

If the mortgagee, pledgee, secured party, or holder fails to give an account within fifteen days or is found to have given a false account, he may, of course, be relieved of the effects of his failure if he brings a petition in equity in the superior court and shows that his error was the result of someone else's fraud or his own accident, mistake, or misfortune and that relief would be just.[205]

---

204 The prior creditor may wait until the collateral has been sold and bring a writ of replevin (Gilmore v. Gale, 33 N.H. 410 (1856)).

205 RSA 511:29. See also New Hampshire Comments, RSA 382-A:9–311.

§ 17.26. New or Additional Attachments—Circumstances Under Which New or Additional Attachments May Be Made

While an action is pending, whether or not one or more attachments have already been granted, the plaintiff may file a motion seeking new or additional attachments.[206]

§ 17.27. —Procedure for Making New or Additional Attachments

The statute is unfortunately ambiguous with respect to the form of pleading that the plaintiff must file in order to effect new or additional attachments. When the attachment is sought after service of the writ but before the defendant has appeared, the prescribed petition forms should be used. After the defendant has appeared, however, there would not seem to be as much need for the warnings mandated by RSA 511-A:2, and a verified motion setting forth the same information required by the form petitions ought to be sufficient for any attachment. A Motion to Attach with Notice need not be served but may simply be mailed to the defendant or his counsel.[207] Although the defendant must file his Objection to the motion within ten days,[208] it would seem to be inconsistent with RSA 511-A:2 and 3 to require him also to set out the grounds for his Objection. But there is no reason why such a Motion could not be granted if the defendant failed to object.[209] The procedure for new or additional attachments is in all other ways the same as for an attachment sought when the writ is served, except that in the case of personal property attachments, due to the actual or constructive possession of an officer resulting from a prior attachment, subsequent attachments may only be made by the prior attaching officer, and subsequent writs of attachment must be delivered to him.[210]

---

[206] RSA 511-A:7.

[207] Super. Ct. R. 21.

[208] Super. Ct. R. 58.

[209] Id.

[210] Odiorne v. Colley, 2 N.H. 66 (1819); Moore v. Graves, Jr., 3 N.H. 408 (1826).

§ 17.28. Priority of Attachments

RSA 511-A:5 provides that "[a]s between attaching creditors, all attachments made in conformity with this chapter shall have priority in the order of service and notice on the defendant as provided by RSA 511-A:2." This section conflicts with and thereby partially repeals the last part of RSA 511:55 which provides that "if there are several attachments, the property shall be holden to the creditors in the order in which their attachments were made."

Strangely enough, RSA 511-A:5, if taken literally, gives priority to an attachment obtained with notice over an attachment granted ex parte if the preattachment notice is served on the defendant before the notice of the ex parte attachment, even though the ex parte attachment may have been granted days before the attachment with notice. This provision contrasts with the other requirements in RSA 511-A:5 that attachments be filed in certain public offices in order to take priority over the claims of third parties. New Hampshire law prior to 1973 provided for priority of attachments based on service of the writs of attachment,[211] an arrangement which made sense in a system where writs signed in blank were filled out and served without any further action by the court. But since 1973, no attachment has been obtainable without a prior court order, and, while it may be reasonable to arrange priorities amongst attachments with notice according to the date of service of the notice rather than the date of entry of the court order granting the attachment, it makes no sense to subordinate ex parte attachments that have already been approved by the court to attachments with notice that are granted by the court at a later date.

It is interesting to note that RSA 511-A:5 establishes priority according to service of notice *only* for "attachments made in conformity with this chapter." Presumably this means that attachments ordered under other provisions of law follow the priority rule of RSA 511:55. It may also provide the basis for an argument by one attaching creditor that another attaching creditor should take a lower priority due to technical defects in his compliance with RSA ch. 511-A.

Library References

CJS Attachment § 226
Right of attachment or judgment creditor, or officer standing in his shoes, to attach older lien or security interest for usury. 70 ALR2d 1409.

---

211 Kittredge v. Bellows, 7 N.H. 399 (1835).

§ 17.29. Plaintiff's Rights After Attachment and Before Judgment— Generally

After making his attachment, unless otherwise ordered by the court,[212] the plaintiff may redeem real estate from any mortgage or encumbrance and may sell perishable goods or living animals in order to preserve their value or reduce his expense.

Library References

CJS Attachment §§ 229 et seq.

§ 17.30. —Redemption of Mortgages on Real Estate

RSA 511:12 authorizes the plaintiff or sheriff to demand that any person entitled to be paid by the defendant under a mortgage, execution, tax lien, or contract for sale of the real estate attached give him a sworn account of the amount due at the time of the attachment.[213] The account must be provided within fifteen days.[214] After receiving the account, the plaintiff may pay or tender the amount due[215] to the person entitled to payment and thereby extinguish all that person's rights in the real estate,[216] including priority over the attachment.[217] That person's priority will also be extinguished if he refuses to give a true account within fifteen days,[218] unless he is relieved by the court upon filing a bill in equity demonstrating that his failure to render a true account within the time allowed is the result of a "fraud, accident, mistake or misfortune."

In addition to giving the plaintiff first priority in the real estate, this procedure allows him to demand a conveyance of the person's interest if the attachment is later dissolved or defeated.[219] If the person refuses to convey that interest, the plaintiff is entitled to recover the sum he has previously paid for the defendant's account.[220] After the person's right is either conveyed or retained, the defendant's rights of redemption are reinstated.[221]

---

212 RSA 511-A:4.
213 Farr v. Dudley, 21 N.H. 372 (1850).
214 RSA 511:12.
215 RSA 511:10.
216 Felker v. Hazelton, 68 N.H. 304, 38 A. 1051 (1895).
217 RSA 511:11.
218 RSA 511:12.
219 RSA 511:14.
220 RSA 511:15.
221 RSA 511:16.

The procedure authorized by RSA 511:10–16 is cumbersome and not very practical for many plaintiffs. It cannot be used to displace other attachment lienholders, but it may be useful in some situations for eliminating persons with a legal interest in the property who are friendly to the defendant.

§ 17.31. —Sale of Personal Property

The owner and all attaching creditors can always agree between themselves in writing that personal property that has been attached will be sold in any manner which will assure a fair return.[222] The proceeds of such a sale are held subject to the attachments in the same priority as they attached to the property.[223] When the parties cannot agree, either to the fact or means of the sale, either one of the parties may ask the sheriff to sell any living animals or any goods which are perishable, which will be "greatly reduced in value by keeping," or which will cost a great deal to store.[224] Upon receiving such an application, the sheriff appoints one examiner, the plaintiff and defendant each appoint an examiner,[225] and the three examiners, after being sworn, examine the property attached and certify what part of it is subject to sale as set forth above.[226] If either party is dissatisfied with the determination that specific property is *not* subject to sale, he may petition the superior court for an order that the property be sold.[227] There is no statutory appeal from the examiners' decision that the property *may* be sold. After notice and hearing, the court may order the sale or affirm the examiners' decision.[228] The sheriff may sell the property as if taken on execution as soon as the examiners or the court authorize him to do so.[229]

Library References

Construction and effect of provision for execution sale on short notice, or sale in advance of judgment under writ of attachment, where property involved is subject to decay or depreciation. 3 ALR3d 593.

---

[222] RSA 511:30.

[223] Grant v. Lathrop, 23 N.H. 67 (1851).

[224] RSA 511:31. The attaching creditor has a common law duty to sell any perishable goods which cannot be preserved. Cilley v. Jenness, 2 N.H. 87 (1819).

[225] RSA 511:32.

[226] RSA 511:33.

[227] RSA 511:34.

[228] *Id.*

[229] RSA 511:30, 33, and 34.

§ 17.32. Release, Dissolution, and Expiration of Attachments— Release of Attachments

(a) *Full Release by Waiver or Agreement.* Any attachment can be waived by the plaintiff [230] or released by agreement of the parties at any time and on any lawful condition.[231] The attachment being for the protection of the plaintiff rather than the court, the plaintiff may waive the protection without the court's approval, and the court will enforce the waiver.[232] Where an attachment involves sureties, bonding companies, receiptors, or other third parties who bear a contingent liability as a result of the attachment, the consent of those third parties to the release must also be obtained.

(b) *Release or Modification by Order of the Court.* The court that granted the attachment also has inherent authority to modify or release it upon such terms as justice requires.[233] In equity actions, there is also statutory authority for the modification or release.[234]

(c) *Involuntary Release Upon Defendant's Petition.* RSA 511:48 permits the defendant to petition the superior court for release of an attachment on his real estate and the substitution of a bond running to the plaintiff in an amount equal to the value of the interest attached[235] and conditioned to pay any judgment and costs. The petition must be filed in the superior court, regardless of which court may have granted the attachment. "[A]ll parties interested" are entitled to notice and an opportunity to be heard. The defendant has no right to have the attachment released, but, if the court finds that justice requires the substitution of a bond for the attachment, it may enter an order to that effect.[236] The defendant must then obtain an attested

---

230 But a waiver is revoked by demand if made before the rights of third parties attach. Johnson v. Lang, 71 N.H. 251, 51 A. 908 (1902).

231 The ability of a plaintiff to abandon an attachment and of the defendant to accept that abandonment has been implicitly recognized by the Court in Houston v. Blake, 43 N.H. 115 (1861), and Wheeler v. Eaton, 67 N.H. 368, 39 A. 901 (1892). But a plaintiff must evidence his abandonment by clear and unequivocal actions; silence or equivocal actions will not be construed to constitute an abandonment. Ela v. Shepard, 32 N.H. 277 (1855); Wheeler v. Eaton, 67 N.H. 368, 39 A. 901 (1892).

232 See Leonard v. Aranosian Oil Company, Inc., 103 N.H. 107, 165 A.2d 593 (1960).

233 The court may also make the continuation of the attachment conditional upon the occurrence of certain events, limit its duration, or otherwise modify the grant of the lien in a fashion which gives it a continuing authority to revoke it. See RSA 511-A:4.

234 RSA 498:21. See Woodland Shores Association v. Kellar, 109 N.H. 538, 257 A.2d 26 (1969) (the court did not abuse its discretion in releasing an attachment which was no longer needed).

235 RSA 511:48 and 49.

236 RSA 511:48.

copy of the petition, pleadings relating to it, and order, and a clerk's certificate that the bond has been filed with the court[237] and record those documents in the Registry of Deeds where the attachment has been recorded.[238] Like the attachment it affects, the release is not effective until these documents have been filed and recorded by the Register in the index of attachments.[239]

There is no statutory procedure for involuntary release of an attachment on personal property.

(d) *Involuntary Release by the Plaintiff.*

(1) *Failing to Enter the Writ.* In the days when actions were begun by service of a combined writ of attachment and summons prior to filing any pleadings in court, it was held that the failure to enter the writ after making an attachment released that attachment.[240] This rule was apparently founded on one or both of two principles: (1) That an attachment is only an aid to a pending action and serves no purpose when no case is pending in court; and (2) that an attachment has not been perfected until the sheriff's return on the writ of attachment has been filed in court.

Today, attachments with notice are allowed only after the Writ of Summons and Petition to Attach with Notice have been served on the defendant and entered in court. However, even though the first justification for the rule no longer applies in attachments granted with notice, there is still a basis to argue that attachments are not fully perfected until the sheriff's return has been filed.[241] And in attachments ordered ex parte, only the Petition to Attach without Notice is filed before the attachment is allowed. Both the Writ of Summons and the Writ of Attachment are served on the defendant before they are entered in court.[242] Thus, it must be assumed that, under the present attachment procedure, the plaintiff's failure to enter the Writ of Summons after an ex parte attachment or to enter the Writ of Attachment with the

---

237 RSA 511:51.

238 RSA 511:52.

239 *Id.*; RSA 511-A:5.

240 Munroe v. St. Germain, 69 N.H. 200, 42 A. 900 (1897).

241 Rules and Procedures to Implement Attachment Law (RSA ch. 511-A) "Attachment With Notice," paragraph 4, "*Ex Parte* Attachment," paragraph 4.

242 Rules and Procedures to Implement Attachment Law (RSA ch. 511-A) "*Ex Parte* Attachments."

sheriff's return after any attachment will act as a release of the attachment effected under the writ.[243]

The date when the attachment will be released by the plaintiff's failure to enter the writ is difficult to establish. Certainly the Writ of Summons and Writ of Attachment should be filed before any hearing, and the defendant ought to be able to take advantage of the plaintiff's failure to do so at that time. However, since the court will only set down a hearing on an attachment after the defendant has objected,[244] in cases where the defendant does not enter an objection to the attachment, it is possible that no hearing will be held before the return day set in the Writ of Summons. In that event, the return day should be the day on which any attachments will be released if the Writs of Summons and Attachment have not been filed.

(2) *Amending the Writ After Attachment.* If the plaintiff amends his writ to increase the ad damnum or to change the substance of the action, with the result that the amended action is not "for the same demand originally sued," his attachment may be released as against any creditor then holding an attachment obtained after the plaintiff's.[245] The same result is achieved by the attaching creditor stipulating to judgment with the debtor on claims which were not recoverable under the writ.[246] "The subsequent attaching creditor has a vested right to the excess beyond the amount of the judgment to be rendered upon the writ of the first attaching creditor as it was when served."[247] However, because the court has statutory authority to

---

243   Only the defendant is entitled to take advantage of this release, however, and, if he waives it, a receiptor whose liability is no greater after the waiver than before the release cannot object. Stevens v. Bailey, 58 N.H. 564 (1879).

244   RSA 511-A:3 and 8(V).

245   Page v. Jewett, 46 N.H. 441 (1866).

246   *Id.*

247   46 N.H. at 445. See also Laighton v. Lord, 29 N.H. 237 (1854), where Justice Woods wrote:

> The obligation of bail and receiptors is to be regarded as entered into with the full understanding of the existence of the right on the part of the plaintiffs to amend and of the power and duty of the court to allow the exercise of that right in all proper cases and it is clear that neither bail nor bailees of property attached nor subsequent attaching creditors have any right in law or justice to complain when the amendment made does not in fact prejudice their rights by increasing the responsibility of bail or receiptors or tend to diminish the surplus property to which such subsequent attaching creditor may be entitled according to the conditions of the action at the time of service of the writ. (29 N.H. at 257, 258.)

And in Brown v. Ellsworth, 72 N.H. 186, 55 A. 356 (1903), Justice Chase balanced the rights of the first attaching creditor (Brown) against the rights of the second (Eaton) as follows:

impose limitations on the scope and extent of an attachment,[248] it presumably also has power to protect and preserve the attachment according to the requirements of justice. It is therefore wise when seeking any amendment to a writ secured by one of several attachments on the defendant's property to ask the court for an order preserving the attachment against the claims of subsequently attaching creditors. In cases where the amendment sought is substantial, the court may be obliged to modify the plaintiff's rights under the attachments or to enter other orders to protect the subsequent attaching creditors from prejudice.[249]

As with other releases caused by errors in the plaintiff's handling of his case, it is difficult to establish the date on which an attachment will be regarded as void due to the allowance of an amendment which broadens or changes the nature of the case. Logically, the attachment ought to be released as of the date of the amendment, but it has been held that when such an amendment has been made and, through accident or mistake the plaintiff eventually takes a judgment no larger than and for the same cause as he could have taken on the original demand, the original attachment will be unaffected.[250] Perhaps the Court has intended by this approach to allow a second attaching creditor who obtained judgment before the first to intervene in the first case, not to defend but solely to test the validity of the first attachment. Whatever the purpose, the effect of this approach is to make an attachment in a case that has been substantially amended voidable but not void at the instance of a subsequently attaching creditor and then only if the first attaching creditor cannot or is not willing to limit his damages to those allowable under his original declaration.

Library References

CJS Attachment §§ 247 et seq.

As against Eaton, the extent of Brown's lien was limited by the amount he was entitled to recover upon the demand for the recovery of which his action was brought. If the declaration in his writ was not sufficient in form or substance to include such demand or if the writ itself was defective in some amendable particular he might amend without prejudicing his rights, but Brown could not enlarge his action by an amendment including other demands and take judgment upon them without sacrificing the superiority of his right under his prior attachment. The law would regard such an amendment as a fraud upon the subsequent attaching creditor and consequently if made would treat the attachment in the prior action as void as against such creditor. (72 N.H. at 188, 55 A. at 357.)

248 RSA 511-A:4.

249 Page v. Jewett, 46 N.H. 441, 445 (1866); RSA 514:9.

250 Brown v. Ellsworth, 72 N.H. 186, 188, 55 A. 356, 357 (1903).

§ 17.33. —Dissolution of Attachments

(a) *Events That Automatically Dissolve Attachments.* Attachments of both real and personal property are automatically dissolved without further order of the court upon the occurrence of any of the following events:

(1) Entry of a final decree that the defendant's estate shall be administered in the insolvent course, if the defendant dies before judgment has been rendered.[251]

(2) Death of the defendant before judgment, if the cause of action in aid of which the attachment was made does not survive the defendant's death.[252]

(3) Entry of final judgment for the defendant.[253]

(4) Settlement of the action by agreement of the parties.[254]

(b) *Dissolution by Court Order for Fraud or Improper Acts.* An attachment which is otherwise good may be dissolved by order of the court upon a finding that either the plaintiff or the sheriff has acted fraudulently or improperly in obtaining it. To some extent, abuses of this sort have been eliminated by the new procedures requiring court approval before any attachment can be obtained.[255] But it is still possible for an attachment to be obtained for fraudulent purposes or through deceitful means. Any fraud in the means by which an attachment is obtained will make the attachment void, and when judgment is taken for the plaintiff "in a way and with intent to defraud, injure or delay other creditors of the debtor"[256] or subject to any secret trust for the benefit of the debtor, the attachment which secures that judgment may be dissolved if the fraud is shown to the court.[257] Similarly, if the sheriff has obtained property, against which an attachment is to be

---

251 RSA 511:46; Blaisdell v. Harris, 52 N.H. 191 (1872); Waitt v. Thompson, 43 N.H. 161 (1861). The attachment will be reinstated as of the date of the original attachment, however, if the defendant's administrator continues to defend. Lyford v. Dunn, 32 N.H. 81 (1855).

252 *Id.*

253 RSA 511:45.

254 *Id.*

255 See, e.g., Buswell v. Davis, 10 N.H. 413 (1839) (where a creditor who knew that his debtor planned to discharge one mortgage to substitute another obtained an attachment after the discharge but before the new mortgage was filed).

256 Page v. Jewett, 46 N.H. 441, 446 (1866).

257 *Id.*

made, by improper or fraudulent means, the attachment will be dissolved on grounds of public policy.[258]

The validity of an attachment obtained by fraud or improper acts may be challenged by the defendant in a Motion to Vacate the Attachment or by subsequently attaching creditors intervening in the action for the purpose of contesting the validity of the attachment.[259]

(c) *Dissolution by Court Order for Noncompliance with RSA ch. 511-A.* Any claimant of property that is subject to a purported attachment may petition the superior court to declare that the property is unencumbered and to vacate the purported attachment on the ground of noncompliance with RSA ch. 511-A.[260] The court's order vacating the purported attachment may apply to all property sought to be attached, even though the claimants to all such property are not before the court.[261]

(d) *Erroneous or Fraudulent Judgment for the Defendant.* An attachment is not dissolved by the entry of a judgment for the defendant which is obtained by fraud or is based on an error of law or abuse of discretion.[262]

(e) *Recording Notice of the Dissolution.* Although the attachment is dissolved as a matter of law upon the occurrence of the events set forth above and can no longer be enforced by the plaintiff, it will remain a record encumbrance on the defendant's title until a discharge has been recorded in all places where the attachment was recorded. Defendant is entitled to obtain a discharge from the plaintiff within thirty days of the dissolution and may record it in all places where the attachment was filed.[263]

Library References

CJS Attachment §§ 217, 336 et seq.

Appealability, prior to final judgment, of order discharging or vacating attachment or refusing to do so. 19 ALR2d 640.

Cross References

Death of a party while action is pending, see § 6.40 *supra.*

---

258 Closson v. Morrison, 47 N.H. 482 (1867).

259 Webster v. Harper, 7 N.H. 594 (1835).

260 Topjian Plumbing and Heating, Inc. v. Bruce Topjian, Inc., 129 N.H. 481, 529 A.2d 391 (1987).

261 Topjian Plumbing & Heating, Inc. v. Bruce Topjian, Inc., 129 N.H. 481, 529 A.2d 391 (1987).

262 Gunnison v. Abbott, 73 N.H. 590, 64 A. 23 (1906).

263 RSA 511:8.

§ 17.34. —Expiration of Attachments

(a) *In General.* Attachments are liens that continue for a fixed time without further action by the plaintiff, but they expire without further action by the defendant at the end of that time, and the lien is then lost unless the plaintiff has previously levied execution.[264]

(b) *Real Estate Attachments.* From the earliest date until 1963,[265] New Hampshire law provided for the expiration of both real estate and personal property attachments at the conclusion of the same period of time following the entry of a judgment on which the plaintiff could take execution.[266] Until 1961, that period was thirty days; from 1961 to 1963, it was sixty days.[267] In 1963, the Legislature amended the statute to provide that real estate attachments would expire at the end of six years, rather than sixty days, after the entry of judgment. But title examiners later pointed out that there was no provision for the expiration of attachments obtained in cases which were "continued for judgment"[268] and were therefore not subject to the provisions of RSA 511:55. In 1975, the Legislature remedied this problem by amending the statute further to provide that a real estate attachment shall expire at the end of ten years from the "date of filing" unless judgment has first obtained

---

[264] Manchester Federal Savings & Loan Association v. Emery-Waterhouse Company, 102 N.H. 233, 153 A.2d 918 (1959).

[265] See Laws of New Hampshire (1805), p. 89; Revised Statutes (1843), 184:33 (p. 371); Compiled Statutes (1854), 195:35 (p. 473); General Statutes (1867), 205:36 (p. 419); General Laws (1878), 224:36 (p. 522); Public Statutes (1900), 220:40 (pp. 706–07); Public Laws (1926), 332:53 (pp. 1341–42); Revised Laws (1942), 388:53 (p. 1651); Revised Statutes Annotated (1955), 511:55.

[266] This may not be the same date as the date of a final judgment. RSA 511:55 and its predecessors provided that an attachment would expire at the end of 30 days "from the time of rendering a judgment in the action in favor of the plaintiff on which he can take execution." For the purposes of these statutes, "the time of rendering a judgment" must generally be regarded as the effective date of the judgment rather than the date on which the court made the order on which the judgment is based. See, e.g., RSA 511:58, which also refers to rendering a judgment and seems to refer to the effective date of that judgment. See also Hackett v. Pickering, 5 N.H. 19 (1829) (where the Court held that a default without judgment preserved the attachment); Nihan v. Knight, 56 N.H. 167 (1875).

[267] In that year, the Legislature doubled the period at the recommendation of the Judicial Council "to protect a judgment creditor against loss of his real estate lien in the event he had inadvertently failed to take out execution within 30 days of judgment." New Hampshire Judicial Council, 8th Report (1960), p. 18; Laws of 1961, ch. 100:3.

[268] See David D. Prugh, *Risks in Title Examinations*, 8 N.H.B.J. 150, 160 (1966). Mr. Prugh suggested a 10- or 15-year maximum on the continuation of any attachment on real estate.

in the action.[269] Use of the date of filing, rather than the date of recording, assures that the date entered in the index may be relied upon without the need to inquire into the procedures by which the index was updated. The statute applies to all attachments, whether filed before or after the effective date of the amendment.[270]

Thus, real estate attachments expire by force of law at the expiration of six years from the entry of judgment or at the expiration of ten years from the date of filing the attachment in the Registry of Deeds if the case has not gone to judgment within that time. The maximum theoretical duration of an attachment is therefore one day less than sixteen years from the date of filing the attachment in the Registry.[271]

(c) *Personal Property Attachments.* Attachments of personal property expire at the end of sixty days from the entry of a judgment on which the plaintiff can take execution.[272] There is no provision for the expiration of an attachment on personal property in cases which have not gone to judgment, but, in light of the record nature of those attachments,[273] there should be.

(d) *Special Rules for a Judgment Nunc Pro Tunc.* RSA 511:58 provides that the starting date for measuring the expiration of an attachment when a judgment is granted nunc pro tunc is the date on which the court makes its order. Unfortunately, the 1963 Legislature appears to have forgotten to amend RSA 511:58 when it was extending the duration of real estate attachments. RSA 511:55 and 58, taken literally, seem to require that real estate attachments expire sixty days after the entry of a judgment nunc pro tunc even if that sixty-day period expires before the end of six years from the nunc pro tunc judgment date. RSA 511:58 also appears to allow an otherwise expired attachment to be revived for sixty days by the entry of a

---

269 Laws of 1975, ch. 105:1 (now RSA 511:55 (II)). See 1975 Senate Journal 270, where Senator Fennelly reported for the Judiciary Committee that the bill "says that if no action on a lien on a property has been taken within six years, this bill would automatically take the lien off."

270 The effect of the statute is only to fix a termination date for rights which had previously been inchoate and uncertain. The statute thus has no retrospective effect (see part 1, article 23) and probably fixes the expiration at a date later than any court would grant judgment on a continuance anyway. See, e.g., Super. Ct. R. 168 (nonjury cases dismissed before trial when three years have expired without any action).

271 If the case goes to judgment on the last day before the expiration of ten years from filing, it will continue for six more years.

272 See note 266, *supra.*

273 RSA 511-A:5.

nunc pro tunc judgment.[274] While it is reasonable to provide a plaintiff with a minimum period of time in which to levy after he knows that he has a judgment on which he can obtain execution, and it may even be reasonable in some cases to revive attachments in order to allow the plaintiff time to take execution, it makes no sense to cut off a plaintiff's six-year period of lien protection simply because he has obtained a judgment nunc pro tunc. RSA 511:58 is a trap for the unwary and bears close attention whenever a judgment is obtained nunc pro tunc.

Library References

CJS Attachment § 208

§ 17.35. Excessive Attachments

In 1953, the Legislature enacted RSA 511:53 and thereby, for the first time, provided a statutory remedy for "excessive or unreasonable attachments."[275] The need for this statute has been greatly reduced by the requirements for court approval of the amount of an attachment before it is obtained and for an automatic right to a hearing upon the defendant's objection.[276]

A petition to reduce or discharge an excessive or unreasonable attachment must be filed in the superior court, regardless of which court granted the attachment, and has the effect of requiring the plaintiff to show that the attachment is not excessive or unreasonable. Interestingly, the statute also provides that the court's conclusion as to whether the attachment was unreasonable or excessive may not be introduced in evidence "for any purpose at any other stage in the proceedings." This suggests a legislative desire to protect overreaching plaintiffs from being prejudiced by their zeal and probably provides an appropriate method of treating ex parte petitions which are denied as well.

---

[274] The statute provides that upon the entry of a nunc pro tunc judgment "property attached shall be holden until the expiration of sixty days." Whether the statute is meant to apply only to attachments still in force or to any attachment in effect on either the date of the nunc pro tunc judgment or the date when the nunc pro tunc judgment is granted is unclear. There is enough ambiguity in the statute to allow the court to give either effect to its order consistent with constitutional guarantees of due process.

[275] Prior to the enactment of RSA 511:53, the defendant's only remedy for excessive attachment was an action against the officer based on malice. There was no provision for reducing the attachment. No statute or case has defined the term "unreasonable attachment," and, although it is generally assumed that the statute refers only to the size of attachments, there is no reason to think that the statute could not also be used to remedy attachments that were obtained by an unreasonable procedure.

[276] RSA 511-A:3 and 8.

Library References

CJS Attachment § 340
Liability of creditor for excessive attachment or garnishment. 56 ALR3d 493.

§ 17.36. Misuse of the Procedures or Forms

RSA ch. 511-A is intended to provide defendants with as much protection as possible against unnecessary or harassing use of attachments. To this end the statute requires court approval of every attachment and provides the defendant with notice and hearing before attachment in all but exceptional cases.[277]

Only two cases have been decided involving intentional misuse of the procedures or forms employed under RSA ch. 511-A. In the first of these, *Jerry's Sports Center, Inc. v. Novick*,[278] the plaintiff's attorney sent the Petition to Attach With Notice and the Writ of Summons to the Registry of Deeds *before* he filed either in court, along with a request that the Register file the document as a lis pendens against the transfer of the defendant's real estate. The Register recorded the notice and writ. When the defendant learned of this procedure, he filed a motion to declare the notice of lis pendens null and void. After a hearing, the superior court found that the procedure violated RSA ch. 511-A, that the plaintiff's attorney intended to encumber the defendant's title when he filed the notice and writ and that the use of a superior court petition form and writ gave substance to his attempt.

---

277 Compare Topjian Plumbing and Heating, Inc. v. Bruce Topjian, Inc., 129 N.H. 481, 529 A.2d 391 (1987), where the plaintiff, relying on RSA 511-A:8(III), recorded a writ of attachment in the Registry without prior judicial approval and served a copy on the record owners of the property. The plaintiff had already commenced an action at law against one of the title holders to recover money due for labor and materials and his purpose in recording the writ was to perfect a materialman's and a mechanic's lien. It is not clear from the opinion whether the writ was marked "lis pendens." The trial court discharged the purported attachments on the owners' application, on the ground that no prior judicial approval had been obtained before the writs were filed. The Supreme Court upheld the trial court, holding that RSA 511-A:8(III) only authorizes a materialman's or mechanic's lien claimant to record a writ of attachment marked "lis pendens" for the purpose of giving notice of an underlying action which may affect the property and does not allow a claimant to encumber the property or obtain the benefits of an attachment without first applying to a court and receiving an order authorizing an attachment.

Although the facts of the case are similar to the facts of *Jerry's Sports Center, Inc. v. Novick, supra*, there was at least a preexisting contract action, which had given the title holder notice of the claim, some support for the plaintiff's actions in the statute, and no indication that plaintiff intended to overreach. These differences may account for the failure of the court to consider or assess sanctions against the plaintiff or his attorney.

278 120 N.H. at 373, 415 A.2d at 331 (1980).

The court ordered that the recordings be expunged and that the plaintiff's attorney pay $300 as the defendant's costs and expenses. The Supreme Court affirmed.

In the second case, the plaintiff's attorney was less creative in his use of forms but more imaginative in his conception of the case. In *P.J. Currier Lumber Company, Inc. v. Stonemill Construction Corporation*,[279] the plaintiff's attorney filed petitions for ex parte attachments on three lots with houses which the defendant had once owned but recently sold. The plaintiff's attorney did not tell the court when he sought the attachments that the lots were no longer owned by the defendant. The court granted the attachments, and the plaintiff's attorney perfected them by recording. After recording the attachments, the plaintiff's attorney mailed copies of the writs of attachment to the owners of the lots. This led one of the owners to petition to intervene and to file a motion that the attachments be declared null and void. After a hearing, the district court clarified the original attachment by saying that it was meant to apply only to property then owned by the named defendant. The plaintiff appealed to the Supreme Court, which again had no difficulty, holding that the plaintiff's attorney had violated RSA ch. 511-A, that the present owner of real estate is a necessary party to any proceedings in which a lien is claimed on that property, and that the owner was entitled to the notice required by RSA 511-A:2 when an ex parte attachment had been obtained on his property.

Library References

CJS Attachment §§ 394 et seq.
Recovery of value of use of property wrongfully attached. 45 ALR2d 1221.
Posting of redelivery bond by defendant in attachment as waiver of damages for wrongful attachment. 57 ALR2d 1376.
Right to recover attorneys' fees for wrongful attachment. 65 ALR2d 1426.
What constitutes malice sufficient to justify an award of punitive damages in action for wrongful attachment or garnishment. 61 ALR3d 984.
Recovery of damages for mental anguish, distress, suffering, or the like, in action for wrongful attachment, garnishment, sequestration, or execution. 83 ALR3d 598.

B. Trustee Process

Cross References

Default, see § 33.11 *infra*.

---

[279] 120 N.H. at 400, 415 A.2d at 869 (1980).

§ 17.37. Introduction

Trustee process is a form of attachment[280] by which the defendant's right to receive money or property from a third party may be held as security for the plaintiff's judgment. Trustee process is sometimes called "foreign attachment" in the older cases and "garnishment" in other jurisdictions. Trustee process may only be used in personal actions.[281]

It has been said that trustee process, like attachment, was unknown at common law and is entirely a creation of statute.[282] However, there is some evidence that, although long regulated by statute, the procedure was used in the seventeenth century without statutory authority.[283] It is said, however, that its "scope and effect do not extend beyond the express provisions which the statutes contain."[284] Unlike attachments, trustee process substitutes for a right to seize and hold property, a right to hold the trustee personally liable for the value of the property or funds in his hands.[285] In *Philbrick v. Philbrick*,[286] Justice Doe wrote for the Court:

> [T]he trustee statute merely provides how a debtor's property may be attached and appropriated towards the payment of his debts in cases where, the property being in the possession of third persons, it would be inconvenient, difficult or impossible to reach it by an ordinary attachment or levy or execution. The statute does not in the least impair the obligation of the trustee to pay his debt, it only directs to whom he shall pay it . . . .[287]

Nearly seventy-five years later, Justice Allen noted another function. "Trustee process," he wrote, "reaches property not subject to ordinary attachment and levy . . . ."[288] Thus, trustee process is a supplement to attach-

---

280 RSA 511-A:1. "The substantial difference between attachment by direct seizure and by trustee process is that the validity of the attachment in the latter case does not depend upon the officer's taking or retaining possession of property, and creates no specific lien upon the defendant's property in favor of the plaintiff." Corning v. Records, 69 N.H. 390, 398, 46 A. 462, 466 (1898).

281 RSA 512:1.

282 Kibling v. Burley, 20 N.H. 359 (1850); Chadbourn v. Gilman, 63 N.H. 353 (1885). It does, however, date from colonial times.

283 See Walsh v. Boulanger, 107 N.H. 458, 225 A.2d 185 (1966).

284 Kibling v. Burley, 20 N.H. 359 (1850).

285 RSA 512:20; Corning v. Records, 69 N.H. 390, 46 A. 462 (1898).

286 39 N.H. 468 (1859).

287 39 N.H. at 474.

288 Dupont v. Moore, 86 N.H. 254, 261, 166 A. 417 (1933).

ment and allows a plaintiff to secure his judgment with property which the defendant has yet to receive.

Trustee process is also "an equitable proceeding in which the rights of the parties are determined on equitable principles."[289]

Trustee process is both a "joint process" against the principal defendant[290] to assess his liability to the plaintiff[291] and against the trustee to determine his liability to the principal defendant. "The two actions raise different questions, on different pleas, determined by different judgments between different parties."[292] As a result, use of trustee process can complicate and prolong litigation.

Library References

CJS Garnishment §§ 1, 2

§ 17.38. Persons Who May Be Summoned as Trustees—Generally

In general, any person who holds property or money under a present obligation to deliver or pay it to the principal defendant may be summoned by trustee process. In addition, persons who have contingent obligations to pay or deliver to the principal defendant may be summoned in trustee process if it is likely that their obligations will become fixed during the course of the litigation. However, a person may not be subjected to trustee process after assets or obligations have been delivered or paid to the principal defendant or for his account. The obligation to deliver or pay need not be a contractual one if it is recognized in law.[293]

Library References

CJS Garnishment §§ 25–31

---

289 Corning v. Records, 69 N.H. 390, 396, 46 A. 462, 465 (1898).

290 In trustee process, the trustee is named as a defendant on the writ of summons although only in his role as a trustee. To avoid confusion, therefore, the person against whom the plaintiff asserts his claim is referred to as "the principal defendant."

291 Jones v. Roberts, 60 N.H. 216 (1880); Ingraham v. Olcock, 14 N.H. 243 (1843).

292 60 N.H. at 218.

293 Canning v. Knights, 71 N.H. 404, 52 A. 443 (1902) (trustee had taken the principal defendant's money for safekeeping while the principal defendant was drunk).

§ 17.39. —Partnerships, Executors, Administrators, and Trustees Under Trusts

A partnership may be charged as a trustee only if the general partners are summoned in their capacities as partners of that partnership.[294] Executors, administrators,[295] and trustees under a trust should also be summoned in the roles in which they are to be charged. However, a plaintiff cannot summon himself even though he does so by naming himself only in a special capacity.[296]

Library References

CJS Garnishment §§ 52, 76
CJS Partnership § 216

§ 17.40. —Persons Jointly and Severally Liable

A person who is jointly liable with another to the principal defendant will not be held liable on trustee process unless his joint obligor is also summoned[297] and the Petition to Attach with Notice or Petition for Ex Parte Attachment states that their liability to the principal defendant is joint.[298] If the trustees are not declared against as being jointly liable, their liability will be determined as if each were summoned singly.[299] However, the plaintiff may move to amend his Petition to Attach with Notice or Petition for Ex

---

294 Keenan v. Perrault, 72 N.H. 426, 57 A. 335 (1904); RSA 512:7. A person who is summoned without any designation of capacity but who is also a general partner in a partnership will not be charged as a partner even though he discloses a debt due to the principal defendant from the partnership. Atkins v. Prescott, 10 N.H. 120 (1839). The partnership may be charged as trustee even though only one partner has been served (Shelters v. Boudreau, 66 N.H. 576, 32 A. 151 (1891); Atkins v. Prescott, 10 N.H. 120 (1839)), but one partner may not be charged as a trustee by another partner prior to winding up the partnership's affairs. Treadwell v. Brown, 41 N.H. 12 (1860).

295 See Palmer v. Noyes, 45 N.H. 174 (1864).

296 Hoag v. Hoag, 55 N.H. 172 (1875) (plaintiff attempted to bring trustee process against himself as administrator of another's estate).

297 Rix v. Elliot, 1 N.H. 184 (1818); Hudson v. Fisk, 5 N.H. 538 (1831) ("It is also settled as a general rule, that one of two joint debtors cannot be charged as a trustee, unless the other debtor is joined with him in the process." 5 N.H. at 539). See Fullerton v. Hayes, 32 N.H. 212 (1855). See also Barker v. Garland, 22 N.H. 103 (1850). Although doubt has been expressed on this point by Justice Sawyer, it seems to be the only reasonable way of proceeding.

298 Ingraham v. Olcock, 14 N.H. 243 (1843).

299 Sleeper v. Weymouth, 26 N.H. 34 (1852). Where the property is a promissory note, the claimant must show that it "was transferred to him in good faith and for a valuable consideration, before the service of the writ upon the trustee. . . ."

Parte Attachment to claim a joint liability if necessary after receiving the trustees' disclosures.[300]

Library References

CJS Garnishment §§ 73, 74

§ 17.41. —Persons Outside New Hampshire

Residents who are temporarily out of state may be summoned by abode service. Nonresidents may be summoned as trustees only if they do business in New Hampshire and only for "money, goods or chattels . . . in this state" or any "rights or credits of the defendant by reason of contracts made or performed within this state."[301] Foreign corporations and companies which "have a place of business or do business within this state" may be subjected to trustee process.[302] Nonresident natural persons may be summoned as trustees either by personal service in state or by service upon a "clerk or agent having charge of [his] business [in New Hampshire]."[303] Foreign partnerships, associations, and corporations may be summoned as trustees in the same way that other service may be made upon them.

Library References

CJS Garnishment § 36

Partnership residence for purpose of statutes authorizing garnishment on ground of nonresidence. 9 ALR2d 471.

Foreign attachment or garnishment as available in action by nonresident against nonresident or foreign corporation upon a foreign cause of action. 14 ALR2d 420.

---

300 Fullerton v. Hayes, 32 N.H. 212 (1855).

301 RSA 512:5. It is important to remember that the standard for summoning a nonresident trustee is not the same as the standard for compelling a nonresident defendant to defend an action begun in this state by trustee process. In the latter situation, New Hampshire will assert jurisdiction over the plaintiff's claim against the defendant only if "the exercise of jurisdiction is reasonable in light of New Hampshire's interest in the litigation" and if "the defendant has sufficient minimum contacts with New Hampshire so that, in the circumstances, the exercise of jurisdiction is consistent with the principles of fair play and substantial justice." Pono v. Brock, 119 N.H. 814, 816, 408 A.2d 419, 420 (1979). The standard for summoning a nonresident as a trustee is also much narrower than the standard for requiring him to defend a cause of action in the New Hampshire courts. A person may be summoned as a trustee in an action between two other persons only if he does business in New Hampshire and then only for property located or contracts made or performable in state. RSA 512:5. But he may be required to respond as a principal defendant if he transacts any business in the state, commits a tort, or owns, uses, or possesses any property in the state. RSA 510:4(I). The distinction arises from the more pressing need to hold nonresidents responsible for their own acts than for the acts of others. When the trustee is a nonresident, the additional requirements of RSA 512:5 must be met. Even when the requirements of Pono and RSA 512:5 have been satisfied, the case may be dismissed under the doctrine of forum non conveniens.

302 RSA 293-A:112.

303 RSA 512:5.

§ 17.42. —Persons Under an Obligation To Account

Persons who are or may soon be under legal obligations to account to the principal defendant may be summoned on trustee process. Thus, an executor, administrator, guardian, or trustee may be summoned as trustee of an heir, legatee, devisee, ward, or trust beneficiary if he is or will shortly be obligated to make a payment or delivery to the heir, legatee, devisee, or beneficiary[304] or if he has entered into a settlement whereby the principal defendant has agreed to make payments to the heirs.[305] And a receiver appointed by the court to wind up a business may be summoned in trustee process for the amount due the principal defendant at the conclusion of his service.[306] Where the executor, administrator, trustee, or receiver is summoned before it is clear what he will be required to pay or deliver to the heir, legatee, devisee, or beneficiary, the action may be continued for a reasonable time until it has been determined.[307]

Library References

CJS Garnishment §§ 49, 52, 53
Garnishment against executor or administrator by creditor of estate. 60 ALR3d 1301.

§ 17.43. —Persons With No Foreseeable Obligation To Pay

A person who has no present or foreseeable obligation to pay or deliver to the principal defendant may not be summoned by trustee process. Thus, the administration of an estate or proceedings for dissolution of a corporation "cannot be embarrassed by . . . trustee process."[308]

A fiduciary who has discretion to decide whether to pay anything to the defendant cannot be summoned on trustee process,[309] unless he has already exercised the discretion but has not completed payment and he either has no discretion to reverse his decision or the case arises under circumstances which make it equitable to compel him to complete the payment. And a partner cannot be summoned in trustee process in an action against his copartner unless there is a liquidated sum due in his copartner's hands.[310]

---

304 See, e.g., Palmer v. Noyes, 45 N.H. 174 (1864); Protective Check Writer Co. v. Collins, 92 N.H. 27, 23 A.2d 770 (1942).

305 Protective Check Writer Co. v. Collins, 92 N.H. 27, 23 A.2d 770 (1942).

306 Willard v. Decatur, 59 N.H. 137 (1879).

307 Palmer v. Noyes, 45 N.H. 174 (1864).

308 Willard v. Decatur, 59 N.H. 137 (1879).

309 Banfield v. Wiggin, 58 N.H. 155 (1877); Brahmey v. Rollins, 87 N.H. 290, 179 A. 186 (1935).

310 Treadwell v. Brown, 41 N.H. 12 (1860).

§ 17.44. —The State

Trustee process, like all other legal compulsions, is barred against the state by the doctrine of sovereign immunity. As a result, trustee process lies against officers and agencies of the state only to the extent authorized by statute.[311] Pursuant to RSA 512:9, the State Treasurer may be summoned as trustee of the salaries and wages of state employees and officials,[312] including members of the Legislature,[313] for work done before service of the writ for which he still retains custody of the check.[314] But no other state official may be so summoned for state funds in his possession.[315] Nearly thirty years ago, the Supreme Court held that the state could not be summoned as a trustee of funds in its possession belonging to the principal defendant even though it held those funds under a contract which allowed the state to withhold payment of the funds pending settlement of claims by third parties.[316] This holding, that the state cannot be trusteed even for funds which it holds for the benefit of third parties, is unaffected by the enactment of RSA ch. 541-B, establishing the Board of Claims.

Library References

CJS Garnishment § 43

§ 17.45. —Units of Local Government

RSA 512:9-a authorizes trustee process to reach wages of county, city, town, and school district officers and employees, designates the treasurer of each unit as the appropriate trustee, and limits the amount to be charged to the amount of any check still in his hands.

§ 17.46. —Attorneys and Sheriffs

An attorney may be summoned in trustee process for money he has collected for his client in the course of his professional work,[317] unless those funds are exempt.[318] Attorneys are not regarded as "employees" within the exemption created by RSA 512:21. And a sheriff or other collecting officer

---

311 Moore v. Dailey, 97 N.H. 278, 86 A.2d 342 (1952); Ladd v. Gale, 57 N.H. 210 (1876).
312 RSA 512:9. See Opinion of the Justices, 103 N.H. 381, 173 A.2d 578 (1961).
313 Klinger v. Cartier, 96 N.H. 180, 71 A.2d 786 (1950).
314 RSA 512:9.
315 Ladd v. Gale, 57 N.H. 210 (1876).
316 Moore v. Dailey, 97 N.H. 278, 86 A.2d 342 (1952).
317 Narramore v. Clark, 63 N.H. 166 (1884).
318 Gagnon v. Marcoux, 85 N.H. 237, 157 A. 82 (1931).

may be summoned for money collected on execution and due to the principal defendant.[319]

Library References

CJS Garnishment §§ 47, 51
Client's funds in hands of his attorney as subject of attachment or garnishment by client's creditors. 35 ALR3d 1094.

§ 17.47. —Banks

When a bank is the trustee, service may be made, at any time or place, on an officer or, during "banking hours," at the bank on any "person in charge, teller or office employee." The bank may not be charged as trustee for any funds or property coming into its hands after service of the trustee writ.[320]

Library References

CJS Garnishment § 62
Attachment and garnishment of funds in branch bank or main office of bank having branches. 12 ALR3d 1088.
Joint bank account as subject to attachment, garnishment, or execution by creditor of one of the joint depositors. 11 ALR3d 1465.

§ 17.48. Assets Which May Be the Object of Trustee Process— Generally

Any "money, goods, chattels, rights or credits[321] of the defendant, not exempted from trustee process"[322] that the trustee has in his possession at the time of service of the writ of attachment may be subject to trustee process. Claims that are contingent or unliquidated at the time of service and remain so at the time of a hearing on chargeability may not be reached

---

319 Willard v. Decatur, 59 N.H. 137 (1879).

320 RSA 512:9-b.

321 The term "credit" includes all manner of indebtedness from the trustee to the principal defendant, regardless of how it arose or in what form it was held. Isabelle v. LeBlanc, 68 N.H. 409, 39 A. 436 (1895). See Hall, Morse, Gallagher & Anderson v. Koch & Koch, 119 N.H. 639, 406 A.2d 962 (1979). The Supreme Court has held that when the DRA enforces a tax assessment, the State, like any other judgment creditor, must use the trustee process to reach the taxpayer's bank accounts through RSA 512:9-b, and not through distraint. Pappalardo v. Bank of Boston, No. 89-273 at 7 (1991); DeLellis v. Burke, 134 N.H. 607 (1991) ("Trustee process is a statutory procedure by which a judgment creditor, in order to satisfy a debt owed him by a debtor, may attach either property owned by the debtor that is presently held by a third party, or the debtor's right to receive property from a third party.").

322 RSA 512:20. Stock certificates may be the subject of trustee process. Dupont v. Moore, 86 N.H. 254, 166 A. 417 (1933).

by trustee process.[323] Claims that become fixed and liquidated by the time of the hearing on chargeability may.[324]

However, money in custodia legis by virtue of being in the hands of an officer of the court pending the outcome of litigation or subject to court order is exempt from attachment. This rule "is based on the policy of avoiding conflicting orders from different courts and . . . practical inconvenience to courts and . . . officers."[325] The rule will not be applied if the funds are only being held awaiting disbursement to the principal defendant,[326] if the funds are only being held by the court to assure their application to the principal defendant's debts[327] or if the equities otherwise require.[328]

Library References

CJS Garnishment §§ 69 et seq.

Retirement or pension proceeds or annuity payments under group insurance as subject to attachment or garnishment. 28 ALR2d 1213.

Garnishment of salary, wages, or commissions where defendant debtor is indebted to garnishee-employer. 93 ALR2d 995.

Funds deposited in court as subject of garnishment. 1 ALR3d 936.

Liability insurer's potential liability for failure to settle claim against insured as subject to garnishment by insured's judgment creditors. 60 ALR3d 1190.

Cross References

Property rights exempt from trustee process, see § 17.07 *supra*.

§ 17.49. —Property Paid or Delivered by the Trustee After Service

When trustee process is attempted with notice, pursuant to RSA 511-A:2, although the plaintiff is required to give the trustee notice of his intention to attach,[329] no provision of RSA ch. 511-A prohibits the trustee from conveying the property in his hands to the principal defendant before the

---

323 McKean v. Turner, 45 N.H. 203 (1864); Bucklin v. Powell, 60 N.H. 119 (1880); Paul v. Paul, 10 N.H. 117 (1839); Foster v. Dudley, 30 N.H. 463 (1855); Getchell v. Chase, 37 N.H. 106 (1858); Rand v. White Mountains Railroad, 40 N.H. 79 (1860).

324 Gove v. Varrell, 58 N.H. 78 (1877); Protective Check Writer Co. v. Collins, 92 N.H. 27, 23 A.2d 770 (1942).

325 Walsh v. Boulanger, 107 N.H. 458, 460, 225 A.2d 185, 187 (1966).

326 *Id.*

327 Cnaeps v. Brown, 101 N.H. 116, 135 A.2d 721 (1957).

328 Walsh v. Boulanger, 107 N.H. 458, 225 A.2d 185 (1966).

329 Rules and Procedures to Implement the Attachment Law (RSA ch. 511-A), "Petition to Attach With Notice." The caption will set forth the trustee's name, and the petition will identify the attachment to be made of the property in his hands.

attachment is granted or the writ of attachment is served.[330] In theory, this omission encourages consolidation of the principal defendant's assets in his hands, but it also has a tendency to produce uncollectible judgments. A trustee who has no defense to payment or delivery to the principal defendant can avoid any further involvement in the case by making that payment or delivery immediately upon receiving notice of the petition to attach and by informing the plaintiff that the payment or delivery has been made.

Library References

CJS Garnishment §§ 95, 96

§ 17.50. —Property Actually in the Trustee's Hands or Due Him

Only property or funds actually in the trustee's possession or due from him at the time of service or thereafter[331] may be attached by trustee process. The trustee is under no obligation to exercise any right he may have to compel conveyance or delivery from a fourth party or to expedite a determination of liability to the defendant and thereby to increase the amount of the principal defendant's property in his possession.[332] By the same token, he may not defeat the trustee process by disclaiming or assigning his interest before collection.[333]

§ 17.51. —Property Held as the Principal Defendant's Debtor

Only property or funds held by the trustee as the principal defendant's debtor can be trusteed.[334] As a result, an exchange of cash or a check for goods presently delivered cannot be interrupted by summoning the payor on trustee process.[335] If the principal defendant makes a profit on the sale,

---

330 RSA 511-A:6 only prohibits the principal defendant from disposing of his assets without fair consideration.

331 Steer v. Dow, 75 N.H. 95, 71 A. 217 (1908); Brown v. Silsby, 10 N.H. 521 (1840); Edgerly v. Sanborn, 6 N.H. 397 (1833); Smith v. Boston, Concord & Montreal Railroad, 33 N.H. 337 (1856).

332 McKean v. Turner, 45 N.H. 203 (1864); Bucklin v. Powell, 60 N.H. 119 (1880).

333 National Revere Bank v. Bay State Shoe Fastening Company, 67 N.H. 371, 40 A. 255 (1892); Fisk v. Aldrich, 59 N.H. 113 (1879).

334 A.E. Nelson & Co. v. Haggett's Sport Shop, Inc., 120 N.H. 515, 418 A.2d 1273 (1980).

335 Paul v. Reed, 52 N.H. 136 (1872) (sale of goods which were from attachment was interrupted by service of trustee process on the buyer); National Revere Bank v. Bay State Shoe Fastening Company, 67 N.H. 371, 40 A. 255 (1892) (buyer who is under an obligation to pay upon delivery, with delivery to be made within 30 days and a deposit to be taken at the time of sale and held until delivery, cannot be trusteed at the time of sale or later).

that profit must be attached in his hands. And a person may not be trusteed for payments which the principal defendant has made in advance, at least when the payee cannot, under any set of circumstances, become obligated to refund those payments.[336]

Library References

CJS Garnishment § 71

§ 17.52. —Exemptions

Certain types of property and funds in certain locations are exempt from trustee process and cannot be attached. A number of statutory exemptions are set forth in RSA 512:21 and listed in Section 17.07, *supra*. A policy and the proceeds of life or endowment insurance also cannot be trusteed as the assets of the principal defendant if the beneficiary has an insurable interest in the life being insured, except to the extent of any premiums (and interest on those premiums) paid by the principal debtor in fraud of creditors.[337] And no "money or other benefit, charity or relief or aid to be paid, provided or rendered" by any fraternal benefit society as defined in RSA 418:1 may be subjected to trustee process.[338] This exemption covers policies of life insurance issued by such societies to their members.[339] An adjusted claim under a fire or casualty insurance policy may be trusteed,[340] but an unadjusted one may not.[341]

A judgment debt can be trusteed.[342]

Library References

CJS Exemptions § 123

Family allowance from decedent's estate as exempt from attachment, garnishment, execution, and foreclosure. 27 ALR3d 863.

Employee retirement pension benefits as exempt from garnishment, attachment, levy, execution, or similar proceedings. 93 ALR3d 711.

---

336 Cowdry v. Walker, 59 N.H. 533 (1880).

337 RSA 408:22.

338 RSA 418:24.

339 Gagnon v. Marcoux, 85 N.H. 237, 157 A. 82 (1931).

340 Swamscot Machine Co. v. Partridge, 25 N.H. 369 (1852). The payment due may be offset by amounts due the insurance company.

341 Bucklin v. Powell, 60 N.H. 119 (1880).

342 Isabelle v. LeBlanc, 68 N.H. 409, 39 A. 436 (1895).

§ 17.53. Limitations on Claims Which May Be Asserted by Trustee Process

Just as a plaintiff can, in general, obtain by attachment no greater rights in the property attached than the defendant possessed, so he cannot by trustee process assert any claim which the defendant himself could not assert against the trustee. Conversely, the plaintiff cannot, by trustee process, authorize a third party to perform an act which that third party could not otherwise perform. A bank, for example, cannot be summoned as a trustee of the contents of a safe deposit box since it has no right in the absence of trustee process to withhold or deliver the contents thereof.[343]

Library References

CJS Garnishment § 99

§ 17.54. Procedure for Obtaining Trustee Process—In General

The procedure by which trustee process is obtained is similar to the procedure for obtaining any other attachment under RSA ch. 511-A.[344]

Library References

CJS Garnishment §§ 191 et seq.

§ 17.55. —Preparation of the Petition To Attach and Writ of Attachment

(a) *In General.* The caption of the Petition to Attach and Writ of Attachment[345] must list the name of the trustee as a defendant, state that he issued in his capacity as a trustee, and identify the source and nature of his

---

343 Dupont v. Moore, 86 N.H. 254, 166 A. 417 (1933).

344 See RSA 511-A:1 and Rules and Procedures to Implement the Attachment Law (RSA 511-A), "Writ Forms." DeLellis v. Burke, 134 N.H. 607 (1991) ("In order to invoke this statutory procedure [for a writ of attachment], a party must comply with the threshold procedural requirement that a trustee writ be filed. RSA 512:3."; a plaintiff who fails to file a writ in accordance with the statute has no standing to maintain an action against a defendant on the theory of equitable trustee process).

345 The Rules and Procedures to Implement the Attachment Law (RSA ch. 511-A) require that, if the petitioner is successful, he complete a "Writ of Attachment" ("attachment with notice," paragraph 4 and *Ex Parte* Attachment," paragraph 4). DeLellis v. Burke, 134 N.H. 607 (1991) ("In order to invoke this statutory procedure [for a writ of attachment], a party must comply with the threshold procedural requirement that a trustee writ be filed. RSA 512:3.").

liability to the defendant.[346] Both the principal defendant and the trustee defendant are named in the caption of the Petition to Attach with Notice or Petition for Ex Parte Attachment and both are served.[347]

The Writ of Attachment[348] and other pleadings should not use a fictitious name but should refer to a specific, identifiable trustee in the capacity in which he is obligated to the principal defendant.

The trustees must be named and their liability asserted in the same way that the principal defendant would be obliged to do if he were asserting the claim on his own behalf. Thus, a person who is jointly liable with another to the principal defendant will not be held liable on trustee process unless his joint obligor is also summoned and the Petition to Attach with Notice or Petition for Ex Parte Attachment states that their liability to the principal defendant is joint. The listing of property to be attached in the petition form should, in the case of tangible property, state that the property is in the hands of the named trustee and, in the case of a claim or right of payment, identify the claim or right of payment by amount and source.

(b) *Use of One or Several Writs.* Trustees may be summoned either together in one Petition to Attach with Notice or Petition for Ex Parte Attachment or severally in separate petitions. It is generally wiser to summon trustees separately, both because it simplifies service and because trustees who are jointly liable to the principal defendant may be charged

---

346 RSA 511-A:5-a provides that trustee process shall be ineffective to attach a principal defendant's interest in real estate unless the caption in all cases names the principal defendant and the trustee and recites their roles and the Writ of Attachment specifically states that the real estate is attached and identifies it.

347 See Gothic Metal Lathing v. Federal Deposit Insurance Corp., which states the three-part test that must be strictly complied with in order for a Writ of Attachment to be sufficient. The writ "must state the purpose for which the attachment is brought, describe the property to be attached with reasonable accuracy and specificity, and direct the officer to attach that specific property." 135 N.H. 262 (1992) (citing Ferns v. American Moore Peg Co., 81 N.H. 283, 283, 125 A. 434 (1924), for three-part test and for principle that court requires strict compliance with test; Rodd v. Titus Construction Co., 107 N.H. 264, 266, 220 A.2d 768, 770 (1966); Wurm v. Reilly, 102 N.H. 558, 563, 163 A.2d 13, 17 (1960); Mathers v. Connelly, 95 N.H. 107, 108, 58 A.2d 510, 511 (1948)).

In *Gothic Metal*, the Court found that the writ of attachment was insufficient as it did not meet any of the three parts of the test. The Court distinguished Manchester Federal Savings & Loan Association v. Letendre, 103 N.H. 64, 164 A.2d 568 (1960), as a case where the required elements were "physically too lengthy to fit on the writ, and this court allowed them to run onto a second page." 135 N.H. at 263.

348 The former writ of trustee process (former RSA 509:18 and 512:3) is no longer in use. All trustee process is now accomplished on a Writ of Attachment. See Rules and Procedures to Implement the Attachment Law (RSA ch. 511-A), "Writ Forms."

jointly, though separately summoned,[349] while, at least in the case of partners, persons who may be charged either singly or jointly will not be charged singly unless separately summoned.[350]

Forms

Writ of Attachment and Trustee Process (Superior Court), see Appendix.
Writ of Attachment and Trustee Process (District Court), see Appendix.

§ 17.56. —Determination of Preference Where Attachment and Trustee Process Are Sought Together

Neither RSA ch. 511-A nor any case which has been decided to date determines whether, if an attachment of tangible property and a trustee process are sought together, preference should be given to one over the other. The issue does not arise, of course, where all of the defendant's property and claims, both in his hands and in the hands of third parties, are insufficient to satisfy the judgment sought. Because the plaintiff often does not know the value remaining in such assets when he petitions for an attachment, he will usually ask for an attachment and trustee process on everything he can find, leaving it to the defendant to justify a lesser attachment. But it may later appear that the assets presently in the defendant's hands, without taking into account any assets held by a trustee, will be more than sufficient to satisfy the plaintiff's judgment should he prevail.

An attachment which gives the plaintiff more security than he needs is subject to reduction under RSA 511:53. In the usual case, the question will be resolved by the court on the principal defendant's or trustee's motion and in a manner which will make enforcement of any resulting judgment as simple as possible. Since the trustee only has to pay and must pay someone in any event, the court may prefer trustee process over attachment.

§ 17.57. —Completing and Serving the Writ

Once the court has granted the trustee process, a Writ of Attachment must be completed, again listing the trustee as a defendant in the caption and identifying the source and nature of his liability to the principal defendant. One original Writ of Attachment should be completed for each trustee and the sheriff should be given that original and *two* service copies. The sheriff

---

349 RSA 512:8.
350 RSA 512:7.

then serves *both* the trustee and the principal defendant with the writ of attachment[351] and return[352] and makes his return on the original to the court.[353]

A person sought to be charged as a trustee may not, however, accept or waive the fact of or defects in service of process, either on his own behalf or for a partnership or copartner of which he is a member or agent, but must insist that he be served formally in the manner provided by the statute.[354] This rule rests on the principle that the trustee has no power, either alone or for others, to avoid his debt or obligation to the principal defendant by a unilateral agreement with a third party. As the Court said in *Nelson v. Sanborn*:[355]

> The debt sought to be attached belonged to the defendant. He had a right to insist that if it was to be taken from him against his will, and applied to satisfy his indebtedness to the plaintiff, it should be done in the mode pointed out by the statute. The trustee could waive his own but not the defendant's rights. He could no more waive an attachment than he could the exemptions from attach-

---

351　In the past, service on the defendant was not a prerequisite for an attachment on trustee process—assets could be attached without the defendant's knowledge and quasi in rem jurisdiction could be obtained where personal jurisdiction could not. Now, however, RSA ch. 511-A requires that the defendant receive immediate notice of the attachments granted ex parte, and, under the doctrine of Pono v. Brock, 119 N.H. 814, 408 A.2d 419 (1979), "the test for *in personam* jurisdiction . . . applies to *quasi in rem* jurisdiction as well." 119 N.H. at 815–16, 408 A.2d at 419, 420. This new doctrine both requires and permits the defendants to be served in all cases where trustee process is sought. See also Hampton National Bank v. Desjardins, 114 N.H. 68, 314 A.2d 654 (1974); Steer v. Dow, 75 N.H. 95, 71 A. 217 (1908); Edgerly v. Sanborn, 6 N.H. 397 (1833); Palmer v. Noyes, 45 N.H. 174 (1864); White v. Fernald-Woodward Company, 76 N.H. 83, 79 A. 641 (1911); McGreenery v. Murphy, 76 N.H. 338, 82 A. 720 (1912).

352　Foster v. Hadduck, 6 N.H. 217 (1833).

353　Rules and Procedures to Implement the Attachment Law (RSA ch. 511-A), "Attachment with Notice," paragraph 4 and "*Ex Parte* Attachment," paragraph 4.

354　Nelson v. Sanborn, 64 N.H. 310, 9 A. 721 (1886); Shelters v. Boudreau, 66 N.H. 576; 32 A. 151 (1891); Clark v. Wilson, 15 N.H. 150 (1844). The rule exists for the benefit of the principal defendant and subsequent attaching creditors, but those beneficiaries may waive its protection by delay. If a defect occurs in the process or service which makes it voidable and the trustee appears and defends along with the principal defendant and any subsequently attaching creditors without raising the objection, it will be waived and the defect may be cured by amendment. Johnson v. Abbott, 60 N.H. 150 (1880). If, however, the trustee refuses to make the objection, subsequently attaching creditors may do so in his place within the time allowed. Pratt v. Sanborn, 63 N.H. 115 (1884).

355　64 N.H. 310, 9 A. 721 (1886).

ment . . . ., or the defendant's right that his property shall not be taken by this process in an action of slander.[356]

Library References

CJS Garnishment §§ 153, 154
Who may serve writ, summons, or notice of garnishment. 75 ALR2d 1437.

§ 17.58. —Addition of Trustees

Notwithstanding the permission contained in RSA 512:6, additional trustees may not be added without permission of the court.[357]

§ 17.59. Effect of Trustee Process—On Venue

Trustee process has no effect on venue.[358]

§ 17.60. —On Personal Liability of the Trustee

Service of the Writ of Attachment makes the trustee personally liable to the plaintiff for the value of "any money, goods, chattels, rights or credits of the defendant, not exempted from trustee process" that are in his possession at the time of service "or at any time after."[359] Service of the writ does not, however, give the plaintiff any lien[360] on the specific funds or property held by the trustee;[361] it "constitutes an attachment of the defendant's property rights in the possession of the trustee,"[362] not an attachment of the defendant's property itself.[363] It also summons the trustee to show cause why

---

356 64 N.H. at 311, 9 A. at 721.

357 RSA 511-A:1 and 7.

358 RSA 512:2.

359 RSA 512:20.

360 A "lien" is a security interest subject to the provisions of RSA ch. 382-A. See RSA 21:43.

361 Although this view contradicts the language of RSA 512:3, it has been repeatedly upheld. See Walcott v. Keith, 22 N.H. 196 (1850); Bufford v. Sides, 42 N.H. 495 (1861); Corning v. Records, 69 N.H. 390, 46 A. 462 (1898); Edgerly v. Hale, 71 N.H. 138, 51 A. 679 (1901).

362 Edgerly v. Hale, 71 N.H. 138, 141, 51 A. 679, 681 (1901).

363 In addition, trustee process may be distinguished from attachment by the fact that in trustee process there is no notice to third parties by a public record filing of the lien. Over the years, the opinions of the Supreme Court have demonstrated some confusion on the issue whether trustee process gives the plaintiff a lien on the property or just a claim against the trustee. In one of its earlier opinions, Blaisdell v. Ladd, 14 N.H. 129 (1843), Justice Gilchrist remarked that service of the trustee writ created an attachment on the property in the hands of the trustee. In Hoag v. Hoag, 55 N.H. 172 (1875), Justice Ladd repeated the argument of counsel, without adopting it, that "trustee process [is] a proceeding in rem." 55 N.H. at 173. And in Nelson v. Sanborn, 64 N.H. 310, 9 A. 721

execution for that amount should not be issued against him.[364]

Library References

CJS Garnishment §§ 175–180

§ 17.61. —On Property or Funds in Favor of the Trustee

Trustee process does, however, give the *trustee* a lien on the goods or funds in his hands, so long as he holds them, to secure the personal liability to the plaintiff which is imposed by the attachment.[365] And it supersedes any obligation or liability which the trustee might otherwise incur to the principal defendant as a result of the delay in paying or delivering the property or funds to him.[366]

(1886), Justice Carpenter cited *Blaisdell v. Ladd*, and the predecessor to RSA 512:3 for the proposition that service of the writ creates an attachment on funds in the trustee's possession.

However, during this same period a parallel line of cases developed the view that trustee process did not create a lien on specific funds or property. In Walcott v. Keith, 22 N.H. 196 (1850), Justice Woods wrote that service of trustee process "gave the creditor no right or lien upon the specific property but . . . only [rendered] the trustee personally liable for its value . . . ." 22 N.H. at 205. In Bufford v. Sides, 42 N.H. 495 (1861), Justice Sargent agreed.

Justice Parsons attempted to reconcile these conflicting holdings in Corning v. Records, 69 N.H. 390 (1898), by saying that "the service of the writ upon the trustee constitutes an attachment on the defendant's property rights" and by denying that it had never been "suggested that any special property . . . accrued to . . . the creditor in the specific chattels in the trustee's possession . . . . 69 N.H. at 398–99, 46 A. at 462, 466. Whatever they may have thought of Justice Sargent's sense of history, his view that property rights rather than specific property were attached by trustee process was subsequently repeated by Justice Chase in Edgerly v. Hale, 71 N.H. 138, 51 A. 679 (1901), Justice Bingham in White v. Fernald-Woodward Company, 76 N.H. 83, 79 A. 641 (1911), and Justice Walker in McGreenery v. Murphy, 76 N.H. 338 (1912). The issue remained thus settled for 30 years until Chief Justice Allen wrote in Protective Check Writer Co. v. Collins, 92 N.H. 27, 23 A.2d 770 (1942), without citation to any authority, that trustee process created a lien on the "money, goods, chattels, rights and credits" in the trustee's possession. In Hampton National Bank v. Desjardins, 114 N.H. 68, 314 A.2d 654 (1974), Chief Justice Kenison reaffirmed the *Edgerly v. Hale* formulation, that trustee process creates "an attachment of the defendant's property rights in the trustee's possession."

364 Edgerly v. Hale, 71 N.H. 138, 51 A. 679 (1901).

365 Swamscot Machine Company v. Partridge, 25 N.H. 369 (1852).

366 Carter v. Webster, 65 N.H. 17, 19, 17 A. 978 (1888); Wentworth Bus Lines v. Windle, 98 N.H. 234, 97 A.2d 228 (1953).

§ 17.62. —On the Principal Defendant's Rights

By means of trustee process, the plaintiff obtains all the rights, but only those rights, which the principal defendant had to require the trustee to pay or deliver the property or funds in his hands.[367]

§ 17.63. Procedure After Service of a Petition for Writ of Attachment—Hearing

The principal defendant has the same rights to a hearing under RSA 511-A:3 and 8 when trustee process is sought as when an attachment of goods in his possession is desired. RSA ch. 511-A does not provide for a hearing at the trustee's request, but there is no reason to think that one would not be granted in an appropriate case.

§ 17.64. —Appearance and Default

The trustee must respond to the Petition to Attach with Notice or Petition for Ex Parte Attachment and Writ of Attachment like any other defendant,[368] with the exception that the substance of his response on the merits may be limited to the issue of whether he has any obligation to the principal defendant which may be the subject of trustee process. If the trustee fails to respond, the court will order special notice[369] in order to make certain that the trustee is aware of the action.[370] If the trustee defaults after that notice has been given, the court will find him chargeable for the amount specified in the petition and will enter judgment against him for so much of that amount as the plaintiff establishes his right to receive from the defendant.[371]

In his response, the trustee can admit or dispute his liability to the principal defendant. He is not obliged to require the plaintiff to prove that

---

367 Palmer v. Duplex Truck Company, 79 N.H. 28, 103 A. 943 (1918) ("The plaintiff in trustee-process proceeds against the trustee upon the strength of the defendant's right and title and in the absence of fraud can recover only what the defendant could against the trustee." 79 N.H. at 30, 103 A. at 944)); Dole v. Farwell, 72 N.H. 183, 55 A. 553 (1903) ("When the trustee process is invoked, the plaintiff stands in the shoes of the principal defendant as respects charging the trustee, and can raise only such questions as are open to the defendant." 72 N.H. at 184, 55 A. at 553).

368 See §§ 17.11 and 17.17, *supra*.

369 RSA 512:10.

370 The trustee should be given an opportunity to defend if he wants it. Rigney v. Hutchins, 9 N.H. 257 (1838).

371 RSA 512:11; Caouette v. Young, 67 N.H. 159, 32 A. 157 (1891); Drew v. Towle, 27 N.H. 412 (1853).

claim since its admission works no prejudice to the principal defendant's right to require that the debt be paid to him.[372]

Library References

Garnishee's pleading, answering interrogatories or the like, as affecting his right to assert court's lack of jurisdiction. 41 ALR2d 1093.

Cross References

Appearances, see ch. 15 *supra*.

§ 17.65. The Trustee's Disclosure—In General

After the Writ of Attachment has been served[373] on the trustee,[374] the plaintiff [375] must require the trustee to disclose whether he holds any funds or property belonging to the principal defendant and, if he does, the nature and amount or value of the same and the terms of his obligation to pay those funds or deliver that property. In most cases, the disclosure is made by completing a "Disclosure of Trustee" form. The plaintiff completes and serves a copy of the Disclosure of Trustee form on the trustee and any party adverse to the plaintiff on the issue of whether the trustee may be charged[376] with a requirement that it be completed and returned to the plaintiff by a particular date.

Library References

CJS Garnishment § 209

Forms

Disclosure of Trustee, see Appendix.

§ 17.66. —Time for Taking the Disclosure

RSA 512:12 provides that the disclosure may be given or taken "at any time after the service of the writ upon the trustee, upon such notice to the adverse party as is required in taking depositions . . . ." There is no statutory

---

372 Edgerly v. Hale, 71 N.H. 138, 51 A. 679 (1901).

373 RSA 512:12. The disclosure may not be taken until the court has approved the attachment.

374 RSA 512:12. The disclosure may be taken before the principal defendant has been served but not without notice to him if necessary under RSA 512:12.

375 RSA 512:12 says that "any party to the action" may take or give the disclosure. This language is broad enough to allow the principal defendant, another trustee, a third party, or an intervenor to require the disclosure. It is also sufficiently broad to authorize the disclosing trustee to make the disclosure voluntarily. In most cases, however, the plaintiff will require the disclosure of the trustee.

376 Jones v. Roberts, 60 N.H. 216 (1880).

limit on the time within which the plaintiff must seek a disclosure if none is given.[377] A disclosure may not therefore be compelled from a trustee any sooner than a deposition might from a principal defendant, and notice must be given to all adverse parties. If the trustee or any party objects to a disclosure by form, the trustee's deposition may be taken either by agreement or pursuant to RSA ch. 517.[378]

Library References

CJS Garnishment § 210

§ 17.67. —Service of the Disclosure Form

The disclosure form and notice should be served on the trustee in the same manner as service of other process.[379] The trustee may attach the affidavits of other persons to his disclosure form as exhibits.[380] The period of time between service and return of the disclosure form to the plaintiff must be "reasonable."[381]

§ 17.68. —Scope of Disclosure by the Trustee

The trustee has a duty to answer any question "material to a correct decision" of whether he should be charged, even though, in so doing, he may furnish evidence which impairs his title to the property sought.[382]

§ 17.69. —Use of Other Means of Obtaining Disclosure From the Trustee

If the trustee refuses to complete and return the disclosure form as required by the notice or fills it out without sufficient detail or with conflicting or confusing statements or if the plaintiff, either before or after the return of the form, has reason to believe that he cannot obtain a full account of the nature of the trustee's liability without a more detailed or

---

377 See, e.g., General Statutes, ch. 230:12; Demeritt v. Estes, 56 N.H. 313 (1876).

378 See Jones v. Roberts, 60 N.H. 216 (1880).

379 RSA 517:4 and 5 and Super. Ct. R. 40 do permit "delivery" rather than service on any "agent" or "attorney" of a nonresident, rather than on the clerk, treasurer, directors, or other specific officers. When the disclosure is sought after the trustee has filed an Appearance, this more general language ought to be relied upon to justify a method of notice less formal than the usual service. But, as a general practice, both for convenience and tidiness of records, it is best to serve the trustee with the disclosure form in the same manner in which he would be served with other process.

380 Giddings v. Coleman, 12 N.H. 153 (1841).

381 RSA 512:12 and 517:4.

382 Bell v. Kendrick, 8 N.H. 520 (1837).

flexible examination of the trustee, he may use other types of pretrial discovery to obtain the trustee's disclosure.[383] When a public body, corporation, or partnership is the trustee, the plaintiff may, except in cases of wage garnishment,[384] specify which agent, member, or officer is to make the disclosure[385] and serve that agent or officer directly as representative of the public body, partnership, or corporation.[386]

Library References

CJS Garnishment §§ 212–224

§ 17.70. —Proceedings Upon Intervention by Third-Party Claimants

Any person, including a subsequently attaching creditor,[387] who claims an interest in the property in issue may petition to intervene and dispute the plaintiff's claim to it.[388] If, from the disclosure form and depositions, it appears that some person other than the trustee or principal defendant claims the property or rights in issue, the court may order that the plaintiff give him notice[389] to appear and defend his claim or be forever barred from asserting it.[390] Any claimant appearing in the action has the same rights as any other party and may move for a jury trial on the respective rights of the plaintiff and claimant to the property in issue.[391]

Library References

CJS Garnishment §§ 267 et seq.

§ 17.71. —Signing and Filing the Disclosure

The disclosure form or the deposition transcript must be signed under oath, the oath stating that the disclosure "contains the truth, the whole truth

---

383 A failure to return a disclosure form may also be treated as a default under RSA 512:10 and 11. In that case the plaintiff must move the court to prescribe further notice which, if unanswered, will result in an order charging the trustee.

384 RSA 512:9 and 9-a.

385 RSA 512:14; Whidden v. Drake, 5 N.H. 13 (1829).

386 RSA 512:14 and 15.

387 Blaisdell v. Ladd, 14 N.H. 129 (1843).

388 RSA 512:26; Webster v. Farnum, 60 N.H. 288 (1880).

389 The notice must be given personally "if practicable," otherwise by publication or in some other appropriate manner.

390 RSA 512:23 and 27.

391 RSA 512:28.

and nothing but the truth, relative to the cause . . . ."[392] The original disclosure form or deposition transcript is returned by the trustee, after execution, to the plaintiff. A copy is sent to each person who received notice of the disclosure or attended the deposition. The plaintiff thereafter files the original with the clerk of court. When trustee process is granted ex parte and the trustee is served before the Writ of Summons is entered in court, the disclosure must be filed in the superior court no later than sixty days and in the district and municipal courts no later than thirty days after the return day specified in the writ.[393] If the trustee was served after the Writ of Summons was entered, it must be filed no later than sixty or thirty days, respectively, after service.[394] The plaintiff should notify the trustee and other persons involved in the disclosure when he files it with the court.

If the plaintiff fails to request or file the disclosure within the time allowed, the trustee or any other party may move to have the trustee discharged from any further claim by the plaintiff.[395]

§ 17.72. —Extension of Time for Taking the Disclosure

The plaintiff, trustee, or any other party may move to extend the time for taking the disclosure.[396] The motion must be accompanied by an affidavit showing "sufficient cause."[397] The plaintiff, trustee, or any other party may also move to extend the time for filing a disclosure which has already been taken[398] based on the moving party's "good cause" for needing to take further

---

392 RSA 517:7. See New Hampshire Explosives and Machinery Corp. v. Morency, 126 N.H. 626, 496 A.2d 338 (1985) (trustee who later disputes accuracy of disclosure form has burden of producing evidence to show that it was wrong).

393 Super. Ct. R. 86; Dist. and Mun. Ct. R. 3.22.

394 RSA 512:17; Super. Ct. R. 86; Dist. and Mun. Ct. R. 3.22. Because the Rules and Procedures to Implement the Attachment Law (RSA ch. 511-A) require that the Writ of Summons be entered "immediately" after the Writ of Attachment has been filed, it is theoretically impossible for a trustee to be served pursuant to authority to make additional attachments before the Writ of Summons has been entered. Note, however, that Rule 86 may have the effect of requiring that the disclosure of the second trustee served be filed before the disclosure of the first if the second trustee is served before the return day.

395 Super. Ct. R. 86. In the District and Municipal Courts, the trustee will be discharged automatically without motion. Dist. and Mun. Ct. R. 3.22. See Demeritt v. Estes, 56 N.H. 313 (1876).

396 Super. Ct. R. 86; Dist. and Mun. Ct. R. 3.22.

397 Id. Presumably, "sufficient cause" will not be shown if the plaintiff has not diligently attempted to obtain the disclosure within the time allowed.

398 RSA 512:17.

depositions of other persons relating to the trustee's liability. Such a motion must also be supported by affidavit.[399]

§ 17.73. —Depositions of Nontrustees

Persons other than the trustee may also be deposed "by any party to the suit" relative to the liability of the trustee.[400] Notice of these nonparty depositions is given in the same way as notice of the deposition of any witness in a civil case.[401]

Cross References

Depositions, see ch. 26 *infra*.

§ 17.74. Determining Whether the Trustee Should Be Charged— Motion To Charge; Objection

When the plaintiff submits the disclosure form and deposition transcripts, he must also file a Motion To Charge the trustee for the amount which the plaintiff believes he had in his possession at the time of service or thereafter.[402] The trustee should file an Objection to the motion, if he has one, and request a hearing, if he needs one, within ten days.[403]

§ 17.75. —Jury Trial

Whether or not the trustee objects to the motion or requests a hearing, either the plaintiff or the trustee may move that the issue of the trustee's liability be tried by a jury[404] if the trustee has denied his liability in the disclosure. In the absence of a motion for jury trial, the court will decide whether the trustee should be charged without a hearing, if none is requested, based on the disclosure forms and deposition transcripts submitted or after an evidentiary hearing, if the defendant requests one.

If either the plaintiff or the trustee moves for a jury trial and the disclosure shows that the trustee has a good faith basis for disputing liability,[405] the

---

399 Super. Ct. R. 57.

400 RSA 512:13.

401 These nonparties, not being trustees, may not be deposed within 20 days of service of the writ or on less than three nor more than 20 days notice. RSA 512:12; Super. Ct. R. 38.

402 See RSA 512:20.

403 Super. Ct. R. 58.

404 RSA 512:18.

405 *Id.* The court will not allow a jury trial if the trustee, in spite of his general denial, has admitted enough facts to make him liable as a matter of law.

423

court will frame an issue for the jury "as to the liability of the trustee."[406] The plaintiff will first be required to give the trustee "a specification stating the ground on which he expects to charge the trustee."[407] The disclosure forms and deposition transcripts,[408] but not the affidavits appended to either,[409] may be introduced in evidence at the trial.[410] The jury may, and sometimes must, return a special, as well as a general, verdict on the issue, finding both that the trustee is chargeable and the basis or limitations of his liability.[411]

Library References

CJS Garnishment §§ 232 et seq.
Issue in garnishment as triable to court or to jury. 19 ALR3d 1393.

§ 17.76. —Verdict and Judgment

The court will enter judgment in accordance with the jury's verdict.[412] If the jury does not return a special verdict on the mode of the trustee's liability, the court will specify the amount and source of that liability in its judgment.

Library References

Form of judgment against garnishee respecting obligation payable in installments. 7 ALR2d 680.

§ 17.77. Procedure Upon a Finding That the Trustee May Be Charged—Trustee's Duty To Hold or Pay Into Court

In general, the trustee is obligated only to hold the sum of money, property, or other claim for which he is adjudged chargeable until he is requested to turn it over to the sheriff upon execution or he receives notice that the suit has been terminated and the attachment dissolved.[413] With respect to any sum of money for which he is charged, he may alternatively pay that sum into court and thereby discharge his liability.[414]

---

406 RSA 512:19. The general issue is whether the trustee had at the time of service of the writ or at any time since or has now any money, goods, chattels, rights, or credits of the plaintiff. Hills v. Smith, 19 N.H. 381 (1849).

407 Wright v. Bosworth, 5 N.H. 400 (1831).

408 *Id.*

409 Amoskeag Manufacturing Company v. Gibbs, 28 N.H. 316 (1854).

410 Depositions cannot be used as evidence in any criminal prosecution except a trial of an indictment for violation of RSA 641:1. See RSA 512:46.

411 Hills v. Smith, 19 N.H. 381 (1849).

412 RSA 512:20.

413 RSA 512:33; Steer v. Dow, 75 N.H. 95 (1908).

414 RSA 512:39.

Library References

CJS Garnishment §§ 293–297

§ 17.78. —Delivery to a Receiver

If the trustee is adjudged chargeable for personal property subject to a mortgage, pledge, or other lien,[415] the court may appoint a receiver, either on its own motion or on the motion of a party, to sell it "so long as more can be obtained for it than the claims upon it."[416] If the trustee is adjudged chargeable for any note, security for the payment of money, or chose in action upon which execution cannot be levied, the court may appoint a receiver, either on its own motion or the motion of a party, to collect it.[417] The trustee must deliver the property, note, security, or chose in action to the receiver in accordance with the court order or be judged personally liable for its value.[418] After the receiver has sold or collected the property, as the case may be, and paid the costs and charges of the sale, he must pay any preexisting mortgages, pledges, or other liens.[419] If the plaintiff obtains judgment, the receiver will pay that judgment from the remainder, without the necessity of an execution, and turn over the excess, if any, to the principal defendant.[420] The receiver must account to the court for his handling of these transactions.

Library References

CJS Garnishment § 193

§ 17.79. —Contingent Liability

When the trustee is charged for a liability which is not yet due, he may move the court to stay further proceedings for the collection of that amount, either by a receiver or the sheriff, "as equity requires."[421] The court can make such a stay conditional on the trustee paying the amount directly into court when it falls due.

---

415 RSA 512:29.

416 *Id.* See Briggs v. Walker, 21 N.H. 72 (1850) (property returned to trustee if more than amount of the lien cannot be obtained on a sale).

417 RSA 512:30.

418 RSA 512:32.

419 RSA 512:31. See Hills v. Smith, 28 N.H. 369 (1854) (pledgee entitled to be paid amount of debt secured plus storage and related costs, if any).

420 *Id.*

421 RSA 512:37.

Library References

Right of garnishee, other than bank holding deposit, to set off claims not due or certain when garnishment is served. 57 ALR2d 700.

§ 17.80. —Discharge and Costs

When the trustee has paid the money or delivered the property for which he is charged to the court, the sheriff, or the receiver, as provided in the statute, he is "discharged of all claim of the defendant for the same."[422] The trustee is entitled to costs "as a party" from the day he enters his Appearance,[423] regardless of the disposition of the case, unless: (1) he is adjudged chargeable on a jury verdict for a sum greater than or for property different from what he would have been charged for on his deposition alone;[424] (2) the court finds that the trustee did any act in relation to the principal defendant's property "with intent to aid him in defeating or delaying a creditor";[425] or (3) the defendant settles before the return day, when only the defendant's wages have been trusteed.[426] In the first two cases, the trustee must pay costs of all parties; in the last case, he must only bear his own. The court may, of course, make an adjustment of costs amongst the parties "as shall seem equitable."[427]

Library References

CJS Garnishment § 264

§ 17.81. Release of Trustee Process

The plaintiff's attachment on the principal defendant's rights in property which the trustee process secures may be released by the plaintiff at any time.[428] It may also be released by order of the court upon petition of the principal defendant and after notice and hearing, if the principal defendant gives the plaintiff a bond to pay, within thirty days of judgment, the amount for which the trustee is chargeable up to the amount of the judgment.[429] The attachment is also discharged by payment into court,[430] payment or delivery

---

422 RSA 512:38.
423 Super. Ct. R. 86.
424 RSA 512:41.
425 RSA 512:42.
426 RSA 512:44.
427 RSA 512:43.
428 RSA 512:16.
429 RSA 512:40.
430 RSA 512:39.

to the sheriff or a receiver as required by order of the court,[431] a decision that the trustee is not chargeable or other discharge of the trustee,[432] or the termination of the suit in favor of the principal defendant. The release of the attachment discharges the trustee, and vice versa. However, the attachment is not discharged by death of the trustee; instead, the court will notify his executor or administrator to come in and defend.[433]

Library References

CJS Garnishment §§ 243, 270, 271, 274, 275

§ 17.82. Recording and Indexing of Trustee Process

Trustee process constitutes an attachment upon real estate only when the Writ of Attachment "specifically recites that the real estate standing in the name of the trustee is attached," is recorded in the Registry of Deeds for the county in which the real estate is located, and names both the trustee and the principal defendant in the caption.[434]

---

431 RSA 512:38.

432 See, e.g., Super. Ct. R. 86 allowing for discharge of trustees upon whom no disclosure form is filed within 60 days after the return day or, in the case of additional attachments, within 60 days after service.

433 RSA 512:4.

434 RSA 511:5-a(I). The Register of Deeds must list the Trustee's, as well as the principal defendant's name in the attachment index. RSA 511-A:5-a(II).

CHAPTER 18. REPLEVIN

§ 18.01. Introduction

Replevin is a procedure by which personal property[1] which has been wrongfully taken or detained[2] may be recovered by a person entitled to its immediate and exclusive possession.[3] Replevin seeks to reestablish a status quo which has recently existed, and a plaintiff's delay will therefore bar his use of the procedure. A replevin proceeding is in rem[4] and, as such, is also a local action[5] which must be commenced in the district or county where the personal property was either unlawfully taken or is being unlawfully detained.[6] Although replevin has been called "a strictly possessory action"[7] which decides only which of the claimants is entitled to possession and what damages, if any, should be assessed for loss of possession,[8] the action has been expanded in the twentieth century to include other issues. Replevin may be brought in conjunction with other claims and actions,[9] and the fact that the plaintiff may recover his damages in an associated action does not prevent him from maintaining replevin solely to recover possession of the

---

1 RSA 536-A:1. Replevin does not lie for the recovery of money, choses in action, or fixtures.

2 RSA 536-A:1.

3 Mitchell v. Roberts, 50 N.H. 486 (1871); Bonney v. Smith, 59 N.H. 411 (1879); Peirce v. Finerty, 76 N.H. 38, 79 A. 23 (1911). In Sanborn v. Leavitt, 43 N.H. 473, 474 (1862), the Court summarized the difference between attachment and replevin as follows:

> The writ of replevin requires the sheriff to take the property, not as in an attachment, for the purpose of retaining it, but for the sole purpose of forthwith delivering it to the plaintiff in replevin, who, by the very nature of the process, claims it as his own. 43 N.H. at 474.

4 Brown v. Smith, 1 N.H. 36, 38 (1817); Mitchell v. Roberts, 50 N.H. 486 (1871).

5 In Claggett v. Richards, 45 N.H. 360 (1864), Justice Nesmith questioned whether replevin might be transitory under the statute then in effect. In Sleeper v. Osgood, 50 N.H. 331 (1870), however, the Court held that the action was local. RSA 536-A says nothing about venue, and it must be assumed that the common law principles still apply and that replevin is still a local action. See Chapter 4, Venue.

6 Sleeper v. Osgood, 50 N.H. 331, 336 (1870). As no section of RSA 536-A prescribes venue for the action, common law principles govern the point. See Chapter 4, Venue.

7 Mitchell v. Roberts, 50 N.H. 486 (1871); Peirce v. Finerty, 76 N.H. 38, 47, 79 A. 23, 24 (1911).

8 RSA 536-A:16 and 18. See Mitchell v. Roberts, 50 N.H. 486, 488 (1871), where Justice Foster quotes *Blackstone* to the effect that a possessory action is " 'such wherein the right of possession only, and not of property, is contested.' "

9 See, e.g., Sleeper v. Davis, 64 N.H. 59, 6 A. 201 (1886) (replevin joined with assumpsit for price of goods which could not be recovered); Burley v. Pike, 62 N.H. 495 (1883) (replevin for hay brought with trespass for damages caused by conversion of the hay).

430

property.[10] Replevin may be commenced at any stage of the proceedings,[11] but may not be used as an alternative to an action already pending.[12]

Library References

CJS Replevin §1

§ 18.02. History of the Procedure

Unlike attachment and trustee process, replevin was known to the common law, and existed in provincial times without benefit of statute. In its original form, replevin was available, with one exception, only for the recovery of property taken by trespass. After the American Revolution, a few statutes were passed prescribing the form of the writ and establishing a period of time within which to bring it.[13] In 1825, the Legislature partially waived a common law exemption for property in custodia legis, and permitted the use of replevin to recover goods which had been subjected to attachment. In 1873, the Legislature further expanded the writ's common law base to include property unlawfully detained. And in 1973, the Legislature required that writs of replevin, like writs of attachment and trustee process, be approved by a judge before being issued. Despite these statutory changes, replevin has, throughout the last two centuries, remained essentially a creature of the common law, and has been developed and refined in the decisions of the New Hampshire Supreme Court. As a result, while powers of attachment or trustee process must be regarded as nonexistent if not specifically created by statute, powers of replevin will be more broadly construed.[14]

§ 18.03. When Replevin Lies—Generally

(a) *Nature of Property Recoverable.*   Replevin lies only for the recovery of personal property.[15] Personal property which is attached to realty, whether fixtures, standing timber, or houses, may not be recovered by means of

---

10 Burley v. Pike, 62 N.H. 495 (1883).

11 RSA 536-A:19.

12 Peirce v. Finerty, 76 N.H. 38, 79 A. 23 (1911).

13 See Laws of N.H. (1805), pp. 83 and 135.

14 Woodward v. Grand Trunk Ry. Co., 46 N.H. 524, 525 (1866).

15 RSA 536-A:1; Peirce v. Finerty, 76 N.H. 38, 79 A. 23 (1911).

replevin.[16] Use of personal property as a residence does not, however, exempt it from replevin.[17]

(b) *Right to Possession and Title.* Replevin lies only on the behalf of one "entitled to possession against one having at the time the suit was begun actual or constructive possession and control of the property."[18] The plaintiff must have an immediate and exclusive right to possession, both at the time of the taking or detention complained of, and at the time the action is begun.[19] Additionally, the defendant must have the property in his possession at the time the complaint is filed.[20] However, the action will not fail simply because the plaintiff loses his right to possession pendente lite.[21]

Replevin tests rights of possession, not title.[22] It is therefore not necessary that either party have title to the property,[23] or that the owner of the property join in the complaint; nor is title in the defendant sufficient to defeat the action if the plaintiff has a superior right of possession at the time of the taking or detention.[24]

Library References

CJS Replevin §§ 9, 42, 43
Conversion as precluded by resort to replevin. 3 ALR2d 230.

---

16 Peirce v. Finerty, 76 N.H. 38, 79 A. 23 (1911).

17 See RSA 536-A:9, which permits replevin of "property . . . used as a dwelling, such as a housetrailer, mobile home or boat. . . ."

18 Mitchell v. Roberts, 50 N.H. 486, 488 (1871); Bowers v. Parker, 58 N.H. 565 (1879); Stevens v. Chase, 61 N.H. 340 (1881). At the time the writ is brought, the plaintiff must have "such a general or special property in the goods as [entitles] him to the exclusive possession against the defendant." Dickinson v. Lovell, 35 N.H. 2, 19 (1857).

19 RSA 536-A:2(I); Peirce v. Finerty, 76 N.H. 38, 79 A. 23 (1911); Stevens v. Chase, 61 N.H. 340 (1881); American Steel & Iron Co. v. Wooster, 95 N.H. 179, 59 A.2d 341 (1948); Mechanicks National Bank v. Parker, 109 N.H. 87, 242 A.2d 69 (1968); Sanford Mfg. Co. v. Wiggin, 14 N.H. 441 (1843). Justice Gilchrist wrote in Sanford:

   To support the action of replevin, the plaintiff must have had at the time of the caption, either the general property in the goods taken, or a special property therein. . . . If the plaintiff has not the immediate right of possession, replevin cannot be supported, but the party must proceed by an action on the case. 14 N.H. at 445.

20 Mitchell v. Roberts, 50 N.H. 486 (1871). See also Carr v. Clough, 26 N.H. 280, 295 (1853).

21 Derry Loan & Discount Co. v. Falconer, 84 N.H. 450, 152 A. 427 (1930). His loss of the right of possession may, however, affect the relief given after trial.

22 Mitchell v. Roberts, 50 N.H. 486 (1871).

23 Mechanicks National Bank v. Parker, 109 N.H. 87, 242 A.2d 69 (1968); Burley v. Pike, 62 N.H. 495 (1883).

24 Stevens v. Chase, 61 N.H. 340 (1881).

Remedy of replevin where agent, employed to purchase personal property, buys it for himself. 20 ALR2d 1149.

Availability of replevin or similar possessory action to one not claiming as heir, legatee, or creditor of decedent's estate; against personal representative. 42 ALR2d 418.

County that may bring replevin, or similar possessory action. 60 ALR2d 487.

Maintenance of replevin or similar possessory remedy by cotenant, or security transaction creditor thereof, against other cotenants. 93 ALR2d 358.

Recovery of value of property in replevin or similar possessory action where defendant, at time action is brought, is no longer in possession of property. 97 ALR2d 896.

§ 18.04. —At Common Law

(a) *Introduction.*   At common law, replevin lay to recover personal property in three types of situations: (1) when the property had been wrongfully taken; (2) when the property had been taken under a legal power of distraint, but the distress had subsequently been handled so unlawfully as to make the distrainor a trespasser ab initio; and (3) when domestic animals (usually cattle), which had escaped from their owner's land to the land of another and had been taken by that other landowner, were not returned upon their owner's tendering the costs of their keeping and the damages caused by their trespass.[25] While the first two situations involved a taking by trespass either in fact or by force of law, the last was actually an unlawful detention. This sole exception to the oft-stated rule that replevin lay at common law only for an unlawful taking apparently had no firmer foundation than English tradition.[26]

(b) *Property Wrongfully Taken.*   The clearest case of a wrongful taking is a deprivation of property by theft. In any such case, the owner may maintain replevin against the criminal to recover his property.[27] Under the present statute, the writ will issue ex parte.[28]

The taking need not be an intentional trespass, however, to be wrongful.[29] Any unprivileged interference with another person's right of possession may constitute a basis for issuance of the writ.[30] Property which is taken on an invalid attachment or replevin, or remains in the sheriff's possession after dissolution of an attachment, is taken on an attachment which is junior to the plaintiff's right of possession,[31] or is taken on a valid attachment but is

---

25 Dame v. Dame, 43 N.H. 37 (1861).

26 *Id.*

27 See Knapp v. Mahurin, 72 N.H. 595, 56 A. 315 (1903).

28 RSA 536-A:12(I).

29 Knapp v. Guyer, 75 N.H. 397, 74 A. 873 (1909).

30 Farley v. Lincoln, 51 N.H. 577 (1872).

31 Mechanicks National Bank v. Parker, 109 N.H. 87, 242 A.2d 69 (1968).

433

either exempt from attachment[32] or does not belong to the defendant debtor, may be replevied.[33] Replevin will also lie to recover furniture and other personal property improperly held by a landlord as security for unpaid rent,[34] as well as to recover property which the plaintiff is entitled to hold as security for payment for his services,[35] or for a debt.[36] Replevin may also be used to recover property which another person purports to hold under legal authority but which has come into his hands as a result of his own fault, rather than the owner's.[37]

Replevin can also be used to recover personal property which has been obtained by means of a fraudulent representation that the defendant will pay for it at a later date.[38] Such a fraudulent purchase has consistently been held to constitute a trespass, even though the property initially appears to be passing into the defendant's possession by lawful means, and to justify the writ's use against the fraudulent vendee[39] or any assignee,[40] vendor,[41] or attaching creditor[42] of the fraudulent vendee who gives no new consideration. The writ cannot be used, however, to retrieve goods from a person who buys them in good faith, without notice of the fraud and for valuable consideration paid before replevin is sought,[43] or to recover property attached by a person who extended his credit to the fraudulent vendee after the fraud.[44] The fraudulent vendee cases are, in this sense, to be distinguished from those cases in which an agent transfers his principal's goods to the

---

32 Carkin v. Babbitt, 58 N.H. 579 (1879).

33 Garvin v. Paul, 47 N.H. 158 (1866).

34 Standish v. Moldawan, 93 N.H. 204, 37 A.2d 788 (1944).

35 Smith v. Marden, 60 N.H. 509 (1881) (pasture owner could recover milch cow held subject to a statutory lien for charges); Commercial Acceptance Corporation v. Hislop Garage Co., 89 N.H. 45, 192 A. 627 (1937) (temporary return of car to owner did not constitute a waiver of the lien).

36 Caraway v. Jean, 97 N.H. 506, 92 A.2d 660 (1952) (equitable mortgagee could recover TV set that had been pledged as security for a debt he had paid).

37 York v. Davis, 11 N.H. 241 (1840) (cattle impounded by the defendant had escaped onto his land because of defendant's failure to maintain a fence).

38 In many cases, this activity will constitute a violation of RSA 637:4 (Theft by Deception) and justify an ex parte writ.

39 Gitterman & Company v. Lynn Modern Shoe Co., 87 N.H. 335, 179 A. 351 (1935); Sleeper v. Davis, 64 N.H. 59, 6 A. 201 (1886); Bradley v. Obear, 10 N.H. 477 (1839).

40 Farley v. Lincoln, 51 N.H. 577 (1872).

41 Sleeper v. Davis, 64 N.H. 59, 6 A. 201 (1886).

42 Bradley v. Obear, 10 N.H. 477 (1839).

43 Sleeper v. Davis, 64 N.H. 59, 6 A. 201 (1886).

44 Bradley v. Obear, 10 N.H. 477 (1839).

agent's creditor, a bailee sells his bailment to a bona fide purchaser without authority,[45] or a person obtains possession from a person with no apparent authority to hold or sell the property.[46] In all of the latter cases, replevin lies to recover the principal's goods.[47]

(c) *Abuse of Distraint.*   At common law, when one person seized another person's property pursuant to a legal power to take, hold and sell that property to satisfy a debt, he could not be held liable in replevin unless he abused the distress or otherwise acted so unlawfully or beyond the scope of his authority as to become a trespasser ab initio.[48] This issue arose most frequently in cases of impounded livestock or goods sold for taxes, but the theory can be applied to any case in which a person has a legal right to seize and hold another's property as security for payment of charges.[49]

The early cases show a great deal of confusion over the question whether a mere failure to comply with a statute which grants the right to seize and hold another's property is sufficient to make the impounder a trespasser ab initio. In 1825, the Supreme Court said that it did not;[50] in 1838, the Court said that it did;[51] in 1847, the Court returned to its original position;[52] and in 1856[53] and 1862,[54] the Court reversed itself again. Throughout this period, the Court seems to have been concerned that a mere failure of technical compliance could be used to strip an impounder of his right to damages or to expose him to a claim for unlawful caption. Today, a mere technical noncompliance with a statute authorizing the seizure and holding of property will not justify the issuance of a writ of replevin, but a substantial noncompliance or an act outside the impounder's authority will. As Justice Green wrote in *Barrett v. White:*[55]

> On the whole, it is believed, that an attentive examination of all
> the authorities will clearly show, that a man may become a

---

45 See Proctor v. Tilton, 65 N.H. 3, 17 A. 638 (1888).

46 Derry Loan & Discount Co. v. Falconer, 84 N.H. 450, 152 A. 427 (1930).

47 Johnson v. Willey, 46 N.H. 75 (1865); Partridge v. Philbrick, 60 N.H. 556 (1881); Gould v. Blodgett, 61 N.H. 115 (1881).

48 Osgood v. Green, 30 N.H. 210 (1855).

49 See RSA 270-B.

50 Kimball v. Adams, 3 N.H. 182 (1825).

51 McIntire v. Marden, 9 N.H. 288 (1838).

52 Young v. Rand, 18 N.H. 569 (1847).

53 Osgood v. Green, 33 N.H. 318 (1856).

54 Cate v. Cate, 44 N.H. 211 (1862). See also Bills v. Kinson, 21 N.H. 448 (1850).

55 3 N.H. 210 (1825).

trespasser *ab initio* not only by using an authority, which the law gives him, for improper purposes, or by pushing the exercise of it beyond its due limits, but by exercising it in an improper and illegal manner to the prejudice of another.[56]

The only case in which the Supreme Court has expressly found an abuse of distraint sufficient to transform a distrainor into a trespasser ab initio is *Blake v. Johnson*.[57] In that case, a federal collector of duties on carriages seized a harness and bells without informing the owner and sold them two hours later at auction without notice and for less than half their value. The federal statute under which the collector was acting authorized distraint and sale but did not specify any procedure to be followed in the exercise of those powers. The Court held that any sale which was made without at least four days' notice to the owner or which was not calculated to bring the best price for the property was unreasonable[58] and that the collector's actions in this case were so unreasonable as to make him a trespasser ab initio. In *Barrett v. White*,[59] the Court also said, in dicta, that a distrainor who makes changes in the goods may become, by that act, a trespasser ab initio and added that a sheriff who attaches goods in a house but who fails to remove them within a reasonable time or who unpacks and searches through items in such a way as to injure them will also be transformed by those acts into a trespasser ab initio.

(d) *Animals Destroying Crops.*   RSA 471 provides that any beast "found doing damage in some inclosure"[60] may be seized as a stray and sets forth a procedure for notifying the beast's owner of the seizure and of the costs of redeeming the animal.[61] If the beasts are trespassing, but have done no damage by the time they are seized[62] or if the finder refuses to release the

---

56 *Id.* at 230. In Butnam v. Wright, 16 N.H. 219 (1844), the Court said: "Whoever abuses an authority derived from the law, thereby becomes a trespasser from the beginning. . . ." 16 N.H. at 221.

57 1 N.H. 91 (1817).

58 Chief Justice Richardson wrote for the Court, as follows:

And we are very clear, that every distress of this kind must be kept a reasonable time before it be sold, that the party whose goods are distrained may have an opportunity to replevy, or to discharge the demand for which they are taken. 1 N.H. at 92.

59 3 N.H. 210 (1825).

60 RSA 471:12.

61 RSA 471:1-8.

62 Osgood v. Green, 33 N.H. 318 (1856).

beasts upon tender of the costs of redemption, the owner is entitled to maintain replevin to get the animals back.[63]

Library References

CJS Replevin §§ 53–55

§ 18.05. —By Statute

(a) *History of the Statute.* In 1873, the Legislature, for the first time, authorized the use of replevin to recover property which had lawfully come into the defendant's possession but was being unlawfully detained by him. The effect of this enactment was to combine the common law writs of replevin and detinue into one statutory writ of replevin.[64] Although of substantial effect, the amendment was only a logical step in the development of the law of replevin during the nineteenth century.

Many cases prior to 1873 had raised the question whether replevin would lie for unlawful detention, some arguing that the common law must have recognized such a doctrine because unlawful detention was a necessary part of any unlawful taking and others attempting to extend the exception for animals damage feasant to other situations. All direct efforts failed, but the door was opened to an expansion of the remedy in the first half of the nineteenth century by the court's adoption of the fiction that certain acts occurring after an apparently lawful taking could relate back and convert the lawful taking into a trespass.[65] In 1861, the court held that the common law writ of detinue existed in New Hampshire, presumably meaning thereby to provide for expansion of the right to recover property unlawfully detained.[66] But in 1873, the Legislature expanded the right by statute and cut

---

63 Kimball v. Adams, 3 N.H. 182 (1825).

64 It did not, however, abolish the common law writ of detinue. See Bowers v. Parker, 58 N.H. 565 (1879).

65 The Court implicitly recognized this evolutionary process in Noyes v. Patrick, 58 N.H. 618 (1879), when it held that replevin would lie for goods unlawfully detained under the 1873 statute to recover property obtained by fraud. Prior to 1873, the Court had held that goods obtained by fraud could be recovered by replevin on the theory that the fraud itself was a trespass and had allowed recovery of goods lawfully taken on distress after the distress had been abused, on the theory that the abuse related back and made the initial taking a trespass. To hold, after the statute was amended, that a fraudulent vendee's refusal to return goods was an unlawful detention, not only admitted that the amendment had legitimized a good deal of the development of case law during the nineteenth century, but also extended replevin for unlawful detention to cases of abuse of distraint.

66 See, e.g., Farley v. Lincoln, 51 N.H. 577 (1872) (detinue would lie to recover goods fraudulently obtained in the guise of a sale).

short the development of detinue as a procedure separate and distinct from replevin.

(b) *Occasions When Replevin Has Been Allowed.* Under the 1873 amendment, replevin has been held to lie to recover goods wrongfully held by a common carrier,[67] to repossess automobiles[68] and consumer goods[69] subject to a security interest upon the owner's default, to recover goods subject to a statutory[70] or common law[71] lien for service charges, and to recover property which the plaintiff was fraudulently induced to transfer.[72] In order to maintain replevin for unlawful detention, however, the plaintiff must be able to show that the defendant is exercising dominion over the property and is intentionally keeping the property from the plaintiff's possession.[73] It is not enough for the plaintiff to show that the defendant is denying him access to the property if he does not also show that the defendant is claiming his own title or right of possession in it.[74] In most cases, proof of the exercise of dominion will require a formal demand for return of the goods and a clear refusal before the writ is brought.[75] While no minimum amount of time is required between the time of demand and commencement of the action,[76] the holder of the property may ask for and is entitled to receive a reasonable time to investigate the plaintiff's claims before responding.[77]

---

67 Hart v. Boston and Maine R.R., 72 N.H. 410, 56 A. 920 (1903).

68 R.C. Hazelton Co. v. Southwick Constr. Co., 105 N.H. 25, 192 A.2d 610 (1963); National Shawmut Bank v. Jones, 108 N.H. 386, 236 A.2d 484 (1967); Mechanicks National Bank v. Parker, 109 N.H. 87, 242 A.2d 69 (1968). In 1986 the Court held, in Dartmouth Motor Sales, Inc. v. Wilcox 128 N.H. 526, 517 A.2d 804 (1986), that if a bona fide purchaser buys a motor vehicle which has a facially valid title, the title that is passed is good.

69 Sears, Roebuck & Co. v. Bonsant, 114 N.H. 270, 319 A.2d 633 (1974); Caraway v. Jean, 97 N.H. 506, 92 A.2d 660 (1952).

70 Smith v. Marden, 60 N.H. 509 (1881).

71 Hiltz v. Gould, 99 N.H. 85, 105 A.2d 48 (1954) (holding that common law lien for charges for work performed in repairing motor vehicle was defense to action of trover).

72 Noyes v. Patrick, 58 N.H. 618 (1879).

73 See, e.g., Partridge v. Philbrick, 60 N.H. 556 (1881) (where defendant claimed title after demand).

74 Peirce v. Finerty, 76 N.H. 38, 79 A. 23 (1911).

75 Farley v. Lincoln, 51 N.H. 577 (1872). Of course, no demand is necessary before seeking replevin of property taken unlawfully (Knapp v. Mahurin, 72 N.H. 595, 56 A. 315 (1903)), or with respect to which the defendant never had a right of possession. Proctor v. Tilton, 66 N.H. 3, 17 A. 638 (1888).

76 One hour was enough in Partridge v. Philbrick, 60 N.H. 556 (1881).

77 Peirce v. Finerty, 76 N.H. 38, 79 A. 23 (1911).

§ 18.06. When Replevin Does Not Lie—In General

Prior to 1873, the Court repeatedly held that replevin would not lie for the wrongful detention of property, with the sole exception of cattle taken damage feasant.[78] Those cases are, of course, no longer reliable. However, a number of other pre-1873 exemptions from replevin are still in force.

§ 18.07. —Property In Custodia Legis

Like attachment and trustee process, replevin will not lie against goods in the possession of the court or its officers (in custodia legis).[79] In 1825, the Legislature removed a portion of this exemption and allowed replevin of goods attached on mesne process.[80] This exemption was reinstated when the replevin statute was revised in 1973. Property in other types of legal custody has always been exempt from replevin. Goods taken by a sheriff on execution from a judgment debtor may not be replevied;[81] neither may goods impounded by the sheriff under statutory authority.[82] Similarly, replevin will not lie to take goods already held by the sheriff under another writ of replevin.[83]

Library References

CJS Replevin §§ 25 et seq.
Replevin or claim-and-delivery: modern view as to validity of statute or contractual provision authorizing summary repossession of consumer goods sold under retail installment sales contract. 45 ALR 3d 1233.

§ 18.08. —Property Replevied by the Plaintiff

Although property may be replevied by a third party after the plaintiff has taken possession of it on replevin,[84] the defendant cannot simply re-replevy goods which have been recovered from him by the plaintiff.[85]

---

78 Woodward v. Grand Trunk Ry. Co., 46 N.H. 524 (1866).

79 Smith v. Huntington, 3 N.H. 76 (1824) (goods held by sheriff on an attachment); Mitchell v. Roberts, 50 N.H. 486 (1871) (property held by sheriff on execution).

80 Melcher v. Lamprey, 20 N.H. 403 (1845). See also Mitchell v. Roberts, 50 N.H. 486 (1871); Carkin v. Babbitt, 58 N.H. 579 (1879); Mechanicks National Bank v. Parker, 109 N.H. 87, 242 A.2d 69 (1968).

81 Mitchell v. Roberts, 50 N.H. 486 (1871); Kittridge v. Holt, 55 N.H. 621 (1875); Kellogg v. Churchill, 2 N.H. 412 (1821); Melcher v. Lamprey, 20 N.H. 403 (1845); Bonney v. Smith, 59 N.H. 411 (1879).

82 State v. Barrels of Liquor, 47 N.H. 369 (1867).

83 Sanborn v. Leavitt, 43 N.H. 473 (1862); Bonney v. Smith, 59 N.H. 411 (1879).

84 Id.

85 Sanborn v. Leavitt, 43 N.H. 473 (1862).

Library References

CJS Replevin § 36

§ 18.09. —Property Subject to a Contract for Sale

The Court has refused to allow a buyer under a contract of sale to use replevin as a means of requiring specific performance. In *Chellis v. Grimes*,[86] the Court held that the proper legal remedy for a seller's breach was damages, not replevin. The Court has also declined to allow sellers who have agreed to accept payment over time to replevy goods before the time for payment has expired.[87]

§ 18.10. —Property Held Pending Investigation of the Plaintiff's Claim

In *Peirce v. Finerty*,[88] the Court held that replevin will not lie for wrongful detention in any case where the holder entertains a reasonable doubt about the plaintiff's right to possession while a reasonable investigation is being made. The Court further held that it is immaterial on what points the doubts may arise, so long as they are reasonable and are resolved in a reasonable time. Where an action is already pending between the plaintiff and holder which tests the parties' respective rights to possession, replevin may not be brought to compel delivery pendente lite.[89]

§ 18.11. —Property Given Away by the Plaintiff's Cotenant

In an unusual case, the Supreme Court has held that replevin will not lie against a donee of the plaintiff's cotenant.[90] A husband, who had recently separated from his wife, gave the family dog to a friend. The wife then sought to recover the dog from the friend by replevin, but the district court denied the use of the writ on the ground that it would have had the effect of revoking her husband's gift of his half of the dog. The Supreme Court upheld the district court's ruling on the ground that replevin will not lie against a

---

86 72 N.H. 104, 54 A. 943 (1903).

87 Kimball v. Farnum, 61 N.H. 348 (1881); Proctor v. Tilton, 65 N.H. 3, 17 A. 638 (1888); Nutting v. Nutting, 63 N.H. 221 (1884). Where the seller has agreed to wait an indefinite period before receiving payment, he cannot maintain replevin without first giving the buyer a demand for payment and waiting it reasonable time for him to complete his title. Kimball v. Farnum, 61 N.H. 348 (1881). Where he has given the buyer a reasonable time to pay, no demand is necessary. Proctor v. Tilton, 65 N.H. 3, 17 A. 638 (1888).

88 76 N.H. 38, 79 A. 23 (1911).

89 *Id.*

90 Sullivan v. Ringland, 117 N.H. 596, 376 A.2d 130 (1977).

donee of the plaintiff's cotenant.[91] It was impossible, no matter what procedure was employed, to reestablish the status quo, and use of the writ obviously could serve no proper purpose.

Library References

CJS Replevin § 49

Maintenance of replevin or similar possessory remedy by cotenant, or security transaction creditor thereof, against other cotenants. 93 ALR 2d 358.

Maintainability of replevin or similar possessory action where defendant, at time action is brought, is no longer in possession of property. 97 ALR 2d 896.

§ 18.12. —Motor Vehicles Purchased in Good Faith

The Court has held that, where a good faith purchaser bought a motor vehicle and the title was facially valid, and the purchaser otherwise had no notice of the adverse claims against the vehicle, that the title procured was a good one.[92]

§ 18.13. Procedure To Obtain a Writ of Replevin—In General

Actions of replevin, like proceedings in equity seeking injunctive relief, consist of two procedural phases. The first phase is the pretrial effort to recover the property in issue from the defendant's possession; the second phase is the case in chief, which seeks to establish the plaintiff's right to possession of the property, to apportion damages and to resolve other related issues. The first stage is regulated largely by RSA 536-A. The second is governed by principles of New Hampshire case law.

Forms

Writ of Replevin (Superior Court), see Volume 6.
Writ of Replevin (District Court), see Volume 6.
Order of Notice—Replevin Proceeding (Superior Court), see Volume 6.

§ 18.14. —Form of the Complaint

Replevin may be brought in either the district courts or the superior court, depending on the value of the property sought to be recovered.[93] Replevin is begun by filling out a complaint which identifies with particularity the

---

91 *Id.*

92 Dartmouth Motor Sales v. Wilcox, 128 N.H. 526, 517 A.2d 804 (1986).

93 RSA 536-A:1. The plaintiff's claim of value, rather than the value proven at trial, forms the basis for jurisdiction in either the district court or superior court. Stevens v. Chase, 61 N.H. 340 (1881); Adams v. Spaulding, 64 N.H. 384, 10 A. 688 (1887). However, the court may examine whether the claim is reasonable at any time before trial, either on its own or the defendant's motion, and may dismiss the complaint if it finds that the claimed value is beyond the jurisdictional amount. RSA 536-A:1.

item sought,[94] states the nature and source of the plaintiff's right to immediate possession,[95] describes how the defendant obtained the article and why,
how and where he is keeping it,[96] and states its value.[97] The complaint must
also give the name and address of the defendant, of any person holding the
property[98] and of any "known lienholder"[99] and state whether the property
is exempt from execution.[100] The complaint must be executed by the plaintiff
under oath.[101]

Library References

CJS Replevin §§ 143–152

§ 18.15. —Filing in Court and Service of the Complaint

An original of the complaint and two service copies for each defendant
must be filed in court before any service is made upon the defendant.[102]
When a writ is sought after notice, the court will, "without delay," issue
orders of notice requiring the plaintiff to serve the defendant by a particular
method within a specified time.[103] The court will include in the order of
notice a requirement that the defendant appear at a hearing between ten and
twenty days after the date of the order and "show cause why the property
should not be taken from the defendant and delivered to the applicant."[104]

---

94 RSA 536-A:2(III); Lewis v. Claggett, Smith 187 (1807). In *Lewis*, Justice Smith listed,
in footnote 1, several descriptions which have been regarded by other courts as
sufficient for replevin.

95 RSA 536-A:2(I). Lewis v. Claggett, Smith 187 (1807). A copy of any bill of sale or
other "written instrument upon which such title or right is claimed" must also be
attached to the complaint.

96 RSA 536-A:2(II).

97 RSA 536-A:2(III). Statements of value may be amended on the plaintiff's motion and
in response to a defendant's objection to the sufficiency of a bond. Briggs v. Wiswell,
56 N.H. 319 (1876).

98 RSA 536-A:2(III).

99 RSA 536-A:2(IV).

100 RSA 536-A:2(IV).

101 RSA 536-A:2.

102 At least as a matter of procedure, replevin is no longer an action at law.

103 RSA 536-A:3. RSA 536-A:3 provides that service "shall be by personal service or
certified mail, return receipt requested, or in such other manner as the Court may
determine under the circumstances appearing from the complaint and affidavit." The
phrase "complaint and affidavit" apparently refers to the verified complaint that begins
the action. No provision is made in the statute for an affidavit specifically addressed to
the issue of service.

104 RSA 536-A:3.

The order of notice will also notify the defendant that he can respond before the hearing by filing affidavits and can appear at the hearing and present testimony and that he can, either before or at the hearing, file a bond to retain possession of the property.[105] Finally, the order will inform the defendant that a writ of replevin will be issued if he defaults,[106] and will order him not to remove, damage, or encumber the property "until further order of the court."[107] The complaint, with orders of notice attached, must be served on the defendant, but need not be served on any other person who happens to be in possession of the property. When a writ of replevin has been issued ex parte, the complaint and writ will be served together on the defendant, and the writ will also be served on any other person having possession of the property. An order of notice, containing substantially the same terms as set out above, will also be issued by the court and served with the complaint. Any defendant or person from whom the property is taken on an ex parte writ may move for an earlier hearing than set out in the order of notice, and the court may shorten the time before hearing to no less than two days from the granting of the motion.[108]

§ 18.16. —Ex Parte Issuance of the Writ

RSA 536-A:12 permits the court to issue a writ of replevin prior to notice and hearing[109] if the plaintiff's complaint and any associated affidavits show probable cause to believe that the property was stolen by the defendant,[110] consists, in part, of credit cards or negotiable instruments,[111] will perish

---

105 *Id.*

106 *Id.*

107 RSA 536-A:4. This is an exception to Superior Court Rule 161(a) and provides much broader protection than is afforded by RSA 511-A:6 in the case of attachments and trustee process. A plaintiff seeking an attachment has stated under oath that he has a good claim, believes there is no defense, and doubts that the defendant will have sufficient assets to pay a judgment or, in an equity proceeding for specific performance to transfer a unique chattel, will have the asset to convey unless it is attached before the case progresses further. In the case of replevin, however, the plaintiff has sworn that the specific article involved is his property or that he has a right to exclusive and immediate possession. In the former case, if the defendant transfers the goods, he may be defrauding the plaintiff as a potential creditor or purchaser. In the latter case, he will be depriving the plaintiff of his property.

   It may also be argued that the court's temporary order prevents any other legal process from attaching to the property while the action is pending.

108 RSA 536-A:13.

109 The Court has stated that it "looks askance" at such orders. Garthe v. Mills, 118 N.H. 270, 385 A.2d 855 (1978).

110 RSA 536-A:12(I).

111 RSA 536-A:12(II).

before any hearing can be arranged, or is in immediate danger, due to the defendant's threats, of being destroyed, seriously harmed, concealed, taken out of state or sold to an "innocent purchaser."[112] Threats to the property itself may be shown by the plaintiff's averments in the complaint or by the affidavit of a third party.[113] The court may also allow the plaintiff to produce physical evidence or testimony.[114]

If the court finds probable cause, it should set forth that finding and the evidence to support it in writing and issue the writ. Unlike the case with attachment and trustee process, in replevin the court completes the writ form and delivers it to the plaintiff, along with an order of notice in the usual form. If the defendant, after service, wishes an earlier hearing date than the one set forth in the order of notice, he may move the court to hold a hearing not less than forty-eight hours after notice to the plaintiff.[115]

§ 18.17. —Preliminary Hearing

The preliminary, or show cause, hearing must be held between ten and twenty days after issuance of the order of notice, unless a sooner hearing is requested by a defendant against whom an ex parte writ has been issued. The plaintiff is not required to carry a heavier burden in order to obtain a preliminary writ of replevin than he would to obtain the writ after a final hearing on the merits, and the parties have the same burden of proof on the respective issues which they would have at a final hearing.[116] The court must decide which party "with reasonable probability, is entitled to possession, use and disposition of the property pending final adjudication of the claims" and, if it decides that the plaintiff is entitled to immediate possession, whether the equities of the situation require issuance of the writ prior to a final hearing.[117]

In an appropriate case, the preliminary hearing may be combined with the final hearing. The defendant can always avoid the preliminary hearing and retain possession of the property during the pendency of the case by

---

112 RSA 536-A:12(III).

113 *Id.*

114 RSA 536-A:12.

115 RSA 536-A:13.

116 The statement in RSA 536-A:5 that the writ will be issued if the defendant "fails to appear at the preliminary hearing" refers to his physical presence in court rather than his filing of an Appearance.

117 RSA 536-A:5.

posting a bond with the court prior to either the hearing or delivery of the property to the plaintiff.[118]

§ 18.18. —Defendant's Responsive Pleadings

(a) *In General.* The defendant must file a pleading in response to the replevin complaint. At common law, the form of the defendant's response was as formalized as the writ; under RSA 536-A, a simple paragraph-by-paragraph answer may be substituted for the traditional common law pleas. But, whatever the form, scrupulous attention must be paid to the issues addressed if the defendant is to avoid inadvertent admissions.

At common law, the writ of replevin alleged an unlawful taking (caption) and the defendant could respond in a number of ways. He could either admit the taking and justify it as lawful (e.g., because he was a sheriff following the command of a writ of attachment[119] or a tax collector acting on a warrant), deny the taking, or deny the plaintiff's right of possession by asserting that the property belonged to the defendant or to a third party.[120] If he admitted but justified the taking, he filed an avowry (i.e., he avowed the taking). If he denied the taking, he entered a plea of non cepit (after 1873, he entered non detinet if he denied the detention).[121] And if he claimed that title lay in someone other than the plaintiff, he filed a plea in bar or plea of property. (After 1825, pleas in bar, including non cepit, could be entered by Brief Statement.) Under common law rules of pleading, the plaintiff could then respond to the avowry with a plea in bar of the avowry (claiming, for example, that the defendant may have taken the property lawfully but that he then acted in such a manner as to make him a trespasser ab initio)[122] or could respond to the plea of property in the defendant with a plea of property in himself. No further plea was required to non cepit or non detinet since they raised the general issue.

It is important to remember that, while these antiquated forms and their Latin titles may have passed from our usage, the essential distinctions in allegations and admissions which they represented have not. The general

---

118 RSA 536-A:14.

119 The sheriff cannot, however, justify actions under a writ when he has not made return within the time allowed. Barrett v. White, 3 N.H. 210 (1825).

120 "There is no doubt that possession is prima facie evidence of property, sufficient to enable a party who has it to maintain replevin. . . . But it is only prima facie evidence and may be rebutted by showing a title in a third person." Brown v. Webster, 4 N.H. 500, 500–01 (1828).

121 Kittredge v. Holt, 55 N.H. 621 (1875); Carter v. Piper, 57 N.H. 217 (1876).

122 See, e.g., Osgood v. Green, 30 N.H. 210 (1855); Kimball v. Adams, 3 N.H. 182 (1825).

issue in replevin is not, as in most other actions, a denial of all material facts alleged in the complaint.[123] It is a denial of the taking or detention only.[124] There are, in fact, two central issues in replevin: (1) whether the defendant took or detained the goods; and (2) whether they are the plaintiff's property.[125] The defendant is free to deny each issue separately. But if he pleads non cepit or non detinet—i.e., denies the taking or detention—he will thereby be deemed to admit the plaintiff's property.[126] And if he pleads property in himself or a third person, he will be deemed to admit the taking or detention.[127] Under modern rules of pleading, the defendant can, of course, plead both, even though they are inconsistent defenses,[128] but if he files only a General Appearance he will be deemed to have denied only the taking or detention, not to have justified it by any special right, and to have admitted the plaintiff's property.

(b) *Sufficiency.* The sufficiency of a defendant's response to a replevin complaint is judged by a well-established set of rules. If the defendant avows the taking or detention, his avowry or answer must meet the standards of specificity and completeness which apply to a declaration in a writ.[129] While the defendant will usually be given a chance to amend to correct deficiencies,[130] by the time he is through, he must have stated the time, place and manner of the taking or detention, the nature and basis of the authority under which he acted in taking each article,[131] and the way in which the taking and subsequent holding complied with that authority.[132]

---

123 Dickinson v. Lovell, 35 N.H. 2 (1857).

124 Sinclair v. Wheeler, 69 N.H. 538, 45 A. 408 (1898).

125 Dickinson v. Lovell, 35 N.H. 2 (1857).

126 Mitchell v. Roberts, 50 N.H. 486 (1871); Chellis v. Grimes, 72 N.H. 104, 54 A. 943 (1903); Lothrop v. Locke, 59 N.H. 532 (1880); Sinclair v. Wheeler, 69 N.H. 538, 45 A. 1085 (1898). This is apparently what happened in Derry Loan & Discount Co. v. Falconer. 84 N.H. 450, 152 A. 427 (1930). The defendant may also plead inconsistent titles. Williams v. Beede, 15 N.H. 483 (1844).

127 Page v. Ramsdell, 59 N.H. 575 (1880).

128 Carter v. Piper, 57 N.H. 217 (1876).

129 Brackett v. Whidden, 3 N.H. 17 (1823).

130 See, e.g., Lothrop v. Locke, 59 N.H. 532 (1880); Sinclair v. Wheeler, 69 N.H. 538, 45 A. 1085 (1898).

131 Lothrop v. Locke, 59 N.H. 532 (1880); Sinclair v. Wheeler, 69 N.H. 538, 45 A. 1085 (1898).

132 When the defendant avows the taking of beasts under RSA 471, he need only allege that they were found in his enclosure and need not also allege his title or right of possession in that enclosure. McIntire v. Marden, 9 N.H. 288 (1838). Detention to enforce a common law or statutory lien is a good defense in a replevin action. Hiltz v.

(c) *Particular Responses.* If the defendant pleads the general issue—non cepit or non detinet—he may deny either the place or manner of taking or detention alleged or both.[133] If he simply files an Appearance, he will be regarded as having denied both.

If the defendant pleads property, he must specify the identity of the owner.[134] He may not simply deny the plaintiff's title. If he claims property in himself, he will thereby be deemed to admit that he had no right to take or hold the property if it turns out that the property belonged to another.[135] The defendant's plea of property must also be sufficient on its face to counter whatever allegations the plaintiff makes of a right to immediate and exclusive possession.

The defendant must be careful, not only that he does not inadvertently admit a fact which he wishes to contest and that he adequately sets forth his defense, but that he does not inadvertently set forth inconsistent defenses in a confusing way. A defendant may, for example, both deny the taking and claim property in himself,[136] but he should not do so by filing a General Appearance (the equivalent of non cepit or non detinet) and a Brief Statement raising title. Such a response will not make clear that the defendant denies the taking or detention. Instead, he should file an Answer expressly denying the taking or detention along with his Brief Statement raising title.

Gould, 99 N.H. 85, 105 A.2d 48 (1954). When the defendant avows the taking under multiple authorities, he need only prove enough authority to justify the taking and will not lose if his additional authority is bad. Brackett v. Whidden, 3 N.H. 17 (1823). But where his justification for the taking relies upon more than just the validity of a process, he must show the additional background facts on which the authority is based. Sanford Manufacturing Co. v. Wiggin, 14 N.H. 441 (1843).

133 Sanford Manufacturing Co. v. Wiggin, 14 N.H. 441 (1843). A denial of both the place and method of taking is called "non cepit modo et forma."

134 Dickinson v. Lovell, 35 N.H. 2 (1857); Sinclair v. Wheeler, 69 N.H. 538, 45 A. 408 (1898). In this respect, Lewis v. Claggett, Smith 187 (1807), has been reversed. If he claims property in himself or another, the defendant must prove, but need not allege in his pleading, the basis of that title. McIntire v. Marden, 9 N.H. 288 (1838); Great Falls Co. v. Worster, 15 N.H. 412 (1844). He may also prove property in a person other than the one he named if he does not claim property in himself. Compare Brown v. Webster, 4 N.H. 500 (1828) and Lewis v. Claggett, Smith 187 (1807). See also Moore v. Stevens, 42 N.H. 404 (1861).

135 Lewis v. Claggett, Smith 187 (1807).

136 A defendant may also enter inconsistent pleas of title. Carter v. Piper, 57 N.H. 217 (1876). In the days of strict common law pleading, this right was at first denied the defendant (see Sanford Manufacturing Co. v. Wiggin, 14 N.H. 441 (1843)), but the Court later confirmed it if each issue was raised by a separate plea. Taylor v. True, 27 N.H. 220 (1853).

The defendant can also move to transfer for improper venue[137] or to dismiss the complaint for lack of jurisdiction[138] as well as for all the usual grounds of facial[139] or procedural[140] insufficiency. One of the most frequently raised grounds for dismissal during the nineteenth century was the defendant's claim that the plaintiff had posted either no bond or an insufficient bond.[141] That problem eventually worked itself out in practice and is largely taken care of today by the requirement in RSA 536-A:7 that the court approve the size and form of the bond before any writ issues. But it is worth remembering that the defendant may move to dismiss the writ or complaint if no bond[142] or an inadequate bond has been filed.[143] And the court always has power to examine the sufficiency of the bond on its own or a party's motion and to require that it be increased.[144]

Library References

CJS Replevin §§ 154–160
Voluntary dismissal of replevin action by plaintiff as affecting defendant's right to judgment for the return or value of the property. 24 ALR3d 768.

§ 18.19. —Plaintiff's Reply

The plaintiff need not respond to the defendant's avowry or plea of non cepit or non detinet. But he must reply to the claim of property because it attacks his right to maintain the action. The plaintiff must reply that he has title or a right of immediate and exclusive possession which is superior to the title alleged by the defendant.[145] The plaintiff may not simply deny the

---

137 Wheeler & Wilson Mfg. Co. v. Whitcomb, 62 N.H. 411 (1882).

138 E.g., when the complaint contains an incorrect statement of the property's value. Lewis v. Claggett, Smith 187 (1807).

139 E.g., when the complaint contains an inadequate statement of the property's value. Lewis v. Claggett, Smith 187 (1807).

140 In Chellis v. Grimes, 72 N.H. 104, 54 A. 943 (1903), for example, the Court stated that if the defendant pleaded non cepit to a writ of replevin seeking to obtain property which the defendant had agreed to sell to the plaintiff, the plaintiff would be nonsuited and in Lothrop v. Locke, 59 N.H. 532 (1880), the Court said that the plaintiff in an action to recover a piano in the possession of a woman should have been nonsuited when he brought the action against the woman's father who replied non cepit.

141 See Sumner v. Steward, 2 N.H. 389 (1819); Briggs v. Wiswell, 56 N.H. 319 (1876); Whittemore v. Jones, 5 N.H. 362 (1831); Chadwick v. Badger, 9 N.H. 450 (1838). However, a plaintiff cannot avoid a bond, which he has voluntarily executed and delivered to the court, on the ground of a technical deficiency.

142 Sumner v. Steward, 2 N.H. 39 (1819).

143 Briggs v. Wiswell, 56 N.H. 319 (1876).

144 Id.

145 Bonney v. Smith, 59 N.H. 411 (1879); Taylor v. True, 27 N.H. 220 (1853).

title asserted by the defendant;[146] he must allege his own title or the complaint will be dismissed.[147] He must "prevail on the strength of his own title and not on the weaknesses of his opponent's."[148] Pleading or proof by the plaintiff of title in a third party[149] or in himself in a manner different from that alleged in the pleadings[150] will defeat his action. At trial, he must then prove his own title.[151]

Library References

CJS Replevin § 164

§ 18.20. —Hearing on the Merits and Issuance of the Writ Generally

The pleadings, of course, determine the issues to be tried and the nature of the relief which the court may grant. If the defendant relies solely on the general issue, the plaintiff will have the burden of establishing the taking or detention but will not be obliged to show his own title or to negative any special privilege to take in the defendant. If the defendant raises title, the plaintiff will have to establish his title or superior right of immediate and exclusive possession. If the defendant admits the taking but seeks to justify it, the plaintiff will have no burden, and the defendant will be required to establish that he enjoyed a special privilege to act and that his actions fell within that privilege. In the first two cases, the plaintiff will open; in the last, the defendant may.[152] If the defendant relies on inconsistent defenses, each

---

146 Dickinson v. Lovell, 35 N.H. 2 (1857).

147 Moore v. Stevens, 42 N.H. 404 (1861).

148 National Shawmut Bank v. Cutter, 105 N.H. 206, 196 A.2d 706 (1963).

149 Dickinson v. Lovell, 35 N.H. 2 (1857). Under the holdings of Dickinson v. Lovell, 35 N.H. 2 (1857) and National Shawmut Bank v. Cutter, 105 N.H. 206, 196 A.2d 706 (1963), a plaintiff in replevin may not recover the property or damages for its taking or holding where property is an issue and he merely proves that the defendant's claim of title is defective but does not also show his own title. (A contrary interpretation of the *Dickinson* and *Lewis* holdings is expressed by the editor of Smith's Reports at 190, note II, but *National Shawmut Bank* would seem to have rejected it.) Lewis v. Claggett, Smith 187 (1807), held that a defendant could not succeed where property was an issue if he claimed property in himself but the proof showed it to be in a third party. In a case, therefore, where the plaintiff and defendant each claim property in themselves but the proof shows it to be in a third person, the court cannot enter a common law judgment but must make an equitable adjustment of the parties' rights as shown by the proof. See R.C. Hazelton Co. v. Southwick Constr. Co., 105 N.H. 25, 192 A.2d 610 (1963).

150 Moore v. Stevens, 42 N.H. 404 (1861) (plaintiffs pleaded that they held the property jointly, when they held it as partners). This type of error can be cured by amendment.

151 Taylor v. True, 27 N.H. 220 (1853); Everett National Bank v. DeSchuiteneer, 109 N.H. 112, 244 A.2d 196 (1968); Moore v. Stevens, 42 N.H. 404 (1861).

152 Bills v. Vose, 27 N.H. 212 (1853); Belknap v. Wendell, 21 N.H. 175 (1850); Chesley v. Chesley, 37 N.H. 229 (1858).

party will carry the burden appropriate to each issue, and the plaintiff will open if there is any affirmative issue for him to prove.[153]

At a preliminary hearing on the complaint, whether held before or after issuance of the writ, the plaintiff must show "with reasonable probability" that he "is entitled to possession, use and disposition of the property" while the case remains undecided.[154] Unless the defendant admits the taking and seeks to justify it, the plaintiff's burden has two parts. He must show "with reasonable probability" both that all the facts stated in his complaint are true and that he is entitled to "possession, use and disposition" of the property while the case is pending. If the plaintiff does not meet this burden by failing either to prove his complaint or to refute the defendant's claim of right to "possession, use and disposition," the writ will not issue. If he meets it, the court will issue the writ "forthwith,"[155] so long as the plaintiff posts a bond or other "written undertaking executed by the applicant and one or more sufficient sureties, approved by the court"[156] equal to twice the property's value"[157] and conditioned on the plaintiff's prosecuting the action to completion, returning the property to the defendant, if required to do so, and paying the defendant any damages or costs awarded in the action.[158] The

---

153 Bills v. Vose, 27 N.H. 212 (1853).

154 RSA 536-A:5.

155 *Id.*

156 RSA 536-A:7. In Briggs v. Wiswell, 56 N.H. 319 (1876), the Court held that the sheriff (who in those days took replevin bonds from plaintiffs) could require the plaintiff to give a bond for twice the actual value, regardless of the plaintiff's allegations of value. As the court now takes and approves the bonds before issuing the writ, that power has devolved upon it. But the sheriff is still responsible for checking the goods when he replevies them to ascertain whether the amount of the bond is adequate and to tell the court in his return if he believes that it is not.

157 In the absence of an agreement, including upon a default, the court must determine the value of the property. RSA 536-A:7.

158 RSA 536-A:7. The bond must be signed by the plaintiff personally and covers payment of damages allowed on set-off. But it is not security for the plaintiff's wrongful acts during the pendency of the case. Derry Loan & Discount Co. v. Falconer, 84 N.H. 450, 453, 152 A. 427, 429 (1930) (stating that the delivery of a replevied car by the plaintiff to a third party while the case was pending would be a conversion if the plaintiff did not have title to the car). Additionally, there is no error in the court excluding evidence of such interim dealings with the property at trial. R.C. Hazelton Co. v. Southwick Constr. Co., 105 N.H. 25, 192 A.2d 610 (1963).

The technical requisites of the replevin bond were long-ago established. In Sumner v. Steward, 2 N.H. 39 (1819), the Court determined that the replevin bond should run to the sheriff, his representatives and assigns, could secure payment of "costs and damages" only, and could be secured by only one surety. Under RSA 536-A:7, the bond must now run to the court. In Whittemore v. Jones, 5 N.H. 362 (1831), the Court held that a bond could include additional term, including one indemnifying the sheriff. Such

defendant may prevent replevy of the goods or recover any of the goods replevied which have not yet been delivered to the plaintiff by posting a similar bond in favor of the plaintiff.[159] The court should make findings of fact to support the issuance of the writ and to assist the sheriff in locating the property.[160]

Library References

CJS Replevin § 170

§ 18.21. —Issuance of the Writ After Default

A writ of replevin will be issued on default after notice.[161]

Library References

CJS Replevin § 245

§ 18.22. Service of the Writ of Replevin—In General

If the court finds that the plaintiff is probably entitled to "possession, use and disposition" of the property pending a final decision, it will issue a writ of replevin[162] directed to the "sheriff, constable or police officer within whose jurisdiction the property is located"[163] directing him to go to a particular place or places, seize the property and hold it.[164] The sheriff or

---

    a term is no longer required in light of RSA 536-A:15. In Chadwick v. Badger, 9 N.H. 450 (1838), the Court held that the bond was not made invalid by the inclusion of surplus description which did not effect the parties' ability to understand its language.

159 RSA 536-A:14. The defendant's bond, however, must be in an amount equal to twice the value of the property "as stated in the verified complaint . . . or as determined by the court" and need not be conditioned on defending the action to the end.

160 RSA 536-A:8 requires the writ to specify "the location or locations where . . . there is probable cause to believe the property or some part thereof will be found. . . ."

161 RSA 536-A:3 and 5.

162 RSA 536-A:5.

163 RSA 536-A:8.

164 *Id.* In the days when the plaintiff delivered his writ and bond to the sheriff before any action had been taken by the court, the Supreme Court stated that the sheriff in replevin acted for both parties—recovering the property for the plaintiff and seeing that the plaintiff posted adequate security for its return to protect the defendant. Sumner v. Steward, 2 N.H. 39 (1819). That theory is, at least in part, no longer correct. Under RSA 536-A:7 and 9, the sheriff's former functions are split, and the court, rather than the sheriff, has the responsibility to examine and approve the bond in the first instance. However, even after the court has approved the bond, the sheriff still has the duty, when serving the writ, "to inquire" as to the value of the property . . . to satisfy himself to a reasonable certainty that the plaintiff has not undervalued them, and that the bond tendered is, as to the amount of the penal sum, a substantial compliance with the statute." Briggs v. Wiswell, 56 N.H. 319, 321 (1876). If he believes the bond to be inadequate,

451

other serving officer is not free to search for the property according to his own instincts or the directions of the plaintiff; he must go only to the places directed by the court in its original order or in subsequent orders endorsed on the back of the writ.[165]

The writ may authorize the sheriff or serving officer to enter a building or "private premises"[166] upon the same findings, but it must do so explicitly.[167] When the writ directs the officer to look for the property inside a "building or enclosure,"[168] he must first identify himself and the purpose of his visit to the person in charge and request that the property be produced.[169] If he is refused, he may either force his way into the building and seize the property or withdraw.[170] He is required to withdraw if he "reasonably believes" that forcible entry and seizure "will involve a substantial risk of death or serious bodily harm to any person."[171] If the sheriff chooses not to enter forcibly, he must immediately make return stating this decision and his reasons for concluding that a substantial risk of death or serious bodily harm would have been presented by a forcible seizure.[172] The court, upon receiving such a return, has full discretion and authority to make any further order to protect the plaintiff's rights to "possession, use and disposition" of the property.[173]

---

he should state that conclusion on his return so that the court may order an increase in bond. See RSA 536-A:7 and 9.

165 The court must make specific findings of fact that "there is probable cause to believe the property or some part thereof will be found" in each location it initially directs the officer to search. RSA 536-A:8. If the property cannot all be found in those locations, the plaintiff, without further notice to the defendant, may file further affidavits or produce testimony to establish probable cause to believe that the property or some part of it is located in another place, and the court may, without a hearing or ex parte, then endorse further orders on the writ directing the sheriff or other officer to search those locations. RSA 536-A:8.

166 For example, an apartment, mobile home, boat, "enclosure," or storage locker. Cf. RSA 536-A:9 and 10.

167 RSA 536-A:6.

168 The term "enclosure," as used in RSA 536-A:10, presumably is meant to refer to "private premises" (RSA 536-A:6) which are supervised or in the possession of another natural person. Thus, the court must specifically authorize an officer to enter "private premises," but when they are an "enclosure," he must just request that the property be brought out to him.

169 RSA 536-A:10.

170 *Id.*

171 *Id.*

172 *Id.*

173 *Id.* The statute says that the court "thereupon shall make such orders and decrees as may be appropriate." Whether the scope of such orders is limited, in the case of district courts, in some way by its jurisdictional limit of $25,000 or $50,000 is not clear.

The sheriff is directed by the writ to seize the property before serving a copy on the defendant.[174]

Library References

CJS Replevin § 117

§ 18.23. —Seizure of the Property and Subsequent Actions

When the sheriff or other serving officer finds the property, he must seize and retain it, "either by removing the property to a place of safekeeping or, upon good cause shown, by installing a keeper."[175] There is no provision for a "bulky article replevin"—the property must be seized and taken out of the defendant or other holder's possession. If the property to be seized is used as a dwelling,[176] the sheriff or serving officer must place a keeper in charge for two days, then evict the persons inside, as well as their possessions which are not subject to the replevin, and take the property.[177]

§ 18.24. —Service of Copies Upon the Defendant or His Agent

The sheriff is not required to serve a copy of the writ of replevin on any person other than the defendant, including a person in whose possession he finds the property if that person is not the defendant's agent. After seizing the property, either by installing a keeper or removing it, the sheriff or other serving officer must "without delay" serve a copy of the writ, bond, complaint, and supporting affidavits on the defendant or any agent of the defendant found holding the property. Service may be in-hand, at the abode of either the defendant or his agent with a "person of suitable age and discretion," or by registered mail to the "last known address" of either.[178] The sheriff must make return to the issuing court within twenty days after seizing the property.[179]

---

174 RSA 536-A:9 and 11.

175 RSA 536-A:9.

176 It must be assumed that this means currently used as a dwelling at the time of seizure, although it may not require that anyone be "at home" at the time the sheriff or other serving officer appears with the writ.

177 RSA 536-A:9. Prior cases held that the defendant was not entitled to a return of the property rather than damages. Bell v. Bartlett, 7 N.H. 178 (1834); Sanborn v. Leavitt, 43 N.H. 473 (1862); Mitchell v. Roberts, 50 N.H. 486 (1871); Ramsey v. Landry, 78 N.H. 612, 102 A. 531 (1917). Those holdings have been reversed by RSA 536-A:18.

178 RSA 536-A:11.

179 RSA 536-A:17. Notwithstanding the language of the last sentence of RSA 536-A:9, the date of placing a keeper in possession is the date of the taking for purpose of making a return.

Library References

CJS Replevin §§ 115, 121

§ 18.25. Retention of Property Seized by the Sheriff; Recovery of Property by the Defendant

After seizing the property, the sheriff must "keep it in a secure place" until the court has decided who is entitled to have it pending the final decision (in the case of a writ issued ex parte) or until the plaintiff pays him his fees and expenses (in the case of a writ issued on notice).[180] During the period when the sheriff has possession, the defendant may recover the property by filing with the court a bond for double the alleged value of the property, payable to the plaintiff if the defendant fails to redeliver the property as required by the court or to pay any damages awarded.[181] Simultaneously with filing the bond in court, the defendant must serve on the plaintiff or his attorney a notice that the bond has been filed and a copy of the bond.[182] A similar notice should be sent to the sheriff or officer in possession to prevent his delivery of the property to the plaintiff, and proof of service must be filed in court.[183]

The plaintiff must file any objections to the sufficiency of the bond within five days,[184] again with a copy to the sheriff. Because the mere filing of objections does not suspend the sheriff's authority to redeliver the property to the defendant, the plaintiff should also ask for an order staying redelivery. The only issues raised by objections to the bond are the amount, the compliance of the bond's conditions with the requirements of the statute, and the sufficiency of the sureties. If the court finds the bond satisfactory, it will either order the sheriff to return the property (if the writ was issued after notice) or cancel the preliminary hearing (if the writ was issued ex parte). If the bond is not satisfactory, the court may permit the defendant to cure its deficiencies within a reasonable time. If the defendant fails to do so, the court will order the sheriff to deliver the property to the plaintiff.

If the defendant does not file a bond before the sheriff delivers the property to the plaintiff, he may not recover the property by doing so thereafter.[185]

---

180 RSA 536-A:17.

181 RSA 536-A:14. Of course, the defendant can also file the bond after the hearing and before a writ has been either issued or executed.

182 RSA 536-A:14.

183 *Id.*

184 *Id.*

185 *Id.*

§ 18.26. Awarding of Damages and Other Relief—In General

The nature of the relief which a court may grant in replevin has undergone some evolution during the past two centuries. At common law, it was originally held that the prevailing party was entitled to some damages, even if they were only nominal.[186] That holding was reversed in *McKean v. Cutter*,[187] and the *McKean* holding was reaffirmed in *National Shawmut Bank v. Cutter*.[188] In *National Shawmut*, Chief Justice Kenison wrote: "The award of damages is not compulsory and necessarily depends on the evidence in the case and the equities of the respective parties."[189]

§ 18.27. —Actual Damages and Return of the Property

While they need not be given, actual, nominal, and exemplary damages may be awarded according to certain established limitations. If the plaintiff wins, the court may order the property returned to him, if it has not already been put in his possession, and may award him damages actually caused by the unlawful taking or detention.[190] If the defendant wins on the general issue, he will receive no damages because he never had the property to begin with and is not entitled to damages solely because he was sued.[191] If the defendant wins on an avowry or on a plea of title, the court must order the

---

[186] Kendall v. Fitts, 22 N.H. 1 (1850). "In the action of replevin, damages should always be assessed, whether the verdict be for the plaintiff or defendant." 22 N.H. at 9–10.

[187] 48 N.H. 370 (1869). "In the nature of replevin, its form, substance, methods, or results, there is no peculiar need of damages as a basis or element of a judgment." 48 N.H. at 372.

[188] 105 N.H. 206, 196 A.2d 706 (1963).

[189] *Id.* at 209, 196 A.2d at 709.

[190] Kendall v. Fitts, 22 N.H. 1 (1850); Derry Loan & Discount Co. v. Falconer, 84 N.H. 450, 152 A. 427 (1930); Messer v. Bailey, 31 N.H. 2 (1855).

[191] Derry Loan & Discount Co. v. Falconer, 84 N.H. 450, 152 A. 427 (1930). "Even when the defendant prevails, there is no wrong against him in bringing the action of replevin." 84 N.H. at 452, 152 A. at 429. See also Mitchell v. Roberts, 50 N.H. 486 (1871); Dickinson v. Lovell, 35 N.H. 2 (1857).

property returned to him if he desires,[192] if it has been taken on a preliminary writ. Whether or not the property can be returned, the court may instead order the plaintiff to pay the defendant the value of the property as of the day it was replevied.[193]

The unsuccessful plaintiff does not have a right to elect to return the property he has replevied[194] and, if ordered to pay the value of the property, must pay the value as of the date of replevin even if the property has since declined in value.[195] In determining the value of the property on the date of replevin, the plaintiff's allegations of value are competent and sufficient,[196] but not conclusive,[197] evidence. The plaintiff will be allowed to show the circumstances under which he claimed the original value and to prove a lower value,[198] even if that proof runs counter to the court's preliminary finding of value implicit in approval of the bond.[199]

Library References

CJS Replevin §§ 263–275
Recovery of damages in replevin for value of use of property detained, by successful party having only security interest as conditional vendor, chattel mortgagee, or the like. 33 ALR2d 774.
Voluntary dismissal of replevin action by plaintiff as affecting defendant's right to judgment for the return or value of the property. 24 ALR3d 768.

§ 18.28. —Nominal Damages

In some circumstances, the defendant may be awarded nominal damages for the infringement of his possessory right.[200] Even nominal damages must

---

192 Return of the property has been called the "ancient judgment." Sanborn v. Leavitt, 43 N.H. 473, 474 (1862). The court may also decline to order the property returned or damages paid. National Shawmut Bank v. Cutter, 105 N.H. 206, 196 A.2d 706 (1963).

193 Dickinson v. Lovell, 35 N.H. 2 (1857).

194 Claggett v. Richards, 45 N.H. 360 (1864); Bell v. Bartlett, 7 N.H. 178 (1834). "The plaintiff in replevin, who has wrongfully sued out the process, cannot complain that he is required to pay the value, instead of having the privilege of returning them again to the defendant." Bell v. Bartlett, 7 N.H. at 190. See also Kendall v. Fitts, 22 N.H. 1 (1850).

195 Ramsey v. Landry, 78 N.H. 612, 102 A. 531 (1917); Carney v. Emerson, 82 N.H. 487, 136 A. 139 (1927). The plaintiff has no right to pay the damages actually sustained by the defendant rather than the value of the property replevied. Claggett v. Richards, 45 N.H. 360 (1864).

196 Sears, Roebuck & Co. v. Bonsant, 114 N.H. 270, 319 A.2d 633 (1974).

197 Briggs v. Wiswell, 56 N.H. 319 (1876).

198 *Id.*

199 See RSA 536-A:7.

200 Sanborn v. Leavitt, 43 N.H. 473 (1862).

be justified by the evidence and equities,[201] and they will only be awarded where the plaintiff's interference with the defendant's possession was not justified and the defendant's right of possession and obligation to account for it has expired before judgment. The most common example of such a defendant is a deputy sheriff holding the property under a writ of attachment or replevin, but any other bailee may also qualify.[202]

Library References

CJS Replevin § 268

§ 18.29. —Exemplary Damages

In extreme cases, where the plaintiff has abused the writ, exemplary damages may be awarded.[203]

Library References

CJS Replevin § 285
Necessity of determination or showing of liability for punitive damages before discovery or reception of evidence of defendant's wealth. 32 ALR4th 432.

§ 18.30. —Separate Judgments on Each Item of Property

A different judgment may be awarded on each piece of property replevied.[204] In that case, the court or jury must separately find the value of each item.[205]

§ 18.31. —Costs

Costs will be taxed to each side according to the issues found, and where some issues are found for each side, a set-off will be allowed and execution for costs will issue for the balance.[206]

---

201 National Shawmut Bank v. Cutter, 105 N.H. 206, 196 A.2d 706 (1963).

202 For example, a lienholder on property whose debt is paid or a receiptor. Sanborn v. Leavitt, 43 N.H. 473 (1862).

203 Dickinson v. Lovell, 35 N.H. 2 (1857).

204 Williams v. Beede, 15 N.H. 483 (1844). "If replevin be brought for divers chattels, the property in all which is in issue if the plaintiff's property be proved in some of the chattels only, he shall have damages for their detention and costs, although the defendant shall have a return of the other chattels and his damages." 15 N.H. at 484–85.

205 Williams v. Beede, 15 N.H. 483 (1844).

206 Jordan v. Cummings, 43 N.H. 134 (1861). "So far as replevin goes, the plaintiff is the prevailing party if he has the antecedent right to possession." Derry Loan and Discount Co. v. Falconer, 84 N.H. 450, 453, 152 A. 427, 429 (1930).

Library References

CJS Replevin § 261
Recovery of fees as damages by successful litigant in replevin or detinue action. 60 ALR2d 945.

§ 18.32. —Other Relief

(a) *Application of Equitable Principles.* In *National Shawmut Bank v. Cutter,*[207] Chief Justice Kenison wrote: "In this state replevin has become impregnated with equitable principles without strict regard to its common-law limitations."[208] The trial court in *National Shawmut Bank* had given judgment to the defendants in a car repossession action but had declined to award damages on the ground that, although replevin would not lie under the financing documents against either defendant, an award of damages, in light of the free use which the defendants had had of the car before repossession, would have constituted an unjust enrichment. The Court held that the trial court was not required to award damages just because the defendant had established a better legal right to possession than the plaintiff, but could instead let the plaintiff's equitable rights make up for the deficiencies in its legal rights and shape the remedy to fit the equities of the case.[209]

The *National Shawmut Bank* case climaxed several decades of development of equitable theories in replevin. In *Kimball v. Farnum,*[210] the Court had held that a transfer of a vendor's interest in a chattel sold under an agreement that the vendee could pay when able could not replevy the goods "until demand was made, and a reasonable time given the defendant after demand to complete his title."[211] In *Proctor v. Tilton,*[212] the Court had limited the *Kimball* holding by allowing replevin by a vendor against a vendee who was put in possession of the property subject to an obligation to complete payment within a reasonable time when the vendee failed to pay within the "reasonable time." The Court noted that the result would have been different if the vendee had expressly been given a period to pay, even an indefinite one, which had not yet expired. In *Partridge v. Philbrick,*[213] the Court had allowed replevin against a vendee whose time for payment had not expired

---

207 105 N.H. 206, 196 A.2d 706 (1963).

208 *Id.* at 208, 196 A.2d at 708.

209 105 N.H. 206, 196 A.2d 706 (1963).

210 61 N.H. 348 (1881).

211 *Id.*

212 65 N.H. 3, 17 A. 638 (1888).

213 60 N.H. 556 (1881).

when the vendee sold the property unconditionally to a third party, holding, in effect, that the Court would recognize and enforce the vendor's equitable right to hold the property as security for the purchase price. The same principle, although applied to an assignee of a vendor's documented security interest, had been recognized seventy years later in *Caraway v. Jean*.[214] The Court had long held that the vendor who sold and delivered goods subject to the vendee's obligation to pay after delivery could rescind the contract and replevy the goods from the vendee or, in some cases, his assignee, if he learned that the vendee's promise to pay was fraudulent when made.[215] In *Partridge v. Philbrick*,[216] the Court had suggested, but had not held, that a person holding property which had come into his possession lawfully might be entitled to request and receive time to investigate a plaintiff's right to possession before the writ could be brought. In *Peirce v. Finerty*,[217] the Court held that he did have such a right, saying that a refusal to deliver until the defendant had had a reasonable opportunity to investigate the plaintiff's claim was proper so long as there was a reasonable doubt on some point (lien, identity, authority, or law) related to the demand. In effect, the Court in *Peirce* had allowed the *defendant* in an action to replevy detained goods to make the inquiry which the trial court would have made at a hearing on a common law writ of detinue. This use of equitable principles to join the two procedures set the tone for the development of replevin in the twentieth century and for the allowance of certain types of collateral relief as part of the proceedings.[218]

In *National Shawmut Bank*, Chief Justice Kenison recognized a trend in replevin cases which had been developing throughout the twentieth century. Just as the nineteenth century saw the gradual evolution of replevin from a remedy to recover property wrongfully taken to a procedure for obtaining property wrongfully detained, so the twentieth century witnessed the application of equitable and quasi-equitable considerations to the decision of replevin actions. It can be argued that the completion of the first development actually brought about the second since, with the acknowledgment, at first of a common law[219] and later of a statutory basis for recovering property

---

214   97 N.H. 506, 92 A.2d 660 (1952). ·

215   See Bradley v. Obear, 10 N.H. 477 (1839).

216   60 N.H. 556 (1881).

217   76 N.H. 38, 79 A. 23 (1911).

218   The Court had also refused to allow the real purchaser of goods to appear and defend in a replevin action when the purpose of such a defense was only to further a scheme of fraudulent purchase. Levy v. Woodcock, 63 N.H. 413 (1885).

219   In the writ of detinue. Dame v. Dame, 43 N.H. 37 (1861).

wrongfully detained, the court was required to decide what notice and waiting period, if any, the plaintiff was obliged to give the defendant before compelling a return of the property.[220] The effect of this infusion of equitable principles into replevin actions will doubtless be magnified by the requirement in RSA 536-A that no writ be issued without prior court approval. Since the enactment of RSA 536-A, equitable principles have been applied before, as well as after, the writ has been issued, with the effect that the force of a plaintiff's purely legal right to possession has been diluted. This tension between the common law presumption that possession not obtained by force was lawful and the statutory ability to recover by force goods whose possession had been lawfully obtained, required the court to announce, as part of the common law, equitable prerequisites for the issuance of the writ in cases of wrongful detention.

(b) *Appointment of a Receiver.* In *Peirce v. Finerty*,[221] the plaintiff sought replevin or the appointment of a receiver to collect the property. The appointment of a receiver would only have substituted a court-appointed collector for the sheriff and given the plaintiff the proceeds rather than the property itself, and the court declined to grant that relief where the issue of the plaintiff's right to possession was as yet undecided, and there was no indication that the defendant would refuse to comply with the court's order once it was made. However, the court did not rule out the use of a receiver in an appropriate case.

(c) *Set-Off.* In 1861, the same year that the Court conceded a right to recover property wrongfully detained under the common law writ of detinue, it recognized that, where several items of property were involved and the plaintiff won with respect to some and lost with respect to others, the defendant could request that the costs allowed to him on the issues he won be set off against the costs allowed to the plaintiff and that execution be issued for the balance only.[222] But it was not until 1945 that the Court agreed that a defendant might, in some circumstances, set off his claims for damages against the plaintiff's claim for unlawful taking or detention. In *Vernon Parts Corp. v. Granite State Machine Co., Inc.*,[223] the Court allowed a defendant in a replevin action for machine parts unlawfully detained to

---

220 This issue arose because under the common law writ of detinue, a plaintiff could not recover property wrongfully detained until after trial whereas under the statute of 1873, he could recover it before trial just as though it had been unlawfully taken from his possession. Dame v. Dame, 43 N.H. 37 (1861).

221 76 N.H. 38, 79 A. 23 (1911).

222 Jordan v. Cummings, 43 N.H. 134 (1861).

223 93 N.H. 315, 41 A.2d 605 (1945).

set off a claim for damages for breach of the same contract under which the plaintiff had delivered the goods sought to be replevied. The Court held that the defendant could have his set-off "where special circumstances exist which entitle the defendant to equitable relief"[224] and "where the cross demands grow out of the same transaction"[225] even if the amount of the defendant's claim exceeded the plaintiff's. The Court found "special circumstances" justifying set-off in that case in the fact that the plaintiff was a nonresident. The Court quoted with approval from the Missouri Court of Appeals, as follows:

> In replevin suits, it is frequently a matter of no small difficulty to properly protect the interests and to equitably adjust the rights of parties. Such suits are said to be in some respects, *sui generis*, and the inclination of the courts . . . has been to give to them a flexibility sufficient to meet exigencies and adjust all equities arising in such actions.[226]

Pleas of set-off must be filed within thirty days of the filing of the complaint.[227]

(d) *Incidental Orders.* In both *Vernon Parts* and *National Shawmut Bank*, the Court recognized and applied equitable principles in a replevin proceeding to mold the remedy to the circumstances proved. In *Vernon Parts*, it approved use of set-off to resolve a defendant's related claim where special circumstances existed, and in *National Shawmut Bank*, it affirmed a refusal to award damages to a victorious defendant where they were not equitably due. In a third case, *Derry Loan and Discount Co. v. Falconer*,[228] the Court stated the broader principle that, in replevin, "justice and convenience of procedure in avoidance of scattered and separate litigation may properly warrant incidental orders in the defendant's favor when he is not the prevailing party."[229] What form those "incidental orders" may take is apparently a question for the discretion of the court. A suggestion is provided by *National Shawmut Bank*, however, where the Court, in dicta, allowed that a defendant in a repossession case might raise breach of warranty as a

---

224　*Id.* at 316, 41 A.2d at 606.
225　*Id.* at 316–17, 41 A.2d at 606.
226　*Id.* at 316, 41 A.2d at 606.
227　Super. Ct. R. 33.
228　84 N.H. 450, 152 A. 427 (1930).
229　*Id.* at 454, 152 A. at 430.

defense but only if it is sufficient to extinguish the debt and, with it, the right of possession.

Cross References

Receivers, see ch. 20 *infra*.
Set-off, see ch. 11 *supra*.

§ 18.33. Entry of Final Orders

Upon satisfaction of its final order,[230] or any other conclusion of the case,[231] the court will vacate the temporary restraining order and release any bonds filed in the case.

---

230 The bonds are automatically released by final judgment in the caption (Bell v. Bartlett, 7 N.H. 178 (1834)), but the court will usually include an order releasing them as part of its judgment.

231 The bond is released by the entry of a nonsuit. Chadwick v. Badger, 9 N.H. 450 (1838).

CHAPTER 19.   INJUNCTIONS

Forms

Petition for Injunction and Declaratory Judgment, see Appendix.

§ 19.01. Definition

An injunction is an order requiring a person subject to the court's in personam jurisdiction to do or to refrain from doing a certain act or series of acts.

463

Library References

CJS Injunctions § 2

§ 19.02. Types of Injunctions

Injunctions are classified according to their duration and effect.

The types of injunctions, classified by duration, are temporary restraining orders, preliminary injunctions, and permanent injunctions. A temporary restraining order (TRO) is an injunction, usually issued ex parte, which expires within ten days. A preliminary injunction is issued only after notice and hearing and lasts until the entry of final judgment. A permanent injunction is issued after the final hearing and lasts until terminated by further court order.

The types of injunctions, classified by effect, are mandatory injunctions and prohibitory injunctions. Regardless of how long it lasts, an injunction may either require that a person do an act ("mandatory") or require that he refrain from doing it ("prohibitory").

Library References

CJS Injunctions §§ 4–10

Power to enjoin canvassing votes and declaring result of election. 1 ALR2d 588.

Removal of child from state in violation of injunction order as affecting jurisdiction of courts of another state to award custody. 4 ALR2d 7.

Injunction against breach of contract for will or conveyance of property at death in consideration of support or services. 7 ALR2d 1178.

Mandatory injunction prior to hearing of case. 15 ALR2d 213.

Enforcement of personal covenant in recorded deed by injunction against grantee's lessee or successor. 23 ALR2d 527.

Injunction against procuring contract. 26 ALR2d 1275.

Mandatory injunction to compel removal of encroachments by adjoining landowner. 28 ALR2d 679.

Injunction as remedy against removal of public officer. 34 ALR2d 554.

Injunction against parking vehicles on private way. 37 ALR2d 944.

Injunction as remedy against defamation of person. 47 ALR2d 715.

Injunction to prevent insured from settling suit against wrongdoer to detriment of insurer. 51 ALR2d 726.

Injunction against repeated or continuing trespasses on real property. 60 ALR2d 310.

Wording injunction in terms of avoiding disclosure of trade secret or the like. 62 ALR2d 530.

Injunction to prevent violation of Sunday law. 76 ALR2d 874.

Right of private sewerage system owner to mandatory injunction for removal of unauthorized sewerage connection. 76 ALR2d 1329.

Injunction to prevent interference with operations under standing timber contract providing that trees to be cut and order of cutting shall be as selected by seller. 79 ALR2d 1243.

Injunction against acts constituting offense of official oppression. 83 ALR2d 1016.

Injunction against exercise of power of eminent domain. 93 ALR2d 465.

Propriety of injunctive relief against diversion of water by municipal corporation or public utility. 42 ALR3d 426.

Preliminary mandatory injunction to prevent, correct, or reduce effects of polluting practices. 49 ALR3d 1239.

Proceedings for injunction or restraining order as basis of malicious prosecution action. 70 ALR3d 536.

§ 19.03. Courts Which May Issue Injunctions

Probate courts,[1] the superior court,[2] and the Supreme Court[3] have the power to issue injunctions. The district and municipal courts have no such power.

Library References

Injunction by state court against action in court of another state. 6 ALR2d 896.

Extraterritorial recognition of, and propriety of counterinjunction against, injunction against actions in courts of other states. 74 ALR2d 828.

§ 19.04. Parties to an Injunction Proceeding

(a) *Petitioners.* Any person who has an interest which is recognized at law or in equity may seek an injunction to prevent harm to that interest.[4]

(b) *Respondents.* All persons whose actions must be restrained in order to give effect to the court's order must be made respondents in a petition for injunction.[5]

Library References

CJS Injunctions § 182

---

1 RSA 547:3-b provides that probate courts may hear and determine certain enumerated cases according to the course of equity and "may grant writs of injunction whenever the same are necessary to prevent fraud or injustice."

2 RSA 498:1 grants to the superior court the "powers of a court of equity in . . . [certain enumerated cases and] cases in which there is not a plain, adequate and complete remedy at law, and in all other cases cognizable in a court of equity [except those which have been assigned to the probate courts as part of their exclusive jurisdiction."

3 RSA 490:4 provides that the Supreme Court "shall have general superintendence of all courts of inferior jurisdiction . . . and may issue all . . . writs and processes to other courts, to corporations and to individuals . . . . See also Boody v. Watson, 64 N.H. 162, 9 A. 794 (1886).

4 See N.H. Bd. of Reg. of Optometry v. Scott Jewelry Co., 90 N.H. 368, 9 A.2d 513 (1939).

5 See Doe v. Doe, 37 N.H. 268 (1858). However, the order must run against some limited and defined group who are capable of being notified of its terms. State v. Gross, 117 N.H. 853, 379 A.2d 804 (1977).

§ 19.05. Requirements and Standards for Issuance of Injunctions Generally

Injunctions are issued as a matter of discretion.[6] Courts are generally reluctant to issue an injunction and, regardless of its duration or effect, no injunction will be issued until a writ, petition, bill, libel, or other process has been filed.[7] Unless the petitioner is presently threatened with irreparable harm, there must also be no adequate, alternative remedy, the injunction must be likely to prevent the threatened harm and promote justice, and it must appear that the injunction will be complied with.

Library References

CJS Injunctions §§ 12–16

§ 19.06. Particular Requirements for Issuance of Injunctions—The Threat Must Be Immediate

A petitioner's need for injunctive relief must be present and immediate.[8] The court will not grant him relief against a threat which may never materialize[9] or which has already passed.[10]

---

6 Bow v. Farrand, 77 N.H. 451, 92 A. 926 (1915); Varney v. Fletcher, 106 N.H. 464, 213 A.2d 905 (1965); Timberlane Reg. School Dist. v. Timberlane Reg. Ed. Assn., 114 N.H. 245, 317 A.2d 555 (1974); Cushing v. Thomson, 118 N.H. 292, 386 A.2d 805 (1978); Vigitron, Inc. v. Ferguson, 120 N.H. 626, 419 A.2d 1115 (1980); Gauthier v. Robinson, 122 N.H. 365, 444 A.2d 564 (1982); Chase v. Joslin Management Corp., 128 N.H. 336, 512 A.2d 434 (1986); UniFirst Corp. v. City of Nashua, 130 N.H. 11, 533 A.2d 372 (1987). (" '[T]he granting of an injunction . . . is a matter within the sound discretion of the Court exercised upon a consideration of all the circumstances of each case and controlled by established principles of equity.' " 122 N.H. at 368, 444 A.2d at 566).

7 Super. Ct. R. 162. The Rules do provide, however, that "when the object of the injunction would be defeated by the delay necessary to file such process, an injunction may issue to expire on a day specified therein, unless such process be filed by such day." *Id.*

8 UniFirst Corp. v. City of Nashua, 130 N.H. 11, 533 A.2d 372 (1987).

9 Johnson v. Shaw, 101 N.H. 182, 137 A.2d 399 (1957); King v. Thomson, 116 N.H. 838, 367 A.2d 1049 (1976); Meredith Hardware Inc. v. Belknap Realty Trust, 117 N.H. 22, 369 A.2d 204 (1977); Private Truck Council of America v. State, 128 N.H. 466, 517 A.2d 1150 (1986) (injunction would not be issued to prevent the "imposition or collection of retaliatory taxes pursuant to any authority" because the "request rest[ed] upon purely speculative grounds and . . . raise[d] serious issues regarding the separation of powers." 128 N.H. at 477, 517 A.2d at 1158).

10 Perley v. Town of Effingham, 94 N.H. 120, 48 A.2d 484 (1946); Keene v. Gerry's Cash Market, Inc., 113 N.H. 165, 304 A.2d 873 (1973); Littlefield v. NHIAA, 117 N.H. 183, 370 A.2d 645 (1977); Vigitron, Inc. v. Ferguson, 120 N.H. 626, 419 A.2d 1115 (1980); Thurston Enterprises v. Baldi, 128 N.H. 760, 519 A.2d 297 (1986).

CJS Injunctions § 22

§ 19.07. —The Threatened Harm Must Be Irreparable

The fact that the petitioner is presently in danger is not enough; he must also be threatened with a harm which cannot be cured by any legal means.[11] The mere threat of danger which can be quantified and compensated by money damages after it occurs will not form the basis for issuance of an injunction.

CJS Injunctions § 27

§ 19.08. —The Petitioner Must Be Without an Adequate, Alternative Remedy

The equitable powers of the court will only be exercised if the petitioner has no other means of protecting himself against permanent damage from the threatened harm.[12] To some extent, this standard is linked to the requirement that the harm be irreparable, since a suit for money damages is regarded as an adequate, alternative remedy except where the wrongdoer is insolvent[13] and, of course, precludes the harm from being irreparable.[14] Even where money damages are not available or appropriate, an injunction will not be issued if there is any other procedure, including administrative appeals[15] and

---

11 Johnson v. Shaw, 101 N.H. 182, 137 A.2d 399 (1957); Timberlane Reg. School Dist. v. Timberlane Reg. Ed. Assn., 114 N.H. 245, 305 A.2d 673 (1974); Murphy v. McQuade Realty, Inc., 122 N.H. 314, 444 A.2d 530 (1982).

12 Winnipissiogee Lake Co. v. Worster, 29 N.H. 433 (1854); Perley v. Dolloff, 60 N.H. 504 (1881); Spaulding v. Mayo, 81 N.H. 85, 122 A. 899 (1923); Timberlane Reg. School Dist v. Timberlane Reg. Ed. Assn, 114 N.H. 245, 317 A.2d 555 (1974); Murphy v. McQuade Realty, Inc., 122 N.H. 314, 444 A.2d 530 (1982); Thurston Enterprises v. Baldi, 128 N.H. 760, 519 A.2d 297 (1986); UniFirst Corp. v. City of Nashua, 130 N.H. 11, 533 A.2d 372 (1987). The general rule does not, however, apply to requests to enforce restrictive covenants on the use of real estate. New Hampshire Donuts, Inc. v. Skipitaris, 129 N.H. 774, 533 A.2d 351 (1987).

13 Amoskeag Mfg. Co. v. Shirley, 69 N.H. 269, 39 A. 976 (1897).

14 Wason v. Sanborn, 45 N.H. 169 (1862).

15 The doctrine of exhaustion of administrative remedies will be applied in such a case. V.S.H. Realty, Inc. v. City of Rochester, 118 N.H. 778, 394 A.2d 317 (1978) ("[T]his sound rule is based on the reasonable policies of encouraging the exercise of administrative expertise, preserving agency autonomy, and promoting judicial efficiency." 118 N.H. at 782, 394 A.2d at 320); Rochester School Board v. N.H. PELRB, 119 N.H. 45, 398 A.2d 823 (1979).

completion of suits pending in other forums,[16] which may be expected to prevent or correct the threatened harm.

The absence of an adequate, alternative remedy must not be due to any fault of the petitioner. Exposure to a threatened harm due to the petitioner's own neglect in failing to claim a protection which was once available will not justify the issuance of an injunction except in cases of the clearest injustice.

The rule that an injunction will not be issued where an adequate, alternative remedy is available at law does not, however, preclude joining an action for damages based on past events with a petition for injunction to prevent their recurrence in the future where it can be established that a continuation of the offense could not be adequately compensated for by money damage.[17]

Library Reference

CJS Injunctions §§ 30, 31
Adequacy, as regards right to injunction, of other remedy for review of order fixing public utility rates. 8 ALR2d 839.

§ 19.09. —The Injunction Must Be Capable of Preventing the Threatened Harm

Even when a petitioner is presently threatened with irreparable harm and has no adequate, alternative remedy, an injunction may not be capable of protecting him. The court will, in all cases, carefully examine whether its order may be expected to accomplish its intended purpose and will shape its order to that end.

Library References

CJS Injunctions § 34

§ 19.10. —It Must Appear That There Will Be Compliance With the Injunction

The orders of a court depend for their effect largely upon the voluntary compliance of persons to whom they are directed. Voluntary compliance with court orders is encouraged in large part by the prestige and general respect in which the public holds courts and the judicial process. Since courts have only limited means of compelling persons to comply with their orders, they are very reluctant to issue injunctions where a danger exists that the person enjoined can effectively refuse to comply with the order. Such a

---

16 The doctrine of abstinence will be applied in these situations.

17 Bailey v. Collins, 59 N.H. 459 (1879). See Tapley v. Crothers, 103 N.H. 46, 164 A.2d 564 (1960).

refusal to comply may result in loss of prestige and public respect for the courts generally and, by forcing the court to become embroiled in a frustrating effort to compel compliance, place the court in an adversary relationship with one of the parties before it.

For these reasons, even when all other conditions for the issuance of an injunction have been met, the court will decline to enter the order unless it affirmatively appears that the procedure will have its intended effect. In analyzing this question, the court will consider whether the person or persons intended to be bound by the injunction can be expected to learn of the order in time to obey it. A court may well decline to issue an injunction, even in an otherwise appropriate case, where the class of persons to be affected by that order is so broad that it is unlikely that they can all be notified of the order before violating it, where the order will come too late to prevent a large portion of the feared harm, or where the respondent has openly proclaimed his implacable refusal to comply with the order if issued.[18]

§ 19.11. —It Must Appear That the Injunction Will Further the Interests of Justice

An injunction will not be issued except to provide a just resolution of the case.[19]

§ 19.12. —The Injunction Must Not Cause More Harm Than It Prevents

Whenever a court is asked to issue an injunction, it will balance the threatened harm to the plaintiff resulting from a refusal to issue the injunction against the harm to the defendant from its issuance.[20] The court will either shape an order that is limited to the protection of the plaintiff's rights[21]

---

18 While the court will not want to reward defiance by a refusal to act and will generally assure that its lawful orders, once known, will be obeyed, if it affirmatively appears that a party will not obey an injunction once issued, the court may try to defer entering such an order until it is clear, after a hearing on the merits, that the petitioner needs such an order and that the respondent has no defense. The court may advance the date for a final hearing on the merits in order to arrive at this juncture quickly.

19 Higgins v. Higgins, 57 N.H. 224 (1876).

20 New Hampshire Donuts, Inc. v. Skipitaris, 129 N.H. 774, 533 A.2d 351 (1987). See also Manchester Dairy System, Inc. v. Hayward, 82 N.H. 193, 132 A. 12 (1926).

21 Dunlop v. Daigle, 122 N.H. 295, 444 A.2d 519 (1982) ("The trial court has broad and flexible equitable powers which allow it to shape and adjust the precise relief to the requirements of the particular situation." 122 N.H. at 300, 444 A.2d at 521); Fisher v. Koper, 127 N.H. 330, 499 A.2d 1001 (1985).

or will refuse to grant the injunction if the defendant will thereby suffer greater harm than is threatened against the plaintiff.[22]

Library References

CJS Injunctions § 35

§ 19.13. Additional Requirements for Particular Types of Injunctions—In General

Beyond the general standard which applies to the issuance of injunctions, there are additional specific prerequisites to the entry of each type of injunction.[23] These additional requirements generally impose a higher standard for orders entered early rather than later in the case, and for orders compelling action rather than inaction.

§ 19.14. —Temporary Restraining Order (TRO)

(a) *Generally.* A temporary restraining order, or TRO, has been characterized as the entry of judgment without trial and is, for that reason, only sparingly issued. A temporary restraining order will be granted only to preserve the status quo against the threat of immediate and irremediable change[24] or when it is certain that the petitioner will prevail on the merits.

(b) *Issuance Ex Parte.*

(1) *Basis*: Temporary restraining orders may be granted either ex parte or after notice and hearing. They may be entered in equity proceedings or in aid of any other form of action in the superior court.[25] When application is made for the issuance of a temporary restraining order ex parte the applicant must accompany his motion with sworn statements of specific facts which "clearly" show "that immediate and irreparable injury, loss or damage will result to the applicant before the adverse party or his attorney

---

22 Johnson v. Shaw, 101 N.H. 182, 137 A.2d 399 (1957); Frost v. Polhamus, 110 N.H. 491, 272 A.2d 596 (1970); Carroll v. Schechter, 112 N.H. 216, 293 A.2d 324 (1972). See also New Hampshire Donuts, Inc. v. Skipitaris, 129 N.H. 774, 533 A.2d 351 (1987); Bogardus v. Zinkevicz, 134 N.H. 527 (1991).

23 See, e.g., Super. Ct. R. 161(e) (labor disputes and liens).

24 Super. Ct. R. 160 and 161(a). See Aetna Cas. & Ins. Co. v. Sullivan, 83 N.H. 426, 143 A. 687 (1928); Poisson v. Manchester, 101 N.H. 72, 133 A.2d 503 (1957).

25 Super. Ct. R. 161(a).

can be heard in opposition."[26] The motion must also be accompanied by a draft order which meets the requirements of Rule 161(a) and (d).[27]

(2) *Notice of Application*: Even when a basis exists for the court to enter a temporary restraining order ex parte, it is a good practice for the applicant to notify his opponent, if possible, of his intention to apply, and of the time and place at which he will do so. This notification can be accomplished in most cases by a simple telephone call to the opposing party or his attorney. If the applicant has a sufficient basis for obtaining the order (i.e., the certainty of success on the merits and a clear and immediate threat of irreparable harm), the presence of his opponent should have no effect on the outcome of the hearing and may only be expected to insure earlier notice of the order. If, as often happens, the opponent is unable or unwilling to attend the hearing even after notice, the applicants representation to the court that he has been notified will only strengthen the application.

It occasionally happens that a person applies for the ex parte issuance of a temporary restraining order precisely to catch his opponent off guard and to obtain a perceived psychological and procedural advantage in the case. In such a case, notice to the opponent before making the application

---

26 Super. Ct. R. 160. In marital proceedings, this requires a showing that "physical or emotional harm" would likely result to the plaintiff. Super. Ct. Admin. R. 7-1. See also N.H. Rules of Professional Conduct, Rule 3.3(d) ("In an *ex parte* proceeding, a lawyer shall inform the tribunal of all material facts known to the lawyer which will enable the tribunal to make an informed decision, whether or not the facts are adverse.").

27 Super. Ct. R. 164 provides that "[t]he attorney of the party, in whose favor an *ex parte* decree will be issued, shall draw the proposed order for the Court to consider." Although the court will review proposed ex parte orders and make amendments and deletions as it sees fit, the court is entitled to rely on the good faith of attorneys to assure that proposed orders meet the requirements of the Rule and are justified in the premises. If the court is nevertheless prevailed upon to sign a proposed form of order which it later turns out was not justified by the case or was beyond its authority, the court will often award the respondent who challenges the order costs and attorneys fees to be paid by the attorney upon whom the court mistakenly relied.

Super. Ct. R. 161(a) and (d) together require that a temporary restraining order contain the following elements:
   (a) The caption;
   (b) The title of the order;
   (c) The date and time when issued;
   (d) A specification of the harm expected;
   (e) A statement of why the harm will be irreparable;
   (f) A statement of the specific facts, established by affidavit or verified petition, that show that the specified harm would result before the respondent or his attorney could be notified;
   (g) A specific statement "in reasonable detail" of the actions which the respondent must take or refrain from taking in order to comply with the order; and
   (h) The Presiding Justice's signature.

would, of course, be regarded as counter-productive. To avoid this misuse of the temporary restraining order procedure, the court will usually ask an applicant who appears without opposition whether he has notified or attempted to notify his opponent. When it discovers that he has not done so, the court may either recess the hearing and require that he do so or direct the clerk to try to reach him by telephone. For all these reasons, the better practice requires that a person notify his opponent that he plans to apply for the ex parte issuance of a temporary restraining order before he does so.

(3) *Requirements of the Order*:   Rule 161(a) requires that, absent a contrary order for good cause shown,[28] any temporary restraining order issued ex parte carry the time and date when it was entered, specifically identify the threatened injury and show why the court considered it irreparable, and state what specific facts established that harm would result before the respondent or his attorney could be notified.

(4) *Expiration of the Order*:   Temporary restraining orders entered ex parte automatically expire at the same time of day as issued, ten calendar days after issuance, unless the court specifies an earlier expiration time and date in the order.[29] A temporary restraining order issued ex parte may be extended to any other time and date by agreement of the parties or may be renewed for successive ten day periods, by order of the court, after hearing, "for good cause shown."[30]

(5) *Service and Notice to Respondent*:   When the court issues a temporary restraining order ex parte, the petitioner must arrange to have the respondent notified of its terms at the earliest possible time. Usually this is accomplished by taking a copy of the motion, temporary restraining order, and order of notice, attested by the clerk, to the sheriff with instructions for service and a request that service be accomplished immediately. In many cases, the Motion for Temporary Restraining Order will be filed at the beginning of the case, on the same day that a Petition for Injunction, Libel for Divorce, or other pleading is filed. In such a case, the petitioner will also take his initial pleading to the sheriff for service with the temporary restraining order.[31]

Whenever possible, the applicant should call his opponent or the opposing attorney and inform him of the substance of the order and the time

---

28 Super. Ct. R. 161(d).

29 Super. Ct. R. 161(a).

30 *Id.*

31 However, service of an attested copy of the court's order alone is enough to subject the recipient to its terms. Fowler v. Beckman, 66 N.H. 424, 30 A. 1117 (1891).

when it was issued. If the applicant can deliver a copy immediately to his opponent or to the opposing attorney, he should do so. Although these forms of notice will not constitute legal service, the time when the respondent became aware of the terms of the court's order will be relevant in any subsequent proceedings for contempt.

(6) *Substituted Service*:   Where the location of the respondents is unknown or they constitute too large a class to be served individually in time to prevent the threatened harm, the applicant should ask the court for permission to notify them by special means, including publication. Such a request will usually be granted.

(7) *Respondent's Objection*:   Once the respondent has received notice of the ex parte temporary restraining order, he may object to its continuation by filing his Appearance[32] and a Motion to Dissolve or to Modify Temporary Restraining Order.[33] The motion must be supported by affidavits, if based on facts not apparent in the record. The court will hold a hearing on the motion within two days of notice to the applicant and will usually enter its order on the motion at the hearing.[34]

(c) *Issuance With Notice.*   Although no rule or statute prescribes the procedure for issuing temporary restraining orders in the presence of an opponent, in such a case the superior court generally follows Rule 161(a), with suitable modifications, and regards the order as limited in time and conditions to the same extent as if issued ex parte. Of course, in some cases where the opponent appears on an application for ex parte temporary restraining order, the hearing will be so complete and the opponent will be so thoroughly able to present his defenses that the hearing will in effect be converted to a hearing on a preliminary injunction. In that case, if the court finds that injunctive relief is appropriate, it will enter a preliminary injunction, rather than a temporary restraining order, and the limitations on that device will pertain instead.

(d) *Hearing on Preliminary Injunction.*   If the court issues a temporary restraining order and the applicant has also prayed the court to issue a preliminary injunction, the court will schedule a hearing on that request for

---

32 The respondent may file either a Special or a General Appearance. If he files a Special Appearance, however, he may not move to modify the temporary restraining order and may not assert any ground for dissolution other than lack of jurisdiction.

33 Super. Ct. R. 161(a). See also Super. Ct. R. 141. The temporary restraining order will automatically be dissolved if the applicant fails to seek further relief by preliminary injunction at a hearing scheduled for that purpose. Super. Ct. R. 161(a).

34 Super. Ct. R. 161(a) requires the court to "proceed to hear and determine such motion as expeditiously as the ends of justice require." See also Super. Ct. R. 141.

a date prior to the scheduled expiration of the temporary restraining order.[35] If the court refuses to issue the temporary restraining order, the hearing will still be scheduled for an early date, but not necessarily within ten days of the date of the application. When the court has issued a temporary restraining order, the parties may agree to continue it pending final judgment and thereby dispense with the hearing on a preliminary injunction. Or, if the court has declined to issue the temporary restraining order, the parties may still avoid a hearing and agree to the entry of a preliminary injunction on certain terms pending final judgment. A hearing on a request for temporary or permanent injunctive relief, like a hearing on motions, may be conducted in the form of offers of proof and arguments on the facts and law, if the court desires and neither party objects.[36]

(e) *Bond.*   A person in whose favor a temporary restraining order has been issued may be required to post a bond to indemnify the respondent against any damages caused by the injunction "in case it shall appear that the injunction was improper."[37]

---

35 Super. Ct. R. 161(a) requires a hearing "at the earliest possible time, and in any event within 10 days."

36 UniFirst Corp. v. City of Nashua, 130 N.H. 11, 533 A.2d 372 (1987).

37 Super. Ct. R. 161(c) and 163. See also Lefebvre v. Waldstein, 101 N.H. 451, 146 A.2d 270 (1958); Allen v. Newmarket Industrial Associates, 96 N.H. 340, 76 A.2d 920 (1950); Fowler v. Taylor, 99 N.H. 64, 104 A.2d 746 (1954); Town of Exeter v. Britton, 115 N.H. 209, 337 A.2d 356 (1975); Merrimack v. Spade, 120 N.H. 922, 426 A.2d 19 (1980) (where damages were allowed on an injunction bond in favor of one who was rightfully, but too broadly, enjoined). Rule 163 provides for a bond "with sufficient sureties conditioned to pay and satisfy all such damages as may be occasioned to the adverse party by reason of the injunction." The Rule also states that a bond "ordinarily shall" be required when a temporary restraining order is issued ex parte (except in marital cases) and "may" be required in other cases.

Rule 161(c) also provides for an injunction bond in any case (except marital cases) "in such sums as the Court deems proper, for the payment of such costs and damages as may be incurred or suffered by any party who is found to have been wrongfully enjoined or restrained." A bond is not required of the State or federal government, but must be provided by cities, towns, counties, and other states or countries. Rule 161(c) goes farther than Rule 163 and says that no Temporary Restraining Order or preliminary injunction may be issued unless such a bond is posted or the court relieves the applicant of the requirement "for good cause shown."

Taking Rules 163 and 161(c) together, it may be concluded that the Superior Court is more inclined to require an injunction bond when a temporary restraining order is issued ex parte than in other cases, that it may require such a bond in any case where an injunction is issued prior to final judgment, that no such bond will be required of the state or federal governments, and that such a bond, if required, will provide for payment to the respondent of any costs or damages which he incurs by reason of the entry of the order if the court later determines that no injunction should have been issued. Presumably, a subsequent refusal to renew a temporary restraining order issued ex parte or a decision not to enter a permanent injunction in a case in which a preliminary

Library References

CJS Injunctions §§ 10, 17, 245

Necessary parties defendant to independent action on injunction bond. 55 ALR2d 545.

Court's lack of jurisdiction of subject matter in granting injunction as a defense in action on injunction bond. 82 ALR2d 1064.

Dismissal without prejudice as breach of injunction bond. 91 ALR2d 1312.

Period for which damages are recoverable or are computed under injunction bond. 95 ALR2d 1190.

Appealability of order granting, extending, or refusing to dissolve temporary restraining order. 19 ALR3d 403.

Appealability of order refusing to grant or dissolving temporary restraining order. 19 ALR3d 459.

Recovery of damages resulting from wrongful issuance of injunction as limited to amount of bond. 30 ALR4th 273.

Forms

Temporary Orders and Notice of Hearing (District Court), see Appendix.

§ 19.15. —Preliminary Injunction

(a) *Differences Between a Temporary Restraining Order and a Preliminary Injunction.* A preliminary injunction differs from a temporary restraining order in three ways: (1) it may not be issued ex parte,[38] (2) it may last until the entry of final judgment, not just ten days,[39] and (3) it may be issued when there is merely a probability, rather than a certainty, that the application will succeed on the merits.[40]

(b) *Consolidation With Final Hearing.* Whenever it appears that a decision is needed at an early date, the court may shorten or eliminate the opportunity for pretrial discovery, advance the date for final hearing on the merits, and combine the hearing on a preliminary injunction with the hearing on a permanent injunction or final hearing on the merits.[41] An order consoli-

---

injunction has been issued will not be regarded as evidence that the respondent was "wrongfully enjoined." A finding of wrongful injunction should be express and restricted to a case in which a temporary restraining order or preliminary injunction is vacated or dissolved during its term.

38 Super. Ct. R. 161(b)(1).

39 But see RSA 498:12 which requires that interlocutory injunctions expire at the end of the term after they are entered in the county where the action is pending.

40 The petitioner is required to show a certainty of success and the absence of any possible legal or equitable defense only when he is seeking the entry of an order before the respondent has been given the chance to present a defense. When the respondent has received notice of the proceedings, the petitioner's burden is reduced to a balance of probabilities.

41 Super. Ct. R. 161(b)(2). See, e.g., UniFirst Corp. v. City of Nashua, 130 N.H. 11, 533 A.2d 372 (1987).

dating the final hearing on the merits with the hearing on a preliminary injunction may be made after a hearing on the preliminary injunction has begun, if it appears that the parties are already fully prepared to present their cases and the case is ripe for determination. A party who fails to object to the court's consolidation of a hearing waives the right to object on appeal.[42]

(c) *Bifurcation for Jury Trial.* When the case involves an issue as to which a party enjoys and has claimed his right to trial by jury, the court may not eliminate that right by its order of consolidation, but may bifurcate the trial and consolidate all equitable issues for hearing at one time.[43]

(d) *Requirements of the Order.* Like a temporary restraining order, a preliminary injunction must specifically state "in reasonable detail" what the respondent is required to do or refrain from doing.[44] It may also require that the petitioner post a bond.[45]

(e) *Notice of the Order.* The court will often issue its preliminary injunction from the bench at the conclusion of the hearing. In cases where the court receives reliable assurances from the respondent that nothing will be done pending its order or where the date for the respondent to act has not yet arrived, the court may take the matter under advisement and issue its decision within a few days.

Although it is not required by the rules, the petitioner should prepare and submit a proposed order for the court's consideration. Not only will this save the court time, but it will focus the court's attention on precisely the relief which the petitioner desires and will assure that nothing is overlooked when the court formulates its order.

A request for a preliminary injunction will never be heard before service and the filing of a General Appearance by the respondent. If the petitioner fails to file the sheriff's return or the respondent files a Special Appearance and Motion to Dismiss based on lack of jurisdiction, the court will not hear the request for injunctive relief until its jurisdiction is clear.

Once the court has decided whether to grant the request for preliminary injunction, the clerk will notify all parties in writing of its decision.

---

42 Johnson v. Nash, 135 N.H. 534 (1992) (citing UniFirst Corp. v. City of Nashua, 130 N.H. 11, 13, 533 A.2d 372, 374 (1987)).

43 *Id.*

44 Super. Ct. R. 161(d).

45 Super. Ct. R. 161(c).

Library References

CJS Injunctions §§ 166 et seq.
Reviewability, on appeal from final judgment, of interlocutory order relating to injunction, as affected by fact that order was separately appealable. 79 ALR2d 1397.
Recovery of damages resulting from wrongful issuance of injunction as limited to amount of bond. 30 ALR4th 273.

§ 19.16. —Permanent Injunction

A permanent injunction is only issued after the applicant has carried his burden of showing the need for and appropriateness of such an order at the final hearing on the merits. A permanent injunction lasts until it is modified or vacated. In all other respects, the same procedures and limitations which apply to the issuance of preliminary injunctions apply to permanent injunctions.

Library References

CJS Injunctions §§ 6, 7, 235, 246, 280
Propriety of permanently enjoining one guilty of unauthorized use of trade secret from engaging in sale or manufacture of device in question. 38 ALR3d 572.

§ 19.17. Effect of an Injunction

An injunction takes effect from the moment the judge announces, signs, or enters the order and will be binding upon "the parties to the action,[46] their officers, agents,[47] servants, employees, and attorneys, and upon those persons in active concert or participation with them who receive actual notice of the order."[48] The injunction will specify those individuals or groups of nonparties whose acts it seeks to control, and the petitioner should have those persons served with a copy of the order. Where that group is too large to effect individual service in-hand or the identity of its members is unknown, the petitioner should seek the court's permission to notify them by means other than personal service. Although the petitioner is always free to notify nonparties of the order by any means he chooses, the court's approval of a particular method may have the effect of making the use of that method constructive notice to nonparties who cannot be personally contacted. Since the order will bind all nonparties who join with parties or their agents in

---

46 This includes not only persons who were parties at the time of the order but persons later added, although in the latter case they are bound only from the date of joinder.

47 The term "agents" may include other professionals such as accountants and, in any given transaction, banks and other persons with a business association with the respondent.

48 Super. Ct. R. 161(d).

violating the order only if they know of the order, it will always be in the petitioner's interest to give as broad a publicity to the order as possible.

Library References

CJS Injunctions § 243

§ 19.18. Dissolution of an Injunction

A temporary restraining order is automatically dissolved at the end of ten days unless renewed.[49] Other injunctions are dissolved by expiration according to their terms or by express order of the court.

Once an injunction has been dissolved it may not be revived without a further order of the court.[50]

Library References

CJS Injunctions §§ 255 et seq.
Dismissal of suit as nullifying previous temporary injunction. 11 ALR2d 1411.
Dismissal of suit as conclusively establishing that temporary injunction had been improvidently granted. 54 ALR2d 505.

§ 19.19. Modification of an Injunction

The court which enters an injunction retains jurisdiction to modify it at any time for good cause.[51]

§ 19.20. Contempt

Knowingly violating an injunction or helping another to do so constitutes a contempt of court.[52]

---

49 Super. Ct. R. 161(a).

50 Allen v. Newmarket Industrial Associates, 96 N.H. 340, 76 A.2d 920 (1950).

51 Town of Durham v. Cutter, 121 N.H. 243, 428 A.2d 904 (1981) (change of law).

52 Fowler v. Beckman, 66 N.H. 424, 30 A. 1117 (1891). See also State Department of Health and Welfare v. Blaisdell, 118 N.H. 4, 381 A.2d 1200 (1978); Town of Nottingham v. Cedar Waters, Inc., 118 N.H. 282, 385 A.2d 851 (1978) (distinguishing between civil and criminal, direct and indirect, contempt); Dover Veterans' Council v. City of Dover, 119 N.H. 738, 407 A.2d 1195 (1979) (the injunction must be clear); Vermont National Bank v. Taylor, 122 N.H. 442, 445 A.2d 1122 (1982) (contempt proceedings cannot be commenced by the *ex parte* issuance of a capias); Town of Epping v. Harvey, 129 N.H. 688, 531 A.2d 345 (1987) (discussing direct and indirect, civil and criminal contempt and holding that a "trial court may impose a continuing fine in a civil contempt proceeding in order to coerce a defendant to comply with its order." 129 N.H. at 692, 531 A.2d at 348); Town of Nottingham v. Bonser, 131 N.H. 120, 552 A.2d 58 (1988) (collateral estoppel prevents relitigating, in a proceeding for contempt, the nonjurisdictional basis for the order which a party is accused of disobeying).

§ 19.21. Costs

Costs may be awarded in proceedings to obtain injunctive relief on the same terms as on other actions.[53]

Library References

CJS Injunctions § 252

§ 19.22. Appellate Review

The Supreme Court has said that it "will uphold the decision of the trial court with regard to the issuance of an injunction absent an error of law, abuse of discretion, or clearly erroneous findings of fact."[54]

---

[53] Allen v. Newmarket Industrial Associates, 96 N.H. 340, 76 A.2d 920 (1950).
[54] UniFirst Corp. v. City of Nashua, 130 N.H. 11, 533 A.2d 372 (1987).

CHAPTER 20. RECEIVERS AND GUARDIANS AD LITEM

A. RECEIVERS

B. GUARDIANS AD LITEM

481

20.30. Confidentiality Privilege
20.31. Termination of Representation

A. Receivers

§ 20.01. Definition

A receiver is a person appointed by the court to take charge of certain property involved in a case pending before it for the purpose of preserving that property until the case is decided.[1]

Library References

CJS Receivers § 1

§ 20.02. Appointment of Receivers—Cases in Which a Receiver May Be Appointed

The Supreme Court and superior court have inherent[2] and statutory[3] power to appoint a receiver when necessary to protect the rights of persons before it in property subject to its jurisdiction.[4] "[W]here there is some evil actually existing, or some evidence of danger to the property, . . . a receiver will be appointed."[5]

In addition, several statutes authorize the superior court to appoint a receiver in specific situations:

---

1 In at least one case, the Supreme Court has also referred to a person appointed by the court to carry out its orders with respect to property in litigation as a "receiver," but this expanded usage of the term has never gained acceptance. See Peirce v. Finerty, 76 N.H. 38, 79 A. 23 (1911).

2 The Court's inherent power to appoint a receiver arises from its equity jurisdiction. See RSA 498:1; RSA 491:7.

3 See RSA 498:8, 12; RSA 293-A:99, 100.

4 Staples v. Dix & Staples Co., 85 N.H. 115, 115, 155 A. 43, 44 (1931) ("Its purpose is to secure and conserve the property for [the] benefit [of persons interested in it]."); Fisher v. Concord R.R., 50 N.H. 200 (1870). See also Munsey v. G.H. Tilton & Son Co., 91 N.H. 51, 13 A.2d 468 (1940); Currier v. Janvrin, 58 N.H. 374 (1878); Petition of Keyser, 98 N.H. 198, 201, 96 A.2d 551, 553 (1953) (receivership is created "principally 'for the benefit of creditors' ").

5 Ladd v. Harvey, 21 N.H. 514, 521 (1850). A receiver may be appointed where the property is in danger due to insolvency (*id.*) or neglect of duty on the part of a trustee. Rockwell v. Dow, 85 N.H. 58, 154 A. 229 (1931); Eastman v. Savings Bank, 58 N.H. 421 (1878) (power "is exercised for the more speedy getting in of a party's estate and securing it for the benefit of those entitled to it . . ."). See also Hale v. Nashua & Lowell R.R., 60 N.H. 333 (1880) (receiver appointed to complete construction of railroad line).

(1) For New Hampshire corporations, when nonresident directors, officers, or agents refuse to appear for a deposition ordered by the superior court.[6]

(2) For property which has been fraudulently conveyed.[7]

(3) For a public housing project, upon an authority's default on its obligations to its bondholders.[8]

(4) For the Water Resources Board, upon its default on bonds.[9]

(5) For property attached on trustee process.[10]

(6) For a business engaging in a violation of RSA 358-A, when the Attorney General brings the action.[11]

Finally, at least one statute allows an administrative agency to appoint itself as receiver of a company that it regulates.[12]

Library References

CJS Receivers § 7

Appointment of receiver in proceedings arising out of dissolution of partnership or joint adventure, otherwise than by death of partner or at insistence of creditor. 23 ALR2d 583.

What constitutes waste justifying appointment of receiver of mortgaged property. 55 ALR3d 1041.

Appointment or discharge of receiver for marital or community property necessitated by suit for divorce or separation. 15 ALR4th 224.

§ 20.03. —Persons Who May Apply for the Appointment of a Receiver

Any party to the proceedings may ask the court to appoint a receiver pursuant to its inherent or general statutory power. If no action or proceeding is pending, any person who can establish a legal or equitable interest in the property may petition the court to appoint a receiver to preserve it. When a statute authorizes the appointment of a receiver, it usually also specifies the persons who may apply for the appointment.[13]

---

6 RSA 516:15.

7 RSA 545-A:7(I)(c)(2).

8 RSA 203:19(II).

9 RSA 481:17(II).

10 RSA 512:29, 33. See Bufford v. Sides, 42 N.H. 495 (1861) (appointment of receiver in trustee process restricted to situations authorized by statute); Fling v. Goodall, 40 N.H. 208 (1860); Hills v. Smith, 28 N.H. 369 (1854).

11 RSA 358-A:4(III-a).

12 RSA 401-B:11 (insurance commissioner, for insolvent domestic insurer).

13 See RSA 203:19(II) (bondholder); RSA 358-A:4(III-a) (Attorney General); RSA 481:17 (trustee appointed by holders of 25% of bonds); RSA 512:29-33 (plaintiff); RSA 545-A:7(I)(c)(2) (creditor).

Library References

CJS Receivers § 11
Appointment of receiver at insistence of plaintiff in tort action. 4 ALR2d 1278.
Propriety of appointing receiver, at behest of mortgagee, to manage or operate property during mortgage foreclosure. 82 ALR2d 1075.

§ 20.04. —Persons Who May Be Appointed a Receiver

Any disinterested person[14] whom the court finds qualified by training, temperament, location, and skill to take possession of, hold, and manage the property may be appointed a receiver. A trust company organized in New Hampshire may be a receiver.[15]

Library References

CJS Receivers §§ 70–73

§ 20.05. —Property for Which a Receiver May Be Appointed

A receiver may be appointed to take and hold any interest in property that it is possible to own and the existence of which is recognized by law. A receiver may be appointed for all or any portion of a person's property.[16]

Library References

CJS Receivers §§ 13, 14

§ 20.06. —Effect of Receivership

A receiver is an officer of the court that appoints him; he is appointed to preserve the existence and benefit of the property until the litigation is concluded and the rights established therein are vindicated.

> Such an appointment freezes the affairs that the court has taken control over at the time of the appointment, pending the orderly reduction of the assets to such form as may be necessary for distribution and judicial determination of the rights and obligations involved. The property is thereby held *in custodia legis*. The

---

14 See Ladd v. Harvey, 21 N.H. 514, 521 (1850) (referring to "indifferent person"). See also Palmer v. U.S. Savings Bank of America, 131 N.H. 433, 441, 553 A.2d 781, 786 (1989) (shareholder could not provide fair and adequate representation for other similarly situated shareholders because he was a judgment creditor of bank who wished to be appointed receiver of bank's assets).

15 RSA 390:13.

16 Fisher v. Concord R.R., 50 N.H. 200, 201–02 (1870) ("It may be in the power of imagination to suppose a case of one hundred and one dollars in a single trust, where a receiver would be necessary for the one dollar, and not for the hundred.").

rights and interests of the parties relate to and become fixed as of that date, as do the right and title of the receiver.[17]

Seizure and control of property by a receiver places the property in the custody of the court,[18] but does nothing to affect or determine any person's permanent right to possession or title.[19] The receiver "takes possession of the property . . . subject to all the liens and equities which existed at the time it was taken over by the receiver. He does not take over any more title than the person, firm or corporation had."[20] He may be authorized to incur expenses which will take priority over preexisting liens and security interests, but only "for the care, preservation and benefit of the estate."[21] Even though the receiver is an officer and agent of the court, his acts, as respect the property and any claims which may be made upon it, are those of the owner, and any liabilities that he incurs in the management and control of the property are chargeable to the owner upon termination of the receivership.[22]

Library References

CJS Receivers §§ 103 et seq.
Action for malicious prosecution based on institution of involuntary bankruptcy, insolvency, or receivership proceedings. 40 ALR3d 296.

§ 20.07. —Procedure for Obtaining the Appointment of a Receiver

If a party wishes to have a receiver appointed in connection with a pending case, he should file a Motion for Appointment of a Receiver. If no action

---

17 Petition of Keyser, 98 N.H. 198, 96 A.2d 551 (1953).

18 Rand v. Merrimack River Sav. Bank, 86 N.H. 351, 353, 168 A. 897, 899 (1933) ("The possession of the receiver is the possession of the court, and the court holds and administers the estate through the receiver.").

19 Staples v. Dix & Staples Co., 85 N.H. 115, 117, 155 A. 43, 44 (1931) ("The appointment of a receiver does not determine the property rights of the persons interested in the subject matter of the receivership."); Eastman v. Sav. Bank, 58 N.H. 421 (1878).

20 National Bank of Bellowes Falls v. Vermont Packing Co., Inc., 90 N.H. 232, 235, 6 A.2d 176, 179 (1939). See also Goudie v. American Moore Peg Co., 81 N.H. 88, 91, 122 A.2d 349, 351 (1923) ("Whenever and upon whatever grounds he was appointed, he took the property subject to all existing liens."); Bellows Falls Trust Co. v. American Mineral Prods. Co., 89 N.H. 551, 3 A.2d 98 (1938). If property subject to a prior lien is sold by a receiver, he holds the proceeds subject to an equitable lien in favor of the original lienholder. Munsey v. G.H. Tilton & Son Co., 91 N.H. 51, 13 A.2d 468 (1940).

21 Standard Oil Co. v. Nashua St. R.R., 88 N.H. 342, 345, 189 A. 166, 168 (1937). The receiver's charges are of this character. "[T]he security of mortgaged property may not be impaired by the allowance from its proceeds of priority in respect to claims for matters not directed to the advantage of the security." 88 N.H. at 345, 189 A.2d at 168.

22 LeBrun v. Boston & Me. R.R., 82 N.H. 170, 131 A. 441 (1925).

for other relief is pending or contemplated, he may file a Petition for Appointment of a Receiver. In either case, the application must state facts from which the court can determine that a receiver is required, what other persons have an interest in the property, the identity and location of the specific property sought to be placed under the receiver's control, the function that the receiver will serve in the case, and the period of time that the receiver will be required to serve.[23] Usually, these facts will not be apparent from the record and the applicant will be required to support his request with affidavits or a verified petition. If the applicant wishes to suggest a particular person for the office of receiver, he may do so, but should first obtain that person's agreement to serve if appointed and state that he has so agreed in the Motion or Petition.

Because the appointment of a receiver is not only a highly intrusive order, but also may be expected to open up several new grounds for dispute and test the court's ability to obtain compliance with its orders, the court must be confident at the outset that the property of which the receiver is taking possession is clearly identified, that the receiver can obtain possession without a breach of the peace, and that he is a person or company of integrity and judgment. The applicant may find it advantageous to attach to his motion or petition, or to produce in court at a hearing, detailed schedules of the property to be held, photographs of the locations where it may be found, evidence of the proposed receiver's qualifications and experience, and other material which will reassure the court on these points.

When the application is set forth by motion, a copy must be sent to the opposing party. When it is by petition, the opponent must be served. In addition, although third persons who have possession of, or an interest in, the property need not be made parties to the case in order to obtain the appointment of a receiver for that property, they should be served with a copy of the motion or petition and given notice of the time set for hearing.

Any nonparty who is notified may file an Appearance and a Motion to Intervene for the purposes of opposing the application, and such a motion will usually be granted. Any party may object to the application for receiver on the ground that a receiver is not necessary, that the proposed receiver is unsuitable, that the court lacks power to appoint a receiver in the case, or that the class of property to be held is too broad.[24]

---

23 Ladd v. Harvey, 21 N.H. 514 (1850).

24 The objection must be made within 10 days if the application is by motion, or within such other period as the court requires in its order of notice if the application is by petition.

The court will always hold a hearing on an application to appoint a receiver. The court may hear and grant the request ex parte,[25] but when it does, it will follow the procedures and time deadlines established for temporary restraining orders.[26] The issues at the hearing will be: the need for a receiver and the possibility of accomplishing the desired purpose by an alternative remedy; the scope of the receiver's authority; the precise identity and location of the property to be taken and held; and the suitability of the person proposed for the post. Any party may participate in the hearing and propose amendments to the plan of receivership or an alternate candidate for the office. The decision to appoint or refuse to appoint a receiver rests in the "sound discretion of the court."[27]

Upon the conclusion of the hearing, the court will announce its decision. If it decides to appoint a receiver, it will issue a written commission in the form of an order identifying the receiver and specifying his duties, his term of office, and the property to be taken and held. The receiver will be required to post a bond with the clerk of court, in an amount and form established by the court and conditioned on "the faithful discharge of [his] duties, payable to the Clerk and his successor, for the benefit of all persons interested."[28] The court may also establish by its order a more frequent obligation to account than once every six months and may place any other conditions on the appointment which it thinks appropriate. The receiver will be sworn and will assume his duties immediately, irrespective of whether any person seeks to challenge his appointment in the Supreme Court.

The court will send a copy of its order to all persons who were notified of the application.

Library References

CJS Receivers §§ 36 et seq.

Costs and other expenses incurred by receiver whose appointment was improper as chargeable against estate. 4 ALR2d 160.

Effect of nonsuit, dismissal or discontinuance of action upon previous order appointing receiver. 11 ALR2d 1426.

Appealability of order appointing, or refusing to appoint, receiver. 72 ALR2d 1009.

Reviewability, on appeal from final judgment, of interlocutory order pertaining to receiver, as affected by fact that order was separately appealable. 79 ALR2d 1390.

---

25 Ladd v. Harvey, 21 N.H. 514 (1850); Fisher v. Concord R.R., 50 N.H. 200 (1870).

26 See Super. Ct. R. 161(a).

27 Eastman v. Sav. Bank, 58 N.H. 421 (1878); Ladd v. Harvey, 21 N.H. 514 (1850) ("The exercise of the power to appoint a receiver, must depend upon sound discretion, and in a case in which it must appear fit and reasonable that some indifferent person under approved security should receive and distribute the issues and profits for the greater security of all the parties concerned.").

28 Super. Ct. R. 165.

§ 20.08. Duties of the Receiver

The receiver has four duties:

(1) To locate and take possession of the subject property in the name of the court.

(2) To preserve and protect the property while the action is pending.

(3) To account to the court by inventories (first within thirty days of his appointment, and thereafter on the first days of January and July)[29] showing the property taken, transactions he has made in the property, and his charges and expenses.[30]

(4) To surrender and deliver the property and any additions thereto upon the court's direction.

The receiver is an officer and agent of the court[31] and draws his authority from and owes his duty to it.[32] In the performance of his duties, the receiver may call upon the sheriff or his deputies for assistance.[33] Although not a

---

29 *Id.*

30 The court "is vested with a sound discretion in fixing the amount of the compensation of a receiver. . . . Ordinarily a receiver is entitled to compensation for authorized services performed by him measured by the reasonable value thereof." In determining what is reasonable, the court may consider "the knowledge and experience of the receiver, the time devoted to his work, and the amount paid as compensation for similar services." Castriano v. Gelardi, 103 N.H. 476, 477, 175 A.2d 390, 391 (1961). The receiver's charges and the expenses of preserving the property are satisfied out of the receivership property and take priority over any other claims. Other expenses incurred by the receiver take priority only over claims not reduced to lien, mortgage, or security interest before the receiver takes possession. Hale v. Nashua & Lowell R.R., 60 N.H. 333 (1880); Standard Oil Co. v. Nashua St. R.R., 88 N.H. 342, 189 A. 166 (1937). See Petition of N.H. Structural Steel Co., 90 N.H. 547, 11 A.2d 713 (1940) (priority over city taxes not reduced to lien prior to seizure). " 'When it becomes the duty of a court of equity to take property under its own charge through a receiver, the property becomes chargeable with the necessary expenses incurred in taking care of and saving it, including the allowance to the receiver for his services. He is the officer and agent of the court, and not of the parties; and it is a right of the court, essential to its own efficiency in the protection of things so situated, to keep them under its control until such expenses and allowances are paid or secured to be paid.'" 90 N.H. at 548.

31 Petition of N.H. Structural Steel Co., 90 N.H. 547, 11 A.2d 713 (1940).

32 Rockwell v. Dow, 85 N.H. 58, 68, 154 A. 229, 234 (1931) ("[A] receiver is the proper officer of the court of equity, and accountable to it."); Eastman v. Sav. Bank, 58 N.H. 421 (1878). In most cases, a person with an interest in the property will not be appointed to the office of receiver. But if he is, the receiver "has the same right to be heard [as respects his individual claims upon the property] as any other litigant." Staples v. Dix & Staples Co., 85 N.H. 115, 117, 155 A. 43, 44 (1931).

33 The receiver's commission from the court gives the sheriff and his deputies authority to act in aid of the receivership.

party to the case, the receiver will be given notice of any proceedings that relate to his appointment, duties or rights.[34]

Library References

CJS Receivers §§ 150–162

Allowance of wage claims of employees of operating receiver. 27 ALR2d 720.

Corporate receiver as affected by statute denying defense of usury to corporation. 63 ALR2d 946.

Receiver's personal liability for negligence in failing to care for or maintain property in receivership. 20 ALR3d 967.

§ 20.09. Ancillary Proceedings Subsequent to Appointment of the Receiver

The court may, but is not required to, hold hearings on the receiver's semiannual inventories. It may also authorize the receiver to sell some part of the property,[35] borrow money and give a security interest in or mortgage on the property as collateral,[36] distribute some part of the assets to creditors,[37] or do any other act reasonably necessary for the preservation of the value of the property committed to his custody or for the payment of creditors. The court may enter injunctions and other ancillary orders to protect the

---

34 Staples v. Dix & Staples Co., 85 N.H. 115, 155 A. 43 (1931).

35 See *id.*

36 Munsey v. G.H. Tilton & Sons, Inc., 91 N.H. 51, 53 13 A.2d 468, 469 (1940) ("The underlying reason for the appointment of receivers is to conserve assets for the benefit of creditors. There may be occasions when this purpose can best be accomplished by continuing the business in operation even though such continued operation entails borrowing by the receivers, but whether, in any particular case, there is occasion for continued operation by receivers and borrowing by them for that purpose depends not so much upon the nature of the business as upon the condition of its affairs."). See also Rand v. Merrimack River Sav. Bank, 86 N.H. 351, 352, 354, 168 A. 897, 898, 899 (1933) ("Power to permit a receiver to borrow money is implied from the inherent right of a court of equity to preserve the receivership property from loss or destruction. . . . It is the general rule that where the security pledged is subject to all prior encumbrances, or where . . . no prior encumbrances exist, the court may, in the exercise of discretion, authorize a receiver to borrow funds for the purpose of continuing the business temporarily, if that is 'the most practical way of preserving the value of the property.' " The purpose of the loan must be " 'to preserve the receivership property from waste, damage, or loss.' ").

37 The court will administer the fund in the receiver's hands equitably and with an equal regard for all creditors having a similar interest. It will not allow one creditor to obtain a greater advantage on distribution because he happens to be holding a part of the fund on the date of appointment. Petition of Keyser, 98 N.H. 198, 96 A.2d 551 (1953) (requiring bank to pay balance in "set-off" account on day of appointment to receiver and to accept pro rata share of whole fund). The court will not allow the payment of a forfeiture or liquidated damages allowed by contract but unrelated to the harm actually suffered by the creditor. Wein v. Arlen's, Inc., 98 N.H. 487, 103 A.2d 86 (1954).

receiver's right of possession.[38] Whenever possible, the court will give notice to all persons interested in the property and hold a hearing before entering any such supplementary orders, but in an appropriate case, the court may enter the order ex parte.[39]

Library References

Consent of court to tax sale of property in custody of receiver appointed by court. 3 ALR2d 893.

Succession of receiver to statutory right of action for recovery of money lost at gambling. 18 ALR2d 1002.

§ 20.10. Removal of the Receiver—In General

The receiver[40] or any person having an interest in the property under receivership may apply to the court by motion to terminate the receivership or to replace the incumbent. If the applicant is not a party, he must file an Appearance and move for leave to appear before making such a motion.

Library References

CJS Receivers §§ 98–100

§ 20.11. —Terminating the Receivership

A Motion To Terminate Receivership must assert that the basis for the appointment no longer exists and that the property may be more suitably protected and dealt with by other means. The motion will require supporting affidavits and may be objected to by any other party within ten days. The court will hold a hearing on the motion. If the receivership is terminated, the property will be returned to the original holder or distributed to such other persons as the court determines have a greater right to it, subject to all obligations incurred by the receiver during the period of his appointment.[41]

Library References

Appealability of order discharging, or vacating appointment of, or refusing to discharge, or vacate appointment of, receiver. 72 ALR2d 1075.

---

38 Goudie v. American Moore Peg Co., 81 N.H. 88, 122 A. 349 (1923).

39 Munsey v. G.H. Tilton & Son Co., 91 N.H. 51, 13 A.2d 468 (1940).

40 See Wein v. Arlen's, Inc., 98 N.H. 487, 103 A.2d 86 (1954).

41 LeBrun v. Boston & Me. R.R., 82 N.H. 170, 131 A. 441 (1925); Watkins v. Boston & Me. R.R., 81 N.H. 363, 127 A. 701 (1924) (claims for personal injuries incurred during receivership).

§ 20.12. —Replacing the Receiver

A Motion To Replace Receiver must be based on the present receiver's desire to be relieved, unsuitability,[42] disqualification, death, or misconduct. This motion, too, must be supported by affidavit, may be the subject of an objection, and will be heard.

§ 20.13. —Notice

Copies of a Motion To Terminate Receivership or Motion To Replace Receiver must be sent to all persons who were notified of the appointment or their successors in interest, persons who have obtained rights in the property since the appointment, and the receiver. The court may order that notice of motions relative to a receivership may be published if the group of potential claimants in the property is large.

§ 20.14. Suits Against Receivers—In Official Capacity

"A receiver can be sued . . . without leave of the appointing court in any case which seeks to recover against the receiver for some act in the conduct of the receivership. But leave is required if the suit involves title to or possession of the property in the receiver's hands, its use, its control, or the liquidation and the distribution of the proceeds."[43]

Upon being served in any case, the receiver will notify the appointing court of the action and file a petition for instructions. A copy of the notice and petition will be sent to all parties to the proceeding and other persons interested in the property. Any interested party may then move that the court instruct the receiver to respond in a particular way. The court may issue its instructions with or without hearing and may, either on its own or a party's motion, issue orders with respect to the maintenance of the new action if it is pending in the same or an inferior court.[44]

Property in receivership is held in custodia legis and may not be attached or seized without permission of the appointing court.[45]

Library References

CJS Receivers §§ 330 et seq.
Lien for storage of motor vehicle, priority as against receiver. 48 ALR2d 924.

---

42 Fisher v. Concord R.R., 50 N.H. 200 (1870).

43 McGreavey v. Straw, 90 N.H. 130, 137, 5 A.2d 270, 275 (1939).

44 The superior court may, for example, order a consolidation of the cases.

45 A receiver may, however, be charged as the owner's trustee for property he holds after his appointment has been terminated. Willard v. Decatur, 59 N.H. 137 (1879).

§ 20.15. —In Personal Capacity

A receiver may be sued personally for breach of his or her duty or for defalcation. He may be sued on his bond in the name of the clerk of court.[46]

B. Guardians Ad Litem

§ 20.16. Guardians Ad Litem—In General

A guardian ad litem is a person appointed by a court or administrative agency to protect the interest of a minor or an incompetent in a proceeding before it.[47] Guardians ad litem may be appointed for children during proceedings for divorce, nullity, or legal separation,[48] for indigent defendants in criminal proceedings,[49] and for parties to litigation who are legally incapacitated.[50]

If it appears that a party to litigation is not legally competent to direct the progress of the case and he or she does not presently have a guardian, the court or administrative agency[51] will appoint a guardian ad litem to represent him or her in the action.[52] If a judicial determination of incompetency has not been made previously, the administrative agency or court must conduct its own hearing to determine incompetency.[53] A guardian ad litem may be

---

46 Super. Ct. R. 165.

47 RSA 170-C:2(VI). See RSA 464-A:41 (appointment of guardian ad litem); RSA 482:71 (condemnation of dams—Water Resources Board); RSA 498-A:23 (eminent domain proceedings—Board of Tax and Land Appeals); RSA 371:6 (eminent domain—Public Utilities Commission).

48 RSA 458:17-a.

49 N.H. GAL Rule 1.1; RSA 604-A.

50 RSA 464-A:41. "The orderly course of justice demands that a party apparently irresponsible should not maintain litigation in his own name. The rights of the adversary as well as his own rights are affected, since a verdict or judgment in favor of the adversary may be set aside by reason of the irresponsibility." Moore v. Roxbury, 85 N.H. 394, 397, 159 A. 357, 359 (1932).

51 RSA 464-A:41. See RSA 482:71 (condemnation of dams—Water Resources Board); RSA 498-A:23 (eminent domain proceedings—Board of Tax and Land Appeals; RSA 371:6 (eminent domain—Public Utilities Commission); Moore v. Roxbury, 85 N.H. 394, 397, 195 A. 357, 359 (1932).

52 RSA 464-A:41. "The orderly course of justice demands that a party apparently irresponsible should not maintain litigation in his own name. The rights of the adversary as well as his own rights are affected, since a verdict or judgment in favor of the adversary may be set aside by reason of the irresponsibility." Moore v. Roxbury, 85 N.H. 394, 397, 159 A. 357, 359 (1932).

53 This appears to be the holding of Armstrong v. Armstrong, 123 N.H. 291, 461 A.2d 103 (1983), in which the Court, although not specifically discussing the statutory powers of administrative agencies to appoint guardians ad litem, did state that it was a violation of a party's constitutional right to due process for the superior court to appoint a

appointed on motion of the incompetent party, the attorney,[54] any other party or the court, at any stage of the proceedings.[55] A guardian ad litem has "none of the rights of the general guardian,"[56] is a "full party to the proceedings,"[57] must be sworn, and may be required to give a bond.[58] The charges incurred by a guardian ad litem will generally be paid by the ward,[59] but in some cases they may be assessed against the party bringing the action which required the appointment,[60] against all the parties proportionately,[61] or

---

guardian ad litem for the purposes of a divorce case when no specific finding of "incapacity" according to the "procedures specified in RSA chapter 464-A" had been made. Because RSA ch. 464-A requires a hearing on "incapacity" before a probate court, it is unclear whether the Court means that administrative agencies and the superior court must stop their proceedings and refer the matter to a probate court for a determination of incapacity. But the Court goes on to note the superior court's statutory power to appoint a guardian ad litem for an insane libelee, so it may be that the Court did not mean to suggest that statutes which confer jurisdiction on administrative agencies or the superior court to appoint guardians ad litem are unconstitutional, but only that guardians ad litem must only be appointed by a court or agency according to the procedures authorized in RSA ch. 464-A. No hearing on the question of incapacity is required prior to the appointment of a guardian ad litem for any child under the age of 18.

54 See N.H. Rules of Professional Conduct, Rule 1.14(b) (motion by incompetent client's lawyer).

55 Super. Ct. R. 141. "If in the progress of the trial it came to the court's notice that her responsibility for bringing and maintaining the litigation was doubtful, the course to take was to suspend the trial and make inquiry which would determine the point." Moore v. Roxbury, 85 N.H. 394, 397, 159 A. 357, 359 (1932).

56 In re Lisa G., 127 N.H. 585, 504 A.2d 1 (1986); RSA 464-A:41 (in general); RSA 477:41 (proceedings to sell real estate with remainder or contingent interests); RSA 559:18 (sale of decedents' real estate); RSA 170-C:8 (termination of parental rights); RSA 458:17-a (divorce); RSA 367:31 (assessment of dissenting shareholder's equity in railroad corporation); RSA 169-A:2(IV) (runaway children); RSA 538:7, 20 (partition of real estate) (*Note*: these statutes simply refer to appointment of "guardian" rather than "guardian ad litem," and the context of proceedings makes clear that full guardian of the type authorized by RSA ch. 464-A was not intended.); RSA 498:5-b (petition to quiet title). See also RSA 464-A:25.

57 Ross v. Gadwah, 131 N.H. 391, 554 A.2d 1284 (1988).

58 RSA 464-A:41.

59 RSA 464-A:43 (in general); RSA 482:56 (condemnation of dams); RSA 371:7 (eminent domain by public utilities).

60 See, e.g., RSA 498-A:31 (condemnor pays in eminent domain proceedings); RSA 477:41 (petitioner pays in proceedings to sell real estate with remainder or contingent interest); RSA 367:31 (dissenting shareholder of railroad corporation in assessment proceedings).

61 See, e.g., RSA 458:17-a(II-a) (divorce proceedings); RSA 538:15 and 20 (partition of real estate).

against the government.[62] Any court may appoint a guardian ad litem,[63] and the selection of a suitable person to fill the office is within the court's discretion.[64] However, a court or agency may only appoint a guardian ad litem to appear in a specific case that is pending before it.

Library References

CJS Adoption of Persons § 54
CJS Divorce §§ 89, 90
CJS Eminent Domain § 236
CJS Equity § 145
CJS Executors and Administrators §§ 848, 849
CJS Infants §§ 222 et seq.
CJS Insane Persons §§ 140 et seq.
CJS Partition § 84
CJS Spendthrifts § 4
Allowance of fees for guardian ad litem appointed for infant defendant, as costs. 30 ALR2d 1148.
Authority of guardian ad litem or next friend to make agreement to drop or compromise will contest or withdraw objections to probate. 42 ALR2d 1361, 1366.
Power of guardian representing unborn future interest holders to consent to invasion of trust corpus. 49 ALR2d 1095.
Maintainability of bastardy proceedings against infant defendant without appointment of guardian ad litem. 69 ALR2d 1379.
Recognition of foreign guardian ad litem. 94 ALR2d 211.
Who is minor's next of kin for guardianship purposes. 63 ALR3d 813.

§ 20.17. —Minor Children in Domestic Proceedings

Guidelines for persons appointed as guardians ad litem for minor children in marital proceedings under RSA 458:17-a,[65] were prepared by the Guard-

---

62 See, e.g., RSA 169-A:8; RSA 464-A:43(II).

63 In re Lisa G., 127 N.H. 585, 589, 504 A.2d 1, 3 (1986) ("A court has jurisdiction to determine whether a guardian *ad litem* is required and to appoint a guardian ad litem if necessary. This jurisdiction is inherent in a court's general jurisdiction."). See also New Hampshire Supreme Court Guidelines and Standards of Practice for Guardians Ad Litem, § 2.3.

64 See, e.g., Public Guardianship and Protection Program (RSA 547-B); RSA 463:6-a (authorizing appointment of either Office of the Director of the Division of Children and Youth Services, Child and Family Service of New Hampshire or New Hampshire Catholic Charities, Inc., as guardian of minor); In re Lisa G., 127 N.H. 585, 592, 504 A.2d 1, 5 (1986) ("While attorneys can be guardians ad litem, it is by no means necessary that such appointments be restricted to attorneys. Courts may use, where available, knowledgeable and concerned citizens as guardians ad litem.").

65 RSA 458:17-a permits the superior court to appoint a guardian ad litem in any divorce, annulment, or legal separation proceeding related to custody or visitation. Failure of the probate court to appoint guardians ad litem to represent financial interests of children being adopted by stepparents is not a denial of due process or unprivileged taking of children's property, even though the adoption results in termination of their rights to inherit from a natural parent. In re McQuesten, 133 N.H. 420, 425, 578 A.2d

ian Ad Litem Committees of the Justices of the Superior Court and the Clerks of the Superior Court, and became effective June 21, 1983.[66] They remained in effect until they were superseded by the "System-Wide Guardian Ad Litem Application, Certification and Practice" guidelines in 1994.[67]

§ 20.18. System-Wide Guidelines for Guardians Ad Litem

The 1994 guidelines were approved by the Supreme Court on a temporary basis, and have been effective since December 15, 1994.[68] They have been referred to the Advisory Committee on Rules for consideration of whether they should be adopted permanently.[69] These new guidelines apply beyond superior court divorce, annulment, and separation proceedings, to guardians ad litem appointed for delinquent children, children in need of services, indigent defendants in criminal cases, and in all of the types of cases listed in the note below.[70]

§ 20.19. Certification—Generally

To serve as a guardian ad litem in the superior, district and municipal, and probate courts, one must be certified.[71] To become certified, the application

---

335, 339 (1990). In its order of appointment, the court may specify the concerns to be addressed and otherwise limit the scope of the guardian ad litem's duties. RSA 458:17-a(I). In cases involving neglected or abused children under RSA 169-C, the court must appoint a guardian ad litem or Court Appointed Special Advocate (CASA) for the child. See RSA 169-C:10 and 10-a.

66 New Hampshire Superior Court Guidelines for Guardians Ad Litem.

67 New Hampshire Court Rules Annotated, System-Wide Guardian Ad Litem Application, Certification and Practice Volume 2, Miscellaneous section.

68 The new guidelines state that "[t]his rule supersedes all previous requirements." New Hampshire System-Wide Guardian Ad Litem Application, Certification and Practice, § 1.1. See also RSA 490:26-e (granting the Supreme Court authority to establish guidelines relative to guardian ad litem appointment); RSA 458:17-a(IV).

69 RSA 458:17-a(IV).

70 The guidelines apply to guardians ad litem appointed in the following cases: RSA 169-B, Delinquent Children; RSA 169-C, Child Protection Act; RSA 169-D, Children in Need of Services; RSA 170-B, Adoption; RSA 170-C, Termination of Parental Rights; RSA 173-B, Protection of Persons from Domestic Violence; RSA 458, Annulment, Divorce and Separation; RSA 463, Guardians of Minors; RSA 464-A, Guardians and Conservators; RSA 604-A, Adequate Representation for Indigent Defendants in Criminal Cases. System-Wide Guardian Ad Litem Application, Certification and Practice, § 1.1. This represents a dramatic broadening of the guidelines' application over the 1983 guidelines which applied only to superior court cases arising under RSA 458:17-a. The 1994 guidelines also explicitly supersede the "Guardian Ad Litem Application, Certification and Practice in New Hampshire Superior Court Domestic Relations Cases," adopted by the Supreme Court earlier in the year, on May 20, 1994.

71 N.H. GAL Rule 1.2.

must be approved by the administrative judge of the respective court, and the applicant must: successfully complete twenty hours of education/training in an approved program; pay an initial certification fee; and meet any other requirements established by the administrative judge of the respective court.[72]

§ 20.20. —Application

Applicants for guardian ad litem certification in the superior, district and municipal, and probate courts must file the following documentation with the administrative judge of the appropriate court:[73] (1) a completed application and questionnaire in the form prescribed by the administrative judge; (2) a writing sample; (3) evidence satisfactory to the administrative judge that the applicant possesses the minimum qualifications and/or education necessary to serve as a guardian ad litem; (4) an application fee as prescribed by the Supreme Court;[74] and (5) such other information as may be required in each individual case by the administrative judge.[75] The administrative judge has complete discretion to approve or to reject any application for certification[76] and may conduct an investigation of the applicant's qualifications and may require a personal interview.[77]

The applicant must waive all rights of privacy with respect to all documentary material filed or secured in connection with the application.[78]

§ 20.21. —Qualifications

Unless waived by the administrative judge, each applicant for certification as a guardian ad litem must meet the following minimum qualifications:[79] (1) have attained the age of twenty-five; (2) have obtained either a bachelor's degree from an accredited college or university or an associate's degree with a concentration or major in the field of human services or a related specialization from an accredited associates' program or a substantially equivalent college education that is deemed adequate by the respective

---

72 N.H. GAL Rules 1.2. and 1.3–1.4.

73 N.H. GAL Rules 1.2. and 1.4.

74 The fee is $25.00.

75 N.H. GAL Rule 1.4.

76 *Id.*

77 *Id.*

78 *Id.*

79 *Id.*

administrative judge;[80] (3) be in "good standing in the community"; (4) not have been found in contempt by any court; (5) not have suffered any conviction for a felony or serious misdemeanor; (6) not have been involved in litigation which could affect the applicant's judgment as a guardian ad litem; (7) possess the ability to evaluate issues objectively; and (8) possess any additional qualifications established by the administrative judge.[81]

§ 20.22. —Training

Once approved for certification, the applicant must complete twenty hours of "education/training" in a program approved by the administrative judge.[82] The training program is designed to enable the applicant to perform his or her duties in a manner which will serve the best interests of the ward.[83]

§ 20.23. —Tenure

Administrative judges of the superior, district and municipal, and probate courts[84] need not state a reason for rejecting any application for certification.[85] Certification may be revoked or other action may be taken against a guardian ad litem if he or she fails to perform the duties and responsibilities of his or her office properly.[86]

§ 20.24. Scope of Representation

Once certified and subsequently appointed for a particular case, a guardian ad litem must represent the best interests of the ward.[87] This requires

---

80 This represents a change from the 1983 Superior Court Guidelines which required guardians ad litem to be attorneys admitted to practice law in New Hampshire except where, in extraordinary circumstances, "the court otherwise ordered." See also In re Lisa G., 127 N.H. 585, 504 A.2d 1 (1986).

81 N.H. GAL Rule 1.4

82 N.H. GAL Rule 1.5.

83 *Id.*

84 New Hampshire Court Rules Annotated, System-Wide Guardian Ad Litem Application, Certification and Practice, Volume 2, Miscellaneous Section, § 1.3. See also N.H. GAL Rule 2.3 ("[t]he guardian ad litem serves at the pleasure of the court.").

85 N.H. GAL Rule 1.4.

86 N.H. GAL Rule 1.3.

87 N.H. GAL Rules 2.4.1, 2.4.2. See RSA 458:17-a(II); Ross v. Gadwah, 131 N.H. 391, 554 A.2d 1284 (1988); Richelson v. Richelson, 130 N.H. 137, 143, 537 A.2d 176, 180 (1987) ("[t]he role of the guardian ad litem is primarily to be an advocate for the best interests of the child, and to assist the court and the parties in reaching a prompt and fair determination, while minimizing the bitterness in the process"). See also Provencal v. Provencal, 122 N.H. 793, 451 A.2d 374 (1982), for a discussion of the role of the guardian ad litem in custody and related proceedings. The guardian ad litem's duty to proper preparation, promptness, diligence, and attention to details and schedules in furtherance of the ward's best interests.[88] The guardian ad litem must also keep the ward reasonably informed regarding the status of the matter, considering the ward's age and maturity level.[89] In some cases, the court may require the guardian ad litem to state an independent position regarding the best interests of the ward.[90] In doing so, the guardian ad litem may consider but it is not bound by the preference of the ward.[91]

§ 20.25. Competence

In performing his or her duties, the guardian ad litem must:

(1) Gather sufficient facts regarding the ward's family history and current situation, both from the ward and from other sources, including the parents of a minor or legal guardian;

(2) Identify material issues, comprehending the legal principles applicable to the ward's situation, and formulate alternative responses for consideration;

(3) Develop "a good faith presentation" to achieve results in the best interests of the ward;

(4) Undertake actions on the ward's behalf in a timely and effective manner, including, where appropriate, associating with other professionals who possess the skill and knowledge required to assure competent representation and problem solving;

(5) When ordered, prepare and present a thorough and timely report with recommendations to the court; and

(6) Employ impartiality, open-mindedness, and fairness while acting in the best interest of the ward.[92]

§ 20.26. Guardian Ad Litem as Advocate

In fulfilling the role of advocate, the guardian ad litem must exercise due diligence and must make reasonable efforts to expedite litigation consistent

---

represent the best interests of the children does not cease on the filing of the guardian ad litem report. Boyle's Case, 136 N.H. 21, 24, 611 A.2d 618, 620 (1992). See also RSA 458:17-a (allowing a court to appoint a guardian ad litem to continue to serve after a final decree of divorce has been granted).

88 N.H. GAL Rule 2.4.2.

89 N.H. GAL Rule 2.4.3.

90 N.H. GAL Rule 2.4.2.

91 *Id.*

92 N.H. GAL Rule 2.4.1.

with the best interests of the ward.[93] The guardian ad litem may be called to testify in the proceeding, by either party, or by the court.[94] However, the parties may agree that the guardian ad litem will not be called as a witness except upon order of the court and may agree to accept the guardian ad litem's report in place of live testimony.[95]

A guardian ad litem must disclose his or her role when dealing with unrepresented persons.[96] A person certified to act as a guardian ad litem is obligated to accept appointment to a reasonable number of publicly funded cases annually.[97] The guardian ad litem must also inform the administrative judge if he or she has knowledge that another guardian ad litem has violated the rules.[98]

Because the guardian ad litem serves as an officer of the court, he or she is subject to all rules, regulations, and standing orders of that court.[99] A guardian ad litem is forbidden from bringing or defending frivolous proceedings,[100] from issuing subpoenas without good cause,[101] from making

---

93 N.H. GAL Rule 2.6.2.

94 N.H. GAL Rule 2.6.3.

95 *Id.*

96 N.H. GAL Rule 2.7.1. This rule also requires a guardian ad litem to make reasonable efforts to correct an unrepresented person's misunderstanding of the guardian ad litem's role in the matter (if the guardian ad litem knows or reasonably should know of the unrepresented person's misunderstanding). The characterization of the guardian ad litem's representation of a "client" in this rule appears to be inconsistent with the holding in Ross v. Gadwah, 131 N.H. 391, 395, 554 A.2d 1284, 1286 (1988) ("[guardians ad litem] do not act as legal counsel for the child but rather as parties to the proceedings").

97 N.H. GAL, Rule 2.8.1.

98 Id. at 2.10.3. A guardian ad litem must also inform the judge if he or she knows that another guardian ad litem has engaged in conduct which raises a "substantial question" as to that guardian ad litem's honesty, trustworthiness, or fitness in any other respect.

99 N.H. GAL Rule 2.4.2; RSA 458:17-a(II). When attorneys serve as guardians ad litem, "they do not act as legal counsel for the child, but rather as parties to the proceedings." Boyle's Case, 136 N.H. 21, 23, 611 A.2d 618, 619 (1992) (quoting Ross v. Gadwah, 131 N.H. 391, 395, 554 A.2d 1284, 1288 (1988)). See also In re Lisa G., 127 N.H. 585, 591, 504 A.2d 1, 4 (1986) (describing guardian ad litem's role as that of substitute decision-maker or concerned parent). Although the guardian ad litem does not act as counsel to the child, he is subject to sanctions for conflicting representation. Boyle's Case, 136 N.H. 21, 24, 611 A.2d 618, 620 (1992) (finding that attorney violated Rules of Professional Conduct in acting as child's guardian ad litem while concurrently representing parent in criminal case). See also N.H. GAL Rule 2.4.6 and 2.4.7 (regarding conflicts of interest).

100 N.H. GAL Rule 2.6.1.

101 N.H. GAL Rule 2.7.2.

public statements relating to pending cases,[102] from making false statements of material facts or failing to disclose facts necessary to correct certain misapprehensions, and from neglecting to respond to lawful demands for information.[103]

A person certified to act as a guardian ad litem may not solicit employment to serve as a guardian ad litem.[104] However, he or she may communicate the fact that he or she along with his or her educational background and professional certification[105] has passed the training course required by the guidelines, and that he or she is certified by the court to serve as a guardian ad litem.

§ 20.27. Guardian Ad Litem Stipulation

Pursuant to New Hampshire Superior Court Standing Order Relative to Guardian Ad Litem Appointment,[106] in every case in which a guardian ad litem is appointed, the parties must file a stipulation regarding the following matters within thirty days of the appointment:

(1) The expenses for which the guardian ad litem will be reimbursed;

(2) The guardian ad litem's hourly billing rate and the total fee, the $60.00 per hour maximum hourly rate, and the $1,000.00 maximum total fee may be waived with court approval if the parties are paying the cost;[107]

(3) The expected frequency of billing and the terms of payment, including whether a retainer is expected;

(4) Identification of the individuals to be interviewed by the guardian ad litem in order of importance, including names, addresses, telephone numbers, and the relationship between the individual and the ward;

(5) The manner in which the guardian ad litem will communicate with each party's references;

(6) The actions which the guardian ad litem will take if he or she is unable to contact a reference;

(7) Whether the guardian ad litem will visit each party's home;

---

102 N.H. GAL Rule 2.10.2.

103 N.H. GAL Rule 2.10.1.

104 N.H. GAL Rule 2.9.1. This rule defines the term "solicitation" to include any "contact in person, by telephone or telegraph, by letter or other writing, or by other communication. . . ."

105 N.H. GAL Rule 2.9.2.

106 New Hampshire Superior Court Standing Order Relative to Guardian Ad Litem Appointment, 3 New Hampshire Bar News 208, (September 23, 1992).

107 N.H. GAL Rule 2.4.4. This standing order has apparently not been affected by the System-Wide Guardian Ad Litem Application, Certification and Practice Guidelines. See also Fees, Section 20.26.

(8) Whether conversations between the guardian ad litem and the children will be considered confidential;

(9) Whether other orders are necessary in order to protect confidentiality; and

(10) The dates by which the parties will execute authorizations for reports and a list of the specific records that will be requested.

If the stipulation is not filed by the date set forth in the Order on Appointment of Guardian ad Litem, either party or the guardian ad litem may request an immediate enforcement hearing and the clerk will schedule it. Any changes to a stipulation must be filed with the writing. After the appointment of a guardian ad litem in a case, the parties are forbidden to stipulate to any issue concerning the represented children without the concurrence of the appointed guardian ad litem.[108]

§ 20.28. Fees

In proceedings for divorce, nullity, or legal separation, unless otherwise agreed, the court will assess the financial situation of each party and the fees for services provided by the guardian ad litem (and others utilized by the guardian ad litem and approved by the court) will be charged against them.[109] The parties may agree to a different arrangement with the guardian ad litem, if they do so in writing.[110] However, the guardian ad litem may not enter into any contingent fee agreement,[111] and he or she must submit itemized fee statements to the court upon the court's request.[112]

Where the parties are indigent, compensation for guardians ad litem is based on the fee schedule for indigent defense counsel established by the

---

108 New Hampshire Superior Court Standing Order Relative to Guardian Ad Litem Appointment, 3 New Hampshire Bar News 208, (September 23, 1992).

109 See RSA 458:17-a(II-a). See also Wheaton-Dunberger v. Dunberger, 137 N.H. 504, 511, 629 A.2d 812, 817 (1993) (fact that a master ordered each party to a custody dispute to pay one-half of the guardian ad litem fees in no way prohibits the master from altering the division of guardian ad litem fees throughout the course of the proceedings). The 1983 guidelines state that "unless otherwise requested and approved, the fees for the Guardian Ad Litem shall be shared equally between parties;" however, the 1994 guidelines contain no similar provision. New Hampshire Superior Court Standing Order Relative to Guardian Ad Litem Appointment, 3 New Hampshire Bar News 208, 218 (September 23, 1992), sets a maximum fee of $1,000.00 applicable to all cases whether paid by the parties or by the Court Fund. This maximum fee cannot be exceeded unless the court approves after a written request is filed and a hearing is held with all parties present. The Standing Order also sets the maximum hourly billing rate for guardians ad litem at $60.00 per hour.

110 N.H. GAL Rule 2.4.4.

111 N.H. GAL Rule 2.4.4.

112 N.H. GAL Rule 2.4.4.

Supreme Court.[113] A guardian ad litem appointed by the court and compensated by public funds may not receive additional payment from any party.[114]

Library References

Allowance of fees for guardian ad litem appointed for infant defendant, as costs. 30 ALR2d 1148.

§ 20.29. Guardian Ad Litem's Recommendation

The guardian ad litem must undertake an investigation of the matter affecting the child and must render a written report in that includes recommendations concerning the ward's best interests. Those recommendations must be supported by reference to specific information obtained by the guardian ad litem in the course of the investigation.[115]

§ 20.30. Confidentiality Privilege

The guardian ad litem must keep confidential all information revealed by the ward and can disclose only such information in accordance with law and court orders.[116] However, during custody proceedings, the attorney-client privilege does not protect communications between the guardian ad litem and the minor child, as due process requires that either parent has the right to challenge any evidence presented.[117] All information which the guardian ad litem obtains from the child may be discovered by either parent prior to the hearing.[118]

---

113 RSA 458:17-a(II-a). See also Supreme Court Rule 48, setting this rate at $60 per hour and RSA 458:17-b, requiring the Supreme Court to establish separate funds for the compensation of guardians ad litem.

114 N.H. GAL Rule 2.4.4.

115 N.H. GAL Rule 2.5.1. However, "the recommendations of the guardian ad litem do not, and should not, carry any greater presumptive weight than the other evidence in the case. The guardian ad litem is appointed to represent the best interests of the child, not to make a conclusive or presumptive determination; that is the province of the court or master." Richelson v. Richelson, 130 N.H. 137, 143, 537 A.2d 176, 180 (1987); Ross v. Gadwah, 131 N.H. 391, 554 A.2d 1284 (1988); Doubleday v. Doubleday, 131 N.H. 250, 551 A.2d 525 (1988); New Hampshire Superior Court Standing Order Relative to Guardian Ad Litem Appointment, 3 New Hampshire Bar News 208, 218 (September 23, 1992), regarding guardians ad litem investigations and reports as well as the suspension and resumption of these guardian ad litem duties.

116 N.H. GAL Rule 2.4.5.

117 Ross v. Gadwah, 131 N.H. 391, 554 A.2d 1284 (1988) (overruling Richelson v. Richelson, 130 N.H. 137, 536 A.2d 176 (1987), Place v. Place, 129 N.H. 252, 525 A.2d 704 (1987), and Provencal v. Provencal, 122 N.H. 793, 451 A.2d 374 (1982)).

118 Ross v. Gadwah, 131 N.H. 391, 554 A.2d 1284 (1988) (overruling Richelson v. Richelson, 130 N.H. 137, 536 A.2d 176 (1987), Place v. Place, 129 N.H. 252, 525 A.2d 704 (1987), and Provencal v. Provencal, 122 N.H. 793, 451 A.2d 374 (1982)).

§ 20.31. Termination of Representation

Once a guardian ad litem has been appointed and has entered an Appearance, continued representation may not be terminated by the parties without the court's permission.[119] Upon termination, the guardian ad litem must take steps to protect the child's best interests, including allowing time for employment of a new guardian ad litem, surrendering papers and property, and refunding any advance payment or fee that has not been earned.[120]

---

119 N.H. GAL Rule 2.4.8. This rule apparently applies to guardians ad litem wishing to discontinue representation because guardians ad litem are "parties to the proceedings." See Ross v. Gadwah, 131 N.H. 391, 554 A.2d 1284 (1988).

120 N.H. GAL Rule 2.4.8.

CHAPTER 21. CONFESSION OF A CLAIM

§ 21.01. Tender to the Claimant's Attorney Before the Return Day

RSA 515:1 allows an opponent to cut off a claimant's further right to costs in any action for a sum certain by tendering[1] the amount which he agrees is due,[2] plus costs to date, to the claimant's attorney prior to the return day. The sum must be tendered after the date of the writ, however, to have its desired effect.[3]

If the plaintiff accepts the amount tendered in full satisfaction of the claim before entry, he will simply not enter the writ and the case will, for all practical purposes, be concluded.

Library References

CJS Tender §§ 1, 4, 8, 13

Repayment or tender of unearned premium as condition precedent to exercise by insurer of right to cancel policy. 16 ALR2d 1200.

Tender as affecting personal liability of executor or administrator for interest on legacies or distributive shares where payment is delayed. 18 ALR2d 1409.

Effect of tender of purchase money or rights as between vendor and vendee under land contract in respect of interest. 25 ALR2d 973.

Interest on consideration returned or tendered as condition of setting aside release or compromise. 53 ALR2d 749.

Timeliness of tender or offer of return of consideration for release or compromise, required as condition of setting it aside. 53 ALR2d 759.

Liability for costs in trial tribunal in eminent domain proceedings as affected by offer or tender by condemnor. 70 ALR2d 804.

Creditor's failure to disclose correct amount due as affecting sufficiency of debtor's tender of amount that debtor believes to be due, but that is less than amount actually due. 82 ALR3d 1178.

Right of judgment creditor to demand that debtor's tender of payment be in cash or by certified cheek rather than by uncertified check. 82 ALR3d 1199.

---

[1] The tender may be unconditional, in which case the claimant may accept the money deposited and pursue his claim for the rest, or the tender may be conditioned upon the claimant taking it in full satisfaction of the claim. See Brown v. Heath, 78 N.H. 180, 97 A. 744 (1916). The tender is an admission. Ashuelot R.R. v. Cheshire R.R., 60 N.H. 356 (1880). But advance payments made as an accommodation to an injured party or his heirs or dependents are not. RSA 508-B:1.

[2] Even if this is less than the amount claimed in the count. Sawyer v. Baker, 20 N.H. 525 (1846).

[3] RSA 515:5; Thurston v. Blaisdell, 8 N.H. 367 (1836).

§ 21.02. Payment Into Court and Confession (Offer of Judgment)

After entry of the writ in any case in which one party asserts that his opponent owes a sum certain, the opponent may file an Answer and Motion To Dismiss, Brief Statement, or Counterclaim[4] which admits that a lesser sum is due but denies the rest, and therewith pay to the clerk[5] the sum which he admits to be due[6] plus costs to that date.[7] In actions to recover the possession of real estate, a similar manner of pleading may be adopted with the same effect, but the opponent need not deliver a deed to the clerk.[8]

If the opponent wishes to confess and pay money into court after filing his Answer or other responsive pleading, he may do so along with a Motion To Amend his prior pleading.[9] At any time thereafter, the claimant may accept the amount tendered in full satisfaction of his claim[10] by filing a Motion To Amend revising his claim to the amount paid. The court will allow the motion as a matter of course. Judgment will be entered immediately upon the allowance of the amendment,[11] and the clerk will enter judgment for that amount plus costs.[12] When the plaintiff accepts the tender but files no pleading, the opponent may file a Motion To Dismiss or a Motion for Summary Judgment with an affidavit and, in the absence of objection, the court will grant the motion without hearing.

---

4 Woodward v. Roberts, 51 N.H. 552 (1872); Thurston v. Blaisdell, 8 N.H. 367 (1836).

5 A tender is no defense unless the money is brought into court. Felker v. Hazelton, 68 N.H. 304, 38 A. 1051 (1895); Allen v. Cheever, 61 N.H. 32 (1881); Heywood v. Hartshorn, 55 N.H. 476 (1875); Frost v. Flanders, 37 N.H. 549 (1859); Colby v. Stevens, 38 N.H. 191 (1859); Bailey v. Metcalf, 6 N.H. 156 (1833).

6 Super. Ct. R. 60, 61; Dist. and Mun. Ct. R. 3.18(A); RSA 515:2. RSA 515:2 does not expressly require payment into court, but the Rules do. When a special plea or set-off, counterclaim, or recoupment is filed, the claimant's costs must be paid with the sum admitted. Super. Ct. R. 61.

7 Thurston v. Blaisdell, 8 N.H. 367 (1836); Dist. and Mun. Ct. R. 3.18(A).

8 RSA 515:2.

9 Merrill v. Mellen, 24 N.H. 258 (1851). Nothing in RSA 515:2 or Super. Ct. R. 60 or 61 limits the filing of a confession or payment into court to the time for filing responsive pleadings.

10 The claiming party may not accept the amount paid and also continue with the action.

11 See Super. Ct. R. 75. There is no need to wait 31 days for the filing of a postverdict motion or a Notice of Appeal as the opponent has waived all exceptions by his admission and payment.

12 Super. Ct. R. 60; Dist. and Mun. Ct. R. 3.18(A).

If the claimant refuses to accept the amount tendered in full satisfaction of his claim within ten days of receiving the responsive pleading,[13] the trial will be on the amount in excess of the amount tendered.[14] When the sum is tendered with an Answer only, the claimant will be denied any costs at all and his opponent will have costs from the date of the payment[15] if the claimant is unable to establish a right to a greater amount than was paid into court. When the sum is paid with a Motion To Dismiss, a Brief Statement, or a Counterclaim,[16] the claimant will be denied any costs and the opponent will be awarded only the costs incurred since the date of payment.[17]

If the claimant establishes a right to a greater amount than was paid into court, he may have judgment for that amount, plus costs.[18] Generally, he will not be allowed to recover interest at the lawful rate on the funds deposited for the period of deposit,[19] but will be given any interest earned thereon while

---

13 Although the Rules do not establish a time within which the amount paid must be accepted in order to cut off the opponent's right to costs, it seems reasonable to follow the period allowed for filing Replications. See Super. Ct. R. 137 ("[a] replication shall be entitled like an answer and shall be filed within ten days after the filing and delivery of the answer").

14 The opponent's right to contest the remainder of the claim will not be affected by his confession of the claimant's right to a partial recovery. If the cause of action is divisible, only the part that is admitted will be closed and the trial will proceed on the others as though no admission had been made. If the cause of action is not divisible, the confession will admit it but leave open to further contest the amount of damages. Hackett v. B.C. & M R.R., 35 N.H. 390, 397 (1857) ("A confession is an admission of a cause of action, as alleged in the declaration to the extent of its terms, and no further."). See also Pittsfield v. Barnstead, 38 N.H. 115 (1859).

15 Super. Ct. R. 60; Dist. and Mun. Ct. R. 3.18(A). See Eastman v. Molineux, 14 N.H. 503 (1843).

16 The question whether the claimant has established a right to a greater sum than admitted is determined with reference to the whole sum recovered, not solely by looking to the amount obtained on the claimant's case in chief. Richey v. Cooper, 45 N.H. 414 (1864).

17 Super. Ct. R. 61; Dist. and Mun. Ct. R. 3.18(B). There is no apparent reason for this distinction, because the opponent is admitting that there is an amount due the claimant.

18 Where the amount paid into court is less than the jurisdictional limit of a lower court, the court will not, for that reason, limit the claimant's costs to the jurisdictional limit. Stevens v. Gilson, 9 N.H. 106 (1837).

19 Beaudry v. Favreau, 99 N.H. 444, 114 A.2d 666 (1955). This is an unfair rule, because it permits an opponent to save a substantial interest liability whenever the market rate is less than the legal rate. The theoretical basis for the rule—that neither party has the use of the funds while in the custody of the court—ignores the fact that, by depositing funds which he knows he will eventually have to pay, at a time when the market rate is less than the legal rate, the opponent is making use of the funds to earn interest on the differential. In earlier days, this rule was rejected. See Drew v. Towle, 30 N.H. 531 (1855).

in the court's possession.[20] After he has either accepted the amount paid, or obtained judgment for a greater amount, the clerk may pay him the amount deposited in court directly without the need of an execution, and an execution may be issued for the excess, costs, and interest.

Library References

CJS Tender §§ 58–64

Rights as between vendor and vendee under land contract in respect of interest as affected by payment into court. 25 ALR2d 1975.

Condemnor's right, as against condemnee, to interest on excessive money deposited in court or paid to condemnee. 99 ALR2d 886.

Appealability of order directing payment of money into court. 15 ALR3d 568.

Payment or deposit of award in court as affecting condemnor's right to appeal. 40 ALR3d 203.

---

20 Super. Ct. Admin. R. 1-4 provides that the clerk will deposit any sum totalling $500 or more in an interest-bearing account and pay the amount deposited plus interest to the prevailing party upon the court's order.

Part VII

DISCOVERY AND DEPOSITIONS

Cross References

Pretrial Procedure, see Part VIII *infra*.

CHAPTER 22. GENERAL PRINCIPLES OF PRETRIAL DISCOVERY

A. IN GENERAL

A. *In General*

§ 22.01. Introduction

From the early nineteenth century pretrial discovery has been a favored procedural device and has been consistently expanded.[1] The power to permit and control pretrial discovery is rooted in the court's equity powers and inherent authority to control the proceedings before it.[2]

---

1 See RSA 498:1; Robbins v. Kalwall Corp., 120 N.H. 451, 417 A.2d 4 (1980). "[T]he remedy is available and has continued to develop for the most part without the aid of statute or special rules of court." Drake v. Bowles, 97 N.H. 471, 473, 92 A.2d 161, 163 (1952). See also Gibbs v. Prior, 107 N.H. 218, 220 A.2d 151 (1966); Ingram v. Boston & Maine Railroad, 89 N.H. 277, 197 A. 822 (1938); Reynolds v. Burgess Sulphite Fibre Co., 71 N.H. 332, 51 A. 1075 (1902).

2 In practice, the rules of discovery in the district and municipal courts are construed in a manner consistent with the Superior Court Rules, and pretrial discovery proceeds according to the same principles in both forums. Prob. Ct. R. 10 provides that discovery in the probate court is governed by the same rules that apply in the superior court, and incorporates by reference Super. Ct. R. 35 through 45A. Discovery in the probate court is also subject to several statutes. See, e.g., RSA 547:11-a (accounting proceedings) and RSA 555:1 (suspected embezzlements). The exercise of power under those statutes is limited to their terms.

§ 22.02. Law v. Equity

The same principles and procedures govern discovery in actions at law and in equity.[3]

§ 22.03. Marital Proceedings

The scope of discovery in marital proceedings is essentially the same as in other actions, although discovery at times is accomplished under more court supervision than in other actions.[4]

§ 22.04. Nature of Pretrial Discovery

Pretrial discovery is frequently referred to as a preliminary,[5] remedial,[6] and discretionary[7] device. As a preliminary device, it exists to aid the parties before any right to relief has been proved. As a remedial device, discovery is applied liberally in a manner designed to accomplish its purposes. It is not confined or restricted by arbitrary limitations but takes any form necessary to accomplish its goals. Finally, as a discretionary device, its application rests entirely in the hands of the trial judge.[8] He determines

---

3 Reynolds v. Burgess Sulphite Fibre Co., 71 N.H. 332, 337, 51 A. 1075, 1080 (1902). Forms of proceedings in equity have survived the adoption of liberal rules of discovery for use in actions at law. Dondero v. Ferranti, 90 N.H. 554, 3 A.2d 831 (1939). See also Super. Ct. R. 35(b)(3)(a)(ii).

4 See, e.g., Vasoli v. Vasoli, 100 N.H. 200, 122 A.2d 533 (1956); Calderwood v. Calderwood, 112 N.H. 355, 296 A.2d 910 (1972).

5 See, e.g., State v. Cote, 95 N.H. 108, 58 A.2d 749 (1948); Reynolds v. Boston & Maine Transportation Co., 98 N.H. 251, 98 A.2d 157 (1953); Lincoln v. Langley, 99 N.H. 158, 106 A.2d 383 (1954).

6 See, e.g., State v. Cote, 95 N.H. 108, 58 A.2d 749 (1948); Reynolds v. Boston & Maine Transportation Co., 98 N.H. 251, 98 A.2d 157 (1953); Lincoln v. Langley, 99 N.H. 158, 106 A.2d 383 (1954); McDuffey v. Boston & Maine Railroad, 102 N.H. 179, 152 A.2d 606 (1959).

7 See, e.g., State v. Cote, 95 N.H. 108, 58 A.2d 749 (1948); Reynolds v. Boston & Maine Transportation Co., 98 N.H. 251, 98 A.2d 157 (1953); Lincoln v. Langley, 99 N.H. 158, 106 A.2d 383 (1954); Staargaard v. Public Service Co. of N.H., 96 N.H. 17, 69 A.2d 4 (1949); Drake v. Bowles, 97 N.H. 471, 92 A.2d 161 (1952); Hartford Accident & Indemnity Co. v. Cutter, 108 N.H. 112, 229 A.2d 173 (1967).

8 New Castle v. Rand, 101 N.H. 201, 136 A.2d 914 (1957); Currier v. Allied New Hampshire Gas Co., 101 N.H. 205, 137 A.2d 405 (1957); McDuffey v. Boston & Maine Railroad, 102 N.H. 179, 152 A.2d 606 (1959); Hardware Mutual Casualty Co. v. Hopkins, 105 N.H. 231, 196 A.2d 66 (1963); Riddle Spring Realty Co. v. State, 107 N.H. 271, 220 A.2d 751 (1966); Hartford Accident & Indemnity Co. v. Cutter, 108 N.H. 112, 115, 229 A.2d 173, 176 (1967) (On the exercise of the trial judge's discretion "rests in great measure the success of pretrial procedures."); Scontsas v. Citizens Insurance Company, 109 N.H. 386, 253 A.2d 831 (1969); Workman v. Public Service Co., 113 N.H. 422, 308 A.2d 540 (1973); Miller v. Basbas, 131 N.H. 332, 553 A.2d 299 (1988);

when, how, and subject to what limitations discovery will be used, and his decision will be overruled only for an abuse of discretion.[9] As a discretionary device, discovery is flexible enough to meet the requirements of justice in each individual case.[10]

Just as pretrial discovery is, by its nature, preliminary, remedial, and discretionary, so is it given a favored,[11] liberal,[12] and broad[13] application in order to accomplish its purposes. Its use has been encouraged,[14] and its availability has been consistently expanded.[15]

State v. DeLong, 136 N.H. 707, 709, 621 A.2d 442 (1993) ("The trial court has the inherent authority to exercise its sound discretion in matters relating to pre-trial discovery.").

9 McDuffey v. Boston & Maine Railroad, 102 N.H. 179, 152 A.2d 606 (1959); Miller v. Basbas, 131 N.H. 332, 553 A.2d 299 (1988); Daigle v. City of Portsmouth, 131 N.H. 319, 553 A.2d 291 (1988).

10 McDuffey v. Boston & Maine Railroad, 102 N.H. 179, 181, 152 A.2d 606, 608 (1959) ("In encouraging use of discovery and depositions . . . it has been pointed out that it operates with desirable flexibility under the discretionary control of the Presiding Justice of the trial court . . . and that this is a logical method of preventing surprise and permitting both court and counsel to have an intelligent grasp of the issues to be litigated and knowledge of the facts underlying them."). See also Hardware Mutual Casualty Co. v. Hopkins, 105 N.H, 231, 196 A.2d 66 (1963); Riddle Spring Realty Co. v. State, 107 N.H. 271, 278, 220 A.2d 751, 758 (1966) ("Hence the Trial Court by the exercise of its discretion plays an important role in maintaining the desired flexibility in this important procedural tool. . . ."); Workman v. Public Service Co., 113 N.H. 422, 308 A.2d 540 (1973).

11 Drake v. Bowles, 97 N.H. 471, 92 A.2d 161 (1952); Reynolds v. Boston & Maine Transportation Company, 98 N.H. 251, 98 A.2d 157 (1953); McDuffey v. Boston & Maine Railroad, 102 N.H. 179, 152 A.2d 606 (1959); Smith v. American Employers' Insurance Co., 102 N.H. 630, 168 A.2d 564 (1960); Yancey v. Yancey, 119 N.H. 197, 399 A.2d 975 (1979).

12 Lefebvre v. Somersworth Shoe Company, 93 N.H. 354, 41 A.2d 924 (1945); Drake v. Bowles, 97 N.H. 471, 92 A.2d 161 (1952); McDuffey v. Boston & Maine Railroad, 102 N.H. 179, 152 A.2d 606 (1959); Hardware Mutual Casualty Co. v. Hopkins, 105 N.H. 231, 196 A.2d 66 (1963); Durocher's Ice Cream, Inc. v. Pierce Construction Co., 106 N.H. 293, 210 A.2d 477 (1965); Hartford Accident & Indemnity Co. v. Cutter, 108 N.H. 112, 229 A.2d 173 (1967); Calderwood v. Calderwood, 112 N.H. 355, 296 A.2d 910 (1972); Yancey v. Yancey, 119 N.H. 197, 399 A.2d 975 (1979); Miller v. Basbas, 131 N.H. 332, 553 A.2d 299 (1988).

13 Drake v. Bowles, 97 N.H. 471, 92 A.2d 161 (1952); McDuffey v. Boston & Maine Railroad, 102 N.H. 179, 152 A.2d 606 (1959); Hardware Mutual Casualty Co. v. Hopkins, 105 N.H. 231, 196 A.2d 66 (1963); Durocher's Ice Cream Inc. v. Pierce Construction Co., 106 N.H. 293, 210 A.2d 477 (1965); Calderwood v. Calderwood, 112 N.H. 355, 296 A.2d 910 (1972); Willett v. General Electric Co., 113 N.H. 358, 306 A.2d 789 (1973); Sawyer v. Boufford, 113 N.H. 627, 312 A.2d 693 (1973); Barry v. Horne, 117 N.H. 693, 377 A.2d 623 (1977); Miller v. Basbas, 131 N.H. 332, 553 A.2d 299 (1988).

14 McDuffey v. Boston & Maine Railroad, 102 N.H. 179, 152 A.2d 606 (1959).

15 See, e.g., Robbins v. Kalwall Corp., 120 N.H. 451, 417 A.2d 4 (1980).

Library References

CJS Discovery §§ 1, 20

§ 22.05. Purposes of Pretrial Discovery

Pretrial discovery serves the following purposes:

(1) Ascertaining the truth at an early stage of the proceedings;[16]

(2) Providing both the court and counsel with "an informed grasp of the issues to be litigated" and of the facts underlying those issues;[17]

(3) Preventing surprise at trial;[18]

(4) Allowing each side to prepare its case or defense properly for trial by permitting each side to have access to all the information favorable to its side of the case;[19]

(5) Probing the other side's claims and knowledge before trial;[20]

(6) Narrowing the issues which must be tried;[21]

---

16 Reynolds v. Boston & Maine Transportation Co., 98 N.H. 251, 98 A.2d 157 (1953); Drake v. Bowles, 97 N.H. 471, 92 A.2d 161 (1952); State v. Cote, 95 N.H. 108, 58 A.2d 749 (1948); Hartford Accident & Indemnity Co. v. Cutter, 108 N.H. 112, 229 A.2d 273 (1967); Sawyer v. Boufford, 113 N.H. 627, 312 A.2d 693 (1973).

17 Calderwood v. Calderwood, 112 N.H. 355, 358, 296 A.2d 910, 912 (1972); Scontsas v. Citizens Insurance Co., 109 N.H. 386, 253 A.2d 831 (1969); Riddle Spring Realty Co. v. State, 107 N.H. 271, 220 A.2d 751 (1966); Hardware Mutual Casualty Co. v. Hopkins, 105 N.H. 231, 196 A.2d 66 (1963); McDuffey v. Boston & Maine Railroad, 102 N.H. 179, 152 A.2d 606 (1959).

18 Calderwood v. Calderwood, 112 N.H. 355, 296 A.2d 910 (1972); Scontsas v. Citizens Insurance Co., 109 N.H. 386, 253 A.2d 831 (1969); Hardware Mutual Casualty Co. v. Hopkins, 105 N.H. 231, 196 A.2d 66 (1963); McDuffey v. Boston & Maine Railroad, 102 N.H. 179, 152 A.2d 606 (1959); Riddle Spring Realty Co. v. State, 107 N.H. 271, 220 A.2d 751 (1966).

19 Scontsas v. Citizens Insurance Co., 109 N.H. 386, 253 A.2d 831 (1969); Hardware Mutual Casualty Co. v. Hopkins, 105 N.H. 231, 196 A.2d 66 (1963); McDuffey v. Boston & Maine Railroad, 102 N.H. 179, 152 A.2d 606 (1959); Drake v. Bowles, 97 N.H. 471, 92 A.2d 161 (1952); Riddle Spring Realty Co. v. State, 107 N.H. 271, 220 A.2d 751 (1966); Calderwood v. Calderwood, 112 N.H. 355, 296 A.2d 910 (1972); Humphreys Corporation v. Margo Lyn, Inc., 109 N.H. 498, 256 A.2d 149 (1969). Pretrial discovery has been described as "an integral part of pretrial procedure." Durocher's Ice Cream Inc. v. Pierce Construction Co., 106 N.H. 293, 294–95, 210 A.2d 477, 478 (1965). See also N.H. Rules of Professional Conduct, Rule 3.4(a) (unprofessional conduct to obstruct access to evidence or to alter or conceal documents or other physical evidence) and Rule 3.4(f) (unprofessional conduct to request witnesses not to give evidence).

20 Hartford Accident & Indemnity Co. v. Cutter, 108 N.H. 112, 229 A.2d 173 (1967); Scontsas v. Citizens Insurance Company, 109 N.H. 386, 253 A.2d 831 (1969).

21 Hartford Accident & Indemnity Co. v. Cutter, 108 N.H. 112, 229 A.2d 173 (1967); Workman v. Public Service Co., 113 N.H. 422, 308 A.2d 540 (1973); Sawyer v. Boufford, 113 N.H. 627, 312 A.2d 693 (1973); In re Estate of Ward, 129 N.H. 4, 11,

(7) Improving the chances for a just settlement;[22] and

(8) Shortening the eventual trial.[23]

All of these purposes are, to one degree or another, interrelated, and it has become common for the Court to state a variety of them together as a preamble to its opinions in discovery cases. Thus, in *McDuffey v. Boston & Maine Railroad*,[24] Chief Justice Kenison wrote:

> Discovery in civil actions has been regarded in this jurisdiction as a proper procedural aid for the parties to prepare their case in advance of trial and has been given a broad and liberal interpretation . . . . In encouraging use of discovery and depositions . . . it has been pointed out that it operates with desirable flexibility under the discretionary control of the Presiding Justice of the trial court . . . and that this is a logical method of preventing surprise and permitting both court and counsel to have an intelligent grasp of the issues to be litigated and knowledge of the facts underlying them.[25]

Perhaps the best explication of the relationship of these purposes was provided by Justice Grimes in *Scontsas v. Citizens Insurance Company*:[26]

> It is the philosophy of the adversary system that the truth will more likely be reached if both sides of the issue are fully presented and that this is more likely to occur if the sides are presented by partisan advocates. To permit the system to have maximum effectiveness, therefore, each of the advocates must be fully informed and have access to all evidence favorable to his side of the issue. This is true whether the issue is one which has been raised by him or by his opponent, and whether the evidence is in the possession of his opponent or someone else. If a party is surprised by the introduction of evidence or an issue or the presentation of a witness previously unknown to him, the trier of fact is likely to be

---

523 A.2d 28, 34 (1986) ("One of the purposes of discovery is to decrease the time and expense involved in litigation.").

22 Hartford Accident & Indemnity Co. v. Cutter, 108 N.H. 112, 229 A.2d 173 (1967); Workman v. Public Service Co., 113 N.H. 422, 308 A.2d 540 (1973); Sawyer v. Boufford, 113 N.H. 627, 312 A.2d 693 (1973).

23 Hartford Accident & Indemnity Co. v. Cutter, 108 N.H. 112, 229 A.2d 173 (1967). See also N.H. Rules of Professional Conduct, Rule 3.2 (lawyer's duty to expedite cases).

24 102 N.H. 179, 152 A.2d 606 (1959).

25 *Id.* at 181, 152 A.2d at 608.

26 109 N.H. 386, 253 A.2d 831 (1969).

deprived of having that party's side of the issue fully presented, and the system becomes less effective as a means of discovering of the truth.[27]

Library References

CJS Discovery § 20

§ 22.06. When Discovery May Be Had—Pending Actions

With some minor limitations, pretrial discovery may begin as soon as the writ or other process has been entered and may continue through the end of trial. The parties have an obligation to seek desired discovery promptly, however, and a party's failure to request discovery until the eve of trial may prevent his obtaining useful material.[28]

Library References

CJS Discovery §§ 3, 23, 24

§ 22.07. —Actions That Have Not Yet Been Brought

Modern pretrial discovery has its roots in the inherent powers of the court and is derived from the early bills of discovery and petitions for an accounting, for specific performance, and to establish a constructive trust. As a result, some early decisions of the Supreme Court seem to recognize a right to obtain discovery in proceedings which are either separate from or antecedent to the actions in which the information disclosed could be expected to be used.[29] Until very recently, however, it was generally understood that a party who had no independent contractual, equitable, or statutory right to information could not commence discovery until his case had been brought. In all cases in which the Supreme Court has allowed a party to obtain information before an action has been commenced, the petitioner

---

27 *Id.* at 388, 253 A.2d at 833.

28 See Talbot v. Catelli-Habitant, Inc., 122 N.H. 517, 446 A.2d 858 (1982).

29 In the 1920s and 1930s, the former bills of discovery were transmuted in practice into discovery motions and the use of a separate equity proceeding for discovery in aid of a pending action at law was discontinued. The process began with LaCoss v. Lebanon, 78 N.H. 413, 101 A. 364 (1917), in which Justice Young, writing for the Court, remarked that a bill of discovery could be treated simply as a motion in the related action at law. Following the decision in *LaCoss*, discovery was at first attempted by "a bill of discovery in the form of a motion" (Davis v. Central New Hampshire Power Co. of Maine, 79 N.H. 377, 109 A. 263 (1920)) and later by a "motion for discovery." Ingram v. Boston & Maine Railroad, 89 N.H. 277, 197 A. 822 (1938).

has had some right to obtain the information which was *independent* of his need to prepare for trial.[30]

However, in *Robbins v. Kalwall Corp.*,[31] the Supreme Court revived the old bills of discovery and, for the first time, allowed their use against third parties in aid of an action at law that had not yet been brought. The plaintiff in *Robbins* had been injured on the job by an oven, had received workmen's compensation, and was barred by statute from suing her employer or his insurance carrier. She sought, however, to bring a products liability action against the manufacturer of the oven, and, to that end, requested her employer to allow her to examine the oven to determine the name of the manufacturer and the nature of its defects. When her employer refused to allow an inspection, the plaintiff brought a petition in superior court against the employer to compel a disclosure and inspection. The employer moved to dismiss for lack of jurisdiction, but the Supreme Court permitted the petition to stand. In a per curiam opinion, the Court found jurisdiction to grant discovery in the superior court's inherent and statutory equity powers. As a result of *Robbins*, it is now possible to bring a bill of discovery in the superior court against a third party prior to the commencement of any action, in order to obtain information which would be discoverable from that person had suit been commenced. Prefiling disclosure from potential parties presumably must still be based on an independent right to have the information.

Robbins raises the question whether, taken together with *Dupuis v. Smith Properties*,[32] the Court may one day regard the commencement of a bill of discovery before the expiration of the statute of limitations as sufficient to preserve the right of action if the intended defendant has notice of the commencement of the bill and of the claim in aid of which it is brought. In a case where such an issue might arise, the plaintiff may find it advisable to state the substance of his intended claim with some completeness in the bill of discovery and to serve the intended defendant at the same time that he serves the third party.

---

30 In Kann v. Wausau Abrasives Company, 81 N.H. 535, 129 A. 374 (1925), for example, the plaintiff sought specific performance of a contractual provision which obligated the defendant to give him information on the estimated capacity of a mine and the defendant's projected annual requirements for the mine's output. Although nonaction for breach of contract had yet been brought and the Court recognized that the relief sought was "akin to discovery" and for the purpose, in part, of computing damages resulting from breach of other contract provisions, it affirmed an order requiring disclosure as the contract required.

31 120 N.H. 451, 417 A.2d 4 (1980).

32 114 N.H. 625, 325 A.2d 781 (1974).

§ 22.08. Persons Who May Be Ordered To Make Discovery

While only a party to a pending or threatened action may seek discovery, any person, whether he will be liable in that action or not, may be required to provide information on the issues involved.[33] "[E]very member of the community has a general and public duty . . . to disclose all matters known to him, to the end that truth may be established in litigation."[34] Because the right to discovery is clear, it should not ordinarily be necessary to seek a court order to obtain information from nonparties. However, when a nonparty objects, the discovering party must bring a bill of discovery in aid of the pending or threatened action and serve it upon the nonparty.[35]

Library References

CJS Discovery §§ 10, 26 28
Compelling party to disclose information in hands of affiliated or subsidiary corporation, or independent contractor not made party to suit. 19 ALR3d 1134.
Absent or unnamed class members in class action in state court as subject to discovery. 28 ALR4th 986.

B. Methods of Discovery

§ 22.09. In General

The following nine methods of discovery are recognized for use in New Hampshire:[36]

    (1) Depositions on oral examination (videotape or stenographic)[37]

    (2) Depositions on written examination[38]

    (3) Written interrogatories[39]

    (4) Request for production of documents

    (5) Request for production of personalty

    (6) Request for permission to enter upon land or other real estate

    (7) Request for physical examination

---

33 Lefebvre v. Somersworth Shoe Company, 93 N.H. 354, 41 A.2d 924 (1945); Therrien v. Public Service Co. of N.H., 99 N.H. 197, 108 A.2d 48 (1954); Yancey v. Yancey, 119 N.H. 197, 399 A.2d 975 (1979); Robbins v. Kalwall Corp., 120 N.H. 451, 417 A.2d 4 (1980); Calderwood v. Calderwood, 112 N.H. 355, 296 A.2d 910 (1972).

34 Robbins v. Kalwall Corp., 120 N.H. 451, 452, 417 A.2d 4, 5 (1980).

35 Lefebvre v. Somersworth Shoe Company, *supra*; Robbins v. Kalwall Corp., *supra*.

36 See Super. Ct. R. 35(a); Prob. Ct. R. 10. See also Claire Murray, Inc. v. Reed, 139 N.H. 437, 439 (1995) (petition for accounting may be used as a discovery device).

37 Super. Ct. R. 37–45; Prob. Ct. R. 10.

38 *Id.*

39 Super. Ct. R. 36, 36-A; Prob. Ct. R. 10.

(8) Request for mental examination

(9) Request for admission.[40]

Although these nine methods of discovery are most commonly used in preparation for trial, they are also available for use in execution and other postjudgment proceedings at the trial court level. The right to discovery by one method is as extensive as by another, and the same principles govern discovery regardless of which method is used.[41]

Library References

CJS Discovery §§ 11(1), 16, 18, 37, 39, 55, 69, 88

Cross References

Depositions generally, see ch. 27 *infra.*
Depositions in Perpetual Remembrance, see ch. 28 *infra.*
Medical Examinations, see ch. 24 *infra.*
Production of Documents and Things, see ch. 25 *infra.*
Requests for Admissions, see ch. 26 *infra.*
Written Interrogatories, see ch. 23 *infra.*

§ 22.10. Frequency of Use

Absent a specific court order to the contrary, there is no limit to the number of methods of discovery that a party may employ in any case or at any one time or to the number of times that any method may be used.[42] The fact that the information sought by one method may be obtained by another method which has already been commenced and is pending does not limit the party's ability to use another method.[43]

§ 22.11. Sequence of Use

Absent a specific court order to the contrary,[44] the nine methods of discovery may be used at the same time or in any sequence. No party need

---

40 Super. Ct. R. 54; Prob. Ct. R. 10.

41 "The right to the discovery of documents, etc., is as extensive as the right to discovery by oral testimony and depends upon the same principles." Reynolds v. Burgess Sulphite Fibre Co., 71 N.H. 332, 336, 51 A. 1075, 1077 (1902). See also Ingram v. Boston & Maine Railroad, 89 N.H. 277, 197 A. 822 (1938); Prob. Ct. R. 10.

42 Super. Ct. R. 35(a); Prob. Ct. R. 10. There is, however, a limit on the number of written interrogatories which either side may propound. See Super. Ct. R. 36; Dist. and Mun. Ct. R. 1.10(D); Prob. Ct. R. 10.

43 Wheeler v. Wadleigh, 37 N.H. 55 (1858).

44 Super. Ct. R. 35(d) provides that the court may regulate the sequence and timing of discovery "for the convenience of parties and witnesses and in the interests of justice."

delay his use of any method because his coparty or opponent has either begun or not begun discovery or is currently using any method.[45]

C. *Scope of Discovery*

§ 22.12. In General

Superior Court Rule 35(b)(1) states the general scope of pretrial discovery as follows:

> Parties may obtain discovery regarding any matter, not privileged, which is relevant to the subject matter involved in the pending action, whether it relates to the claim or defense of the party seeking discovery or to the claim or defense of any other party, including the existence, description, nature, custody, condition and location of any books, documents, or other tangible things and the identity and location of persons having knowledge of any discoverable matter. It is not ground for objection that the information sought will be inadmissible at the trial if the information sought appears reasonably calculated to lead to the discovery of admissible evidence.[46]

The superior court has inherent equitable authority to broaden or narrow this general scope of discovery in any case.[47] The right to pretrial discovery, however, is limited to obtaining information and does not extend to an award of pretrial relief.[48] Thus, while a discovery of money received and expenses paid may be had in many contract actions as a matter of course, where the parties dispute the existence of any relationship entitling the plaintiff to such information, the relationship will have to be established before the accounting is ordered.[49]

---

45 Super. Ct. R. 35(d); Prob. Ct. R. 10.

46 See, e.g., Phillips v. Verax Corp., 138 N.H. 240, 637 A.2d 906 (1994) (trial court well within its discretion to require a deposition 24 hours in advance of a witness's testimony where plaintiff lacked pretrial access to witness). Although the scope of discovery is wide, "it is subject to limitations, mainly for the protection of the parties against harrassment." Jarvis v. Prudential Ins. Co. 122 N.H. 648, 654 (1982).

47 See RSA 498:1; Super. Ct. R. 35(b).

48 Currier v. Concord Railroad Corporation, 48 N.H. 321 (1869). Pretrial discovery should not be construed so liberally as to permit a party to avoid the necessity of proving his right as a condition to obtaining the requested relief.

49 Cf. Rosenblum v. Judson Engineering Corp., 99 N.H. 267, 109 A.2d 558 (1954). However, if the defendant admits the existence of a relationship which entitles the plaintiff to an accounting or if such a relationship is clear as a matter of record on the court's docket, he cannot object to providing it without a trial and in the course of

Library References

CJS Discovery §§ 1, 20, 22
Discovery of defendant's sales, earnings, or profits on issue of punitive damages in tort action. 54 ALR4th 998.
Discovery of identity of blood donor. 56 ALR4th 755.

§ 22.13. Information Regarding the Opponent's Case

Until very recently, it was generally held that discovery could not be used to obtain information about the opposing party's case or method of proving that case.[50] A party was restricted in discovery to obtaining information to establish his own case or defense. This rule was supported by an 1858 statute (now set forth as RSA 516:23) which permitted a party to decline, on deposition, "to disclose the names of the witnesses by whom [and] the manner in which he proposes to prove his case" or to "produce any writing which is material to his case or defense, unless the deposition is taken in his own behalf."

Over the years, it became clear that this attempt to restrict a party to the discovery of information which related to his defense, but not to his opponent's claim, was both artificial and calculated to permit a continued reliance on trial by surprise. Accordingly, these restrictions were gradually eased. In *Gibbs v. Prior*,[51] the Supreme Court affirmed an order which required a defendant on deposition to identify a person whose home he had left shortly before an accident. In *Hartford Accident & Indemnity v. Cutter*,[52] the Court allowed the trial court to require the defendant to produce at

---

discovery. Kann v. Wausau Abrasives Co., 81 N.H. 535, 129 A. 374 (1925); Bay State Iron Company v. Goodall, 39 N.H. 223 (1859); Treadwell v. Brown, 44 N.H. 551 (1863); Brooks v. Goodwin, 70 N.H. 281, 47 A. 255 (1900).

50 See, e.g., LaCoss v. Lebanon, 78 N.H. 413, 101 A. 364 (1917); Ingram v. Boston & Maine Railroad, 89 N.H. 277, 197 A. 822 (1938); Reynolds v. Boston & Maine Transportation Company, 98 N.H. 251, 98 A.2d 157 (1953). A typical statement of this limitation was set forth by Justice Marble in Ingram v. Boston & Maine Railroad, *supra*, as follows:

> The fundamental rule on this subject is, that the plaintiff's right to a discovery does not extend to all facts which may be material to the issue, but is confined to facts which are material *to his . . . cause of action*; it does not enable him to pry into the defendant's case, or to find out the evidence by which that case will be supported.

89 N.H. at 278 79, 197 A. 823. As late as 1960, Justice Blandin wrote in Smith v. American Employers' Insurance Co., 102 N.H. 530, 163 A.2d 564 (1960), "The moving party cannot be allowed to pry indiscriminately into the opponent's case to ferret out the evidence by which the case will be proved." 102 N.H. at 535, 163 A.2d 568.

51 107 N.H. 218, 220 A.2d 151 (1966).

52 108 N.H. 112, 229 A.2d 173 (1967).

deposition a written statement signed by a nonparty insured. Writing for the Court, Justice Lampron said:

> Discovery, together with depositions, interrogatories, and pretrial hearings, are important procedures for probing in advance of trial the adversary's claims and his possession or knowledge of information pertaining to the controversy between the parties.

* * *

> These pretrial devices have supplanted the "older notion which dominated trials at common law . . . the right of each party to keep from disclosure the facts which he intended to show at trial beyond the very limited disclosure he was required to make in his pleadings or by an occasional order for particulars."[53]

In *Scontsas v. Citizens Insurance Company*,[54] the Court held that an insurance company defendant could be required to produce all documents it had generated in issuing the policy. In announcing the Court's decision in *Scontsas*, Justice Grimes formulated the lengthy rationale for full disclosure, which is set forth elsewhere in this chapter, in which he transmuted the old rule allowing access to information necessary to the *preparation* of a party's case into a rule permitting discovery of information *favorable* to the party's position, as follows:

> To permit the system to have maximum effectiveness, therefore, each of the advocates must be fully informed and have access to all evidence favorable to his side of the issue. This is true whether the issue is one which has been raised by him or by his opponents and whether the evidence is in the possession of his opponent or someone else.[55]

In *Humphreys Corporation v. Margo Lyn, Inc.*,[56] the Court said that the trial court could permit discovery despite the objection that the request pried into an opponent's case "if the evidence sought would aid the party either in his own case or in defending against the case of the other party."[57] Finally, in

---

53 *Id.* at 113–14, 229 A.2d at 175.

54 109 N.H. 386, 253 A.2d 831 (1969).

55 *Id.* at 388, 253 A.2d at 833.

56 109 N.H. 498, 256 A.2d 149 (1969).

57 *Id.* at 500, 256 A.2d 150.

Willett v. General Electric Co.[58] and *Workman v. Public Service Co.*,[59] the Court held that the facts and conclusions known by a party's experts and their reports could be discovered as a matter of course when the experts are expected to testify and upon a showing of necessity when they are not.

Throughout the period when these decisions were being made, the Court was also cutting back on the effectiveness of RSA 516:23 in shielding a party's case from disclosure on deposition. In *Gibbs v. Prior*[60] and *Roy v. Monitor-Patriot Co.*,[61] the Court announced that the statute did not restrict the superior court's power in equity "to compel discovery in accordance with established principles."[62] In *Riddle Spring Realty Co. v. State*,[63] the Court held that RSA 516:23 could not be used as an objection to written interrogatories propounded to the state in an eminent domain case. In *Humphreys Corporation v. Margo Lyn, Inc.*,[64] the Court decided that the statute had no application to a corporation or its agents. In *Barry v. Horne*,[65] referring to RSA 516:23 as an antiquated statute which was inconsistent with modern-day discovery, the Court held that while a party could object to giving the names of his witnesses at a deposition, the trial court could order him to give those names as a matter of course and without any showing of necessity. The Court thereby effectively repealed RSA 516:23 by judicial decision.

Thus, in the period from 1966 to 1977, the Supreme Court expanded the subjects of discovery from matters which help to establish a party's own case or defense to any matter relevant to either party's case or defense. This is the general scope of discovery today and is set forth in Superior Court Rule 35(b)(1) and Probate Court Rule 10.

§ 22.14. Demonstration of Necessity for Information—History

In the early days of this century, it was occasionally remarked that the right to discovery "depends upon the necessity for discovery in the admini-

---

58 113 N.H. 358, 306 A.2d 789 (1973).

59 *Id.* 422, 308 A.2d 540 (1973).

60 107 N.H. 218, 220 A.2d 151 (1966).

61 112 N.H. 80, 290 A.2d 207 (1972).

62 107 N.H. at 222, 220 A.2d at 154.

63 107 N.H. 271, 220 A.2d 751 (1966).

64 109 N.H. 498, 256 A.2d 149 (1969).

65 117 N.H. 693, 377 A.2d 623 (1977).

stration of justice."[66] But even as originally conceived, this standard of necessity was meant to apply in only the broadest sense. Thus, in *Reynolds v. Burgess Sulphite Fibre Co.*,[67] Justice Chase went on to say that "[t]o warrant discovery, it is not necessary that there should be absolutely no means of proving the plaintiff's case without it. . . . A party may maintain a bill of discovery, 'either because he has no proof, or because he wants it in aid of other proof.' . . . 'When the plaintiff has any case to make out, he has a right to discovery of anything that may assist him in proving his case, or even the smallest tittle of it.' "[68] Superior Court Rule 35(b)(1) and Probate Court Rule 10 impose no general standard of necessity on a party seeking discovery.

Library References

CJS Discovery §§ 2, 11(3)

§ 22.15.   —Modern Practice

Under modern practice, a party need only show actual necessity in the following situations:

(a) *For Information Subject to a Qualified Privilege.*   Where a party seeks disclosure of information which is subject to a qualified privilege and his opponent objects, the court will normally require that the party show why he needs the information in order to prepare his case. While the standard of need is not high, it must exceed the responding party's recognized right to maintain the privacy of his information.

(b) *For Materials Prepared for Trial.*   Superior Court Rule 35(b)(2) permits a party to obtain discovery of "documents and tangible things . . . prepared in anticipation of litigation or for trial . . . upon a showing that [he] has substantial need of the materials in preparation of his case and that he is unable without undue hardship to obtain the substantial equivalent of the materials by other means." The court is required to "protect against disclosure of the mental impressions, conclusions, opinions or legal theories of an attorney or other representative of a party" concerning the litigation. Any person who has made "a statement concerning the action or its subject

---

66 Reynolds v. Burgess Sulphite Fibre Co., 71 N.H. 332, 339, 51 A. 1075, 1078 (1902). See also State v. Cote, 95 N.H. 108, 58 A.2d 749 (1948).

67 71 N.H. 332, 51 A. 1075.

68 *Id.* at 339, 51 A. at 1078.

matter"[69] is entitled to have a copy of that statement upon request, without filing a motion or making any showing of necessity.[70]

(c) *For Facts Known to or Opinions Held by Experts Not Expected To Testify.* Superior Court Rule 35(b)(3)(b) allows a party to discover "facts known or opinions held by an expert, who has been retained or specially employed by another party in anticipation of litigation or preparation for trial and who is not expected to be called as a witness at trial, only upon a showing of exceptional circumstances under which it is impracticable for the party seeking discovery to obtain facts or opinions on the same subject by other means." This Rule does not authorize a party to obtain his opponent's expert reports simply in order to save expense.[71]

Library References

CJS Discovery §§ 5, 72

§ 22.16. Relevancy of Information

Both Superior Court Rule 35(b)(1) and Probate Court Rule 10 allow a party to obtain discovery of any information "which is relevant to the subject matter involved in the pending action," and the Supreme Court has remarked that the "scope of discovery is generally limited to relevant material that is 'not privileged'."[72] In *Durocher's Ice Cream, Inc. v. Pierce Construction,*

---

69 A statement concerning the action or its subject matter may be obtained if it is "a written statement signed or otherwise adopted or approved by the person making it" or "a stenographic, mechanical, electrical, or other recording, or a transcription thereof, which is a substantially verbatim recital of an oral statement by the person making it and contemporaneously recorded." Super. Ct. R. 35(b)(2).

70 Super. Ct. R. 35(b)(2).

71 Workman v. Public Service Co., 113 N.H. 422, 308 A.2d 540 (1973). In Johnston v. Lynch, 133 N.H. 79, 574 A.2d 934 (1990), the Supreme Court held for the first time that a party may discover the identity of an expert the opposing party has retained but does not intend to call to trial, absent evidence that the information is irrelevant, upon making the showing provided by Rule 35(b)(3)(b). The Court rested its decision both on Federal Rule of Civil Procedure 26(b)(4)(B) ("the identity of an expert whom the opposing party has retained but does not expect to call as a witness is discoverable without any special showing of exceptional circumstances") and on the Court's preference for liberal discovery. See also Wheeler v. School Administrative Unit 21, 130 N.H. 666, 669, 550 A.2d 980, 982 (1988) (plaintiff not allowed to obtain deposition of psychiatrist not expected to be called at trial even though psychiatrist was the only expert in that field in the state; plaintiff was required to show that expertise in that field was necessary to the proof of his case and that "similarly qualified individuals from other states were not available to supply the opinions needed").

72 Willett v. General Electric Co., 113 N.H. 358, 359, 306 A.2d 789, 790 (1973). See also Jarvis v. Prudential Insurance Company of America, 122 N.H. 648, 448 A.2d 407 (1982) (advertising material and information on other lawsuits denied).

Co.,[73] Chief Justice Kenison wrote that "it is impossible to state in advance the precepts of relevancy"[74] but went on to hold that the relevancy of evidence requested on discovery does not depend upon its admissibility at trial so long as it is reasonably calculated to lead to the discovery of admissible evidence.[75] Chief Justice Kenison's statement in this regard has been adopted in the second sentence of Superior Court Rule 35(b)(1) and the fourth sentence of Probate Court Rule 10.

It is clear, however, that the information sought must be relevant *to the pending action*. A party may not use discovery in one case to ascertain the merits of another, whether that other is pending or anticipated.

Library References

CJS Discovery §§ 4, 34

§ 22.17. Cumulativeness of Information

It has long been the case that information may be discovered even though it is not strictly necessary for the presentation of the requesting party's case. As Justice Marble wrote in *Ingram v. Boston & Maine Railroad*,[76] "It is no objection that the evidence sought may be merely cumulative. . . . Its

---

73 106 N.H. 293, 210 A.2d 477 (1965).

74 *Id.* at 294, 210 A.2d at 477. Materiality and competency are, in this regard, just alternative terms for "relevancy," and the Supreme Court has often held that materiality of information sought on discovery need not be clear in order for a party to be allowed to obtain it. In Ingram v. B & M Railroad, 89 N.H. 277, 279, 197 A. 822, 823 (1938), the Court stated: "Nor need its materiality be definitely established. Its production will be ordered if the court can fairly find that it may in any way be material to the plaintiff's cause." See also Lefebvre v. Somersworth Shoe Co., 93 N.H. 354, 41 A.2d 924 (1945) (Justice Johnston wrote that the term "material to the plaintiff's cause" means material to the *proper preparation* of his case); Reynolds v. B & M Transportation Co., 98 N.H. 251, 98 A.2d 157 (1953); Rosenblum v. Judson Engineering Corp., 99 N.H. 267, 109 A.2d 558 (1954). In McDuffey v. B & M Railroad, 102 N.H. 179, 152 A.2d 606 (1959), Chief Justice Kenison observed that, if facts were material to the proper preparation of the party's case, the fact that they would not be admissible at trial was of no consequence. Information sought by discovery need not be competent evidence if it is calculated to lead to evidence which is competent. Lefebvre v. Somersworth Shoe Co., *supra*; Staargaard v. Public Service Co. of N.H., 96 N.H. 17, 69 A.2d 4 (1949).

75 This was a refinement of Justice Johnston's statement in Staargaard v. Public Service Co. of N.H., 96 N.H. 17, 69 A.2d 4 (1949), that the propriety of questions asked on deposition depends not on their admissibility but on whether the matters inquired into may become relevant and competent, and of Justice Duncan's observation in Therrien v. Public Service Co. of N.H., 99 N.H. 197, 108 A.2d 248 (1954), that documents could be discovered which, although not themselves admissible, might give clues to the existence or location of relevant facts or be useful for impeachment or corroboration.

76 89 N.H. 277, 197 A. 822 (1938).

production will be ordered if the court can fairly find that it may in any way be material to the plaintiff's cause."[77]

§ 22.18. Discovery of Facts Known to and Opinions Held by Experts

Except in unusual cases, a party may obtain discovery of the facts known to and opinions held by an expert[78] retained by another party who has acquired that information or developed those opinions in anticipation of litigation or for trial only if the expert is expected to be called as a witness at trial.[79] Facts known to and opinions held by experts who were not retained or did not develop their opinions in anticipation of litigation or for trial are discoverable in the same ways as the facts known to and opinions held by other potential witnesses.

With regard to experts expected to be called at trial, a party may, by interrogatory, require another party to give their names and addresses, the subject matter of their expected testimony, the facts and opinions on which they will testify, and the grounds for those opinions.[80] A party may request his opponent[81] to provide a Disclosure of Expert Witnesses giving the names and addresses of "each person, including any party" whom the opponent expects to present as an expert witness at trial, a brief statement of that person's education and experience, the subject matter of his expected testimony, and "a summary of the facts and opinions to which the expert is expected to testify and a summary of the ground for each opinion."[82] The Disclosure of Expert Witnesses must be produced within thirty days of the request or within such other period as the court orders after a discovery conference, and it must include as attachments all reports from the expert

---

77 *Id.* at 279, 197 A. at 823.

78 Not every person with expertise, even on the subject in litigation, is an "expert" for the purposes of Superior Court Rule 35. Gelinas v. Metropolitan Property and Liability Insurance Co., 131 N.H. 154, 167–68, 551 A.2d 962, 970 (1988) ("Where a person who might otherwise be qualified as an expert testifies as to personal or first-hand knowledge, such a witness should be treated as an ordinary witness and not as an expert.").

79 But a party can call as a witness at trial an expert who was originally consulted by his opponent to evaluate the case and can require him to testify to facts learned and opinions formed during his original consultation with the opponent. Fenlon v. Thayer, 127 N.H. 702, 506 A.2d 319 (1986). See also Wheeler v. School Administrative Unit 21, 130 N.H. 666, 550 A.2d 980 (1988).

80 Super. Ct. R. 35(b)(3)(a)(i); Prob. Ct. R. 10.

81 A party has no right, absent a court order, to obtain a Disclosure of Expert Witnesses from a coparty.

82 Super. Ct. R. 35(f).

relating to the case.[83] If a party wishes to depose an expert, he must either obtain the other party's agreement to the additional discovery or convince the court to order it.[84] The court's order in such a case may place limits on the scope of such further discovery.

A party seeking discovery from another party's expert must pay the expert "a reasonable fee . . . unless manifest injustice would result."[85] A party seeking discovery of the facts known to or opinions held by an expert who is not expected to testify at trial or of an expert witness's reports may also be required to pay "a fair portion of the fees and expenses reasonably incurred by the latter party in obtaining facts and opinions from the expert."[86]

Library References

CJS Discovery §§ 5, 18, 71(2)

Pretrial deposition—discovery of opinions of opponent's expert witnesses. 86 ALR2d 138.

Right to elicit expert testimony from adverse party at pretrial discovery proceeding. 88 ALR2d 1190.

Discovery: right to ex parte interview with injured party's treating physician. 50 ALR4th 714.

Propriety of allowing state court civil litigant to call expert witness whose name or address was not disclosed during pretrial discovery proceedings. 58 ALR4th 653.

§ 22.19. Discovery of Privileged Information—Generally

Parties and witnesses have some limited rights to withhold relevant information both before and during trial[87] under fifteen[88] recognized doctrines of privilege.[89] While a party or witness may not use the shield of privilege indiscriminately, he is not required to disclose the privileged

---

83 *Id.* See also Wheeler v. School Administrative Unit 21, 130 N.H. 666, 550 A.2d 980 (1988) (defendant's failure to file supplementary reports as agreed was no basis to exclude expert's testimony at trial where plaintiff was aware of the reports and did not file motion to compel).

84 Super. Ct. R. 35(b)(3)(a)(ii); Prob. Ct. R. 10.

85 Super. Ct. R. 35(b)(3)(c)(i); Prob. Ct. R. 10.

86 Super. Ct. R. 35(b)(3)(c).

87 Privileges may be asserted during discovery as well as at trial. State v. Miskell, 122 N.H. 842, 451 A.2d 383 (1982). NHRE 512(b) requires that "[i]n jury cases, proceedings shall be conducted, to the extent practicable, so as to facilitate the making of claims of privilege without the knowledge of the jury."

88 The Court has also suggested the existence of a sixteenth privilege in RSA 632-A:6 (the "Rape Shield Law"), but apparently this privilege only applies to criminal prosecutions. See State v. Miskell, 122 N.H. 842, 451 A.2d 383 (1982).

89 For a more thorough discussion of the law of privilege in New Hampshire, see Richard B. McNamara, *The Hierarchy of Evidentiary Privilege in New Hampshire*, 20 N.H.B.J. 1 (1978).

information in order to show his right to claim the protection. He need only disclose enough for the court to see that the claim has a reasonable basis in fact.[90] A claim of privilege must, however, be asserted at the time when information which it seeks to protect is withheld.[91] The fact that a party has claimed a privilege is "not a proper subject of comment by judge or counsel" and may not form the basis for any inference.[92]

Statutory privileges[93] are, however, strictly construed and will be applied only as their terms specifically require.[94]

Library References

CJS Discovery §§ 5, 35

§ 22.20. —Testimonial Privileges

(a) *In General.* Testimonial privileges may be divided into two groups: absolute and qualified. Absolute privileges apply as a complete protection at all times unless waived; qualified privileges do not prevent disclosure but form the basis for objection and the imposition of conditions on disclosure.

(b) *Absolute Privileges.* Three absolute privileges are recognized under New Hampshire law. Those privileges relate to:

(1) *Self-Incrimination:* The privilege against disclosing information which will incriminate the person making the disclosure is founded on the Fifth Amendment to the United States Constitution and the 15th article,

---

90 State (ex rel.) Eaton v. Farmer, 46 N.H. 200 (1865); Currier v. Concord Railroad Corporation, 48 N.H. 321 (1869). The preliminary question of the existence of a privilege is to be determined by the court. NHRE 104(a) provides that "the existence of a privilege . . . shall be determined by the court," and that in making its determination, the court "is not bound by the rules of evidence except those with respect to privileges." See also State v. O'Connell, 131 N.H. 92, 94, 550 A.2d 747, 749 (1988) ("Witnesses may not claim the privilege against self-incrimination to create an all-inclusive immunization of their testimony. Rather, the privilege should be raised separately with respect to each question propounded, and the witness should present the court with adequate information upon which it can determine if the privilege applies.").

91 Daigle v. City of Portsmouth, 131 N.H. 319, 328, 553 A.2d 291, 296 (1988) ("A party cannot determine by itself that material is exempt because of a privilege and fail to inform the other party that it is withholding specific information.").

92 NHRE 512(a). "Upon request, any party against whom the jury might draw an adverse inference from a claim of privilege is entitled to an instruction that no inference may be drawn therefrom." NHRE 512(c). See also RSA 173-C:8.

93 The privileges created by statute are: priest/penitent (RSA 516:35), physician/surgeon/psychiatrist/patient (RSA 329:26), psychologist and related professionals/patient (RSA 330-A:19), and sexual assault counselor/domestic violence counselor/victim (RSA 173-C:2).

94 In re Brenda H., 119 N.H. 382, 402 A.2d 169 (1979); State v. LaRoche, 122 N.H. 231, 442 A.2d 602 (1982).

part I, of the New Hampshire Constitution. It permits any person to refuse to produce any evidence of "the principal fact, or any one of a series or chain of facts, which may constitute or establish a criminal charge against him."[95] The privilege cannot be claimed by "organizations or companies, incorporated or unincorporated, whose character is essentially impersonal rather than purely private and personal," or by individual officers, directors or agents of such organizations to shield personal records which are commingled with the organization's records.[96]

(2) *Exposing to a Charge of Moral Turpitude or to a Penalty or Forfeiture:* This privilege springs from the same principles of natural justice as the privilege against self-incrimination.[97] It was recognized at the turn of the century[98] but has apparently not been applied recently, and its continued vitality must be doubted. Presumably a corporation or other impersonal organization has no more right to claim this privilege than to claim the privilege against self-incrimination.

---

95 Noyes v. Thorpe, 73 N.H. 481, 482, 62 A. 787, 787 (1906); State v. O'Connell, 131 N.H. 92, 94, 550 A.2d 747, 748 (1988) ("The privilege . . . extends not only to answers that in themselves would support a conviction, but also to any information sought which would furnish a link in the chain of evidence needed to prosecute.") See also Bay State Iron Company v. Goodall, 39 N.H. 223 (1859); State (ex rel.) Eaton v. Farmer, 46 N.H. 200 (1865); Winsor v. Bailey, 55 N.H. 218 (1875); Reynolds v. Burgess Sulphite Fibre Co., 71 N.H. 332, 51 A. 1075 (1902); State v. Merski, 121 N.H. 901, 437 A.2d 710 (1981); Caledonia, Inc. v. Trainor, 123 N.H. 116, 459 A.2d 613 (1983) (deposition transcript used when defendant refused to testify at trial on basis of privilege against self-incrimination); Maine v. Latshaw, 137 N.H. 665, 663 A.2d 952 (1993) (privilege against self-incrimination invoked in civil proceeding where answers would support a conviction and where information sought would furnish link in chain of evidence needed to prosecute).

96 State v. N.H. Retail Grocers' Ass'n, 115 N.H. 623, 348 A.2d 360 (1975).

97 See Reynolds v. Burgess Sulphite Fibre Co., 71 N.H. 332, 334, 51 A. 1075, 1076 (1902); Currier v. Concord Railroad Corp., 48 N.H. 321 (1869).

98 In Reynolds v. Burgess Sulphite Fibre Co., 71 N.H. 332, 334 51 A. 1075, 1079–80 (1902), Justice Chase wrote:

> It is true . . . that a person cannot be called upon to furnish testimony in aid of such an action or any other which tends to show that he has committed a crime or misdemeanor, or that he is liable to a penalty or a forfeiture of property. Testimony of this kind is excepted from the operation of the remedy in deference to the fundamental law that no subject shall be compelled to accuse or furnish evidence against himself in a criminal proceeding. It is also said that this equitable jurisdiction will not be exercised in controversies involving moral turpitude and arising from acts clearly immoral, even though brought for the purpose of recovering pecuniary compensation.

The Court went on to hold that a claim of negligence in the maintenance of a machine did not involve a charge of moral turpitude which would justify use of the privilege.

(3) *Priest/Penitent:*   Confessions or confidences to a "Priest, rabbi, or ordained or licensed minister of any church or a duly accredited Christian Science practitioner" are privileged from disclosure unless the penitent "waives the privilege."[99] The privilege does apply to suspected child abuse or neglect.[100]

(c) *Qualified Privileges.*   Twelve qualified privileges are recognized in New Hampshire practice. Those privileges relate to:

(1) *State Secrets:*   This privilege finds support in only two cases. The state's privilege against disclosure is limited to information which, if disclosed, would harm the state,[101] or be "prejudicial to the community."[102] The disclosure of such "state secrets" may be required under appropriate court-imposed conditions.

(2) *Trade Secrets:*   A party has a qualified privilege not to disclose trade secrets. The privilege cannot be used to prevent disclosure of information necessary to decide the case,[103] but can be raised as a barrier to inquiries which have strayed from the central issues in the case. A claim of trade secret privilege requires the inquiring party to show at least that he cannot properly prepare his case without disclosure.[104] In cases where trade secrets are truly in issue, it is customary for the parties to enter into stipulations limiting disclosure of the information produced to the parties, their experts and the court and to provide, upon settlement, for the return or

---

99 RSA 516:35; NHRE 505. The confidence or confession must, however, be made to the priest, rabbi, minister, or practitioner "in his or her professional character as spiritual advisor." *Id.*

100 See RSA 169-C:32 (which does not include the priest/penitent privilege within its provisions).

101 Lefebvre v. Somersworth Shoe Company, 93 N.H. 354, 41 A.2d 924 (1945).

102 Reynolds v. Burgess Sulphite Fibre Co., 71 N.H. 332, 334, 51 A. 1075, 1076 (1902). See also Lefebvre v. Somersworth Shoe Company, 93 N.H. 354, 41 A.2d 924 (1945).

103 "The privilege not to disclose trade secrets is a limited one which cannot be exercised to prevent a disclosure which is 'indispensable for the ascertainment of the truth.' " Lincoln v. Langley, 99 N.H. 158, 160, 106 A.2d 383, 385 (1954) (defendant who sought disclosure against claim of trade secret required to show that it was unable to properly prepare defense without it and that production was necessary in interest of justice). See also Spain v. United States Rubber Company, 94 N.H. 400, 54 A.2d 364 (1947); NHRE 507 (privilege will not be allowed if to do so would "tend to conceal fraud or otherwise work injustice").

104 Lincoln v. Langley, 99 N.H. 158, 106 A.2d 383 (1954); Farnum v. Bristol Myers Company, 107 N.H. 165, 169, 219 A.2d 277, 280 (1966) ("If it appears from competent evidence that disclosure of the formula in advance of trial is 'essential' or 'urgently necessary' . . . the Trial Court has the authority to order it subject to suitable conditions calculated to prevent public disclosure or improper use of the information.") See also NHRE 507 (disallowing the privilege where it would "work injustice").

destruction of all documents setting forth that information. If the parties cannot agree on restrictions, the court may impose appropriate safeguards to prevent disclosure.[105]

(3) *Informers:*   The United States, the state, and units of local government have a qualified privilege against disclosing the identity of an informer.[106] The privilege covers persons who have given information "relating to or assisting in an investigation of a possible violation of a law to a law enforcement officer or member of a legislative committee or its staff conducting an investigation."[107] The privilege may be waived by "an appropriate representative of the public entity to which the information was furnished,"[108] by disclosure of either the informer's identity or "the informer's interest in the subject matter of his or her communication,"[109] or by presenting the informer as a witness for the government.[110] In addition, the trial court may order disclosure in a civil case in which the public entity entitled to claim the privilege is a party when it appears that the informer "may be able to give testimony relevant to . . . a fair determination of a material issue on the merits."[111] The court must first give the public entity "an opportunity to show *in camera* [and outside the presence of other counsel and parties] facts relevant to determining whether the informer can, in fact, supply that testimony."[112] It is unclear whether a similar disclosure may be compelled in a case in which the public entity is not a party.[113]

---

105 Lincoln v. Langley, 99 N.H. 158, 106 A.2d 383 (1954) (Court suggested that samples be delivered to recognized expert retained by defendant with requirement that any unused portions be returned to plaintiff upon completion of tests). See also NHRE 507.

106 See State v. Thorp, 116 N.H. 303, 358 A.2d 655 (1976); Richard B. McNamara, *The Hierarchy of Evidentiary Privilege in New Hampshire*, 20 N.H.B.J. at 11–13 (1978); NHRE 509.

107 NHRE 509(a). Note that the privilege is not restricted to the identity of persons who give information relating to the violation of a criminal statute.

108 NHRE 509(b).

109 NHRE 509(c)(1)(A).

110 NHRE 509(c)(1)(B). The language of this subsection suggests that the privilege is not waived by the government entity allowing the informer to be deposed (under appropriate safeguards) but only by its presentation of the informer as a witness at the trial or final hearing.

111 NHRE 509(c)(2).

112 NHRE 509(c)(2).

113 The scope of the privilege as set forth in Rule 509(a) is broad enough to permit assertion by government entities even when they are not parties to litigation. But Rule 509(c)(2), authorizing a court to order disclosure of an informer's identity, is limited to situations in which the government entity is a party in the case. In the absence of case law supporting a broader common law power to compel disclosure, there is at least some

(4) *Journalists:*   The Supreme Court has recognized a qualified privilege against forced disclosure of a journalist's sources.[114] A journalist is justified in refusing to respond to requests for discovery of his sources until adequate safeguards have been imposed.[115]

(5) *Work-Product of Attorneys or Other Representatives:*   Except in the case of experts retained for and expected to testify at trial,[116] a party cannot be required to disclose what his attorney or other representative has prepared or has had prepared in the course of work on the case except upon a showing that the discovering party has "substantial need of the materials in the preparation of his case and that he is unable without undue hardship to obtain the substantial equivalent of the materials by other means."[117]

(6) *Federal Income Tax Returns:*   In *Currier v. Allied New Hampshire Gas Co.,*[118] Chief Justice Kenison wrote:

> We adopt the majority view that federal income tax returns are not privileged as a matter of law in civil litigation where the returns are material to the claims of the parties. We recognize that discovery of federal income tax returns is discretionary with the Trial Court, but it should not be used as a means of harassment or impertinent intrusion. The Trial Court may, if circumstances warrant it, in any particular case impose stringent requirements upon

---

doubt whether the trial court could require that a government entity which was not a party to an action identify its informer.

114 Downing v. Monitor Publishing Co., Inc., 120 N.H. 383, 415 A.2d 683 (1980).

115 In *Downing, supra,* Chief Justice Grimes wrote that "there is no absolute privilege allowing the press to decline to reveal sources of information when those sources are essential to a libel plaintiff's case," but went on to say that, before ordering disclosure, the plaintiff must "satisfy the trial court that he has evidence to establish that there is a genuine issue of fact regarding the falsity of the publication." 120 N.H. at 386–87.

116 See 22.18 *supra.*

117 Super. Ct. R. 35(b)(2). See Johnston v. Lynch, 133 N.H. 79, 574 A.2d 934 (1990) (citing Riddle Spring Realty Co. v. State, 107 N.H. 271, 275, 220 A.2d 751, 756 (1966)). Formerly, the work product of nonlawyers, such as investigators and insurance adjusters, was not privileged and had to be disclosed. See State v. Cote, 95 N.H. 108, 58 A.2d 749 (1948); Ingram v. Boston & Maine Railroad, 89 N.H. 277, 197 A. 822 (1938). Super. Ct. R. 35(b)(2) now restricts disclosure of materials prepared by or for nonlawyers who are a "party's representative (including his . . . consultant, surety, indemnitor, insurer or agent)" unless the discovering party can show hardship. If there are persons who have prepared materials for a case and do not come within this definition, their work product may still be subject to disclosure without a showing of hardship. In Therrien v. Public Service Co. of N.H., 99 N.H. 197, 200, 108 A.2d 48, 51 (1954), Justice Duncan said that the test is whether their "work product . . . is . . . so far akin to that of a lawyer as to merit like protection from disclosure . . . ."

118 101 N.H. 205, 137 A.2d 405 (1957).

the moving party to establish grounds for the production of federal income tax returns.[119]

Thus, tax returns have a status somewhere between information which must be disclosed as a matter of course and information to which a qualified privilege may be raised requiring the court to impose restrictions on its production, dissemination, and use.

In cases where lost income is claimed, the claimant must give his opponent's counsel his federal income tax returns for the year of the incident, the previous two years, and the year after (or written authorization to obtain them from the Internal Revenue Service) within six months of entry.[120] In other cases, tax returns are usually produced without objection in cases in which the information they contain is material. But, under the *Currier* holding, a party in such a case may require his opponent to satisfy the court that the returns are necessary to the preparation of his case.

(7) *Bank Records:*   Although the Legislature has recognized the need for confidentiality in a bank's dealings with its customers,[121] the Supreme Court has decided that a party's bank records enjoy no privilege against disclosure in a case where the financial dealings or resources of a party are in issue.[122] However, a party's financial resources are not put in issue simply by his being named a defendant in an action and the court will not allow the plaintiff to explore on discovery the extent to which the defendant could respond to a judgment in excess of his insurance coverage.[123] But where a party's financial resources or dealings are in issue, the Court has not chosen to require in the case of bank records, as it has with tax returns, that upon his opponent's objection, the moving party may be required to meet "stringent conditions" for establishing the relevancy of the records before he can obtain them.

(8) *Marital Communications:*   "Husband and wife are competent witnesses for or against each other in all cases . . . ,"[124] except that: (a) neither spouse may "testify against the other as to any statement, conversation, letter

---

119 *Id.* at 207, 137 A.2d at 407. Presumably, state and local tax returns enjoy no greater privilege against disclosure than federal returns.

120 Super. Ct. R. 63(B).

121 See RSA ch. 359-C (Right to Privacy Act).

122 Calderwood v. Calderwood, 112 N.H. 355, 269 A.2d 910 (1972). See also State v. Sands, 123 N.H. 570, 467 A.2d 202 (1983).

123 Sawyer v. Boufford, 113 N.H. 627, 312 A.2d 693 (1973).

124 NHRE 504; RSA 516:27.

or other communication" made to anyone,[125] and (b) neither spouse may "testify as to any matter which in the opinion of the court would lead to a violation of marital confidence."[126] The privilege may not be claimed in cases of child abuse or neglect[127] or of adult abuse.[128]

(9) *Physician/Surgeon/Psychiatrist/Patient:*   A physician or surgeon licensed in New Hampshire may not be compelled to disclose information obtained in the course of and for the purposes of providing professional care.[129] In addition, no person working under the supervision of a physician or surgeon licensed in New Hampshire[130] may be compelled to disclose communications "that are customary and necessary for diagnosis and treatment."[131] The privilege does not apply to chiropractors or other quasi-medical practitioners who are not licensed as physicians or surgeons in New Hampshire, but does protect confidences to a psychiatrist.[132] "The purpose behind the . . . privileges is to encourage full disclosure by the patient for the purpose of receiving complete medical and psychiatric treatment. . . . However, the privileges . . . are not absolute and must yield when disclosure of the information concerned is considered essential."[133] The privilege may not be claimed in disciplinary hearings conducted by the State Board of Registration in Medicine, the Board of Nursing Education and Nurse

---

125   NHRE 504; Clements v. Marston, 52 N.H. 31, 38 (1872).

126   NHRE 504. For an illuminating discussion of this privilege, see Richard B. McNamara, *The Hierarchy of Evidentiary Privilege in New Hampshire*, 20 N.H.B.J. at 69 (1978). The Supreme Court has defined the term "marital confidence" to include "something confided by one [spouse] to the other, simply and specially as husband and wife, and not what would be communicated to any other person under the same circumstances." Clements v. Marston, 52 N.H. 31, 38 (1872). Purely business matters are usually held not privileged because they are not marital confidences. See Maine v. Latshaw, 137 N.H. 665, 553 A.2d 952 (1993).

127   RSA 169-C:32.

128   RSA 161-D:3-b.

129   RSA 329:26;. NHRE 503(a). But see RSA 161-D:7 (access by investigators from the Division of Elderly and Adult Services).

130   To come within the privilege, the assistant must be working directly and presently under the physician or surgeon's supervision. See State v. LaRoche, 122 N.H. 231, 442 A.2d 602 (1982) (EMT's in ambulance on the way to a hospital did *not* qualify); In re Kathleen M., 126 N.H. 379, 493 A.2d 472 (1985) (statements made to psychiatrist in the presence of a mental health worker held protected).

131   RSA 329:26, 330-A:19; NHRE 503(a). See also State v. Thresher, 122 N.H. 63, 442 A.2d 758 (1982).

132   In re Kathleen M., 126 N.H. 379, 493 A.2d 472 (1985).

133   State v. Kupchun, 117 N.H. 412, 415, 373 A.2d 1325, 1327 (1977); In re Field, 120 N.H. 206, 412 A.2d 1032 (1980); In re Kathleen M., 126 N.H. 379, 493 A.2d 472 (1985); Nelson v. Lewis, 130 N.H. 106, 534 A.2d 720 (1987).

Registration, the Board of Examiners of Nursing Home Administrators, "or any other statutorily created medical occupational licensing board conducting disciplinary hearings."[134] The privilege also does not apply in cases of suspected child abuse or neglect[135] or of adult abuse.[136]

Similarly, the privilege does not apply to information concerning "reportable communicable diseases" which must be reported or provided to the Director of the Division of Public Health Services,[137] to any information which is relevant to the involuntary admission of a person to a mental health treatment facility,[138] or to information which must be communicated in order to warn of or take precautions against a patient's "violent behavior."[139]

The privilege is partially waived by the commencement of a medical malpractice action.[140] But the waiver is not so broad as to allow the defendant or his attorney to interview the plaintiff's treating physician outside the formal discovery process.[141]

(10) *Psychologist and Related Professional/Patient:* Communications between a patient and a psychologist, associate psychologist, pastoral counselor, or certified clinical social worker and any person working under the supervision of any such person, if the communications are "necessary for diagnosis and treatment," are privileged from compulsory disclosure

---

134 RSA 329:26.

135 RSA 169-C:32. But see In re Brenda H., 119 N.H. 382, 402 A.2d 169 (1979) (where the Court said, in construing the slightly different wording of a prior statute, that the court should "carefully exercise [its] discretion in admitting these communications" so as to protect the privilege's purpose of building confidence in relationships necessary to the treatment of illness).

136 RSA 161-D:3-b.

137 RSA 141-C:10(III).

138 RSA 329:26. Cf. RSA 135-C:27 54.

139 RSA 329:31(III).

140 Nelson v. Lewis, 130 N.H. 106, 110, 534 A.2d 720, 722 (1987) ("Disclosure of the plaintiff's treatment-related statements relevant to claimed negligence is essential if the defendant is to challenge such a claim or the court is to evaluate it. . . . The Legislature certainly did not intend to prevent just resolution of such claims by giving the plaintiff the right to deprive the defendant of relevant information.").

141 Nelson v. Lewis, 130 N.H. 106, 111, 534 A.2d 720, 723 (1987) ("[A] plaintiff who places her medical condition at issue in an action for medical negligence does not waive the physician-patient privilege so as to permit defendants to interview treating physicians *ex parte*. The plaintiff waives her privilege to the extent necessary to provide the opposing party information essential to defending the action. However, the fact that statements irrelevant to the action remain privileged requires that we recognize the plaintiff's right to limit the defendant to obtaining such information through formal discovery.").

"unless such disclosure is required by a court order."[142] The privilege may not be claimed in cases of suspected child abuse or neglect[143] or of adult abuse.[144] The privilege also does not apply to any information which is relevant to the involuntary admission of a person to a mental health treatment facility[145] or to information which must be communicated in order to warn of or take precautions against a patient's "violent behavior."[146] It is not clear whether the privilege prevents information disclosed by a patient concerning sexual misconduct by a previous psychologist, certified clinical social worker, or certified pastoral counselor from being disclosed to a licensing board.[147]

(11) *Lawyer/Client:* The lawyer/client privilege has recently been extensively revised and expanded by the adoption of NHRE 502. The new rule extends the privilege to the following seventeen categories of confidential communications:[148]

(A) Between a client[149] and his lawyer;[150]

(B) Between a client and his lawyer's representative;[151]

---

142 RSA 330-A:19; NHRE 503(b). But see RSA 161-D:7 (access by investigators from the Division of Elderly and Adult Services). The privilege does not extend to psychological assistants, except when they are working under the supervision of a psychologist or other certified professional, because they are "registered" rather than certified under RSA ch. 330-A.

143 RSA 169-C:32. But see In re Brenda H., 119 N.H. 382, 402 A.2d 169 (1979).

144 RSA 161-D:3-b.

145 RSA 330-A:19.

146 RSA 330-A:22.

147 RSA 330-A:25(III).

148 NHRE 502(a)(5) defines the term "confidential communication" to be a communication which is "not intended to be disclosed to third persons other than those to whom disclosure is made in furtherance of the rendition of professional legal services to the client or which is reasonably necessary for the transmission of the communication." See also N.H. Rules of Professional Conduct, Rule 1.6(a) ("A lawyer shall not reveal information relating to representation of a client unless the client consents after consultation, except for disclosures that are impliedly authorized in order to carry out the representation. . . ."), Rule 2.3(b) (disclosure in connection with evaluations for third parties), and Rule 3.3(b) (disclosure to court of later acquired information).

149 NHRE 502(a)(1) defines the term "client" to include "a person . . . who is rendered professional legal services by a lawyer, or who consults a lawyer with a view to obtaining professional legal services from him."

150 NHRE 502(a)(3) defines the term "lawyer" to include "a person authorized, or reasonably believed by the client to be authorized, to engage in the practice of law in any state or nation."

151 NHRE 502(a)(4) defines the term "representative of a lawyer" to be "one employed by the lawyer to assist the lawyer in the rendition of professional legal services."

(C) Between a client's representative[152] and his lawyer;

(D) Between a client's representative and his lawyer's representative;

(E) Between a client's lawyer and the client's lawyer's representative;

(F) By a client to a lawyer for another party regarding a matter of common interest;

(G) By a client to a lawyer's representative for another party regarding a matter of common interest;

(H) By a client's representative to a lawyer for another party regarding a matter of common interest;

(I) By a client's representative to a lawyer's representative for another party regarding a matter of common interest;

(J) By a client's lawyer to a lawyer for another party regarding a matter of common interest;

(K) By a client's lawyer to a lawyer's representative for another party regarding a matter of common interest;

(L) By a client's lawyer's representative to a lawyer for another party regarding a matter of common interest;

(M) By a client's lawyer's representative to a lawyer's representative for another party regarding a matter of common interest;

(N) Between the client's representatives;

(O) Between the client and the client's representative;

(P) Between two or more lawyers representing the same client; and

(Q) Between two or more of a client's lawyer's representatives.[153]

In order to be privileged, the communication must be "made for the purpose of facilitating the rendition of professional legal services to the client."[154] The privilege survives death or dissolution of the client and may be claimed by the client directly or by his representative, successor, lawyer, or lawyer's representative on his behalf.[155]

---

152 NHRE 502(a)(2) defines the term "representative of a client" to be "one having authority to obtain professional legal services, or to act on advice rendered pursuant thereto, on behalf of the client."

153 The extent of the privilege is set forth in NHRE 502(b). Information which members of the New Hampshire Bar Association receive "during the course of their work on behalf of the Professional Conduct Committee which is indicative of a violation of the Code of Professional Responsibility" is also protected by the privilege. Sup. Ct. R. 37(d).

154 NHRE 502(b).

155 NHRE 502(c).

Information which is otherwise discoverable cannot, however, be protected from disclosure simply by communicating it to a party's attorney.[156] Although the lawyer/client privilege is subject to no statutory exception or abrogation,[157] it will not prevent disclosure in six situations:

(1) "When there is a compelling need for the information and no alternative source is available";[158]

(2) If the lawyer was consulted for advice or aid with respect to a future "crime or fraud";[159]

(3) In disputes between the client's heirs or grantees;[160]

(4) In cases involving a claimed breach of duty between the lawyer and client;[161]

(5) In matters relating to the attestation of a document by the lawyer;[162] and

(6) In an action "between or among" persons who were formerly joint clients of the lawyer.[163]

(12) *Sexual Assault Counselor/Domestic Violence Counselor/Victim:* Information disclosed by a person claiming to be the victim of criminal sexual assault or domestic violence to a trained sexual assault or domestic violence counselor "in the course of that relationship and in confidence" is privileged from compulsory disclosure except in cases where a criminal

---

156 See, e.g., LaCoss v. Lebanon, 78 N.H. 413, 414, 101 A. 364, 365 (1917): ("[A] party cannot escape his duty of discovering material documents by merely handing them to his attorney.").

157 Compare RSA 169-C:32, 529:26 and 330-A:19.

158 McGranahan v. Dahar, 119 N.H. 758, 764, 408 A.2d 121, 125 (1979).

159 NHRE 502(d)(1); N.H. Rules of Professional Conduct, Rule 1.6(b)(1) (disclosure may be made by lawyer "to prevent client from committing a criminal act that lawyer believes is likely to result in death or bodily harm or substantial injury to financial interest or property of another"); Rule 1.13(c).

160 NHRE 502(d)(2).

161 NHRE 502(d)(3); N.H. Rules of Professional Conduct, Rule 1.6(b)(2) (disclosure may be made "to establish a claim or defense on behalf of the lawyer in a controversy between the lawyer and the client, to establish a defense to a criminal charge or civil claim against the lawyer based upon conduct in which the client was involved, or to respond to allegations in any proceeding concerning the lawyer's representation of the client"). See also N.H. Rules of Professional Conduct, Rule 1.9(b).

162 NHRE 502(d)(4).

163 NHRE 502(d)(5). The communication must have been made by one of the clients to the lawyer during the former joint representation and must have been "relevant to a matter of common interest between or among two or more clients" at that time.

defendant's right to a fair trial and to confront witnesses will be affected.[164] RSA 173-C:1(I) extends the sexual assault counselor/domestic violence counselor/victim privilege to communications made "in confidence by means which, so far as the victim is aware, does not disclose the information to a third person." The privilege does not prevent the counselor from reporting cases of child abuse.[165]

(d) *Extension of the Privileges by Special Circumstances.* RSA 330-A:19 and 329:26 both provide that communications made to a person who is working under the supervision of a licensed or certified professional will be privileged as though made to the professional if they "are customary and necessary for diagnosis and treatment." NHRE 502 similarly provides that communications made to "one employed by the lawyer to assist the lawyer in the rendition of professional legal services" are protected by the lawyer/client privilege. RSA 521-A:11 also provides that when a deaf person communicates to a person with whom communications are privileged through the assistance of an interpreter, the privilege extends to the communication with the interpreter as well. In other cases, a communication which would otherwise be privileged will become subject to compulsory disclosure if communicated in the presence of or through a third party.[166]

(e) *Effect of Disclosure of Privileged Matter.* A knowing and voluntary disclosure or consent to disclosure of "any significant part of the privileged matter" by a person holding the privilege is a waiver of that privilege as to the whole of the "privileged matter," and the waiver is binding on the party holding the privilege and his successors in interest.[167] However, the privilege is not waived by a "disclosure that was compelled erroneously or . . . that was made inadvertently during the course of discovery."[168]

(f) *Effect of Asserting a Privilege.* A claim of privilege, once asserted, stands as a barrier to disclosure of the privileged matter until such time as the privilege is waived or the trial court enters an order compelling disclosure. In jury cases, claims of privilege should be raised outside the presence and "without the knowledge" of the jury.[169] Neither the judge nor the jury is

---

164 RSA 173-C:2. The statute goes on to say, however, that "the location and the street address of a rape crisis center or domestic violence center" may not be disclosed under any circumstances.

165 RSA 173-C:10.

166 State v. LaRoche, 122 N.H. 231, 442 A.2d 602 (1982).

167 NHRE 510. But see RSA 173-C:4 (waiver to "specific portion" is no waiver to "other portion").

168 NHRE 511.

169 NHRE 512(b).

permitted to draw any inference from the fact that a privilege has been claimed,[170] and a party is entitled to a jury instruction to that effect "[u]pon request."[171] It naturally follows that neither the judge nor the lawyers may comment upon the fact that a privilege has been claimed.[172]

Library References

CJS Discovery §§ 5, 18, 35, 37, 67, 71(1)–(9), 72, 73

Discovery or inspection of trade secret, formula, or the like. 17 ALR2d 383.

Privilege of communications or reports between liability or indemnity insurer and insured. 22 ALR2d 659.

Court's power to determine, upon government's claim of privilege, whether official information contains state secrets or other matters disclosure of which is against public interest. 32 ALR2d 391.

Privilege of custodian, apart from statute or rule, from disclosure, in civil action, of official police records and reports. 36 ALR2d 1318.

Privilege against disclosure of matters arising out of transactions or relationship between accountant and client. 38 ALR2d 670.

Discovery and inspection of income tax returns in actions between private individuals. 70 ALR2d 240.

Privilege or immunity as affecting statements of parties or witnesses as subject of pretrial or other disclosure, production, or inspection. 73 ALR2d 84, 133.

Work product or confidential privilege as affecting discovery, inspection, and copying of photographs of article or premises the condition of which gave rise to instant litigation. 95 ALR2d 1063, 1273.

Commencing action involving physical condition of plaintiff or decedent as waiving physician-patient privilege as to discovery proceedings. 21 ALR3d 912.

Application of privilege attending statements made in course of judicial proceedings to pretrial deposition and discovery procedures. 23 ALR3d 1172.

Pretrial testimony or disclosure on discovery by party to personal injury action as to nature of injuries or treatment as waiver of physician-patient privilege. 25 ALR3d 1401.

Development, since *Hickman v. Taylor*, of attorney's "work product" doctrine. 35 ALR3d 412.

Assertion of privilege in pretrial discovery proceedings as precluding waiver of privilege at trial. 36 ALR3d 1367.

Privilege against self-incrimination as ground for refusal to produce noncorporate documents in possession of person asserting privilege but owned by another. 37 ALR3d 1373.

Physician-patient privilege as extending to patient's medical or hospital records. 10 ALR4th 552.

Applicability of attorney-client privilege to communications made in presence of or solely to or by third person. 14 ALR4th 594.

Work product privilege as applying to material prepared for terminated litigation or for claim which did not result in litigation. 27 ALR4th 568.

Extent and determination of attorney's right or privilege against self-incrimination in disbarment or other disciplinary proceedings—post-*Spevack* cases. 30 ALR4th 243.

Attorney-client privilege as extending to communications relating to contemplated civil fraud. 31 ALR4th 458.

---

170 NHRE 512(a). See also RSA 173-C:8.

171 NHRE 512(c).

172 NHRE 512(a).

Privilege as to communications between lay representative in judicial or administrative proceedings and client. 81 ALR4th 1226.

Applicability of marital privilege to written communications between spouses inadvertently obtained by third person. 32 ALR4th 1177.

Presence of child at communication between husband and wife as destroying confidentiality of otherwise privileged communication between them. 39 ALR4th 480.

§ 22.21. Duty To Respond to Requests for Discovery

A party is obligated to respond to requests for discovery honestly, "fully and responsively."[173] He must refresh his recollection, find out what information is in his records and what is known to his agents and employees, and, in general, attempt in good faith to give his opponent the information he has requested. He need not volunteer information which has not been requested, but neither should he be evasive and rely upon technicalities of semantics or defects in the request to avoid producing information which he knows that his opponent is seeking and is entitled to receive. The fact that the agents from whom answers are sought or the documents or other property to which access is sought are out of state does not insulate them from discovery so long as the party from whom discovery is sought has access to them and is subject to the in personam jurisdiction of the court.[174]

Library References

CJS Discovery §§ 12, 13
Answer to interrogatory merely referring to other documents or sources of information. 96 ALR2d 598.

§ 22.22. Duty To Supplement Responses—Generally

If a party has made a full, honest, and responsive answer to a discovery request, he need not supplement that response to include additional infor-

---

173 See, e.g., Super. Ct. R. 36; Dist. and Mun. Ct. R. 1.10(A); Kearsarge Computer, Inc. v. Acme Staple Co., 116 N.H. 705, 366 A.2d 467 (1976). "Subject only to the limitations of full or qualified privileges full discovery, under the discretionary control of the Trial Judge to prevent harassment, has 'supplanted the older notion . . . [of] the right of each party to keep from disclosure the facts which he intended to show at trial' . . . and those which he intended not to show." Scontsas v. Citizens Insurance Company, 109 N.H. 386, 388, 253 A.2d 831, 833 (1969). "Absent some privilege and subject to control to prevent harassment, full discovery is favored . . . ." Yancey v. Yancey, 119 N.H. 197, 198, 399 A.2d 975, 976 (1979). See also N.H. Rules of Professional Conduct, Rule 3.4(d) (unprofessional conduct to "fail to make reasonably diligent effort to comply with a legally proper discovery request by an opposing party"); Daigle v. City of Portsmouth, 131 N.H. 319, 553 A.2d 291 (1988).

174 A decree for discovery is in personam (Davis v. Central New Hampshire Power Co. of Maine, 79 N.H. 377, 109 A. 263 (1920)), and can require the party to bring anything movable, discoverable, and within his control into the state or to a location outside of the state at which his opponent can examine it. See Therrien v. Public Service Co. of N.H., 99 N.H. 197, 108 A.2d 48 (1954).

mation which he acquires thereafter, except as required by the continuing effect of any court order mandating the response or as indicated in Sections 813 through 817. A party's duty to supplement responses continues through trial and must be fulfilled as quickly as possible but, in any event, in time for his opponent to make appropriate use of the new information.

Library References

CJS Discovery §§ 12, 13
Propriety of discovery interrogatories calling for continuing answers. 88 ALR2d 657.

§ 22.23. —Identity and Location of Witnesses Generally

A party must provide additional or corrective information on the identity and location of "persons having knowledge of discoverable matters" as soon as he learns of their existence or location. Because such persons may not, in all cases, be competent to testify at trial, this obligation to supplement requires more than that a party disclose only the names of persons who are potential witnesses at trial.[175]

Library References

CJS Discovery § 4
Identity of witnesses whom adverse party plans to call to testify at civil trial, as subject of pretrial discovery. 19 ALR3d 1114.

§ 22.24. —Identity and Testimony of Expert Witnesses

A party must provide additional or corrective information on the identity of expert witnesses who are expected to be called at trial,[176] and the subject matter and substance of their testimony as soon as he has determined that they will testify.[177] He must also "promptly" provide his opponent with any additional expert reports which become known or available to him.[178]

Library References

Propriety of allowing state court civil litigant to call expert witness whose name or address was not disclosed during pretrial discovery proceedings. 58 ALR4th 653.

---

175 Super. Ct. R. 35(e)(1)(a); Prob. Ct. R. 10.

176 "An expert is 'expected to testify' if and when it becomes reasonably probable that he will be called as a witness." Workman v. Public Service Co., 113 N.H. 422, 425, 308 A.2d 540, 542 (1973).

177 Super. Ct. R. 35(e)(1)(b); Prob. Ct. R. 10.

178 Super. Ct. R. 36.

§ 22.25.   —Correction of Mistakes

If a party later discovers that a response was incorrect when made or was then correct but is no longer true, he must "seasonably" amend his original response to make it accurate.[179]

§ 22.26.   —Effect of Court Order or Agreement of the Parties

The court may impose or the parties may agree upon a greater obligation to supplement responses with respect either to all discovery or to a particular request.[180] The court will enforce the parties' agreement in this regard.

§ 22.27.   —Effect of New Request

In the absence of a court order or agreement of the parties, a party may be obligated to supplement his responses to include additional after-acquired information if, at any time before trial, his opponent specifically requests a supplementary response.[181] Such a request must, however, comply in all respects with the rules applicable to the original request.

D. Judicial Enforcement and Supervision of Discovery

§ 22.28. Motions To Compel Production

In *Humphreys Corporation v. Margo Lyn, Inc.*[182] Justice Griffith wrote:

> Discovery is a two-way street and ordinarily will be best accomplished by direct exchange between counsel with only occasional resort to the Trial Court. In opposing discovery in the Trial Court counsel should exercise discrimination as to the limitations sought.[183]

The Court prefers that the parties work out the sequence, timing, and scope of discovery by agreement[184] and that they refer disputes to the trial court as infrequently as possible. At a minimum, this preference requires that the

---

179 Super. Ct. R. 35(e)(2); Prob. Ct. R. 10; Daigle v. City of Portsmouth, 131 N.H. 319, 553 A.2d 291 (1988).

180 Super. Ct. R. 35(e)(3); Prob. Ct. R. 10; Daigle v. City of Portsmouth, 131 N.H. 319, 553 A.2d 291 (1988).

181 Super. Ct. R. 35(e)(3); Prob. Ct. R. 10.

182 109 N.H. 498, 256 A.2d 149 (1969).

183 *Id.* at 500, 256 A.2d at 151.

184 N.H. Rules of Professional Conduct, Rule 3.2 (lawyer's obligation to expedite case). See also N.H. Rules of Professional Conduct, Rule 3.4(d) (obligation to make reasonably diligent effort to comply with discovery requests).

parties talk to each other before filing motions in court[185] and make concessions in areas which are not vital to their cases in order to avoid involving the court in the discovery process. A party who fails or refuses to attempt to reach a reasonable agreement on discovery matters, with the result that either he or his opponent files a motion with the court, risks being assessed costs and attorneys fees.[186]

When a party is unable to obtain discovery of information necessary for the preparation of his case, he may file a Motion To Compel answers or production. The Motion should summarize the nature of the case and identify the information sought in such a way that the court can determine whether discovery is reasonably necessary and what has been done to obtain it voluntarily. The opponent may file an Objection, if he has any, within ten days, specifying the reasons for his belief that discovery of this information is not necessary or appropriate. In his Objection, a party may alternatively object to the scope or timing of the discovery sought, but in that case he should show how the issues in the case or progress of the case to date make a limitation on scope or timing appropriate. Both the moving party and his opponent should endeavor to set forth the issues in their pleadings to a sufficient degree that the court can decide the Motion without hearing. Even in those cases where a party's Motion To Compel or Objection has a sufficient basis to avoid the imposition of costs and attorneys fees, his request for a hearing or his lack of specificity in pleading which requires a

---

185 See, e.g., Super. Ct. R. 35(b)(2), which requires a prior request. See also Prob. Ct. R. 10. The modern policy of pretrial cooperation is obviously different from that which prevailed in the nineteenth century. A century ago, the gamesmanship theory of trials was thought to support the adversary system, and, while a party's right to have discovery of certain information relevant to his case was recognized, the Court expected that parties would resist even allowable discovery to the maximum extent and that the trial court would be required to rule on almost every attempt to obtain discovery. Thus, it was held that a party need not make demand for voluntary discovery before seeking the court's aid. Treadwell v. Brown, 44 N.H. 551 (1863). The scope of permissible discovery is much broader now than it was at the 19th century, and this fact, coupled with the modern preference for cooperation and minimal resort to the trial court, requires today that demand be made before a motion to compel discovery is filed. Of course, Super. Ct. R. 57-A requires that a party certify he has made a good faith attempt to obtain his opponent's concurrence in the relief sought by a motion to compel.

186 See Super. Ct. R. 59; Prob. Ct. R. 9 and 10. When a party refuses to make discovery specifically required by the Rules or a pretrial order, costs will be assessed upon the filing of a motion. See, e.g., Super. Ct. R. 35(b)(2). See also N.H. Rules of Professional Conduct, Rule 3.2 (lawyer's duty to expedite the case) and Rule 3.4(d) (lawyer's duty to make reasonably diligent response to discovery requests).

hearing may subject him to an order for costs and attorneys fees.[187] The failure to file a Motion To Compel when the other side is not cooperating in discovery can result in prejudice to a party's case.[188]

Library References

CJS Discovery §§ 13, 53

Dismissal of action for plaintiff's failure or refusal to obey court order in aid of discovery or inspection. 4 ALR2d 348.

Appealability of order pertaining to pretrial examination, discovery, interrogatories, production of books and papers or the like. 37 ALR2d 586.

Mandamus or prohibition as available to compel or to prevent discovery proceedings. 95 ALR2d 1229.

Judgment in favor of plaintiff for defendant's failure to appear, or to answer questions or interrogatories, in pretrial proceedings. 6 ALR3d 713.

§ 22.29. Motion for Protective Order

As the old categorical limits on the use of pretrial discovery have been put aside and the permissible scope of pretrial discovery has been steadily expanded during the last several decades, a feeling has grown that some substitute method of limiting the use of discovery should be developed. As early as 1959, Chief Justice Kenison warned that "[w]hile the use of discovery in this state has been regarded as a remedial device which has been given a liberal application, we have attempted to indicate that it is subject to limitations."[189] The next year, in *Smith v. American Employers' Insurance Co.*,[190] the Court referred to the need to keep the process "within reasonable limits."[191] Thus, while the Court has, on the one hand, been stripping away most of the former restrictions on the use of pretrial discovery and has resisted all efforts to impose other clearly determined limita-

---

187 The Supreme Court has held that a motion can be granted but not denied without a hearing. Yancey v. Yancey, 119 N.H. 197, 399 A.2d 975 (1979). Thus, costs may be assessed against a moving party for filing a motion which is so doubtful as to require a hearing or against an opponent whose Objection is groundless.

188 See, e.g., Wheeler v. School Administrative Unit 21, 130 N.H. 666, 550 A.2d 980 (1988) (even though defendant did not forward two supplementary expert reports to plaintiff as promised, plaintiff's motion to strike expert's testimony at trial was denied because he had not attempted to compel production of reports).

189 McDuffey v. Boston & Maine Railroad, 102 N.H. 179, 181, 152 A.2d 606, 608 (1959).

190 102 N.H. 530, 163 A.2d 564 (1960).

191 *Id.* at 535, 163 A.2d at 568. This point was echoed in a number of subsequent cases. See, e.g., Hardware Mutual Casualty Co. v. Hopkins, 105 N.H. 231, 196 A.2d 66 (1963); Hartford Accident & Indemnity Co. v. Cutter, 108 N.H. 112, 229 A.2d 173 (1967).

tions[192] in their place, it has also recognized that some limitations may be appropriate from time to time and has adopted a balancing test approach to determining when those occasions occur.[193]

Limitations have been imposed in three ways. First, in cases of qualified privilege or in which a party seeks information which is outside the general scope of discovery as set forth in Superior Court Rule 35(b)(1), the Court has required that a party bear the burden of establishing that the information is relevant to the issues in the case and necessary to his preparation for trial. In the case of material which is not subject to a full privilege but either enjoys a qualified privilege or is generally regarded as confidential, the trial court may "impose stringent requirements upon the moving party to establish grounds for the production."[194]

Second, in cases where the disclosing party can show good cause, the trial court may order that the discovery proceed either under the control of a special master[195] or subject to suitable safeguards designed to limit inquiry into contested areas[196] or further disclosure.[197]

Lastly, the trial court may limit a party's access to any information, whether within the general scope of discovery set forth in Superior Court

---

192 The Court has said that it will not place "any crippling limitations on the use of discovery." McDuffey v. Boston & Maine Railroad, 102 N.H. 179, 181, 152 A.2d 606, 608 (1959). See Hartford Accident & Indemnity Co. v. Cutter, 108 N.H. 112, 229 A.2d 173 (1967).

193 The modern need for limitations is said to arise from "competing policies," rather than from fixed rules. Willett v. General Electric Co., 113 N.H. 358, 306 A.2d 789 (1973); Sawyer v. Boufford, 113 N.H. 627, 312 A.2d 693 (1973). The modern process of limiting discovery is always expressed as a balancing of the public policy in favor of full and open discovery against any other policy urged as a basis for refusal of the right.

194 Currier v. Allied New Hampshire Gas Co., 101 N.H. 205, 207, 137 A.2d 405, 407 (1957). See Downing v. Monitor Publishing Co., Inc., 120 N.H. 383, 415 A.2d 683 (1980).

195 A discovering party has no right to supervise the selection of documents produced by his opponent. If the discovering party distrusts his opponent in a case in which a special master has not been appointed to supervise the production, he may inquire about the methods of selection, move for further disclosure, and ask for sworn representations regarding the selection. Staargaard v. Public Service Co. of N.H., 96 N.H. 17, 69 A.2d 4 (1949). A special master serves to assure both that the disclosures are made and that the requesting party does not examine any matter "not legitimately necessary" to enable him to prepare for trial. Ingram v. Boston & Maine Railroad, 89 N.H. 277, 197 A. 822 (1938). This procedure was employed in State v. Cote, 95 N.H. 108, 58 A.2d 749 (1948).

196 Smith v. American Employers' Insurance Co., 102 N.H. 530, 163 A.2d 564 (1960); Workman v. Public Service Co., 113 N.H. 422, 308 A.2d 540 (1973).

197 Lincoln v. Langley, 99 N.H. 158, 106 A.2d 383 (1954); Workman v. Public Service Co., 113 N.H. 422, 308 A.2d 540 (1973); Downing v. Monitor Publishing Co., Inc., 120 N.H. 383, 415 A.2d 683 (1980).

Rule 35(b) or not, if it appears that the request has been made with the purpose or effect of harassing,[198] embarrassing,[199] annoying,[200] or invading the privacy[201] of or to impose an undue burden or expense[202] or an oppressive hardship[203] on a party.

Of course, the traditional power of the court to keep a party within the general scope of discovery remains. When a party begins to stray outside the realm of relevant information, to engage in a "fishing expedition,"[204] the court may limit his inquiry or cut him off and order him to return to the

---

198 Currier v. Allied New Hampshire Gas Co., 101 N.H. 205, 207, 137 A.2d 405, 407 (1957) ("[Discovery] should not be used as a means of harassment or impertinent intrusion."); Hardware Mutual Casualty Co. v. Hopkins, 105 N.H. 231, 196 A.2d 66 (1963); Farnum v. Bristol-Myers Company, 107 N.H. 165, 167, 219 A.2d 277, 279 (1966) ("The right of a party to be free from the burden of discovering records which could have no possible 'legitimate bearing' on the issues of the case . . . and from unjustified harassment or impertinent intrusion . . . is well established."); Riddle Spring Realty Co. v. State, 107 N.H. 271, 220 A.2d 751 (1966); Scontsas v. Citizens Insurance Company, 109 N.H. 386, 253 A.2d 831 (1969).

199 Hardware Mutual Casualty Co. v. Hopkins, 105 N.H. 231, 196 A.2d 66 (1963); Yancey v. Yancey, 119 N.H. 197, 399 A.2d 975 (1979). See also N.H. Rules of Professional Conduct, Rule 4.4 (unprofessional conduct to take action with "no substantial purpose other than to embarrass, delay, or burden a third person").

200 Yancey v. Yancey, 119 N.H. 197, 399 A.2d 975 (1979).

201 Riddle Spring Realty Co. v. State, 107 N.H. 271, 220 A.2d 751 (1966); Sawyer v. Boufford, 113 N.H. 627, 312 A.2d 693 (1973) (inquiring into defendant's personal net worth to determine ability to pay judgment exceeding insurance coverage deemed invasion of privacy).

202 Yancey v. Yancey, 119 N.H. 197, 399 A.2d 975 (1979). See also N.H. Rules of Professional Conduct, Rule 4.4.

203 Yancey v. Yancey, 119 N.H. 197, 399 A.2d 975 (1979). See also New Castle v. Rand, 101 N.H. 201, 204, 136 A.2d 914, 917 (1957) ("Whether the depositions in perpetual remembrance were a necessary and expedient method of preparation for trial as claimed by the plaintiff, or whether they were unnecessary, oppressive and burdensome as claimed by the defendant rested primarily in the sound discretion of the Trial Court under the circumstances and facts of that particular case.").

204 Use of the term "fishing expedition" has an interesting history. In England's chancery courts, bills of discovery that were used oppressively to inquire into the names of a party's witnesses or into the manner of proving his case were referred to as "fishing bills." In State (ex rel.) Eaton v. Farmer, 46 N.H. 200, 202 (1865), Justice Bellows called attention to this bit of history and remarked that the New Hampshire Supreme Court would "not be inclined to favor a fishing deposition any more than a fishing bill" and would move to limit inquiry at a deposition which seemed to intrude on the areas protected by the predecessor to RSA 516:23. In the days when a party was not allowed to inquire into his opponent's case on discovery, any attempt to learn the theory of the defense or facts relating exclusively to the defendant's case was called a "fishing bill." Reynolds v. Burgess Sulphite Fibre Co., 71 N.H. 332, 342, 51 A. 1075, 1081 (1902).

subjects about which he is allowed to inquire.[205] The court may enjoin the use of any specific discovery device upon the motion of a party.[206]

However, the trial court has very little role in supervising modern discovery, and the Supreme Court has encouraged counsel to cooperate in the accomplishment of discovery and not to bother the trial court with frequent objections and motions.[207] If appropriate, a Motion for Protective Order may be made by any person from whom discovery is sought, whether he is a party or not, or by the party himself and the court may grant the motion "for good cause shown."[208] The court's protective order may take any form "which justice requires,"[209] and may prohibit discovery, limit its scope, terms, or conditions,[210] require use of a different method than the one chosen, or limit the persons who may participate or learn of the discovery.[211] Motions for protective orders are not favored,[212] and the court may assess reasonable attorney fees and costs against a party or witness who files such a motion without substantial justification.[213]

Library References

CJS Discovery §§ 2, 17, 36, 47
Protective orders limiting dissemination of financial information obtained by deposition or discovery in state civil actions. 48 ALR4th 121.

---

205 Robbins v. Kalwall Corp., 120 N.H. 451, 417 A.2d 4 (1980); Staargaard v. Public Service Co. of N.H., 96 N.H. 17, 69 A.2d 4 (1949).

206 New Castle v. Rand, 101 N.H. 201, 136 A.2d 914 (1957).

207 Humphreys Corporation v. Margo Lyn, Inc., 109 N.H. 498, 500, 256 A.2d 149, 151 (1969):

> The immovable object resistance to discovery with intermediate appeal to this court does not advance the law of discovery. Discovery is a two-way street and ordinarily will be best accomplished by direct exchange between counsel with only occasional resort to the Trial Court. In opposing discovery in the Trial Court counsel should exercise discrimination as to the limitations sought.

208 Super. Ct. R. 35(c).

209 Id.

210 It may, for example, require a party to pay the cost of producing the requested information if the process of assembling that information proves "unreasonably burdensome." Kann v. Wausau Abrasives Company, 81 N.H. 535, 129 A. 374 (1925).

211 Super. Ct. R. 35(c).

212 Cf. Humphreys Corporation v. Margo Lyn, Inc., 109 N.H. 498, 256 A.2d 149 (1969).

213 Super. Ct. R. 35(c), 59; Prob. Ct. R. 9, 10. See also N.H. Rules of Professional Conduct, Rule 3.2 (lawyer has a duty to expedite litigation). Even in the 19th century, a party who requested the court's aid in obtaining discovery before attempting to obtain disclosures by agreement could be ordered to pay costs. See Dennis v. Riley, 21 N.H. 50 (1850).

§ 22.30. Special Orders Relating to Discovery

A party may move at the start of a case that the court enter an order limiting or specifying the scope, sequence, manner, or timing of discovery to be followed by the parties.[214] The moving party should set forth in such a motion the nature of the case and the facts or circumstances which he thinks warrant the court's regulation of the discovery process. The moving party will generally bear the burden of convincing the trial court that its regulation of discovery is necessary, and this can be more difficult at an early stage of the proceedings when the exact nature of a party's requests or objections cannot be foreseen.

A Motion To Regulate discovery may be made as soon as discovery may begin.[215] The court will not generally enter an order regulating discovery without a hearing or until a Structuring Conference has been held. If the moving party's opponent objects to regulation of discovery in general or to any particular terms which might be included in such an order, he should file an Objection within ten days setting forth the reasons for his objections and alternative terms which he could accept. Whether objecting to a Motion To Compel or to a Motion To Regulate, a party should "exercise discrimination as to the limitations sought"[216] and, whenever possible, propose alternative terms which he could accept. The necessity for cooperation in pretrial discovery does not stop at the courthouse door.

Although it is more common to request the court to enter an order regulating future discovery at the beginning of a case, a motion for such an order can be made at any time.

Library References

Propriety of discovery order permitting "destructive testing" of chattel in civil case. 11 ALR4th 1245.

Propriety of allowing state court civil litigant to call expert witness whose name or address was not disclosed during pretrial discovery proceedings. 58 ALR4th 653.

§ 22.31. Sanctions

In an appropriate case, the court may impose sanctions on a party or his attorney for a failure to cooperate in discovery or to obey court orders

---

214 The court has inherent equity power to regulate discovery in the interests of justice and may enter an order setting forth discovery procedure in any case.

215 Super. Ct. R. 62.

216 Humphreys Corporation v. Margo Lyn, Inc., 109 N.H. 498, 500, 256 A.2d 149, 151 (1969).

relating thereto.[217] The question of whether to impose sanctions and, if so, against whom and in what form they should be imposed are matters assigned to the discretion of the trial court.[218] Sanctions may consist of an award of attorneys fees and costs, regardless of who eventually prevails in the case,[219] dismissal of the action[220] and other orders.

Library References

CJS Discovery § 53

E. Completion of Discovery

§ 22.32. The General Rule

There is no longer any rule which places a deadline on the completion or discovery.[221] Pretrial discovery deadlines are generally now included in the Court's Structuring Conference Order.[222]

§ 22.33. Continuation of Discovery

Under modern principles of liberal discovery and cooperation, a party should be able to continue discovery even during trial if necessary to the preparation of his case and, although his opponent may reasonably object

---

217 Daigle v. City of Portsmouth, 131 N.H. 319, 326, 553 A.2d 291, 295 (1988) ("Action or inaction by a party may provide the basis for the imposition of sanctions. . . . Sanctions are appropriate in part to deter parties from disregarding discovery requests . . . and to compensate others for costs associated with a party's failure to act in accordance with such requests. These purposes would not be served if we were to hold that sanctions could be imposed only for attorney wrongdoing, and that a party was therefore free to disregard instructions from counsel regarding proper compliance with discovery requests"); Miller v. Basbas, 131 N.H. 332, 553 A.2d 299 (1988).

218 Daigle v. City of Portsmouth, 131 N.H. 319, 553 A.2d 291; Miller v. Basbas, 131 N.H. 332, 553 A.2d 299.

219 Daigle v. City of Portsmouth, 131 N.H. 319, 327, 553 A.2d 291, 296 (1988) ("The imposition of attorneys fees may be used as a sanction for a failure to comply with discovery requests. . . . It is not dispositive in determining whether to impose sanctions whether a claim ultimately prevails. We refuse to 'fashion a rule whereby legal fees are awarded against intransigent defendants only to the extent of expenses incurred on prevailing claims.' ").

220 Miller v. Basbas, 131 N.H. 332, 553 A.2d 299 (1988).

221 Former Super. Ct. R. 62(E) (amended in May 1994) provided that pretrial discovery had to be completed within 11 months of the return day. The Rule was frequently ignored.

222 Super. Ct. R. 62.

if the discovering party, either out of neglect or a desire to harass, seeks late discovery which he could have obtained earlier, the objection will in most cases result in a regulation on, rather than prohibition of, the discovery sought.

CHAPTER 23.   WRITTEN INTERROGATORIES

Library References

Discovery by written interrogatories, generally. 4 Am Jur Trials, pp. 1–117.
Interrogatories in actions involving trade secrets. 14 Am Jur Trials, pp. 1–100.
Use of interrogatories in libel actions by public officials. 17 Am Jur Trials, pp. 223–403.

Forms

Interrogatories Propounded by Defendant To Be Answered by Plaintiff, see Appendix.

§ 23.01. Introduction

Written interrogatories are one of the recognized methods of discovery in New Hampshire practice.[1] They may be used in aid of any proceeding[2]

---

1 Super. Ct. R. 35 and 36; Dist. and Mun. Ct. R. 1.10; Prob. Ct. R. 10. (Probate Court Rule 10 incorporates Superior Court Rules 35–45A which include the rules regarding interrogatories.)

2 There is no restriction on the use of written interrogatories in marital matters, administrative proceedings, or ancillary proceedings (e.g., execution).

(except small claims actions[3]) in any court in the state.[4] The purpose of interrogatories "is to narrow the issues of the litigation . . . and prevent unfair surprise by making evidence available in time for both parties to evaluate it and adequately prepare for trial."[5]

A. Propounding Written Interrogatories

§ 23.02. When Interrogatories May Be Propounded

Written interrogatories may be propounded to a party only after the writ or other process has been served.[6] They may not be served with the writ. When interrogatories are propounded immediately after service of the writ, or at any time before the return day, they are not returnable until thirty days after the return day.

Library References

CJS Discovery § 58
Time for filing and serving discovery interrogatories. 74 ALR2d 534.

§ 23.03. Persons Who May Propound Interrogatories

Only a party to the action may propound written interrogatories.[7]

Library References

CJS Discovery § 59

§ 23.04. Persons Who May Be Required To Answer Interrogatories

Only parties to the action may be required to answer written interrogatories.[8] When the answering party is a corporation, partnership, association,

---

3 Dist. and Mun. Ct. R. 4.21.

4 Super. Ct. R. 35, 36, and 44; Dist. and Mun. Ct. R. 1.10; Prob. Ct. R. 10.

5 Kearsarge Computer, Inc. v. Acme Staple Co., 116 N.H. 705, 707, 366 A.2d 467, 469 (1976). See also Hubbard v. Panneton, 121 N.H. 526, 433 A.2d 1246 (1981) (defendant's failure to provide information bearing on his only defense until the day of trial prevented plaintiff from adequately preparing for trial).

6 Super. Ct. R. 36; Dist. and Mun. Ct. R. 1.10(A); Prob. Ct. R. 10.

7 *Id.*

8 *Id.* The District and Municipal Court Rules state that interrogatories may be served on an "adverse party," but it is doubtful that the Rules intend to limit discovery only to a party's opponents. The District and Municipal Court Rule is apparently derived from an earlier form of Superior Court Rule 36. One commentator, when considering this earlier language, was of the opinion that, since codefendants and coplaintiffs would not be adverse parties, interrogatories could probably not be propounded to them. See Edward P. McDuffee, *Interrogatories*, 9 N.H. BAR JOURNAL 79, 80 (1967). The change in the wording of the Superior Court Rule and the liberalization of discovery generally suggest that a different conclusion must be arrived at today.

or public agency, it may designate any officer or agent who has access to "all information available to the party" to answer the interrogatories on its behalf.[9] The propounder may not require that any particular officer or agent answer his interrogatories, but may ask whether a particular person has knowledge of an event or material fact.

Library References

CJS Discovery § 59

Taking deposition or serving interrogatories in civil case as waiver of incompetency. 23 ALR3d 389.

§ 23.05. Limitations on the Number of Interrogatories Which May Be Propounded

Each party to an action in the superior court or the probate courts is limited to fifty written interrogatories[10] and in the district and municipal courts to not more than thirty.[11] These limitations apply to the total number of questions asked, regardless of whether the opponent successfully declines to answer one or more of them, and they apply to each period of discovery, not to the life of the case. Thus, a party to an action in the superior court or the probate courts may propound fifty written interrogatories during pretrial discovery, fifty more if a new trial is granted on the basis of newly discovered evidence, and fifty more during the process of execution. There is no limit on the number of times a party may propound interrogatories if his total on all occasions combined does not exceed the established limit.

The Rules of the Superior Court, Probate Courts, and District and Municipal Courts all state that, "[i]n determining what constitutes an interrogatory . . . it is intended that each question be counted separately, whether or not it is subsidiary or incidental to or dependent upon or included in another question, and however the questions may be grouped, combined or arranged."[12] A question is not rendered multifarious by its requirement that more than one fact or document be identified in response.

This principle may be illustrated by the following questions, the first of which would be counted as one question and the second as two:

Question 1. Please identify all persons who have examined the subject ladder since the date of the accident and give the dates of their examination?

---

9 Super. Ct. R. 36; Dist. and Mun. Ct. R. 1.10(A); Prob. Ct. R. 10.

10 Super. Ct. R. 36; Prob. Ct. R. 10.

11 Dist. and Mun. Ct. R. 1.10(D).

12 Super. Ct. R. 36; Dist. and Mun. Ct. R. 1.10(D); Prob. Ct. R. 10.

Question 2. Please identify all persons who have examined the subject ladder since the date of the accident and list the defects in manufacture which you claim it included on the date of the accident?[13]

The court may permit a party to propound more than the usual limit of written interrogatories "for good cause shown."[14] But in such a case the propounding party must file the proposed additional interrogatories with his motion.[15] There is no provision in the Rules for the court to grant an expanded number of interrogatories at the beginning of discovery or before seeing the proposed additional questions.

§ 23.06. Form of Interrogatories

Written interrogatories must be in the form of a question or a request to identify and must be in a form which could be asked in open court. Written interrogatories are individually typed on plain paper, headed with the caption of the case and a title of the pleading which identifies the propounding and responding parties. Each interrogatory must be followed by a "blank space reasonably calculated to enable the answering party to have his answer typed in."[16] The interrogatories are concluded in the same form as any other pleading, but an additional line is added for the answering party's signature and a jurat is appended to evidence his oath.

Library References

CJS Discovery § 57

§ 23.07. Serving Interrogatories

In the superior court and the probate courts, an original and two copies,[17] and in the district and municipal courts one copy only,[18] of each set of

---

13 One commentator, while adopting a stricter view of the separability of questions than is followed in this treatise, discerns a distinction between the courts' treatment of so-called "preliminary questions," as to which a number of connected queries are counted loosely as one question, and questions going to the substance of the case, which are rigidly broken down in the counting. Edward P. McDuffee, *Interrogatories*, 9 N.H. BAR JOURNAL 79, 82 (1967). However, the Supreme Court has not adopted this view since it was first advanced, and it seems safer to adopt one system of counting which applies to all questions.

14 Super. Ct. R. 36; Dist. and Mun. Ct. R. 1.10(D); Prob. Ct. R. 10.

15 *Id.*

16 Super. Ct. R. 36; Prob. Ct. R. 10.

17 *Id.*

18 Dist. and Mun. Ct. R. 1.10(A). This is but the first of several differences between the Superior and District and Municipal Court Rules relating to written interrogatories. In almost all cases, the variances are pointless and appear to be the result of inadvertence

interrogatories must be mailed or hand-delivered to the party whose response is requested.[19] When the responding party is represented by an attorney who has filed an Appearance, the interrogatories may be mailed first class or hand-delivered to the attorney. When the answering party appears pro se or has not yet filed an Appearance, the interrogatories should either be hand-delivered by a person over eighteen or mailed by registered or certified mail to the responding party.

B. Response to Written Interrogatories

§ 23.08. Form and Time for Submission of Responses to Interrogatories

Written interrogatories must be answered "fully and responsively."[20] The responding party "must fully disclose all requested information which he has at the time of the demand. . . . Although the duty to investigate is not unlimited, a party must find out what is in his own records and what is within the knowledge of his agents and employees concerning the occurrence or transaction."[21] If the responding party needs more than the time allowed by the court or Rules to make such an investigation, he may request that his opponent agree to an extension[22] or he may move the court for an order expanding the time for response.[23] Any question which is not objected to must be answered within the time allowed.[24] A party's response should also "be free of argumentation, impertinence or irrelevancy."[25]

---

rather than intention. The practice in the two court systems is much more alike than the Rules would suggest, and there is clearly a need for revision of the Rules to reflect this similarity.

19 Super. Ct. R. 36; Dist. and Mun. Ct. R. 1.10(A); Prob. Ct. R. 10.

20 *Id.* It has been suggested that a responsive answer is one which "[offers] only to answer what is asked for." Edward P. McDuffee, *Interrogatories*, 9 N.H. BAR JOURNAL 79, 80 (1967). But the requirement that the questions be answered "fully," and the general requirement that discovery be open and complete should also be kept in mind.

21 Kearsarge Computer, Inc. v. Acme Staple Co., 116 N.H. 705, 707, 366 A.2d 467, 469 (1976). See also N.H. Rules of Professional Conduct, Rule 3.4(d) (professional obligation to make a reasonably diligent effort to comply).

22 Kearsarge Computer, Inc. v. Acme Staple Co., 116 N.H. 705, 707, 366 A.2d 467, 469 (1976). Neither the Superior Court Rules, the District and Municipal Court Rules, nor the Probate Court Rules refer to motions to extend or prescribe any procedure for their filing or consideration.

23 Super. Ct. R. 36 and Prob. Ct. R. 10 provide that the parties may extend the time for providing answers by written agreement.

24 Super. Ct. R. 36; Dist. and Mun. Ct. R. 1.10(A); Prob. Ct. R. 10.

25 Edward P. McDuffee, *Interrogatories*, 9 N.H. BAR JOURNAL 79, 80 (1967).

When an interrogatory requests a copy of any document, that copy must be attached to one of the sets of answers which are returned to the propounder.[26] If an expert's or physician's report is requested, an "exact copy" of the whole report must be provided and the answering party must certify, along with his oath, that he is not aware of any other oral or written reports by that expert or physician.[27]

Superior Court Rule 36, District and Municipal Court Rule 1.10, and Probate Court Rule 10 "[contemplate] full disclosure by a party . . . except where the information sought is subject to privilege or answer is excused by statute."[28] However, a responding party may only be required to provide facts in response to written interrogatories and is under no duty to disclose the opinions or conclusions of any person other than an expert whom he expects to call at trial.[29]

The answering party must answer each question separately[30] in the space provided on the original or copy of the interrogatories with which he is served.[31] If the space provided on the original or copy is not sufficient for his answer, the responding party may either continue on additional pages which he then attaches to the set delivered to him or he may retype the set of interrogatories with the questions followed by his answers.[32] The answering party must then sign the interrogatories and swear that the answers are true and complete.[33]

---

26 Super. Ct. R. 36; Prob. Ct. R. 10. The District and Municipal Court Rules do not speak to the question of document production, but the practice is the same as in superior court.

27 Super. Ct. R. 36; Prob. Ct. R. 10.

28 Farnum v. Bristol-Myers Company, 107 N.H. 165, 168, 219 A.2d 277, 280 (1966).

29 *Id.*; Humphreys Corporation v. Margo Lyn, Inc., 109 N.H. 498, 256 A.2d 149 (1969). See also Bronson v. Hitchcock Clinic, 140 N.H. 798, 677 A.2d 665 (1996) (plaintiff's failure to include in interrogatories one question regarding his theory of liability did not render testimony of plaintiff's expert unfairly surprising to defendant).

30 If the responding party combines his answers in a confusing manner, the propounder may move to compel a more specific answer. Edward P. McDuffee, *Interrogatories*, 9 N.H. BAR JOURNAL 79, 80 (1967).

31 Super. Ct. R. 36; Dist. and Mun. Ct. R. 1.10(A); Prob. Ct. R. 10.

32 Super. Ct. R. 36; Prob. Ct. R. 10.

33 Super. Ct. R. 36; Dist. and Mun. Ct. R. 1.10(A); Prob. Ct. R. 10. It has been suggested that the responding party's attorney may not sign the responses. Edward P. McDuffee, *Interrogatories*, 9 N.H. BAR JOURNAL 79 (1967). Note that Superior Court Rule 36, Probate Court Rule 10, and District and Municipal Court Rule 1.10(A) allow a public agency, corporation, partnership, or association to cause its responses to be signed by "an agent," and the attorney who represents that party could be such an agent. Nevertheless, it will rarely be advisable for the responding party's attorney to sign interrogatory answers for his client. Even if he could be satisfied that he had received sufficient disclosure from his client to justify swearing to the completeness and accuracy of the responses, the attorney's signature would make him a potential witness,

Within thirty days of receipt of the interrogatories, the answering party must either hand-deliver or mail his responses to the propounding party.[34] In the superior court, the responding party may wait until thirty days after the return day if the interrogatories were propounded before that date.[35] However, where the responding party's answers may be expected to discourage the propounder from even entering his writ, it may be to the responding party's advantage to answer before the return day.[36] The parties can, of course, agree to an earlier or later deadline without the court's approval.[37] In the absence of an agreement between the parties, the court may either grant an extension or shorten the time for response upon a party's motion, after notice and for good cause shown.[38] The original and a copy of the responding party's answers must be given to the propounding party.[39]

Library References

CJS Discovery §§ 63, 65

---

either on deposition or at trial, and would thereby severely hamper his ability to continue to serve as trial counsel.

34 Super. Ct. R. 36; Dist. and Mun. Ct. R. 1.10(A); Prob. Ct. R. 10.

35 Super. Ct. R. 36.

36 See Edward P. McDuffee, *Interrogatories*, 9 N.H. BAR JOURNAL 79, 80 (1967).

37 Super. Ct. R. 36; Dist. and Mun. Ct. R. 1.10(A); Prob. Ct. R. 10. In the superior and probate courts, that agreement must be in writing. Super. Ct. R. 36 and Prob. Ct. R. 10. For some reason, the Superior Court and Probate Court Rules do not expressly authorize an agreement to shorten the time for response, but such an agreement would certainly be enforceable.

38 Dist. and Mun. Ct. R. 1.10(A). Super. Ct. R. 36 and Prob. Ct. R. 10 do not provide for a motion to shorten or enlarge time or explicitly authorize the court to order any change in the time limits for responding to written interrogatories. They do refer to "thirty days, or any enlarged period," but, while this suggests a power to extend, it may refer as well to extensions by agreement. Nevertheless, it is clear that the court has the inherent authority to shorten or extend the time for answering upon motion for good cause shown, and this variance between the Superior Court and Probate Court Rules and District and Municipal Court Rules appears to have no purpose.

39 In another example of apparently pointless variance, the Superior Court and Probate Court Rules require that the propounder give the responding party an original and two copies of the interrogatories and that the responding party keep one of the copies and return the original and the other copy to the propounder with his answers on both (Super. Ct. R. 36 and Prob. Ct. R. 10), while the District and Municipal Court Rules require that the propounder give only one copy to the responding party but that the responding party return "the original and a copy of his answers" to the propounder. Dist. and Mun. Ct. R. 1.10(A).

§ 23.09. Objecting to Interrogatories

The responding party may make the same objections to written interrogatories which he could make if the questions were posed orally at a discovery deposition.[40] The Rules of the Superior Court, the District and Municipal Courts, and the Probate Courts provide that the responding party "shall ordinarily be required to answer all questions not subject to privilege or excused by the statute relating to depositions [i.e., RSA 516:23],[41] and it is not grounds for refusal to answer a particular question that the testimony would be inadmissible at the trial if the testimony sought appears reasonably calculated to lead to the discovery of admissible evidence and does not violate any privilege."[42]

Whether RSA 516:23 retains any force in light of the decision in *Barry v. Horne*[43] is still questionable. The defendant in *Barry*, a defamation action, invoked RSA 516:23 and refused to reveal during his deposition names of people from whom he had obtained information about the plaintiff, because some or all of them might become witnesses at trial. The trial court, however, granted plaintiff's motion to compel disclosure of witnesses, and the Court upheld, with Chief Justice Kenison writing that "[t]he secrecy permitted by RSA 516:23 is somewhat inconsistent with the policies underlying new Superior Court Rule 35(b)(1), which . . . allows very broad discovery."[44]

The decision in *Barry* certainly deprived RSA 516:23 of its ultimate power to protect a party's witness list and plan of proof from court-ordered discovery.[45] A responding party can still refuse to provide information voluntarily which he thinks pries into the manner of proving his case, but in most cases he will be required to produce that information on his opponent's motion.[46] Whether a refusal to produce the information volun-

---

40 Super. Ct. R. 36 and 44; Dist. and Mun. Ct. R. 1.10(E); Prob. Ct. R. 10.

41 RSA 516:23 provides as follows:

> No party shall be compelled, in testifying or giving a deposition, to disclose the names of the witnesses by whom nor the manner in which he proposes to prove his case, nor, in giving a deposition, to produce any writing which is material to his case or defense, unless the deposition is taken in his own behalf.

42 Super. Ct. R. 44; Dist. and Mun. Ct. R. 1.9(G); and Prob. Ct. R. 10.

43 117 N.H. 693, 377 A.2d 623 (1977).

44 Barry v. Horne, 117 N.H. 693, 694, 377 A.2d 623, 624 (1977).

45 Roy v. Monitor-Patriot Co., 112 N.H. 80, 290 A.2d 207 (1972). See also State v. Drewry, 139 N.H. 678, 681, 661 A.2d 1181, 1183 (1995) "[W]itness lists are an exception to the work product doctrine and . . . must be disclosed upon request or order.").

46 Humphreys Corporation v. Margo Lyn, Inc., 109 N.H. 498, 256 A.2d 149 (1969).

tarily would be regarded as frivolous in light of *Barry v. Horne* depends upon the circumstances of the case.

Thus, the only cognizable objections to individual written interrogatories are the following:

(1) The question is put in an improper or unclear form or language.[47]

(2) The matter inquired into is irrelevant *and* cannot be expected to lead to relevant evidence.

(3) The witness is incompetent to respond to the question asked.

(4) The question exceeds the maximum number allowed by Rule or court order.

(5) The question calls for burdensome research.[48]

(6) The witness enjoys a privilege against responding to the question.

In addition, the responding party may object to the entire set of interrogatories on the ground that they are propounded too early, to a nonparty or at a stage or in a form of proceedings in which written interrogatories are not allowed. The responding party may also object to the production of copies of documents which are requested by the interrogatories, either because they are too bulky or inconvenient to duplicate, or because he has a privilege against their production. In the former case, his answer will be regarded as responsive, despite his failure to provide copies, if he states a time and a place where the propounder may review the originals. Within twenty days, the propounder can move for an order that the originals be produced at another time or place or be copied on terms. If the responding party objects on the basis of privilege, the objections may be raised and disposed of in the same manner as objections to substantive questions.[49]

In the superior court and the probate court, the responding party may raise his objection to an individual's interrogatories in two ways: (1) by stating in the space provided for his answer that the question is improper; or (2) by moving within twenty days of receipt to strike the improper interrogatories.[50] No express provision is made in the District and Municipal Court Rules for a Motion To Strike, but there is no reason to think one would not

---

47 "Questions that are ambiguous or create misunderstanding in the mind of the answering party serve no useful purpose and refusal to answer such questions is probably justified." Edward P. McDuffee, *Interrogatories*, 9 N.H. BAR JOURNAL 79, 83 (1967).

48 Kearsarge Computer, Inc. v. Acme Staple Co., 116 N.H. 705, 366 A.2d 467 (1976).

49 Super. Ct. R. 36; Prob. Ct. R. 10. The District and Municipal Court Rules state that the adverse party shall have the same privileges in answering written interrogatories as the deponent in the taking of a deposition. Dist. and Mun. Ct. R. 1.10(E).

50 Super. Ct. R. 36; Prob. Ct. R. 10.

be entertained. In either case, the responding party should state why he believes the interrogatories to be improper.[51] Whenever a party objects to an interrogatory, "before there is any court hearing regarding said objections, counsel for the parties shall attempt in good faith to settle the objections by agreement."[52] The objecting party has the obligation to start discussions to resolve the objections and to notify the clerk, at the conclusion of the discussions, whether a hearing is required.[53]

In his Motion To Strike, the responding party should also give the court an idea of the issues involved in the action and should set forth verbatim the interrogatories to which he objects.[54] Because the court can assess costs against the responding party if either his refusal to answer or his Motion To Strike is without foundation, the responding party will object by failing to answer only when he is certain that the question need not be answered, and will move to strike whenever he is not. Even when he is not certain that the question need not be answered and files a Motion To Strike to determine the issue, he may still be assessed costs if he has no substantial basis for the Motion.

If the responding party objects by refusing to answer, he should state the objection among his other answers and return both objections and answers at the end of thirty days. If he objects by moving to strike, he must do so within twenty days. If the court denies his motion and orders a response, he must serve the response within ten days[55] or within such further time as the court allows by specific order.[56] If the responding party simply objects to the question without moving to strike, the propounder may move to compel an answer.[57] The Motion To Compel must state the nature of the action and recite the interrogatories and answers in issue. The propounder must make the Motion within twenty days after receipt of the answers.[58] If the court orders a response, it will set a time within which it must be made.[59]

---

51 Id.

52 Super. Ct. R. 36-A; Prob. Ct. R. 10. See also N.H. Rules of Professional Conduct, Rule 3.2 (duty to expedite litigation).

53 Super. Ct. R. 36-A; Prob. Ct. R. 10.

54 Super. Ct. R. 36; Prob. Ct. R. 10.

55 Super. Ct. R. 36-A; Prob. Ct. R. 10.

56 Super. Ct. R. 36; Prob. Ct. R. 10.

57 Id.

58 Id.

59 Id.

The District and Municipal Court Rules are not as specific or detailed as the Superior Court Rules on this point and say only that sanctions may be applied against a responding party who neither answers nor files "written objection" to the interrogatories within thirty days of receipt.[60] Nevertheless, there appears to be nothing in the District and Municipal Court Rules which compels the adoption of a different procedure from the one which is followed in the superior court.

Library References

CJS Discovery § 61

§ 23.10. Filing Responses to Interrogatories

In the superior court and the probate courts, written interrogatories and their answers need not be filed with the clerk of court unless the court enters a specific order requiring it.[61] Although Superior Court Rule 36 and Probate Court Rule 10 provide only that an order for filing may be entered at the final pretrial or at trial, the courts have inherent authority to order their filing at any time.

Similarly, there is no rule in the district and municipal courts which requires interrogatories and answers be filed with the court, although the court has inherent authority to require such a filing at any time.

§ 23.11. Moving To Compel a Response to Interrogatories

In the superior court, district and municipal courts, and probate court, if a party refuses to make any response to written interrogatories within thirty days, the propounding party must send a further written request that he respond immediately. If no response is made within twenty days of that request, a Motion To Compel Answers may be filed.[62]

When a party responds, but in an incomplete or vague way, the propounding party may file a Motion To Compel a more specific answer. Superior Court Rule 36 and Probate Court Rule 10 require that Motions To Compel more specific answers include a statement summarizing the nature of the action and the exact form of the questions propounded and the answers to which objection is taken. No time limit for the filing of such motions is set forth. The District and Municipal Court Rules make no reference to Motions

---

60 Dist. and Mun. Ct. R. 1.10(B) and 1.9(G) authorize the propounder of unanswered questions to apply by motion for an order to compel.

61 Super. Ct. R. 36; Prob. Ct. R. 10.

62 Super. Ct. R. 44; Dist. and Mun. Ct. R. 1.9(G); Prob. Ct. R. 10.

To Compel more specific answers, but the same procedure should be followed there as in the superior court.

A Motion To Compel a more specific or complete response is addressed to the trial court's discretion[63] and must, in the final analysis, be based on the answering party's duty to respond. Because the answering party must respond fully, within the time allowed, to all interrogatories to which he does not state a written objection (either in his response or by Motion To Strike) and because the scope of an answering party's permissible objections is limited, when considering a Motion To Compel the court will place the burden on the answering rather than on the moving party. If the question propounded appears on its face not to have been answered fully or responsively, the court will require the responding party to show that, in fact, it has been. If the answer appears to be evasive or vague, the court will require the responding party to show that it was the best answer that could have been made under the circumstances. Only when the answer appears to be full and responsive will the court first require the propounder to explain why he is entitled to a different answer. In such a case, the propounder should anticipate the inquiry and set forth his justification in the Motion.

Motions To Compel can, in most cases, be decided without a hearing. The responding party should set forth his objection to the motion, if any, within ten days of the filing and state therein the reason why his response is all that may be required under the circumstances. In all but the most unusual situations, the merits of the parties' positions can be weighed without the necessity of oral testimony or arguments.

Neither the Rules of court nor any decision of the Supreme Court has determined whether a responding party may raise objections to interrogatories for the first time in response to a Motion To Compel. Probably the same guidelines should apply here as apply to objections raised for the first time after no response has been made. The courts should neither reward a party who saves his objections until forced to present them, nor strip a responding party of a substantial objection when he has attempted in some manner to respond.

---

63 Riddle Spring Realty Co. v. State, 107 N.H. 271, 220 A.2d 751 (1966); Farnum v. Bristol-Myers Company, 107 N.H. 165, 219 A.2d 277 (1966) (extent of "rigid compliance" with Rule 36 is left to discretion of trial court); Hartford Accident and Indemnity Co. v. Cutter, 108 N.H. 112, 115, 229 A.2d 173, 176 (1967) ("Discretion should be exercised, however, in a manner consonant with the concept that the orderly dispatch of judicial business is accomplished more efficiently when the parties are given adequate opportunity to properly prepare their case in advance of trial.").

§ 23.12. Sanctions for Failure To Respond to Interrogatories

In the superior court and the probate court, if a party fails either to answer interrogatories or to object (by Motion To Strike or by responding that the question is improper) within the time allowed, the propounder may move that the clerk enter a conditional default.[64] Although the language of Superior Court Rule 36 (and therefore Probate Court Rule 10) indicates that the clerk *must* enter a conditional default as a matter of course, in practice it is more common for the clerk to notify the answering party of the motion and to request a response. If the clerk nevertheless does enter the conditional default and notifies the answering party of the order, the answering party has ten days from the date of receipt of such notice to answer the interrogatories and move to strike the default.[65] If he does not answer the interrogatories within that time, the default may become final and the action may be terminated in favor of the propounder.[66]

Superior Court Rule 36 and Probate Court Rule 10 do not permit the answering party to object to the interrogatories after the entry of a conditional default, and it is therefore unclear whether the unexcused failure to object or answer within the time allowed constitutes a waiver of objections. Certainly, a failure to answer cannot amount to a waiver of objections which arise from the interrogatories themselves (e.g., ambiguous question) or which the answering party himself is not competent to waive (e.g., an attorney's obligation to maintain the confidentiality of his client's communications). But it might be regarded as a waiver of insubstantial or optional objections (e.g., relevancy or questions exceeding the maximum number permitted) or of waivable privileges (e.g., a client's right to relate his communications with his attorney). To date, the Supreme Court has not considered any of these questions and the only safe conclusion is that a

---

64 Super. Ct. R. 36; Prob. Ct. R. 10.

65 *Id.* The Supreme Court has said that "both notice and an opportunity for hearing should be given to a party in default prior to the entry of judgment and assessment of damages." Donovan v. Canobie Lake Park Corp., 127 N.H. 762, 763, 508 A.2d 1043, 1044 (1986). Query whether this requirement is met by notice from the clerk that a conditional default has been entered and a delay of 10 days before the entry of a further order during which the party may file his answers and a Motion To Strike the Conditional Default.

66 See American Board of Trade, Inc. v. Dun & Bradstreet, Inc., 122 N.H. 344, 444 A.2d 550 (1982) (default will not be vacated because it resulted from attorney's misconduct, rather than client's); Barton v. Barton, 125 N.H. 433, 480 A.2d 199 (1984) (judgment on default for failure to answer written interrogatories barred subsequent action for same cause); Donovan v. Canobie Lake Park Corp., 127 N.H. 762, 508 A.2d 1043 (1986) (default does not constitute a judgment for purposes of res judicata where there was neither notice nor an opportunity for a hearing).

failure to answer or object within the time allowed may, in some circumstances, be regarded as a waiver of objections.

Even in cases where a failure to answer is regarded as a waiver of objections, an answering party who is prevented from answering by accident or misfortune can always move to be relieved of the waiver.

It must be remembered, however, that the entry of a conditional default for failure to answer or object to interrogatories within the time allowed is not automatic. If the propounder fails to call the clerk's attention to his opponent's omission, the clerk need do nothing. And no matter how long the propounder waits to seek a conditional default, his opponent will always be entitled to another ten days to answer after receiving notice of the entry of the conditional default. Thus, although the Rules give a party just thirty days, or as much additional or lesser time as the court in an individual case orders, in fact, the answering party has as much time as the propounder will give him, and it is up to the propounder to assure, by making immediate objection, that he receives timely answers.

Moreover, it is important for the answering party to remember that the clerk who has entered a conditional default has no way of knowing that the interrogatories have subsequently been answered unless the answering party tells him by filing a Motion To Strike the Default. Neither the Rules nor any case decided by the Supreme Court has addressed the question whether the conditional default becomes final as a matter of law if no Motion To Strike Default is filed before the expiration of ten days. In the usual case, no further action is taken by the court until either a Motion To Strike Default or a Motion for the Entry of Judgment on the Default is filed. No doubt in many cases where the interrogatories are answered within the ten days and the failure to move to strike is inadvertent or excusable and is called to the court's attention before third parties have been affected, the answering party will be relieved of the default. But there may be cases, particularly where the Motion To Strike is filed several weeks or months after the end of the ten days and other persons have by then relied on the state of the docket, in which the answering party will not and should not be relieved of the default.

When a responding party makes no response or makes an incomplete or nonresponsive answer without justification, and his opponent is aware of the deficiency and seeks an order compelling a more complete answer, the court may also order the responding party to pay costs.[67] Where the response is incomplete but the responding party has a basis for objecting, the court may simply order an answer without imposing costs. But where the respond-

---

67 Super. Ct. R. 36; Dist. and Mun. Ct. R. 1.9(G); Prob. Ct. R. 10.

ing party submits answers that are incomplete, but not known to be incomplete until trial, or that are complete when made, but require supplementation which the responding party fails to provide, the court may impose additional sanctions on the answering party which disadvantage that party at trial. For example, in *Kearsarge Computer, Inc. v. Acme Staple Co.*,[68] the defendant counterclaimed for breach of contract and the plaintiff posed an interrogatory seeking the dates of all breaches claimed. In its response, the defendant listed eleven breaches. But at trial two years later, it sought to prove additional breaches which occurred before the date for response to the interrogatories. Although it apparently had had all the information regarding the additional breaches in its files at the time it responded to the interrogatories, the files had been in disarray and the information had not been readily accessible. However, the defendant offered no explanation for its failure to supplement the responses during the two years after it responded to the interrogatories but before trial began. On these facts the trial court refused to permit the defendant to introduce evidence of the additional breaches at trial. The *Kearsarge* case illustrates the principle that when a responding party fails to respond at all or responds only at a time when the propounder can no longer use the information to prepare his case, but his opponent does not move to compel an answer, the court may still impose sanctions, including a continuance, new trial, and costs.[69] When the court is made aware of a party's failure to meet its obligations to discover, even when his opponent has been slow to complain, it will take steps to deprive the uncooperative party of the tactical advantage sought by his failure to discover and to put the parties in the same position as if discovery had proceeded in the appropriate fashion.

In the district and municipal courts, the procedure is less clearly delineated by rule than in the superior court, but is essentially the same. The Rules provide that upon a party's failure to answer within the time allowed,[70] the propounder may "inform the *Court*" (emphasis supplied) and that the court "shall make such orders as justice requires including the entry of a conditional default.[71] The rule does not limit the time for answering, but, in

---

68 116 N.H. 705, 366 A.2d 467 (1976).

69 See Hubbard v. Panneton, 121 N.H. 526, 433 A.2d 1246 (1981) (defendant's failure to provide information bearing on his only defense until day of trial prevented plaintiff from adequately preparing for trial).

70 Dist. and Mun. Ct. R. 1.10(B) actually refers only to the standard period of 30 days, but it must be assumed that the answering party is intended to have whatever time was granted by agreement or court order pursuant to Dist. and Mun. Ct. R. 1.10(A).

71 Dist. and Mun. Ct. R. 1.10(B).

practice, the defendant is usually given ten days to respond to the propounder's notice to the court. District and Municipal Court Rule 1.10 also specifically recognizes the court's right to enter sanctions other than a conditional default.

Library References

CJS Discovery § 68
Judgment in favor of plaintiff for defendant's failure to appear, or to answer questions or interrogatories, in pretrial proceedings. 6 ALR3d 713.
Dismissal of state court action for failure or refusal of plaintiff to answer written interrogatories. 56 ALR3d 1109.
Judgment in favor of plaintiff in state court action for defendant's failure to obey request or order to answer interrogatories or other discovery questions. 30 ALR4th 9.

Cross References

Conditional default, see § 33.26 *infra*.

§ 23.13. Sanctions for Frivolous or Delaying Actions

Both the propounder and the answering party have ample opportunity to file frivolous or delaying motions. The propounder can file a Motion To Compel more specific or complete answers or to compel a response when he knows or should know that the answering party is not required to respond further than he has. A responding party can move to strike interrogatories when it is clear that they must eventually be answered.

Both sides also have the opportunity to take frivolous or delaying actions which will cause their opponents to file a motion which they should not have to file. The propounder may pose more than the allowed number of interrogatories, may propound them too early or too late, or may ask for information to which he is clearly not entitled.[72] The responding party may fail to make any answer or may submit a clearly nonresponsive answer.

In all cases where a party has filed a motion which is frivolous or for the purpose of delay or has himself acted in such a frivolous or delaying way as to cause his opponent to file a motion, the court may and should require the frivolous or delaying party or his attorney to pay the costs and attorneys fees which his opponent has incurred.[73] The determination of whether a party has acted frivolously or for the purpose of delay will ordinarily require a hearing.

---

72 In most such cases, the responding party can avoid the trouble of a Motion To Strike by simply objecting to the questions in his response. If the propounder then moves to compel, *his* motion is frivolous.

73 Super. Ct. R. 36; Dist. and Mun. Ct. R. 1.9; Prob. Ct. R. 10. See also N.H. Rules of Professional Conduct, Rules 3.1, 3.2, and 3.4(d).

§ 23.14. Duty To Supplement Responses to Interrogatories

An answering party has the same duty to supplement his responses to written interrogatories as he has to supplement any other response to a request for discovery. His duty to supplement "is implicit in the duty of full disclosure" and is especially clear "when failure to disclose newly discovered information would substantially prejudice the other party."[74] In the superior court and the probate court, in the case of expert or physician reports, if additional reports become known to the answering party after he has made his initial response, or if additional experts become expected witnesses,[75] he must provide that information to the propounder "promptly," but, in any case, "not later than ten days prior to the pretrial settlement conference."[76] When an answering party is obliged to supplement a prior response, he must do so in writing in the form of a pleading specifically identifying the interrogatory originally posed, and he must either hand-deliver or mail the response to the propounder.[77]

Library References

CJS Discovery § 57
Propriety of discovery interrogatories calling for continuing answers. 88 ALR2d 657.

Cross References

Duty to supplement responses in discovery generally, see §§ 22.22–22.27 *supra*.

§ 23.15. Use of Answers to Interrogatories

Written interrogatories and their answers are used at oral depositions and at trial in the same manner and subject to the same limitations as responses in oral depositions.[78]

---

74 Kearsarge Computer, Inc. v. Acme Staple Co., 116 N.H. 705, 708, 366 A.2d 467, 469 (1976). See also Daigle v. City of Portsmouth, 131 N.H. 319, 553 A.2d 291 (1988).

75 See Workman v. Public Service Co., 113 N.H. 422, 425, 308 A.2d 540, 542 (1973) ("An expert is 'expected to testify' if and when it becomes reasonably probable that he will be called as a witness."). See also Bronson v. Hitchcock Clinic, 140 N.H. 798, 677 A.2d 665 (1996) (plaintiff's failure to include in interrogatories one question regarding his theory of liability did not render testimony of plaintiff's expert unfairly surprising to defendant.).

76 Super. Ct. R. 36; Prob. Ct. R. 10. But see Wheeler v. School Administrative Unit 21, 130 N.H. 666, 550 A.2d 980 (1988) (defendant's failure to provide two supplementary expert reports before trial not sufficient ground to strike expert's testimony because plaintiff knew reports existed and had not moved to compel production).

77 The District and Municipal Court Rules do not specifically provide for supplementation of responses, but in practice the same procedure is followed in the district courts as in the superior and probate courts.

78 Super. Ct. R. 36 and Prob. Ct. R. 10 provide that:

Library References

CJS Discovery § 67

Propriety of considering answers to interrogatories in determining motion for summary judgment. 74 ALR2d 984.

Party's right to use, as evidence in civil trial, his own testimony given upon interrogatories or deposition taken by opponent. 13 ALR3d 1312.

Answers to interrogatories as limiting answering party's proof at state trial. 86 ALR3d 1089.

Propriety of allowing state court civil litigant to call expert expert witness whose name or address was not disclosed during pretrial discovery proceedings. 58 ALR4th 653.

Cross References

Use of depositions, see § 9.16 *infra*.

Interrogatories and answers may be used at the trial to the same extent as depositions. If less than all of the interrogatories and answers thereto are marked or read into evidence by a party, an adverse party may read into evidence any other of the interrogatories and answers or parts thereof necessary for a fair understanding of the parts read into evidence.

The District and Municipal Court Rules specify only that interrogatories may be used at trial to the same extent as depositions, and do not specify as do the Superior and Probate Court Rules what happens if less than all of the interrogatories and answers are marked and read into evidence.

CHAPTER 24.   MEDICAL EXAMINATIONS

A. PHYSICAL EXAMINATION

B. MENTAL EXAMINATION

Library References

Power to require physical examination of injured person in action by his parent or spouse to cover for his injury. 62 ALR2d 1291.

Right of party to have his attorney or physician present during his physical examination at instance of opposing party. 84 ALR4th 558.

Court's power to order physical examination of personal injury plaintiff as affected by distance or location of place of examination. 71 ALR2d 973.

Physical examination of allegedly negligent person with respect to defect claimed to have caused or contributed to accident. 89 ALR2d 1001.

Right of party to have his attorney or physician, or a court reporter, present during his physical or mental examination by a court-appointed expert. 7 ALR3d 881.

Timeliness of application for compulsory physical examination of injured party in personal injury action. 9 ALR3d 1146.

Right of defendant in personal injury action to designate physician to conduct medical examination of plaintiff. 33 ALR3d 1012.

Right to require psychiatric or mental examination for party seeking to obtain or retain custody of child. 99 ALR3d 268.

A. Physical Examination

§ 24.01. Right To Obtain a Physical Examination

A party[1] is entitled to a physical examination[2] of another party or witness, or another party or witness's plants, animals, or real estate before trial if some aspect of the physical condition of that person or that person's plants, animals, or real estate[3] is related to an issue which is involved in the action.[4] In actions for personal injuries, the physical examination may even be requested and obtained by the defendant *during* trial.[5]

Library References

CJS Discovery § 37

§ 24.02. Rights of Parties and Witnesses to Protection From Physical Harm, Unnecessary Intrusion, and Embarrassment

The purpose of a physical examination is to provide facts and expert opinions on the basis of which a party can evaluate his case for settlement and prepare his case for trial. The examining agent must, therefore, have sufficient credentials in the subject matter of the examination to qualify as an expert witness in a New Hampshire court. In addition, any party or witness being examined has a right to be protected from physical harm, embarrassment, and unnecessary intrusion.

Although the examining agent need not be a licensed physician, he should, in the case of human beings, be a licensed health care professional and have sufficient qualifications to assure that the party or witness or his plants or animals will not suffer physical harm due to incompetence. And

---

1 Because any physical examination of a person is, to some extent, intrusive and embarrassing, a person should not be permitted to require such an examination until he has commenced an action.

2 Medical examinations are not generally available as a means of pretrial discovery in the district and municipal courts. See generally Dist. and Mun. Ct. R. 1.9 and 1.10.

3 Physical examination of plants and animals is governed by the same principles as physical examination of parties and witnesses, with the exception that plants and animals are unlikely to suffer embarrassment or be as concerned about unnecessarily intrusive examinations. Nevertheless, their owners have a right to assure that the examination does not cause unnecessary pain or physical injury. The owner of a plant or animal being examined is entitled to be reimbursed for the expenses he actually incurs in producing the plants or animals for examination.

4 Super. Ct. R. 35(a). "Physical and mental examinations conducted pursuant to statutory authority or judicial order have been sustained as not violating the privilege against self-incrimination in civil litigation. . . ." In re Miller, 98 N.H. 107, 108, 95 A.2d 116, 117 (1953).

5 Super. Ct. R. 63(D).

the examination should be conducted in such a way that the party or witness is protected from unnecessary intrusion and embarrassment. While the party or witness being examined has no right to choose the person who will perform the examination[6] or to establish conditions for its performance,[7] he may object and seek a protective order if either the examining agent's qualifications or the conditions under which the examination is to be performed give rise to a reasonable concern for his safety or privacy. He may also object, absent unusual circumstances, to being required to submit to more than one physical examination.

§ 24.03. Necessity for a Court Order

A party or witness who is asked to submit himself or his plants, animals, or real estate to a physical examination as part of pretrial discovery should do so without a court order unless he has a substantial objection to the relevancy of the examination, the qualifications of the examining agent or the scope or conditions of the examination. The trial court should not be required to order a party or witness to submit to a routine examination, and costs will ordinarily be assessed against a party or witness whose refusal to cooperate necessitates the entry of such an order.[8]

Where the party or witness to be examined does have a substantial objection, which is brought before the trial court by either a Motion To Compel or Motion for Protective Order,[9] the court will address the parties' valid concerns in light of the New Hampshire preference for full and liberal discovery.[10] If there are any conditions or limitations under which the examination may be conducted which will protect the party's or witness's right to physical safety and privacy, the court will order that the examination proceed subject to those conditions and limitations.[11]

Library References

CJS Discovery § 37

---

6 Krook v. Blomberg, 95 N.H. 170, 59 A.2d 482 (1948) (plaintiff could not object to physical examination on ground that physician chosen to perform exam disliked plaintiff's counsel; plaintiff in such a case is adequately protected by his right to cross-examine defendant's physician and to produce his own, presumably more friendly, physician).

7 Drake v. Bowles, 97 N.H. 471, 92 A.2d 161 (1952) (plaintiff could not refuse to submit to physical examination on ground that defendant would not agree to provide her with copy of resulting report).

8 Super. Ct. R. 59.

9 See Super. Ct. R. 35(c).

10 Drake v. Bowles, 97 N.H. 471, 92 A.2d 161 (1952).

11 *Id.*; Super. Ct. R. 35(c).

§ 24.04. Autopsies

In an appropriate case, an autopsy may be had if the deceased person or animal's physical condition at death is relevant to the issue being tried and that physical condition can be determined by an autopsy at the time requested.[12] Although the right to the examination may seem to be clear, it is unlikely that a refusal to permit an autopsy of a human being without a court order would ever be regarded as sufficiently unreasonable to warrant the assessment of costs.

In balancing the parties' interests on a Motion To Compel an autopsy, the trial court will consider all the issues which would normally arise if the person or animal were still living and, in the case of an autopsy of a human being, the surviving relatives' interest in preserving the remains of the deceased. In those cases where an autopsy requires disinterment, the moving party must show good and substantial reasons to disinter, but the fact that the moving party has other ways of obtaining evidence on the person's physical condition at death, by itself, is not sufficient to defeat his Motion if the information which can be obtained from an autopsy is necessary to the preparation of his case or defense.[13]

Library References

CJS Dead Bodies §§ 2, 4(1), (3)
Power of court to order disinterment and autopsy or examination for evidential purposes in civil case. 21 ALR2d 538.

§ 24.05. Costs of and Access to Reports

In the ordinary case, a party requesting a physical examination of another party or witness or his plants, animals, or real estate pays the costs of that examination[14] and, subject to Rules 35(b)(3)(b) and 63(E), has no obligation to disclose the results unless and until the examining agent becomes an expected trial witness.[15]

When the examining agent does become an expected witness at trial, the party must disclose the substance of the facts known and opinions held by that expert and the grounds for those facts and opinions *only* if he is

---

12 Kusky v. Laderbush, 96 N.H. 286, 74 A.2d 546 (1950) (plaintiff died 11 months after accident and 1½ months after bringing suit, in which claim was that disability and impending death resulted from accident; defendant had reason to believe that plaintiff's death was caused by cancer).

13 Kusky v. Laderbush, 96 N.H. 286, 74 A.2d 546 (1950).

14 The party or witness being examined receives only witness fees and mileage and has no right to compensation for time lost.

15 Super. Ct. R. 35(b)(3).

requested to do so by written interrogatories,[16] subject, however, to the requirement of Rule 63(E) that copies of all medical reports be furnished upon receipt. Except as provided in Rule 63(E), a party need not provide a copy of the expert's written report unless ordered to do so by the trial court, and the trial court will only make such an order if the other party shows both a "substantial need" for the materials and an inability to obtain their "substantial equivalent" without "undue hardship."[17] And the trial court will not require a party to state the facts known and opinions held by an expert who is not expected to be a witness at trial, even in response to written interrogatories, unless "exceptional circumstances" exist which make it "impracticable" for the other party "to obtain facts or opinions on the same subject by other means."[18] In either case, the court will ordinarily require that the requesting party reimburse the examining party for a "fair portion" of the costs of making the examination and report.[19]

Library References

CJS Discovery § 37
Right to copy physician's report of pretrial examination where there is no specific statute or rule providing therefor. 70 ALR2d 384.

B. Mental Examination

§ 24.06. Right To Obtain a Mental Examination

A party may obtain a mental examination[20] of another party or a witness if some aspect of the mental or emotional condition of that person is related to an issue which is involved in the case.[21]

---

16 Super. Ct. R. 35(b)(3)(a)(i) and 36.

17 Super. Ct. R. 35(b)(2). The court will not order production of the report simply to satisfy the opponent's curiosity or to save him trouble or expense. Drake v. Bowles, 97 N.H. 471, 92 A.2d 161 (1952).

18 Super. Ct. R. 35(b)(3)(b).

19 Super. Ct. R. 35(b)(3)(c).

20 The term "mental examination," as used in this section, means any attempt to obtain information directly from a person, whether by scientific, religious, parapsychic, or other means, about that person's manner of thinking, general beliefs or values, emotional concerns or reactions to stress. It must be distinguished from an examination of the physical workings of the brain and nervous system.

21 Super. Ct. R. 35(a). "Physical and mental examinations conducted pursuant to statutory authority or judicial order have been sustained as not violating the privilege against self-incrimination in civil litigation. . . ." In re Miller, 98 N.H. 107, 108, 95 A.2d 116, 117 (1953); In re Fay G., 120 N.H. 153, 412 A.2d 1012 (1980).

§ 24.07. Rights of Parties and Witnesses to Protection From Physical or Mental Harm, Unnecessary Intrusion, and Embarrassment

Like examinations of the body, mental examinations are intended to provide a party with facts and expert opinions on the basis of which he can evaluate his case and prepare for trial. Mental examinations are, however, much more intrusive, embarrassing and potentially harmful than physical examinations. For this reason, the party being examined has a right to insist that some showing of mental illness or disturbance be made before the examination is required,[22] that the examining agent possess unobjectionable professional credentials, that the scope, nature and duration of the examination be appropriately limited and that the disclosure of facts by the examining agent and the eventual use and dissemination of the examining agent's opinions be restricted. He may also object if more than one mental examination is requested in preparation for a case, and he may, at any time during the examination, refuse to answer questions on the ground of privilege.[23] A discovering party's refusal to comply with a party or witness's reasonable requests for protection in these areas is a sufficient ground for a Motion for Protective Order.

§ 24.08. Necessity for a Court Order

In most cases, a party or witness will be understandably reluctant to undergo a mental examination, particularly if the proposed examination involves testing or the administration of drugs or treatments. However, the New Hampshire preference for full and liberal discovery is just as pronounced in this area as elsewhere, and it is incumbent upon a party or witness to cooperate with reasonable requests for discovery by mental examination.

In extreme cases, a party or witness who refuses to submit to a reasonable request for mental examination, with the result that the trial court must enter an order requiring the examination to be held, may be subjected to an assessment of costs. However, where a party or witness has a substantial basis for objecting and files a Motion for a Protective Order, the trial court, in deciding the motion, will balance the interests of the parties and give substantial weight to the party or witness's need to be protected from

---

22 In re Fay G., 120 N.H. 153, 412 A.2d 1012 (1980).
23 See In re Miller, 98 N.H. 107, 95 A.2d 116 (1953).

unnecessary intrusion, disclosure or embarrassment. If the court can adequately protect these interests by imposing restrictions or conditions on the examination, it will order that the examination take place subject to those limitations.

Library References

CJS Discovery § 37

§ 24.09. Costs of and Access to Reports

Mental examinations are paid for and their results are distributed in the same manner as physical examinations.

Library References

CJS Discovery § 37

Cross References

Costs of and access to reports of physical examinations, see § 24.05 *supra*.

CHAPTER 25. PRODUCTION OF DOCUMENTS AND THINGS

Library References

Discovery and inspection of article or premises the condition of which is alleged to have caused personal injury or death. 13 ALR2d 657.

Applicability of order pertaining to pretrial examination, discovery, interrogatories, production of books and papers, or the like. 37 ALR2d 586.

Pretrial discovery to secure opposing party's private reports or records as to previous accidents or incidents involving the same place or premises. 74 ALR2d 876.

Taxation of costs and expenses in proceedings for discovery or inspection. 76 ALR2d 953.

Discovery, inspection, and copying of photographs of article or premises the condition of which gave rise to instant litigation. 95 ALR2d 1061.

Pictures of litigant taken by opponent or latter's investigator as subject of pretrial disclosure, production, and inspection. 95 ALR2d 1084.

Pretrial discovery of engineering reports of opponent. 97 ALR2d 770.

Discovery and inspection of articles and premises in civil actions other than for personal injury and death. 4 ALR3d 762.

Who has possession, custody, or control of corporate books or records for purposes of order to produce. 47 ALR3d 676.

Discovery of hospital's internal records or communications as to qualifications or evaluations of individual physician. 81 ALR3d 944.

Photographs of civil litigant realized by opponent's surveillance as subject to pretrial discovery. 19 ALR4th 1236.

Judgment in favor of plaintiff in state court action for defendant's failure to obey request or order for production of documents or other objects. 26 ALR4th 849.

Dismissal of state court action for failure or refusal of plaintiff to obey request or order for production of documents or other objects. 27 ALR4th 61.

§ 25.01. Right to Production

A person[1] may require another person to produce originals and copies of documents and other items of personal property for his inspection and copying prior to trial.[2]

Library References

CJS Discovery § 69

§ 25.02. Conditions of Production—Convenient Time and Place

The obligation to produce documents and personal property requires only that the producing person make them available for inspection and copying at a reasonably convenient time and place. Production during business hours at the place where the documents or personal property are normally kept will, in most cases, be all that is required.

Library References

Time and place, under pretrial discovery procedure, for inspection and copying of opposing litigant's books, records, and papers. 83 ALR2d 302.

§ 25.03. —Examination for a Reasonable Period of Time

A discovering party is entitled to examine, for a reasonable period of time, the documents or personal property produced. What is considered reasonable depends upon the circumstances, and it must take into account the producing party's need for access to the documents or personal property, as well as the discovering party's right to review their contents.

§ 25.04. —Marshalling, Sorting, and Organizing Documents

The producing person has no obligation to sort through documents or to organize them in preparation for inspection, but he does have an obligation to bring together all the documents in his possession or under his control for inspection in one or a few locations. If the producing person chooses to sort through the documents, the discovering party may question him on his methods in order to ensure that nothing has been held back, but the discovering party may not sort through the files which have not been

---

1 A present or potential party or witness, or a person who will never be either, may be required to produce documents or personal property. In some cases, a person may require production of personal property from a third person before any action has been commenced. See Robbins v. Kalwall Corp., 120 N.H. 451, 417 A.2d 4 (1980).

2 Super. Ct. R. 35(a); Prob. Ct. R. 10; Dist. and Mun. Ct. R. 1.9(G).

produced.[3] The producing person must represent only that all of the documents in his possession, or under his control of the type requested have been shown to the discovering party. If this representation is disputed, the examining party may require him to make the representation under oath.

§ 25.05. —Photographing and Copying

The discovering party will ordinarily not be permitted to have unrestricted possession of the documents or of personal property produced for his inspection. Normally, he will be required to make his inspection or to conduct his review on the producing party's premises and under his watchful eye. The discovering party is entitled, however, to make copies of any documents produced and to take photographs or make other passive and nondestructive records of the personal property produced. Once a discovering person has identified the documents he wants copied, he may either ask the producing person to copy them for him, or he may make arrangements for them to be copied at his office or at a commercial duplicating establishment. One set of copies is generally made for each person and at his own expense.

§ 25.06. —Taking of Samples

Samples may be taken from personal property produced on discovery if the discovering party needs them for further analysis and if to do so will not materially alter or destroy evidence necessary for trial.

Library References

Propriety of discovery order permitting "destructive testing" of chattel in civil case. 11 ALR4th 1245.

§ 25.07. —Protection of Privileged Matter

The producing person, whether he is a party or not, has the same privileges against production of documents and personal property as he has against other discovery.

---

3 See Staargaard v. Public Service Co. of N.H., 96 N.H. 17, 19, 69 A.2d 4, 5 (1949), in which Chief Justice Johnston wrote:

> If [the plaintiffs] are distrustful of selection of appropriate records by the defendant, it will be open to them to inquire concerning the method of selection, and to seek further production if occasion is disclosed. It is not to be presumed that the defendant will not comply with a proper order, and no reason appears why the plaintiffs' right to have access to records of a particular type should be extended to supervision of the selection of such records from the defendant's files.

Cross References

Privileged matter in discovery generally, see § 22.19 *supra*.

§ 25.08. Procedure for Obtaining Production—By Agreement or By Response to Written Interrogatories or Deposition Subpoena

Documents and personal property may be requested by any method which is sufficient to identify the materials sought. It is not necessary that the request be in writing or in any particular form, but it must be clear. Production of documents may be requested of a party as part of a response to written interrogatories. In that instance, the responding party must provide one copy of each document sought within thirty days of receipt of the request. Production of documents or other personal property may also be required by a subpoena duces tecum served upon a person prior to a deposition. The documents and personal property must then be produced at the time of the deposition.[4]

4　At one time, production of a broader range of documents could be required at a deposition than for general pretrial inspection. The theory was that a deponent might need more of his notes and other papers to refresh his recollection at deposition than he could be required to produce in normal document discovery. For a case in which this distinction was raised, see Staargaard v. Public Service Co. of N.H., 96 N.H. 17, 69 A.2d 4 (1949). Modern practice, however, favors document production as inexpensive and nonintrusive and permits the same scope of discovery by all methods of discovery. In most cases today, there will not be any documents which a deponent finds useful or necessary to refresh his recollection which the discovering party cannot compel him to produce, either before or at the time of the deposition. The sole exception may be documents that contain privileged matter (e.g., trade secrets), and even those documents may be produced subject to a protective order, on stipulations or under the supervision of a special master or the court.

　　Accordingly, the modern practice is to combine document discovery and depositions and to subpoena a deponent and his records together, then to inventory the deponent's response to the subpoena duces tecum at the beginning of the deposition, marking and copying all papers produced and noting his objections to production on the transcript. If the discovering party distrusts the deponent's selection process, he may inquire about it at that time. Staargaard v. Public Service Co. of N.H., 96 N.H. 17, 69 A.2d 4 (1949).

Library References

Necessity and sufficiency under statutes and rules governing modern pretrial discovery practice of "designation" of documents, etc., in application or motion. 8 ALR2d 1134.

Form, particularity, and manner of designation required in subpoena duces tecum for production of corporate books, records and documents. 23 ALR2d 862.

Subpoena duces tecum for production of items held by a foreign custodian in another country. 82 ALR2d 1403.

§ 25.09. —By Court Order

Production of documents or personal property may be compelled by court order.[5] In balancing the interests of the parties involved, the court will try to find some way to permit the requested discovery by imposing sufficient limitations and conditions to protect the producing person. In some cases it may be necessary to appoint a special master to supervise the selection, production, examination, and copying of documents, or the testing, photographing, and sampling of personal property. The court may also require that information obtained by this means not be disclosed, or that only certain designated persons be present when the documents or personal property are produced. In an extreme case, the court may even order that documents or personal property be taken into the custody of the court, or that they be examined by an expert appointed by the court.

In light of the general New Hampshire preference for full and liberal discovery, the wide latitude given to requests for documents and personal property, and the obligation the parties have to try to resolve discovery disputes without reference to the court, there are few occasions when a Motion for Protective Order will be justified. A person who has been requested to produce documents or personal property should, if he thinks that the request is too broad, be able to agree with the discovering party either to narrow the request to documents which may actually be useful, or to meet the request in stages. The most important documents should be produced first, with the ultimate expectation that the full request will not be pressed when the insignificant nature of later documents becomes clear.

Even if the parties cannot agree to limit the request for documents and personal property, the producing person should immediately produce anything to which he cannot object. He should then drop all but his most substantial objections recognizing the tendency of trial courts to favor liberal discovery.[6] Only if the discovering party is demanding production of documents or property that would materially affect a substantial and recognized

---

5 Super. Ct. R. 36; Prob. Ct. R. 10; Dist. and Mun. Ct. R. 1.9(G).

6 See generally N.H. Rules of Professional Conduct, Rules 3.1 and 3.4.

interest of the producing person, and no compromise can be reached, should he refuse to produce and bring the matter to the court's attention. If the trial court is obliged to order production of documents or personal property in a situation where the producing person has not attempted to resolve his objections, or if there is no substantial objection to be resolved, costs will be assessed.[7]

Library References

CJS Discovery §§ 81–84

---

7 See Super. Ct. R. 36; Prob. Ct. R. 10; Dist. and Mun. Ct. R. 1.9(G).

CHAPTER 26. REQUESTS FOR ADMISSIONS

Library References

Time for filing responses to requests for admissions; allowance of additional time. 93 ALR2d 757.

Formal sufficiency of response to request for admissions under state discovery rules. 8 ALR4th 728.

§ 26.01. Right To Make Requests for Admissions

A party may make requests for admissions to another party[1] at any time after the return day[2] and prior to trial.[3]

Library References

CJS Discovery § 88

§ 26.02. Procedure for Making Requests for Admissions—In the Writ, Petition or Libel

A plaintiff's first requests for admissions are contained in his writ, petition, or libel. Any facts that are properly pleaded and not denied are admitted.[4] Any documents that are either described in the writ and relied upon to support material allegations of fact, or are attached to the writ, and

---

1 Only a person who has commenced an action or who has been joined as a party in an action is entitled to demand, or may be required to make judicial admissions. Persons who have not yet been made parties, persons as to whom an action has been discontinued, or witnesses cannot be required to make admissions, nor can they require others to make admissions.

2 The first request for admission is made by service of a writ, petition, or libel. Upon being served, the defendant's first obligation is to respond to either the substance or the procedure of the action. Until this initial exchange has been completed, it is impossible for either the parties or the trial court to know exactly what issues will be disputed, or who may eventually be involved as parties and, therefore, what further admissions should be requested. Requests for admission should not, therefore, be made until issue has been joined.

3 Super. Ct. R. 35(a); Prob. Ct. R. 10(A).

4 Super. Ct. R. 133. But see Bernier v. Bernier, 125 N.H. 517, 484 A.2d 1088 (1984); Weeks v. Weeks, 124 N.H. 252, 469 A.2d 1313 (1984).

the signatures and endorsements on any documents that are attached to the petition or libel and incorporated by reference into its allegations[5] are admitted unless the defendant files a Notice of Dispute within thirty days of the return day denying their genuineness.[6]

§ 26.03. —By Either Party Upon a Separate Pleading

At any time after the return day, but preferably not before the issue has been joined, any party may file a Request for Admissions with the clerk of court and mail or hand-deliver a copy to either the party from whom admissions are sought, or to his attorney.[7] The Request for Admissions may relate to: (1) the genuineness of relevant signatures or endorsements; (2) the genuineness of relevant documents; or (3) the truth of relevant facts.[8] The originals of any documents involved must be attached to the original Request for Admissions which is filed with the clerk of court.[9] Each signature, document, or fact as to which an admission is sought should be set forth in a separate paragraph in the Request for Admissions. There is no

---

5 Super. Ct. R. 53 refers to "written instruments declared on." In Yeaton v. Skillings, 100 N.H. 316, 125 A.2d 923 (1956), the defendant claimed that the Rule required that a copy of the full instrument be attached or set out at length in the writ or petition. The Supreme Court held that the Rule made no such requirement and that it was enough if the specification contained "all essential facts including dates, amounts, interest and payments on account" and that the instrument was adequately identified and described to "apprise the defendant . . . of all necessary facts to enable him to decide whether he should contest the signatures." *Id.* at 318, 125 A.2d at 925. Although *Yeaton* is helpful if the plaintiff, for some reason, does not have a copy of the written instrument, it will always be the best practice to attach a copy of the instrument to the writ or petition whenever possible. *Id.*

6 Super. Ct. R. 53; Dist. and Mun. Ct. R. 3.16(A). There is no similar provision in the Probate Court Rules. See also NHRE 1004(3) (permitting use of something other than original document if opponent had original in his control when pleadings notified him that it would be "a subject of proof at the hearing").

7 Super. Ct. R. 53; Dist. and Mun. Ct. R. 3.16(B). In the probate courts, this request may be filed at "any time during the proceeding." Prob. Ct. R. 11. It is unclear whether a Request for Admission is an "affirmative pleading" within the meaning of RSA 508:4-c, which prohibits a party prosecuting a personal action from specifying the amount of damages in his "declaration or other affirmative pleading." If it is an affirmative pleading, the proponent of the cause of action cannot request admissions on the various amounts of damages suffered nor, perhaps, on the genuineness of medical and other bills.

8 Super. Ct. R. 54; Dist. and Mun. Ct. R. 3.16(B). The standard of relevancy in making requests for admissions is the same as in other discovery.

9 Super. Ct. R. 54; Dist. and Mun. Ct. R. 3.16(B). In the probate courts, the original Request for Admission, with the original documents, is filed with the register. Prob. Ct. R. 11.

limit to the number of items as to which admissions may be sought or to the number of times that admissions may be requested.

The party from whom admissions are sought may decline to respond, in which case he will be deemed to have made all of the requested admissions, or he may respond to some or all of the requests, under oath, either by objecting that they call for privileged information or are otherwise improper,[10] or by denying the genuineness or truth of the matter.[11] If a signature, document or fact cannot be wholly denied, he must distinguish what can be admitted from what must be denied.[12] Any response must be filed with the clerk of court and hand-delivered or mailed to the requesting party within thirty days of receipt.[13] If the party from whom admissions are requested fails to respond within thirty days, the requests will be deemed admitted for the purposes of any dispositive motion at trial.[14]

Library References

CJS Discovery §§ 95–101

§ 26.04. Necessity for a Court Order

A party who, "without good reason or in bad faith" either requests an admission which he later fails to prove, or denies a request which is later proved against him may be "ordered to pay the reasonable expense, including attorney's fees, incurred by such other party in the signature or fact or in denying the request, as the case may be."[15] But the court has no power to compel a response to a Request for Admissions.[16]

10　The party from whom admissions are requested may make the same objections as a party to whom written interrogatories are propounded.

11　Super. Ct. R. 54; Dist. and Mun. Ct. R. 3.16(B); Prob. Ct. R. 11.

12　Super. Ct. R. 54; Dist. and Mun. Ct. R. 3.16(C).

13　Super. Ct. R. 54; Dist. and Mun. Ct. R. 3.16(B); Prob. Ct. R. 11.

14　Super. Ct. R. 54; Dist. and Mun. Ct. R. 3.16(B). In the probate courts, the response must be filed with the register. Prob. Ct. R. 11; Peaslee v. Koenig, 122 N.H. 828, 453 A.2d 832 (1982); Smith Cove Association v. Special Board, 116 N.H. 24, 352 A.2d 726 (1976).

15　Super. Ct. R. 54; Dist. and Mun. Ct. R. 3.16(D). See also N.H. Rules of Professional Conduct, Rules 3.1 and 3.4(d).

16　Estabrook v. American Hoist and Derrick, Inc., 127 N.H. 162, 498 A.2d 741 (1985).

CHAPTER 27. DEPOSITIONS

Forms

Notice To Take Deposition, see Appendix.
Subpoena, see Appendix.

§ 27.01. Right To Take Depositions

A party may take the deposition[1] of another party[2] or witness[3] at any time

---

1 The Court has defined a deposition as the "testimony of a witness reduced to writing, under oath or affirmation, by oral examination or in response to written interrogatories, and with the opportunity of cross-examination." Manchenton v. Auto Leasing Corp., 135 N.H. 298, 605 A.2d 208 (1992).

2 Depositions are so expensive, time-consuming, and intrusive that only a person who has brought an action or has been named a party to an action should be permitted to require another person to submit to them.

3 Any person with information relating to the parties' claims or the case who is subject to the in personam jurisdiction of the court may be compelled to give his deposition.

on or after the twentieth day after service of the writ, petition, or libel,[4] for use in any action or proceeding.[5]

Library References

CJS Depositions § 3 et seq.
Admissibility of Depositions under Federal Evidence Rule 804(b)(1). 84 ALR Fed 668.

§ 27.02. Methods of Taking Depositions

Depositions may be taken by posing questions orally or in writing.[6] Oral depositions are by far the most common. Although much used in the nineteenth century, depositions upon written interrogatories are today reserved for the deaf and persons who are not fluent in English.

Library References

CJS Discovery §§ 39, 50, 51

§ 27.03. Methods of Recording Depositions

Depositions, whether taken upon oral or written interrogatories, may be recorded and preserved by stenographic transcript, mechanical voice re-

---

4 Super. Ct. R. 35(a) and 38. Depositions may only be taken in connection with a pending case. Swinglehurst v. Busiel, 84 N.H. 327, 150 A. 485 (1930). But they may be taken at any stage of the proceedings, including after verdict (Super. Ct. R. 35(a) and 38; Huey v. West Ossipee Mines Inc., 81 N.H. 103, 122 A. 334 (1923)) or on petition for a new trial. B & M Railroad v. Watkins, 80 N.H. 102, 113 A. 796 (1921); Amoskeag-Lawrence Mills, Inc. v. State, 101 N.H. 392, 144 A.2d 221 (1958).

5 RSA 517:1, which formerly covered the taking and use of depositions, has been replaced by NHRE 804(b)(1), the "former testimony" exception to the hearsay rule. If the declarant is unavailable as a witness, testimony given in a deposition is not excluded in a civil action if the party against whom the testimony is offered, or a predecessor in interest with a similar motive and opportunity, developed the testimony by direct, cross or redirect examination. It was previously, but is no longer required that dispositions in marital proceedings be taken under court supervision. Calderwood v. Calderwood, 112 N.H. 355, 296 A.2d 910 (1972); former Super. Ct. R. 148, repealed effective June 1, 1982). See also Wessels v. James J. Parle Co., 89 N.H. 230, 196 A.763 (1938) (depositions in municipal court).

6 Super. Ct. R. 35(a); Prob. Ct. R. 10. Probate Court Rule 10 now states that "discovery shall be governed by the same rules as apply in the Superior Court" and incorporates Super. Ct. R. 35-45A into Prob. Ct. R. 10.

cording,[7] videotape,[8] or any other "form of verbatim reporting approved by the court."[9]

Library References

Use of videotape to take depositions for presentation at civil trial in state court. 66 ALR3d 637.

Permissibility and standards for use of audio recording to take depositions in state civil case. 13 ALR4th 775.

§ 27.04. Time for Taking Depositions—Of a Party

Depositions of a party may be taken at any time from the twenty-first day after service until the last Monday before the first day of the term in which the case is to be tried.[10] The court may permit depositions of a party at other times upon motion, for good cause shown, and upon terms.[11] The parties can agree to the taking of a deposition at any time without a court order.

---

7 Super. Ct. R. 41; Prob. Ct. R. 10.

8 Super Ct. R. 45; Prob. Ct. R. 10. The Rules provide for the use of videotape depositions that have been taken by agreement. But the court has the power to require that a deposition be recorded on videotape in an appropriate case. Super. Ct. R. 45; Prob. Ct. R. 10; Dist. and Mun. Ct. R. 1.9(H).

Super. Ct. R. 45, Probate Court Rule 10, and Dist. and Mun. Ct. R. 1.9(H) provide, in part:

> At the commencement of the videotape deposition, counsel representing the deponent should state whose deposition it is, what case it is being taken for, where it is being taken, who the lawyers are that will be asking the questions, and the date and time of the deposition. Care should be taken to have the witnesses speak slowly and distinctly and that papers be readily available for reference without undue delay and unnecessary noise. Counsel and witnesses shall comport themselves at all times as if they were actually in the courtroom. If any problem arises as to the admissibility or inadmissibility of evidence, this should be handled in the same manner as written depositions.

Objections may be made at videotape depositions on the same grounds and are handled in the same manner as objections at any other deposition. Super. Ct. R. 45; Prob. Ct. R. 10; Dist. and Mun. Ct. R. 1.9(H). In addition, Super. Ct. R. 45-A and Prob. Ct. R. 10 have been amended to state explicitly that, "[t]he provisions . . . with respect to objections to testimony or evidence shall also apply to a videotape deposition." See also Bronson v. Hitchcock Clinic, 140 N.H. 798, 677 A.2d 665 (1996) (no error for trial court to allow plaintiff to compel videotape deposition of medical witness and not to compel plaintiff to present videotape at trial).

9 Super. Ct. R. 41; Prob. Ct. R. 10.

10 Super. Ct. R. 37 and 38; Prob. Ct. R. 10; Dist. and Mun. Ct. R. 1.9(A).

11 Super. Ct. R. 37; Prob. Ct. R. 10; Dist. and Mun. Ct. R. 1.9(A). In the district and municipal courts, no deposition may be taken within 30 days of the scheduled trial or hearing date. Dist. and Mun. Ct. R. 1.9(B).

Library References

CJS Depositions § 69
CJS Discovery § 50
Party's right to use, as evidence in civil trial, his own testimony given upon interrogatories or depositions taken by opponent. 13 ALR 3d 1312.

§ 27.05. —Of a Witness

Depositions of a witness who is not a party may be taken at any time after the twentieth day after service.[12] The court may permit depositions of a witness prior to the twenty-first day after service upon motion for good cause shown and on terms.[13] The twenty-day delay is for the benefit of the defendant, not the witness, and, if the parties are willing to agree to take the deposition of a witness prior to the twenty-first day without a court order, the witness cannot object.[14]

§ 27.06. Procedure for Scheduling Depositions—By Agreement

The parties have a responsibility to cooperate in discovery[15] and should arrange to take depositions by mutual agreement, at times and places that are convenient for all sides and for the witnesses, and without the formalities imposed by RSA 517. When depositions are arranged by agreement, it is not necessary to serve a notice or subpoena upon parties or witnesses. The superior court generally takes the position, however, that Motions To Compel may not be filed in connection with depositions taken by agreement. If a party is unable to obtain an answer to a question posed in such a case, he must compel attendance at a second deposition taken under RSA 517 and, if he is still unable to obtain a response, may then file a Motion To Compel.

Library References

CJS Discovery 30

---

12 Super. Ct. R. 38; Prob. Ct. R. 10; Dist. and Mun. Ct. R. 1.9(A).

13 Super. Ct. R. 38; Prob. Ct. R. 10. In the district and municipal courts, no deposition may be taken within 30 days of the scheduled trial or hearing date. Dist. and Mun. Ct. R. 1.9(B).

14 Philips v. Verax Corp., 138 N.H. 240, 637 A.2d 906 (1994) (trial court had discretion to bar testimony of defense witness unless he submitted to discovery deposition 24 hours prior to testifying, as witness had not been available to be deposed by plaintiff earlier).

15 N.H. Rules of Professional Conduct, Rules 3.2 and 3.4(a) and (d).

§ 27.07. —In the Absence of Agreement

(a) *By Notice and Subpoena.*

(1) *In General:*   When the parties cannot mutually agree to arrange their depositions, the party wishing to take the deposition must either mail or hand-deliver a notice of the taking of the deposition to the other parties[16] or to their attorneys[17] and must serve a subpoena on the party or witness whose deposition is to be taken.[18] A deposition that has been duly scheduled by notice and subpoena may be continued from day-to-day until concluded without the necessity of serving additional notices or subpoenas. A deposition that has been scheduled may be cancelled by giving a written notice that it will not be taken, signed by the person who signed the original notice, to the other parties[19] and by notifying the witness in writing, signed by the justice of the peace, that the subpoena is withdrawn.

(2) *Requirements of the Notice:*   The notice of the taking of a deposition must be in writing, it must bear the caption of the case, identify the witness and the party taking his deposition, state the place where the deposition will be taken, and the day and time when it will begin;[20] it must also identify the stenographer who will record the testimony and the magistrate who will supervise the deposition.[21] The notice must be signed by a justice of the peace or notary public,[22] who may be the attorney of the

---

16 Clement v. Brooks, 13 N.H. 92 (1842). Where the action is in the name of a nominal party and the identity of the real party in interest is known, the real party in interest or his attorney should receive notice. Super. Ct. R. 40; Prob. Ct. R. 10; Dist. and Mun. Ct. R. 1.9(D). RSA 517:4 permits a party to serve the notice on "the adverse party, or one of them." Taken literally, this allows a party to send a notice to only one of several codefendants and third parties. In order to avoid a subsequent claim that a codefendant received insufficient notice, a party should attempt to send notice to all other parties. See Eastman v. Coos Bank, 1 N.H. 23 (1817). In the case of a corporation, service must be on an officer. Great Falls Mfg. Co. v. Mathes, 5 N.H. 574 (1832).

17 Super. Ct. R. 40; Prob. Ct. R. 10; Dist. and Mun. Ct. R. 1.9(D). The notice need not be given to the witness. The notice can be left at the adverse party's abode if he lives in New Hampshire within 20 miles of the party taking the deposition or of the place of taking (RSA 517:4) or at his agent's or attorney's abode if he does not. RSA 517:5. Abode service should never be relied upon, however, if it is possible to serve in-hand.

18 RSA 516:5. It is not clear whether depositions may be compelled in the probate courts by notice and subpoena or only by court order based on a petition filed by the party seeking discovery. RSA ch. 517 has never been regarded as applying to proceedings in the probate courts. See also Rules of Professional Conduct 4.5 ("A lawyer shall not issue or obtain the issuance of a subpoena without good cause.").

19 RSA 517:12.

20 RSA 517:4.

21 Super. Ct. R. 39; Prob. Ct. R. 10; Dist. and Mun. Ct. R. 1.9(C).

22 RSA 517:4.

party taking the deposition. A separate notice must be given for each person whose deposition is to be taken.

(3) *Requirements of the Subpoena:*   The subpoena must follow the form prescribed by RSA 516:1 and must be signed by a justice or notary public.[23] The subpoena, when completed, will bear the caption of the case, the witness's name, the day and hour when the deposition will commence, and the place of the taking. It will briefly describe the subject of his testimony, and it will be dated. The information in the subpoena must be consistent with the notice of the taking of the deposition. The subpoena must be served in-hand or read to the witness, at some place in New Hampshire,[24] by a person eighteen years of age or older.[25] The witness must be given, at the time of service, cash or a check covering one day's witness fees and mileage to the place of taking and back.[26]

(4) *Time for Serving the Notice and Subpoena:*   The notice must be served "a reasonable time before the taking" of the depositions.[27] Superior Court Rule 38, Probate Court Rule 10, and District and Municipal Court Rule 1.9 provide that twenty days' notice shall be reasonable in all cases unless the court orders otherwise. The same rules further provide that nothing less than three days' notice shall ever be regarded as reasonable without a court order.[28] Subpoenas should be served equally far in advance, but may be served at any time before the day of the deposition.

(b) *By Court Order.*   As an alternative to giving notice, a party may request the court to schedule a deposition and to appoint a magistrate to supervise the taking.[29] The notice and subsequent court order must contain the same information as required for a notice of deposition. No further service of a subpoena need be made on a party witness, but a subpoena must be served on any non-party whose testimony is desired. The minimum time periods for notice and the requirement that witness fees and mileage be

---

23 RSA 516:4.

24 "Out-of-state witnesses are beyond the subpoena powers of the State courts." Moore v. Conifer Corp., 130 N.H. 795, 800, 547 A.2d 298, 301 (1988).

25 RSA 516:5.

26 *Id.* If the deposition continues past the day specified in the notice, the witness must continue to attend without advance payment of additional witness fees and mileage.

27 RSA 517:4.

28 Super. Ct. R. 38, Prob. Ct. R. 10, and Dist. and Mun. Ct. R. 1.9 refer to the minimum notice period as "at least three days, exclusive of the day of service and the day of caption, before the day on which they are to be taken." The notice periods are counted in calendar days.

29 RSA 517:2.

tendered in advance apply to court ordered depositions unless the court grants an exception for good cause shown.

Library References

CJS Discovery §§ 29–38
CJS Discovery §§ 40–49

§ 27.08. Procedure for Conducting Depositions—Stipulations

It is customary to enter into the following stipulations at the commencement of a deposition, particularly when the deposition has been scheduled by agreement:

> It is stipulated and agreed that the deposition may be taken in the first instance by stenograph and, when transcribed and then signed by the deponent, may be used for all purposes for which depositions are competent under the laws of the State of New Hampshire. Form, filing, notice, caption, and other formalities are waived. All objections are waived to the time of trial except as to form. Copy of the deposition to be furnished to deponent's counsel.

> It is further stipulated and agreed that if the deposition remains unsigned thirty (30) days after delivery to deponent's counsel, signature shall be deemed waived; and the deposition may be used the same as if signed.

Library References

CJS Deposition § 66
CJS Discovery § 51

§ 27.09. —Posing Questions

The deposition is usually attended by the attorneys for all parties and the witness. The witness is entitled to be represented by counsel, and the parties themselves may also be in attendance unless excluded by order of the court for good cause shown.[30] In an appropriate case, a party's witness may attend to hear the testimony and advise the questioning attorney. Depositions are not public events, however, and care should be taken to keep the number of additional persons to a minimum. If a person attending a deposition becomes unruly or interferes with the witness, the party calling the deposition may insist that he leave. If a party or his attorney has been duly notified of the deposition but does not appear, the deposition may be conducted and used as though he were in attendance.

---

30 Marston v. Brackett, 9 N.H. 336 (1838).

When a magistrate has been designated or appointed to supervise a deposition, he swears the witness. In all other cases, the attorney who is taking the deposition administers the oath. The oath is the same at depositions and at trial.

The attorney for the party who is taking the deposition begins the questioning.[31] He is permitted to continue his questioning as long as necessary, even continuing it beyond the day of beginning, so long as it does not appear that he is prolonging the deposition merely to cause inconvenience to the witness or other parties. Any other party or the witness may object to the questions, and the witness may refuse, either on his own initiative or on instruction of his counsel, to answer any question upon stating his reason for so refusing. Upon the conclusion of the deposing party's questions, every other party may ask questions, and the questioning will continue to alternate until all sides have finished.

§ 27.10. —Review and Signature of Transcript

Once the transcript has been prepared, the original and one copy for each party are sent to the party conducting the deposition. At the end of the original and the copies of a transcript of a deposition scheduled pursuant to RSA 517, the magistrate will certify that the transcript is accurate and will set forth the time and place of the deposition, the case in which it is to be used, the parties notified and present, and the stipulations or circumstances under which it was taken.[32] At the end of the originals and copies of a transcript of a deposition scheduled by agreement, the stenographer will certify to the accuracy of the transcript and identify the case in which it is to be used. When a deposition is scheduled pursuant to RSA ch. 517 and conducted in the absence of an adverse party, a copy of the notice and proof of service produced by the deposing party will also be attached, and the transcript will be sealed by the magistrate and delivered directly to the court.[33] In other cases, the deposing party will submit the transcript to the witness for his review. The witness then has a reasonable time—usually thirty days—to review the transcript, note the errors he claims, and sign it under oath.[34] If the witness finds errors, he may not make the changes on the transcript but must set them out on a separate sheet of paper and attach

---

31 Super. Ct. R. 41; Prob. Ct. R. 10; Dist. and Mun. Ct. R. 1.9(E).

32 RSA 517:8. See Fabyan v. Adams, 15 N.H. 371 (1844); Currier v. B & M Railroad, 31 N.H. 209 (1855); Field v. Tenney, 47 N.H. 513 (1867); Carter v. Beals, 44 N.H. 408 (1862); Powers v. Shephard, 21 N.H. 60 (1850); Burnham v. Porter, 24 N.H. 570 (1852).

33 RSA 517:9 and 10.

34 RSA 517:7.

that sheet to the original and copies.[35] His signature under oath on the original and copies is then an adoption of the transcript as altered by his proposed changes. After the deposition has been signed or any agreed time for review and signature has passed, the deposing party must submit a copy to each of the parties who were notified of the deposition.

Library References

CJS Depositions § 71

§ 27.11. —Filing in Court

Deposition transcripts are not generally filed in court prior to trial.[36] Any party may move that a deposition be filed,[37] however, and the court will, in such a case, generally order the filing as a matter of course.[38]

Library References

CJS Depositions § 73 et seq.

§ 27.12. —Costs

The party taking a deposition pays all costs, including witness fees, mileage, and the preparation of an original and one copy for every other party in the case.[39] If a party wants additional copies he must make arrangements with the stenographer directly and bear the expense himself.

Library References

CJS Discovery § 38

§ 27.13. Objections To Taking Depositions—To the Caption

A party may object to taking the deposition at the time or place or in the manner prescribed. He may also object to the stenographer or magistrate chosen or the notice given before the taking. Objections of this sort are called objections to the caption, and they are waived if not raised promptly.

In the case of the stenographer or magistrate, a party must object in writing to the deposing party or to the court before the day of the deposi-

---

35 Super. Ct. R. 41; Prob. Ct. R. 10; Dist. and Mun. Ct. R. 1.9(E).

36 See NHRE 804(b)(1) regarding the admission in evidence of a deposition transcript. See also NHRE 803(5).

37 Super. Ct. R. 41; Prob. Ct. R. 10; Dist. and Mun. Ct. R. 1.9(E).

38 Carr v. Adams, 70 N.H. 622, 45 A. 1084 (1899). If a party fails to obey such an order, the court "may take such action as justice may require." Super. Ct. R. 41; Prob. Ct. R. 10; Dist. and Mun. Ct. R. 1.9(E).

39 See Dist. and Mun. Ct. R. 1.18.

tion.[40] The parties are entitled to a stenographer and a magistrate who are "as nearly impartial as the lot of humanity will admit."[41] In most cases this is not a problem, and the stenographer or magistrate chosen by the deposing party or appointed by the court is readily accepted. If it appears that an objection may be raised, the deposing party should seek the other parties' agreement to the stenographer or magistrate before sending the notices or beginning the deposition.[42] If the parties cannot agree before the notices are sent or if an objection is raised after notice, the trial court can appoint a stenographer or magistrate on the motion of any party.[43] If a party has an objection to the court's appointment, he must preserve it in the same manner as he would any other objection. If a party does not object in writing to the choice of a stenographer or magistrate before the day scheduled for the deposition, his objection is waived.[44]

When the usual deposition stipulations are not adopted, objections to the notice period,[45] to the substance of the notice,[46] or to the time, place, and manner of conducting the deposition should be raised immediately and on the record, either by filing a Motion To Quash the notice of deposition or deposition subpoena, an Objection to the Petition for Deposition, or by stating the objections on the record.[47] A party will not be permitted to save his objections for several weeks or months while his opponents rely on the regularity of their proceedings. While it is doubtful that any court would allow a party who participated in a deposition without objection to raise these objections later, a party who wishes to flush out any such objections in an action in superior court or probate court may do so by filing the deposition in court on the first day of a term and notifying the other parties

---

40 Super. Ct. R. 41; Prob. Ct. R. 10. The objection may be raised later if the party was not then aware of the bases for it. Edmunds v. Griffin, 41 N.H. 529 (1860); Whicher v. Whicher, 11 N.H. 348 (1840). In the district and municipal courts, the objection must be made within five days of the filing of the petition for deposition. Dist. and Mun. Ct. R. 1.9(C).

41 RSA 517:3; State v. White, 105 N.H. 159, 161, 196 A.2d 33, 34 (1963).

42 Super. Ct. R. 41; Prob. Ct. R. 10; Dist. and Mun. Ct. R. 1.9(E).

43 Id.

44 Id.

45 See Ellis v. Lull, 45 N.H. 419 (1864); Gerrish v. Pike, 36 N.H. 510 (1858) (notice must be sufficient to give the witness time to reach the place of deposition).

46 See Ballou v. Tilton, 52 N.H. 605 (1873); Bundy v. Hyde, 50 N.H. 116 (1870); Kingsbury v. Smith, 13 N.H. 109 (1842).

47 Adams v. Adams, 64 N.H. 224, 9 A. 100 (1886); City Bank v. Young, 43 N.H. 457 (1862); Wendell v. Abbott, 45 N.H. 349 (1864); Barlett v. Hoyt, 33 N.H. 151 (1856); Spence v. Smith, 18 N.H. 587 (1847).

or their attorneys in writing of the filing. Any objections not filed with the court within seven days of receipt of the notice of filing will then be waived.[48]

If a party or witness objects to the deposition for any substantive reason, he may file a Motion To Quash Deposition Subpoena or Objection to Petition for Deposition at any time before he is required by the subpoena to appear. In the case of a Petition for Deposition, the filing of an objection will usually cause the court to hold a hearing before permitting the deposition to be taken. In the case of a deposition subpoena, however, the mere filing of a Motion To Quash does not defeat the legal force of the subpoena, and unless the court enters an order before the time set for response which excuses his appearance, the witness must appear and put his objection on the record. If it is not possible to proceed in the face of the objection, the deposition will be recessed, and the objection certified to the court. The court may punish a witness's failure to appear as contempt.[49]

Library References

CJS Discovery §§ 14, 36
Dismissal of state court action for failure or refusal of plaintiff to appear or answer questions at deposition or oral examination. 32 ALR4th 212.

§ 27.14. —To the Questions or Conduct of the Deposition

Superior Court Rule 41, Probate Court Rule 10, and District and Municipal Court Rule 1.9(E) provide that the magistrate must note on the record any objections to questions or answers and any complaint of interference with a witness.

Superior Court Rule 44, Probate Court Rule 10, and District and Municipal Court Rule 1.9(G) provide that a deponent "shall ordinarily be required to answer all questions not subject to privilege or excused by the statute relating to depositions, and it is not grounds for refusal to answer a particular question that the testimony would be inadmissible at the trial if the testimony sought appears reasonably calculated to lead to the discovery of admissible evidence and does not violate any privilege."[50]

When a party or witness objects to a question asked and states his objection on the record, the witness may either answer it or not. If the witness answers it, the party objecting may still object at trial to its use in

---

[48] Super. Ct. R. 43; Prob. Ct. R. 10.

[49] Super. Ct. R. 142. See Miller v. Basbas 131 N.H. 332, 553 A.2d 299 (1988) (trial court had discretion to dismiss with prejudice tort action unless plaintiffs could assure court that they would allow their young child, the alleged victim of sexual abuse by defendant, to be deposed).

[50] Super. Ct. R. 43; Prob. Ct. R. 10.

evidence. If the witness refuses to answer it, and the deposition has been compelled under RSA ch. 517 or by court order, the deposing party may move to compel him to answer.[51]

In extreme cases, the deposing party may suspend the deposition in order to file the motion or may even adjourn the deposition to the courthouse so that he may readily appeal to a Justice. In most cases, he will push on with the deposition and await receipt of a copy of the transcript before filing a Motion To Compel.

When the witness or an opposing party objects to a question, his refusal to answer it will usually resolve the matter for the time being. However, where the deposing party continues to ask objectionable questions and, though warned, refuses to change the manner or subject of his questions, the witness or opposing party may suspend the deposition and either file a Motion for Protective Order or wait for the deposing party to file a Motion To Compel.

Objections to the form of questions must be made at the deposition or they are waived.[52] Objections to the admissibility of the deponent's responses may be made for the first time at trial.[53]

As with other methods of discovery, so too in depositions, a refusal to cooperate or unreasonable conduct which necessitates the court's intervention may result in an assessment of costs against a party or witness. In the case of depositions, however, the assessment may run against the attorneys as well as the client.[54]

§ 27.15. —Objections by Party After Failure to Attend

A party who has been duly notified of a deposition but fails to attend may not object to lawful procedures followed at the deposition[55] or to its use like any other deposition in the action.[56]

---

51 Super. Ct. R. 44; Prob. Ct. R. 10; Dist. and Mun. Ct. R. 1.9.

52 Willey v. Town of Portsmouth, 35 N.H. 303 (1857); Whipple v. Stevens, 22 N.H. 219 (1850).

53 Page v. Parker, 40 N.H. 47 (1860).

54 Super. Ct. R. 44; Prob. Ct. R. 10; Dist. and Mun. Ct. R. 1.9.

55 Bowman v. Sanborn, 25 N.H. 87 (1852) (but the deposition must still be conducted according to the usual procedures). See also Philips v. Verax Corp., 138 N.H. 240, 637 A.2d 906 (1994) (trial court had discretion to bar testimony of defense witness unless he submitted to discovery deposition 24 hours prior to testifying, as witness had not been available for plaintiff to depose earlier).

56 Lowd v. Bowers, 64 N.H. 1, 3 A. 431 (1885).

§ 27.16. Use of Depositions

Depositions, once signed under oath, may be used by any party[57] at other depositions and may be used at trial if the party offering the deposition first shows that the witness is unavailable to testify due to a testimonial privilege, lack of memory, death or physical incapacity, refusal, or absence from the hearing despite the efforts of the offering party.[58] The party against whom the testimony is offered, or a predecessor in interest, must have had an opportunity and similar motive to develop the testimony by direct, cross, or redirect examination.[59] Depositions taken in connection with one case may be used against the deponent in another case.[60] Once offered into evidence, depositions cannot be challenged upon review if a reasonable person could interpret the testimony as the trial court did.[61]

Library References

CJS Discovery § 14

Admissibility of depositions under Federal Evidence Rule 804(b)(1). 84 ALR Fed. 668.

Admissiblity in evidence of deposition as against one not a party at time of its taking. 4 ALR3d 1075.

Dismissal of state court action for failure or refusal of plaintiff to appear or answer questions at deposition or oral examination. 32 ALR4th 212.

§ 27.17. Liability of Party for Neglect or Refusal To Take Deposition

If a party gives notice of the taking of a deposition but then neither rescinds the notice nor takes the deposition at the time and place prescribed,

---

57   Hyland v. Hines, 80 N.H. 179, 116 A. 347 (1921); Taylor v. Thomas, 77 N.H. 410, 92 A. 740 (1914).

58   NHRE 804(a). The deposition may not be used, except to impeach (Carter v. Beals, 44 N.H. 408 (1862)) when the deponent testifies. Cote v. Sears, Roebuck & Company, 86 N.H. 238, 166 A. 279 (1933); Hayward v. Barron, 38 N.H. 366 (1859); Angelowitz v. Nolet, 103 N.H. 347, 172 A.2d 103 (1961). Deposition transcriptions that contain notes or underlinings may not be admitted in evidence. Knight v. Coleman, 19 N.H. 118 (1848). See Caledonia, Inc. v. Trainor, 123 N.H. 116, 459 A.2d 613 (1983) (defendant's deposition properly admitted into evidence after he invoked the privilege against self-incrimination and refused to testify at trial); Manchenton v. Auto Leasing, 135 N.H. 298, 605 A.2d 208 (1992) (defendant's submission of a deposition of witness with motion for summary judgment satisfied the affidavit requirement).

59   NHRE 804(b)(1).

60   *Id.* See Brewer v. Hyndman, 18 N.H. 9 (1845); Great Falls Bank v. Farmington, 41 N.H. 32 (1860); Leviston v. French, 45 N.H. 21 (1863); Gove v. Lyford, 44 N.H. 525 (1863).

61   Kellison v. McIsaac, 131 N.H. 675, 559 A.2d 834 (1989) (citing U.S. Fidelity & Guaranty Co. v. Johnson Shoes, Inc., 123 N.H. 148, 153 (1983)).

any party or witness who attends may have judgment and execution for his "equitable" costs, up to 25 cents per mile per person.[62]

§ 27.18. Taking of Depositions in Another State, Territory, or Country

If a party wishes to take depositions outside of New Hampshire, he must file a motion with the superior court to have some "suitable person" appointed commissioner to take the depositions[63] or, for matters pending in a probate court, file a petition or motion to have a person authorized to take the deposition.[64]

§ 27.19. Taking of Depositions in This State for Use in Another State, Territory, or Country

If a court of record in any other state, territory, or country appoints a person to take depositions in New Hampshire for use in that other state, territory, or country, that person has, by virtue of his appointment and without approval from the courts of this state, the same power to subpoena witnesses and papers that justices of the peace in this state enjoy.[65]

---

62 RSA 517:12. See Miller v. Basbas, 131 N.H. 332, 553 A.2d 299 (1988) (trial court did not abuse its discretion by ordering videotape deposition of young child in tort action where defendant was accused of sexually abusing the child and parents had previously refused to schedule child's deposition).

63 RSA 517:15. The district and municipal courts and the probate courts have no power to appoint commissioners to take depositions out of state, and the superior court cannot appoint such commissioners to take depositions for use in actions pending in the district and municipal courts and the probate courts. RSA 517:15. But the district and municipal courts and the probate courts will recognize the prima facie authority of someone who takes a deposition out of state. Dist. and Mun. Ct. R. 1.9(F).

64 RSA 547:26.

65 RSA 517:18; State v. Ingerson, 62 N.H. 437 (1882).

CHAPTER 28. DEPOSITIONS IN PERPETUAL REMEMBRANCE

Library References

Right to take depositions in perpetual remembrance for use in pending action, where statute does not expressly grant or deny such right. 70 ALR2d 674.

§ 28.01. Purpose

Depositions in Perpetual Remembrance preserve a witness's testimony on the public record, for possible use in a later trial or administrative proceeding.

§ 28.02. Situations in Which Depositions in Perpetual Remembrance May Be Taken

Depositions in Perpetual Remembrance may be taken only with the permission of a court of record.[1] Permission will be granted only if the court is satisfied, in the exercise of its discretion, that the requested depositions are necessary.[2] The question of necessity turns on three subsidiary issues: (1) the likelihood that the witness whose testimony is sought to be preserved will be available at the time and place where the issue is eventually tried;

---

1 RSA 518:2.

2 Because Depositions in Perpetual Remembrance involve time and expense for persons who may otherwise never be called to testify in any proceeding, and because they require a recording of the witness's statements on the public record, a higher standard of necessity is required to justify their use than is required to support the use of other methods of discovery. A person seeking permission to take Depositions in Perpetual Remembrance must show some reason why he needs them to protect his interests. See New Castle v. Rand, 101 N.H. 201, 136 A.2d 914 (1957).

603

(2) the importance of the witness's expected testimony to the petitioner's rights or interests; and (3) the significance of the interest that the petitioner is seeking to protect. Advanced age, enfeebled health, or imminent departure of a witness from the state may be sufficient grounds for the use of Depositions in Perpetual Remembrance if the witness's testimony is important to the protection of the petitioner's interests. Even when the witness is expected to be available for the foreseeable future, the importance of his testimony, coupled with uncertainty of whether any case may ever be brought involving the point, may also justify use of the device (e.g., a case involving lost or missing official records). The likelihood of the court to approve the taking and recording of the depositions is dependent upon the importance of the interest the petitioner seeks to protect, the precariousness of the continued availability of the testimony needed to protect it, and how critical the intended witness's testimony is to the preservation of that interest.

Library References

CJS Depositions § 5

§ 28.03. Persons Who May Take Depositions in Perpetual Remembrance

Any person with a cognizable interest in the subject of the expected testimony may petition to take Depositions in Perpetual Remembrance.[3] Persons who are, or who expect to be, parties or witnesses in cases that are either pending,[4] or may be brought in any jurisdiction, or persons whose property or other legal rights may be affected by the expected testimony (even though no case may ever be brought) may seek the right to take Depositions in Perpetual Remembrance. Particularly in cases involving disputes over interests in real property, a person may wish to take and to record Depositions in Perpetual Remembrance for the purpose of avoiding, rather than prosecuting, future litigation.

§ 28.04. Rules Governing the Taking and Use of Depositions in Perpetual Remembrance Generally

Once permission has been given for the taking, and the statutory notice has been given, Depositions in Perpetual Remembrance are conducted in

---

3 RSA 518:2.

4 Depositions in Perpetual Remembrance may be taken for use in pending cases if "there is a likelihood that the testimony may not be subsequently available due to the age or physical condition of the prospective witness." New Castle v. Rand, 101 N.H. 201, 203, 136 A.2d 914, 916 (1957).

the same manner and are subject to the same rules as other discovery depositions.[5] They may be used at other depositions or at trial, in any case involving the same questions, in the same manner as any discovery deposition.[6]

Cross References

Depositions generally, see ch. 27 *supra.*

§ 28.05. Procedure for Taking Depositions in Perpetual Remembrance—Obtaining Permission of the Court

A court of record may grant permission to take Depositions in Perpetual Remembrance, on motion for use in any pending case,[7] or on petition if no case is pending.[8] The motion or petition must be supported by sworn allegations of fact showing the issues involved, the petitioner's interest, the relationship of the expected testimony to the issues and to the petitioner's interest in them, the names and addresses of the proposed witnesses and of other interested persons, and the reasons why a Deposition in Perpetual Remembrance is necessary.[9] Upon receipt of a petition, the clerk will issue orders of notice requiring the petitioner to notify all interested persons of the petition.[10] Where the interested persons cannot be served in hand, the clerk may order notice by publication and public notice.[11] The notice will specify a time by which response must be made. If the request is made in connection with a pending case, all interested persons will, in most cases,

---

5 RSA 518:6 provides: "All such depositions shall be written, signed and sworn to as provided in case of depositions in actions pending, with the necessary variation in the form of the oath."

6 RSA 518:9.

7 See New Castle v. Rand, 101 N.H. 201, 136 A.2d 914 (1957).

8 RSA 518:2.

9 *Id.* If the names and addresses of other interested persons are unknown, the petitioner should so state.

10 Where any interested person is a minor, his guardian must be notified, if he has any; otherwise the petitioner or moving party must petition for the appointment of a guardian by the probate court and that guardian must be notified. RSA 518:4.

11 RSA 518:5. RSA 518 is an old statute and does not provide for notice to interested parties before a request to take Depositions in Perpetual Remembrance is acted upon. However, New Hampshire courts now routinely give notice and hold a hearing before granting such relief. See New Castle v. Rand, 101 N.H. 201, 136 A.2d 914 (1957).

already be involved as parties or witnesses,[12] and they may file their objections, if any, within ten days of the filing of the motion.

Upon completion of service and the expiration of the time for objections, the court will ordinarily hold a hearing on the request at which the interested parties and witnesses may appear and submit oral argument. If the court concludes that the requested depositions are necessary, it will appoint a commissioner to supervise their taking[13] and establish the time, place, and circumstances of the deposition.[14]

Library References

CJS Depositions §§ 23, 24

§ 28.06. —Giving Notice of the Deposition

The commissioner must give notice of the time and place of the depositions to all interested persons in the same manner as notice is given in other discovery depositions.[15] The notice must include a copy of the petition or motion.[16] When the names or addresses of interested persons are not known, notice of the deposition must be published once each week for three successive weeks, beginning at least eight weeks before the deposition, in a newspaper printed in Concord and a newspaper published in the county where the petition was filed.[17] If the deposition "relates to land," the notice

---

12 If a person affected by the proposed Deposition in Perpetual Remembrance has not yet been made a party, he must be served with the motion and given an opportunity to join and either to object or to participate in the deposition.

13 RSA 518:1 provides that Depositions in Perpetual Remembrance in general, "may be taken before a court of record, or before two justices, one of whom shall be of the quorum" and that any such depositions relating to "the burning, destruction or loss of any public files or records" shall be taken before the superior court or a commissioner appointed by it. In practice, Depositions in Perpetual Remembrance are never taken before a court, and courts of record always appoint a commissioner to oversee the process. See New Castle v. Rand, 102 N.H. 16, 148 A.2d 658 (1959).

14 A Deposition in Perpetual Remembrance is subject to the same regulations as other discovery. A Deposition in Perpetual Remembrance can be taken at a location out of state.

15 RSA 518:3.

16 Although due process may not require that persons previously served with a copy of the petition or motion receive a second copy with the notice of deposition, because Depositions in Perpetual Remembrance are recorded for later use and their authentication depends upon the commissioner's strict compliance with the statute, the second and redundant notice should be sent.

17 RSA 518:5.

must also be posted "in some public place" in the county seat of the county in which the land lies.[18]

§ 28.07. —Conduct of the Deposition

Depositions in Perpetual Remembrance may be recorded by any means used in other discovery depositions and approved by the court, except videotape.[19] Any person receiving notice may pose questions. In cases in which the witness may become unavailable before the normal period for review and signature has expired, special arrangements may be made for his early subscription or acceptance of the transcript. The transcript is authenticated by the commissioner's certificate stating the time and place of the deposition, the name of the petitioner or moving party, and the names of all persons who were notified and who attended. The certificate must also have attached to it a copy of the notice and evidence of its service.[20] The commissioner delivers the transcript with his certificate to the petitioner or moving party for filing.

Cross References

Methods of recording depositions, see § 27.03 *supra*.

§ 28.08. Filing or Recording the Record of the Deposition

The petition, order of notice, returns of service, court's order, commissioner's certificate and attachments, and transcript must be filed or recorded together in the public records to which they relate.[21] If the deposition relates to the records of a court or "public office," the proceedings must be filed there.[22] If it relates to real estate, the proceedings must be recorded in the Registry of Deeds for the county in which the land is located.[23] Depositions in Perpetual Remembrance that do not relate to matters of public record *may*, but need not, be recorded in the Registry of Deeds for the county in that the court that ordered the depositions is located.[24] Depositions in Perpetual Remembrance that relate to real estate should be recorded within

---

18 *Id.* If the land lies in more than one county, the notice must be published and posted in both.

19 RSA 518:6 provides that "[a]ll such depositions shall be written. . . ."

20 RSA 518:6.

21 The purpose of recording is "to preserve its purity and integrity, as well as the testimony itself." New Castle v. Rand, 102 N.H. 16, 21, 148 A.2d 658, 661–62 (1959).

22 RSA 518:7.

23 RSA 518:8.

24 *Id.*

ninety days of their taking.[25] There is no suggested time deadline for filing or recording other deposition transcripts. Regardless of when the transcript is filed or recorded, however, it may thereafter be used at trial if no other party at trial has been prejudiced by the late recording.[26] A copy of any recorded or filed transcript may be used if a party does not have the original in his possession.[27]

---

25 *Id.*

26 New Castle v. Rand, 102 N.H. 16, 148 A.2d 658 (1959).

27 RSA 518:9.

9907